6

Race, Ethnicity, and Leisure

Perspectives on Research, Theory, and Practice

Monika Stodolska, PhD

University of Illinois at Urbana-Champaign

Kimberly J. Shinew, PhD

University of Illinois at Urbana-Champaign

Myron F. Floyd, PhD

North Carolina State University

Gordon J. Walker, PhD

University of Alberta

Editors

HUMAN KINETICS

Library of Congress Cataloging-in-Publication Data

Race, ethnicity, and leisure : perspectives on research, theory, and practice / Monika Stodolska, PhD, University of Illinois at Urbana-Champaign, Kimberly J. Shinew, PhD, University of Illinois at Urbana-Champaign, Myron F. Floyd, PhD, North Carolina State University, Gordon J. Walker, PhD, University of Alberta, editors.
      pages cm
   Includes bibliographical references and index.
   1. Leisure--Social aspects. 2. Leisure--Research. 3. Racism. I. Stodolska, Monika.
   GV14.45.R34 2014
   790.1--dc23

                              2012047544

ISBN-10: 0-7360-9452-0 (print)
ISBN-13: 978-0-7360-9452-8 (print)

Copyright © 2014 by Monika Stodolska, Kimberly J. Shinew, Myron F. Floyd, and Gordon J. Walker

The web addresses cited in this text were current as of April 17, 2013, unless otherwise noted.

Acquisitions Editor: Gayle Kassing, PhD; **Developmental Editor:** Melissa Feld; **Assistant Editor:** Rachel Fowler; **Copyeditor:** Joyce Sexton; **Indexer:** Alisha Jeddeloh; **Permissions Manager:** Dalene Reeder; **Graphic Designer:** Joe Buck; **Graphic Artist:** Dawn Sills; **Cover Designer:** Kim McFarland; **Photo Asset Manager:** Laura Fitch; **Visual Production Assistant:** Joyce Brumfield; **Photo Production Manager:** Jason Allen; **Art Manager:** Kelly Hendren; **Associate Art Manager:** Alan L. Wilborn; **Illustrations:** © Human Kinetics; **Printer:** Sheridan Books

Printed in the United States of America   10 9 8 7 6 5 4 3 2 1

The paper in this book is certified under a sustainable forestry program.

Human Kinetics
Website: www.HumanKinetics.com

United States: Human Kinetics
P.O. Box 5076
Champaign, IL 61825-5076
800-747-4457
e-mail: humank@hkusa.com

Canada: Human Kinetics
475 Devonshire Road Unit 100
Windsor, ON N8Y 2L5
800-465-7301 (in Canada only)
e-mail: info@hkcanada.com

Europe: Human Kinetics
107 Bradford Road
Stanningley
Leeds LS28 6AT, United Kingdom
+44 (0) 113 255 5665
e-mail: hk@hkeurope.com

Australia: Human Kinetics
57A Price Avenue
Lower Mitcham, South Australia 5062
08 8372 0999
e-mail: info@hkaustralia.com

New Zealand: Human Kinetics
P.O. Box 80
Torrens Park, South Australia 5062
0800 222 062
e-mail: info@hknewzealand.com

E5154

CONTENTS

PART I   Theories, Methods, and Practice   7

The editors of and contributors to this book could not have found a more appropriate time to examine the critical issues relating to the intersection of race, ethnicity, and leisure. The importance of this work is suggested both by the central role of race and ethnicity in the diversification of population growth and by the growth in the depth and breadth of scholarship regarding the demographic and social factors that are seen as resulting from, or at least affected in major ways by, racial and ethnic change.

Although this is only one of the areas of interest to the authors of this work, the patterns of change in the United States clearly demonstrate why race and ethnicity are likely to be of increasing importance to scholars in leisure studies and elsewhere. For example, 2010 U.S. Census data showing population growth in the United States by race-ethnicity document the dominant role of minority population growth in the total increase in the United States. Thus, of the net addition of 27.3 million persons to the population of the United States between April 1, 2000, and April 1, 2010, about 3.7 million were African American (i.e., non-Hispanic Blacks), 6.1 million were non-Hispanic Asian or Other, and about 15.2 million were Hispanic. Non-Hispanic Whites accounted for only 2.3 million of the net change. In sum, Hispanics accounted for 55.5% of the net change, non-Hispanic Asian and Others for 22.5%, non-Hispanic African Americans for 13.7%, and non-Hispanic Whites for 8.3% of the net change in the U.S. population from 2000 to 2010. By 2010, the U.S. population was about 64% non-Hispanic White (down from nearly 70% in 2000), 12% non-Hispanic African American (virtually unchanged since 2000), 8% non-Hispanic Asian and Other (compared to about 6% in 2000), and nearly 16% Hispanic (compared to about 12% in 2000).

Recent U.S. Census Bureau projections suggest that this diversification, especially the growth of Hispanic populations, will continue. Middle-scenario projections made in 2012 (U.S. Census Bureau, 2012) suggest that the total U.S. population will become less than one-half non-Hispanic White by about 2042. By 2060 the projected U.S. population of 420 million will be 43% non-Hispanic White (compared to 64% in 2010), 13% non-Hispanic African American (compared to 12% in 2010), about 14% non-Hispanic Asian and members of Other racial and ethnic groups (compared to about 8% in 2010), and 30% Hispanic (compared to 16% in 2010). What is particularly telling is that 111.5 million people are projected to be added to the population between 2010 and 2060. This growth will result from an increase of 78.3 million who will be Hispanic, 33.5 million who will be Asian and Other, and 17.6 million who will be African American, while the non-Hispanic White population decreases by 17.9 million.

Of particular importance for those interested in many forms of leisure styles is the fact that over 50% of all persons less than 18 years of age will be minority population members by about 2023. It is clear, then, that it is increasingly important to examine activities among minority populations who will soon form the majority of all young persons in the United States.

Differentiation by race and ethnicity clearly is important in a number of ways that affect leisure activities. Recognition of socioeconomic disparities by race and ethnicity is also important. For example, due to a variety of historical, discriminatory, and other factors, minority populations have tended to have fewer resources to devote to leisure activities because they have substantially lower incomes. An American Community Survey report for 2010 shows income data by race and ethnicity for 2009 (DeNavas-Walt, Proctor, & Smith, 2010). These data point to large income differences among racial and ethnic groups. The 2009 median household income for non-Hispanic Whites was $54,671 compared to $39,923 for Hispanics and $33,463 for African Americans. Asians had median household incomes of $68,780. What is evident in these same data is that the economic downturn of the last part of the 1999 to 2009 decade disproportionately disadvantaged African American and Hispanic minorities who already had markedly lower incomes. Thus, non-Hispanic White incomes declined by $3,852 from 1999 to 2009, Black incomes declined by $4493, and Hispanic incomes declined by $3,519, while Asian incomes actually increased by $1,819 during that decade in 2009 constant dollars. As a proportion of income in 1999, these 1999 to 2009 changes represent real income declines of 6.6% for non-Hispanic Whites, an increase of 2.7% for Asians, and declines of 11.8% for African Americans and 8.1% for Hispanics in 2009 dollars.

As a result of differences in socioeconomic resources and the range of experiences in natural and other settings, there are also clear racial–ethnic differentials in participation in leisure activities. For example, data from the 2011 National Survey of Fishing, Hunting, and Wildlife-Associated Recreation show that over 90% of all persons participating in fishing, hunting, and wildlife watching were non-Hispanic Whites. Similarly, the rates of participation among these groups were 2 to 2.5 times greater for non-Hispanic Whites than for either African Americans or Hispanics.

Data from the Forest Service (U.S. Forest Service, 2004) show that even for activities that are less resource intensive, large differences occur in participation rates by race-ethnicity. For example, activities such as viewing natural scenery, sightseeing, visiting wilderness areas, and general sightseeing showed rates of participation that were 20% to 30% lower for Hispanics than for non-Hispanic Whites. Clearly, then, socioeconomic characteristics as well as potential cultural and other factors create important differences in leisure activity that merit concerted scholarly attention.

In sum, little doubt exists that understanding how race and ethnicity associate with various forms and extents of leisure involvement will be of increasing importance as leisure participant populations diversify and expand. Understanding the implications of such diversity is important demographically, socially, economically, and relative to the equality of opportunity and access to resources essential to establishing greater racial and ethnic equality in the world. The authors of the chapters in this book provide a comprehensive examination of such issues. Major theoretical frameworks, methodological issues in the analysis of racial and ethnic dimensions of leisure research, and racial and ethnic issues affecting the field of leisure research and teaching are examined. Detailed analyses of leisure activities among diverse populations including African Americans, Latinos, Asians, American Indians, and religious minorities are

also presented. The authors examine not only participation differences among such groups but also needs, motivations, and constraints on their leisure activities and the effects of discrimination on leisure experiences and participation. Different forms of leisure such as sport, physical activity, and recreation in natural areas are examined. A broad set of geographic areas in addition to North America is represented. Leisure scholarship in Europe, Australia and New Zealand, and East Asia is included as well. Finally, the work provides an excellent examination of continuing and emerging issues that will affect leisure research involving racial and ethnic minorities in the coming decades.

This book provides an overview of race and ethnicity as they influence leisure activity. I know of no current work that is more inclusive, is more careful in its examination of both the theoretical and the empirical, or explores the topic with a higher level of scholarship and attention to the theoretical as well as the empirical information available. The reader will gain substantive empirical and theoretical knowledge of the current importance of race and ethnicity to understanding differentials in leisure activities but will also gain insight into the likely future role of race and ethnicity in leisure research and theory development. For anyone interested in either leisure or the importance of race and ethnicity in substantive areas of human activity, I highly recommend this text. I predict that it will become a valued part of the library of persons in both leisure studies and social sciences in general.

Steve H. Murdock is the Allyn R. and Gladys M. Cline Professor of Sociology at Rice University. He previously served as director of the U.S. Census, having been nominated by President Bush and unanimously confirmed by the U.S. Senate in 2007 and then serving until the change in administration in January 2009. Before his appointment at Rice, he was the Lutcher Brown Distinguished Chair in Demography and Organization Studies at the University of Texas at San Antonio (UTSA) and director of the Institute for Demographic and Socioeconomic Research. Before UTSA, Murdock was a Regents Professor and head of the Department of Rural Sociology at Texas A&M University.

INTRODUCTION

Treatment of Race and Ethnicity in Leisure Research

Monika Stodolska, Kimberly J. Shinew, Myron F. Floyd, and Gordon J. Walker

In the second decade of the new millennium, the United States and Canada are more diverse than at any time in recent history. According to the 2010 U.S. Census, more than one-third of the American population were classified as racial or ethnic minorities, while at the same time the proportion of the non-Hispanic Whites had decreased (Humes, Jones, & Ramirez, 2011; Pew Research Center, 2010). In 2010, already four of the U.S. states (California, Hawaii, New Mexico, and Texas) and the District of Columbia had minority–majority populations, and several more were destined to join this list in the near future (Humes et al., 2011). Similar trends are observable in Canada, where between 1981 and 2011 the number of visible minorities increased almost fourfold, from 5% of the total population to approximately 19% of the total population, with Chinese and South Asians being the largest visible minority groups[1] (Statistics Canada, 2013).

The proportion of ethnic and racial minorities in the United States and Canada is projected to continue to grow in the future (Passel & Cohn, 2008; Statistics Canada, 2010). Between 2000 and 2010, racial and ethnic minorities accounted for 91.7% of the U.S. population growth, with most of that increase attributed to Latinos (Passel, Livingston, & Cohn, 2012). In 2011, the Census Bureau announced that for the first time non-Hispanic Whites accounted for a minority of births in the United States and almost half of children younger than five years old belonged to minority groups (Passel et al., 2012). It is projected that if the current trends continue, Whites will become a minority (47%) by 2050. In Canada, by 2031 the visible minority population is expected to reach 12.8 million or one in three Canadians (Statistics Canada, 2010).

This rapid increase of ethnic and racial minorities in both countries can be attributed to high fertility rates and immigration (Passel et al., 2012; Statistics Canada, 2010). For instance, the foreign-born population in the United States grew from 11.1% in 2000 to 12.9% in 2010 (39.9 million people) and is expected to increase to 19% by 2050 (Passel & Cohn, 2008; Pew Research Center, 2010), with the majority of immigrants coming from Mexico and South and East Asia. Since the early 1990s, immigration has also been the main contributing factor to the Canadian population growth. According to Statistics Canada (2013), in 2011, two-thirds of population growth in the country was attributable to international immigration. In the 25 years between 1986 and 2011, the immigrant population in Canada increased from 3.9 million (15.6% of the total population) to 6.8 million (20.6% of the total population). More than 60% of the immigrants came from Asia (Statistics Canada, 2013). The proportion of immigrants in Canada is expected to exceed 25% by 2031 (Statistics Canada, 2010).

Ethnic and racial minorities not only constitute a numerically growing segment of the U.S. and Canadian populations; they also play important roles in the culture, politics, and economies of these countries. Diversity and immigration lay at

[1]Census Canada defines visible minorities as "persons, other than Aboriginal peoples, who are non-Caucasian in race or nonwhite in colour. The visible minority population includes those reporting themselves as Chinese, South Asian, Black, Arab/West Asian, Filipino, Southeast Asian, Latin American, Japanese, Korean and Pacific Islander" (Statistics Canada, 2001, p. 3).

the historic foundation of the U.S. and Canadian societies, and these countries are seen across the world as ethnic mosaics. Ethnic and racial minorities contribute to U.S. and Canadian economic wealth, are important political voting blocks, and are vital parts of the two countries' vibrant cultural tapestries. At the same time, issues surrounding minority populations are at the center of political, economic, social, and cultural debates. Racial tensions, bilingual education, rising health care costs, racial profiling, intergroup conflict, border security, and illegal immigration are just some of the topics that dominated the news in the first decade of the 21st century. Similar issues are drawing attention in Europe, where immigration from North Africa, South Asia, and the Caribbean has led to debates surrounding cultural change, religious freedoms, gender equality, assimilation policies, and socioeconomic deprivation. The history of racism in the United States and Canada, as well as oppression, slavery, and colonialism throughout the world, has also sparked dialogues about White privilege and social responsibility.

SCHOLARSHIP ON RACE AND ETHNICITY

Over the last 40 years, leisure researchers have paid increasing attention to leisure behavior of ethnic and racial groups. This literature has explored a number of distinct but interrelated topics including leisure needs, motivations, and constraints among ethnic and racial minorities; types of recreation participation (e.g., physical activity, sport); recreation in natural environments; and factors affecting their leisure behavior (e.g., acculturation, discrimination, and socioeconomic status). Although this body of research is noteworthy, it is comparatively smaller than other topics of inquiry within the leisure discipline. In their comprehensive review of leisure research on race and ethnicity in five primary leisure journals, Floyd, Bocarro, and Thompson (2008) found that only 4.5% of articles published in these outlets had race or ethnicity as a main research focus. The authors identified 19 thematic categories that included, among others, activity participation and preferences, outdoor and forest recreation, interracial interaction/race relations, leisure

constraints, racial/ethnic identity, and gender and race issues. Floyd and colleagues commented that this research still remains limited in relation to the leisure literature as a whole, and critiqued it for its inability to keep up with developments in other social sciences, lack of sophisticated theoretical grounding, and narrow focus.

The scholarship on race and ethnicity has been a focus of a number of special issues of the main disciplinary journals in the field, including the *Journal of Leisure Research* (in 1993 and 1998), *Leisure Sciences* (in 2002 and 2005), and *Leisure/Loisir* (in 2007). Moreover, a number of book chapters have appeared on the topic: Jackson's (2005) *Constraints to Leisure;* Jackson and Burton's (1999) *Leisure Studies: Prospects for the Twenty First Century;* and Kleiber, Walker, and Mannell's (2011) *A Social Psychology of Leisure.* Allison and Schneider's *Diversity in the Recreation Profession: Organizational Perspectives* (2000, 2008) also offers extensive treatment of issues of ethnic and racial minority populations. Although the volume of literature on racial and ethnic minority groups is growing, there has not been a comprehensive treatment of these topics in book form. In particular, the various pieces have not been woven together to offer the perspective necessary to provide solid grounding for faculty, graduate, and upper-level undergraduate students and professionals attempting to better understand these issues. Thus, the purpose of this book is to provide a comprehensive overview of the existing research on leisure behavior of ethnic and racial minorities—the core theories, concepts, and research findings that have advanced understanding of how race and ethnicity affect individuals' daily lives, their use of leisure resources, and the provision of leisure services.

CENTRAL CONCEPTS

Three concepts central to this book are leisure, ethnicity, and race. Following the 1975 definition of Kaplan, a leisure theorist, *leisure* in this book is broadly conceptualized as a "relatively self-determined activity-experience that falls into one's economically free-time roles, that is seen as leisure by participants, that is psychologically pleasant in anticipation and recollection . . . and that provides opportunities for recreation, personal growth, and service to others" (p. 26). The U.S. Census and other federal programs in the United States follow the classifications of *race* and *ethnicity* revised by the U.S. Office of Management and Budget (OMB) in 1997 (U.S. Office of Management and Budget, n.d.). The revised OMB standards specify "five minimum racial categories for data on race: American Indian or Alaska Native, Asian, Black or African American, Native Hawaiian or Other Pacific Islander, and White. There will be two categories for data on ethnicity: 'Hispanic or Latino' and 'Not Hispanic or Latino.'" The OMB states, "The categories represent a social-political construct designed for collecting data on the race and ethnicity of broad population groups in this country, and are not anthropologically or scientifically based." In the U.S. Census, responses to questions about race and Hispanic origin are based on self-identification. Respondents are allowed to select more than one racial category.[2] Sociological and ethnic studies literature defines *ethnicity* in a number of ways. According to Berry (1958, quoted by Anderson and Frideres, 1981, p. 36), an ethnic group is a group of people possessing, among others,

> Ties of cultural homogeneity; a high degree of loyalty and adherence to certain basic institutions such as family patterns, religion, and language; distinctive folkways and mores; customs of dress, art, and ornamentation; moral codes and value systems; patterns of recreation; some sort of object to which the group manifests allegiance, such as a monarch, a religion, a language, or a territory; a consciousness of kind, a wefeeling; common descent (perhaps racial), real or imagined; and a political unit.

Hutchison (1988) defined ethnicity as "membership in a subcultural group on the basis of country of origin, language, religion, or cultural traditions, different from the dominant society" (p. 18). In many projects grounded in the positivist tradition, *race* has been defined in terms of biological characteristics (Kivel, Johnson, &

Scraton, 2009). However, contemporary research recognizes that race is a constantly evolving social construct "grounded in ideological and cultural discourses" and related to "relations of power and processes of struggle" (Kivel et al., pp. 478-479). Floyd (1998) argued with respect to race that biological characteristics are not related to one's leisure behavior patterns but that "phenotypic characteristics demarcate social boundaries and structure social interaction. Such characteristics carry meaning and provide cues about social standing and behavioral expectations relative to others who possess similar and dissimilar phenotypic traits" (p. 11). Because the concepts of race and ethnicity are interconnected, the authors of the chapters in this book refer to racial–ethnic groups throughout. Moreover, various terms may be used by different researchers to refer to the same group of people. For example, the terms *Anglo American, European American,* and *White* are used to refer to White people of European ancestry. *Black* is sometimes used instead of *African American,* and *Latino American* is used in the chapter on Latino Americans although *Latino* and *Hispanic* are used elsewhere. In general, the authors of these chapters have tried to use the terms employed by the researchers when citing their work.

ORGANIZATION AND STRUCTURE OF THE BOOK

Race, Ethnicity, and Leisure provides an in-depth overview of the research in the field of leisure studies and its allied disciplines that focuses on various aspects of leisure behavior of four minority populations—African Americans, Latino Americans, Asian North Americans, and Indigenous peoples. Although the major emphasis of the book is on racial and ethnic minority populations in the United States and Canada, a section is devoted to leisure among minority populations in Europe, Australia and New Zealand, and East Asia. The book consists of 19 chapters, including Introduction and Conclusions. It is divided into five major content areas. Following the Introduction chapter,

---

[2]Definitions of specific racial categories are presented by Humes and colleagues (2011).

part I examines theories, methods, and practice in research and the provision of leisure services to racial and ethnic minority populations. In chapter 1 on theoretical frameworks, Myron F. Floyd and Monika Stodolska provide a critical examination of past and current theoretical approaches used to frame research on race and ethnicity and identify opportunities for the development and application of new approaches for understanding race and ethnicity in leisure contexts. In chapter 2 on methods, Karla A. Henderson and Gordon J. Walker examine the philosophical issues associated with conducting ethnic and racial leisure research, discuss the use of various qualitative and quantitative methods to collect data, and explore some of the methodological concerns associated with conducting research on ethnic and racial minority groups. In chapter 3, "Race, Ethnicity, and Leisure Services: Can We Hope to Escape the Past?", David Scott examines how race and ethnicity affect North Americans' access to park and recreation services. He begins by describing how park and recreation agencies have historically positioned themselves vis-à-vis immigrants and people of color. He then summarizes research showing that people of color do not use public park and recreation resources to the same extent as Whites and do not enjoy the same access to public park and recreation services. Lastly, he explains how institutional barriers contribute to inequities in park and recreation service delivery and proposes how leisure service organizations can better serve people of color.

The focus of part II is extant scholarship on leisure among specific minority populations in the United States and Canada. In chapter 4 on leisure among African Americans, Myron F. Floyd and Rasul A. Mowatt examine historical and contemporary influences on leisure patterns among Black Americans; emerging issues related to the evolving social and demographic contexts of race relations in 21st-century American society that will affect future leisure research concerning Black Americans; current trends in theory and research related to Black leisure experiences; and emerging research needs associated with changing social and demographic contexts. In chapter 5 on leisure among Latino Americans, Monika Stodolska and Kimberly J. Shinew discuss the

history of the Latino immigration to the United States, provide information on the current and projected size of this group, and describe the cultural background of Latinos in the United States. They then provide a comprehensive overview of the history and current status of leisure research involving Latinos, including definitions and meanings of leisure, leisure participation preferences and styles, motivations for participation, and benefits of participation. The chapter also discusses factors responsible for unique leisure behavior patterns among Latinos (including culture and acculturation, access to recreation opportunities, socioeconomic disadvantage, discrimination, immigration experience, legality of status, and transnational arrangements).

In chapter 6 on leisure among Asian North Americans, Gordon J. Walker and Jinyang Deng analyze the term "Asian North American" and present demographics of this group in the United States and Canada. They then provide a comprehensive review of the history and current status of leisure research on Chinese and Korean North Americans, including the meaning of leisure, leisure attitudes, leisure needs and motivations, leisure participation, and leisure constraints. The authors also make intragroup comparisons of Asian North Americans' leisure and provide recommendations for future research and practice. In chapter 7, "Leisure Among Alaskan Natives, American Indians, First Nations, Inuit, Métis, Native Hawaiians, and Other Pacific Islanders," Karen Fox, Leo McAvoy, Xiye Wang, and Daniel A. Henhawk discuss the presence of and the terms used to refer to Indigenous peoples of North America and associated lands. They then examine the history, politics, economics, postcolonial forces, and outcomes of interactions between Euro-North Americans and Indigenous peoples and their effect on current leisure behavior and attitudes among this diverse group. They also identify challenges and conflicts facing Indigenous peoples and leisure practitioners and other professionals in the delivery of and participation in leisure. Lastly, they describe and summarize the rationale for holistic and collaborative approaches to future research and services focused on leisure and Indigenous peoples. Chapter 8, by Paul Heintzman and Monika Stodolska, explores leisure among religious minority groups, specifically focusing on the relationship between religion and leisure and on leisure behavior of Christian, Muslim, and Jewish minority groups in the United States and Canada. The review includes information on the size and cultural background of religious minority populations and suggestions for future research and practice.

Part III of the book examines specific topics and issues related to leisure behavior of ethnic and racial minorities: leisure needs and motivations, leisure constraints, and discrimination in leisure contexts. In chapter 9 on leisure needs and motivations, Gordon J. Walker describes what needs (e.g., autonomy, belonging, competence) and motivations (e.g., intrinsic, extrinsic) are and explains how these concepts are related. He also provides a comprehensive review of research on racial and ethnic similarities and differences in needs, motivations, and explanatory frameworks such as self-determination theory, and identifies specific leisure research areas or topics that are in particular need of further study. In chapter 10 on leisure constraints, Ingrid E. Schneider, Kimberly J. Shinew, and Mariela Fernandez provide an overview of definitions and models of constraints and negotiation strategies and review research on constraints among racially and ethnically diverse groups. This review specifically focuses on access to resources, immigration factors, and history and discrimination issues. The authors conclude by outlining implications for recreation managers. In chapter 11 on discrimination in leisure contexts, Iryna Sharaievska, Monika Stodolska, and Myron F. Floyd provide a brief overview of discrimination in the United States, define the terms racism and discrimination, including terms for different types of discrimination, and focus in detail on discrimination in leisure contexts. Their review examines types of discrimination experienced in leisure and responses to discrimination. The chapter concludes by providing recommendation for future research on discrimination in leisure.

In part IV, the focus is on special types of leisure and leisure settings. In chapter 12, "Wilderness in the U.S. Immigrant Mind," Cassandra Johnson-Gaither addresses immigrant interaction with wildlands and wilderness by examining the environmental worldviews of Latino and

Asian cultures in the United States. She provides an assessment of how congruent these various ontologies may be with North American ideals of nature interaction and preservation. The chapter ends with a discussion of the implications of growing diversity in American society for managing wildlands and wilderness. In chapter 13 on race, ethnicity, and physical activity, Kindal A. Shores and Kimberly J. Shinew provide an overview of research on leisure-time physical activity and discuss obesity as a public health concern in the United States. They then review conceptual models used to examine physical activity and focus in detail on research on leisure-time physical activity among African Americans, Latinos, and Asian North Americans. Chapter 14 on race, ethnicity, and sport, by Louis Harrison Jr. and Albert Y. Bimper Jr., provides a critical analysis of the persistent beliefs of racial superiority in sport. The chapter examines racial and ethnic sport participation patterns and provides an overview of theoretical frameworks and historical explanations for overrepresentation of African Americans in sport. The authors discuss the influence of stereotypes in sport, issues of identity as they relate to sport, socialization into sport, and activity choices and health. The chapter concludes with a discussion of future directions for research that would help elucidate the impact that race and ethnicity have on choices in sport leisure activities.

The last section of the book, part V, focuses on international perspectives and examines scholarship on racial and ethnic minorities in Europe, Australia and New Zealand, and East Asia. In chapter 15, "Research in Europe," Karin Peters provides an overview of the history of migration to Europe and the current status of ethnic and racial groups in the Netherlands, France, Great Britain, Germany, Sweden, and Denmark. She discusses the position of non-Western immigrants in Europe, including their socioeconomic, sociocultural, and spatial distribution. The main thrust of the chapter is on reviewing studies on leisure participation and behavior among minorities in the United Kingdom, Germany, the Netherlands, and the Scandinavian countries. The chapter ends with research and practical recommendations for the future. In chapter 16, "Research in Australia and New Zealand," Eva Hiu-Lun Tsai,

Grant Cushman, Bob Gidlow, and Michael Toohey review research related to leisure of Indigenous peoples and migrants in Australia and New Zealand. They examine the settlement histories, including changes in the ethnic populations of the two countries and their subsequent ethnic policies. The chapter provides an overview of leisure and sport participation patterns of Indigenous peoples and migrants, and also discusses the meanings and roles of traditional and modern Indigenous games, leisure, and sport. The review leads to recommendations for improving current practices to meet challenges in the management of leisure in multicultural communities and identifies gaps and limitations in the Australian and New Zealand ethnic leisure research. In chapter 17 on research in East Asia, Erwei Dong, Monica Li, and Junhyoung Kim provide an overview of the history of migration to East Asia and the current status of ethnic minority groups in China, Japan, and Korea; discuss the meanings of leisure in these three countries; and overview research on leisure of ethnic minority groups and immigrants in China, Japan, and Korea. The book's Conclusions chapter provides a summary of the existing knowledge on the topic and offers suggestions for future research.

THE BOOK'S CONTRIBUTORS

This book has been a collaborative project among 28 researchers representing six countries, Australia, Canada, China, the Netherlands, New Zealand, and the United States. Because of their vision, perseverance, and hard work, this project can be passed into the hands of faculty, students, and professionals interested in issues related to the leisure of racial and ethnic minorities. We hope that this project will be helpful in making a difference and that the day will come when the diversities of our cultures are embraced, animosities are forgotten, wrongs are remedied and forgiven, and we all get to enjoy the beauty and richness that leisure brings to our lives.

Theories, Methods, and Practice

This part of the book introduces and discusses the main theoretical frameworks, methods, and issues related to the provision of leisure services to racial and ethnic minority populations. The section consists of three chapters. Chapter 1 examines past and current theoretical approaches used to frame leisure research on race and ethnicity and discusses how these approaches have shaped the emergence of the subfield of ethnic–racial leisure research. The chapter also explores possibilities for and challenges related to the development of new theoretical approaches in the field. Chapter 2 analyzes the use of quantitative and qualitative methods to collect data in research on leisure among ethnic and racial minorities and discusses philosophical and methodological issues associated with conducting such research. Chapter 3 examines how race and ethnicity affect access to park and recreation services among residents in the United States and Canada. The chapter provides a historical overview of struggles that minorities have experienced with accessing park and recreation resources, examines research on minorities' use of and access to park and recreation resources, and explores how institutional barriers contribute to inequalities in service delivery.

CHAPTER 1

Theoretical Frameworks in Leisure Research on Race and Ethnicity

Myron F. Floyd and Monika Stodolska

OVERVIEW

With the growing diversity of societies around the world, this is an exciting time for those interested in the leisure behavior of ethnic and racial minorities. The purpose of this chapter is fourfold. One aim is to examine past and current theoretical approaches used to frame leisure research on race and ethnicity; another is to discuss how these approaches have shaped the emergence of the race and ethnicity subfield in leisure studies. The authors have also sought to identify opportunities for the development and application of new approaches to understanding race and ethnicity in leisure contexts. A final purpose is to speculate on challenges to theoretical development related to race and ethnicity in leisure.

Learning Outcomes

After reading this chapter, readers will be able to

- explain the major theories used to explain racial and ethnic variation in leisure behavior,
- describe strengths and limitations of the major theories used to study ethnicity in leisure, and
- identify emerging theories and new approaches for studying race and ethnicity in leisure contexts.

He who loves practice without theory is like the sailor who boards ship without a rudder and compass and never knows where he may cast.

Leonardo da Vinci

Turner (1986) defined theory as a process of developing ideas that help to explain "how and why events occur" (p. 4). Theoretical frameworks provide context for understanding data derived from empirical studies. They are useful for organizing research activities, including determining research questions, methods, and the variables in studies. This chapter presents the major theoretical perspectives used to explain and contextualize how and why race and ethnicity matter in leisure settings. Although theorizing on race and ethnicity and leisure has been criticized for failing to recognize the complexities of concepts such as *race* and *ethnicity* and how they intersect with broader social–cultural structures (Floyd, 1998; Hutchison, 1988; Kivel, Johnson, & Scraton, 2009; West, 1989), significant progress has occurred over the past four decades. The chapter highlights these developments as well as opportunities for improvements.

MARGINALITY AND ETHNICITY

The marginality–ethnicity framework represents the earliest theoretical perspective employed in leisure literature that focused specifically on understanding racial differences in leisure behavior (Washburne, 1978); this framework guided much of the empirical work of the 1970s and 1980s. With the aim of explaining differences in rates of wildland recreation participation between Whites and Black Americans, Washburne offered two perspectives with contrasting policy implications. These are presented separately here.

The Marginality Hypothesis

The marginality hypothesis held that low participation rates in wildland recreation activities among Black Americans were associated with limited access to socioeconomic resources (e.g., education and employment), which in turn resulted from past discrimination. The research community was receptive to this perspective mainly because the ramifications of de jure and de facto discrimination were blatantly obvious during the 1960s and 1970s. In addition, testing for marginality effects in recreation participation using indicators such as educational attainment, income, and access to transportation appeared to be straightforward. Typically, the marginality hypothesis was tested through comparison of rates of participation between Whites and African Americans while income, education, or other socioeconomic variables were controlled (Floyd, 1999; Johnson, Bowker, English, & Worthen, 1998). If any observed differences attenuated substantially or disappeared, this was treated as evidence of marginality effects, since the hypothesis assumes that intergroup differences can be explained by access to socioeconomic resources. Differences that might persist signaled that intergroup variation was associated with other factors.

Limitations of the marginality hypothesis are well documented. First, it does not explicate the processes related to how historical racism and discrimination influence contemporary behaviors and preferences. As a result, researchers have relied on use of proxy variables (i.e., substitute variables such as racial categories) that are actually poor representations of what Washburne originally articulated. Only recently have researchers attempted to go beyond racial categorical comparisons and incorporate historical race relations between Blacks and Whites and institutional discrimination into empirical studies (e.g., Arai & Kivel, 2009; Erickson, Johnson, & Kivel, 2009). Second, the marginality hypothesis does not recognize class differences within racial–ethnic groups (Floyd, 1998; Hutchison, 1988). Thus, it cannot account for intergroup variation (differences) when income or related factors are not a constraint to participation. Third, and similarly, the hypothesis does not account for intragroup variation associated with cultural factors (e.g., strength of ethnic identity, level of acculturation). Finally, and more recently, the assertion of race as a social construct (Floyd, 1998; Hylton, 2005) has focused attention on the need to deconstruct racial categories and group differences. This view, aligned with critical theory, holds that marginality does not provide necessary perspective for analyzing "structural inequalities, power, ideology, and white hegemony" (Kivel et al., 2009, p. 464).

The Ethnicity Hypothesis

Washburne offered the "ethnicity hypothesis" (also known as the subcultural hypothesis) as an alternative to marginality. To explain intergroup variation, it directs attention to cultural factors such as cultural norms, values systems, and socialization practices within racial–ethnic groups independent of socioeconomic status. As discussed by Floyd (1999), subcultural influences have been interpreted as "processes which lead to the preservation or maintenance of ethnic identity" (p. 4). The ethnicity hypothesis fits with established ideas about how cultural identity is expressed in leisure behavior (Allison, 1988). For example, Kelly (1987) suggested that because leisure is subject to fewer normative pressures to conform to external group standards, ethnic identity is more likely to be expressed in leisure than in other social settings. Empirical documentation of ethnicity effects relied on an indirect and imperfect analytical strategy. If differences in participation remained after socioeconomic factors were controlled, this was treated as evidence for ethnicity or subcultural effect (Floyd, Shinew, McGuire, & Noe, 1994; Johnson et al., 1998). While the hypothesis added cultural perspective, early studies failed to go further to identify specific aspects of ethnic culture that are associated with leisure participation. Additionally, the concepts of race and ethnicity often have been

confounded and used interchangeably. As a result, studies were not able to distinguish ethnic effects, stemming from social and cultural norms and mores (Stodolska & Jackson, 1998), from effects that are associated with race (e.g., discrimination based on skin tone). Another limitation of the ethnicity hypothesis, similar to the situation with the marginality hypothesis, was that it perpetuated "a static and monolithic view of minority groups" (Floyd, 1998, p. 6) by neglecting diversity within racial and ethnic minorities.

Subsequent theory development occurred as a reaction to the shortcomings of these perspectives as well as to changing demographics in the United States and Canada. In the United States, as Latino and Asian Americans became increasingly visible in public parks and forest recreation areas, researchers explored alternative theoretical perspectives to characterize the diversity in leisure styles (e.g., on-site behaviors, activity preferences) exhibited by members of these population groups, particularly new immigrants. Not only the participation, but also the types of and meanings associated with leisure activities began to draw academic attention.

ADAPTATION THEORIES

Several theoretical perspectives have been used to explain how processes involved in adapting to new cultural environments influence leisure behavior among immigrant groups. Four specific concepts have been applied in this regard: assimilation, acculturation, segmented assimilation, and selective acculturation.

Assimilation and Acculturation

Much of the research in the 1990s on ethnicity was informed by Gordon's (1964) theory of assimilation. His framework described the processes by which minority groups overcome cultural and structural impediments to enjoy full participation in society (Aguirre, Saenz, & Hwang, 1989). Among the key subprocesses he outlined were cultural assimilation (or acculturation) and structural assimilation. Cultural assimilation refers to minority group acquisition of dominant group cultural characteristics (e.g., language). Structural assimilation refers to the extent of social interaction between majority and minority group members in primary, face-to-face interactions (e.g., friendship and family) and in secondary social groups such as the workplace and community (Gordon, 1964). These two concepts have been employed in several studies in leisure research. For example, Floyd and Gramann (1993) and Carr and Williams (1993) used these concepts to examine outdoor recreation use patterns among Mexican Americans. Further, Carr and Williams demonstrated that acculturation was more advanced among Mexican Americans than among Central American forest visitors, even though the majority of both groups were foreign born. Such studies were important in shattering the perception that the "Hispanic population" was a monolithic group. This research also gave U.S. Forest Service resource managers important information for planning for Latino recreationists. For example, recreation use patterns among less acculturated Latinos reflected larger groups and more extended families than among other, more acculturated Latino users and non-Hispanic Whites.

Assimilation theory has also been used to describe discrimination experiences of immigrant groups in leisure settings. Floyd and Gramann (1995) applied this framework in a study of Mexican Americans in Arizona, and Stodolska and Jackson (1998) focused on perceived discrimination among Polish immigrants to Canada. Both studies suggested that because leisure activities and locations are often self-selected and "ethnically enclosed," which limits contact with other groups, ethnic minority groups may experience less discrimination during leisure than in other social settings such as work or school. At the same time, ethnic enclosure can be a coping strategy for avoiding leisure-related, work, and other discrimination in public places (Stodolska, 2007).

Segmented Assimilation and Selective Acculturation

Gordon (1964) noted that complete assimilation is not inevitable. Moreover, the idea of Anglo conformity—that is, that minority groups would lose their cultural distinctiveness—has received a lot of criticism (Alba & Nee, 1997), giving rise to different models for characterizing adaptation processes of immigrant groups (Portes & Zhou, 1993). For example, the concept of segmented assimilation suggests that because the United States is stratified socioeconomically and racially, multiple "assimilation outcomes" are possible (Portes & Rumbaut, 1996; Portes & Zhou, 1993). Selective acculturation refers to the strategic retention of core cultural values and practices among minority groups (Keefe & Padilla, 1987). According to Shaull and Gramann (1998), "[l]eisure behavior may be a major contributor to the selective–acculturation process" (p. 49).

Stodolska and Alexandris (2004), using segmented assimilation theory, examined the role of recreational sport participation in the adaptation of Korean immigrants. Their findings showed that Korean Americans followed three distinct patterns of adaptation: acculturation to the White mainstream, acculturation to the Korean American ethnic community, and preservation of their own ethnic traditions. Gramann and colleagues used selective acculturation to examine perceived benefits of outdoor recreation among Mexican Americans (Gramann, Floyd, & Saenz, 1993; Shaull & Gramann, 1998). Gramann et al. (1993) found that perceived benefits related to family cohesion were highly rated among Mexican Americans who exhibited the most acculturation compared to Anglo Americans and less acculturated Mexican Americans. They concluded that this finding followed a pattern of selective acculturation since many of the Mexican American respondents exhibited "substantial assimilation" on other cultural variables (e.g., language). In other words, it appeared that a core cultural value among Latinos—strong attachment to family—was resistant to assimilation pressures. In contrast, Shaull and Gramann's (1998) findings from California showed little support for a "selective acculturation" effect in perceived family-related benefits. They noted that the Latino community in central and southern California was large and well established, creating a more pluralistic condition in which Anglos and Latinos exhibited more similarity than difference.

TRANSNATIONALISM

A few investigations have examined the concept of transnationalism and its influence on leisure behaviors of immigrant groups. Transnationalism refers to sustained interaction and exchanges across borders through which immigrants maintain social networks in the "home and host" society. This perspective was introduced to leisure studies by Stodolska and Santos (2006) and Li and Stodolska (2006). In their study of temporary Mexican migrants, Stodolska and Santos identified several factors that conditioned the leisure of immigrants, including separation from family, unique work arrangements, their social and cultural networks, and legal status. The authors also contrasted the social structure of temporary migrants and permanent Mexican immigrants. For example, temporary migrants were mostly male and young. On the other hand, permanent immigrants arrived with nuclear and possibly extended families. These socioeconomic characteristics were some of the main determinants of differences in leisure behaviors between transnational and permanent immigrants. The authors proposed the concept of transnational leisure, defined as leisure maintained by temporary migrants to "foster their ties with their countries and communities of origin" (p. 162), to refer to how immigrants used their leisure efforts to stay connected to their families and home country. In their study of Chinese graduate students attending a U.S. university, Li and Stodolska (2006) found that the students' temporary residence and their desire to succeed in their studies were the major factors affecting their leisure. Specifically, leisure was limited given the higher priority placed on academic success and travel restrictions due to their legal status (e.g., visa restrictions).

ETHNIC BOUNDARY MAINTENANCE

The concept of ethnic boundary maintenance has appeal for understanding ethnic patterns in leisure behavior. However, it has received little research attention in the leisure studies literature. Boundary maintenance involves "a set of prescriptions governing situations of contact, and allowing for articulation in some sectors or domains of activity, and a set of proscriptions on social situations preventing interethnic interaction in other sectors, and thus insulating parts of the cultures from confrontation and modification" (Barth, 1969, p. 16). Boundary maintenance relates to two previously discussed concepts, the ethnicity hypothesis and selective acculturation. As Gramann and Allison (1999) and Gramann and colleagues (1993) suggested, leisure may play a role in creating and maintaining social boundaries between ethnic groups. Washburne and Wall (1980) introduced the idea that leisure activities and locations can be used by ethnic groups as a way to set themselves apart from other groups. Furthermore, leisure activities and settings might be defined as inappropriate because they do not reinforce an ethnic group's collective identity (Floyd, 1999). Such ideas present possibilities for investigating conditions under which leisure is more or less salient in boundary maintenance processes. Data reported by Stodolska and Jackson (1998) and Stodolska (2007) suggest that discrimination experiences lead to ethnically enclosed leisure (locations and activities). Given the close association between boundary maintenance and the ethnicity hypothesis, the lack of development around this association is surprising and unfortunate.

DISCRIMINATION THEORY

It is generally assumed that actual or perceived discrimination is a constraint to participation in certain activities or use of particular locations. Unlike the marginality hypothesis, which references historical discrimination, more recent studies examine contemporary sources of discrimination affecting minority groups associated with interactions between ethnic groups or institutions. West (1989) can be credited with providing the first empirical analysis of the effect of discrimination in leisure. Over the last two decades, a number of studies have documented perceived discrimination against racial and ethnic minority groups in urban parks (Blahna & Black, 1993; Gobster & Delgado, 1993; Sharaievska,

Stodolska, Shinew, & Kim, 2010; West, 1989), national forest recreation areas (Chavez, 1993; Johnson et al., 1998), and golf courses (Gobster, 1998). Researchers have also shown how discrimination affects quality of leisure experiences (Livengood & Stodolska, 2004; Philipp, 1995), choices of recreation settings (Johnson et al., 1998; West, 1989), and choices of coparticipants (Livengood & Stodolska, 2004). Discrimination against racial and ethnic minority groups in public recreation settings has also been thoroughly documented through historical analysis (Murphy, 1972; Woodward, 1974). Specific models to explain discrimination experiences in leisure were developed by Floyd and colleagues (1993), Gómez (2002), and Stodolska (2005).

Using the concept of social distance (Bogardus, 1933) and behavioral receptional assimilation (Gordon, 1964), Floyd and colleagues (1993) hypothesized that decreased social distance between Mexican Americans and Anglo Americans increased the likelihood of visiting national parks, forest recreation areas, and city parks in the Phoenix area. Social distance indicators were perceived discrimination, socioeconomic status, and acculturation. Educational attainment (one aspect of socioeconomic status) was the most consistent predictor of outdoor recreation use. Perceived discrimination was not significant across 13 recreation settings studied. However, a subsequent analysis found that perceived discrimination was more likely to be reported among Mexican Americans with higher levels of educational attainment and acculturation (Floyd & Gramann, 1995). This finding is consistent with the ethnic competition hypothesis articulated by Portes (1984). This view holds that minority group members' movement from ethnic enclaves and neighborhoods, as well as socioeconomic mobility, leads to greater awareness of cultural differences and heightened awareness of discrimination.

Perceived discrimination was also examined as a component of Gómez's Ethnicity and Public Recreation Participation (EPRP) Model (Gómez, 2002) and Stodolska's (2005) Conditioned Attitude Model of Individual Discriminatory Behavior that will be described later in this chapter. Despite numerous studies examining perceived discrimination and attempts to develop conceptual models

of individual-level discrimination, relatively less effort has been directed toward exploring institutional discrimination and racism (see chapters 3 and 11 on leisure services and discrimination in leisure contexts, respectively).

MULTIPLE STRATIFICATION HIERARCHY THEORY

One of the limitations of the marginality hypothesis (Washburne, 1978) is that it overlooks class differences within minority groups. In addition, with few exceptions (e.g., Floyd et al., 1993, Gómez, 2006; Gómez & Malega, 2007), studies on race and ethnicity do not consider how multiple sources of stratification (e.g., class, gender, age) along with race and ethnicity affect leisure behavior among racial and ethnic minorities. Building on theory from social gerontology (Markides, Liang, & Jackson, 1990), several studies over the past two decades have applied the multiple stratification hierarchy perspective to examine how combined sources of disadvantaged statuses condition various domains of leisure behavior. Specifically, the multiple stratification hierarchy theory (MSHP) is an extension of the double-jeopardy hypothesis developed to examine the effect of race–ethnicity and age on quality of life among older adults. According to the double-jeopardy hypothesis, members of racial–ethnic minority groups who are of older age face a double disadvantage with respect to access to societal benefits and rewards (e.g., housing, health care, leisure resources) (Markides et al., 1990). Inclusion of additional stratification factors presents an opportunity to examine how membership in multiple disadvantaged statuses associates with leisure behaviors (e.g., low income, female, minority, older adult). Following this approach, leisure researchers have applied the multiple stratification hierarchy perspective in analyses of activity preferences and participation (Cutler, Riddick, & Stewart, 1994; Shinew, Floyd, McGuire, & Noe, 1995), leisure benefits (Philipp, 1997), visitation to local and state parks (Lee, Scott, & Floyd, 2001), constraints to park use (Arnold & Shinew, 1998; Shores, Scott, & Floyd, 2007), and participation in fishing- and wildlife-related recreation (Floyd, Nicholas, Lee, Lee, & Scott, 2006; Lee & Scott,

2011). In general, findings from these studies follow predictions of the MSHP. Variables indicating disadvantaged statuses were associated with lower probability of participation and increased likelihood of leisure constraints. The studies also suggest that the combined or cumulative effect of stratification variables exerts more influence on leisure constraints and participation than their separate effects.

Although the MSHP offers a way to consider race and ethnicity in relation to other stratification variables, findings have been most robust when the high and low ends of the MSHP continuum have been contrasted. For example, differences in the probability of state park visits are usually observable when White men of upper income and younger age are compared to lower-income African American women who are older adults (e.g., Lee et al., 2001). The theory is less precise about occupants of middle strata (e.g., older, lower-income White males). Researchers have also not considered how multiple sources of disadvantage affect domains of leisure behavior over the life course. Current applications of the perspective occur in cross-sectional studies with age as a predictor variable. Thus, the extent to which race and ethnicity and other stratification variables change in their effect on leisure over the life course is unknown.

THE CONDITIONED ATTITUDE MODEL OF INDIVIDUAL DISCRIMINATORY BEHAVIOR AND THE ETHNICITY AND PUBLIC RECREATION PARTICIPATION MODEL

Two theoretical frameworks have been developed *within* the leisure studies field with the study of leisure among racial and ethnicity minorities specifically in mind. Stodolska's (2005) Conditioned Attitude Model of Individual Discriminatory Behavior focused on the decision-making process leading to discrimination against minority groups. It conceptualized discrimination as a sequential process consisting of three stages. First, a person uses her information set to derive beliefs about a group or an evaluation of its characteristics. Second, she combines these beliefs with any new information received about a group and forms an attitude that signifies the degree of hostility or a favorable attitude toward the group members. Lastly, she weighs benefits and consequences of discrimination and chooses whether or not to engage in a discriminatory behavior. Based on the predictions of the model, Stodolska proposed several policy recommendations aimed at reduction of discrimination in leisure settings.

The other theoretical framework, the Ethnicity and Public Recreation Participation (EPRP) Model, was developed by Gómez (2002). Gómez conducted an extensive review and synthesis of theories and models applied to recreation and leisure participation among racial and ethnic minority groups. Five major concepts were distilled from the review and synthesis and incorporated into the EPRP: acculturation, socioeconomic status, subcultural identify, recreation benefits, and perceived discrimination. The model did not include other key variables representing social group influences, place variables (e.g., place of residence or place perception), gender, or age.

In the EPRP model, perceived discrimination was treated as a mediating variable between subcultural identity and recreation participation, and between socioeconomic status and participation. Using a sample of respondents with Puerto Rican ancestry, an empirical test of the model showed that perceived discrimination exerted a direct and negative effect on perceived benefits rather than a direct effect on participation (Gómez, 2006). Similarly, Gómez and Malega (2007) reported that increased perceived discrimination was associated with perceptions of fewer benefits from using public parks. These findings highlight the importance of specifying how perceived discrimination conditions leisure experiences.

SELF-CONSTRUAL

Gordon J. Walker

Self-construal refers to how a person thinks about himself in relation to others. Markus and Kitayama (1991) proposed two main types of self-construal: (a) *independent (or individualistic),* in which one endorses being unique, asserting oneself, expressing one's inner attributes, and promoting one's own goals; and (b) *interdependent (or collectivistic)*, in which one endorses belonging, fitting in, maintaining harmony, restraining oneself, and promoting others' goals. Research (Coon & Kemmelmeier, 2001) has indicated that African and Asian Americans are higher in collectivism compared with European Americans, with some studies (e.g., Freeberg & Stein, 1996) suggesting that Latino Americans are also more likely to endorse this type of self-construal than European Americans. Interestingly, Coon and Kemmelmeier found that African Americans were also higher in individualism than Asian and European Americans. Although it may initially seem incongruent that African Americans are both more individualistic *and* collectivistic than European Americans, this could reflect two different ways in which the former group has endeavored to deal with systemic racial discrimination.

Triandis (1995) largely concurred with Markus and Kitayama's (1991) conceptualization of self-construal, although he felt that equality (i.e., the belief that people are equal in status) and hierarchy (i.e., the belief that people differ in status, and that rank has its privileges) were also major factors. Thus, he proposed four main types of self-construal: (a) *vertical collectivism* (i.e., hierarchy and interdependence); (b) *horizontal collectivism* (i.e., equality and interdependence); (c) *horizontal individualism* (i.e., equality and independence); and (d) *vertical individualism* (i.e., hierarchy and independence). A study (Su & Hynie, 2011) of Chinese and European Canadian mothers found that the former group endorsed vertical individualism and vertical collectivism more than the latter group. Moreover, another study (Hunter & Joseph, 2010) discovered intragroup differences in self-construal among African Americans. For example, one group of African Americans (i.e., multiculturalists) was found to endorse horizontal collectivism more than three other groups of African Americans. This finding led the researchers to suggest that "members of the multicultural group feel a sense of attachment and interdependence toward both in-group and out-group members" (Hunter & Joseph, p. 500).

Self-construal is important because it can affect people's needs and motivations (Markus & Kitayama, 1991; Triandis, 1995)—including during their leisure (Kleiber, Walker, & Mannell, 2011). (The role of self-construal is discussed further in chapter 9.) Walker, Deng, and Dieser (2001) examined the effect of self-construal on the expressed leisure needs of Chinese Canadian and Euro-North American outdoor recreationists. The results led the researchers to state that, rather than ethnicity *directly* affecting the perceived importance of most expressed needs, it generally did so *indirectly,* in one of three ways. Either (a) ethnicity affected independence, which in turn influenced the importance of a need; (b) it affected interdependence, which in turn influenced the importance of a need; or (c) it affected both types of self-construal, and both in turn influenced a need's importance. For example, Chinese Canadians were found to be more interdependent than Euro-North Americans; and this, in turn, meant that members of the former group were more likely to rate social security, group autonomy, group membership, humility or modesty, attention to others, and respect for or sensitivity to others higher than members of the latter group.

Walker and Virden (2005) proposed that because self-construal impacts needs and motivations during leisure, it likely affects constraints to leisure as well. Although cross-cultural support for this proposition has existed for some time (Walker, Jackson, & Deng, 2008), only one study to date has examined the influence of ethnicity and self-construal on leisure constraints. Hudson et al. (2013) found that both Chinese- and Anglo-Canadian skiers who endorsed horizontal collectivism reported lower levels of intrapersonal and interpersonal constraints. Hudson and associates speculated that this might be because this type of self-construal emphasizes equality, cooperation, and social cohesion and all factors that seem congruent with a concept called "interpersonal compatibility and coordination" in the hierarchical constraints model (Crawford, Jackson, & Godbey, 1991). Thus, it appears that the self-construal framework could contribute to our broader understanding of ethnic and racial similarities and differences in leisure.

EMERGING FRAMEWORKS

Recent efforts to steer theorizing about race and ethnicity in leisure in new directions are informed by the theory of planned behavior, social and cultural capital theories, and critical race theory. The strongest critiques of theories of race–ethnicity and leisure originate with proponents of critical perspectives.

Theory of Planned Behavior

Although Ajzen's (1991) theory of planned behavior (TPB) has been used frequently in research on leisure behavior and physical activity (e.g., Blanchard et al., 2004, 2007; Nigg, Lippke, & Maddock, 2009), Walker, Courneya, and Deng (2006) have been the first and the only leisure researchers so far to employ it to examine the behavior of minority populations. Walker and colleagues examined motivations for playing the lottery and ethnic and gender-based differences in the TPB constructs. They proposed seven hypotheses to examine why some Chinese Canadians and British Canadians play the lottery. Their findings showed that injunctive norm (i.e., normative beliefs about what others think one should do and motivation to comply) was an important predictor for playing the lottery for Chinese Canadian males and that controllability was an important predictor for Chinese Canadian females. The authors concluded that the study supported the cross-cultural applicability of the TBP and that TPB constructs vary in importance for different ethnic–racial groups.

Social Capital Theory

Social capital theory appears throughout the social sciences as a framework to understand social structures and social networks and how they facilitate purposive action (Glover, 2004). Social capital can be defined as the resources (tangible or symbolic) embedded in social networks that can be used to achieve individual or collective goals (Lin, 2002; Portes, 1998; Putnam, 2000). Researchers applying social capital theory to race–ethnicity and leisure have addressed two primary concerns: (1) the potential of public leisure spaces to bridge racial divides and promote social capital (Shinew, Glover, & Parry, 2004) and (2) the extent to which social capital is equally distributed and how its distribution associates with racial inequality (Glover, 2004).

Although Shinew and colleagues (2004) did not frame their study in terms of social capital, their findings demonstrated that public community gardens provided neighborhood spaces for increasing neighborhood cohesion, fostering friendships between African Americans and Whites, and thus offering opportunities to build social capital. In his study of community gardeners, Glover (2004) reported both positive and negative outcomes related to social capital. He observed that the gardening network was organized by race and socioeconomic status and that these factors led to differential access to social capital, creating advantaged and disadvantaged positions among the gardeners. Those in disadvantaged positions were not able to "appropriate resources associated with the garden network" (p. 157) such as keeping keys to locked garden gates and having meaningful influence in the decision making about the garden.

Cultural Capital Theory

Cultural capital is another form of social capital recently employed to frame a study of race and leisure. Associated with the writings of Pierre Bourdieu (e.g., Bourdieu, 1986), cultural capital consists of knowledge, skills, education, and "material objects and media (e.g., writing, paintings, monuments, instruments, etc.)" (p. 50) that convey higher social status. Erickson, Johnson, and Kivel (2009) used Bourdieu's concepts of cultural capital and habitus as the theoretical basis for understanding nonvisitation to Rocky Mountain National Park among African American residents of Denver. Erickson and colleagues described the cultural and historical context surrounding local African Americans' relationship to Rocky Mountain National Park. They reported that African Americans were not frequent visitors to the park because the idea of visiting national parks was not something passed down from their parents, because memories of and experience with legal segregation still existed, and because recreating in "the outdoors" held negative connotations (e.g., lynching and rural servitude). The authors concluded that "the cultural capital learned as a result of years of historical oppression" (p. 543) helped shape the current recreational preferences and behavior among the study participants. While others have made similar observations (e.g., Meeker, Woods, & Lucas, 1973; Taylor, 1989), Erickson and colleagues offered a compelling alternative account by linking their analysis to broader socio-historical, economic, and political contexts associated with the local Black community and the national parks.

Critical Race Theory

At its core, critical race theory (CRT) represents an aggressive and "unapologetic focus on 'race,' racism and anti-subordination" (Hylton, 2005) or (anti)racism (Arai & Kivel, 2009). According to Glover (2007), three principles guide CRT research:

1. Recognition of race as a social construct rather than as biological given

2. Rejection of the notion of a color-blind society in which merit supplants race in distribution of societal rewards and privileges

3. Preference for a "racial epistemology that privileges story telling" by minority communities (p. 197) over traditional social science epistemologies that reproduce dominant discourses and maintain "hegemonic order" (p. 917)

Glover's (2007) study of racism in youth baseball is one of a few empirical studies to apply CRT in leisure studies. Glover examined the formation of an urban recreational baseball league that was intentionally created to provide opportunities for African American youth. His interviews with league founders revealed the type of encounters with park agency youth leagues that led to the formation of a separate African American league. For example, teams were selected by a draft system, which often meant that there was only one Black youth on a team; games and practices

were located outside of Black neighborhoods; and Black role models (coaches and instructors) were often lacking. Furthermore, the idea of separate neighborhood teams that would be all Black was strongly resisted by the park agency. In his analysis, Glover examined what was generally perceived as a color-blind, fair, and open system (little league baseball) and exposed a set of racist practices that ultimately "privilege(d) white youth while disadvantaging youth of color" (p. 195). Consistent with CRT, he used the findings to argue for a new model for distributing youth sport programs to address these constraints. His theoretical and methodological approach (e.g., use of storytelling) provided an example of how CRT can be used to identify and reform racist practices in leisure services.

CONCLUSION

This review indicates that two theoretical approaches (marginality and ethnicity) (Washburne, 1978) dominated much of the research on leisure behavior of ethnic and racial minorities. It was not until the early to mid-1990s that researchers began to look to disciplines such as sociology, psychology, and ethnic studies for other frameworks that may be helpful in modeling leisure of minority populations. The decade of the 1990s was dominated by the assimilationist frameworks, and it has been only within the last 10 to 13 years that more contemporary approaches to ethnicity and race have begun to be incorporated.

One could argue that we have made progress in the theoretical sophistication of the subfield but still there is a long way to go. In particular, researchers need to ensure that they pay particular attention to cutting-edge developments in the cognate disciplines (e.g., sociology, psychology, ethnic studies, geography) so that their research is informed by up-to-date discourses in other social sciences. Calls for the development of unique theoretical frameworks particular to the entire field are not new, and such work would certainly enhance the credibility of ethnic leisure research. Future advances in theory development related to race and ethnicity will also depend on the ability to synthesize existing frameworks within the field. This creative task would be one strategy to develop perspectives for understanding the racial and ethnic dynamic in leisure contexts. According to Crawford and Jackson (2005, p. 161), one "desirable characteristic of theory is that it be *integrative*—that it bring together its constructs and statements in coherent fashion." The next decade would seem to be particularly conducive to the incorporation, or perhaps development, of such novel theoretical frameworks as increased globalization, realignment of the existing racial and ethnic hierarchy, and shifting migration patterns may call for new ways of understanding the dynamics of leisure behavior of minority populations.

CHAPTER 2

Ethnic and Racial Research Methods

Karla A. Henderson and Gordon J. Walker

OVERVIEW

Most disciplines—including the subfield of race, ethnicity, and leisure—face methodological problems and challenges. The good news is that such challenges open up many opportunities for creativity and innovation. Thus, this chapter begins by briefly explaining what research is and the various types (e.g., exploratory, descriptive, explanatory, predictive) and methods (e.g., quantitative, qualitative) that exist. The use of quantitative (e.g., mail, on-site surveys) and qualitative (e.g., in-depth interviews, focus groups) methods to collect data, using examples from earlier race, ethnicity, and leisure research studies are examined next. The future of quantitative (e.g., experience sampling method, multilevel linear modeling) and qualitative (e.g., participatory inquiry, creative analytic practice) race, ethnicity, and leisure research is subsequently considered, including a special section on mixed methods. Discussion then ends by outlining four conclusions reached after discussing this chapter.

Learning Outcomes

After reading this chapter, readers will be able to

- articulate what is meant by the term *research* and the various paradigms and approaches that can guide it;
- explain the different types of methods that have been used in past research on race, ethnicity, and leisure, and the adequacies and inadequacies of this research; and
- design and implement better qualitative and quantitative studies on this topic in the future.

From this analysis . . . a perspective can be offered on how methods have structured the literature and what methodological strategies are needed to advance the literature.

Floyd, Bocarro, and Thompson (2008, p. 4)

In their comprehensive review of race, ethnicity, and leisure articles, Floyd, Bocarro, and Thompson (2008) found that quantitative methods were predominant. They recognized that studies using quantitative approaches possessed some inherent benefits (which will be outlined later in this chapter), but they reiterated other researchers' (e.g., Allison, 1988) proposition that qualitative approaches might provide more contextually rich data. Based on this chapter's quote, the chapter focuses on the methods that have been employed in the past and presents recommendations regarding methods that can be used in the future. But first it is important to understand what research is and what can guide it.

WHAT IS RESEARCH?

Research is a systematic process of discovering and interpreting data to understand reality. The goal of social research is to discover, understand, and communicate truths about people in society. Research may be exploratory (i.e., what is happening?), descriptive (i.e., what are the salient behaviors?), explanatory (i.e., what is shaping a behavior and why?), or predictive (i.e., what will occur in the future?) (Babbie, 2003). Further, research should lead to knowledge about the realities of the world. These perceptions of reality are socially constructed, and research provides a process for analyzing reality in all its dimensions, including aspects related to race, ethnicity, and leisure behavior.

The dimensions surrounding research are the nature of truth (i.e., ontology) and the ways in which truth is known (i.e., epistemology; Henderson, 2006). Social research involves ontological paradigmatic issues as well as epistemological methodological approaches. To understand race and ethnicity more fully, different methodologically innovative approaches are necessary. In leisure studies during the past 20 years, both quantitative and qualitative approaches have been used to ascertain truths about leisure behavior and how people experience it based on markers such as race or ethnicity.

Henderson (2006) saw these approaches to research as *yin-yang*—the symbol of polar energies in harmony with one another. Within every aspect of life, a counterforce interacts with a major force to create a balance. This interdependency appears to exist between the ontology and epistemology associated with research. Although some argue that this dualism is outmoded, the contrast of qualitative and quantitative approaches offers ways to think about how to understand race and ethnicity relative to leisure behavior. The focus is not on quantitative *versus* qualitative approaches but on how both approaches might enable people to arrive at truths in multiple ways. The worldview or paradigm held, the general approaches to research design chosen, and the specific methods applied must all be considered in any research project undertaken in the study of race and ethnicity related to leisure behavior.

PARADIGMS AND APPROACHES TO STUDYING RACE AND ETHNICITY

A paradigm describes ontology or the nature of the social world. Paradigms fundamentally provide a model that organizes a view of something. The two dominant paradigms (i.e., the yin and yang) that have provided a basis for leisure studies are positivism and interpretive social science. These two have typically been considered opposites in many ways. In reality, much of the research done today might be better termed postpositivist because elements of both paradigms might be used (Henderson, 2011). Much of the meaningful research, especially on a fluid topic like race and ethnicity, demonstrates the importance of using the strengths of both worldviews in a given study.

Traditionally, positivism has meant seeking facts or causes of social phenomena with the idea that truth can be obtained objectively and that it is singular and external to the individual. Interpretivism enables researchers to examine themselves subjectively in relation to others to describe and explain how ideas reflect the social reality of the world. The assumptions of the interpretive paradigm are that meanings are important, social behavior can best be understood in its natural environment, reality is the meanings attributed to experiences, and social reality is not the same for all people (Bullock, 1983). Postpositivism is emerging in a number of disciplines as a means to understand and interpret research. Postpositivism provides a paradigm that can move positivism from a narrow perspective into a more encompassing way to examine real-world problems (Henderson, 2011) and an opportunity to enhance social justice within communities (Parry, Johnson, & Stewart, 2013). It emphasizes meanings, not unlike interpretivism, but also seeks to bring together theory and practice and the possibilities for using mixed and multiple methods (Ryan, 2006). As a third integrative paradigm, postpositivism allows for a broader yet more targeted view of any topic.

Henderson (2006) used the term *approaches* to refer to the foundations or traditions of applying methods to conduct research. Approaches describe epistemology or the science of knowing. They encompass the assumptions, interests, and purposes that shape the way research questions are addressed. The epistemological categories for research have typically been described as quantitative and qualitative. Quantitative approaches emerge almost solely from the positivist worldview and involve the testing of theory, the use of controlled data collection, and an analysis using statistics. Qualitative approaches are usually interpretive or postpositivist and expropriate emerging research designs, use the natural environment, focus on determining the meaning attached to phenomena, acknowledge the researcher as the instrument in interaction with the phenomena being studied, and use words as the primary symbols for generating emerging theory specific to the

context in which the research occurs. Qualitative approaches used in much of the leisure research have tended to be postpositivist. Further, many traditions might constitute a particular qualitative epistemology (e.g., phenomenology, ethnography, case study; Creswell, 1998).

Methodology is the science of finding out (Babbie, 2003). Methods are used to denote specific procedures such as surveys, interviews, or observations. These methods might be used to collect qualitative or quantitative data. Techniques involve the specific tasks undertaken to discover and interpret data within a given method. Methods are neither qualitative nor quantitative but depend on how data are used. Regardless of the method used, the bottom line is whether or not the research makes something more understandable. Therefore, different paradigms, approaches, methods, and strategies are needed to understand the meanings of leisure behavior as experienced by individuals and communities comprising people with diverse racial and ethnic identities.

PAST QUANTITATIVE RESEARCH USED TO STUDY RACE, ETHNICITY, AND LEISURE

The comprehensive review mentioned earlier (Floyd et al., 2008), of five leading North American leisure research journals, showed that less than 5% of all published articles were related to race and ethnicity. Moreover, slightly less than half of these used quantitative methods, primarily mail and telephone surveys (35%), followed by on-site surveys (7%) and then secondary data analyses (4%). The remainder of this section identifies some of the key quantitative race, ethnicity, and leisure studies that have been conducted to date, as well as some of the major issues associated with conducting quantitative research.

Floyd and colleagues (2008) held that the benefit of quantitative methods included standardization of measures, identification of causal factors, and wider generalization of findings. Barnett's (2005) study of four aspects of the leisure experience (i.e., awareness, boredom, challenge, and distress), using an on-site survey distributed to African, Asian, European, and Hispanic American undergraduate students, is a good example of measure standardization. Barnett examined the psychometric properties of the four corresponding scales, including their internal consistency (based on Cronbach's coefficient alphas) and their distinctiveness (using principal components analysis). Results of these statistical analyses led her to conclude that the scales and their associated items were applicable for all four racial and ethnic groups.

Another on-site study, this one with Chinese and European Canadian park visitors, illustrated both the difficulties that can arise when only traditional measures are used and the insights that can be gained through examination of previously untested causal factors. Walker, Deng, and Dieser (2001) proposed that (a) cultural groups can hold different perceptions about what the appropriate relationship is between an individual and others (or what Markus & Kitayama, 1991, called *self-construals*); and (b) depending on the type of self-construal a person has, his motives for engaging in leisure can differ. On the basis of

these two propositions the researchers developed five new social interdependence (SI) scales, which they believed were more consistent with Chinese Canadians' *interdependent* self-construals. These scales complemented four recreation experience preference scales (REP; Driver, 1977), which they believed were more congruent with Euro-Canadians' *independent* self-construals. According to Walker and colleagues, the SI results suggested that leisure researchers should use caution when considering employing quantitative measures previously used with only majority group recreationists. On the other hand, a series of regressions revealed that although ethnicity did influence some of the SI and REP motivations directly, these effects were often mediated by self-construal. This finding not only supported the idea of future research using this concept, but also addressed calls (e.g., Hutchison, 2000) for more research on the variables that intervene between ethnicity, race, and leisure.

Quantitative studies, which often focus on participation and visitation rates, can result in the standardization of measures, identification of causal factors, and wider generalization of findings.

© Terry Wild Stock

Other leisure scholars (e.g., Floyd, 1998) have recommended that instead of focusing on one or two intermediary factors, researchers need stronger theoretical frameworks. In the leisure field, for instance, Gómez (2002, 2006) created and tested the Ethnicity and Public Recreation Participation (EPRP) Model. Using mail surveys sent to Puerto Ricans living in the United States, he found that acculturation affected recreation participation both directly and indirectly through socioeconomic status and subcultural identity more proximally, and perceived benefits and perceived discrimination more distally (see chapter 1 on theoretical frameworks). Rather than develop new leisure-specific schemes, other researchers have examined how more generic theories work in the leisure domain and with different ethnic and racial group members. For example, using the theory of planned behavior (TPB; Ajzen, 1991), Walker, Courneya, and Deng (2006) conducted a telephone survey of British and Chinese Canadians to learn more about their attitudes toward, subjective norms regarding, and perceived behavioral control over playing the lottery (see chapter 1). Their results suggested that while TPB overall is potentially applicable across ethnic and racial groups, differences in how its variables are valued, and perhaps even related, could exist. Similarly, with self-determination theory (SDT; Deci & Ryan, 1985), Walker (2008) found that Chinese Canadians were more intrinsically motivated (i.e., interested, joyful) when they participated in leisure activities than when they were doing work-related, unpaid work, or self-care activities. These results, in conjunction with comparable findings in a study of Canadian and Mainland Chinese students (Walker & Wang, 2008), led Walker to conclude that though SDT overall is potentially applicable across ethnic and racial groups, differences in how motivations are valued, and perhaps even conceptualized, could exist.

Another attribute of quantitative research that Floyd and colleagues (2008) identified was generalizability. A quantitative study's generalizability can be evaluated based on how well three questions are answered (Brewer, 2000): *Is it representative? Can it be replicated? And does it matter?* The first question concerns ecological validity, or whether an association or mean difference occurs under *real-world* conditions (Brewer, 2000). This concern is key in mainstream psychology because laboratory-based studies are common. However, this type of study is rare in leisure research (Kleiber, Walker, & Mannell, 2011) and nonexistent in racial and ethnic leisure research (Floyd et al., 2008). Arguably, ecological validity is less a concern for on-site surveys. Mail and telephone surveys, which are typically answered in a person's home, fall somewhere in between the artificiality of a lab and the reality of an individual's social world.

An additional issue related to generalizability in quantitative research is robustness, or whether an association or mean difference replicates across people, groups, and contexts (Brewer, 2000). This issue is important in quantitative leisure research because (a) the practice of using nonrandom samples, for example when undergraduate students, recreation participants, or park visitors are selected based on convenience, is common; and (b) there is inherent difficulty in determining what exactly constitutes a group in terms of either its boundaries, its characteristics, or both. Regarding the first issue, Visser, Krosnick, and Lavrakas (2000) admonished that random sampling (i.e., in which everyone has the same chance of being chosen) is required before an outcome can be generalized to the entire population. Similarly, stratified random sampling (i.e., in which everyone in a stratum has the same chance of being chosen) is required before an outcome can be generalized to the entire group. Li and associates (2007) reiterated this point in stating that because few leisure studies have used random samples, "generalization of results is difficult, if not impossible. Nevertheless, authors tend to state their results as if they are generalizable to the ethnic groups in question" (p. 537). Concerning the second issue, quantitative leisure researchers typically have participants report their self-identity by using either a question composed of limited commonly accepted categories (e.g., those listed in the census) or an open-ended question. The former is advantageous in that comparability across studies is possible, whereas the latter is useful because of its specificity (e.g., a person can select Vietnamese Chinese American). However, both may lump people together either initially (e.g., by providing only an Asian category) or subsequently if a researcher has to construct larger groups (e.g., by combining Chinese, Japanese, and Koreans into an Asian category) to perform the planned statistical analyses.

A related concern is what characteristics actually make a group a group and thus distinct from other groups. Li and colleagues (2007) employed cultural consensus analyses (CCA) to examine whether Anglo, Hispanic, and Asian Americans, as well as some of the subgroups within these larger groups, were distinguishable based on four of Hofstede's (1980) value dimensions. From the 12 CCAs conducted, only Hispanic Americans overall, the two subgroups within this group (i.e., Hispanic and Mexican Americans), and Vietnamese Americans were deemed *culturally homogeneous* by the researchers. By empirically demonstrating within-group homogeneity, quantitative ethnic and racial leisure researchers may be better able to answer Brewer's (2000) "Can it be replicated?" question. As a result, some of the conflicting research findings commonly found in the leisure field may be avoided, according to Li and colleagues.

The final question speaks to relevance. In its broader sense, relevance concerns whether an association or mean difference is "potentially useful or applicable to solving problems or improving quality of life" (Brewer, 2000, p. 12). Gobster (2002) found that 1 in 10 visitors to Chicago's Lincoln Park reported discrimination, with the perpetrators largely perceived to be other users and police officers (see chapter 11 on discrimination in leisure contexts). He added that although discrimination was a sensitive issue and therefore difficult to address in an on-site survey, "it is likely . . . that the findings identified the principal sources and types of discrimination, and that park managers can begin to take positive steps to counteract some of them" (p. 156).

A quantitative study's relevance, however, can also be evaluated more narrowly in terms of its practical significance. "Statistical significance is concerned with whether a research result is due to chance or sampling variability; practical significance is concerned with whether the result is useful in the real world" (Kirk, 1996, p. 746). The importance of reporting and interpreting a study's practical significance—or what is also referred to as explained variance or effect size—has long

been recognized in the leisure studies field generally (Smale, 1996) and, more recently, in the race, ethnicity, and leisure area specifically (Li et al., 2007). Unfortunately, Li and colleagues identified a number of ethnic and racial leisure studies that focused on statistically significant group differences at the expense of explained variance. In most of these cases, the problem did not appear to be that the amount of explained variance was not reported. Rather, because the magnitude of the effect size was not properly interpreted, practical significance was exaggerated.

Cohen (1992) provided a useful heuristic for appraising effect size (ES). A medium ES represents an effect that is visible to an expert's naked eye. A small ES is noticeably smaller but not trivial, and a large ES shows the same distance above a medium ES that a small ES is below it. Other ES measures exist (Kirk, 1996), but, regardless of which metric is selected, race and ethnic leisure researchers should remember that "For the reader to appreciate the magnitude or importance of a study's findings, it is almost always necessary to include some measure of effect size" (American Psychological Association, 2009, p. 34). Matsumoto, Kim, Grissom, and Dinnel (2011) concurred; however, they also contended that it is ultimately the reader who must decide whether a study's results are, or are not, meaningful.

Li and colleagues (2007) described a related methodological concern. The more multiple comparisons conducted (e.g., a chi-square test, *t*-test, or analysis of variance or multiple analysis of variance test), the more likely that a Type I error (i.e., finding a statistically significant difference by chance) will occur. Use of the Bonferroni procedure (i.e., dividing $p < .05$ by the number of comparisons and then using this new alpha level) is one way of dealing with this issue. As Li and associates added, however, this procedure can lead to the occurrence of a Type II error (i.e., not identifying a difference that does, in fact, exist). Moreover, Gregoire and Driver (1987) proposed that this type of error was sometimes preferable, at least in the exploratory stage of research. Because of these conflicting viewpoints, we suggest that, at a minimum, race and ethnic leisure researchers should describe how and why they did—or did not—deal with Type I and II errors when they conduct multiple-comparison tests.

These last two matters raise an important question regarding whether quantitative leisure researchers, either by omission (e.g., by not interpreting the magnitude of an effect size) or commission (e.g., by using $p < .05$ regardless of the number of multiple comparisons), have overstated ethnic and racial differences and understated ethnic and racial similarities. Li and colleagues (2007), as well as others (e.g., Hutchison, 2000; Walker, Dieser, & Deng, 2005), have suggested this possibility. The follow-up question is then "Why have these errors occurred?" One answer can be found in a response from Mannell (2005) to a refereed article on culture, self-construal, and leisure (Walker, Deng, & Dieser, 2005). Mannell began by describing a three-generation model of cross-cultural psychological research (Hoshino-Browne, Zanna, Spencer, & Zanna, 2004). The *first generation* of research was intent on identifying cross-cultural similarities to demonstrate the prevalence of psychological constructs. The *second generation* of research was intent on identifying culture-specific phenomena to demonstrate differences in psychological constructs. Finally, the *third generation* of research synthesized the two to develop a more comprehensive and more realistic view of the effect that culture has, and does not have, on psychological functioning. With few exceptions, Mannell maintained that leisure researchers have largely remained at the second generational level. Researchers using both quantitative and qualitative approaches would be wise to consider Mannell's claim when conducting their literature reviews, discussing their results, and summarizing their conclusions.

PAST QUALITATIVE RESEARCH USED TO STUDY RACE, ETHNICITY, AND LEISURE

The early research on race, ethnicity, and leisure behavior relied almost exclusively on quantitative approaches. This positivist research focused on testing theories about why people of color were not involved in certain types of leisure activities, such as those in the outdoors. For example, Floyd (1998) summarized the need to move beyond marginality or ethnicity (Washburne, 1978) as explanations for nonparticipation in leisure activities. Much of the early research described categorical

differences between Blacks and Whites, with White people unconsciously considered the norm. This emphasis on differences due to racial categories was expanded to include other racial and ethnic groups, but remained largely quantitative with comparisons of differences. More recently, Floyd (2007) suggested that the research on race and ethnicity was moving toward understanding how leisure practices can create, perpetuate, and reinforce racism. Arai and Kivel (2009) observed this movement toward the contextualizations of race and the underpinnings associated with the meanings of race as a construct. This emerging focus requires that the study of race, ethnicity, and behavior include qualitative approaches. Allison (1988) admonished that cross-cultural research in leisure must go beyond surveys, but few qualitative data were evident in this leisure literature until the past 10 to 15 years. Even so, based on the results of Floyd and associates' review (2008), only 20% of the race, ethnicity, and leisure studies conducted to date used direct observation, in-depth interviews, case studies, ethnography, or other qualitative methods, with an additional 3% using mixed methods. The remainder of this section identifies some of the key qualitative studies that have been conducted, as well as some of the major issues associated with conducting qualitative research.

Qualitative approaches can be helpful in numerous ways. They can assist in understanding some of the inconsistencies in quantitative research, since qualitative data often allow for better interpretations of the context of responses. The value of this approach also lies in how the focus can be on user characteristics, the recreation site itself, and the setting (e.g., physical, cultural, social, and political) where opportunities are located (McCormack, Rock, Toohey, & Hignell, 2010). Further, this research approach relies on the participant's language and action by using purposeful sampling. For example, a specific population (e.g., aging African American women, Latina adolescents) can be targeted so that in-depth data can be collected. Therefore, qualitative approaches can enable exploration of localized and contextualized aspects of leisure events and processes. McAvoy, Winter, Outley, McDonald, and Chavez (2000) also suggested that for minority groups, using verbal methods may be more successful in collecting data because of the oral traditions of groups such as American Indians. Kivel, Johnson, and Scraton (2009) further argued for epistemologies such as memory work, critical analytic practice, and critical ethnography that move beyond differential racial categories. These tools can assist with better understanding of people's experiences and especially the often invisible lives of people of color.

Although quantitative approaches can allow for wider generalization and standardization of methods and results, which is sometimes imperative, quantitative data can also reinforce stereotypes and power structures, and may further alienate minority groups. Researchers using qualitative approaches are not immune to potentially silencing racial and ethnic minorities; but because of the characteristics of this approach (e.g., using the natural environment, focusing on determining the meaning attached to phenomena, using oral traditions), the possibilities for negative outcomes can be minimized. As discussed later in this chapter,

emerging concerns such as intersectionality (i.e., multiple identities or characteristics such as race, gender, and income) are challenges regardless of the method used.

THE FUTURE OF QUANTITATIVE RESEARCH AND RACE, ETHNICITY, AND LEISURE

Predicting the future is almost always a fool's game, but the authors believe that at least three areas of quantitative research will or must change in regard to race, ethnicity, and leisure. Specifically, there is a need to (a) expand the methodological toolbox; (b) acknowledge three potential measurement issues; and (c) employ, when appropriate, more sophisticated statistical techniques.

Methodological Tools

Experimental research is currently nonexistent in the racial and ethnic leisure area, even though

Qualitative research, which often focuses on experiential phenomena, can target a specific population and in-depth data can be collected.

Floyd and colleagues (2008) noted that prejudice and discrimination have been successfully manipulated in lab settings. As mentioned earlier, however, an experiment's representativeness is quite low. Thus, mainstream psychologists often argue that an experiment's real value is in testing predictions and that other methods should subsequently be used to establish ecological validity (Brewer, 2000). Still, racial and ethnic scholars may want to consider conducting rigorous experimental research.

Floyd and colleagues (2008) also recommended greater use of *secondary data sets*, holding that are more generalizable than experiments, but also acknowledging that they may be limited because some of the variables a researcher may want to study were not measured. Another advantage of secondary data sets is that data are often collected repeatedly over many years. This longitudinal approach allows researchers the opportunity to verify causal factors in a way cross-sectional studies cannot.

Longitudinal research can also be conducted with traditional on-site, mail, and telephone survey methods. With use of a prospective panel (i.e., data are collected more than once but from the same cohort; Gravlee, Kennedy, Godoy, & Leonard, 2009), not only can causality be ascertained (e.g., "What effect does leisure satisfaction have on Hispanic Americans' quality of life?"), but important trends can also be identified (e.g., "How does immigrants' leisure participation change over time?"). Difficulties are associated with longitudinal studies (e.g., time, resources, attrition, data management; White & Arzi, 2005), and these problems may be exacerbated by changes currently taking place with mail (e.g., junk mail increasingly masquerading as legitimate research) and telephone surveys (e.g., reduced response rates because of greater use of caller identification, the abandonment of landlines in favor of cell phones).

Correspondingly, *e-mail* and *Internet-based surveys* have become increasingly common outside the racial and ethnic leisure area. Although concerns about minority group members' computer access were once common, a recent study (Pew Internet & American Life Project, 2010) found that 74% of non-Hispanic Whites, 70% of non-

Hispanic Blacks, and 64% of English- and Spanish-speaking Hispanics now have Internet access. Because these and other types of surveys (e.g., on-site, mail, telephone) have certain advantages and disadvantages, researchers using quantitative approaches may also want to consider a *mixed-mode approach* (Dillman, Reips, & Matzat, 2010) in which potential participants are contacted by mail and asked to complete an online survey.

Finally, although the *experience sampling method* (ESM) has long been used to study leisure phenomena (e.g., Ellis, Voekl, & Morris, 1994), the present authors are aware of only one race, ethnicity, and leisure study (Walker & Wang, 2009) that has used this method to date. Given ESM's high ecological validity (albeit low generalizability), as well as that of other everyday experience protocols (e.g., interval- and event-contingent recording; Reis & Gable, 2000), race and ethnicity leisure researchers should also consider adding these strategies to their methodological toolboxes.

Measurement Issues

At least three measurement issues should be noted. First, Iwasaki, Nishino, Onda, and Bowling (2007) proposed that because leisure and recreation are Western-centric concepts, researchers should avoid their use and instead encourage non-Westerners to "openly talk about their lives within nonwestern contexts and use their natural non-western lens and thinking so that their leisure-like phenomena are described within their own original cultural contexts" (p. 116). Because many immigrants to Canada, England, Australia, New Zealand, and the United States are non-Western in origin, this proposition may be pertinent for leisure researchers in these countries as well. On the other hand, Liu, Yeh, Chick, and Zinn (2008) argued that the Chinese concept of *xiuxian* was quite similar to the Western concept of leisure. One potential solution to this problem is a recently developed measure called the Leisure Ten Statements Test (LTST; Ito & Walker, in press). The LTST asks participants to provide 10 open-ended responses to a prompt (e.g., Leisure _____). Ito and Walker had university students in Japan and Canada complete the LTST. Their responses were classified and statistical analyses were conducted on the 26 resulting categories' proportions. Results indicated that (a) leisure conceptualizations differed not only between Japan and Canada but also within Japan depending on terminologies; (b) the loanword *rejā* has different meanings from its original English word *leisure* suggesting that it has adapted Japanese cultural contexts; and (c) the Japanese leisure-like term that best compares with the English word *leisure* varies depending on which specific aspect of leisure is of interest. Replication with the LTST is needed, but regardless of whether or not it is employed, race and ethnicity leisure researchers—both quantitative and qualitative—must remain cognizant of this ongoing discussion of the appropriate and equivalent terminology.

The article by Iwasaki and associates (2007) is also relevant in terms of a second measurement issue. Although these investigators appear to privilege oral communication, some psychological research suggests that the often assumed linkage between thinking and talking is itself Western-centric, and may be in direct contrast with East Asian cultural traditions in which "states of silence and introspection are considered beneficial for high levels of thinking" (Kim, 2002, p. 829). Kim's study of Asian and European American students supported this hypothesis. Although the generalizability of these findings is a concern because all the Asian American participants were second-generation immigrants, this effect may remain potent even after acculturation. Kim suggested that the reason for this tendency toward quietude may be that talking draws attention to oneself. In cultures that emphasize the group over the individual, this personal attention can result in social disharmony and feelings of stress. In sum, Kim's findings should give pause to quantitative ethnic and racial leisure researchers who use telephone surveys (as well as qualitative ethnic and racial leisure researchers who use in-depth interviews and focus groups) with people who have an East Asian background.

The third measurement issue concerns the potential effect that a survey participant's race or ethnicity can have on how she answers a scale item. Marin and Marin (1991), for instance, stated that Hispanic survey respondents may be more likely to provide extreme (e.g., 1s and 7s on a 7-point scale), acquiescent (or "yea-saying"), and

socially desirable (e.g., reporting that they vote, do not smoke) responses than White Americans. Similarly, Bachman and O'Malley (1984) found that extreme responses were more common among Black than White Americans. However, only one race, ethnicity, and leisure study (Johnson, Bowker, English, & Worthen, 1998) has examined this possibility and it did not find any differences in how members of these two groups responded. Response style differences have also been found among East Asian and North American students (Chen, Lee, & Stevenson, 1995), with the former more likely to use the midpoint of a scale possibly because moderation is highly valued in Confucian-influenced cultures (Davis, 1983). One study (Walker et al., 2001) did take this potential response bias into account. Walker and colleagues standardized their Chinese and European Canadian participants' scale items by group. (See van de Vijver & Leung, 1997, and Johnson, Shavitt, & Holbrook, 2011, for more on the advantages and disadvantages of this procedure.) In conclusion, quantitative researchers should be aware of how race and ethnicity can influence the ways in which participants respond. These responses can potentially affect the results ultimately obtained.

Statistical Techniques

Statistical techniques are another area ripe for potential change in future studies of race, ethnicity, and leisure. However, with regard to employing more sophisticated statistical techniques, a counterpoint is necessary:

> The enormous variety of modern quantitative methods leaves researchers with the nontrivial task of matching analysis and design to the research question. Although complex designs and state-of-the-art methods are sometimes necessary to address research questions effectively, simpler classical approaches often can provide elegant and sufficient answers to important questions. *Do not choose an analytic method to impress your readers or to deflect criticism.* (Wilkinson & Task Force on Statistical Inference, 1999, p. 598; italics added)

The authors concur with Wilkinson and colleagues' call to choose minimally sufficient analyses when appropriate. However, the increasing complexity of quantitative research also suggests that advanced statistical techniques may be beneficial in some cases and crucial in others. Oh and Ditton (2009), for instance, examined Anglo and Hispanic American anglers' conservation attitudes by using *structural equation modeling* (SEM) to test whether the two groups shared (a) comparable underlying structures (i.e., test of the equality of the measurement model) and (b) the same causal relationships among the latent variables (i.e., test of the equality of the causal structure). Oh and Ditton discovered not only that their hypothesized model's structure was invariant but also that, for example, although recreation specialization affected activity preferences for both groups, it influenced willingness to pay only for Anglo Americans. Structural equation modeling, therefore, resulted in a more valid and exact framework than would have been possible if, as was common in the past, an exploratory factor analysis (EFA) and a series of regressions were conducted. (For more on EFA in this context, see van de Vijver and Leung, 1997 and for more information on the difficulties in detecting interactions and moderator effects, see McClelland and Judd, 1993.)

Multilevel linear modeling (MLM) is currently uncommon in the leisure field but offers countless opportunities for researchers (Nezlek, 2011). Multilevel linear modeling is apt when data are organized hierarchically. Wu and Van Egeren (2010), for example, looked at participation in after-school programs using individual-level (e.g., race-ethnicity) and program-level (e.g., racial–ethnic diversity) variables. In another MLM study, Walker (2010) examined how Chinese Canadians' intrinsic motivation was facilitated at the situational level (i.e., through autonomy and competence satisfaction) and the personal level (i.e., depending upon a person's self-construal) during both leisure and nonleisure. Walker, citing Reis and Gable (2000, p. 211), noted that MLM's advantages included its ability to

- simultaneously estimate between- and within-person effects and their interaction;
- handle multiple continuous predictors with an unbalanced number of cases per person, for example, because of missing data;

- use maximum likelihood estimation, which is a more precise and efficient method than least squares estimation; and
- treat predictor variables as random, which most analysis of variance (ANOVA) programs cannot.

Another of Floyd and colleagues' (2008) recommendations was for more integrative reviews of theories, populations, and findings. Although such narrative reviews are valuable, the authors of this chapter also recommend that *quantitative research synthesis* or *meta-analysis* be considered. Quantitative research synthesis statistically cumulates "the results of independent empirical tests of a particular relation between variables" (Johnson & Eagly, 2000, p. 496). Johnson and Eagly listed seven quantitative research synthesis stages; four are briefly described here. The first stage, conceptual analysis of the literature, involves determining which variables define the phenomenon and identifying how they have been operationalized in the past. The second stage, setting boundaries for the sample of studies, entails establishing what criteria will be used to select studies for the sample. The fifth and sixth steps, estimating effect sizes (ES) and analyzing the database, occur after relevant studies have been located and their results have been entered into a meta-analytic database. The former involves determining each study's ES, while the latter entails calculating a composite ES as well as identifying the factors found to moderate it. In summary, using quantitative research synthesis could help make sense of the conflicting research findings that currently exist in the race, ethnicity, and leisure area. In addition, the practical significance overall of the mean differences that have previously been reported should be ascertained, along with identification of the key variables responsible for this variation.

The last statistical technique—*cluster analysis*—while not nearly as sophisticated as the preceding three, could still prove useful. Cluster analysis uses preselected variables to examine whether distinct subgroups exist within an ethnic or racial group. In a study of Canadian and Mainland Chinese students (Walker, Jackson, & Deng, 2008), separate cluster analyses based on participants' self-construal were performed to determine whether the resulting subgroups experienced different leisure constraints. Findings indicated that both the Canadian and Chinese subgroups differed in terms of their intrapersonal constraints (e.g., perceived social support). These results supported recommendations by other race and ethnicity leisure researchers for greater attention to be paid to intragroup variation (Li et al., 2007; Sasidharan, 2002).

THE FUTURE OF QUALITATIVE RESEARCH AND RACE, ETHNICITY, AND LEISURE

Given the limited research of the past (Floyd et al., 2008) as well as the complexity of doing research (Floyd, 2007), many opportunities exist for future qualitative research approaches connected to race and ethnicity. Researchers should always be concerned about how to make the research with any group more reliable, valid, and trustworthy. Unfortunately, past researchers have sometimes used culturally inappropriate techniques (Parker & Lynn, 2002).

Some qualitative researchers, however, have challenged the dominant focus on quantitative racial categories, for several reasons (e.g., Arai & Kivel, 2009; Henderson, 2007). For example, Stansfield and Dennis (1993) cautioned against the myth of internal sameness across race categories, as well as the fallacy of monolithic identity within a group. Categorical research has constructed race as a biological, independent variable focused on differences compared to other races, and at the same time has suggested that individuals within particular racial and ethnic groups are the same. Arai and Kivel emphasized that racial categories are socially constructed and may need reexamination in light of multiracial identities and the influence of intersectionality. In addition to acknowledging the impact of an overemphasis on categorical differences, qualitative researchers have a number of challenges and opportunities in conducting leisure behavior research in the future.

Because so much is yet to be learned about leisure behavior for all groups, many approaches will be needed. Within these approaches, however, some particular issues must be acknowledged.

The issues identified here include researchers' racial identities, participant recruitment, intersectionality, participatory action research, creative analytic practice, and the use of theory and context to expand understandings.

Racial Identity

The racial identity of researchers has been discussed in the past (e.g., McAvoy et al., 2000) and may be especially important when the researcher's positionality is considered. One school of thought holds that it is important, and sometimes essential, for the researcher to be of the same racial or ethnic identity as the research participants, since understanding worldviews different than one's own is difficult. Others suggest that sometimes researchers with different identities see aspects of phenomena that would otherwise be overlooked.

One's identity, whether White or as a person of color, cannot help but influence conscious and unconscious personal views. All research, regardless of the approach, requires that researchers be self-reflective. Researchers, apart from their own racial or ethnic identity, must examine themselves to understand potentially internalized racism, classism, and social oppression (Huang & Coker, 2010; McAvoy et al., 2000). Understanding one's positionality on any issue, as well as being consummately self-reflective, is essential for future qualitative research (Henderson, 2006), and likely applies to quantitative research as well. The ideal solution for research on race and ethnicity may be to have teams of diverse researchers who can represent and be culturally sensitive to the racial and ethnic groups they are studying.

Recruitment

Participant recruitment in racial and ethnic communities is a topic that has been widely discussed among researchers. For example, Huang and Coker (2010) identified factors that affect African American participation in research studies: distrust owing to historical research abuse and institutional racism, lack of information and understanding of research studies and what signing informed consent means (i.e., these forms are sometimes seen as too technical for lay audiences), insufficient recruitment efforts by researchers, and financial considerations on the part of the participants. Huang and Coker recommended that researchers examine their motivations and understanding of racial and ethnic sociocultural contexts. According to Huang and Coker, a culturally sensitive approach places any minority group at the center rather than at the margins of inquiry and enables them to situate based on their own cultural knowledge, especially when qualitative or mixed-methods approaches are used. Banks-Wallace and Conn (2002) emphasized that research must be consistent with shared beliefs, values, and practices of the target populations. Participants in studies must be able to see that the research is going to make a difference in their lives and is not simply being done for a researcher's gain in money or status. Understanding the communal reasons that result in participation by community residents requires that the researcher recognize perceived benefits to participants such as acquiring knowledge or contributing to welfare of the family, community, or both (Huang & Coker, 2010).

Further, recruitment and retention should be based on gaining or strengthening credibility and respect within a racial or ethnic community. Banks-Wallace and Conn (2002) suggested that recruiting and retaining research participants include concern for timing (e.g., around other community events), as well as the use of culturally appropriate incentives. Ammerman and colleagues (2003) found, for example, that a research partnership with pastors and lay leaders of African American churches was effective in recruiting research participants. The investigators learned that honest and frequent communication, sensitivity to the cultural environment, interacting as partners and not within a power structure, and willingness to share results were essential. Other strategies for addressing some of the concerns when qualitative data are being collected might be to focus on structural factors (e.g., community constraints) rather than just focusing on individuals; acknowledging the diversity within any racial or ethnic population; and allowing participants to be coresearchers in interpreting data (Beatty, Wheeler, & Gaiter, 2004). Gibson and Abrams (2003) contended that with cultural awareness and understanding of participant recruitment and

retention in diverse communities, researchers of all racial and ethnic backgrounds can make positive contributions to building knowledge about a topic such as leisure behavior.

Intersectionality

Intersectionality, according to Cole (2009), includes "analytic approaches that consider the meaning and consequences of multiple categories of social group membership" (p. 170). This approach might include examining how identity, difference, and disadvantage may be jointly associated with explaining results obtained in research studies. Shinew and colleagues (2006) noted that few studies have examined the complexities of race related to power and inequality, which might be further evidenced in characteristics such as gender or income level. Models of research tend to be simplified for parsimony, which can result in important aspects being unintentionally ignored.

In the leisure research field, the term *multiple stratification hierarchy* (Shores, Scott, & Floyd, 2007) has also been used to describe the complexity of measuring and negotiating multiracial identity as well as other demographic characteristics such as gender and socioeconomic level (see chapter 1). Importantly, McDonald (2009) suggested that intersectionality works through and against binary framings. The reality of the world is that all people have multiple identities, and to understand a behavior such as leisure requires that more than one dimension be examined. As noted earlier, a monolithic identity is simply not a reality of any racial or ethnic group's experience.

Participatory Inquiry

Participatory inquiry, which is also known as participatory action research (PAR), is another area in which only limited application has occurred in work with racial and ethnic groups in exploring leisure behavior. These research methods focus on integrating knowledge with participant action. Community members and researcher(s), are brought together to address a topic or problem and work collectively to find solutions. The data collected are based on the interactions that occur and on ways in which people use information and become empowered to bring about social change.

Participatory action research forces researchers away from an elitist position suggesting that they alone hold the power and know best how to advance the welfare of others (Whyte, 1995). It can be a strategy for making research contributions while at the same time achieving practical results.

The emphasis of PAR is on empowering and representing individuals, as well as honoring the views and lived experiences of participants by actively collaborating with them in the research process. Research and action go hand in hand. Whyte (1995) noted that the ultimate test of a good theory is what can be done with it. The importance of this participatory inquiry method for examining race and ethnicity lies in how it enables people to have a voice in their actions. The development of theory associated with practical application also offers models for other situations. Participatory inquiry has been used minimally in leisure research, with a few exceptions (e.g., Arai & Pedlar, 1997; Higgins & Rickert, 2005), but offers a rich area for future research examining race, ethnicity, and leisure.

Creative Analytic Practice

Creative analytic practice (CAP) is another emerging area for representing and legitimizing qualitative data (Parry & Johnson, 2007) related to leisure behavior. Creative analytic practice allows for the imaginative and creative representation of qualitative data that might include visual images, stories, poetry, media, or performance. Parry and Johnson described how the processes and products of qualitative inquiry are inextricably linked. They guest-edited a special issue of *Leisure Sciences* that introduced the possibilities of CAP for research on a variety of issues. Two of the articles in that special issue included topics related to race and ethnicity. Lashua and Fox (2007) described research done with Aboriginal Canadian youth through portrayal of the rap music that they created about their leisure and culture. Glover (2007) examined the elements of racism embedded in the policies of little league baseball and portrayed that issue using a short story.

Theory and Context

Arai and Kivel (2009) indicated that race matters, but what may be more important is how race is theorized and contextualized regarding the ideological underpinnings that give meanings to it. Kivel and colleagues (2009) emphasized the need to examine how individuals perform ideologically based identities and how context influences performativity in any leisure area studied. This contextualized application of theory and context to research is essential. Among other aspects, Floyd (2007) challenged researchers to focus more on discussions of history, status, limitations, and potentials of race research within theoretical frameworks that move beyond simple categorical explanations. Kivel and colleagues recommended research on theorizing people and identity without *othering* them (i.e., making them appear deficient or not normal). Additional areas in need of exploration are values and ideologies conveyed through the research, as well as descriptions of power and inequalities regarding such questions as how White privilege and Whiteness affect people of color (e.g., Arai & Kivel, 2009; Roberts, 2009). Critical race theory, for example, is emerging in some fields as a means for moving beyond descriptions of categorical differences to explain the underlying theoretical structures and contexts of racism (see chapter 1 on theoretical frameworks).

Parker and Lynn (2002) argued for how critical race theory (CRT) as a discourse of liberation should be used as a tool and theory to examine ways in which race and racism have influenced the experience of people of color in the United States. Proponents of CRT and its related method of critical race ethnography (Kivel et al., 2009) contend that racism is a system of racial inequality and oppression that transcends acts of individual prejudice (see chapter 11 on discrimination in leisure contexts). According to Parker and Lynn, CRT uses narratives such as those advocated in creative analytic practice to examine race and racism, to argue for eradicating racial subjugation while acknowledging that race is a social construction, and to draw the relationships between race and other forms of domination (i.e., intersectionality). Qualitative research, therefore, offers an important means for the use of critical race strategies to ensure that leisure practices do not reinforce racism (Arai & Kivel, 2009). Glover's (2007) article using creative analytic practice provided a compelling example of how CRT can be used to expose the unconscious racism evident in youth baseball. Critical race theory combined with qualitative approaches and action clearly holds potential for the use of research as a means to address social justice through leisure.

Kivel and colleagues (2009) discussed social justice further by describing how theorizing and contextualizing people's lives in research can be instrumental in understanding how leisure experiences have been conceptualized and how race has been represented in leisure literature. They noted that much of the research on leisure has focused on individual experiences and not at ideological levels. They advocated for shifting from biological identity markers to ways in which these markers are socially and culturally constructed, produced, and reproduced. Kivel and colleagues recognized how methodological strategies such as critical race ethnography and collective memory work can provide important insights for (re)theorizing leisure, experience, and race. For example, in collective memory work, a small group of people engage in a process of analysis to unravel how they may see themselves in social structures that may oppress them. As with participatory inquiry and CRT, this collective memory method has not been widely used in leisure studies especially relative to race issues. As the leisure field moves into what Floyd (2007) called the fourth wave, these emerging methods for a broader theorizing of race, ethnicity, and leisure have great potential. Floyd suggested that the fourth wave is bringing attention to "how leisure practices create, reinforce, and perpetuate racist practices in contemporary society" (p. 249) and how "... understandings of race and leisure contribute to formation of social policies designed to foster constructive engagement and goodwill" (p. 250) across racial and ethnic groups.

USING MIXED DATA TO STUDY RACE, ETHNICITY, AND LEISURE

The influence of postpositivism related to epistemology and methodology and the issues previously discussed all have implications for using mixed methods or mixed data in studying race, ethnicity, and leisure behavior. This mixing is sometimes called linking or triangulation (Henderson, 2006). Regardless of the name, the idea offers a means for combining methods, data, or sources of data in a single study. The strategy can safeguard against accusations that a study's findings are simply an artifact of a single method, a single data source, or a single investigator's biases.

According to Denzin (1978), four types of triangulation exist:

1. Data triangulation (i.e., the use of a variety of data sources)
2. Investigator triangulation (i.e., the use of several researchers)
3. Theory triangulation (i.e., the use of multiple perspectives to interpret data)
4. Methodological triangulation (i.e., the use of multiple methods)

All these types of strategies have been described in this chapter. Methods or data obviously can build upon other methods or data to enable better understanding of the leisure behavior of individuals or groups. Since all methods and types of data have nuances, mixed data, if collected and analyzed properly, can provide more valid and more reliable information.

Several techniques can be used in linking data (Henderson, 2006). These include antecedent or sequential, encapsulated or nested, concurrent, and primary–secondary combinations. Sequential linking of data means collecting one type of data followed by use of a second method. Generally the second method uses information gained in the first data analysis as a guide. Encapsulated or nested techniques include embedding one method within another, for example collecting survey data from a large sample and simultaneously using a subsample of that group to conduct in-depth interviews. Data might also be collected concurrently, such that data are collected at the same time from two related sources (e.g., participants and nonparticipants). The primary–secondary combination may be a variation of any of the other techniques but generally means that one type or source of data is acknowledged as the most important one. Any of these techniques can be used, but they must be carefully planned.

Several cautions, however, must be considered in linking or mixing data. First, the data must be collected and analyzed rigorously. Sometimes qualitative data are dismissed or considered only secondary, resulting in incomplete explanations of methods and analysis. These omissions should not occur. The use of mixed methods or mixed data requires that all data be valid and reliable (i.e., trustworthy).

This admonition about rigor links closely to another caution in that using mixed data may require more time and expertise than using a single approach. Doing a study well requires time; and if two methods are used, presumably the time will be doubled. Related to time is the necessity that a researcher using mixed data has the expertise, or is able to work with a team, to ensure that data are appropriately and rigorously collected and analyzed.

Third, the researchers who desire to link the data should consider whether the data are to be collected simultaneously or whether one set of data will be analyzed first to inform future data collection. In addition, it is important to consider how the data will be linked.

This linking also relates to a final aspect regarding the congruence or compatibility of data (Henderson, 2006). If the data are congruent, there is no problem. Researchers, however, should always consider the possibility of divergence of data and the potential need for explanation of that outcome. Linking more than one data source or method can result in evidence that is confirming or confounding or somewhere in between.

None of these cautions are reason not to undertake a study on race, ethnicity, or leisure behavior using mixed methods or mixed data. However, as much sense as linking or using mixed data makes, especially within the postpositivist paradigm, these strategies must be carefully designed if they are to be useful.

CONCLUSION

This chapter describes the types of research methods that exist and that have been used in past research on race, ethnicity, and leisure. It has also addressed the adequacies and inadequacies of previous research. The hope is that readers will be able to design and implement better quantitative and qualitative studies on this topic in the future. Several conclusions seem evident. First, although studies have been conducted on race, ethnicity, and leisure behavior, not nearly enough has been done to date given the growing diversity in society. Second, both quantitative and qualitative approaches have been used, with mixed results, in contributing to the body of knowledge regarding this topic. Third, new methods and strategies are emerging in other fields that hold promise for further research related to leisure, race, and ethnicity. Finally, many opportunities exist for future research to bring about a much deeper understanding of what differences and similarities among and within racial and ethnic groups mean, as well as how that information can ensure social justice related to leisure and recreation opportunities for all.

CHAPTER 3

Race, Ethnicity, and Leisure Services: Can We Hope to Escape the Past?

David Scott

OVERVIEW

The Public Broadcasting Service described its popular television series *The National Parks: America's Best Idea* as a story of "people from every conceivable background," including "rich and poor," "famous and unknown," and "natives and newcomers" (PBS, 2009). This chapter proposes that access to and use of park and recreation spaces across racial and ethnic groups, past and present, has been a different story. The purpose is to examine how race and ethnicity affect North Americans' access to park and recreation services. Historically, public park and recreation agencies saw their role as Americanizing people of color and immigrants. Both in the past and today, ethnic and racial minorities have been barred from using a wide range of these services. Inequalities in park and recreation delivery are perpetuated by practices that are highly embedded in how agencies routinely do business. If agencies are to better serve ethnic and racial minorities, they will have to ensure that agency offerings are affordable, accessible, culturally relevant, safe, and welcoming. Agencies will need strong and influential political allies as they advocate for improved park and recreation delivery for minorities in the future.

Learning Outcomes

After reading this chapter, readers will be able to

- explain how park and recreation providers historically saw their role in Americanizing immigrants and people of color,

- describe how the Civil Rights era changed service providers' ideas about service delivery toward African Americans and other people of color,

- explain how ethnic and racial minorities historically were barred from park and recreation amenities and how they continue to experience problems of access,

- explain how inequalities in service delivery are perpetuated over time by embedded and taken-for-granted agency practices and beliefs, and

- identify the challenges facing service providers as they seek to diversify program offerings and make park and recreation amenities more accessible.

> *If minorities do not like going to the parks, it is their loss. But please don't let us be duped into thinking it is our loss. Many of us look to the parks as an escape from the problems ethnic and minorities create. Please don't modify our parks to destroy our oasis.*
>
> *Letter to the editor,* National Parks *(September/October, 1994)*

The quote is an excerpt from a letter to the editor published in *National Parks* magazine (September/October, 1994). The letter was written in response to an article in a previous issue of the magazine that described the National Park Service's efforts to promote ethnic and racial diversity in the national parks. Three other letters appeared along with the one quoted, and all the other writers likewise blasted the National Park Service for what they believed was a misguided initiative. Although the letter writers' criticisms were directed at the National Park Service, their views may well apply to how many Whites in North America feel about practitioners' efforts to diversify local, regional, and state park and recreation facilities. Many Whites are uncomfortable sharing public spaces with people of color (Phillip, 2000), and this antipathy creates problems for park and recreation agencies as they seek to provide programs and amenities to a broad spectrum of constituents.

The purpose of this chapter is to examine how race and ethnicity affect people's access to public park and recreation services. The focus is largely on the experiences of minorities who live in the United States. The first section examines how park and recreation agencies have historically positioned themselves vis-à-vis immigrants and people of color. A historical perspective provides insights into prevailing attitudes about service delivery and the struggles that minorities have experienced, and continue to experience, in accessing park and recreation facilities and programs. The second section summarizes research demonstrating that people of color do not use public park recreation resources to the same extent as Whites and do not enjoy the same access to public park and recreation services. The third section is an examination of how institu-

tional barriers contribute to inequities in service delivery. Many of these barriers are in the form of agency practices that are deeply embedded, are not outwardly discriminatory, and are regarded by many stakeholders as legitimate and free of bias. The chapter concludes by putting forth some ideas about how leisure service organizations can better serve people of color.

HISTORY OF PARK AND RECREATION DELIVERY

To understand how leisure service agencies serve people of color, it is useful to take a long view. No comprehensive history exists that addresses how public park and recreation agencies have delivered programs and services to people of color. Such a history waits to be written. The closest anyone has come to writing such a history is James Murphy (1972), whose dissertation was on the history of municipal recreation service for Blacks between 1906 and 1972.[1] What is known about the delivery of leisure services comes from a range of sources and pertains mostly to the experiences of African Americans. Provision of services to other people of color—such as Hispanics—is new enough that the historical record is incomplete and still unfolding.

Assimilation

To understand issues related to leisure service delivery for people of color, it is useful to understand the *philosophy* underlying service provision. Up until the Civil Rights era in the United States, many park and recreation leaders justified services, in part, as instruments of social control; and these services were believed to help Americanize

---

[1]Floyd and Mowatt (chapter 4) draw heavily on Murphy's dissertation.

ethnic groups and people of color. Robert Moses, longtime commissioner of New York parks, was blunt with regard to his view of the people who used parks and beaches under his jurisdiction: "It [the public] needs to be bathed, it needs to be aired, it needs recreation, but not for personal reasons—just to make it a better public" (Caro, 1974, p. 318). Although harsh, Moses' point of view provides an illuminating glimpse into some pre-Civil Rights–era practitioners' view of people of color and the role park and recreation services played in improving (and controlling) their lives.

One such group was early supporters of municipally owned playgrounds. It is important to note that early playgrounds were highly organized spaces for play and recreation. Playground advocates promoted organized play because they felt it contributed to moral and cognitive development and integrated youth into American culture. Social reformers and play advocates, like Jane Addams, believed that organized play would teach working-class and immigrant youth skills that would aid them in their *assimilation* into America (Hose, 1983). To accomplish this goal, play leaders provided programs that were highly structured and oriented toward inculcating middle-class values. In an early inspection of Chicago playgrounds, Zueblin (1896) observed that "no pains were spared to interest the children and educate them in rational play" (p. 151). Cavallo (1981) stated concisely the goals of early play leaders: "The player's behavior, his willingness to obey the rules of the game, and his ability to get along with teammates were more important than his ethnic origin" (p. 6). Thus, organized play and recreation were promoted and justified, in part, as helping immigrants shed their ethnic identities in favor of becoming Americans.

Similarly, advocates of parks have long justified green spaces because of their potential to edify. Byrne and Wolch (2009) observed that early defenders of urban parks "imbued . . . [them] with the power to overcome anarchy, immorality, crime and indolence" (p. 746). Park advocates clashed, however, with working-class and immigrant visitors over appropriate behavior in parks (Rosenzweig & Blackmar, 1992; Taylor, 1999). To ensure that middle-class mores prevailed in parks, elites established rules, dress codes, and acceptable behavior in parks. Police routinely patrolled parks to ensure that visitors conformed to rules and regulations. In this way, urban parks in the United States mirrored prevailing middle-class values and were believed to be important social spaces for instilling these values.

Early pioneers of recreation education also defended organized recreation on the basis of its ability to assimilate ethnic and racial groups into the mainstream of America. One such individual was George Butler, who served as research director of the National Recreation Association for over 40 years. In his classic text, *Introduction to Community Recreation,* published in 1949, Butler stated that municipal recreation was "one of the most powerful agencies for absorbing the various nationality and racial groups into American life" (p. 400). He added that within the context of community recreation programs, immigrants and non-Whites were encouraged to participate "not as members of a particular race or nationality but as neighbors and members of the community" (p. 400). These sentiments were echoed by Harold D. Meyer and Charles K. Brightbill (1948) in the first edition of their text, *Community Recreation:* "Recreation provides a powerful influence in the assimilation of nationalities and races for social well-being. Programs of Americanization, the integration of immigrant groups, the promotion of wholesome race relations, and the constant process of infiltration and blending, find in recreation a strong ally" (p. 638). In subsequent editions of *Community Recreation,* Meyer and Brightbill (1956, 1964, 1969)[2] continued to endorse the role of organized recreation as a mechanism for Americanizing minority group members. This emphasis on assimilation would change in the fifth edition of the book, when H. Douglass Sessoms became lead author and the title of the book was changed to *Leisure Services* (1975). As noted later, the Civil Rights era led many practitioners and educators to rethink their ideas about the role of park and recreation delivery, and many adopted a service delivery perspective based on principles of cultural pluralism.

---

[2]The fourth edition of *Community Recreation* (1969) included H. Douglass Sessoms as a third author.

Although assimilation was espoused as a goal of park and recreation delivery in the late 19th century and for the first 60 or so years of the 20th century, practitioners and educators were not unmindful of ethnic and racial groups' desire to preserve aspects of their culture. Jane Addams, for example, was sensitive enough to cultural diversity that she organized parties and events celebrating the ethnic heritage of immigrant groups who lived in neighborhoods surrounding Hull House (Diliberto, 1999). Educators such as George Butler (1949) advised practitioners that it was sometimes important to consider ethnic and racial groups' heritage and interests when planning recreation services. Early playground and recreation advocates also grasped the importance of enlisting members of ethnic and racial groups in the administration, planning, and organization of recreation services for ethnic communities and people of color (Meyer & Brightbill, 1948; Settle, 1916).

Segregation

If assimilation was a goal of organized park and recreation delivery up until the 1960s, the reality is that many immigrants and people of color were denied access to a wide range of public settings and facilities used by Whites. African Americans in particular were deemed "undesirable," and communities across the United States excluded them or discouraged them, legally or extralegally, from visiting places reserved for Whites,

Courtesy of the National Park Service.

De jure segregation of a recreation facility at Lewis Mountain in Shenandoah National Park, Virginia, circa 1940. According to National Parks Traveler, racial segregation was part of the park's original master plan (www.nationalparkstraveler.com/item/national-park-mystery-photo-31-revealed-lewis-mountain-negro-area-sign-exhibit-shenandoah).

including vacation destinations (Aron, 1999; Rugh, 2008), public swimming pools and beaches (Caro, 1974; Wiltse, 2007), amusement parks and commercial amusement centers (Nasaw, 1993; Wolcott, 2006), YWCA facilities (Verbrugge, 2010), and parks and historic sites (Creighton, 2005; Frazier, 1940). African Americans were also barred from Major League Baseball until the late 1940s. One explanation for owners' reluctance to desegregate Major League Baseball was their fear that integrated baseball would result in their parks being "overrun by black fans" (Tye, 2009, p. 187).

Much has been written about the subordination of and discrimination toward African Americans in the South (Dollard, 1937, Myrdal, 1944; Woodard, 1966). Segregation (also known as Jim Crow) laws legally assigned African Americans second-class status across the South by barring them from interacting with Whites in public settings and accommodations. Although the National Recreation Association (a precursor to the National Recreation and Park Association) sought to meet the needs of African Americans via the Bureau of Colored Work,[3] few Southern cities or communities allocated sufficient funds to provide adequate park and recreation amenities for their Black residents (Frazier, 1940; Jones, 1927; Woofter, 1928). Consequently, throughout the South, Whites enjoyed far greater access to public recreation and park amenities than African Americans and other people of color.

Provision of park and recreation services for African Americans in the North was often not much better than it was in the South. Many communities and cities provided their African American residents limited opportunities for organized recreation and access to parks (Holland, 2002). Many of the restrictions encountered by Blacks and other people of color in the North were imposed by practitioners who were racist and lacked empathy for ethnic and racial minorities. One such individual was Robert Moses. According to his biographer, Robert Caro (1974), Moses used his position and influence to restrict Blacks from using a wide range of public park and recreation amenities and spent little money on parks

in Harlem and other areas where Blacks lived. He was particularly committed to keeping Blacks and Puerto Ricans, whom he regarded as "dirty," from intermingling with Whites in public facilities. Caro describes how Moses kept the water in one swimming pool deliberately cold because he believed "that its temperature, while not cold enough to bother white swimmers, would deter any 'colored' people who happened to enter it once from returning" (p. 514). Moses also discouraged Blacks and other people of color from using pools and beaches "reserved" for Whites by employing White lifeguards and attendants. Moses was remiss regarding investment in public transportation and even banned public buses from using parkways designed to transport New Yorkers to newly opened beaches on Long Island. Moses' bias against mass transit exacted a huge cost on residents living in poor neighborhoods. According to Caro, Moses effectively barred Blacks, Puerto Ricans, and other poor New Yorkers from accessing a wide range of city and regional parks.

Wiltse's (2007) social history of swimming pools in the United States also provides vivid insight into how African Americans were excluded extralegally from using public spaces in Northern cities. The simplest method of keeping Blacks and Whites apart was to locate pools in neighborhoods that were racially homogeneous. In instances in which African Americans sought legal entry into pools used by Whites, city officials gave White swimmers tacit approval to harass and assault Black interlopers. Wiltse placed two factors at the core of Whites' aversion to swimming with Blacks. One pertained to perceived cleanliness and hygiene of Blacks. The other had to do with what he described as the *eroticization* of swimming pools. Whites were fearful that "black men would act upon their supposedly untamed sexual desire for white women by touching them in the water and assaulting them with romantic advances" (p. 124). In cities throughout the North, African Americans struggled to achieve admittance to swimming pools and a whole range of other publicly funded recreation and park facilities.

[3]This branch of the National Recreation Association existed from 1920 through 1954 (Murphy, 1972).

Discrimination in the Civil Rights Era

The Civil Rights era in the United States (1954-1965)[4] struck down segregation laws and made it illegal to bar African Americans and other people of color from using commercial and publicly funded park and recreation sites. Several important Supreme Court decisions opened up publicly funded park and recreation facilities to Blacks and other people of color (Murphy, 1972). In 1955, the Court ruled it illegal to provide segregated beaches in Maryland (*Mayor and City Council of Baltimore v. Dawson U.S. 877*). The Court also ruled in 1955 that the city of Atlanta could no longer assign golf courses to Blacks and Whites on different days of the week (*Holmes v. Atlanta U.S. 879*). A 1963 Supreme Court ruling expanded prior rulings by desegregating all public park and recreation facilities in Memphis (*Watson v. Memphis U.S. 373*). As noted by Murphy, this included parks and playgrounds, libraries and museums, and publicly owned stadiums and community centers. The 1964 Civil Rights Act went even farther and made it illegal for governmental entities to prohibit access to facilities on the basis of race, religion, gender, or nationality. It also outlawed discrimination in hotels, restaurants, resorts, movie theaters, and other commercial enterprises.

The Civil Rights era also resulted in heightened awareness of the depressed state of park and recreation provision in minority communities, particularly those in urban areas (Murphy, 1972; National League of Cities, 1968; Nesbitt, Brown, & Murphy, 1970). This would lead governmental entities to acquire and develop park and recreation programs near minority communities. One important example was the National Park Service's establishment of recreation areas (e.g., Golden Gate National Recreation Area in San Francisco and Gateway National Recreation Area in New York and New Jersey) in and around urban areas as a means of "bringing parks to people." The new awareness would also lead to a proliferation of minority outreach programs, as well as increased efforts by park and recreation agencies to hire and train members of minority groups (Hutchison, 1983; Kraus, 1968).

The Civil Rights era also ushered in new ideas about practice based on the notion of cultural pluralism and inclusion. Educators, in particular, downplayed Americanizing immigrants via public parks and recreation. Sessoms and colleagues (1975) noted that "America became aware of its cultural mosaic, that all of its citizens were not alike and did not want to be treated alike" (p. 233). A similar point of view was voiced by Dahl (1993), who encouraged practitioners to acknowledge the cultural integrity of ethnic and racial communities: "All cultures are rich, varied, and provide *meaning* for those within, irrespective of how fractured or dispossessed others from the outside may judge a culture to be" (p. 156). She also advised practitioners to be open to cultural differences and empower community members by helping them draw upon resources and strengths within their community. An emphasis on inclusion has prompted some writers to argue that recreation and parks can provide safe places for disparate groups to intermingle and learn about other people's cultures (Gobster, 1998; Low, Taplin, & Scheld, 2005). Far from being viewed as a mechanism for absorbing ethnic and racial minorities, recreation and parks became increasingly seen as spaces for preserving and celebrating culture.

Although Civil Rights laws struck down segregated recreation programs and parks, some cities actually avoided desegregation by closing or selling public parks, swimming pools, and other public amenities to private organizations (Murphy, 1972). Just as troubling was the fact that many Whites withdrew from recreation programs and abandoned public spaces so they would not have to interact with Blacks and other people of color (Kraus, 1968; Nasaw, 1993; Wolcott, 2006). Nowhere was this more apparent than in municipal swimming pools. Wiltse (2007) documented that many middle-class Whites in the 1960s abandoned public swimming pools in favor of residential and private club swimming pools. Private pools enabled White Americans "to exercise greater control over whom they swam with than was possible at public pools . . . [and] ensured that other swimmers would be of the same social class and race" (p. 183). Significantly, privatization of swimming pools and other public spaces has

[4]This time frame coincides with the work of Williams (1987).

been accompanied by erosion of public support of municipal facilities and a decline in the quality of existing facilities. By the end of the 20th century, Wiltse observed, many "Americans who could not afford to join a swim club or install a backyard pool had less access to swimming and recreation facilities than did previous generations" (p. 183).

Today, public park and recreation agencies throughout North America continue to wrestle with how best to serve people of color. The situation is made more complicated by the fact that a growing proportion of the population includes immigrants from Latin America and Asia. Many of these new immigrants use park and recreation amenities as a vehicle for keeping ethnic traditions alive and strengthening interpersonal ties with friends and family. Problems arise, however, when their use of space conflicts with park rules or traditional ideas about service delivery (Low et al., 2005). Problems also stem from the fact that many Americans regard immigrants, particularly Latinos, as trespassers and feel they have no right to use municipal park and recreation amenities. Conflicts over soccer provide a case in point (Price & Whitworth, 2004). In some North American communities, Latino immigrants have clashed with park and recreation officials about accessing fields and what constitutes proper use of park land. Accustomed to playing soccer on *any* open area, many Latinos have been chased off fields because they lacked official permits, because fields were restricted for other uses, or because impacts on fields from soccer play were regarded as unacceptable (McKenna, 2009). Issues like this are made more contentious as communities seek to limit park and field use to "legal" residents. As noted in the next section, Latinos and many other people of color continue to experience enormous problems when it comes to accessing public park and recreation amenities.

MINORITY VISITATION AND ACCESS TO SERVICES

A great deal of research has been conducted on patterns of leisure and outdoor recreation among people of color. Several studies have also focused on describing and explaining patterns of use among ethnic and racial minorities when

they visit public park and recreation areas. Collectively, these studies indicate variation among ethnic and racial groups with regard to types of activities pursued, facility and management preferences, and companion choices. Less is known about whether or not people of color visit public parks as frequently as their White counterparts, or about the extent to which people of color have comparable access to public park and recreation amenities near where they live. This section summarizes literature on the ethnic and racial composition of public park and recreation visitors. Also summarized are findings from studies that show the extent to which different ethnic and racial groups have access to public park and recreation amenities.

Americans' Use of Public Park and Recreation Services

Are different ethnic and racial groups in the United States equally likely to visit public parks and participate in public recreation programs? The answer to this question depends on whether one is talking about local parks, regional parks, state parks, or national parks. The best data available indicate that Whites and people of color are equally likely to visit local parks and participate in locally sponsored recreation programs. In a nationwide survey conducted in 1992, Godbey, Graefe, and James showed that three out of four Americans reported visiting community parks, playgrounds, or open spaces occasionally or frequently. Thirty-five percent of Americans reported participating in recreation activities organized by their local park and recreation department within the last 12 months. Godbey and colleagues observed that rates of park visitation and program participation did not vary by race or ethnicity. No national surveys have been conducted since this 1992 study to document Americans' use of community parks and participation in locally sponsored recreation programs.

A few states have conducted studies that include demographic information on their state park visitors. These studies indicate that Whites represent a disproportionate fraction of park visitors in these states. Using data collected from a telephone survey of Texas residents, Lee, Scott, and Floyd

(2001) reported that Anglos were 1.4 times more likely to visit Texas state parks than people of color. This was true even after controlling for the effects of gender, age, household income, and level of education. In Minnesota, nearly 98% of visitors to state parks are White (Kelly, 2008). Whites make up 89% of that state's population. A similar pattern is evident in Pennsylvania. Approximately 93% of visitors to state parks in Pennsylvania are White (Mowen, Kerstetter, Graefe, & Miles, 2006). Eighty-two percent of Pennsylvania residents are White. Importantly, people of color made up a relatively large proportion of visitors to state parks in Pennsylvania that are within the Philadelphia and Harrisburg metropolitan areas. Each of these urban areas has large minority populations.

Studies at the national level suggest that people of color are far less likely to visit national forests and parks compared to their White counterparts. The focus in this discussion is limited to national parks. In a nationwide survey conducted by Northern Arizona University's Social Research Laboratory (Solop, Hagen, Ostergren, 2003), 32% of Americans reported visiting a park or unit under the administration of the National Park Service during the previous two years. Whites (non-Hispanics) reported the highest rate of visitation (36%), followed by Native Americans (33%), Asian Americans (29%), and Hispanics (27%). Only 13% of African Americans reported that they had visited a National Park Service unit in the last two years.

Data collected by the Visitor Services Project (VSP) at the University of Idaho corroborate that people of color represent a relatively small fraction of national park visitors.[5] On average, Whites represented 93% of visitors to 32 national parks for which race–ethnic information is available. Hispanic Americans and Asian Americans each composed less than 5% of visitors. Less than 3% of visitors were African Americans. Although Whites make up the vast majority of national park visitors, it is important to note that some parks are visited heavily by people of color. For example, 31% of visitors to Manzanar National Historic Site in California were Asian American. This unit was the site of one of 10 Japanese American internment centers during World War II and was founded to preserve this painful chapter in American history. Likewise, 17% of visitors to Booker T. Washington National Monument in Virginia were African American. This park was established to honor the birthplace of one of America's most prominent African American educators and orators in the late 19th and early 20th centuries.

This brief review indicates that Whites and people of color are equally likely to visit local parks and participate in locally sponsored recreation programs. Numerous studies, however, show that people of color do not visit remotely located parks to the same extent as their White counterparts. There are some important exceptions. Many people of color visit state and national parks that are within easy reach of urban areas and are historically or culturally meaningful.

Americans' Access to Public Park and Recreation Amenities

Park and recreation officials across North America have long espoused the idea that park and recreation services should be accessible to all community residents. Park and recreation amenities are often touted as integral to what makes cities and neighborhoods livable (Wolch, Wilson, & Fehrenbach, 2005). Indeed, a variety of individual and community benefits are associated with park and recreation use. People who live within close proximity to parks report higher rates of physical activity, health, and psychological well-being (Mowen & Baker, 2009). People who live close to park and recreation areas also benefit by getting to know their neighbors. Social ties and a feeling of security are enhanced in neighborhoods with public parks (Boone, Buckley, Grove, & Sister, 2009). Parks and recreation also foster environmental stewardship, enhance real estate values, combat youth crime, and increase community pride (Crompton & Kaczynski, 2004; Hunt, Scott, & Richardson, 2003). Equality of access to public park and recreation amenities implies that groups have meaningful choices; that there is equity in

---

[5]VSP studies are conducted on-site at National Park Service units. A handful of VSP studies collect information about the ethnic and racial background of visitors. The author examined all 223 reports listed on the VSP website (through August 2010) and found that 32 studies collected race–ethnicity data. VSP reports can be obtained at www.psu.uidaho.edu/vsp.htm.

Whiting Park, an example of accessible recreation areas in a mixed-race community in Whiting, Indiana.

the distribution of services; and that all residents, irrespective of their ethnic and racial background, have access to amenities that contribute to personal and community well-being (Nicholls & Shafer, 2001).

Supply of Recreation Services

One way researchers have sought to determine whether groups have equal access to park and recreation amenities is by comparing the *supply* of recreation resources across neighborhoods or census tracts within a given geopolitical area. Supply measures include the number of parks, amount of park acreage, park congestion (i.e., number of people per park acre), and the type of facilities (e.g., swimming pools, athletic fields, playgrounds) available to residents. Access is generally defined as living within a quarter-mile of a park or recreation facility. This is the equivalent of about a 5-minute walk (Boone et al., 2009). Analytic procedures for determining equality of access have been greatly facilitated in recent years with the introduction of geographic information system

(GIS) technologies (Nicholls & Shafer, 2001). GIS allows researchers and practitioners to integrate spatial data with demographic information and thereby make decisions about potential inequalities in service provision (Wicks, Backman, Allen, & Van Blaricom, 1993).

To what extent do different ethnic and racial groups have equal access to public park and recreation amenities near their homes? The best data available indicate that there is indeed inequality in access. People of color are more likely than Whites to live in communities and neighborhoods that are relatively bereft of parks, open spaces, and recreation amenities. These inequities are most apparent in large urban areas.

Mladenka (1980) was one of the first researchers to examine groups' access to park and recreation facilities. He correlated park acreage and number and type of recreational facilities with ethnic and racial characteristics of wards in the city of Chicago in 1967 and 1977. While park acreage was equally distributed throughout the city in 1967 and 1977, Whites were more likely than Blacks and Latinos to live closer to large city parks. While Blacks and Latinos had access to parks, the parks close to their homes were smaller than the parks Whites had access to. Furthermore, Black and Latino wards had significantly fewer recreational facilities (e.g., athletic fields, swimming pools) than did White wards. Blacks' and Latinos' access to recreational facilities improved between 1967 and 1977, which Mladenka attributed to city officials' becoming more responsive to minority demands (particularly from Blacks) for improved recreation facilities.

Wolch and colleagues (2005) examined access to parks and open space in Los Angeles among Whites, Latinos, Asian Pacific Islanders, and African Americans. Los Angeles residents who lived within White-dominated neighborhoods[6] had far more acres of park land (31.8) per thousand people compared to residents who lived in predominantly Latino (0.6), Asian (0.3), or African American neighborhoods (1.7). Residents of White-dominated neighborhoods had even more park land for children under 18 years of age. There were 193 acres of park land per thousand children in neighborhoods dominated by Whites, compared to only 1.6 acres in Latino neighborhoods, 6.3 acres in African American neighborhoods, and 1.9 acres in Asian neighborhoods. Spending of park bond money also tended to favor neighborhoods with large proportions of Whites and White children. This latter finding led Wolch and colleagues to conclude that new funding of parks in Los Angeles exacerbated rather than ameliorated existing inequities in park and open space access.

Similar findings are evident in a study that examined the distribution of parks in the Baltimore metropolitan area (Boone et al., 2009). On the one hand, African American residents, on average, lived closer to parks than any other racial group. White residents, on the other hand, had far more access to park land than Black residents. White-dominated neighborhoods had more than 50 acres of park land per thousand people; Black-dominated neighborhoods had less than 13 acres. African Americans throughout the Baltimore metropolitan area tended to live in areas that were densely populated. As a result, the parks in these areas were far more congested than parks in White-dominated areas (particularly those outside the city limits). Boone and colleagues showed that existing access inequities in the Baltimore metropolitan area reflect and are linked to longstanding segregation ordinances and racial covenants. Many Blacks continue to be consigned to neighborhoods in and around Baltimore that have long been impoverished and deprived of park and recreation amenities.

Several other studies confirm that minorities and people living in socioeconomically deprived areas have lower access to public recreational resources. This is true in medium-size cities (Estabrooks, Lee, & Gyurcsik, 2003; Nicholls & Shafer, 2001), as well as small and rural communities (Edwards, Jilcott, Floyd, & Moore, 2011; Patterson, Moore, Probst, & Shinogle, 2004). Collectively, these studies indicate that the supply of publicly funded park and recreation amenities favors Whites and socioeconomically affluent communities.

Other Factors Influencing Access

It is important to note that access to park and recreation resources is not limited to their supply and distribution. Access is also influenced by socioeconomic status, safety considerations, information about park and recreation amenities, cultural factors, and how people are treated when they use park and recreation amenities. Each of these factors constrains ethnic and racial minorities' use of park and recreation resources.

In general, minorities have lower levels of discretionary income than Whites. As a result they are more likely to lack financial resources to travel, purchase recreational equipment, and pay admission and program fees. Increases in the costs of travel and admission prices are likely to inordinately affect minorities' access to park and recreation resources. Such changes may result in minorities being "priced out" of the recreation and travel market (Bowker & Leeworthy, 1998).

Because ethnic and racial minority groups are disproportionately represented among the poor,

---

[6]Neighborhoods with a dominant racial–ethnic group were ones that included 75% or more residents who were members of a single race-ethnicity.

many people of color live in neighborhoods and communities that are impoverished. Park and recreation resources in these areas are comparatively run-down and unsafe. Crime and safety considerations are major factors that make public park and recreation resources inaccessible to people who are economically disadvantaged (Scott & Munson, 1994).

Minorities and low-income communities are also more likely than others to be hemmed in by highways, railroad tracks, and other physical features that make easy access to nearby parks and open space problematic (Noonan, 2005). Simultaneously, members of minority groups are more likely than others to rely on public transportation and many public park and recreation areas are not readily accessible via public transportation.

Ethnic and racial minorities are more likely than Whites to report that they lack information about public park and recreation resources (Shores, Scott, & Floyd, 2007; Solop et al., 2003). Many people of color obtain information about community events that are outside the mainstream of traditional park and recreation advertising (Lee, Floyd, & Shinew, 2002; Thapa, Graefe, & Absher, 2002). This problem is exacerbated for immigrants and others who speak English sparingly or not at all.

Cultural factors may also contribute to why some ethnic and racial groups do not find park and recreation amenities accessible. Muslims, for example, are unlikely to mix with non-Muslims in public settings because of restrictions related to modesty, consumption of alcohol, and mixed-gender interactions (Dagkas & Benn, 2006; Stodolska & Livengood, 2006). In other situations, ethnic and racial groups may feel that agencies or park areas have ignored or have even erased their histories (Low et al., 2005). In some cases, activities promoted in parks are seen as White pastimes and irrelevant to the interests and needs of minority groups (Gobster, 1998).

Ethnic and racial minorities have long suffered the indignity of second-class status in the United States. Studies have shown that members of minority groups too often experience suspicion, harassment, and discrimination when they visit park and recreation facilities (Falk, 1995; Feagin, 1991; West, 1989). Past exclusion and racism

explain why some members of minority groups continue to eschew visiting park and recreation destinations irrespective of their proximity (Erickson, Johnson, & Kivel, 2009; Harris, 1997; Tierney, Dahl, & Chavez, 2001) (see chapter 11 on discrimination in leisure contexts).

Access to park and recreation resources is a major problem for people of color, particularly those who are economically disadvantaged and who live in large urban areas. The discussion in this section has shown that access is a function of the supply and distribution of park and recreation amenities and is influenced by economic, cultural, and safety considerations. As the next section shows, inequality in service delivery is deeply embedded in the everyday functioning of public park and recreation agencies, in how they do business.

INSTITUTIONAL BARRIERS AND RECREATION NEED

Public park and recreation agencies today face enormous challenges as they seek to provide equitable services to ethnic and racial minorities. Many of these challenges are hardly new and reflect pervasive problems in service delivery that both mirror and reinforce tensions in ethnic and racial relations in society as a whole. It is the author's contention that inequity in service delivery has been perpetuated over time by established practices and beliefs that are firmly embedded in the normal, everyday functioning of society and how agencies do business. The aim in this section is to show how institutional barriers systematically contribute to inequities in service delivery. The ideas here are based in modified form on ones published elsewhere (Scott, 2000, 2005).

The framework for the discussion borrows from ideas about institutional discrimination and systemic racism (Baron, 1969; Feagin, 2006; Feagin & Feagin, 1986; Williams, 1985). These two perspectives assert that inequalities within major institutional spheres (the economy and labor market, education, housing, and politics) are mutually reinforcing and that they restrict minorities' access to a whole range of opportunities, including park and recreation resources. These perspectives also assume that organizational practices are outwardly neutral yet systematically reflect or perpetuate the effects of preferential treatment in the past. Together, the frameworks compel one to examine inequities in access as a product of longstanding structural arrangements, policies, and past decisions. Reducing inequities in service delivery is all the more difficult because everyday practices are deeply rooted and are perceived by practitioners and laypeople as legitimate.

Perhaps the most insidious institutional barrier that prevents people of color from using park and recreation resources is age-old practices of segregating groups along ethnic and racial lines. Segregation along color lines has been systematic and fueled by lending practices, racial covenants, steering by real estate agents, and White flight from racially mixed communities (Feagin & Feagin, 1986; Massey & Denton, 1993). Problems associated with segregation are complicated by the fact that communities are increasingly becoming segregated by wealth (Massey, 2007). As wealth and potential tax revenues migrate to affluent suburbs, poorer cities and communities struggle to provide residents basic services. Many people of color, African Americans and Latinos in particular, are restricted to communities that are poor and have substandard municipal park and recreation services. Importantly, *because of land acquisition decisions made in the past,* many of these same communities are ones that have been historically deprived of parks and open space. A troubling consequence of all this is that many people of color grow up lacking formative experiences and knowledge of parks, outdoor recreation, and other pastimes.

Other institutional barriers to equitable service delivery are practices and beliefs adopted by park and recreation agencies and practitioners. One of these is an entrepreneurial approach to service delivery, which entails revenue production through the generation of fees and charges and the privatization of services. The latter is characterized by the divestiture of public facilities and programs. As noted in a previous section, many people of color are overrepresented among the poor and are often unable to afford modest program and facility fees. Likewise, many people of color are barred from accessing private facilities

(e.g., swimming pools) and programs (e.g., club sports and select teams) via eligibility requirements, steep program costs, or both. In communities where these practices are used, social equity has become less important in decisions regarding the allocation of resources and services (Godbey, Caldwell, Floyd, & Payne, 2005). While revenue production and privatization of services have greatly aided public park and recreation delivery (Crompton, 1999), these practice have disproportionately and negatively affected ethnic and racial minorities.

A less obvious organizational practice is promoting customer loyalty. Loyal patrons are desired because they are believed to provide park and recreation agencies with long-term sources of income and support for bond measures that potentially expand recreational services (Selin, Howard, Udd, & Cable, 1988). Emphasizing customer loyalty is a laudable, if not a necessary, goal, but it also contributes to agencies' deemphasizing concern over social equity and inclusion. The reason is that the practice gives primacy to the interests of individuals and groups who have historically used an agency's facilities and services. Some park and recreation agencies, for example, send advertisements about agency offerings only to past customers (Harnik, 2010). The vast majority of interpretive exhibits at historic sites celebrate White American experiences, conquests, exploration, and heritage (Taylor, 2000). Missing are stories reflecting the experiences of African Americans, Chinese Americans, Mexican Americans, and so on. The recreation needs of many people of color have been subordinated and sometimes erased as park and recreation agencies continue to provide popular and established programs and services to White constituents.

A closely related practice is embracing a *White racial frame.* According to Feagin (2006), this is "an organized set of racialized ideas, stereotypes, and inclinations to discriminate" (p. 25). Feagin added that a White racial frame is "consciously or unconsciously expressed in the routine operation" of American institutions (p. 25). In everyday practice, White people, White behavior, and White institutions are viewed positively and provide the standard for evaluating what is good and moral, whereas non-Whites and their behavior are regarded with suspicion, subjected to stereotyping, and subjected to negative publicity (Cavin, 2008).

One way a White racial frame permeates the delivery of park and recreation resources is by *equating public spaces to White spaces.* Notwithstanding Civil Rights laws that expressly forbid the exclusion of people of color from public facilities, many parks and public areas are the province of Whites and off limits, at least unofficially, to people of color. Many Whites have developed what Austin (1997-1998) calls a *proprietary* attitude about the public places they occupy and the rules for appropriate behavior. Non-Whites who venture into White spaces may be treated rather coolly and, not surprisingly, feel unwelcome and remain on their guard (Carter, 2008; Erickson et al., 2009; Falk, 1995). If non-Whites are treated coolly, their behavior in White spaces often comes under stringent scrutiny. Leisure among young African American males, in particular, is often viewed as pathological, disruptive, and a major source of disturbance in public settings (Austin, 1997-1998). This has led to no small amount of racial profiling and monitoring in public park and recreation areas.

Another factor that keeps many leisure service agencies from better serving people of color is the fact that employees do not resemble the population at large. According to Allison (1999), diversity policies and practices have historically been more symbolic than substantive. Agencies have also historically engaged in selectively hiring and promoting ethnic and racial minorities (Shinew & Hibbler, 2002). People of color who are hired or promoted in park and recreation agencies sometimes experience White resentment and amazement (Shimoda, 1988). These feelings stem from a longstanding belief that people of color are hired or promoted because of their ethnic–racial identity rather than their job-related skills (Allison, 1999). Lack of diversity in park and recreation agencies means that personnel are likely to embrace White racial frames as normal and to be insensitive to minority interests, viewpoints, and struggles (Allison, 2000; Allison & Hibbler, 2004; Feagin, 2006).

Finally, inequities in access to park and recreation resources are reinforced by a narrow conception of recreation need that is based on the long, highly trusted American belief that people are fully capable of self-determination. As noted by Henderson (1997), this belief prevents practitioners from acknowledging that many people face formidable constraints that stymie their access to park and recreation resources. She noted, "[The] onus is always on individuals. . . . In North American society, we are socialized to 'pull ourselves up by the bootstraps' and to be personally responsible for our fate" (p. 456). In effect, leisure practitioners tend to believe that constituents have equal means and access to park and recreation resources. History has seemingly proved them right—many park and recreation managers are quick to point out that their facilities, swimming pools, programs, and campgrounds are already at capacity or near capacity. Accordingly, they can readily explain nonuse of park and recreation resources on the part of minorities as stemming from alternative interests.

CONCLUSION: ARE AGENCIES CAPABLE OF CHANGE?

Public park and recreation agencies have struggled, since their inception, to provide programs and services to immigrants and people of color. What hope is there that leisure service agencies can do better in the future? Research summarized in this and other chapters suggests that service provision for ethnic and racial minorities can be improved through ensuring that programs and facilities are affordable, accessible, culturally relevant, safe, and welcoming. These principles are straightforward and apply to all people irrespective of their race and ethnicity. Indeed, most Whites, particularly affluent Whites, can generally take for granted that these principles are being followed routinely by leisure service agencies throughout North America.

If leisure service agencies are to better serve people of color, they must first broaden their conception of recreation need. What this means is that they should not assume that people of color are unfettered by social and structural circumstances. The reality is that ethnic and racial minorities are often treated as second-class citizens in North America and that they encounter far more constraints to accessing leisure services than Whites. In many cases they lack sufficient resources to effectively negotiate constraints by themselves. To more effectively serve immigrants and people of color, Allison (2000) argued that leisure service agencies must become antidiscriminatory as opposed to simply being nondiscriminatory. Organizations that are antidiscriminatory are ones that strive to develop an organizational culture in which ideas about diversity, inclusion, and social justice are fundamental to their mission and how they *routinely* do business (Scott, 2005).

Leisure service organizations can also better serve immigrants and people of color by ensuring that their voices are heard in the planning and delivery of programs and services. To state this differently, leisure service organizations need "translators" who effectively communicate the needs of minority communities. There are at least three ways this can be accomplished. First, agencies can be far more aggressive in hiring people of color and including them in advisory capacities. Having a workforce that resembles the population will go a long way in establishing trust between leisure service agencies and minorities. Second, diversity training must be more substantive than symbolic (Allison, 1999). All employees must be committed to principles of inclusion and social justice. Inclusion must permeate the organiza-

tion from top to bottom. Finally, agencies must expand their outreach programs. This is particularly important for agencies that manage outdoor recreation programs or facilities. Many people of color lack formative experiences in outdoor pursuits, but interest can be generated via agency-facilitated programs.

The biggest challenge to improved service delivery is political. This chapter began with a quote from a letter in *National Parks* magazine. Many Whites do not want leisure service agencies to reach out to minority communities. Some of these individuals believe that leisure programs and facilities are available to all people and that agency efforts to diversify program offerings are both unnecessary and financially irresponsible. Others are against diversifying leisure service offerings because they *do not want to share leisure spaces with people of color.* Many of these same individuals feel that illegal immigrants have no right to access public services in the United States. Given the extensive antipathy many people of color encounter in everyday life, leisure service agencies will need strong and influential political allies as they advocate for improved park and recreation delivery for minorities. Short of this, agencies will lack the political mandate to diversify, and many people of color will continue to struggle to access park and recreation programs and facilities.

PART II

Leisure Among Specific Racial, Ethnic, and Religious Populations in the United States and Canada

This part of the book reviews extant research on leisure behavior among specific minority populations in the United States and Canada, including African Americans, Latino Americans, Asian North Americans, Indigenous peoples of North America, and members of religious minorities. Chapter 4 examines historical and contemporary influences on leisure patterns among African Americans, emerging issues related to race relations in the United States, and current trends in theory and research related to leisure experiences among African Americans. Chapters 5, 6, and 7 provide a comprehensive review of the history and current status of leisure research involving Latino Americans, Asian North Americans, and Indigenous Americans, respectively; provide practical recommendations on how to provide leisure services to these populations; and identify areas for future research on these groups. Chapter 8 reviews the literature on the effects of three major religious doctrines (Christianity, Islam, and Judaism) on leisure behavior in the United States and Canada and assesses the current state of empirical research on minority religious groups in these two countries.

Leisure Among African Americans

Myron F. Floyd and Rasul A. Mowatt

OVERVIEW

This chapter takes a close look at race and leisure among Black Americans, past and present. In particular, the authors examine historical and contemporary influences on leisure patterns among Black Americans, as well as emerging issues related to the evolving social and demographic contexts of race relations in 21st-century American society that will affect future leisure research on this group. The discussion then turns to current trends in theory and research related to Black leisure experiences and finally to emerging research needs associated with changing social and demographic contexts.

Learning Outcomes

After reading this chapter, readers will be able to

- identify social forces in the Black society leading to leisure research on Black populations;
- describe the historical development of research literature on Black people, specifically understanding the significance of African Americans as representatives of a larger Black diaspora and their leisure;
- describe the current demographic characteristics of Black people in the United States;
- identify prevailing trends in research on leisure participation among Black populations; and
- describe research needs related to leisure trends among Black populations.

Slavery has always been a problem, for it is based on self-evident existential absurdity: that one human being can be a simple extension of the will of another.

Barbara J. Fields, "Ideology and Race in American History" (1992, p. 161)

All paradises, all utopias, are designed by who is not there, by the people who are not allowed in.

Toni Morrison, PBS NewsHour interview (March 9, 1998)

SLAVERY: BLACK LIFE OR BLACK EXISTENCE?

As one looks at leisure, and in particular the work–life oppositions it often raises, thinking about Black life in the pre-1865 United States presents a quandary. As the industrial revolution yielded lifestyle changes for many people in the United States due to the marvels of manufacturing and industry, the enslavement of Black people funded much of the advancements within the industrial revolution and in turn was expanded by it. From 1654 to 1865, for the vast majority of Black people in the United States, Canada, and the Caribbean, slavery was a way of existence that loomed over all whether they were enslaved or not. The term *existence* applied instead of *life*, as being a slave was not a matter of choice but a harsh reality meaning that one's daily reason for being was servitude to another. The social reality of slavery meant that the very notion of one person's "being a simple extension of the will of another" forever contorted how social interactions in the United States would be formed; it also shaped how social roles and behaviors would be enacted and even included methods of continuous self-enforcement in society (Fields, 1982, p. 161; Nunn, 2008). Historians are still tallying "hard" numbers of those who were systematically captured from various parts of the African continent. Estimated numbers begin at 12 million Africans shipped to the Americas, with nearly 700,000 shipped directly to what would become the United States (Behrendt, 1999; Lovejoy, 1989; Segal, 1995). However, the numbers are only increasing as researchers further analyze ships' logs, census figures, population growth, diaspora dispersion patterns, and African underdevelopment (Behrendt, 1999; Perry, 2009; Rodney, 1982). Thus, the quandary is that the industrial revolution ushered our modern conventions of leisure but at a terrible human cost.

Throughout this chapter, the term "Black" is used to refer to the shared political histories of persons of African descent, born and residing in the United States, who have been affected by the policies and the experiences of living in the United States. Although the term "African American" is more appropriate in specific geographical contexts, the chapter addresses the experiences of Black Canadians traveling in the United States, Africans who immigrated to the United States, those of mixed parentage including one parent who is Black, those who also claim Native American and European ancestry, and longstanding citizens of Caribbean and Latin American descent who do not culturally identify as African American.

In considering the period of slavery, leisure researchers fail on two counts. They fail (1) to acknowledge that American slavery was at its peak at the same period of time when the field originated and (2) to imagine what "living" in slavery could be like. While during her childhood Jane Addams, who would later found Hull House in Chicago, was admiring her father's political work, Black men and women were still being shipped to ports along the southern East Coast (Brown, 2004; Knight, 2005). As the physical culture movement came into being to combat the "disease of affluence" spawned by the advantages of the industrial revolution, this reality of affluence was a direct by-product of having an enslaved labor force of millions and the capital earned from their labor (Conrad, Whitehead, Mason, & Stewart, 2005;

Russell, 2009). At the time when Henry David Thoreau, a lifelong abolitionist, was writing about the splendor of the natural environment that contributed to the idea of national parks, African men and women were being sold, bred, and then sold again into slavery (Berlin, 2003; Thoreau, 2007).

As the field of leisure research was developing, it failed to take slavery and its consequences into account, and it has also neglected to ponder the "quality of life" of this enslaved population. The vast numbers of enslaved Black people inhabiting the United States toiled endlessly on a range of plantations based on corn, indigo, sugar, rice, cotton, and slave breeding (plantations geared specifically toward the production of slaves) (Buzinde & Santos, 2008). There are stories of the enslaved on these plantations creating music and dance, as well as forming unique religious and social customs (Allen, Ware, & Garrison, 1996; Blassingame, 1979; Will, 1999). There are also stories of widespread rape of enslaved women and the violent suppression of independent thought and action (Durant & Knottnerus, 1999; Gunning, 1996; Mowatt, 2008). Those fortunate enough to escape slavery in the Southern states, no longer to be counted among the 3.5 million enslaved, lived as nearly 500,000 freed Black people in constant fear of being sent back to the South or captured under false pretenses (The Civil War Home Page, 2000; Douglass, 2001). This fear was based on the reality of slavery and a belief that one's very existence as a human being was in constant question. The minstrel show tradition that began in the 1830s, in mainly Northern centers, was founded on caricatures of Black people by White performers wearing "blackface" (Mahar, 1998). The minstrel tradition became the first and most popular American stage or theatrical form distinct from European art forms. Science, sociology, psychology, religion, and history were all twisted and used to argue that the Black population was less than human and worthy of whatever treatment anyone was inclined to use (Berlin, 2003; Washington, 2006).

The Three-Fifths Compromise of 1787 further legitimized these beliefs. In the debate over how to enumerate the slave population in the United States, Southern and Northern states entered into a compromise according to which anyone among the vast numbers of enslaved people in the South could not be counted as a full person. This represented the two underlying beliefs that Northerners believed enslaved people were not full human beings and Southerners, who held the same belief, had to count their numbers in order to increase their representation. This would tip the balance of representation in the U.S. House of Representatives toward the Southern states (Taylor, 2009). The Three-Fifths Compromise would leave these words in the U.S. Constitution:

> Representatives and direct Taxes shall be apportioned among the several States which may be included within this Union, according to their respective Numbers, which shall be determined by adding to the whole Number of free Persons, including those bound to Service for a Term of Years, and excluding Indians not taxed, three fifths of all other Persons. (Article 1, Section 2, Paragraph 3)

With this compromise articulated in the Constitution, the very nature of Black humanity was sealed as forever in question. "Free" states wanted only free inhabitants to be counted among their population to determine representation, while "slave" states wanted to count those who were enslaved so that their representation could be greater in the House of Representatives and the Electoral College. Thus the compromise: "All other persons" (enslaved Black people) were to be counted as three-fifths of a person rather than a whole person. It was not until ratification of the 13th and 14th Amendments to the U.S. Constitution that Article 1, Section 2, Paragraph 3 was overturned.[1]

RECONSTRUCTION: HOPE, BETRAYAL, AND FAILURE

The 13th and 14th Amendments during the Reconstruction era (1865-1877) overturned the Philadelphia Three-Fifths Compromise by

---

[1]The 13th Amendment abolished slavery; the 14th Amendment established civil rights and contains the citizenship, due process, and equal protection clauses.

granting citizenship to all Black people in the United States (Foner, 1987). However, the 14th Amendment also symbolized Reconstruction in its hope and failure as the United States underwent a painful restructuring of the economic system, political organization, and geographic boundaries. Leading up to this period, the Emancipation Proclamation (1863) freed all enslaved Black people, which increased the Northern states' population and military conscription. (Guelzo, 2004; Silver, 1998). This act found its way into the present as a Black celebration called Juneteenth, the day news of the Proclamation may have reached Texas, some two years after it was signed. The newly created Freedmen's Bureau embarked on integrating formerly enslaved Black people into areas of employment, education, housing, and social life. The Freedmen's Bureau was very important in that it was developed to determine how to integrate a population that had been enslaved for over 200 years into the fabric (politics, education, employment, and leisure) of the United States. However, as a result of Lincoln's assassination and the fact that the bureau had no appointed head, these intentions were never actualized (Colby, 1985). At the same time, the granting of civil rights to Blacks met with widespread resistance as Southern leaders regained some of the power and influence they had lost during the Civil War. The resistance was also embodied in the Ku Klux Klan (Baker, 2007).

As the Klan and Klan-like sentiment grew, so did the prevalence of lynching throughout the country (Mowatt, 2008). A congressional investigation found that "during a span of a few weeks in 1868 more than 2,000 Black people were murdered by mobs in Louisiana; an incomplete count in Texas revealed that 1,035 were lynched between the end of the Civil War and 1862" (White, 1992, p. xii). This violent unrest and the economic collapse known as the Panic of 1873, the long depression due to the fall in demand of silver, led to the politically corrupt agreement during the presidency of Rutherford Hayes that overturned Reconstruction policies (DeSantis, 1982). The hope and sense of possibilities that had begun with Reconstruction ended for Black people—although slavery no longer existed, they would now have to forage on their own. The ending of this era developed a strong sense of independence among Black people as they dispersed throughout the country after the failure of the Freedmen's Bureau or remained and gathered together in communities such as Atlanta, New Orleans, Birmingham, and Durham. Many Blacks left racism and violence in the East and moved west to Oklahoma, Nebraska, and other destinations to develop businesses in order to take advantage of new economic opportunities (Wilson & Wallace, 2004). Despite the failure of the Freedmen's Bureau and the reinvigoration of the South because of the reversal of the Reconstruction, many Black communities began to flourish in locations like these but also in states such as Florida and Oklahoma and cities like Chicago and East St. Louis.

ASSESSING THE IMPACT OF JIM CROW ON BLACK LEISURE

Under Emancipation, new forms of social control were deployed to enforce separation of the races. Alternative means of controlling free Blacks were necessary because of the ability of Blacks to move freely, a fear of insurrection and revenge among Southern Whites, and the need to secure labor (Woodward, 1974). Widespread beliefs and stereotypes about the inferiority of Blacks pervaded both North and South. As Woodward noted, it was common during the 1880s and 1890s for Northern editorialists and former abolitionists to espouse "the shibboleths of white supremacy regarding the Negro's innate inferiority, shiftlessness, and hopeless unfitness for full participation in the white man's civilization" (p. 70).

The U.S. Supreme Court decision *Plessy v. Ferguson* (1896) provided the legal structure for de jure racial segregation (i.e., segregation by law rather than custom) in the United States. In this case, the Supreme Court upheld Louisiana's Separate Car Act (1890), which required all passenger trains in the state to provide "separate but equal" seating cars for White and Black passengers. According to Foster (1999), segregation of railroad cars was sought to placate White passengers who were offended by the growing presence of prosperous "well-dressed" Black passengers using trains for pleasure travel. In the decision, the Court ruled against Homer A. Plessy, who claimed that

Louisiana violated his right to equal protection under the 14th Amendment to the Constitution. The court followed the doctrine that "legislation was powerless to eradicate racial instincts" and thus provided the legal basis for the application of the separate-but-equal principle to all public facilities (Woodward, 1974, p. 71). The Plessy case was the formal beginning of discrimination by law, the so-called Jim Crow era.

By embracing the separate-but-equal doctrine, the Supreme Court established the rules governing how Black people and White people would interact in public spaces, including schools, churches, restaurants, hospitals, hotels, resorts, theaters, lecture halls, parks, prisons, and even cemeteries (Woodward, 1974). As many Black people would testify, separate public facilities were never equal in quality. The Plessy decision stood until 1954, the year it was overturned in *Brown v. Board of Education of Topeka, Kansas*.

The immediate impact of the Plessy decision on leisure expression among Black people in the late 19th and early 20th centuries can be assessed in a number of ways. In the broadest sense, de jure segregation prescribed psychological, social, and geographic boundaries for leisure among Black people during this time. The next section examines specific ways in which the racism of the period conditioned leisure experiences among Black people.

Racialized Spaces

One of the most obvious ways de jure segregation affected leisure among Black people in the United States was in the physical and temporal separation of "the races." In the era when recreation began to be recognized as a social good, Jim Crow laws "proliferated" (Murphy, 1972; Woodward, 1974). By 1900, most Southern states had adopted Jim Crow laws that applied to passenger trains and waiting areas in the stations. Among these were South Carolina (in 1898), North Carolina (in 1899), and Virginia (in 1900). As a sign of things to come, a Montgomery (Alabama) ordinance set a precedent for providing "completely separate" streetcars for its Black citizens. It was during this era that the "Whites only" and "Colored" signs for water fountains, bathrooms, waiting rooms, and other public places became part and parcel of everyday life for Whites and Blacks, not to be eliminated until the 1960s and 1970s.

Jim Crow laws separated recreation spaces by race.

The first Jim Crow law governing park use appeared in 1905 as "the Separate Park Law of Georgia" (Woodward, 1974). Louisiana required traveling shows such as circuses, carnivals, and tent shows to have "separate entrances, exits, ticket windows, and ticket sellers that would be kept at least twenty-five feet apart" (Woodward, 1974, pp. 99-100). Further, the "city of Birmingham [Alabama] applied the principle to 'any room, hall, theatre, picture house, auditorium, yard, court, ball park, or other indoor or outdoor place' and specified that races be 'distinctly separated . . . by well defined physical barriers'" (p. 100).

As Murphy (1972) observed, there was no indication that organizations such as the Playground Association of America (PAA), established in 1906 (it would later become the National Recreation and Park Association), were concerned about the lack of adequate recreation facilities for Black people in the nation's cities. Efforts to address the lack of playgrounds in Northern cities ignored the needs of Black youth, focusing instead on the White youth. One report cited by Murphy showed that in 1921, a total of 428 municipalities in the United States operated 3,969 playground and recreation centers. Of this number, 56 (or about 13%) reported having a playground available for use by Black children, and only 14 cities operated "integrated" playgrounds. In 1922 the Playground and Recreation Association of America (PRAA, formerly the PAA) hired Ernest T. Attwell, an African American, to direct field service programs that would develop recreation opportunities for urban Black communities. Attwell, employed by the Tuskegee Institute, was selected because of his reputation as a statesman and his association with Booker T. Washington (Murphy, 1972). The change at PRAA came in response to a combination of historical events.

The onset of World War I in 1914 brought significant numbers of Black and White troops to cities where they were stationed. In 1917, organized recreation programs for troops were coordinated by the War Camp Service and the PRAA with separate facilities, activity programs, and staff for White and Black troops (Murphy, 1972). The war also stimulated the movement of Black civilians from the South to Northern cities in search of work in manufacturing industries

supporting the war efforts (Farley & Allen, 1989). The collapse of cotton production in the South caused by the boll weevil infestation between 1906 and 1916 disrupted the region's economy, which was heavily dependent on rural Black labor. Many Black citizens went north looking for jobs. Lastly, intensification of Jim Crow and racial violence were major push factors for Black migration to Northern cities (Mitchell, 2001). The Great Migration, as it came to be called, resulted in a massive shift of the Black population (2 million people) from the rural South to Northern cities. The concentration of these immigrants in segregated slums in Northern cities brought into clearer focus the need to develop recreation programs for Black citizens. One of Attwater's first assignments was to convert the War Camp Service facilities into community recreation centers for Blacks in several cities, including Philadelphia and Harrisburg in Pennsylvania and Mobile in Alabama (Murphy, 1972). Besides offering activities, a key aspect of public recreation programs conducted by Attwell focused on training recreation leaders within Black communities to design and administer organized programs.

The aftermath of the Plessy decision also brought about institutional and individual responses from the Black private sector. Few accounts from slavery into the early 20th century bring attention to status differentiation or class differences within the Black community (Landry & Marsh, 2011; Ruef & Fletcher, 2003). During slavery, men who were skilled as blacksmiths, masons, and carpenters enjoyed greater freedoms and privileges than those who were common field laborers (Ruff & Fletcher). While social mobility was extremely limited for freed men during Reconstruction, a professional class consisting of clergy, teachers, tradesmen, and business owners did emerge (Ruef & Fletcher). In the classic study *The Philadelphia Negro*, DuBois (1899) documented the presence of a small community of "learned professions" consisting of clergy, teachers, doctors, lawyers, and other professionals. As pointed out by Landry and Marsh (2011), DuBois argued that the professional class within the Black community—that is, the "Talented Tenth"—should assume a greater leadership role in promoting the welfare of Black citizens. With the emergence of "parallel institutions" (Hine, 2003), the Black professional class mobilized social and economic resources to provide some social services as well as leisure opportunities to fellow Black citizens.

Parallel Institutions and Black Leisure

The idea of parallel institutions is borrowed from Hine (2003), who used the concept to reflect the "innovative resistance strategies" that Black physicians, nurses, and lawyers deployed to "crack" White supremacy and desegregate these professional communities. (Examples of parallel organizations include the National Medical Association and National Bar Association, for Black doctors and lawyers, respectively.) Hine stated, "Segregation provided blacks the chance, indeed, the imperative, to develop a range of distinct institutions they controlled." Further, she argued that "parallel institutions offered black Americans not only private space to buttress battered dignity, nurture positive self-images, sharpen skills, and demonstrate expertise. These safe havens sustained relationships and wove networks across communities served" (p. 1280).

The economic resources of professional and affluent Blacks were important in establishing parallel institutions (Hine, 2003) for promoting leisure and recreation opportunities for Black communities during the early Jim Crow era. One of the best examples of Black business development is the Greenwood area of Tulsa, Oklahoma, or "Black Wall Street" (Johnson, 1998). Greenwood was dubbed "the Black Wall Street" because of the concentration of Black-owned businesses in the area (Johnson). It would become one of the wealthiest communities in the United States due to the economic boom created by the discovery of oil in the region. White residents failed to see these developments as economic success (e.g., two newspapers and paved roads) achieved by their Black neighbors. Tensions developed in 1921 after a racial encounter in downtown Tulsa. A mob formed, grew, and began to burn down Greenwood. Firemen were held at gunpoint and ordered to not respond. Black residents of Greenwood were shot as they fled from burning structures.

At the conclusion of the riot, the 10,000 Black residents of Greenwood suffered a loss of nearly 30 lives, with over 650 businesses, over 1,200 homes, some 20 churches, nearly 30 restaurants, a couple of movie theaters, schools, libraries, and gymnasiums totaling $1.5 million in property damage (Madigan, 2001; White, 1921).

The violence in 1921 Greenwood that resulted in deaths and devastating property loss was not unique in the U.S. landscape. As lynching continued from the Reconstruction era, race riots involving White violence perpetrated on Black people sprung up in 1871 Meridian, Mississippi; 1891 Omaha, Nebraska; 1898 Wilmington, North Carolina; 1908 Springfield, Illinois; 1917 East St. Louis, Illinois; 1923 Rosewood, Florida; and 1943 Detroit, Michigan (Mowatt, 2008; Tuttle, 1996; Tyson & Cecelski, 1998). Over the course of one year, eight race riots occurred in cities such as Chicago and Omaha (for a second time) and Washington, DC (Dray, 2002; Ifill, 2007; Tuttle, 1996). Racial violence was something that Black communities slowly began to understand as a way of life. The inability to thrive and grow meant that opportunities to self-determine their future, which included self-protection, were seemingly forever out of grasp. In this kind of turmoil, parallel institutions were critical to the development and survival of Black businesses, community solidarity, and leisure expression.

Foster's (1999) sources and historical accounts of leisure among "prosperous" African Americans show that that during Reconstruction (before Plessy), Black service and fraternal organizations in New Orleans arranged day trips and extended excursions that were not reserved only for the affluent. After the Plessy decision, the makings of a Black resort industry emerged as White resort areas increasingly closed their gates to Blacks. Foster's (1999) research shows that by the late 1890s, Black resorts opened in Atlantic City and Cape May, New Jersey; Newport, Rhode Island; Silcott Springs, Virginia; and Harpers Ferry, West Virginia. By the 1920s, resorts sprouted in the Midwest, including the West Michigan Resort (near Benton Harbor) and perhaps the most famous, Idlewild (Michigan). Visitors enjoyed common recreation activities associated with the outdoors such as hiking, horseback riding, boating, and fishing as well as indoor activities like cards, readings, and partying. From the 1920s to the 1950s, some of the biggest names in entertainment performed at Idlewild nightspots, including Count Basie, Duke Ellington, and Sammy Davis Jr. (Wilson, 1981). Other resorts opened in the 1920s and '30s, for example Fox Lake in Indiana; Lake Adney in Minnesota; Cedar Country Club, near Cleveland, Ohio; and Winks Panoramic Lodge, established in the Rocky Mountains and used by the Black community in Denver.

Other forms of parallel leisure institutions developed around specific activities such as tennis, golf, and baseball. Foster's (1999) historical research shows that as early as 1917, Black golf clubs were being formed. One source from 1922, *The Crisis* (the official publication of the National Association for the Advancement of Colored people, NAACP), documented the existence of the Shady Rest Country Club in Westfield, New Jersey. According to *The Crisis*, the club had 200 members and a nine-hole course. Another newspaper reported that the club was the first private club for Black members in the United States. Other clubs that opened in the early 1920s included the Colored Country Club of Bucks County, Pennsylvania; the National Capital Country Club in Baltimore, Maryland; and a golf club in Corona, California (Foster, 1999).

Tennis (compared to golf) was more popular in terms of numbers of Blacks participating in the 1890s (Foster, 1999). The Black press (e.g., *The Defender* and *The Crisis*) documented interstate and national tennis tournaments for Black players. Foster noted that the level of Black participation in tennis was sufficient for the formation of the American Tennis Association (ATA) in 1916. The first national ATA tournament was held in 1917 in Baltimore. Between 1916 and 1924, the ATA grew to consist of 79 local ATA groups in 25 states with about 1,000 members.

Finally, one of the more prominent forms of parallel institutions involving sport was the formation of the Negro baseball leagues, which existed in some form from 1887 to 1952 (Negro League Baseball Players Association, 2012), ending five years after Jackie Robinson signed with the Brooklyn Dodgers to become the first African American to play in Major League Baseball.

In his analysis, Foster (1999) was careful to note that the accommodations at most Black resorts were not on par with amenities found in White resorts. Moreover, it would be safe to conclude that the quality of golf, tennis, and organized sport facilities and venues did not surpass that of amenities available to White participants given the era. Despite their modest provisions, these parallel leisure spaces provided opportunities for leisure expression when other public and private opportunities were off limits to Blacks. Over and above the immediate fun and enjoyment that might have been experienced, they offered Blacks emotional succor and "private space to buttress battered dignity" (Hine, 2003, p. 1280) with their own people in their own leisure community. Damage to the personal and collective psyche from racial oppression and intimate experience with the subtle and blatant racism during that era also altered the way Black Americans conceived of and expressed themselves during leisure.

Psychic Impacts of Racial Oppression

A key part of the legal strategy for the plaintiffs in *Brown v. Board of Education* (1954), which would overturn *Plessy v. Ferguson,* was to show the psychological damage of racial segregation in Black children. This was highlighted by the famous dolls study in which Black children assigned negative attributes to Black dolls and exhibited positive reactions toward White dolls (Clark & Clark, 1947). These findings were used to show that internalized racial stereotypes and self-hatred were produced by racial segregation. Perhaps the most damaging impact to leisure among Black Americans was the psychic cost of enduring racism. The institution of Black codes through the Jim Crow laws and social customs required constant vigilance (e.g., not looking a White man in the eye, not allowing an eye to wander in the direction of a White woman, giving Whites the right of way on a sidewalk).

There are no studies from this era on the effects of the stress associated with constant self-monitoring and surveillance to avoid racism and discrimination. However, current studies indicate that "chronic vigilance" may prolong acute stress and that chronic stress increases allostatic load

(McEwen, 2003). Allostatic load refers to "the wear and tear on the body produced through chronic or repeated activation of the stress-response systems" and "predisposes individuals to a number of health problems, including memory impairment, neural atrophy, and heart disease" (Sawyer, Major, Casad, Townsend, & Mendes, 2012). Many current studies link discrimination experiences with psychiatric symptoms and also report positive associations between discrimination and chronic diseases including heart disease, stroke, diabetes, cancer, and low birth weight babies (Sawyer et al., 2012).

The impact of "constant vigilance" on Black leisure experiences surfaced in Carter's (2008) interviews with Black travel agents and their experiences with White spaces. Black travelers often find themselves in situations in which they have to determine whether a racial slight or some discriminatory treatment carries a racist intent. Carter drew upon Foucault's (1977) theorizing on internalization of discipline by prisoners to illustrate how "Blacks are guarded in White spaces even when they need not be because how would they know if the thoughts and intentions of those around them (Whites) are benign or malevolent?" (p. 279). Carter (2008) described this as "rational paranoia – fearing the unknown with some amount of justification." Even more during the early 20th century, without the protections currently enjoyed, this kind of paranoia and constant vigilance were indeed justified. Black people in that era were well aware of the threat of physical violence from White people, lynching in particular. Tolnay and Beck (1995) found that a disproportionate number of Black people in the United States died by lynching between Emancipation and the Great Depression in comparison to other populations subjected to lynching. A significant number of the lynchings occurred in rural or wooded areas (Mowatt, 2008; 2012; Raper, 1933). Some researchers (e.g., Cloke, 2004; Johnson, 1998) have attributed the low participation of Black people in wildland recreation today to this legacy of violence (see chapter 11 on discrimination in leisure contexts).

AFTER *BROWN V. BOARD OF EDUCATION*

Just as the *Plessy v. Ferguson* ruling was significant for providing the legal framework supporting Jim Crow laws, *Brown v. Board of Education (Topeka, Kansas)* was powerful in dismantling de jure segregation and leveled a strong blow to its core ideological beliefs: White supremacy and Black inferiority. The impact of the Brown decision was far reaching. Although the decision required that public schools be desegregated "with all deliberate speed," all public institutions and most aspects of community life were set on a course toward inevitable desegregation. The process of desegregation of public institutions was not swift. Over the decade following the *Brown v. Board* ruling, a quick succession of civil rights policy changes ensued, with slow implementation. Several specifically targeted desegregation of parks and recreation facilities.[2]

One of the first legal actions related to recreation involved a lawsuit filed by a Black family who were made to leave a municipal beach in Baltimore, Maryland (Murphy, 1972). A federal district judge hearing the case ruled that the family had no right to use the beach because the city operated a separate swimming area for Black citizens (i.e., "separate, but equal"). However, the U.S. Fourth Circuit Court of Appeals overturned the ruling, and that decision was upheld by the U.S. Supreme Court in 1955 (*Mayor and City Council of Baltimore v. Dawson*). According to Murphy,

> The court held that racial segregation in recreational activities could no longer be sustained as a proper exercise of the police power of the state. It reasoned that if that power cannot be invoked to sustain racial segregation in the schools where attendance is compulsory, it therefore cannot be sustained with respect to public beach and bathhouse facilities, the use of which is entirely optional. (p. 118)

Supreme Court rulings on other state-level segregation laws specific to parks and recreation

---

[2]Much of the material here comes from James F. Murphy's (1972) dissertation *Egalitarianism and Separatism: A History of Provision and Leisure Service for Blacks, 1906-1972*, an excellent resource for students of race and leisure service provision.

included *Homes v. Atlanta,* which ruled against segregation on public golf courses. The 1963 case *Watson v. Memphis* reversed Memphis' plan to gradually desegregate parks, playgrounds, and pools over a 10-year period. The city was ordered to desegregate immediately. Murphy's account shows the ways in which Whites, particularly in Southern states, opposed and resisted desegregation of parks and recreation areas (see also chapter 3 on race, ethnicity, and leisure services). Alabama closed all of its state parks and playgrounds in 1958. Arkansas, Mississippi, and Louisiana defied the rulings and maintained the separate-but-equal policy. In some cases, municipalities sold facilities such as swimming pools and wading areas to private citizens for exclusive use by Whites. The rise of White Citizens Councils, a group devoted to preserving segregation, and the threat of Klan activity were also part of the White resistance to desegregation. Thus, what had been de jure segregation became de facto segregation. In other words, separation was imposed by will or custom, and in some cases enforced through violence.

Civil Rights and the 1960s

Despite vigorous opposition, noteworthy progress was made in opening a broader spectrum of recreation opportunities to African Americans. Perhaps the second most important policy change affecting Blacks' access to recreation opportunities was the Civil Rights Act of 1964. Title III of the act prohibited racial discrimination in publicly owned facilities such as parks and recreation facilities, libraries, and sport stadiums. Also during the early 1960s, concern about the "leisure opportunities gap" between Blacks and Whites took on new urgency in national policy affairs. Grievances related to inadequate parks and recreation facilities were identified as a major source of conflict in large cities around the country (National Advisory Commission on Civil Disorders, 1967).

It is important to revisit other key events from the 1960s that are typically left out of leisure texts. From this period, the use of "Black" as a political expression emerged; the term would come to represent all persons of African descent in the following period and become an integral aspect of identity. Disenfranchised and disenchanted youth of the Civil Rights movement branched off and created the Black Power movement for social advancement. They saw that civil rights were not enough. In their view, the development of a new identity via language, appearance, and food (birth of "soul food") was also necessary (Ture & Hamilton, 1992; Van DeBurg, 1992). This led to efforts by organizations such as the Black Panther Party, the Black Liberation Army, and the US Organization to create social services such as providing free breakfast programs, blood pressure screenings, and community gardens within Black communities throughout the country. They also created recreational opportunities through theatrical performances, after-school and weekend youth programming, baseball leagues, and camping excursions (Joseph, 2006). However, the ever-looming presence of violence perpetrated on Black communities was actualized when many of these groups and the individuals associated with them lost their lives, were wrongfully incarcerated for alleged crimes, or became addicted to drugs such as heroin and crack that flowed heavily into the communities. Remnants of those efforts became a part of the Afrocentric movement in the mid-1980s and early 1990s aimed at adult awareness and youth rites of passage programs (Asante, 1998, 2002).

Responses From the Research Community

In response to urban unrest, social protests, and inequality in other social sectors due to racial tensions on the rise in the 1960s, federal, state, and local governments sponsored studies to determine the level of racial disparity in access to recreation opportunities, as well as to identify other factors associated with access (Hutchison, 1974, cited in Johnson, Bowker, English, & Worthen, 1997). Data provided by the Outdoor Recreation Resources Review Commission (ORRRC) (1958-1962), in the first major national study of outdoor recreation in the United States, further illuminated racial disparity in access to outdoor leisure opportunities for Black Americans (Mueller & Gurin, 1962) and identified significant differences in the extent of outdoor recreation participation of Blacks and Whites. With the addition of statistical controls for "income, education, occupational status, and place of residence" (p. 25), racial differences persisted. In a separate ORRRC report (Report 22), Hauser (1962) stated that "non-white (all black) participation in these activities is relatively low apparently by reason of their high cost or the unavailability to the individual of suitable facilities" (pp. 56-57). This pattern of findings would be the focus of studies on race and leisure in the 1970s and 1980s.

The next section reviews research on Black Americans and leisure within the leisure studies field, but first, attention is given to the first empirical sociological study of Black social life that includes specific analyses of leisure patterns. W.E.B. DuBois' analysis in *The Philadelphia Negro* is important for two primary reasons. First, it introduces an earlier starting point for research on leisure among Black Americans. Although the leisure field began to take up research questions pertaining to the Black experience during the 1960s and 1970s, DuBois had contributed important groundwork on urban leisure among Blacks decades before. His work provides important context for better understanding Black leisure in the post–Civil Rights era that has yet to be examined in leisure research. Second, his study provides context for better understanding the contemporary disparities in recreation and park allocation in urban, predominantly Black locations and the systemic impact of those disparities on the quality of life and well-being of communities. Without this historic context, researchers consider the duration of such disparities as spanning only a couple of decades, rather than nearly a century of park policy that left many communities of color poor, underfunded, and lacking in the wide array of recreational programming that White communities possessed.

W.E.B. DuBois' *The Philadelphia Negro: A Social Study*

DuBois' *The Philadelphia Negro* (1899) was the first empirical sociological study on Black Americans. A recognized classic in sociology, the book dealt with social life in Philadelphia's seventh ward, an area largely inhabited by Blacks, using a combination of survey methods and ethnography. Although his insights are largely unknown to students in leisure studies, DuBois examined issues that are relevant to leisure scholars today. It is instructive to review some of his key findings related to leisure experiences.

One aspect of DuBois' research addressed how leisure was practiced in the various social classes within the Black community. He developed four class categories:

1. Lowest; those at the bottom of the status structure—street criminals, prostitutes, and loafers
2. The poor; honest people not able to earn enough "to keep them at all times above want" (p. 311)
3. Working class, whose members were respectable and in "comfortable circumstances" (p. 311) and had nice homes, who could read and write
4. Those at the top who earned enough to live well, with a "wife engaged in no occupation" (p. 311) and children who were not required to be breadwinners and were in school

DuBois reported that the activities of the lowest class consisted mostly of gambling, attending balls, excursions, and drinking. Church and secret societies (e.g., Masonry) were the central activity of the poor and working classes. For the working class, he observed that this class was most identified with the church—"Sunday dinners and small parties, together with church activities, make up their social intercourse" (p. 316). The "upper class" was distinguished by the fact that the home was the "centre of recreation and amusement" (p. 320). Activities such as parties, receptions, and social events related to music and social clubs were most common.

A companion analysis of the seventh ward in *The Philadelphia Negro* by Isabel Eaton focused specifically on the leisure available to domestic servants. In "Special Report on Negro Domestic Service," Eaton surveyed "colored domestics" on the "amount of leisure time usually granted to colored domestics they had for leisure and how this leisure is employed" (p. 468). She noted that domestic service was a less desirable form of employment because of its "flavor" of slavery and because it required workers to give up so much of their personal freedom. However, in most cases, these were the only jobs available. Her report, based on 51 men and 206 women, showed that most were given "one afternoon each week and the evening of alternate Sundays . . . some were allowed one afternoon and every third Sunday or one afternoon and every fourth Sunday. Still a considerable number are given the usual afternoon of a week day and *every* Sunday afternoon as well. Some have their afternoon and alternate Sundays and one or more evenings, and a considerable number have this arrangement with the freedom of *all* their evenings" (pp. 468-469). When respondents were asked "Where do you get your amusements?" (see table 4.1), church activities was the nearly universal response. Women were more likely to say church activities (church and church entertainment) and home resting; men spent most of their off time between home resting, church, and visiting with friends.

Anticipating empirical studies to be conducted in the future, and reflecting the social tenor of the progressive era, DuBois (1899) concluded that "among all classes of Negroes there is a large unsatisfied demand for amusement. . . . The churches supply this need partially, but the institution which will supply better and add instruc-

tion and diversion, will save many girls from ruin and boys from crime" (pp. 320-321). DuBois recognized, and sought to capture empirically, the ways in which the use of leisure contributed to human development. Underlying his criticisms of the lower classes, he saw constructive leisure as a positive mechanism for individual growth and institutional development within the Black community. In particular, he urged those of the upper class (those representing the Talented Tenth) to use voluntary associations and social clubs for the betterment of all classes of Black citizens. In effect, he advocated for parallel institutions that would serve the needs of Black people and provide a buffer against White oppression.

BLACK AMERICA: CURRENT SOCIOECONOMIC AND DEMOGRAPHIC CONTEXT

Historically, Black Americans have lagged behind White Americans on most measures of socioeconomic status and other measures of well-being. With improved societal conditions, however, African Americans currently enjoy unprecedented access to all sectors of society. In 2008, it was truly historic that a person of African descent was elected president of the United States. Over the last several decades, the number of Black Americans joining the middle class has grown significantly (Pattillo-McCoy, 2000). At the same time, there is a widening gap between upper and

Table 4.1   Leisure Time of Colored Domestics—How Employed

Usual recreation	MALE		FEMALE	
	Number	Percent	Number	Percent
Church and church entertainments at home	4	7.8	69	33.5
Church and visits to friends	11	21.6	22	10.7
Church and home (occasional concert or theater)	4	7.8	15	7.3
Church and study	10	19.6	29	14.1
Theater, concerts, balls, and bicycling, for example	5	9.8	10	4.8
Home resting (women "home sewing")	17	33.4	61	29.6
	51		206	

Reprinted from W.E.B. DuBois, 1899, *The Philadelphia Negro* (Baltimore: Lippincott).

lower income groups among Blacks (Landry & Marsh, 2011). Before examining research and theory, this section presents a review of current socioeconomic and demographic conditions of Blacks with a view toward identifying challenges and opportunities for leisure service providers and future research.

Population Size and Geographic Distribution

The 2010 Census indicated that there were 38.9 million African Americans in the United States, representing 12.6% of the total population (Rastogi, Johnston, Hoeffel, & Drewery, 2011). Since the preceding census, Latinos (16.3%, 50.5 million) had surpassed Blacks to become the country's largest racial or ethnic minority group (see chapter 5 on leisure among Latinos). While the rate of growth among African Americans did not rival that of Latinos or Asian Americans, two trends are worth noting that will certainly add to diversity within the Black population. First, with the addition of the option to identify with more than one race, the 2010 Census showed that the largest Black or African American "multiple race" category was "Black-White" (59%) (Rastogi et al., 2011). This was the fastest-growing segment among Black individuals also identifying as multiracial. A second noteworthy trend is the increase in the Black population from African and Caribbean countries, which constitutes 13.3% of all foreign-born populations (Grieco et al., 2012).

As described earlier, Blacks migrated in large numbers to northern cities in the early part of the 20th century (Farley & Allen, 1989). Recent years have seen a "return migration" of African Americans to Southern states. Currently, 22 million Black Americans reside in the Southern region of the United States, up from 18.9 million in 2000. Nearly 60% live in 10 states; four Southern states (Florida, Texas, Georgia, and North Carolina) are among the top six states with the largest Black population. These same four states experienced the fastest growth rates for Blacks. The Black population increased 29% in Florida, 28% in Georgia, 27% in Texas, and 21% in North Carolina (Rastogi et al., 2011). These same states

also experienced substantial growth among Latinos. For example, Latinos in Georgia and North Carolina increased by 96% and 111%, respectively (Ennis, Ríos-Vargas, & Albert, 2011). Given the presence of Blacks in the Southern region, it will be important for researchers and practitioners to understand how changes within these populations will affect demand for leisure services.

Income and Poverty

To give a sense of the current socioeconomic well-being of African Americans, it is useful to describe household income and poverty rates by race-ethnicity. Median income for Black households for 2010 was $32,068 compared to $33,122 in 2009. Median income declined for all race and ethnic groups between 2009 and 2010 (DeNavas-Walt, Proctor, & Smith, 2011). Median incomes for Blacks and Whites (non-Hispanics) declined between 2009 and 2010 at statistically significant rates. Black median income declined approximately three times the rate for Whites (–3.2% vs. –1.3%) (see also the Foreword). Poverty measures show that African Americans experienced the highest rates of poverty relative to Whites, Latinos, and Asian Americans (DeNavas-Walt et al., 2011). Poverty rates in 2010 for Blacks and Latinos were 25.8% and 25.3%, respectively. Thus, one-fourth of households representing the two largest populations were in poverty. Asian American households were the lone group that did not see an increase in poverty between 2009 and 2010; their rates declined from 12.5% to 12.1%.

Educational Attainment and Employment

A way to characterize educational attainment is through examination of percentage of the population with bachelor's degree or higher. Estimates based on the 2006-2010 American Community Survey (Ogunwole, Drewery, & Ríos-Vargas, 2012) show that among all groups, 27.9% of the population 25 or older held a bachelor's degree or higher. Estimates for Latinos were the lowest (13%); estimates for Whites (non-Hispanics) and Blacks were 29.3% and 17.7% respectively. Within the Asian population, half (50.2%) of the population 25 or older held a bachelor's degree or higher. Data for annual rates of unemployment by race and educational attainment show that at every level of education, Blacks and Latinos were more likely to be unemployed. For example, the unemployment rate for persons with a bachelor's degree or higher was 4.3% for Whites (non-Hispanic) and 7.9% and 6.0% for Blacks and Latinos, respectively.

Age Structure and Household Composition

In addition to socioeconomic differences, another key difference between the Black population (and Latinos) and Whites (non-Hispanic) is the youthful age structure of the population. As reported in 2012, the median age for Blacks was 31.3, compared to 41.2 for Whites (non-Hispanics) and 27.4 for Latinos (U.S. Census Bureau, 2012). From another perspective, the percentage of Whites under age 25 was 30%; among Blacks, 40% of the population was younger than 25 years. The percentage for Latinos was 46. Finally, compared to other major racial and ethnic groups, African Americans showed the lowest percentage of "husband–wife" households at 28.5. All other groups were above 50%: Latinos, 50.1%; Whites (non-Hispanics), 51.2%; and Asians, 59.7%. Three in 10, or 30%, of Black American householders were single female with no spouse present.

Overall, current demographic and socioeconomic conditions indicate opportunities and challenges related to providing leisure services for the Black population. Increases in the numbers of Black Americans (and other diverse groups) in Southern states represent opportunities for business development to meet the needs of diverse market segments and for cultivating innovation in community and economic development (Murdock, 1995). Growth among populations exhibiting a youthful age profile may also lead to justification for expanding public recreation opportunities. Challenges center on persistent disparities in income, educational attainment, and employment. In particular, single-parent and female-headed households will continue to face constraints on a number of fronts, including lei-

sure. Maintaining affordable leisure options will be important in this regard.

CURRENT TRENDS IN RESEARCH AND THEORY

This part of the chapter reviews theories and identifies research trends focused on Black leisure experiences, primarily highlighting research published in peer-reviewed journals (with a few exceptions, e.g., Washburne & Wall, 1980). A select list of studies with description of their populations and research settings, primary dependent variables, and theories accompanies this review (table 4.2).

In general, studies from the 1970s were oriented toward documenting disparities in activity participation between White and Black people and the extent to which race or socioeconomic status explained disparities. Few studies appeared in peer-reviewed journals during this era. Activity participation served as the primary dependent variable in most studies in the 1970s and 1980s. A seminal study published at this time was conducted by Washburne (1978). The article provided the formal hypotheses—the marginality and ethnicity hypotheses—that could be applied to findings reported by the ORRRC on racial differences in outdoor recreation participation. Washburne pointed to marginality as a factor related to poverty and socioeconomic discrimination linked to historical discrimination. Ethnicity or subcultural style reflected different values, social organization, and norms. Based on a telephone sample of California residents, his data showed that higher percentages of White participants engaged in travel and outdoor activities (e.g., camping and hiking) compared to Black respondents; higher percentages of Black participants engaged in urban forms of leisure (e.g., sports and community or neighborhood events). When residence and socioeconomic status were controlled (by matched subsamples), these patterns persisted, leading Washburne to conclude that *ethnicity* was the most viable explanation for racial differences in outdoor recreation participation. The hypotheses from the study and the general procedure of controlling socioeconomic and demographic

Table 4.2 Selected Studies Involving Black Americans in Leisure Studies and Support for Alternative Theories

Study	Population/Setting	Primary dependent variable	Theory supported
Craig, 1972	Black American, rural Louisiana	Activity participation	Ethnicity-subculture
Wagner & Donahue, 1976	African American and White households, New Orleans	Activity participation	Marginality and ethnicity-subculture
Washburne, 1978	Black American and White households, California	Activity participation	Ethnicity-subculture; partial support of marginality
Washburne & Wall, 1980	Black American and White households, United States	Activity participation	Ethnicity-subculture
Edwards, 1981	Black American and White households, Lynchburg, VA	Activity participation and preferences	Ethnicity-subculture
Stamps & Stamps, 1985	Black American and White households/ Northern urban community	Activity preferences	Ethnicity-subculture
Hutchison, 1987	Black American, Latino, and White park visitors, Chicago	Park use and social groups of users	Ethnicity-subculture
Woodard, 1988	Black American households, Chicago	Activity participation	Marginality and intragroup stratification
West, 1989	Black American households, Detroit	Park use	Discrimination; partial support for marginality
Floyd et al., 1994	Black American and White households, United States	Activity preferences	Class identification
Shinew et al., 1995	Black American and White households, United States	Activity preferences	Multiple stratification hierarchy
Shinew et al., 1996	Black American, United States	Activity preferences	Intragroup class polarization
Johnson et al., 1997	Black American and White households, rural Florida counties adjacent to a national forest	Wildland recreation visitation	Sociocultural and place attachment
Toth & Brown, 1997	Black American and White households, Mississippi Delta region	Meanings of recreational fishing	Sociocultural and place meaning
Bialeschki & Walbert, 1998	Black American and White women, workers in Southern textile and tobacco factories	Leisure experiences and meanings	Leisure as a site of solidarity and resistance
Johnson et al., 1998	Black American and White households, rural Florida counties adjacent to a national forest	National forest visitation	No support for marginality or ethnicity-subculture
Johnson & Bowker, 1999	Black American and White households, rural Florida counties adjacent to a national forest	On-site activity at a national forest	Partial support for ethnicity-subculture
Floyd & Shinew, 1999	Black American and White park users, Chicago	Activity preferences	Interracial contact hypothesis
Philipp, 1997	Black American and White households, urban Southern city	Perceived leisure benefits	Partial support for marginality, ethnicity, and discrimination
Arnold & Shinew, 1998	Black American and White park users, Chicago	Park use constraints	Discrimination
Philipp, 1999	Black American and White households, urban Southern city	Leisure constraints; activity importance among children	Ethnicity; discrimination

(continued)

Table 4.2   *(continued)*

Study	Population/Setting	Primary dependent variable	Theory supported
Johnson et al., 2001	Black American and White households, United States	Leisure constraints	Mixed; support for interpersonal and structural factors
Lee et al., 2001	Black American, Latino, and White households, Texas	Local and state park use	Multiple stratification hierarchy
Outley & Floyd, 2002	Children from a low-income neighborhood, Houston, TX	Activity participation	Family systems theory, social networks
Payne et al., 2002	Black American and White households, Cleveland, OH	Park preferences and use	Marginality
Tinsley et al., 2002	Black American, Latino, and White park users, Chicago	Perceived leisure benefits	Ethnicity-subculture
Glover, 2007	Black American volunteer youth baseball coaches, Champaign, IL	Racism in little league baseball	Critical race theory
Martin, 2004	Advertisements from three national magazines	Race of models engaged in outdoor leisure	Racialized outdoor identity and place meaning
Shinew et al., 2004	Black American and White park users, Chicago	Constraints to park use and leisure activities	Marginality not supported; ethnicity-subculture
Wolch & Zhang, 2004	Black American, Latino, Asian, and White households, Los Angeles, CA	Beach use rates	Marginality and environmental attitudes
Floyd et al., 2006	Black American, Latino, and White households, Texas	Fishing participation	
Shinew et al., 2007	Volunteers for community center in a Black American neighborhood, Chicago	Volunteer activity	Racial identity
Hunt et al., 2007	Black American and White anglers, Texas	Catch-related motives for fishing	Ethnicity-subculture
Santos & Rozier, 2007	Black American and Latino park visitors and park staff, Chicago	Perceptions of intercultural competence and communication	Conflict negotiation style
Shores et al., 2007	Black American, Latino, and White households, Texas	Park use constraints	Multiple stratification hierarchy
Erickson et al., 2009	Black American residents, Denver, CO	Visitation to Rocky Mountain National Park	Cultural capital, historical discrimination

Adapted from Manning 2011; Johnson et al. 1997.

factors to attempt to attenuate race effects became the benchmark for subsequent studies of Blacks and other populations of color through the 1990s (Floyd, 2007).

During the 1980s and 1990s, two important trends became evident. First, dependent variables other than activity participation (e.g., leisure preferences, local park use) began to attract greater attention. Research interest shifted to activity preferences (e.g., Edwards, 1981; Floyd & Shinew, 1999; Floyd, Shinew, McGuire, & Noe, 1994; Stamps & Stamps, 1985) and use of local, regional parks (Hutchison, 1987; West, 1989) and national forests (Johnson, Bowker, English, & Worthen, 1998). Leisure constraints related to activity participation and park use also attracted research attention (e.g., Arnold & Shinew, 1998; Philipp, 1995). As a final example, perceived benefits and meanings associated with leisure activity and environments among Blacks were also deemed worthy of examination (Bialeschki & Walbert, 1998; Philipp, 1997, 1999; Toth & Brown, 1997). For example, among recreational anglers in the Mississippi Delta, Toth and Brown (1997) found that fishing for sport was more salient among White anglers while subsistence meanings were more important among Black people. This development is significant in three respects. First, to examine leisure from different perspectives is an indication of maturity within the race–ethnicity subfield. Second, the use of additional dependent variables such as perceived benefits, constraints, and place meaning allowed for integration and cross-fertilization with other areas within the literature (Floyd, 2007). Third, focusing on these additional dimensions of leisure experiences can provide new insights and can potentially give leisure service providers information enabling them to better serve the needs of their constituents.

A second trend is the emergence of alternative methodologies and more diverse settings for research on Black leisure. Whereas several earlier studies had been based on household surveys (e.g., Edwards, 1981; Washburne, 1978), studies conducted on-site in parks became more common (e.g., Arnold & Shinew, 1998; Hutchison, 1987; West, 1989). Bialeschki and Walbert (1998) drew upon oral histories from historical archives to analyze the meanings of leisure of Black and White women who worked in textile and tobacco factories from 1910 to 1940. In this fascinating account from the early Jim Crow era, they show how the role of leisure varied by race and gender. For White women, leisure opportunities were mostly social and were limited compared to those of their husbands and other men. However, use of leisure "for its own sake" (p. 98) was evident among these women. Among Black women, leisure centered on church and the labor union and was connected to the struggle for equality at work and in the broader community. Similar themes appeared in DuBois' (1899) and Johnson's (1934) studies.

One of the most significant developments beginning in the late 1980s was the application of more diverse theoretical strategies for understanding leisure among Black people. Woodard (1988) explored the role of geographic regionality (Southern rural birth and residence vs. urban) and discrimination in explaining leisure participation patterns among Black residents of Chicago. Although socioeconomic status was the most consistent predictor of a range of leisure activities, he found that "urban northern" respondents participated more than others in "night life" and entertainment activity. Contrary to expectations, urban respondents also were more involved in informal or home-based leisure. This ran counter to Woodard's idea that origins in the rural South, where informal and home-based leisure are more common, would be reflected in current lifestyles. A key contribution of Woodard's study was the addition of relevant concepts representing the unique socio-historical context associated with Black experiences in the rural South. He also provided the first "intragroup" study of Black leisure.

West (1989) introduced an explicit treatment of prejudice and discrimination in a study of park use in Detroit. West measured "interracial factors" by coding open-ended responses to questions about reasons for not using parks (i.e., racism, racial—anti-Black, racial—anti-White, race relations, and uncomfortable-unwelcome). Data from the study showed that Black residents were more likely to use city parks but less likely to use regional parks. Although transportation was a limiting factor, Black residents were significantly more likely than White residents to report experiences of interracial hostility when asked about their reasons for not using parks. Subculture was not found to be an important factor in park use among Black residents in Detroit. West's findings prompted other researchers to incorporate perceived discrimination in studies of populations of color (e.g., Blahna & Black, 1992; Gómez, 2002; Floyd, Gramann, & Saenz, 1993); see chapter 11 on discrimination in leisure contexts.

Class identification was introduced by Floyd and colleagues (1994). Building on class awareness theories (Centers, 1949; Jackman & Jackman, 1983), Floyd and colleagues examined whether Black and White survey respondents who perceived themselves similarly related to social class would also exhibit similar preferences for leisure activities. As hypothesized, respondents who identified as middle class were similar in their leisure preferences. However, there was less similarity among Blacks and Whites who identified as working class or poor, particularly women. The latter result stimulated interest in exploring the intersection of race, gender, and class awareness in relation to leisure preferences. Shinew and colleagues (Shinew, Floyd, McGuire, & Noe, 1995, 1996) picked up on this theme and applied multiple stratification hierarchy to better understand the source of differences in leisure preferences associated with Black people who identified as poor or working class. In the 1995 study, it became clear that this group (Black women who identified as poor) occupied a unique position in the status hierarchy. That is, their leisure preferences were similar only to those of other women and poor working-class Black men.

Further examination (Shinew et al., 1996) using an exclusively Black subsample revealed positive associations between preferences among men identifying as middle class and working class or poor. Women who identified as middle class exhibited preferences different from those of women in the poor or working-class group. These findings gave support to the emerging idea that individuals who are poor, members of minority groups, and females are subject to multiple stratification effects and that these effects are reflected in their leisure preferences, constraints, and participation. A series of studies provided evidence of multiple stratification effects in leisure and park use constraints (Arnold & Shinew, 1998; Shores, Moore, & Yin, 2010; Shores, Scott, & Floyd, 2007), local and state park visitation (Lee, Scott, & Floyd, 2001), and participation in fishing- and wildlife-related recreation (Floyd, Nicholas, Lee, Lee, & Scott, 2006; Lee & Scott, 2011).

Moving beyond marginality and ethnicity theory, researchers concerned with Black participation in wildland recreation have increasingly turned to place-based perspectives such as place attachment (e.g., Johnson et al., 1998; Johnson, Horan, & Pepper, 1997; Martin, 2004; Toth & Brown, 1997). Johnson and colleagues (1997), for example, investigated activity participation in natural resource settings (camping, hiking, hunting, and fishing) among a sample of rural Southern residents. In this study, wildland meaning was modeled as a mediating variable between race, sex, and education and visitation. Wildland meaning for Black respondents was conceptualized as having multiple components: a collective or group orientation, preference for developed settings, heightened concern for safety, and an affective component reflective of place attachment. These components were based on a review of the race and leisure literature. Using a one-dimensional wildland meaning score, the researchers' statistical model confirmed the role of wildland as a mediator. Race (identifying specifically as African American) was negatively correlated with participation. Wildland meaning was the strongest predictor of wildland activity participation. The importance of such findings rests with their demonstration of ways in which the subjective meaning of outdoor recreation places should be considered. As Woodard (1988) demonstrated the importance of incorporating historically relevant concepts to study urban leisure patterns among Black people, Johnson and colleagues' inclusion of place meaning indicators reflected symbolic meanings that Black people associated with the outdoors. Martin's (2004) study draws on a similar perspective while using a different methodology to examine race and wildland recreation.

Martin (2004) developed the argument that "there exists a stereotyped leisure identity that is associated with wildland leisure activities that results in fewer Black Americans participating in outdoor recreation" (p. 514). He advanced the idea of a "racialized outdoor identity" that operates as a deterrent to outdoor recreation activity among those who do not share this identity. This identity, Martin maintained, is stereotypically young, male, and White. Martin content-analyzed over 4,000 advertisements from three major magazines (*Ebony, Outside,* and *Time*) to determine the frequency of White models in ads relative to Black models and the frequency of outdoor ads in the three magazines. As hypothesized, White models were most likely to appear in ads featuring the outdoors, whereas Black models appeared more frequently in urban environments. Moreover, the lowest percentage of ads focused on the outdoors appeared in *Ebony,* a monthly magazine devoted to Black issues. What Martin brought to light cuts in two directions. On one hand, the racialized outdoor identity reinforces to Blacks and other minority groups that people who look like them are not accepted in wildland settings. In essence, such places become reserved "for Whites only." As Martin suggested, this can create apprehension and fear among individuals who may be interested in outdoor experiences. At the same time, others internalize these expectations and buy into the stereotypes that such places are not part of a Black identity. On the other hand, among White Americans, racialized outdoor identity can legitimize their sense of ownership and entitlement to outdoor spaces as well as reinforce "Whiteness" as a normalizing practice as described by Roberts (2009). Extending arguments developed by McDonald (2009), Roberts interpreted Martin's (2004) finding as evidence of Whiteness as a normalizing practice. As a result of such practices, "Whiteness" becomes the norm, taken for granted, or a standard of reference for all other perspectives and serves to "[stigmatize] the 'other,' but also bolster White 'normality'" (McDonald, p. 13). This line of discussion called to mind the idea of "White supremacy–Black inferiority" undergirding de jure segregation (Aguirre & Turner, 1998; Austin, 2004). Researchers have responded to calls for more direct and critical assessments to expose racist ideologies in relation to leisure experiences of Black people.

Indeed, Arai and Kivel (2009) view the movement of research in this direction as a signal moment, the emergence of a new "wave" of studies focused on "how researchers contextualize race and the ideological underpinnings that give meaning to this construct [race]" (p. 463). Elaborating on the intent of this emerging scholarship, Arai and Kivel state that "this wave contextualizes discussions of race and racism within theoretical frameworks which enable broader discussion of social and structural inequalities, power, ideology and white hegemony" (p. 464). Studies in this vein vigorously challenge categorical definitions of race (and ethnicity), recognizing that race (and ethnicity) represent social, cultural, historical, and political constructions (Kivel, Johnson, & Scraton, 2009). As an illustration, Erickson, Johnson, and Kivel (2009) sought to illuminate how historical racism and discrimination play out in visitation among Black people in Denver. They argued that historic oppression was "absent" in

existing theory. Building on Bourdieu's (1977) concepts of cultural capital and habitus, Erickson and colleagues identified five major historical factors associated with low visitation to the park: lack of a history of park going; affordability related to past discrimination in areas of society (e.g., work, employment); racism and historical legacy of the Jim Crow era; negative images of wildlands; and tradition of visiting family and friends. Finally, study participants made comments such as that visiting national parks is not "a Black thing" or "Black people don't do that" (p. 540). These comments are clear examples of Martin's (2004) reference to racialized outdoor identity and Roberts' (2009) idea of "whiteness as normalizing practice" from the perspective of Black people when interviewed about their park experiences.

FUTURE DIRECTIONS

Over the past four decades, a substantial body of research has focused on the leisure experiences of Black Americans. As previously noted, more is known about a wider set of dependent variables; a more diverse set of methodological approaches and research settings (e.g., household surveys, on-site, geographic locations) is reflected in the literature; and a modest degree of theoretical innovation has occurred. Thus, in several ways the leisure studies field has progressed in building new knowledge about leisure in the Black American experience. Based on the review in this chapter of historical factors, current demographic characteristics, and the current literature, several recommendations are offered for future research.

Several topics for further study of leisure among African Americans are suggested by the review of historical factors, demographic trends, and research themes. The review of history reveals how little is known about Black leisure experiences during Reconstruction and immediately after the beginning of Jim Crow. Historical analysis from this time period would have much to teach us about leisure constraints and negotiation (Jackson, Crawford, & Godbey, 1993) from this era. Such historical data not only would be valuable for their own sake but also could help to make sense of current leisure practices. Thus, further study of parallel institutions (Hine, 2003) applied to leisure would be a productive line of inquiry in understanding Black leisure perspectives. Parallel institutions were important in providing resources for alternative leisure opportunities during the Jim Crow era. Examples of these were documented in Foster's (1999) descriptions of Black resorts and activity associations. Samdahl (2011) provided an account of African American resorts focusing on the development of American Beach, a historic Black beach in Georgia that became popular in the 1940s and 1950s. Bialeschki and Walbert's (1998) use of archived oral histories from the Jim Crow era to study leisure among Black and White women factory workers in the South provides another example of historical research.

Another historic factor with relevance to the present is the role of the Black church as a source of leisure (see chapter 8 on leisure among religious minorities). Historically, the church has been a primary institution within the Black community (DuBois, 1899; Waller, 2010). During slavery, church was one of only a few social settings where Blacks could meet and organize with some freedom (Frazier, 1963). DuBois (1899) documented that the church was the primary source of leisure for working-class Blacks in Philadelphia. From the same study, Isabel Eaton's companion analyses showed that church was the primary activity for limited leisure time of domestic servants. Church was also central in the lives of Black women factory workers in the study by Bialeschki and Walbert (1998). Floyd and coauthors (1994) found that Blacks expressed a greater preference for church as a leisure activity than did Whites. The dearth of research on leisure and religion, particularly the Christian churches, among Black Americans is surprising given the historic presence of the church in Black communities. Perhaps as society has changed and in the absence of legal discrimination, the church now serves a different role in the Black community. Additionally, the proliferation of integrated "mega-churches" offers alternatives to traditional Black churches. There is a need for research on leisure and the Black church as a historical subject and as a source of leisure and community development in the present. For example, Johnson, Jang, Li, and Larson (2000)

found that involvement in religious activities was important in deterring African American youth from serious crimes.

Other potential topics emerge from the demographic data, particularly household composition and the youthful age structure. Clearly, some straightforward analysis of how leisure is organized and arranged within low-resource households is needed. Outley and Floyd's (2002) study of parenting strategies within low-income families in Houston identified the importance of peer groups and kinship networks in facilitating children's leisure. However, the focus of the study was not single-parent families. Few such studies appear in the literature (e.g., Azar, Naughton, & Joseph, 2009; Quarmby & Dagkas, 2010). One study that focused on leisure, with a majority African American sample, found that certain family management practices (e.g., discipline, routines, and mother's constructive use of time) were associated with children's constructive use of leisure time (Larson, Dworkin, & Gillman, 2001). More studies are needed to elucidate ways in which single-parent families negotiate constraints to support parents and to inform providers of leisure services.

The emergence of hip-hop and house music culture (stemming from the youth culture) has gone mostly unnoticed by leisure scholars focused on race and leisure. In viewing both as art forms and not just music played on the radio, one finds a significant amount of history and experience relating to their impact on urban landscapes (graffiti), the creation of parallel venues due to the discrimination at mainstream disco clubs, and the development of styles of dance (e.g., B-Boy and B-Girl, which are the proper terms associated with a breakdancer and breakdancing). Since the late 1970s, hip-hop and house music have grown from a street-level culture among African American, Caribbean, and Latino/a straight and gay youth to major music industry status. In particular, hip-hop is part of the popular culture and has become a globalizing force (Brooks & Conroy, 2011). There are no accounts of the rise of either art form in the leisure literature. Through autoethnography, Lashua and Fox (2006) observed how the creation and performance of hip-hop music composed by Aboriginal youth (Canada) was used as a form of communication, to connect with their peers, and express their leisure preferences (see chapter 7 on leisure among First Nations).

As Quillian (2006) observed, a "number of questions face those trying to understand the nature and extent of discrimination in the post–Civil Rights era" (p. 299). Discrimination as a matter of policy is illegal, and societal attitudes have shifted such that racist behaviors are quickly condemned. Yet many studies show that African Americans continue to experience discrimination in public places (Feagin, 1991; Feagin & Vera, 1995; Philipp, 2000) and in recreation settings (e.g., Blahna & Black, 1993; Erickson et al., 2009; West, 1989). The majority of studies of discrimination against racial and ethnic minorities in recreation settings target individual and interpersonal discrimination (e.g., visitor-visitor or visitor-staff). Additional work is needed to show how historical and institutional discrimination embedded in leisure service organizations, informal settings, and landscapes (e.g., Erickson et al., 2009; Glover, 2007; Martin, 2004) shape leisure experiences among Black Americans.

Researchers should pursue incorporation of a wider use of other fields, paradigms, methodologies, and methods that would facilitate new ways of knowing the experiences of Black populations. For example, the literary criticism and cultural critique that are a fundamental part of cultural studies could enable researchers to construct and deconstruct the lived experiences of Black people, as for many, the influence of slavery and colonialism is still evident today. Another useful framework could be through the use of presentism, a form of historical analysis, in which present-day experiences are discussed with interpretation of the past (this chapter is an example). With a full understanding of the origins of critical race theory, some of the tenets of its social critique of the intersection of race, law, and power can be used to elevate the importance of highlighting White supremacy (which is far different from White privilege) and seeking the end of racial subordination (Bell, 1995). In addition, actively working with Black communities as partners in research formulation, data collection, data analysis, and presentation of findings through community-based participatory research could

inform the field of both appropriate research practices and nuances in Black leisure experiences. Lastly, it is appropriate to take a stand against racial injustice and invoke beliefs, thoughts, and actions that are in line with social justice when it becomes evident that discrimination is occurring at a research site, among a population of color, or on the part of an institution perpetuating racial disparities (Young, 1990).

Although not treated extensively in this chapter, a growing body of research in public health and leisure studies examines racial patterns in the availability of parks and recreation facilities. Parks are increasingly viewed as critical spaces for promoting physical activity and healthy lifestyles (Godbey, Caldwell, Floyd, & Payne, 2005). The lack of parks and recreation facilities in Black neighborhoods has been associated with high obesity rates among Black Americans (Gordon-Larsen, Nelson, Page, & Popkin, 2006; Taylor, Floyd, Whitt-Glover, & Brooks, 2007). In cases in which parks are equally available, they often lack high-quality facilities and amenities (Powell, Slater, & Chaloupka, 2004). Bringing the underlying principles of environmental justice to this research and practice will be important in order to promote equality and equity in the placement and quality of recreation facilities and to engage communities in the process of planning and decision making about the facilities. Thus, in addition to conducting studies of spatial location and availability, researchers should identify ways to effectively engage socioeconomically disadvantaged Black communities in public participation processes. Advancing environmental justice necessitates ensuring the full participation of communities that are disproportionately and adversely affected by environmental decision making, as well as ensuring that solution-based policies benefit all and not just those who are privileged enough to sit and discuss at the "table" (Bryant, 1995).

Finally, structural issues within the leisure studies academy should also be studied. Specifically, the continued underrepresentation of Black students in leisure studies programs throughout North America warrants research attention. Whether they are African American, African Canadian, African Caribbean, or African international students, the number of students in the "pipeline" spells future underrepresentation and disparities with respect to Black leisure professionals and Black faculty. For instance, in Hibbler's (2002) edited book, *Unsilencing the Dialogue: Voices of Minority Faculty,* Floyd (2002) questioned the capacity of the field to make significant contributions to race scholarship. He stated, "I remain unconvinced that we in leisure studies have the requisite faculties (i.e., skills and training) to undertake serious critique of our treatment of diversity. . . . Critique is also thwarted by institutional barriers which may be associated with the small presence of scholars of color . . . there is no one solution" (p. 81).

CONCLUSION

This chapter reviews a number of historical factors impinging on the emergence of leisure in the Black experience, from slavery, Emancipation, and Reconstruction through to the early Jim Crow era of the 1920s and into the late 20th century. A specific aim was to illustrate how these factors shaped different aspects of leisure, particularly its expression in terms of leisure spaces, institutions, and activity participation. The chapter also highlights the current socioeconomic and demographic characteristics of Black Americans. For nearly four decades, researchers within leisure studies have attempted to apply a variety of theoretical perspectives to understand forms of leisure expression with origins in the legacy of slavery and Jim Crow, and they continue to do so. These perspectives also are now confronted by challenges in studying race and leisure at a time when de jure discrimination no longer exists, as society is becoming more pluralistic and multiethnic, and as globalization increases. Researchers will be challenged to make sense of Black leisure in this new and evolving culture of diversity. In addressing this challenge, it is imperative that future leisure research build on the rich history of the Black American cultural experience.

Out from the gloomy past
Till now we stand at last where the
Bright gleam of our bright star is cast.

James Weldon Johnson, "Lift Every Voice and Sing"
(also known as the Negro National Anthem)

CHAPTER 5

Leisure Among Latino Americans

Monika Stodolska and Kimberly J. Shinew

OVERVIEW

Research on leisure behavior among Latino Americans has developed rapidly over the last 30 years. Beginning as simple cross-ethnic comparisons, it has matured to in-depth examinations of the effects of factors such as assimilation–adaptation patterns, discrimination, socioeconomic disadvantage, cultural uniqueness, immigration experience, and transnational arrangements on recreation participation. Moreover, the research has examined a plethora of distinct but interrelated issues tied to the leisure behavior among Latinos, which include the use of natural environments for recreation, benefits of recreation participation, recreation styles, motivations for recreation, and meanings of leisure and recreation. The number of studies on physical activity among Latinos is also increasing in the fields of leisure studies, public health, and kinesiology. The purpose of this chapter is threefold. The authors have sought to explain the relevant terms, provide a brief history of Latino immigration to the United States, and outline the current and projected size of this group in the United States. They also provide a comprehensive review of the history and current status of leisure research involving Latinos, identify leisure research areas in particular need of further study, and present practical recommendations on how best to provide leisure services to Latinos.

Learning Outcomes

After reading this chapter, readers will be able to

- understand the history of Latinos in the United States,
- identify major trends in current leisure research on Latinos in the United States,
- identify research needs when it comes to investigating leisure behavior among Latinos, and
- offer practical recommendations on how to provide leisure services to Latinos.

Paso del norte,	*Step to the North,*
que lejos te vas quedando	*How far you are staying,*
tus divisions	*Your divisions*
de mi se estan alejando	*from me they are getting far.*
Mis padres y mis hermanos	*My parents and my brothers*
de mi se estan acordando	*are remembering me*
Ay que destino!	*What a destiny!*
para ponerme a llorar	*Just to start crying.*

Alejandro Fernandez

In the last 30 years, the number of Latino immigrants in the United States has increased dramatically. Between 2000 and 2010 alone, the Latino population in the United States grew 56%, bringing its total to 50.5 million (Ennis, Rios-Vargas, & Albert, 2011). Research on leisure behavior of Latino Americans has been conducted for over 30 years, and has expanded from basic analysis of recreation participation patterns among Latinos to in-depth examinations of a myriad of factors that shape their leisure behavior. Before one delves into a detailed examination of the extant knowledge on this topic, however, an understanding of the history of the Latino migration to the United States, as well as the cultural and socioeconomic background of specific Latino populations, is needed. First, however, a number of terms need to be defined.

DEFINITION OF TERMS

A variety of terms have been used to refer to the Latino population in the United States. The term *Hispanic* was coined by the federal government in the 1970s to describe people who were born in any of the Spanish-speaking countries of the Americas or those who could trace their ancestry to Spain or former Spanish territories. Although the term Hispanic is widely used in local and federal employment, mass media, and academic literature, it has been criticized by some for its focus on Spanish ancestry of Latinos and its lack of acknowledgment of the Indigenous roots of

the population. Moreover, not all Latinos in the United States speak Spanish, and some Spanish-speaking Americans do not identify themselves with other Hispanics as a group. *Latino,* which is a shortening of the Spanish word *latinoamericano,* refers more exclusively to persons or communities of Latin American origin. Because of the popularity of the term in the western portion of the United States, the government used it in the 2000 Census along with the designations "Spanish" and "Hispanic" (Grieco & Cassidy, 2000). Neither term refers to race, as people of Latino and Hispanic origin can be of any race. The U.S. Office of Management and Budget uses the terms Hispanic and Latino interchangeably and defines Hispanics or Latinos as those of "Cuban, Mexican, Puerto Rican, South or Central American, or other Spanish culture of origin regardless of race" (Grieco & Cassidy, p. 2). Federal agencies are required to use a minimum of two ethnicities in data collection and presentations: "Hispanic and Latino" and "Not Hispanic or Latino."

The term *Chicano* is used to refer to Latinos of Mexican descent in the United States. Although the term can be found in the early and mid-20th century literature, it gained popularity during the Civil Rights struggles of the 1960s. The movement brought together Latinos of all classes and from all regions of the United States and was an origin of unique forms of art, literature, and a plethora of other organizations whose goal was to improve social, political, economic, and cultural conditions of Chicanos. The term's meanings are highly debatable. For some it has pejorative connotations, while for others it evokes ethnic pride and self-determination and has clear political overtones (Anzaldua, 1999; Castillo, 1995). Some have also argued that usage of the term depends on generational status and gender, with the more assimilated, younger, male, and more politically radicalized third-generation Mexicans more likely to describe themselves as Chicanos (Herrera-Sobek, 2006; Ruiz & Sanchez, 2006).

HISTORY AND BACKGROUND INFORMATION ON SELECTED LATINO POPULATIONS IN THE UNITED STATES

Latino Americans are the largest and one of the two fastest-growing minority groups in the United States. Due to their sheer numbers, growth rate, and the attention given by the media to immigration issues, many people ignore the long history of Latinos in the United States and consider Latino immigration a recent phenomenon. However, the history of Latinos in the United States spans more than 400 years and predates Jamestown, Virginia (founded in 1607), and the Plymouth Colony. The first European who arrived in 1513 to the area of present-day Florida was Spaniard Juan Ponce de León. A large number of Spanish explorers, including Hernando de Soto, Francisco Vázquez de Coronado, Lucas Vásquez de Ayllón, and Pánfilo de Narváez, explored the lower 48 states, established cities, and named rivers and mountains years before English settlers arrived in Jamestown (Gonzalez, 2011).

At the end of the American Revolutionary War, Spain controlled roughly half of today's continental United States. Following the Louisiana Purchase in 1803 and the Adams-Onís Treaty of 1819, in which Spain relinquished Florida to the United States and set a boundary between the United States and Mexico, the large section of formerly Spanish territory was transferred to the United States (Gonzalez, 2011). The Mexican-American War, followed by the Treaty of Guadalupe-Hidalgo in 1848 and the Gadsden Purchase in 1853, further extended U.S. control over a wide range of territory once held by Spain and later Mexico, including the present-day states

of California, Arizona, New Mexico, and Texas, along with parts of Colorado, Nevada, and Utah (Gonzalez). The vast majority of Mexican populations in those states chose to remain on their lands and become U.S. citizens.

The Latino population in the United States is very diverse. The following subsections provide a more detailed account of the migration of the three main groups that make up the Latino American population in the United States—Mexican, Cuban, and Puerto Rican Americans. Their histories and unique backgrounds play an important role in shaping their experience in the United States and, to a large extent, their leisure behaviors.

Mexican Americans

Although Latinos have been present in the United States since its beginning, the Latino population continues to be renewed by waves of immigrants from Latin America and the Caribbean. More than two-thirds of Latinos currently residing in the United States are immigrants or children of immigrants. Most are of Mexican American background and share Spanish, other European, Indigenous, and sometimes African heritage. According to Massey, Durand, and Malone (2003), nearly all of today's Mexican Americans trace their origin to people who immigrated to the United States after the Treaty of Guadalupe-Hidalgo that ended the Mexican-American War (1846-1848) and established the Mexico–U.S. border at the Rio Grande. In the second half of the 19th century, the border between Mexico and the United States was poorly demarcated and usually unprotected, and the majority of cross-border movement involved short trips by residents of cross-border towns. Thus, one cannot speak of "international migration" between Mexico and the United States until the 20th century.

Durand, Massey, and Capoferro (2005) identified four major periods in the modern (referring to the 20th and 21st centuries) Mexican migration to the United States: the Classic Era of open immigration until the implementation of the restrictive policies of the 1920s; the Bracero era (1942-1964); the undocumented era between the end of the Bracero program and the implementation of the Immigration Reform and Control Act

(IRCA) of 1986; and the post-IRCA era (from 1987 to the present). During the Classic Era, about half of Mexican immigrants lived in Texas, between 17% and 22% in California (based on the 1910 and 1920 censuses), and between 12% and 14% in Arizona (Durand et al.). The end of the prosperous era under President Porfirio Díaz (1876-1910) in Mexico and the beginning of 10 years of revolution and civil war served as the "push factors" propelling Mexican emigration. At the same time, there was a rapid growth in labor demand in the United States due to a growing economy and developing industries in the cities of the Northeast. Loss of some traditional labor sources as a result of implementation of the Chinese Exclusion Acts of the 1880s, the Gentlemen's Agreement with Japan in 1907, and curtailed East European immigration at the time of World War I and the Soviet Revolution increased labor shortages in the United States (Durand et al.; Massey et al., 2003). To meet these demands, U.S. railroads, mining companies, and agricultural growers began recruiting Mexican workers.

In the 1930s, in the wake of the Great Depression and mass deportations, the population of Mexicans in the United States fell sharply. Due to World War II labor shortages, however, in 1942 the United States negotiated the so-called Bracero Accords that involved annual importation of Mexican farm workers (Durand et al., 2005). The term *bracero* was derived from the Spanish word *brazo* or "arm" and denoted a farmhand (Massey et al., 2003). Although the program was supposed to be temporary, it was renegotiated several times until its termination in 1964. The program led to an unprecedented increase in the number of Mexican farm workers, many of whom settled in California (Durand et al.). The size of the Bracero program was significantly increased in the wake of the 1954 paramilitary Operation Wetback that led to a massive roundup and deportation of over 1 million undocumented migrants (Massey et al.). The operation led to severe labor shortages that angered the U.S. agricultural lobby, resulting in bureaucratic pressures to resume the flow of needed labor from across the border. The Bracero program was ultimately dismantled in 1964 as a result of Civil Rights–era pressures from labor unions, Civil Rights groups, and religious organizations (Cerrutti & Massey, 2004).

The period subsequent to the termination of the Bracero program up until enactment of the IRCA legislation, labeled by Durand and colleagues (2005) the "Undocumented Era," marked continued expansion of Mexican immigration primarily through illegal channels. Steady demand for unskilled labor in the United States made California the primary destination for Mexican migrants. By 1970, 53% of Mexican migrants resided in that state (Durand et al.). In 1965, the U.S. Congress passed the Hart-Celler Act, which was signed into law by President Lyndon Johnson. The act removed the discriminatory quota system and replaced it with a new formula under which each country in Europe, Asia, Africa, and the Pacific qualified for 20,000 visas per year. Visas were to be allotted based on a system that gave preference to skilled migrants and relatives of U.S. citizens and resident aliens (Cerrutti & Massey, 2004). Countries in the Western Hemisphere were not allotted individual visa quotas; instead, immigration from the entire hemisphere was capped at 120,000 per year. Subsequent amendments to the act (in 1976, 1978, and 1980) further reduced the numbers of Latinos permitted to legally immigrate to the United States. The Hart-Celler Act and its subsequent amendments for the first time imposed quantitative restrictions on immigration from Latin America and led to a rise in undocumented migrations. Consequently, the number of people expelled from the United States rose to 1.8 million in 1986 from 87,000 apprehensions in 1964 (Cerrutti & Massey).

Passage of the IRCA in 1986 granted legal permanent residence to approximately 2.3 million undocumented Mexicans between 1988 and 1992 (Durand et al., 2005). Many of the Mexicans who were granted freedom and mobility as a result of the act left traditional Latino enclaves in search of better job opportunities in other areas of the United States. The law also made it illegal for employers to hire undocumented workers, which led many companies to shift responsibility for ensuring the legal status of workers to subcontractors for the services they were providing. For absorbing the risks, subcontractors kept a share of the earnings while lowering the wages among immigrants (Durand et al.). Additionally, IRCA increased the U.S. Border Patrol budget by 50% and offered a separate legalization program to undocumented agricultural workers, the majority of whom resided in Texas and California (Cerrutti & Massey, 2004).

The post-IRCA period has been linked to the selective militarization of the U.S.–Mexico border. In particular, Operation Blockade in El Paso, Texas, in 1993 and Operation Gatekeeper in Tijuana (Mexico) in 1994 deflected migratory flows from these two sectors toward more remote, desert or mountainous crossing points in Arizona and New Mexico (Durand et al., 2005). Several other factors shaped Mexican migration in the post-IRCA period. Freedom of mobility granted to previously undocumented immigrants, anti-immigration politics that culminated in the passing of Proposition 187, and deterioration of California's economy drove a large portion of Mexican immigrants away from California. At the same time, the booming U.S. economy of the 1990s that led to strong labor demand and a rise in wages shifted the immigration flows toward nontraditional destination states such as Florida, Idaho, Nevada, Iowa, New York, New Jersey, Georgia, and North Carolina (Durand et al.). Rogelio Saenz (1991) referred to these areas as "the periphery of Chicano migration" away from the "core areas" of California, Colorado, Texas, New Mexico, and Arizona. Post-1994 economic crises in Mexico furthered strong immigration flows in this era.

The post-2008 worldwide economic crisis seems to have caused other important changes in Mexican immigration. Data from population surveys taken in the United States and Mexico indicate that the economic crisis late in the first decade of the century has led to a significant flow of migrants back to Mexico. As the Pew Hispanic Center (2009) estimates, based on data from Mexico's National Survey of Employment and Occupation, 433,000 Mexican migrants returned home between February 2008 and February 2009.[1] At the same time, the number of new arrivals from Mexico to the United States has substantially decreased. In fact, both the official estimates and those coming from the U.S. Border Patrol, and also based on apprehensions of Mexicans attempting to cross illegally into the United States,

show that the inflows began to diminish in the middle part of the decade. According to the Pew Hispanic Center, the Mexican-born population in the United States, which had been growing earlier in the decade, was 11.6 million in 2008 and 11.5 million in early 2009. In 2010, there were close to 31.8 million people of Mexican origin in the United States (Ennis et al., 2011). Patterns of migration between the United States and Mexico are varied; while some Mexicans come to the United States to settle permanently, others fall in the "transnational" category and move across the U.S.–Mexico border, sometimes staying in the United States for only a few months. Mexican–U.S. migration also tends to be seasonal, with larger northbound flows in the spring and summer and larger southbound flows in the fall and winter.

Cuban Americans

Although the majority of the 1.8 million Cuban Americans residing in the United States (Ennis et al., 2011) arrived after 1959 when Fidel Castro assumed control of the Cuban government, Cuban migration to the United States is not a recent phenomenon (O'Reilly Herrera, 2007). According to Garcilaso de la Vega's chronicle of Hernando de Soto's exploration, the first recorded instance of Cubans on American soil dates back to 1539 when two of de Soto's men, Pedro Morón and Diego de Olivia, swam ashore to what is present-day Florida (Perez, 2005). The first mass migrations of Cubans to the United States occurred between 1868 and 1898, when approximately 100,000 Cubans left the country as a result of the Ten Years' War (*Guerra de los Diez Años*) and settled in several cities along the U.S. East Coast: Key West, Tampa, Ocala, Jacksonville, Pensacola, St. Augustine, New Orleans, Philadelphia, Wilmington, and New York City (O'Reilly Herrera; Perez; Poyo, 2005). Southern Cuban enclaves, many of which were supported by the booming cigar industry, became the financial center of the Cuban émigré community. At the same time, New York City became known as the intellectual center of the diaspora and a hub of movements for independence (*independista*), *anexionista* (advocating that Cuba become a part of the United States), and abolition (Perez). The

---

[1]Adjustment struggles of children of these return migrants have been poignantly described by Cave (2012).

Spanish-Cuban-American War of 1898 and a brief occupation of the island increased U.S. economic presence in Cuba and fostered emigration of Cubans to the United States (Poyo).

The modern history of Cuban migration to the United States began with the exodus sparked by the 1959 overthrow of Fulgencio Batista's regime and takeover by Fidel Castro and his 26th of July Movement (*Movimiento 26 de Julio*). In the 50 years that followed, more than 1/10 of the present-day Cuban population migrated to the United States in response to social, political, and economic restructuring within Cuba (O'Reilly Herrera, 2007).

Perez (2005) divided the 20th century migration of Cubans to the United States into four major periods. In the first period, which began with the 1959 Castro takeover, approximately 200,000 Cubans fled to the United States. Those fleeing included businesspeople and government officials tied to the previous regime, soldiers, lawyers, and educated professional elites. This wave also included more than 14,000 children, unaccompanied by their parents, who were airlifted to the United States in Operation Peter Pan—a controversial effort to provide them an opportunity for a better life abroad (Paris, 2002). Although approximately one-third of the Cuban population was Black or Mulato, almost all the people who emigrated in the first wave were White. Owing to their educational and economic wealth, they became known as America's "Golden Exile." Their hard work and determination, as well as social and economic supports from the government (Cuban Refugee Program established by the Kennedy administration in 1961) and the existing Cuban émigré community, allowed them to establish banks and develop major construction firms and other small businesses in Florida and beyond (O'Reilly Herrera; Perez). Many members of the first wave never lost the hope that someday they would return to their home country. They perceived themselves as exiles rather than immigrants (O'Reilly Herrera). The 1965 Cuban Adjustment Act gave Cubans special preference in U.S. immigration law, virtually guaranteeing their access to the United States (Poyo, 2005).

In the second wave of Cuban immigration, which occurred between 1965 and 1973, approxi-

mately 300,000 Cubans came to the United States (Perez, 2005). In September 1965, for propaganda purposes, Castro announced that those who had relatives in the United States were allowed to leave by boat from the port of Camarioca. At the end of the same year, the "Freedom Flights" began from Varadero Beach. Many people who emigrated on the Freedom Flights came to the United States via Spain, Mexico, and Venezuela. This wave of immigration consisted of well-educated middle-class professionals with high school or college education. Although most of them were White, this group also included many people of Jewish and Chinese backgrounds (Perez).

The third wave of immigration from Cuba took place in 1980 and brought the most heterogeneous group of exiles to the United States (Perez, 2005). This exodus began in March of 1980 when a group of Cubans crashed through the gates of the Peruvian and Venezuelan embassies in Havana. They were followed by approximately 10,000 others who flooded the embassies demanding political asylum. Castro's regime responded by announcing that those who wanted to leave the island could do so through the port of Mariel. This resulted in 125,000 Cubans, later dubbed "Marielitos," exiting to the United States, many of whom were rescued by the U.S. Coast Guard. A large percentage were of African descent, poor, and young, and almost 70% were men (Perez). Although only a small percentage of these groups were criminals and mental patients who were released by the regime and encouraged to leave the island, this immigration wave has long been negatively stereotyped.

The fourth wave occurred after the fall of the Soviet Union and the end of its political and economic support of Cuba. This resulted in massive food shortages, civil unrest, and heightened political repression by the Castro regime. In order to relieve some of the internal pressures, in 1994 Castro announced that he would not stop anyone wishing to leave the island. This led to a mass exodus of people using rafts (or *balsas*) made from inner tubes or empty oil drums or other makeshift floating devices (Perez, 2005). It has been estimated that several hundred *balseros* perished during their journey from Cuba. The exodus forced the United States to change its immigration policy toward Cubans. Under the new rules, immigrants intercepted in the Florida Straits would be returned to the island, while those who reached U.S. shores were given the right to remain. Moreover, the annual quota for Cubans seeking to legally enter the United States was increased (Poyo, 2005).

Almost two-thirds of the people of Cuban origin currently residing in the United States are foreign born. As some have argued, they have assimilated at a faster rate than other Latino Americans, and many have intermarried with Americans of other ethnic backgrounds (Perez, 2005). They are also more educated and earn higher salaries than most other Latino groups in the United States. The vast majority of Cuban Americans live on the East Coast in Florida, New Jersey, and New York.

Puerto Rican Americans

The history of Puerto Rican migration to the mainland United States is much different than that of Mexican Americans or Cubans. The Treaty of Paris (ratified by the U.S. Senate on February 6, 1899) marked the end of the Spanish-Cuban-American War. Spain ceded to the United States the island of Puerto Rico and other islands under Spanish sovereignty in the West Indies. Puerto Ricans, however, were not granted American citizenship until 1917, when the Jones Act conferred U.S. citizenship on the people of Puerto Rico by way of collective naturalization (Fuentes-Rohwer, 2005). Economic hardships and two world wars forced many Puerto Ricans to migrate from the island in search of better life opportunities. In addition, American colonial authorities promoted policies that allowed American companies to recruit agricultural and industrial workers from among the island's impoverished population (Acosta-Belén, 2005). By 1910 there were 1,513 Puerto Ricans in the continental United States. This number grew to almost 12,000 in 1920, to 50,000 in 1930, and to almost 70,000 by 1940 (Fuentes-Rohwer). Migration from the island increased in the wake of World War II. The 1940-1950 exodus, called the Great Migration, was sparked by the U.S.-led industrialization of Puerto Rico that began with Operation Bootstrap (*Operación Manos a la Obra*), which ultimately led to major displacement of the

island's agricultural workforce. The migration was also fueled by the need for low-wage labor in agricultural and manufacturing industries on the mainland, and promoted by cheap airfare from San Juan to New York and other major U.S. cities (Acosta-Belén). By 1950, the number of Puerto Ricans in the United States reached 300,000; it grew to 1.4 million in 1970 and to more than 4.6 million in 2010 (Ennis et al., 2011). The majority of Puerto Rican immigrants settled in New York City. In the 1980s and 1990s, however, Puerto Ricans began to settle in smaller and medium-size cities, including Orlando, Florida; New Haven and Hartford, Connecticut; and Jersey City, New Jersey. Chicago, Boston, and Philadelphia have also witnessed growing populations of Puerto Ricans (Fuentes-Rohwer). Many Puerto Ricans maintain transnational relationships with their country of origin that contribute to socioeconomic dynamics in both communities (Acosta-Belén).

SOCIOECONOMIC CHARACTERISTICS OF LATINO AMERICANS

According to the 2010 Census, 50.5 million Latinos resided in the United States in 2010, and they constituted 16.3% of the total population of the country (Ennis et al., 2011). Latinos of Mexican origin constituted the majority of Latino residents of the United States (63.0%), followed by those of Puerto Rican (9.2%) and Cuban descent (3.5%) (see table 5.1 and figure 5.1). This distribution, however, is likely to change in the future, as the states with the highest Latino growth rate in the 2000s were Arkansas, Georgia, South Carolina, Tennessee, and North Carolina (Ennis et al., 2011).

The Latino population accounted for over half the growth of the total population in the United States between 2000 and 2010 (Ennis et al., 2011). According to the census projections, by 2050 the Latino population in the United States is expected to grow to 102.6 million and to account for 24.4% of the total population (see table 5.2). According to other projections, the Latino population is expected to reach 128 million or 29% of the U.S. population in 2050 (Passel, Livingston, & Cohn, 2012). However, these projections may be revised

Table 5.1   Hispanic or Latino Origin Population in the United States by Type, 2010

Country	Number	Percent
Total population	308,745,538	100.0
Hispanic or Latino	50,477,594	16.3
Not Hispanic or Latino	258,267,944	83.7
Hispanic or Latino by type total	50,477,594	100.0
Mexican	31,798,258	63.0
Puerto Rican	4,623,716	9.2
Cuban	1,785,547	3.5
Other Hispanic or Latino	12,270,073	24.3
Dominican (Dominican Republic)	1,414,703	2.8
Central American (excludes Mexican)	3,998,280	7.9
Costa Rican	126,418	0.3
Guatemalan	1,044,209	2.1
Honduran	633,401	1.3
Nicaraguan	348,202	0.7
Panamanian	165,456	0.3
Salvadoran	1,648,968	3.3
Other Central American	31,626	0.1
South American	2,769,434	5.5
Argentinean	224,952	0.4
Bolivian	99,210	0.2
Chilean	126,810	0.3
Colombian	908,734	1.8
Ecuadorian	564,631	1.1
Paraguayan	20,023	–
Peruvian	531,358	1.1
Uruguayan	56,884	0.1
Venezuelan	215,023	0.4
Other South American	21,809	–
Spaniard	635,253	1.3
All other Hispanic or Latino	3,452,403	6.8

Based on Ennis et al. 2011.

in light of slowed immigration associated with the economic downturn that began in 2007 and pending legislation proposed in 2013 that outlines a path to citizenship for more than 11 million undocumented immigrants, most of whom are from Latin America.

Several noteworthy facts and comparisons can be made based on the report of Ennis and colleagues (2011). For example, 26.3% of Hispanics work in service occupations, compared to 14.9% of non-Hispanic Whites. In the managerial or professional occupations, the comparisons in

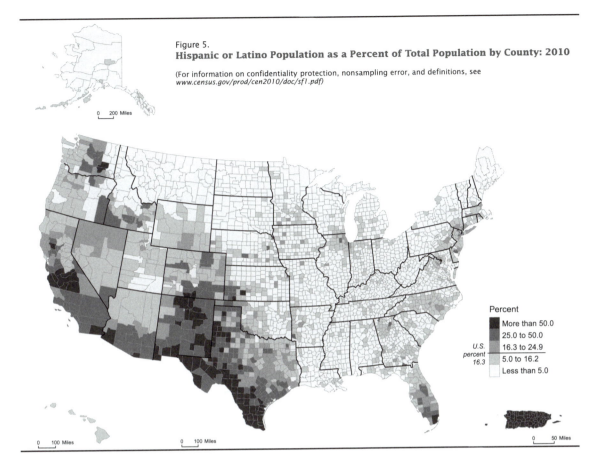

Figure 5.
Hispanic or Latino Population as a Percent of Total Population by County: 2010

(For information on confidentiality protection, nonsampling error, and definitions, see www.census.gov/prod/cen2010/doc/sf1.pdf)

Percent
More than 50.0
25.0 to 50.0
U.S.
percent — 16.3 to 24.9
16.3
5.0 to 16.2
Less than 5.0

0   200 Miles

0   100 Miles   0   100 Miles   0   50 Miles

Figure 5.1   Geographic distribution of the Latino population in the United States.

Reprinted from U.S. Census Bureau 2010.

Table 5.2   Latino Population in the United States, 1970 to 2050

Source of data and year	Hispanic population (in millions)	Percent Hispanic of the total population
CENSUS		
1970	9.6	4.7
1980	14.6	6.4
1990	22.4	9.0
2000	35.3	12.5
2010	50.5	16.3
PROJECTIONS		
2020	59.7	17.8
2030	73.0	20.1
2040	87.7	22.3
2050	102.6	24.4

U.S. Census Bureau, 1970, 1980, 1990, 2000, and 2010 Decennial Censuses; Populations Projections, July 1, 2010 to July 1, 2050.

2010 were 18.6% for Hispanics and 39.6% for non-Hispanic Whites. Among full-time year-round workers, the average Hispanic–Latino family median income was $37,359 in comparison to $54,620 for non-Hispanic White families. In 2011, Ennis and colleagues reported that 26.6% of Hispanics in comparison to 9.9% of non-Hispanic Whites were living at or below the poverty level. Additionally, 61% of Hispanics in comparison to 90% of non-Hispanic Whites have a high school diploma, and 12.6% of Hispanics compared to 31% of non-Hispanic Whites have a bachelor's degree. Language fluency varies among Hispanic subgroups. Census 2010 data show that 76% of Hispanics speak a language other than English at home (76% of Mexicans, 66% of Puerto Ricans, 82% of Cubans, and 92% of Salvadorans). Moreover, 37% of Hispanics state that they are not fluent in English. Another significant point is that in 2010, 34.9% of Hispanics were under the age of 18, compared to 20.9% of non-Hispanic Whites. Among Hispanics, Mexicans have the largest proportion of people under the age of 18, at 38%.

CULTURAL BACKGROUND OF LATINO AMERICANS

Latinos in the United States represent a wide variety of countries and ethnic groups with different social, political, and emotional experiences. Latino culture is very heterogeneous, not only because of cultural differences among source countries of immigrants, but also because of the varied cultural styles that different waves of newcomers brought to the United States and cultural changes they underwent after several generations of residence (Vigil, 1998). Moreover, unique personal values, social class, and racial background are likely to contribute to further diversification of Latino residents of the United States.

Despite significant diversity among Latino Americans, Tann (2005) believed that some degree of shared ethnic identity does exist within the Latino population and that certain broad cultural traits can be identified that are common to many Latinos. For instance, Triandis (1989) asserted that Latino cultures are collectivist in nature and that Latino people place higher value on the family and the larger community than they

do on the individual. Latinos typically have close relations with their families and have a tendency to maintain intensive contacts and affectionate relationships with extended family members that include *abuelos* and *abuelas* (grandfathers and grandmothers), *tios* and *tias* (uncles and aunts), and *sobrinas* and *sobrinos* (nieces and nephews) (Kirschner, 2005). Purnell and Paulanka (2003) indicated that such close kinship often leads to multigenerational Latino households, while Kirschner argued that it constitutes an important force behind minority cultural preservation. Familism, in general, has been widely described as a core value of the Latino culture (Sabogal, Marín, Otero-Sabogal, Marín, & Perez-Stable, 1987; Zinn, 1982). Many authors have described familism as a multidimensional construct that is composed of at least three dimensions: structural, behavioral, and attitudinal (Steidel & Contreras, 2003). Structural familism "marks the spatial and social boundaries within which behaviors occur and attitudes acquire meaning," while the behavioral dimension refers to "those behaviors associated with the feelings and attitudes about the family" (Steidel & Contreras, p. 313). Burgess, Locke, and Thomes (1963) defined *attitudinal familism* as

> 1) the feeling on the part of all members that they belong preeminently to the family group and that all other persons are outsiders; 2) complete integration of individual activities for the achievement of family objectives; 3) the assumption that land, money, and other material goods are family property, involving the obligation to support individual members and give them assistance when they are in need; 4) willingness of all members to rally to the support of a member if attacked by outsiders; and 5) concern for the perpetuation of the family as evidenced by helping adult offspring in beginning and continuing an economic activity in line with family expectations and in setting up a new household. (pp. 35-36)

Niemeyer, Wong, and Westerhaus (2009) identified and measured a number of components of *familismo,* including familial support (the belief that family members have an obligation to support each other in all circumstances); familial interconnectedness (the belief that family members must remain close both physically and emotionally); familial honor (the belief that each person has an obligation to uphold the family's honor and reputation); and subjugation of self to family (the belief that the individual must be submissive and yield to the family as a whole).

Vigil (1998) also believed that family is of central importance to Latinos and that they have a strong tendency to stress work and the production of goods for the group rather than the individual. Referring to Mexicans, he explained that the Mexican work ethic seems to be different from the one in the United States, as work and production of goods are aimed to benefit the group rather than the individual, the present is valued more than future savings, and people are valued for who they are rather than what they do.

Patriarchal family relations and subordination of females to males have also been attributed to the Latino culture. Traditional gender roles and attitudes are reflected in concepts such as *machismo, hembrismo,* and *marianismo* (Vigil, 1998). In a negative sense, *machismo* has been defined as the "traditional Latino cult of virility and aggressive masculinity, which is characterized by arrogant sexist attitudes, heavy drinking, domestic violence, male-to-male competition, and of having a large family (frequently in more than one household) as a signifier of virility, homophobia, and violence that includes notions of bravery, honor, and respect" (Kirschner, 2005, p. 54). Comas-Diaz (1987) argued that machismo puts men in a privileged position and demands that they be treated as authority figures, providers, and the ones responsible for the welfare and honor of the family. In a positive sense, according to Kirschner, machismo refers to an "idealized form of masculinity, that is, a way of life; a set of ethical tenets where inner strength, self-respect, responsibility, assertiveness, generosity, courage, pride, honesty, respect, humility, and striving for excellence are desirable personal traits and cultural values that should be aimed at" (p. 54). In the contemporary context, machismo is often seen as responsible for double standards that allow husbands to enjoy extramarital sex while their spouses are expected to be submissive, respectful, and faithful to their husbands (Kirschner).

Hembrismo, which literally means femaleness, has been described by Comas-Diaz (1987) as connoting strength, perseverance, flexibility, and ability for survival. Comas-Diaz suggested that Puerto Rican women who reside in the mainland United States may adhere to the *hembrista* norms in order to preserve their identity and cultural beliefs while simultaneously creating a more flexible role for themselves in American society. *Marianismo* refers to traditional Latino cultural values associated with female gender-role socialization demanding that women sacrifice their personal lives for their families; be kind, submissive, humble, nurturing, virtuous; never put their own needs first; and not wish for more in life than being a housewife (Gil & Vasquez, 1996; Santiago-Rivera, 2005). Marianismo has its roots in Roman Catholic religion and is associated with the Virgin Mary. It places expectations on Latina mothers to be responsible for providing religious and spiritual strength to their families and on young Latina women to remain virgins until they marry (Santiago-Rivera). However, as Comas-Diaz stated, despite the restrictive role of such beliefs, a certain degree of power can be achieved through passivity and conformity to the *marianista* role. Due to the sacredness of motherhood, older Latina women attain a semi-divine status, such that adult offspring revere them and often ally themselves with their mothers' struggles, especially against their fathers.

The extent to which Latinas in the United States today conform to the *marianista* behaviors is a topic of much debate in the contemporary literature (Santiago-Rivera, 2005). Similarly, as many authors have argued, the acculturation process resulting from increased exposure to the host culture, higher levels of women's education, and the rising participation of Latina women in the labor force have challenged the perceptions of femininity and masculinity and stereotypical gender roles among Latino families (Santiago-Rivera; Vazquez-Nuttall, Romero-Garcia, & de Leon, 1987). Cromwell and Ruiz (1979) even went as far as claiming that the prevailing notion of Latino male dominance is a myth that has been "based almost exclusively on simple descriptions or subjective impressions, disseminated in essay form, and seldom subjected to the scrutiny of empirical inquiry" (p. 370).

Some authors have also suggested that Latino cultures adhere to a certain degree of inevitability and determinism related to people's future, including their health, and that they consider the future to be related to luck or the will of a higher power (Davison, Frankel, & Smith, 1992; McCarthy, Ruiz, Gale, Karam, & Moore, 2004; Welch, Comer, & Steinman, 1973). Additionally, health and overall quality of life are believed to be closely linked to personal relationships *outside* one's self with those in the larger community (Tann, 2005) and may include feelings of safety, trust, and community well-being. Vigil (1998) also stressed that formal respect accorded to a person, the sense of loyalty to family and nation, the spiritualism that undergirds religious beliefs, and the strength that assists in overcoming burdens and obstacles also typify many Latinos. Some of those cultural values are clearly represented in Latinos' unique leisure behaviors.

OVERVIEW OF PAST AND PRESENT RESEARCH ON THE LEISURE OF LATINOS

This section provides an overview of the existing research on leisure behavior among Latino Americans. It begins with an analysis of how Latinos define and conceptualize leisure, then examines leisure participation preferences and styles among Latinos and analyzes motivations and benefits from participation. The final subsection provides an overview of factors responsible for unique leisure behavior patterns among Latinos.

Definitions and Meanings of Leisure

Information on how Latinos define and conceptualize leisure is scarce. Acevedo (2010) was one of the first to conduct a cross-national (United States–Mexico) comparison of ways in which Mexicans define leisure, the meanings they ascribe to leisure engagements, and changes that their leisure undergoes as a result of immigration. His study showed that both Mexicans living in Guerrero, Mexico, and Mexican immigrants in the Midwestern United States defined leisure as

tiempo libre, a term similar to the Western notion of leisure as it refers to a subset of time, free from obligations and compulsory activities. Leisure was also considered a state of being in which the individual is free to participate in a given activity, desires to participate in the activity, and strives to obtain positive outcomes from participation. Interestingly, however, strong family values among this population exempted family responsibilities from the notion of "tasks" or "chores" and equated them with true leisure. Only a few of the study participants referred to leisure as *ocio*—a term having negative connotations and meaning laziness in Spanish. When asked to identify the functions and properties of the most satisfying leisure experiences, the majority of Mexicans living in their home country commented that leisure allows for relaxation, satisfaction, enjoyment, and freedom and that it provides relationship opportunities. In general, Mexicans in both Mexico and the United States believed that one of the most important functions of leisure is helping to create and foster interpersonal relationships. Among immigrants, however, leisure took on the function of helping them to develop new social contacts in the host country and to explore new activities and places.

Juniu (2000) explored leisure behavior among immigrants from South America, including Argentina, Colombia, Chile, Ecuador, Paraguay, Peru, and Venezuela. Her findings were somewhat different from those obtained by Acevedo (2010) from a sample of working-class Mexicans. She suggested that the meanings of leisure and recreation differ between middle- and upper-class Latinos and those of a working-class status. Juniu's middle-class respondents saw leisure in a positive light and considered it a time for relaxation and rest, a time to recover energy, and freedom to do what they wanted. In general, perceptions of choice and freedom were critical to defining an experience as leisure. Conversely, working-class Latinos had unfavorable views on leisure and described it as idleness, as "boring," "not productive," and "wasting time" (p. 374). Working-class respondents placed value on work and productive activities. Juniu commented that "In their homeland, they had learned that leisure was wasting time, and they could not relate the concept of leisure and free time. For them, the idea of free time was independent of the notion of leisure. Free time implied the use of time in a productive way. They defined free time as 'time away from work,' 'time without pressures,' and 'time to do something productive'" (pp. 374-375).

Leisure Participation Preferences and Styles

The literature on leisure behavior of Latinos has significantly expanded since the publication of McMillen's study (1983) 30 years ago. As Floyd, Bocarro, and Thompson (2008) commented, "the increasing presence of Hispanic Americans in parks and forests . . . created a need among recreation resource managers for research to understand more diverse outdoor recreation preferences" (p. 11). Research in this area has investigated various aspects of recreation behavior of Latinos and identified their unique leisure participation preferences and styles, motivations for participation, and meanings attached to natural environments. The literature has consistently documented Latinos' preference for participation in family-oriented social activities such as picnicking, visiting with others, relaxing, being

with family, and playing with children (Chavez, 1991; Cronan, Shinew, & Stodolska, 2008; Gobster, 2002; Hutchison, 1987; Hutchison & Fidel, 1984; Stodolska, Shinew, & Li, 2010).

At the same time, in general, Latinos have been found to engage in sport and other physically active leisure pursuits less frequently than members of other groups (Crespo, 2000; Gobster, 2002; Hutchison; Hutchison & Fidel) (see chapter 13 on race, ethnicity, and physical activity). For instance, in a study of Chicago neighborhood parks, Hutchison observed that Latinos were more likely to engage in passive activities, while non-Hispanic Whites and African Americans were more likely to be involved in active pastimes such as jogging and biking. Similar findings were obtained by Gobster (1992, 2002). In his study of recreation use of Chicago's Lincoln Park, Gobster (2002) observed that non-Hispanic Whites were more likely to engage in active, individual sports, while Latinos participated more in passive and social park activities. Most of the studies have also shown that Latino men tend to participate in sport and physically active recreation more often than Latina females. For instance, Stodolska and colleagues (2010) revealed that Latino men who

According to Gobster's (2002) study, Latinos in Chicago's Lincoln Park area participated more in passive and social park activities.

recreated in city parks, in sport complexes, and on trails were more likely to be involved in all active pastimes (other than walking) than Latina females, and that women were more likely to be involved in walking and all passive activities other than barbecuing or picnicking. Results of the study by Barnett (2006) revealed that Latinos showed lower levels of sport involvement than African Americans and European Americans and that, unlike African Americans and Caucasians, none of the Latino males listed watching sports as their favorite leisure activity. Moreover, Latinos, in general, did not list health and fitness activities as their favorite ways of spending free time.

Research has also provided evidence that Latinos' recreation styles are significantly different from those typical of members of other ethnic groups. For instance, Latinos have been found to recreate in large, multigenerational, family-oriented groups with a significant proportion of women, children, and older adults, while individual or peer-group participation is rare (Gobster, 2002; Hutchison, 1987; Hutchison & Fidel, 1984; Irwin, Gartner, & Phelps, 1990; Stodolska et al., 2010).

Juniu (2000) observed, "In these [Latin American] societies less concern is given to the productive use of time and people tend to be more flexible and spontaneous when it comes to socializing" (p. 368). Unlike members of other groups, Latinos have been found to prepare most of their foods on-site and to spend significantly longer amounts of time in recreation places (often in excess of 5 or 6 hours) (Chavez, 1991, 1993; Cronan et al., 2008). Recreational groups of Latinos are large enough that they often exceed capacities of small backyards in many urban communities, making city parks and nature preserves preferable places for spending family time (Stodolska, Shinew, Acevedo, & Izenstark, 2011). The larger average size of the recreation party among Latinos, however, causes them also to exceed the designated capacity of many campsites in national forests (Irwin et al., 1990). When asked about their recreation site preferences, Latinos indicated that they preferred well-developed and -maintained places that included fire rings, toilets, and camping space at each site (Irwin et al.). Similarly, Chavez, Larson, and Winter (1995) documented that Latino visi-

tors to San Bernardino National Forest wanted more parking spaces and playgrounds to accommodate their extended families.

Motivations for Participation and Benefits of Participation

A significant number of studies have examined motivations for recreation participation among Latinos. Most of this research has shown that Latinos are motivated in their leisure by strong family values, including the desire to be with their children, to share experiences with their families, and to increase bonds among extended family members (Acevedo, 2009; Floyd & Gramann, 1992; Hutchison, 1987; Hutchison & Fidel, 1984; Irwin et al., 1990; Pfister & Ewert, 1993; Walker & Virden, 1992). As Juniu (2000) indicated, "Latin American cultures place high value on group-oriented activities and human interaction. For these cultures, social interaction is stressed during leisure time and considered an important recreational activity" (p. 368).

These observations were consistent with the findings of Shaull (1993), who reported that Latinos from California rated "doing something with your family" and "bringing the family together more" as significantly more important to their outdoor recreation enjoyment than did Anglos. Similarly, Tinsley, Tinsley, and Croskeys (2002) found that affiliation or "the opportunity to be with other people" (p. 210) was rated as a more important benefit of visiting parks by older Latinos than by Anglos. In a study of middle-class Latinos from Texas, Dunn (1999) commented, "Many resource managers have observed that Hispanic users seem to be motivated primarily by 'social' experiences and are less interested in the natural resources of the area" (p. 6). Latino interviewees in Stodolska and colleagues' (2011) study of Chicago park users mentioned opportunities to be with family, celebrate family events (e.g., birthdays, graduations), and connect with extended family members as important reasons for visiting urban parks. Such outings were particularly important for newcomers to the United States who used leisure events as a way to reestablish their social networks. Acevedo's (2009) work confirmed that such strong family values

Courtesy of Juan Carlos Acevedo.

Many observations show that Latinos like to bring the family together and connect by celebrating family events and having social experiences at parks.

are the primary driving force of leisure not only among Mexican immigrants in the United States, but also among Mexicans in their home country. His findings have also shown that many immigrant Mexicans in the United States felt isolated, segregated, and lonely and that as a result they used leisure to make new friends and to establish contacts with extended family members.

Factors Responsible for Unique Leisure Behavior Patterns Among Latinos

A number of factors have been discussed in the literature that shape leisure patterns among Latinos. These include culture and acculturation, access to recreation opportunities, immigration experience, legality of status, transnational arrangements, socioeconomic disadvantage, discrimination, and perceptions of welcomeness.

Culture and Acculturation

Differences in recreation behavior between Latinos and members of other groups have been traced to a number of factors; the most prominent are Latinos' culture and changes in their cultural patterns toward those of the "American mainstream"

(i.e., acculturation). Cultural differences, including changes in Latinos' cultural patterns resulting from direct and sustained contact with members of the White mainstream and other ethnic groups in the United States (Gordon, 1964), have been one of the most often cited reasons for the distinct recreation patterns among members of this group. For instance, Gramann, Floyd, and Saenz (1993) compared Mexican Americans and Anglo Americans in terms of social–psychological benefits they received from recreation participation. Following suggestions of Sabogal and colleagues (1987), they proposed that "Mexican American familism may express itself in greater importance on family togetherness as a recreation benefit" (p. 72). Their findings confirmed this hypothesis and showed that people of Mexican ancestry rated family togetherness, as a recreation benefit, much higher than did Anglos. Interestingly, Mexican Americans with the highest acculturation and structural assimilation scores gave the highest importance ratings for this item, which were significantly greater than those of Anglos and of the least acculturated Mexican Americans. The authors speculated that this resulted from disruptive effects of migration on the family structure of Latino(a) migrants. Recreation benefits were also examined by Shaull and Gramann (1998) in their study of Latinos from California. Their findings showed that the least acculturated Latinos rated nature-related benefits as more important than either Anglos or the most acculturated Latinos. Moreover, bicultural Latinos (i.e., those who identified strongly with both native and new culture) placed more importance on family-related benefits than did Anglos and the least acculturated Latinos.

Christenson, Zabriskie, Eggett, and Freeman (2006) examined the relationship between acculturation and family leisure involvement and aspects of family functioning from the perspective of Mexican American parents, youths, and families. Their findings showed that involvement in family leisure played an important role in the acculturation of Mexican American youth. The bicultural youth participated more frequently in core family leisure activities (i.e., activities that are common, inexpensive, and spontaneous) than highly acculturated youth. The authors speculated that bicultural youth had a strong commitment to their families and that they considered involvement in family leisure as important either for themselves or for other family members. On the other hand, highly acculturated youth participated in more balanced family leisure (i.e., activities that happen primarily outside of the home and require more interaction with mainstream Americans). According to Christenson and colleagues, such involvement was likely to play a role in the acculturation of the youth who identify more with the dominant society.

Cultural differences surface quite clearly not only with respect to Latino familism, but also in attitudes toward natural environments and nature-based recreation. Quoting Lynch (1993) and Gramann (1996), Dunn (1999) commented that "Hispanic Americans' environmental perspectives differ from those of Anglo-Americans in that Hispanic culture does not isolate people from the natural landscape [see chapter 12 on wilderness in the U.S. immigrant mind]. The ideal Hispanic landscape is 'peopled and productive' and does not include the notion of an uninhabited wilderness" (p. 6). The "productive" attitude toward the natural environment seemed to be confirmed in studies of recreational fishing

among Latinos and other minority groups (see Oh & Ditton, 2009). The authors observed that unlike Anglo anglers who viewed fishing "from a naturalistic perspective," many Latinos of lower socioeconomic status took part in recreational fishing for "product-driven reasons such as fish consumption" (p. 56).

It has been hypothesized that individuals born in Latin America display a much closer relationship to nature than do mainstream Americans and that they see themselves as a part of nature rather than owners of it (Lynch, 1983; Noe & Snow, 1990; Schultz, Unipan, & Gamba, 2000) (see chapter 12). According to Stodolska and colleagues (2011), this close relationship with nature is often evident in Mexicans' spending large portions of their leisure outdoors as well as in traditional Mexican symbolism (e.g., many Mexican sport teams are named after animals; animals also play important roles in traditional holiday celebrations). Interestingly, it has been found that Latinos' attitudes toward natural environments evolve with their acculturation levels and that Latinos born abroad display more pro-environmental attitudes than those born in the United States (Schultz et al., 2000). On the other hand, in their study comparing conservation attitudes between Anglos and Latinos, Oh and Ditton (2009) found that Latino anglers generally showed a pattern of fostering conservation attitudes similar to that of their Anglo counterparts.

The effects of acculturation and structural assimilation on the outdoor recreation behavior of Latinos also have been investigated in other research projects. For instance, Floyd and Gramann (1993) showed that the greater the level of acculturation, the more similar Mexican Americans were to Anglos in outdoor recreation participation. Moreover, less structurally assimilated Mexican Americans participated in fewer outdoor recreation activities and visited national forests less often than both their more assimilated counterparts and Anglos. Acculturation has also been shown to affect preferred leisure companions. For instance, Carr and Williams (1993) found that more acculturated Latinos with longer generational tenure were more likely to visit outdoor recreation sites with their friends, while recreationists of Mexican ancestry and those with lower acculturation scores were more likely to visit the sites with their immediate or extended families.

Access to Recreation Opportunities

The effects of access to recreation opportunities as determinants of leisure behavior among Latinos have been addressed from a number of different perspectives (see chapter 10 on leisure constraints for additional discussion of this topic). As Gobster (2002) indicated, findings from past research show a general tendency for White recreationists to travel farther and to visit urban and wildland parks and natural areas more frequently than members of minority populations. He further suggested that these findings "raise questions about various dimensions of access to recreation sites" (p. 144), such as physical distance from the place of residence, as well as the cost and availability of transportation, that may constrain the use of natural environments among minorities. Interestingly, and contrary to expectations, in his study of Chicago's Lincoln Park in the upscale downtown district, it was the minority park users who came from farther away and were more likely to travel to the park by car or to use public transportation. Similar findings were obtained by Stodolska and

colleagues (2010) and by Tinsley and colleagues (2002), who reported that Latinos traveled to Chicago's Lincoln Park primarily by car and that it took them significantly more time to reach the destination than it did Caucasian visitors. This has raised issues of cost of access related to parking facilities, gas, and potentially an inability to access the site among minorities who do not own cars. It also raises the question of the quality of parks that are located near their residences.

Gómez and Malega (2007) measured access to outdoor environments by geo-referencing respondents' home street address and the location of a selected recreation area, allowing them to calculate the objective distance between the two locations. The authors explored whether this distance from the park, among other factors, affected Puerto Ricans' uses of parks and perceived park benefits. The findings showed that the distance from the park was not a significant predictor of its use but was a significant predictor of perceived benefits associated with park usage.

Many studies have demonstrated that minorities have less access to recreation facilities and outdoor recreation spaces than non-Hispanic Whites (Floyd, Taylor, & Whitt-Glover, 2009; Taylor & Lou, 2011; Wolch, Wilson, & Fehrenbach, 2005)

© Monika Stodolska

Studies show that non-Hispanic Whites have more access to recreation opportunities than minorities and the quality of parks near Latino residences might be questionable.

(see also chapter 3 on leisure services). Similarly, in Stodolska and colleagues' (2011) study, insufficient access to parks was one of the important leisure constraints identified by Latino urban residents. Some of the natural environments in inner-city Latino communities were described as "wastelands," replete with trash and graffiti-filled walls that served as convenient settings for drug dealing among gangs.

Similar to Floyd and Johnson's (2002) analysis, an investigation by Stodolska and colleagues (2011) highlighted issues of environmental justice that manifest themselves in minorities' lack of access to quality natural environments. The authors argued that Latino residents of lower socioeconomic status often lack political clout to fight environmental degradation in their communities, and that undocumented status among many Latinos hinders advocacy efforts to secure more quality park space. Access to parks in Latino communities was also restricted due to a lack of information about programs in Spanish; the inability of the staff to communicate in Spanish; and perceptions of interracial conflict and dis-

crimination from the park staff, police, and other visitors. Problems with park access were exacerbated by the racial makeup of the surrounding communities that often led to interracial conflict, which in turn limited Mexican Americans' access to other nearby parks. Access to suburban park spaces, on the other hand, was hindered by the lack of automobiles and inability to afford gas (or to obtain a driver's license due to undocumented status).

Crime also has been mentioned as an important factor limiting access of Latinos to recreation environments. In their analysis of physical activity patterns among adolescents, Gordon-Larsen, McMurray, and Popkin (2000) reported that the highest percentage of White adolescents lived in low-crime areas while the highest percentage of Latinos lived in high-crime areas, and that crime was negatively associated with physical activity. Similar results were obtained by Stodolska and colleagues (2009, 2010), who showed that gang activity in Latino inner-city neighborhoods and parks was the major obstacle to Latinos' visiting local public recreation areas.

Gang graffiti and warning signs in Piotrowski Park, Chicago.

In contrast to findings from research that focused only on Latino residents of the United States, findings presented by Acevedo (2009), who compared leisure behavior among Mexicans in the Mexican state of Guerrero and in the United States, showed that leisure opportunities among immigrants actually *increased* after resettlement. His interviewees praised leisure facilities and programs available to them in the United States and, in particular, opportunities for organized leisure activities available to their children. High entrance fees and price of club membership were the factors limiting their ability to take full advantage of the new leisure options.

Immigration Experience, Legality of Status, and Transnational Arrangements

Other possible explanations for differences in leisure patterns among Latinos and members of other ethnic groups may be related to their immigration experience, transnational arrangements, and lack of legal status in the United States (see also chapter 10 on leisure constraints). Changes in the social networks of immigrants and in their work patterns attributable to the effects of immigration have been documented in several research projects (Acevedo, 2009; Juniu, 2000; Stodolska & Santos, 2006a, 2006b). For instance, in their study of Latino day laborers, Stodolska and Santos (2006a) illustrated how immigration led to the breakdown of families and traditional social networks of immigrants and made their leisure less family oriented than in their home country. Similar observations were made by Juniu (2000) in her study of immigrants from South American countries. Juniu's interviewees remarked that socialization in their home countries was easier and that after coming to the United States they tended to spend more time alone and lived more isolated lives.

Juniu's (2000) findings were consistent with Acevedo's (2009) results, which showed that because immigrants came to the United States by themselves or with few friends or family members, many felt lonely and isolated after arrival. Long work hours and lack of knowledge of the activities and recreation resources additionally constrained their leisure. In Acevedo's study, the main differences between residents of Guerrero, Mexico, and Mexican immigrants in the Midwest related to the type of activities they participated in, the feeling of having more freedom to engage in leisure, and more opportunities to be involved in structured leisure pastimes after immigration. Despite the fact that some machismo attitudes were present among Mexican men after immigration, many women were able to work outside of the home and thus had more discretionary income to spend on their leisure. Nonetheless, most were still the main caretakers of their households, and the long work hours and lack of culturally sensitive activity options constrained their leisure. Similarly, Mexican immigrant men worked long and strenuous hours and were often too exhausted to be able to enjoy their time off. After settling in the United States, Mexican immigrants still took part in many "old" leisure activities and celebrations; but in the new environment, many of their old pastimes were reinvented and infused with new American elements.

Stodolska and Santos (2006b) also showed that hardships related to the immigration process, demanding physical labor, and broken family networks made many single male Latino migrants fall into the pattern of substance abuse and passive recreation (watching TV, playing cards), only rarely interrupted by occasional soccer and basketball games. Hard working conditions of Latino immigrants, many of whom are employed in the manufacturing, maintenance, and agricultural sectors, were also seen as a cause for their more passive recreation (Crespo, 2000).

Transnational arrangements among many Latino migrants, for whom residence in the United States is perceived as only temporary and who channel much of their financial resources back to the home country, also severely affect their leisure behavior. A Mexican interviewee in Stodolska and Santos' (2006b) study commented on his financial situation and spending preferences and stated, "A beer is like a tile on my floor," meaning that he would rather use money that could be spent on drinks to finish his house in Mexico. Other Latino participants who were undocumented migrants revealed that they refrained from visiting distant recreation sites for fear of being stopped by the police and deported. Lack of legal status also contributed to transportation problems, as undocumented migrants could not obtain an American driver's license.

Socioeconomic Disadvantage

Since many Latino immigrants live in poor central-city neighborhoods, their leisure behavior is also conditioned by the same factors that affect recreation of other minority populations residing in such areas—crime, lack of access to quality natural environments, and inadequate provision of recreation facilities. Lack of resources for leisure is also related to the low-wage jobs held by many Latinos, the necessity to support larger families, the expectation to contribute to the welfare of the extended family, and transnational arrangements. These factors were discussed in detail earlier in this chapter. Lower socioeconomic status has been shown not only to constrain leisure *participation* among Latinos, but also to shape their leisure *preferences*. This issue is particularly pronounced among working-class Latinos in their home country who feel that, as a result of their lower social status, they are not entitled to participate in leisure activities reserved for the upper class and thus do not expose their children to similar leisure opportunities after immigration to the United States (Acevedo, 2009).

Discrimination and Perceptions of Welcomeness

Discrimination experienced by Latino recreationists has also been shown to significantly affect their recreation behavior. Issues of discrimination against Latinos are discussed in detail in chapter 11 on discrimination in leisure contexts and in chapter 10 on leisure constraints. In addition to perceived discrimination, Stodolska and colleagues' (2011) study identified perceptions of welcomeness as an important factor affecting park visitation and benefits that Latinos could derive from park use. The authors suggested that perception of welcomeness can play a particularly important role among Latinos since in many Latino countries it is an established custom to provide a warm welcome to people who are new to an area. Lack of welcomeness can be considered an insult and akin to a "loss of face" from family to family.

Stodolska and colleagues argued that perception of welcomeness may be related to the ethnic and racial background of park users, park staff, and people who live in the vicinity of parks. It may also be based on visitors' past experiences with discrimination in the park or on their way to the park, past failed attempts to access park programs, or word-of-mouth in the community that labels a park in a particular way (e.g., "Hispanic park" or "African American park"). Promotional materials distributed by the park and types of activities organized in parks are also likely to play a role in how welcome Latinos feel in park spaces.

RECOMMENDATIONS FOR FUTURE RESEARCH AND PRACTICE

Although research on the leisure behavior of the Latino population has developed rapidly in recent years, there are some gaps in the literature that should be addressed. It would be useful to have a greater understanding of leisure behavior among Latinos in their home countries. Much of the research on Latinos has occurred after their emigration. Having a greater appreciation of their leisure behavior in their home countries could provide insight into the adaptations and adjustments they make after emigration. Chick (1991) conducted a rare study on festival sponsorship in traditional Central American communities. He noted that the acculturation of small, rural villages to the national Mexican culture, and away from their traditional Indian background, has had strong negative correlations with the cargo system that provides community-wide recreational opportunities in traditional villages. This led residents of these communities to seek recreational opportunities outside their villages. More in-depth analyses of leisure experiences and opportunities in Latinos' home communities, as well as the effects of globalization trends on their leisure culture at home, would be helpful for understanding the changes they experience as a result of relocation and acculturation.

Additional research is also needed on differences within Latino subpopulations. For example, studies on social class differences among Latinos would be useful. The majority of the existing research focuses on working-class immigrants, while there is a paucity of research on the leisure behavior of middle- and upper-class Latinos who were born in the United States. Other within-group comparisons might include immigrants who reside in urban communities and those who reside in the suburbs or rural communities. Research on leisure behavior in rural communities in general is limited (Edwards & Matarrita-Cascante, 2011), and this type of research would help fill that gap in the literature. Differences among transnational migrants and those who have settled in the United States permanently, as well as comparisons between documented and undocumented immigrants, would also be useful.

Researchers also need to appreciate and acknowledge that there is no such thing as a static Latino culture. Latino cultures are dynamic in that they are constantly evolving and adapting to new circumstances related to the world's economy and global social and cultural processes. Latino communities are shaped and reshaped by the cultural, political, and economic changes in the United States and in the host countries of immigrants. The majority of immigrants are in constant contact with their families "back home" and with their communities of origin. The amount and the type of contact (including remittances) are likely to influence their leisure. Another area of concern relates to the issue of quality of life of those returning to their home countries, especially the welfare of children born in the United States and returning to places and ways of life that are largely unfamiliar to them.

It is important for leisure practitioners to recognize that the Latino population in the United States is diverse and that important differences exist based on people's region of origin, gender, age, and marital and immigration status. Practitioners need to appreciate that these types of factors may affect Latinos' recreation participation. For example, many Latinos (especially undocumented immigrants) are wary of authority figures, and this may affect their willingness to register for scheduled programs for fear of being reported. Moreover, certain forms of organized leisure pastimes often do not exist in their countries of origin, where play among the youth tends to be unstructured. Thus parents are not accustomed

to the formal structure and organization of leisure and recreation programs typical of most community park and recreation agencies in the United States. As noted by Acevedo (2009), although competitive sports and other leisure activities typical of the American society are not common in their home culture, many parents are glad to have their children learn these activities. However, parents may not be aware that such opportunities exist or may be unfamiliar with the registration process required for participation. It is also important for practitioners to recognize the obligations placed on children to spend time with their families. Latino culture is much more collectivistic than the Anglo culture, and thus the majority of leisure takes place in the context of families. Leisure programming for Latinos should reflect and support this aspect of their culture. For example, practitioners could provide programs suited for entire families in order to encourage participation by all members of the family, including women and children. It is also important for practitioners to remember that culturally appropriate child care must be provided so that women feel comfortable participating without their children.

The design and layout of parks and recreation areas should be another important consideration for practitioners. Park designs that better integrate parks with the local communities, such as *plaza*-style design with *kioskos* (small, open-sided pavilions usually located in parks or plazas), help connect parks with the community. Research suggests that it is also important to be mindful of maintenance and safety issues in parks and open spaces and that gang boundaries may prohibit people from moving freely in their communities and accessing recreation spaces (e.g., Stodolska et al., 2009, 2013). Moreover, providing safe, well-maintained, and welcoming recreation areas is vital to participation. Research has shown that providing large family-friendly picnic areas with adequate access to parking, rest rooms, water, and waste receptacles helps encourage use among Latinos.

General operating procedures and their relationship to the Latino population should be considered as well. For example, it is important to determine appropriate and effective ways to distribute information. Thapa and colleagues

(2002) suggested that with regard to information sources, Latinos prefer brochures and fliers and infrequently seek advice from rangers and park staff. Given that 37% of Hispanics state that they are not fluent in English (Ennis et al., 2011), brochures and signs should be translated into Spanish. Information should be distributed through appropriate sources such as Spanish-language radio stations, public schools, churches, and community organizations. Additionally, it is important for staff to represent the community and be either Latino or at least able to communicate in Spanish, have adequate knowledge of Latino cultures, and be sensitized to Latinos' issues.

CONCLUSION

This chapter (1) overviews the history of Latino immigration to the United States, defines relevant terms, and discusses the current and projected size of this group in the United States; (2) provides a comprehensive review of the history and current status of leisure research involving Latinos; (3) identifies leisure research areas in particular need of further study; and (4) provides practical recommendations on how to provide leisure services to Latinos. The research examined shows that Latinos have leisure participation preferences, styles, and benefits that are quite distinct from those of the Anglo mainstream and that their leisure behavior patterns are shaped by an array of factors. These include, but are not limited to, their culture, access to recreation opportunities, immigration experience, and discrimination. Given the size and the rapid growth of the Latino population in the United States, it is critical that leisure researchers and practitioners have a sound understanding of the leisure behavior of members of this group. However, such understanding cannot be achieved if one fails to appreciate Latino history, struggles, concerns, and lifestyles. Although a fair amount of research has been devoted to Latinos, additional research is warranted, and the new findings should be used to inform practitioners on how to better serve this important constituent group.

CHAPTER 6

Leisure Among Asian North Americans

Gordon J. Walker and Jinyang Deng

OVERVIEW

This chapter begins by providing a brief explanation of the term Asian North American (i.e., who is included and why) and then describes the current and projected size of this group in the United States and Canada. A comprehensive review of the history and current status of leisure research involving Asian North Americans follows. Lastly, the authors identify leisure research areas that are in particular need of further study before offering practical recommendations on how to best provide leisure services for Asian North Americans.

Learning Outcomes

After reading this chapter, readers will be able to

- define the terms Asian and Asian North American, as well as describe the current and projected size of the latter group;

- integrate past and present research on leisure among the two most studied Asian North American groups, Chinese and Koreans;

- integrate past and present research on leisure among other Asian North American groups; and

- summarize what leisure scholars and recreation professionals should consider in terms of future research and practice when working with Asian North Americans.

After Confucius asked his disciples what they would do once their talents were recognized, one replied: '. . . I would like to take five or six young men, and six or seven youngsters to go for a swim in the Yi river, enjoying the cool breeze at the Rain Dance Festival, and make our way back home, singing.' To which Confucius replied: 'Ah lovely. I am with you. . . .'

Adapted from Muller (2005)

Some readers may be familiar with the original version of this story in Confucius' *The Analects,* whereas others may remember a slightly longer version in *Leisure Sciences* (Liu, Yeh, Chick, & Zinn, 2008). But while use of this narrative to begin a chapter on leisure among Asians in North America may seem apt, there are some concerns. For example, by looking only at this account rather than Confucius' work as a whole, one could inadvertently misrepresent his overall philosophical stance. Perhaps more importantly, even though singing, swimming, and attending a festival may seem comparable with what people in the West would call leisure, one cannot assume that this concept is identical to that in Confucian-influenced (e.g., Chinese, Korean) cultures. Moreover, because of acculturation (i.e., changes as a result of contact with another cultural group; Berry, Poortinga, Segall, & Dasen, 2002), a Chinese person's or a Korean North American's leisure may look both similar to and different from that found in China or Korea *and* that found in Canadian or American majority group culture. The good news in these two instances is that a modicum of research has been conducted on the leisure of Chinese and Korean people as well Chinese and Korean North Americans. Unfortunately, as will soon be made evident, this is not the case for many other Asian North Americans.

First, however, we must answer the question "What is Asia?" before proceeding to the chapter's main query "What is leisure among Asian North Americans?"—the latter being so sufficiently challenging that it might even lead Confucius to consider returning to his swimming hole.

DEFINITIONS AND DEMOGRAPHICS

It was not Asians but rather ancient Greeks who first used the word "Asia" (Emmerson, 1984). In fact, Bowring (1987) held that the term "Asian" became common in the western and northern part of Eurasia only when self-described "Europeans" decided to distinguish themselves from those living in the eastern and southern part of this same landmass (whom they referred to as Asians). Concurrently, those living in the eastern and southern part of Eurasia, as a consequence of European colonization, began adopting the word Asian to describe themselves.

This intermixing of geography and geopolitics helps explain why it is not always clear who is Asian; and this issue is made even more complex because, at the individual level, the term is often used in a locale-specific fashion (e.g., a Chinese person may consider a Korean, but not a Pakistani, person to be Asian; Bowring, 1987). Additionally, at the organizational level, (a) a country may "straddle" Asia and Europe (e.g., Turkey) and so be considered a part of either the former (e.g., Statistics Canada, 2006) or the latter (e.g., United Nations, 2013); and (b) a person who states, for example, that he is from Lebanon would be classified as White in the United States (U.S. Census Bureau, 2001), as Arab in Canada (Statistics Canada), and as Western Asian by the United Nations (2013). Given the definitional difficulties described here, as well as in another part of this book (see chapter 8) on Muslim North Americans (whose origins are often from what the United

Nations calls Western Asia), this chapter uses the U.S. Census Bureau's (2007) parsimonious definition of who is Asian North American, specifically:

> People having their origins in any of the original people of the Far East (e.g., Chinese, Japanese, Korean, Mongolian, Taiwanese), Southeast Asia (e.g., Cambodian, Filipino, Hmong, Indonesian, Laotian, Malaysian, Thai, Vietnamese), or the Indian subcontinent (e.g., Asian Indian, Bangladeshi, Nepalese, Pakistani, Sri Lankan).

Asians have lived in North America for over a century and a half, beginning when Chinese people started arriving in Canada and the United States around 1850. Poor economic conditions in China, in conjunction with gold rushes in California and British Columbia and, subsequently, construction of cross-continental railway systems, were largely responsible for this migration (Li, 1998; Wong, 2006). Other Asian group members began immigrating shortly thereafter, and as their numbers increased, so too did the frequency and intensity of personal (e.g., the Vancouver riots of 1887 and 1907) and institutional (e.g., the U.S. Immigration Act of 1917, specifically its Asiatic Barred Zone provision; the Chinese Immigration Act of 1923 in Canada) discrimination. The latter policies continued well into the mid-20th century, whereas instances of the former, though diminished, have never entirely disappeared (Stodolska, 2010; Wong).

In the United States, 5.6% of the population is either Asian alone or in combination with another race (U.S. Census Bureau, 2011). Noteworthy here is that the Asian-alone population increased 46% between the 2000 and 2010 censuses, more than any other racial group (U.S. Census Bureau). The five largest Asian groups were Chinese, 22.0%; Filipino, 18.5%; Asian Indian, 16.2%; Vietnamese, 9.8%; Korean, 9.2%; and Japanese, 7.5% (U.S. Census Bureau). For comparative purposes, 19.1% of Canadians were visible minority group members in 2011 (Statistics Canada, 2013). South Asians were the largest group (25.0%; Statistics Canada); however, it is worth noting that this category was composed of over a dozen subgroups, including

those from very different cultural backgrounds (e.g., East Indians, Sri Lankans, and Pakistanis). Chinese were the second largest visible minority group (21.1%), with other large Asian groups including Filipinos (9.9%), Southeast Asians (5.0%; e.g., Vietnamese, Cambodian), West Asians (3.3%; e.g., Afghan, Iranian), and Koreans (2.6%).

Importantly, projections suggest that the percentage of Asians in America will increase significantly, with those reporting being Asian either alone or in combination rising to 9.2% by 2050 (U.S. Census Bureau, 2008). Similarly, in Canada, visible minority group members are expected to nearly double in less than two decades, from 16.2% in 2006 to 30.6% in 2031 (Statistics Canada, 2010). At this future time, 8.7% of the country will be South Asian, 6.4% will be Chinese, and 2.4% will be Filipino (Statistics Canada).

ASIAN NORTH AMERICANS IN LEISURE RESEARCH

To date, most of the research on Asian North Americans' leisure has focused on Chinese and, to a slightly lesser extent, Korean people. The reason for the former may be that Chinese people were the earliest immigrants to Canada and the United States and are the largest (relatively) homogeneous group in both countries. The reason for the latter may be that, although fewer Koreans live in Canada and the United States compared with members of some other Asian groups, there appears to be a considerable number of scholars, both in North America and in East Asia, who are actively engaged in Korean-focused leisure research. Thus, the next two subsections focus on the most well-researched aspects of leisure among Chinese and Korean North Americans, while the last subsection provides an overview of the very limited research that has examined other Asian North American groups' leisure.

Chinese North Americans' Leisure

This section begins by discussing the meaning of leisure for Chinese North Americans, then examines their attitudes, needs and motivations, constraints to, and actual participation in leisure.

Meaning of Leisure

To better understand the Chinese meaning of leisure, it is worthwhile to first look at what is implied by the two characters that make up the word for leisure: "休闲" (*xiu xian*, in simplified Chinese) or "休閑" and its variant "休閒" (in traditional Chinese). The Chinese words for leisure, "休闲" or "休閒," are associative compounds of two Chinese characters: "休" and "闲" or "休" and "閒" (Liu et al., 2008). The word "休," a combination of "人" (*ren,* person) and "树" (*shu,* tree), symbolizes a person leaning against a tree for a rest (Liu et al.). It conveys an image in which a farmer leans on or sits beside a tree to take a break or rest after a hard day of working in the field (Liu et al.). In this sense, "休" has several connotations, including

- the labor of ordinary working-class people;
- utilitarianism, as in helping a person relax and recover after work (Liu et al.);
- an outdoor setting;
- being nature based; and
- being passive in form.

Because "休" also suggests a positive feeling or a moment of happiness after engaging in hard work, this character also means "beauty," "fine quality," "preciousness," and "virtue" as defined in the first Chinese dictionary, "尔雅" (*Er Ya;* Liu et al.).

In terms of one of the other characters associated with the Chinese word for leisure, "閒," is a combination of "門" (*men,* door) and "月" (*yue,* moon or moonlight) and "represents moonlight coming into a house through cracks between the planks of a door" (Liu et al., 2008, p. 487). This implies that the door is closed and, because it is evening, it is safe to rest or relax indoors. Additionally, this may explain why the word "閒" is a variant of the word "閑," which is a combination of "門" (door) and "木" (*mu,* wood or tree), and depicts the door as secured with a wooden bar, a traditional Chinese way of locking the entranceway from inside the house. This character represents, therefore, a protected and undisturbed space (Liu et al.). In this sense the word "閒" or "閑" has several connotations, including that leisure is

- free and unoccupied;
- not related to, or is the opposite of, work;
- indoor based; and
- safe and peaceful.

Thus, although the word "休" denotes taking a break or rest beside a tree in an outdoor setting after work, the word "閑" (and its variant "閒") has a connotation of leisure performed indoors that is free of obligation. In this sense, the Chinese meaning of "閑" is quite close to the classic definition of leisure in Western societies, that is, the opposite of work, free time, or a state of being or mind pursued by citizens in both ancient Greece and feudal officials and the literati in ancient China. Arguably, it is this class difference that leads to leisure being viewed, in most of Chinese history, by the general public (i.e., lower- or working-class people) as "游手好闲" (*you shou hao xian,* idle hand) or "不务正业" (*bu wu zheng ye,* lazing about and not doing anything productive). Therefore, "閒," as the opposite of work, to some extent has a derogatory connotation from the perspective of traditional Chinese agrarian society, in which labor is highly valued.

Unfortunately, empirical research on the Chinese meaning of leisure is rare. One exception is an experience sampling method (ESM) study conducted with Chinese Canadians. Walker and Wang (2009) had 35 Chinese Canadians respond to a watch alarm randomly programmed to ring seven times a day for 12 days. When the alarm rang, participants reported what activity they were doing and whether it was work, leisure, both, or neither (Shaw, 1984). Walker and Wang found that their participants differentiated between leisure and nonleisure primarily in that the former (a) involved certain motivations but not others, (b) satisfied certain needs but not others, and (c) was less effortful. Needs and motivations are discussed shortly, but first it will be useful to examine Chinese people's leisure attitudes more fully.

Leisure Attitudes

The derogatory meaning of leisure associated with the word "閑" and the higher value traditionally placed on work in Chinese society may explain why Chinese people tended to view leisure as a less important aspect of their lives (Ap, 2002; Wang & Stringer, 2000; Xiao, 1997). Hall and

Rhyne (1989) found that Chinese Canadians displayed "leisure lack," which means that they participated in fewer activities, expressed less satisfaction with their leisure, and placed less value on leisure in general. Ho and Card (2001) also found that Chinese American older adult women did not "view leisure as [being] important to them" (p. 295). Rather, they emphasized the traditional Chinese women's roles of wife, mother, grandmother, and daughter (see also Allison & Geiger, 1993). Moreover, the concept of leisure did not change pre- and postimmigration, in that these older adult women viewed taking care of children and grandchildren as leisure. Additionally, in a study of the Chinese experience of "入迷" (*rùmí*, or absorption), a number of participants reported feeling guilty about enjoying themselves (Walker & Deng, 2003/2004). This finding is consistent with Schutte and Ciarlante's observation that "Asians have a generally negative attitude towards leisure . . . [and they feel] a sense of guilt in using leisure time to satisfy only their personal needs" (as cited in Ap, 2002, p. 13).

Leisure attitudes held by Chinese North Americans may change during the process of acculturation. That is, as the Chinese people become more acculturated, their attitudes, preferences, and behaviors may become more like those in the majority group culture. In a study (Deng, Walker, & Swinnerton, 2005) that compared the leisure attitudes of Chinese in Canada and Anglo Canadians, Anglo Canadians' affective and cognitive leisure attitudes were found to be significantly more positive than those of Chinese. However, the two groups' behavioral leisure attitudes did not differ significantly. Interestingly, on the cognitive and affective attitudinal dimensions, high-acculturated Chinese were more different from Anglo Canadians than were low-acculturated Chinese. Deng and associates called this phenomenon "leisure shock," a term they created to describe a situation in which new immigrants with lower levels of acculturation held more positive leisure attitudes than those who had lived in Canada for a longer time versus those who had higher levels of acculturation and who tended to put more emphasis on education, employment, or both, and less on leisure. Lin (2010) conducted a comparable study of Chinese people who had lived in Canada—on average—for more than 10 years. (The number of years postarrival is a commonly used proxy for acculturation.) She found that, while her participants strongly agreed that leisure contributed to one's health and happiness, there was considerable disagreement on whether it was a high priority compared to other pursuits. Arguably, one reason for the differences between Lin's findings and those of earlier researchers (e.g., Allison & Geiger, 1993; Hall & Rhyne, 1989) is that China's economy began to boom in this century and, consequently, Chinese people's—and Chinese immigrants'—leisure attitudes may have become more positive.

Leisure Needs and Motivations

As noted earlier, leisure is highly related to rest and relaxation for Chinese people. Potentially, therefore, leisure could be construed in terms of satisfying the *physiological* need for optimal arousal (Kleiber, Walker, & Mannell, 2011). For example, Ho and Card (2001), in examining the leisure of Chinese female immigrants in the United States, found that "more than half the women thought relaxation was the first and foremost thing to experience leisure. The main concern for the women in experiencing leisure was how they perceived the experience (e.g., relaxing, enjoyable and satisfying)" (p. 295). Similarly, Li and Stodolska (2006) discovered that Chinese graduate students in the United States primarily referred to leisure as a feeling of relaxation. Finally, in a study (Zhang & Gobster, 1998) of Chinese people residing in Chicago, relaxing (including walking, people-watching, sitting, and chatting) was the primary (47.4%) outdoor activity mentioned by participants.

Leisure could also function as a way of satisfying Chinese people's *psychological* needs, both "core" (i.e., needs deemed by psychologists to be pan-human) and "expressed" (i.e., needs offered by recreationists when asked) (see chapter 9 for more on this topic). In the latter case, Walker, Deng, and Dieser (2001) used four Western-based recreation experience preference scales (REP; Manfredo, Driver, & Tarrant, 1996) and developed five new Asian-focused "social interdependence" (SI) scales. Walker and associates found, as they had hypothesized, that Anglo North Americans rated REP autonomy/independence higher than did Chinese North Americans, whereas Chinese

Relaxation is considered one of the first things necessary to experience leisure by many Chinese female immigrants.

North Americans rated SI group membership and humility/modesty higher than did Anglo North Americans. In the latter case, Walker and Wang (2009) had Chinese Canadians use the ESM to report what activity they were doing (i.e., work, leisure, both, or neither; Shaw, 1984) and how well it satisfied their core needs for autonomy, competence, and relatedness (Deci & Ryan, 2000). The researchers found that when their participants were alone, autonomy was satisfied the most during leisure and the least during neither (e.g., doing household chores, driving to work), whereas competence was satisfied the most during work and the least during neither. In contrast, when participants were with others, autonomy and competence were satisfied the most during leisure and the least during work.

Needs are related to, but distinct from, motivations. Thus, a Chinese North American may also be motivated to participate in a leisure activity for intrinsic (i.e., because the activity is interesting, enjoyable, and done for its own sake) or extrinsic (i.e., to obtain internal or external rewards or to avoid internal or external punishments) reasons,

or a combination of the two. For instance, Walker and Deng (2003/2004) compared the Chinese experience of "入迷" (rùmí, or absorption) with the Western subjective leisure experience (Kleiber et al., 2011) and found very high intrinsic motivation during rùmí. Similarly, in an ESM study of Chinese Canadians (Walker, 2008), intrinsic motivation was significantly higher during leisure activities than during work-related, unpaid work, and personal care activities. On the other hand, two types of extrinsic motivation—introjected (e.g., pride or guilt) and external (e.g., others being proud or ashamed of you)—were significantly higher during work-related and unpaid work activities than during leisure activities.

Results from other studies involving Chinese North Americans are congruent with the findings just discussed. For example, Allison and Geiger (1993) found that gardening meant different things for Chinese American older adults compared with their White counterparts. For Chinese Americans, gardening was more production oriented. In addition, many of their other leisure activities (e.g., reading, watching television) were used as a means to learn more about the language and ways of the majority group culture. However, another study (Hirschman, 1982) comparing the leisure activities and motives of six ethnic groups living in New York, reported that seeking fun or pleasure (i.e., intrinsic motivation) through physical activities was rated second lowest by the Chinese participants. In this case, pursuing physical activities to perfect one's performance (i.e., extrinsic motivation) was rated highest by the Chinese participants. Finally, the utilitarian use of leisure is also evident in outdoor recreation settings. Consumptive use motives, for example, were rated higher by Chinese participants compared with other Asian participants (i.e., Japanese, Korean, and Filipino) in a study conducted by Winter, Jeong, and Godbey (2004).

Leisure Participation

Although research on Chinese North Americans' leisure participation dates back more than a century (Burgess, 1909), most studies have been conducted in the last few decades. One common finding across several studies involving diverse ages, settings, and methodologies is that Chinese North Americans' leisure participation is largely passive. For example, a qualitative study (Allison & Geiger, 1993) with Chinese American older adults, many of whom had lived in the United States for most of their adult lives, found that these individuals were involved in a wide range of passive leisure activities including mah-jong, watching television, walking, reading, gardening, and sewing. Though it is not too surprising that the leisure activities reported by these older adults would largely be sedentary, the passive pursuit of leisure activities is also evident in studies conducted with adolescent and middle-aged Chinese North Americans. For instance, a quantitative study (Yu & Berryman, 1996) of Chinese high school students living in New York reported that home/indoor activities (e.g., watching Chinese programs on television) were the most popular.

The preference for passive outdoor leisure activities was also found among Chinese Americans living in Chicago (Zhang & Gobster, 1998), with 71.9% of participants preferring picnic/passive activities, and 47.8% reporting that they were interested in having amenities related to passive

use and nature appreciation built in a proposed park. Similarly, in a study (Walker et al., 2001) at a Canadian national park, Chinese individuals reported viewing wildlife as their most important activity (23%, vs. 15% of Euro-North Americans), followed by viewing scenery (17%, vs. 3% of Euro-North Americans), whereas Euro-North Americans reported camping (18%, vs. 10% of Chinese) and walking/day-hiking (21%, vs. 10% of Chinese). In terms of frequency of visitation, Chinese respondents were also significantly more likely to be visiting the park for the second or third time (45%, vs. 20% of Euro-North Americans), whereas Euro-North Americans were more likely to be visiting the park for the fourth time or more (45%, vs. 13% of Chinese). The latter result concurs with that of Deng, Walker, and Swinnerton (2005), who found that Anglo Canadians were more likely than Chinese Canadians to visit national parks, with the former visiting an average of 2.08 times during the previous 12 months versus 1.57 times for the latter.

These findings suggest that Chinese immigrants are likely to do what they are familiar with, or what they did previously, as long as the conditions in their adopted countries permit. This postimmigration continuation in certain leisure activities has been empirically supported. For instance, Zhang and Gobster (1998) found that swimming, a popular outdoor activity in the Chinese province of Guangdong, and tai chi, a traditional Chinese exercise, were often still practiced by Chinese Americans originally from that province. Other empirical studies have shown that Chinese North Americans' leisure participation changes over time as a result of acculturation. For example, Cheng (1948), Emery (1984), and Kwong (1987) all found that the Chinese immigrants to the United States who were more acculturated became more similar to Westerners in their recreation participation (as cited in Yu & Berryman, 1996). Additionally, Yu and Berryman discovered that Chinese immigrant adolescents in New York who had a lower level of acculturation tended to associate less often with non-Chinese people for recreation purposes; those with a higher level of acculturation tended to participate more often in recreation activities with non-Chinese people. Finally, Hung (2003) found that Chinese in

Vancouver who had higher acculturation levels visited wilderness areas more frequently than those with lower acculturation levels, and that they also participated in more physically demanding or "hard adventure" activities.

Leisure Constraints

Several studies indicate that Chinese North Americans' leisure is often constrained. For example, income was identified as the primary factor that limited frequency of visits to national parks for both Chinese Canadians and Anglo Canadians, but particularly for the former (Deng et al., 2005). Also in Deng and associates' study, a number of Chinese respondents indicated that earning more money to survive had prevented them from pursuing leisure activities. One noted, "Canada has a unique natural environment. [However], work and family prevent me from enjoying it." This result is generally consistent with work by Hall and Rhyne (1989), who found that Chinese living in Ontario were more likely than Anglo Canadians and members of other ethnic groups to mention having no time because of family to pursue either their favorite (25% of Chinese respondents mentioned this constraint vs. 13% of all others) or second favorite (30% vs. 13%, respectively) leisure activities. Yu and Berryman (1996) also reported that lack of money was an important leisure constraint for Chinese adolescents living in New York, but so too were poor English proficiency and lack of opportunity, partners, and knowledge about sites and information about activities. Similar findings were reported in two other studies of Chinese college students living in the United States (Li & Chick, 2007; Li & Stodolska, 2006).

Discrimination has also been reported to constrain Chinese North Americans' leisure participation. Zhang and Gobster (1998), in a study of Chinese living in Chicago, found that 7.9% of their respondents reported that discrimination was a "big problem" while another 24.1% said that it was "somewhat of a problem." In addition, this study showed that while Chinese Americans felt quite comfortable within the homogenous Chinatown core area, they felt uneasy visiting parks outside this area because of "tensions" with Anglo and African American group members. More recently, Jeremy Lin, the son of Taiwanese

immigrants to the United States, was profiled in a *Time* magazine article titled "Harvard's Hoops Star Is Asian. Why's That a Problem?" The author, Gregory (2009), wrote,

> Some people still can't look past his ethnicity. Everywhere he plays, Lin is the target of cruel taunts. 'It's everything you can imagine,' he says. 'Racial slurs, racial jokes, all having to do with being Asian.' Even at the Ivy League gyms? 'I've heard it at most of the Ivies if not all of them,' he says. Lin is reluctant to mention the specific nature of such insults, but according to Harvard teammate Oliver McNally, another Ivy League player called him a *C* word that rhymes with *ink* during a game last season. . . .

Finally, Walker, Halpenny, and Deng (2011) found that Chinese Canadians who reported being more satisfied with their leisure-time physical activity experienced *greater* stress as a function of perceived discrimination. They speculated that this could be because interethnic tension often arose when there was competition for scarce resources, such as goals on a sports field or equipment at a fitness center.

Culture, too, may act as a leisure constraint for Chinese North Americans. For example, in Zhang and Gobster's (1998) study, older Chinese people remarked that sunbathing was an activity that Chinese (and Asians more generally) did not participate in for cultural reasons. Physical activity may also be constrained because of culture. Qin, Way, and Rana (2008), for instance, stated, "In the Chinese culture, physical strength is often contrasted negatively with mental or intellectual capacities. The Chinese idiom 'strong limbs, simple mind' clearly shows a bias against physical size and strength" (p. 36).

It is important to add that acculturation has also been found to affect leisure constraints. For instance, Tsai (2000) found that less acculturated Chinese immigrants in Australia were more susceptible to leisure constraints than their more acculturated counterparts. Similarly, Yu and Berryman (1996) reported that acculturation had a significant negative correlation with the total number of constraints reported by Chinese adolescent immigrants in New York and, perhaps as a consequence, acculturation also had a significant positive correlation with these teenagers' total level of recreation participation.

Similarities in Chinese Americans' and Euro-Americans' leisure participation could result not only from acculturation but also from constraints. For example, native Chinese prefer to pursue leisure activities alone and are less likely to be with family members at leisure (Wang & Stringer, 2000). Traditionally, Chinese do not view leisure as an effective way for family members to be spiritually, emotionally, and mentally united as is often the case for Westerners (Wang & Stringer). This customary leisure pattern may change postimmigration because the absence of an established social network may mean that Chinese North Americans have to participate in social leisure activities with family members. This may explain, for example, why Hall and Rhyne (1989) found that Chinese living in Canada were significantly more likely to play or spend time with their children compared with Canadians,

© Ou Fei | Dreamstime.com

Due to an absence of a social network postimmigration, Chinese North Americans tend to participate in social leisure activities with family members as compared to native Chinese who prefer to recreate alone.

and Yu and Berryman (1996) reported that Chinese adolescents living in New York often recreated with family members.

In conclusion, research indicates that Chinese North Americans tend to participate in passive and appreciative leisure activities and to use leisure for relaxing, self-development, and other utilitarian purposes. In addition, they often participate in leisure activities that they are familiar with or did frequently before they immigrated. Having said this, acculturation does appear to have an effect on their leisure participation over time, in that the more acculturated a Chinese person becomes, the more likely it is that he will participate in leisure activities that are popular among the majority group culture.

Korean North Americans' Leisure

This section begins by characterizing the meaning of leisure for Korean North Americans, then examines their constraints to and actual participation in leisure.

Meaning of Leisure

Whereas an earlier section presented an in-depth discussion of the etymology of the Chinese word for leisure, the authors uncovered little about the origin of the Korean word for leisure. However, in contrast with the lack of empirical research on the meaning of leisure for Chinese and Chinese North Americans, at least three studies have empirically examined its meaning for Koreans and Korean North Americans. Kang and Davenport (2009), for instance, began their literature review by noting that a Korean online dictionary defined leisure in two ways: first, in terms of time away from work, and second, in terms of "utilizing leisure in the right way" (p. 184). Based on in-depth interviews conducted with Koreans and Americans, they documented three key aspects:

1. Koreans generally identified more passive, socially approved activities whereas Americans identified more active, individually directed activities.

2. Koreans preferred doing leisure activities in groups, whereas social interaction was generally unnecessary or even irrelevant for Americans.

3. Koreans were more extrinsically, whereas Americans were more intrinsically, motivated.

The last aspect could include self-development, a proposition consistent with one of the personal perspectives that Kim, Kleiber, and Kropf (2001) found when they asked older Korean Americans about the meanings they associated with leisure *(Yeo-Ga)*. Leisure as self-development, participants reported, was performed to abet intellectual, physical, psychological, and spiritual growth as well as familiarization with the host culture. In this respect, leisure seems to reflect the Confucian principle of developing one's mind and moral character (Kang & Davenport, 2009). The other personal perspective, *Ki-Bun-Chun-Whan,* was more experiential, however, and involved feelings of refreshment and transcendence. This "shift in emotional atmosphere" (Kang & Davenport, p. 114) occurred during a variety of leisure activities, including those that were social, casual (Stebbins, 1992), and absorbing (i.e., enabling flow; Csikszentmihalyi, 1975). Interestingly, the results of Lee, Oh, and Shim's (2000) study at a U.S. university indicated that affect was actually a less important aspect of leisure for Korean than for American students, though it is unclear whether this difference was a function of the role of emotion generally or the level of emotional intensity (i.e., high-arousal positive emotion such as enthusiasm vs. low-arousal positive emotion such as relaxation; Tsai, Knutson, & Fung, 2006) specifically. Conversely, perceived freedom was rated much higher by Korean than American students, which could mean that the former had come to view leisure less in terms of socially approved and self-development activities and more in terms of a way to escape these demands and obligations (cf. Spiers & Walker, 2009; Tafarodi, Lo, Yamaguchi, Lee, & Katsura, 2004).

Leisure Constraints

Monika Stodolska

According to Stodolska (2010),[1] eight major types of constraints affect Korean North Americans' leisure, specifically

1. those related to economic hardships and the necessity to reestablish themselves after immigration,
2. lack of time,
3. high cost of leisure,
4. cultural differences,
5. lack of English-language fluency,
6. changes in family dynamics and family separation,
7. intergenerational conflict, and
8. discrimination.

Because many of these constraints have already been discussed in relation to Chinese North Americans (e.g., lack of time, money, English-language skills), this section focuses on three of the other barriers Stodolska identified. First, while Confucian thought privileges work over leisure (and thus the introductory story is somewhat misleading), Stodolska (2010), citing Lee (2005), contended that the perspective of "neo-Confucianism" is even stronger in Korea than in other East Asian countries. Consequently, it would follow that Korean North Americans might be even more likely to emphasize intellectual pursuits and education; have a cultural preference for passivity rather than activity; and focus on collectivity rather than individuality at the expense of, or in regard to, leisure. Second, citing some of her own earlier work (Stodolska, 2008), Stodolska noted that Korean men often send their families overseas in search of quality education for their children while they stay behind and provide for the family from abroad. Adolescents who eventually reunited with their families were often faced with severe adjustment problems, including those related to their leisure. Stodolska (2008) found that over time, these same teens began enjoying a more North American form of family relationship, one that contrasted sharply with the traditional Korean form in which child raising was almost the sole responsibility of the mother. Third, and related to this last finding, intergenerational conflict seemed to be more pronounced among Korean North American teenagers than among many other immigrant adolescents. This was

---

[1] Readers interested in learning more about Korean Americans' leisure should refer to Monika Stodolska's chapter in *Korean Leisure: From Tradition to Modernity* (Dong & Yi-Kook, 2010).

especially true in terms of parents' preferring (or even pressuring) their children to spend time with other Korean children and to eventually marry other Koreans. These social restrictions could have an effect on younger Korean North Americans' leisure, especially with respect to learning about and participating in the majority group culture's activities.

Leisure Participation

Monika Stodolska

Stodolska (2010), citing Stodolska and Alexandris (2004), found that while many middle-class Korean Americans reported that they had increased their participation in active recreation postarrival, the leisure of working-class members of this group remained relatively passive, home oriented, and highly ethnically enclosed. Kim (2012) also reported on the existence of distinct interethnic boundaries, but added that some of the Korean women in his study reported that leisure participation had led to cross-ethnic group friendships, increased cultural understanding, and reduced life challenges resulting from the acculturation process. This contrasted somewhat with the situation for Korean American teenagers. According to Stodolska and Yi's (2003) research, it appeared that some young people tended to have more leisure time in the United States than in Korea, in part because they were not allowed to work and were not required to attend private tutoring schools. Moreover, the less competitive nature of the American education system positively affected their leisure experience, allowing them greater opportunity to just "hang out" after school or to play computer games. The situation appeared somewhat different again, however, for Koreans studying at a U.S. university. In this case, Heo and Lee (2007) found that adjustment was fostered not only by playing basketball but by playing basketball *seriously;* that is, athletic endeavors were consistent with many of the other qualities (e.g., perseverance, durable benefits) that are characteristic of serious leisure (Stebbins, 1992). Examined holistically, these results suggest that, as with Chinese North Americans, there is both continuation and change in Korean Americans' leisure and this is often a function of other factors such as age, social class, and acculturation level.

Other Asian North Americans' Leisure

Stack and Iwasaki (2009) pointed to "a gap in understanding the adaptation processes of minor, less established, immigrants, including the potential contribution of leisure pursuits to these processes" (p. 239). This lacuna is clearly evident with non-Chinese and non-Korean Asian North Americans; only limited research has been conducted, for example, with Hmong, Japanese, Filipinos, and South Asians living in Canada and the United States.

Much of the leisure research involving "Other" Asian North Americans has focused on outdoor recreation and park visitation. In the case of the Hmong, who mainly arrived in the United States from Laos after the Vietnam War, Bengston and Schermann (2008) provided an overview of the extant research and some of the opportunities and challenges faced by natural resource managers. Sasidharan, Willits, and Godbey (2005) investigated differences in the outdoor recreation characteristics of six subgroups using a mail survey. Most importantly for the discussion here, the researchers found that Japanese were less likely than White, Hispanic, and Korean people to participate in physical activities, and less likely than Korean, Hispanic, and African Americans to participate in food-related activities (e.g., picnicking), during their park visits.

Two other multigroup studies, both of which involved Filipino North Americans, suggest that this seldom-examined group may differ at least somewhat from other Asian North Americans. First, although Fuligni and Masten (2010) found no difference in the amount of leisure time Filipino Americans spent with their families compared with Latino, East Asian, and European Americans, they did discover that time duration had a greater effect on daily happiness for Filipinos compared with European Americans. Second, Afable-Munsuz, Ponce, Rodriguez, and Perez-Stable (2010) found that, overall, Filipino Americans engaged in more leisure-time physical activity (LTPA) than Chinese Americans (33.8% vs. 22.6%, respectively); further, while LTPA grew between the first and third generations for both groups, this increase was much greater for Filipinos (from 32.5% to 48.4%) than for Chinese (from 20.4% to 32.2%). Taken together, these findings suggest that Filipino North Americans may associate family togetherness and physical activity more with their leisure than do other East Asian North Americans.

At least three studies have examined South Asian Canadian women's and adolescents' leisure. According to Tirone and Shaw (1997), women who had immigrated from India reported that "since families, children, and husbands were their source or desired source of fulfillment, enjoyment, satisfaction and relaxation they had little need for time for themselves" (p. 242). As a consequence, the researchers concluded, "private time" was not seen as something positive or desirable by their respondents as it typically is for members of the majority group culture. Tirone (2000) also discovered that South Asian teenagers reported experiencing numerous discriminatory acts during community recreation programs and competitive sport activities and at YMCAs and summer camps. Four of these individuals participated in a follow-up study conducted approximately 10 years later (Tirone & Goodberry, 2011). According to the researchers, leisure played an important part in their participants' identity development as it helped them bridge Canadian and South Asian cultures (see chapters 8 and 11 for more in-depth discussion of the series of studies by Tirone et al.). This outcome is reflected in how South Asians have adopted what is sometimes called *Canada's Game*. Specifically, a survey showed that while roughly half of all Canadians reported they were hockey fans, 61% of South Asian Canadians considered themselves hockey fans (Friesen & Perreaux, 2010). Moreover, a few years ago, the television show *Hockey Night in Canada* began broadcasting not only in English and French but also in Punjabi (Cities of Migration, n.d.). During an interview on the show's success, the two Punjabi hockey announcers reported that the show was popular with fans because "We're connecting generations here" (i.e., grandmothers, parents, and grandchildren all watching together). Also, a recent immigrant from India commented, "Watching and understanding the Saturday night hockey game gives me something in common to talk to my colleagues about on Monday morn-

ings—it makes me feel more at home and a part of the group" (Cities of Migration).

INTRAGROUP COMPARISONS OF ASIAN NORTH AMERICANS' LEISURE

To date, only a few studies have examined both similarities and dissimilarities in the leisure patterns of various Asian North American groups. One of the most interesting of these is a recent survey (Pew Research Center, 2012) of how important having free time was for Chinese, Filipino, Indian, Japanese, Korean, and Vietnamese Americans. Of these six groups, Korean and Vietnamese Americans placed the highest value on having free time (30% and 29%, respectively), followed by Indian, Filipino, and Japanese Americans (19%, 19%, and 18%, respectively) and then by Chinese Americans (15%). (For comparative purposes, while 20% of Asian Americans overall reported that having lots of free time was one of the most important things in their life, only 10% of all Americans did so.) Based in part on this limited research, the next section, in addition to presenting a number of recommendations, points to the importance of recognizing that both similarities and differences exist among Asian North American groups.

RESEARCH AND PRACTICE RECOMMENDATIONS

Given the paucity of past research on Asian North Americans' leisure, the authors are initially inclined to simply recommend "more of everything with everyone." The problem with such an investigative strategy is that personal interest, convenience sampling, or both often trump sociodemographic trends, theoretical application, and practitioners' needs. Thus, because Chinese, South Asians, and Filipinos are and will remain the largest percentage of Asian North Americans, researchers should (at least for now) focus their attention on these three groups. This would seem especially important with regard to South Asians and Filipinos, as at the time of this writing, only one leisure studies researcher (Tirone) had examined the former while none had examined the latter. This having been said, researchers should be cautioned not to "homogenize" these three groups as they may exhibit important differences as a function of religion, social class, and so on. Because past race, ethnicity, and leisure research has largely focused on description at the expense of explanation (Stodolska & Walker, 2007), researchers who intend to study Asian North Americans in the future should not repeat this failing. Rather, given the strength of existing theoretical frameworks (e.g., leisure constraints theory, Crawford, Jackson, & Godbey, 1991; self-determination theory, Deci & Ryan, 2000; theory of planned behavior, Ajzen, 1991), as well as the potential contribution grounded theory could make, taking a more systematic—but still culturally informed and appropriate—approach is strongly suggested (see chapter 1 on theoretical frameworks). Finally, while the authors agree with Lewin's (1951) statement that "there is nothing more practical than a good theory" (p. 169), they also recognize that many scholars (including themselves) often find it difficult to translate abstract results into concrete policies, programs, and services. They recommend, therefore, that future investigators include either a practice-proficient researcher or a research-conversant practitioner (along with a well-informed member of the group being studied; see chapter 2 on methods) as part of their team.

Related to this last point, some recommendations regarding how recreation practitioners could better facilitate Asian North Americans' leisure seem appropriate. First, practitioners should become more knowledgeable about the various Asian North American groups in their community and be careful not to lump them all together. As noted earlier, for example, South Asian is a very broad category that can (and should) be further subdivided based on country of origin, religion, language, and so on. Second, it is incumbent on practitioners to become more cognizant of the constraints these individuals face, both those that are relatively universal but likely more intense (e.g., lack of money) and those that are likely more group specific (e.g., lack of English proficiency), and then to develop strategies to help overcome both types of barriers. Third, practitioners should increase Asian North Americans' awareness of the programs and services they provide (e.g., through intermediaries such as Korean churches or Chinese community centers), and then follow up by providing brochures, website information, and so on in multiple languages. Fourth, practitioners should evaluate whether there is a need for new culture-specific leisure programs (e.g., for Chinese people, opportunities to participate in tai chi, mah-jong). Fifth, a culturally appropriate leisure education program that describes the positive outcomes of engaging in leisure, ways to negotiate leisure constraints, and the need for physically active as well as relaxing activities, might prove beneficial. Lastly, practitioners must be aware of the importance of having culturally competent frontline staff. This may be especially true for law enforcement employees, as many Asian North American immigrants come from authoritarian countries and consequently may be more likely to feel threatened compared to a majority group member when approached by a person in uniform.

CONCLUSION

When the limited research on Asian North Americans' leisure is examined generally, it appears that leisure has generally been viewed less positively by Asian North Americans, especially those who have more recently immigrated to the United States and Canada. This perception of leisure, in conjunction with the high level of constraints these individuals often face (e.g., lack of time because of the need to work multiple jobs, English-language difficulties, perceived discrimination), may limit their actual leisure participation. Having stated this, it is important to add that when Asian North Americans do engage in leisure, certain attributes—such as need satisfaction and intrinsic motivation—are often reported at levels comparable to those in the majority group culture. Generalities such as these, however, are tenuous at best given the paucity of research on Asian North Americans' leisure to date; thus it seems only fitting to conclude with a Chinese adage: *lu chang er dao yuan* ("there is a long way to go"; Gao, Ting-Toomey, & Gudykunst, 1996).

CHAPTER **7**

Leisure Among Alaskan Natives, American Indians, First Nations, Inuit, Métis, Native Hawaiians, and Other Pacific Islanders

Karen Fox, Leo McAvoy, Xiye Wang, and Daniel A. Henhawk

OVERVIEW

The Indigenous peoples of North America and associated lands are not one group, but many groups with widely differing histories and worldviews. The purpose of the chapter is fourfold. One aim is to briefly explain the term Indigenous peoples of North America (i.e., who is included and why; common terminology used) and the current and projected size of this group in the United States and Canada. The authors also provide a comprehensive review of the history and current status of leisure research involving Indigenous peoples of North America, speculate on the future of leisure research involving Indigenous peoples, and identify leisure research areas in particular need of further study. A final purpose is to present practical recommendations on how to provide leisure services to Indigenous peoples of North America.

Learning Outcomes

After reading this chapter, readers will be able to

- explain the presence of and terms used to describe Indigenous peoples of North America and associated lands;
- summarize the history, politics, economics, postcolonial forces, and outcomes of the interactions between Euro-North Americans and Indigenous peoples as they influence and shape current behavior and attitudes surrounding current Indigenous peoples and leisure in North America and associated territories;
- identify challenges and conflicts facing Indigenous peoples and leisure practitioners and professionals in the delivery of and participation in leisure; and
- describe and summarize the rationale for a holistic approach and collaborative approaches to future research and services focused on leisure and Indigenous peoples.

Aboriginal peoples throughout the world have survived five centuries of the horrors and harsh lessons of colonization. [However,] they are emerging with new consciousness and vision.

Battiste (1998, p. 16)

European concepts of leisure and recreation may seem self-evident within Indigenous cultures and practices. For example, events such as the North American Indigenous Games, the Northern Games, and the Makahiki Games, on the surface, seem similar to the Olympics or Pan American Games. Aboriginal people are reviving traditional arts, dances, and crafts, as well as participating in mainstream sports such as hockey and Indigenous hip-hop. The superficial similarity of activities belies differences in worldviews, underlying philosophies and values, ways of knowing and being, and the contexts for physical practices. According to Indigenous scholars (Grande, 2004; Henhawk, 2009, 2010), the relationship between Eurocentric leisure and Indigenous peoples must be conceptualized within the framework of historical and political interactions, especially conquest, exploitation, and colonialism, and inclusive of Indigenous knowledge, self-government, and self-determination. Within this larger panorama, any discussion is haunted by the fluidity of the concepts, the difficulty in formulating precise definitions of leisure or recreation, the political investment of non-Indigenous peoples in positioning Indigenous identity, and questions about what counts as knowledge and who controls resources.

The dominant leisure framework, scholarship, and practice within Canada and the United States are Eurocentric and Euro-North American. The concept of dominant culture is influenced by Williams' (1980) contention that "in any society, in any period, there is a central system of practices, meanings and values, which we can properly call dominant and effective" (p. 38). In this chapter, "Eurocentric" refers to scholarship grounded in the Enlightenment perspectives of ancient history and European authors and theories, and "Euro-North American" indicates scholarship conceptualized from Eurocentric perspectives with North American historical and political values and discourses.

The processes of identifying indigeneity maintain the Eurocentric framework of separating people by identity and from nature. From Indigenous points of view, the process of European expansion and colonization constructed them as different and apart from Europeans and the "lifeworld." Grande (2004) argued that Indigenous struggles have been misrepresented or misframed as struggles for identity rather than as resistance to colonization and as a search for links to Indigenous history and culture that have been obscured or ignored by non-Indigenous peoples.

Therefore, all attempts to separate and identify Indigenous peoples within non-Indigenous systems embody an inherent conundrum and rest on political, economic, social, or legal agendas. Pan-Indigenous movements resulted from residential school experiences in which non-Indigenous people forcibly schooled Aboriginal children from different tribes together without regard for tribal or language differences. The legal frameworks and definitions of identity (e.g., based on blood quanta) of national non-Indigenous governments emerged through processes of dislocating, controlling, and exploiting Indigenous peoples and lands. The collaborative process within the United Nations used four factors to position Indigenous peoples within a Eurocentric international political arena: (a) priority in time with respect to occupation and use of a territory; (b) struggles to perpetuate cultural distinctiveness, self-identify or recognition by others as a distinct collectivity; (c) experiences of subjugation, marginalization, or dispossession; and (d) self-identification. This legal framework leaves invisible those urban Indigenous people who may or may not connect with a specific territory or various issues around "traditional peoples" living in the midst of contemporary societies.

The preferences for and attached meanings of any of the universal categories (i.e., Indigenous, Aboriginal, Native, or Indian) vary with regions and groups. A recent move by Indigenous scholars and peoples is to self-identify using original languages, tribal, band, and clan names (e.g., Cree, Navajo, Ojibwe, Nuu-chah-nulth) or kinship relationships, rather than First Nation or American Indian. With thousands of affiliations in North America and its associated territories, this practice makes it difficult to address common problems or pan-Indigenous commonalities and movements. Therefore, this chapter uses "Indigenous peoples" as "shorthand" that encompasses all of the groups in continental North America and associated territories. Consistent with the terminology used by the Royal Commission on Aboriginal Peoples (1996) in Canada, "Aboriginal peoples" refers generally to the Indigenous inhabitants of Canada, including First Nations, Métis, and Inuit peoples. The commission noted that the term Aboriginal peoples "refers to organic political and cultural entities that stem historically from the original peoples of North America, rather than collection of individuals united by so-called 'racial' characteristics" (p. xii). "First Nations" replaces "Indian," and "Inuit" replaces "Eskimo," although the older terminology continues to be used in federal legislation and policy and in government reports and statistical data sets. Indigenous peoples in the continental United States use various terms, including Native Americans, Indians, and American Indians, in addition to specific tribal affiliations. Based on current literature, American Indian is a more appropriate term and is used in U.S. Census material. Indigenous peoples in Alaska are categorized as Alaska Natives or Native Alaskans inclusive of various tribes, including Aleuts. Native Hawaiian and other Pacific Islanders are officially defined in the U.S. Census as persons "having origins in any of the original peoples of Hawaii, Guam, Samoa, or other Pacific Islands. This includes people who indicate their race as 'Native Hawaiian,' 'Guamanian or Chamorro,' 'Samoan,' and 'Other Pacific Islander'" (www.census.gov/population/race/about).

For all of the Indigenous groups associated with North America, there are strong legal battles around status, land treaties, sovereignty, self-governance, and self-determination, as well as relationships with dominant non-Indigenous power structures (Friesen & Friesen, 2008; Grossman, 2005; Kauanui, 2008; Warry, 2007). Many Native Hawaiians support a sovereignty movement arguing that Hawaii has never been a lawful part of the United States given the illegal overthrow of the Hawaiian Kingdom (Coffman, 2009; Kidani, 2006; Sai, 2011).[1] Native Alaskans have come together to protect their land claims and ability to provide social services to their own people. The government of Canada has a number of outstanding treaties and land claims with ongoing differences around governance, the role of Indian Affairs, and financial accountability for First Nations peoples. American Indian tribes (562 recognized tribes) are involved with federal and state governments in various controversial and legal issues including sovereignty, treaty rights, land claims, Indian gaming, and compensation for the government's past discrimination against American Indians. In addition, various agencies have emerged in Canadian urban settings to provide recreation and community development (e.g., Métis Friendship Centres or Canadian Native Friendship Centres), Aboriginal child and family social services, and coalitions within municipalities (e.g., Western Municipalities Aboriginal Gathering, Wichitowin). Pan-Indian and international Indigenous movements and organizations (e.g., All Indian Pueblo Council, American Indian Movement, Indigenous Media Dialogue Conference, or World Indigenous Peoples Conference on Education) provide political leverage and models for services, legal agreements and challenges, and political organization (Wutzke, 1997/1998).

Given Indigenous peoples' suspicions of the Eurocentric quest for universal definitions and a desire not to be assimilated into Eurocentric categories, the concept of Eurocentric leisure itself is problematic. Although Eurocentric leisure is obviously relevant within a modern globalized world, the use of this category for understanding the worldviews of Indigenous peoples risks appropriating and deforming Indigenous knowledge

---

[1]Where feasible, this chapter identifies Indigenous authors. In many cases, though, this was not feasible. The following are Indigenous authors: Native Hawaiian—Kidani and Sai; Aboriginal—McDonald and Lavallée (Algonquin, Cree, and French ancestry).

and practices. Very few Indigenous languages have words for leisure or recreation. Hawaiian is an Indigenous language with words that suggest very different concepts of leisure (Bates et al., 2001; Fox, 2001). Other Indigenous languages and worldviews do not separate work and leisure or posit work as the antithesis of leisure. Given that much of the conceptualization and scholarship related to the extant leisure literature have evolved without Indigenous voices, and without substantial critiques of Euro-North American theories and practices, the extant leisure literature must be used with critical reflection, decolonizing processes, and caution (Fox, 2006b; Henhawk, 2010). For the discipline of leisure studies or sciences to address issues related to Indigenous peoples, a conceptualization of leisure (Fox & Klaiber, 2006) that is useful and appropriate across historical eras and worldviews and inclusive of multiple research, languages, and knowledge paradigms will be necessary. The use of "leisures" implies multiple frameworks, concepts, and values that frame any set of activities, states of mind, time, relationships, and contexts as leisure. This allows for comparison and critique of the dominant Eurocentric leisure concept grounded in the Enlightenment understanding of Greek philosophy and language.

ABORIGINAL PEOPLE, AMERICAN INDIANS, NATIVE ALASKANS, NATIVE HAWAIIANS, AND OTHER PACIFIC ISLANDERS IN EXTANT LEISURE LITERATURE

Little attempt has been made to understand leisure practices from an Indigenous perspective, especially in leisure literature. The earliest scholarship on "elements" (i.e., games, physical activity, or sport) connected to Eurocentric categories of leisure and recreation was Culin's (1898, 1899, 1903, 1907) categorization of American Indian games as involving chance, skill, or dexterity. Cushing (1896) connected some games with actual ceremonies, and Mooney (1896, 1898a, 1898b) contributed to a refinement of classifications of games. Focusing on rules, structures, and equipment, they suggested but never fully addressed the

mythological, ceremonial, and political contexts inherent in the diversity of tribal games.

More recent work, such as Salter's (1972) doctoral research, provided a rich context for the macro-Siouxan and macro-Alqonquian Aboriginal games and connected them to ceremonies associated with death, sickness, weather, and fertility. Other aspects of the games—such as redistribution of goods and food, alternatives to raiding and warfare, and social, ceremonial, and spiritual interconnections—continued to be unexplored (Cajete, 2005; Gabriel, 1996; Nabokov, 1981). Fox (2001) and Bates and colleagues (2002) suggested that Indigenous leisure is grounded in very different epistemologies, ontologies, and practices as they explored the Hawaiian concept *manawa nanea,* one of the few Indigenous terms connected with the Eurocentric and Euro-North American leisure framework. Detailed investigations of "leisure" relevant to Indigenous perspectives or from a decolonizing point of view are mostly absent (Henhawk, 2009; McDonald & McAvoy, 1997a).

Substantial attention and scholarship have been devoted to comparisons between Indigenous "games" and Eurocentric sport constructions (Forsyth, 2007; Paraschak, 2007). Sport has been a site of regulation and colonization of Indigenous peoples as well as an avenue for resistance and expressive activities. Researchers (Cohen, 2002; Giles, 2004, 2008; Giles & Forsyth, 2007; Rose & Giles, 2007) challenged a straightforward understanding of Indigenous "games" and "sport." To fully explore the paradoxical existence of colonialism and resistance within sport, it is necessary to address aspects such as traditional Indigenous gender roles, modern ideals of beauty and racism, contrasting Indigenous and non-Indigenous concepts of competition and cooperative strategies, present-day Indigenous women's desire to participate in sport and physical activity, postcolonial perspectives, and concepts of equity.

There have been four "state of knowledge" reviews of leisure literature on North American Indigenous peoples. These include work by Fox (2006a, 2006b, 2007) and McDonald and McAvoy (1997a). Multiple publications on Eurocentric leisure, Aboriginal peoples, American Indians, Native Alaskans, and Native Hawaiians have been connected with specific scholars (Henhawk,

2009; McDonald & McAvoy, 1997b; Lashua & Fox, 2006, 2007) or special issues of journals (*Journal of Applied Recreation Research* [1998], *Journal of Leisurability* [1998], and *Leisure/Loisir* [2007—subsumed under ethnicity]). The work by McAvoy (2002) focused primarily on the intersection of American Indian and Aboriginal peoples on park lands; Lashua and Fox worked with urban Aboriginal young people in connection with their participation in Aboriginal hip-hop; and Fox focused on meta-analysis of extant literature about Indigenous peoples and leisure and missionary interpretations of Hawaiian "leisure." Distressingly, most of this work is by non-Indigenous authors grounded in Eurocentric frameworks and methodologies. A new leisure scholar from Six Nations at Grand River, Henhawk (2009), grounds his critique of non-Indigenous leisure in lived experience, Indigenous epistemologies and ontologies, critical and postcolonial Indigenous methodologies, and critical race theories.

INDIGENOUS PEOPLES AND WILDERNESS, NATURAL LANDSCAPES, AND PARKS

Wilderness, natural landscapes, and parks are important economic engines for both Canada and the United States, and millions of recreation users and tourists visit these areas once inhabited by Indigenous peoples. The history of interaction between Europeans and Indigenous peoples in the Americas has been called a "legacy of conquest" by the noted historian Limerick (1987) and others (Mann, 2006; Wilkinson, 1997). Public parks and forests were established in both countries through dubious European and Euro-North American land practices that restricted Indigenous peoples' access to lands where they had lived for centuries, raised their families, hunted, fished, conducted spiritual ceremonies, and buried their ancestors. In Canada, Aboriginal people were typically removed from most of their lands and placed on small reserves or forced to move into urban areas. The appropriated Aboriginal lands became Crown lands for use as national and provincial parks, timber licenses, mineral extraction, and other Euro-North American–owned economic and residential developments. In the United States,

where treaties were signed in the 1800s, American Indian tribes "agreed" to give up vast tracts of land and to move to designated reservations. After the treaties were completed, American Indian tribes owned about 136 million acres on these reservations. With the Dawes Act of 1887, enacted without the consent of or consultation with American Indians, land owned by American Indians was reduced by 66%, to a mere 46 million acres (Keller & Turek, 1998); some American Indian tribes lost over 95% of their reservation lands. The effects of the Dawes Act fractured the American Indian land base and made agriculture almost impossible. National parks such as Glacier National Park and Grand Canyon National Park were established through questionable land deals with the Black Feet and Havasupai tribes, respectively. Hawaii Volcanoes National Park (including the summit of Maunaloa and the most active volcano on earth, Kilauea) encompasses sacred land illegally appropriated from the Hawaiian Kingdom.

The history of Indigenous peoples' relationships (or kinship) with their traditional lands, as well as Euro-North American political practices that stripped Indigenous peoples of access to those same lands, influences how Indigenous peoples view outdoor recreation, resource management, and their claims to land use and management. Indigenous peoples confined to small reservations and reserves and fighting for treaty rights or self-governance are demanding access to their traditional lands for ceremonial, subsistence, and spiritual practices and a voice in the management of such areas.

A climate of tension exists between many Indigenous peoples, on the one hand, and government agencies and adventure recreation or tourism entities, on the other, regarding the management of once traditional homelands as major outdoor recreation and tourism destinations. These "contested terrains" (Said, 1979, 1994) are where a dominant society's view of place competes with a minority's experience of place, where different realities inhabit overlapping territories and intertwined histories. British anthropologist Ingold's (2000) concept of "building" and "dwelling" practices helps frame these differences.

The "building perspective" frames the earth as an opaque solid globe where humans, other species, and objects occupy the outside surface. This view assumes the existence of one environment identified with the order of nature and profoundly alien, if not, hostile to humans. The building perspective designates specific parts of nature for things such as national or federal parks, wilderness, protected areas, or natural landscapes. Ingold (2005, p. 504) argued that consistent with the building perspective, "regions of so-called untouched wilderness are deliberately set up to be untouched, and their subsequent monitoring is more akin to conducting a scientific experiment than abandoning the world to look after itself." All of these constructed spaces with Euro-North American–delimited place meanings imply a nature–human split in which humans live apart from and "superior" to nature. Euro-American wilderness zones are areas that visitors enter to escape modern life (e.g., use of motors, noise, crowds), that they stay in only briefly, and that are "wild" and different from everyday life.

The "dwelling perspective" positions humans within inextricable lived relationships inclusive of ecosystems and built surroundings, and highlights the interconnections and disconnections among all environments including rural, urban, and "wild" lands as humans travel *through* the world. Dwelling assumes that humans always already interact with and inhabit (rather than simply occupy) a changing environment that *surrounds* them. Instead of one environment, Ingold (2000) suggested "zones of entanglement" with intermingling flows of air, water, and soil in which plants and rocks, as well as humans and nonhuman animals, grow and intertwine along trails. Landscapes are not tabula rasa but are continually changing as they embody human and environmental processes and interactions. Dwelling is a lived practice of embedding oneself in the world and having the world embed itself on oneself or one's group.

Indigenous people see wilderness and associated enclosed parks as Euro-North American constructions. These "natural areas" are places where Indigenous communities were intimate with nonhuman entities; where they historically lived, may live now, or are struggling to live; where they carry on their regular activities; and where they are part of the natural environment rather than separated

from it. Furthermore, Indigenous peoples view the idea of restoring land to its state before human contact as naïve. Euro-North American concepts such as restoration or preservation of parks and protected areas typically imply restoring parks to precontact conditions. To most Euro-North Americans, that means a mythical and romantic concept of an 1850 landscape before Euro-North American development and land changes. This erases the lived practices of Indigenous people and their significant impacts on natural resources over thousands of years before the arrival of Euro-North Americans (Cronon, 1996; Denevan, 1992; Mann, 2006).

Indigenous peoples' historical relationship with the earth encompasses a deep respect for the earth and all life and a lengthy cultural relationship with land and waters (Deloria, 1992, 2003; Redmond, 1996). Such life practices resonate with dwelling as natural forces support a deep emotional, symbolic, and spiritual attachment with former traditional lands now within or near national, provincial, or state parks, forests, and wildlife refuges (Davis, 2009; Stoffle, Halmo, & Austin, 1998). For the Nuu-chah-nulth communities of Clayoquot Sound in British Columbia, these long-held attachments to land influence the lifestyles, environment, and perceived quality of life of Indigenous people (McAvoy, McDonald, & Carlson, 2003). This depth of meaning and daily lived practice help explain the emotion and enduring connection on the part of Indigenous peoples and why they continue to make at least cultural claims to those places. Indigenous peoples struggle to understand why former homelands are desecrated by management and incorporate practices that affront their traditions, religion, and histories (Dustin, Schneider, McAvoy, & Frakt, 2002; McAvoy, 2002).

On the other hand, park managers, tourism operators, outdoor recreation organizations, and park visitors, with different historical understandings of the conflicts or ignorant of them, struggle to understand the depth of attachment Indigenous peoples have to traditional lands that are now parks or tourism destinations (Dustin et al., 2002; McAvoy, 2002). Non-Indigenous park and tourism managers, caught between two worlds, struggle to accomplish their mandate and maintain what they see as necessary controls connected to management responsibilities.

In both Canada and the United States, Indigenous peoples are demanding a role in managing or comanaging structures for natural resources on traditional lands as part of cultural reclamation and self-determination processes (Burnham, 2000; Keller & Turek, 1998; Torgerson, 1999). These symbolic and spiritual practices include decision-making processes with elders and spiritual leaders; reciprocal relationships with nature; ceremonies and rituals to respect Mother Earth/Father Sky; impact assessments related to the health of tribe, community, and nature; and a concern for the health and well-being of future generations. Comanagement processes struggle to construct an interplay or dialectical relationship between the "dwelling" and "building" perspectives; such dynamics are supported by the scholarship of Ingold (2000) and Mullins (2011).

Managers of public parks and forest areas in both Canada and the United States are starting to work more cooperatively with Indigenous peoples to manage areas of traditional importance. Lemelin and Bennett (2010) provide a comprehensive review of the literature concerning the involvement of Indigenous people in comanagement of protected areas. Indigenous groups are gaining experience and expertise in non-Indigenous resource management as they integrate traditional Indigenous values with politics and economics. As an example, the eight coastal First Nations and the Council of the Haida Nation have created an alliance to work with environmental, commercial, and governmental organizations toward an ecosystem-based management of coastal areas, which include national parks and provincial forests in British Columbia (Davis, 2009). The coastal First Nations include Wuikinoxv Nation, Heiltsuk, Kitasoo/Xaixais, Nuxalk Nation, Gitiga'at, Haisla, Metlakatla, Old Masset, and Skidegate. The Council of the Haida Nation is the Aboriginal Sovereign Authority and Government of the Haida Nation. A number of national parks in the United States are working with local tribal groups to comanage park units to accommodate the traditional uses and provide employment opportunities for local tribal members. A number of wilderness and wilderness-like areas have been designated in both Canada and the United States with the approval, cooperation, and in some cases cooperative management of local Indigenous groups (McDonald, McDonald, & McAvoy, 2000; Rutledge & Vold, 1995). Examples include the Gwaii Haanas South Moresby National Park Reserve and the Marine Conservation Area Reserve, in Canada, and the Mission Mountains Wilderness located on the Flathead Reservation in Montana, homeland of the Confederated Salish and Kootenai Tribes in the United States.

OUTDOOR RECREATION, ENVIRONMENTAL EDUCATION, AND INDIGENOUS PEOPLES

Limited research has been conducted on Indigenous peoples' leisure use of national parks and forests or other outdoor recreation places. Cordell (1999) conducted a major national study in the United States that included American Indians and found that they participate in outdoor recreation activities similarly to other Americans. Conducting survey research like this with Indigenous peoples is somewhat problematic because of the small numbers of American Indians typically included in the surveys; the impersonal mode of the research; and the questions grounded in Euro-North American leisure perspectives, practices, and measurements. Chick (1998), Fox (2001, 2006b), and McDonald and McAvoy (1997a) indicated that the holistic and interconnected understandings of Indigenous people do not cohere with the work–leisure dichotomy in the Euro-North American perspectives. Rather than being fragmented, work, leisure, family, and spiritual categories blend together in a holistic rhythm of life. Activities like hunting, fishing, and trapping and gathering of berries, mushrooms, and wild rice, which may typically be termed outdoor recreation by Euro-North Americans, seem to Indigenous peoples to be associated with subsistence, family, culture, and tradition. In this context "outdoor recreation" is a cultural expression different for Euro-North Americans and Indigenous peoples (McAvoy, Shirilla, & Flood, 2004).

In other cases, American Indians considered outdoor recreation a "White–European concept" irrelevant to their lives; American Indians participate in "gathering" activities (Flood & McAvoy, 2007a, 2007b; McAvoy et al., 2004). All of these activities continue to tie the Indigenous peoples to special places in their traditional homelands, even as these differences illustrate problematic aspects of Euro-North American leisure research as well as management strategies for national forests or parks and protected areas.

Indigenous people often encounter racism on the part of management staff, enforcement officers, and visitors as a constraint to accessing national and state forests or parks or participating in outdoor recreation and subsistence activities (McAvoy et al., 2004; McDonald & McAvoy, 1997b) (see chapter 11 on discrimination in leisure contexts). Both previous experiences of discrimination and the anticipation of such behavior inhibit Indigenous peoples from fully participating in opportunities available in public lands. Those interviewed believed that Euro-North Americans (staff and visitors) in parks and forests showed a general lack of respect for Indigenous people and their lawful uses of these areas, including treaty rights and other agreements around harvesting of certain game and plants.

Conflicts and debates over the proper use of and outdoor behavior in protected areas are conditioned by different historical, political, and economic understandings of these spaces and relationships with nonhuman entities (Dustin et al., 2002; Gladden, 1999; McAvoy, 2002). For example, non-Indigenous people, on the basis of Leave No Trace principles, advocate travel by foot or paddle in Arctic wilderness areas, while Native Alaskans argue that motorized vehicles are essential to maintain hunting and gathering traditions in a modern world (Gladden, 1999). Flood and McAvoy (2007a, 2007b) demonstrated that tribal members of the Confederated Salish and Kootenai tribes of the Flathead Reservation in Montana accessed national forests for hunting, fishing, berry and mushroom gathering, camping, hiking, and collecting medicinal plants, which can conflict with preservation and Leave No Trace practices.

Outdoor recreation and environmental education programming, envisaged by non-Indigenous peoples as grounded in Eurocentric science or military concepts of citizenship, leadership, and fitness (Lowan, 2009), have little resonance with traditional Indigenous perspectives and practices that exist alongside natural processes or view humans as part of nature—even as "younger siblings" to animals or plants (Sanford Kanahele, 1986). Although outdoor recreation and environmental education have included aspects of Indigenous practices (e.g., the solo or "vision quest," "sweat lodges," tracking skills), the underlying assumptions situate humans as separate from nature, appropriate Indigenous traditions, and use the natural world as a vehicle for personal and group development (Sibthorp, 2011). Lowan's (2009) analysis of a Canadian Outward Bound program (*Giwaykiwin*) for Aboriginal youth is one of the few critical analyses that takes Aboriginal scholarship seriously. Although the program was directed toward Aboriginal youth, the youth struggled with Outward Bound's agenda, which had Aboriginal components but did not seriously engage with the fundamental differences between Indigenous and Eurocentric epistemology and ontology—and which included a human–nature separation framework and goals related to middle-class, Euro-North American citizenship.

Since most traditional outdoor recreation and environmental education programs are historically tied to Euro-North American notions of wilderness travel and residential camping, Indigenous practices, Indigenous self-determination efforts, and relationships with nonhuman entities find little substance in these programs. Furthermore, these programs offer non-Indigenous people little education or political awareness about the complicity of outdoor recreation or education and environmental education with hegemonic forces detrimental to Indigenous lives. Although not specific to Indigenous political goals, Mullins' (2009, 2011) use of Ingold's (2000) critique of dominant paradigms of outdoor recreation is a move in this direction.

With over half of the Indigenous populations living in urban areas and seeking ways to "walk within multiple worlds," urban Indigenous people seek information regarding Indigenous claims and histories embedded in both natural and urban landscapes, spaces (e.g., urban parks) to continue traditional practices such as smudge ceremonies or use of sweat lodges, and strategies for creating an urban Indigenous ethic. One of the few to explore these questions is Swayze (2009), who analyzed an urban environmental learning program for Indigenous youth. Swayze suggested that these types of programs need to distinguish between "residing in" and "inhabiting" places, recognize the dependency of urban residents on nature, and speak of Indigenous practices and knowledge in the present tense and as a relevant critique and map for environmental behavior. In addition, outdoor recreation and environmental education programs need to incorporate cultural decolonization and ecological reinhabitation grounded in community-based processes with Indigenous peoples (Briggs & Sharp, 2004). Such a framework moves beyond the short-course format focused on abstract knowledge to processes of how people inhabit and care for urban or nature environments and occupy a "coming to knowing" (Aikenhead, 2011) knowledge that is established through relationships of trust over time.

Photo courtesy of Karen Fox.

Photo courtesy of Karen Fox.

Native Hawaiian *kupuna* (Hawaiian for elder or grandparent) teaching young people to weave and ways to live that sustain the environment and Native Hawaiian culture.

INDIGENOUS PEOPLES AND TOURISM

Tourism[2] within contemporary North America is primarily a Eurocentric behavior, since most Indigenous peoples traveled and lived within a local contiguous ecosystem that informed their language, culture, and lived practices. In the late 19th century, Eurocentric tourism objectified and exoticized Indigenous peoples (Raibmon, 2005), especially through display of Indigenous people to the "tourist gaze," and conspicuously commercialized Indigenous tourism products. In addition, tourism often damaged Indigenous communities through displacement, conflict and violence, and interruptions of social and cultural practices (Colchester, 2004). Currently, tourism related to Indigenous peoples carries both the legacy of these harms and the potential for establishing an Indigenous presence within non-Indigenous economic arenas with, potentially,

some control over their culture, representations, and environmental practices. Non-Aboriginal scholars Butler and Hinch (2007) suggested that tourism can represent hegemonic subjugation and cultural degradation or potential economic independence and cultural rejuvenation, depending on policy initiatives, consultant services, and financial assistance.

Although Indigenous communities have struggled with and managed change in unique ways (Fox, 2006b; Hokowhitu, 2010), the forces of globalization place severe strains on Indigenous peoples with respect to self-governance, cultural retention, and self-determination. Debates rage about whether the development of Indigenous tourism is an essential element of self-determination or a process of assimilation into mainstream culture (Nepal, 2004). When tourism and leisure research are interwoven with concepts of globalization, sustainability, development, self-governance, sustaining ecological systems, and

Photo courtesy of Karen Fox.

Native Hawaiian youth practicing hula for the Hookuikahi i Puʻukohola Heiau (The Culture of Ancient Hawaii) beneath the Puʻukohola Heiau National Historic Site. Only Native Hawaiian and other Indigenous guests are allowed to enter the heiau proper (a Native Hawaiian sacred place or temple).

---

[2]Tourism is typically considered a modern phenomenon. However, Perrottet (2003) and Balsdon (2002) demonstrated that ancient Roman tourists kept travel journals, rated eating establishments and accommodations, created themed trips, and promoted specific tourist practices. In addition, forces of colonialism and oppression are implicated in almost all tourism.

A Word About Aboriginal and American Indian Gambling

As Culin (1898, 1899, 1903, 1907), Gabriel (1996), and others have noted, games of chance are an integral part of many Indigenous groups throughout North America. The recent involvement of Aboriginal and American Indian groups in the Euro-North American gambling industry related to bingos and casinos is a permutation and modern incarnation of Indigenous gambling practices. The debate surrounding the benefits of gambling within and surrounding Indigenous communities mirrors the ambivalent nature of casinos (Mullis & Kamper, 2000) and criteria and moral judgments from Euro-North American perspectives. Legal and political difficulties between American Indian and state and national governments are complicated by power, economic, and racial agendas (Ackerman, 2009). However, there is evidence that gambling contributes to self-determination and improved economic status (Schaap, 2010). Momper (2010) concluded that the social and economic gains are positive for American Indian communities even as there is a major gap in objective research on the prevalence of gambling and gambling treatment needs in American Indian communities.

cultural identity, the research is murky. Often, "[s]ustainability is as much to do with ensuring continued profits through more flexible patterns of capital accumulation, or middle-class lifestyles in the First World and the ability of these social groups to experience (sustained) Indigenous cultures while holidaying in the Third World, as it is to do with ecology and environment" (Mowforth & Munt, 2005, p. 30). Ecotourism raises a critical threat to Indigenous peoples because it endangers culture and biodiversity by condoning Western industrial development (Johnston, Hixon, & Anton, 2009), extending capitalism and exploitation of Indigenous peoples and their land, or judging Indigenous practices against non-Indigenous environmental standards grounded in a human–nature split without regard to cultural differences and political power imbalances. Scholarship on ecotourism as entrepreneurial activity and an extension of capitalism has yet to address issues such as exploitation, cultural erosion, Indigenous rights, land agreements, prior informed consent for access to Indigenous lands, intellectual property (e.g., authentic handicrafts), and failed rural development initiatives, among many others (Fennell, 2008).

Tenuous potentials exist within ecotourism, such as opportunities for Indigenous youth to learn and share traditional ways of life (e.g., hunting, fishing, tracking wildlife, gathering, agricultural processes, and aquaculture) or develop guiding and interpretive skills (Nepal, 2004).

Although there are educational moments, such as sharing Aboriginal cultural heritage through musical experiences within interpretative settings, these moments are highly ambivalent and problematic. Since they are situated within a cultural hegemony governed by middle- and upper-middle-class White Euro-North Americans who do not favor political tourism products (Mason, 2004), the benefits of ecotourism are far from clear for Aboriginal peoples. Notzke's (2004) research in southern Alberta showed that market demands were small, that resources were insufficient, and that sharing of the Aboriginal hosts' culture without compromising integrity was problematic for Aboriginal tourism development.

INDIGENOUS PEOPLES IN URBAN AREAS, LEISURE, AND A GLOCALIZED WORLD

In Canada and the United States, currently over half of Indigenous peoples live in urban areas creating modern, globalized yet localized (i.e., glocalized) Indigenous life practices. They range from strict adherence to traditional practices to accommodation, acculturation, or assimilation with modern society and variations among all these options. Challenging stereotypes of "traditional, authentic Indians connected to the land" and situated within non-Indigenous expectations that Indigenous people address only Indigenous issues and traditions, urban Indigenous people struggle to find a place in non-Indigenous structures or develop alternative political avenues such as Indigenous protocols, talking circles, Indigenous sport associations, expressive arts, and tourism while honoring obligations to connect and protect traditional knowledges and environmental practices (Alvord, 1999; Lashua, 2005). Although there are indications that training and education in recreation and leisure provide benefits for Aboriginal youth in both rural and urban contexts (Nadjiwan & Blackstock, 2003), many of the well-intentioned programs deliver "generic activities based on a standard benefits model for middle-class Euro-Canadian consumers, with no specific adaptation to Aboriginal cultures" (Wall, 2008, p. 78).

Indigenous peoples are actively seeking connections between traditional knowledge and practice and the current technological world, yet little research has been done in this area as it applies

Aboriginal B-Boy performing at the Edmonton "The Works" Festival.

Photo courtesy of Karen Fox.

to leisure (Feeser, 2001). This gap is especially troubling given the number of urban Indigenous people; the need for recreation and leisure among urban Indigenous youth; the emergence of grassroots forms of Indigenous technological leisure; the potential of recreation and leisure to address the major health issues facing urban Indigenous people; and the lack of Indigenous people as participants, professionals, or university students in recreation and leisure.

Lashua (2006a, 2006b, 2010), Lashua and Fox (2006, 2007), Fox and Lashua (2010/2011), and Fox's (2006a, 2006b) research with urban Aboriginal youth and their involvement in Indigenous hip-hop addressed not only the attraction of technology and arts (Smith & Warke, 2000), but also the creativity and resiliency of urban Aboriginal youth as they straddle the worlds of reserve or band and urban communities, connect technology with their traditional practices and values (Smith & Warke, 2000), and express or integrate the reality of their lives and their hopes for the future.

There are numerous arguments for digital media as culturally appropriated, and the web and cyberspace resonate with social patterns of tribalism (Pannekoek, 2006; Sanchez, Stucky, & Richard, 1998; Wall, 2008; Wheeler, 2002). This modern incantation of chanting, storytelling, and dance reflects the resiliency and ability of urban Indigenous youth to create their own leisure practices inclusive of physical, expressive, and healing forms outside of and different from dominant Euro-North American recreation programming. Similar to the way Andrews and Olney (2007) understand the powwow and potlatch in modern life, urban Aboriginal hip-hop artists see modern variations of traditional practices as a link to the past and a resource for managing and negotiating challenges of the present.

Although traditional hunting, gathering, and agricultural and aquacultural practice form a focal point for tourism connected to Indigenous communities on reserves and reservations or near major protected areas, recreation programs in urban areas have been slow to create substantial and ongoing programs that include Indigenous subsistence skills, arts, and dance, not to mention modern forms such as hip-hop. There is even less research on either the need for these programs or successful initiatives in urban areas, rural communities, and reserves. Henhawk's (personal communication, May 19, 2010) current research around a Six Nations of the Grand River community garden and market project (similar to non-Indigenous community garden projects) addresses the role that gardening can play in the decolonization of the Haudenosaunee people. Six Nations of the Grand River is located in southern Ontario, represents 5% of the land granted by the 1784 Haldimand Treaty, and includes six Iroquois nations: Mohawk, Oneida, Onondaga, Cayuga, Seneca, and Tuscarora. Henhawk's research interest is in the narratives that community members have created and in traditional Haudenosaunee agricultural knowledge as practiced by Haudenosaunee people before the arrival of European colonists and contemporary garden practices. He theorizes that such narratives can be used to help the Haudenosaunee people in the Six Nations of the Grand River community reenvision space to be Indigenous. His research resonates with the Native Hawaiian community and tourism initiative, Ka Welina (www.kawelina.net), which integrates sustainable land use, community practices and integrity, and daily practices for living gently on the land with a Native Hawaiian tourist framework. Moving past simple connections to community development, Henhawk articulates processes of decolonization, moving away from consumption of plastic and processed foods if not questioning all consumptive models, and remaking everyday lived experiences of Aboriginal people in today's world.

Traditionally, leisure researchers have not specifically considered Indigenous practices connected to the arts (e.g., poetry, drawing, painting, jewelry, song, chanting, music, and dancing). There are a number of reasons for this absence, including the fact that these Indigenous practices are connected to Euro-North American constructs of work or subsistence, spirituality, and ceremonies, and thus "not leisure," as well as the conceptual heritage of Euro-North American leisure and the fact that recreation focuses predominantly on a specific Euro-North American form, physical activity and mastering the body. Either way, the Euro-North American approach to Indigenous practices of arts is misleading if not oppressive. This absence of Indigenous arts,

dance, and music in both urban spaces and rural or tribal lands in current leisure research is troubling given the healing and empowering forces of these practices (Johnston et al., 2009; Kwaku, 1999; Mitchell, 2000; Wishart Leard & Lashua, 2006). The emerging power of music, dance, chants, and spoken-word poems in traditional and modern versions (e.g., hip-hop and rap) is important for understanding Indigenous urban culture and leisure (Dimitriadis, 2001a, 2001b; Hollands, 2004; Lai, 2005; Lashua, 2005, 2006a, 2006b, 2010; Lashua & Kelly, 2008; Mitchell, 2000). Crossing boundaries, Navajo youth employ "Navajo-ized" break dancing and heavy metal performances to resist racial discrimination, express hopes for equity, and "sing" traditional worlds "into existence" within the modern and racist world (Deyhle, 1998). Traditional hula dances bring Native Hawaiian social and natural history, philosophy, literature, scientific knowledge, and religious beliefs into the modern world (Rowe, 2008).

Finding space to be an Indigenous person in a society dominated by Eurocentricism is perhaps the greatest challenge that faces Indigenous peoples. Maintaining a sense of indigeneity while navigating the gauntlet of neocolonization is perhaps best illustrated through Anzaldua's work on *nepantla*. Jaramillo and McLaren (2008) note that "*nepantla* signified an intermediary space *sin rumbo* (a "borderland" of "betwixt and between"), as las indigenas shifted their cultural and spiritual practices to accommodate the Christian doctrines being imposed upon them" (p. 197). In short, *nepantla* offered a way for Indigenous peoples in Mexico to maintain their culture in the face of annihilation and assimilation; "remaining faithful to their hearts and in honor of their spirits, they acquired the determination and ability to resist the religious practices and rituals not of their own making" (p. 197). This, however, is not particularly easy given the ubiquity and force of dominant neocolonial forces. As Henhawk, member of Six Nations, stated in his blog Critical Reflections:

When I started my master's thesis . . . I was adamant that I did not want to engage in 'native' research because . . . 'native issues' were a product of *their* own doing. I did not once stop to consider that my conceptualization of a 'they,' meaning my own people, was a product of *my* colonization. . . . My master's thesis journey was an awakening to a raised consciousness about the struggle of being an indigenous person in a society that historically subjugated indigenous cultures and continues to perpetuate the belief in European (read Canadian and American or 'Western') cultural superiority.

Jaramillo and McLaren (2008) suggested that *nepantla* is a way people can operate between theory and practice, to understand that it is important to identify Indigenous peoples' ways of knowing and being in all contexts, both historical and present day.

INDIGENOUS PEOPLES' DESIRE FOR AND COMMITMENT TO HOLISTIC APPROACHES

Overwhelmingly, scholarship across numerous domains (e.g., park management, health promotion and sciences, tourism, recreation programming, the sciences, and environmental education) underscores the calls by Indigenous peoples for holistic models, approaches, and practices in the recreation and leisure field (Hunter, Logan, Goulet, & Barton, 2006; Perkins, 2007; Transken, 2005). Indigenous epistemologies and ontologies are grounded in a situated self intimately connected with other humans, nonhumans, natural forces, and spiritual cosmologies (Brant, 1990; Meyer, 2003). The various holistic models refer to traditional ceremonies; respect for spiritual protocols; inclusion of "all their relations" including land, water and sky, spirits, family and tribal relationships; and collaborative or "circle" governance. Native Hawaiian scholar Oneha (2002) argued that issues of Native Hawaiian health were inseparable from issues of land and water. Navajo physician Alvord (1999) identified diabetes as an illness of colonialism and oppression. Lavallée (2007) (of Cree, Algonquin, and French ancestry), Iwasaki and Bartlett (2006), and Iwasaki and colleagues (2009) explored whether terms such as "leisure," or "physical health" could be meaningfully applied to Indigenous peoples positioned by Euro-North American concepts of illness and healing. They suggested that health, leisure, and

quality of life did not translate well; processes of identifying Indigenous youth as "youth at risk" or focusing on "stereotypical" illness (e.g., diabetes or alcoholism) lead to partial, not holistic, solutions. They also argued that these processes typically reinforce negative and stereotypic concepts of Indigenous peoples, use non-Indigenous assessment frameworks, and leave Indigenous peoples divorced from "all their relations." Emerging Indigenous and non-Indigenous research calls for holistic models (i.e., spiritual, emotional, mental, and physical realms of health); employs a concept of self enmeshed in human and nonhuman communities; and identifies historical, economic, political, spiritual, and cultural contexts as central to the health of Indigenous populations.

Clearly, Euro-North American biomedical and leisure research focused on beneficial causal or correlative links between physical activity and the mitigation (if not prevention or cure) of specific health problems such as diabetes, heart conditions, stress, and obesity with predominantly non-Indigenous peoples and smaller Indigenous samples has yielded promising results (DeRenne et al., 2008; Kirk & De Feo, 2007). However, varied research in Canada has consistently shown that Aboriginal peoples continue to experience substantial health status disparities and barriers to accessing health care and related services necessary for healthy living and also congruent with Indigenous worldviews (Browne, Smye, & Varcoe, 2005; Newbold, 1998; Wilson & Young, 2008; Young, 2003).

Leisure literature has predominantly focused on the link between Euro-North American leisure forms and health. Less is known about Indigenous forms of leisure and health, although research with Native Hawaiian peoples suggests a strong correlation between the two. Native Hawaiian Mokuau (2002) recommended that interventions integrate "mainstream" and culturally specific strategies and attend to non-Indigenous critiques of mainstream approaches in work with Native Hawaiians. This approach is relevant to most Indigenous peoples. An Indigenous person may want to be healthy but not participate in Eurocentric or Euro-North American leisure activities or institutions.

"Poor adherence" as understood by non-Indigenous peoples may be directly related to a dissonance between Euro-North American belief systems (i.e., goals, objectives, expert knowledge) and biomedical structures and Indigenous peoples' worldviews and historical experiences of oppression. When high adherence rates have been demonstrated, they are related to health regimens that include traditional herbal medicines and diets; connection with elders and traditional practices; relationship frameworks that include all relations; culturally appropriate treatment plans; and respectful and reciprocal working relationships between Indigenous and non-Indigenous healers, professionals, and communities (Benoit, Carroll, & Chaudhry, 2003; Heffeman et al., 1999; Mau et al., 2001; Pargee, Lara-Albers, & Puckett, 1999).

FUTURE RESEARCH: INDIGENOUS PEOPLES AND THE SCHOLARSHIP, PRACTICE, AND STUDY OF LEISURE

There is a tremendous need within leisure studies to integrate Indigenous epistemologies and ontologies, postcolonial theoretical perspectives, postcolonial Indigenous knowledge, and critical theories at foundational and theoretical levels. Indigenous scholars critique and call for "decolonizing" (Grande, 2004; Meyer, 2003; Smith, 1999, 2005) Eurocentric and Euro-North American disciplines (e.g., psychology, social psychology, leisure and recreation, sociology, economics) with respect to their assumptions of "objective" or "neutral" knowledge; lack of inclusion of Indigenous knowledges; separation of human beings from nonhuman entities, natural forces, and the cosmos; and emphasis on distant, logical research rather than local, collaborative, and participatory processes (Grande, 2004; Henhawk, 2010; Meyer, 2003; Smith, 1999, 2005; Urion, 1991).

Revitalization of Indigenous languages is a part of many self-determination efforts and has major implications for the quality of scholarship. The Native Hawaiian experience sheds light on numerous issues. The accepted Native Hawaiian canon is based on a total of seven books with problematic translations embedded in political and religious agendas. These books represent the work of four Native Hawaiian authors: the columns or articles of Samuel Mānaiakalani Kamakau and John Papa

'Ī'ī, from Hawaiian-language newspapers, and unpublished manuscripts by Davida Malo and Kepelino Keauokalani. However, Native Hawaiians enthusiastically embraced reading and writing as soon as the Native language was rendered into written form. Between 1834 and 1948, Native Hawaiian writers filled nearly 100 Hawaiian-language *"nupepas"* (or newspapers) with over 125,000 pages (approximately a million or more typescript pages of text). While other Hawaiian texts have been published in English and less than 2% of Hawaiian *nupepas* have been translated or used in academic scholarship, "the translated works of these four authors have become an articulated bastion of Hawaiian reference, and have been granted an overwhelming and far-reaching authority about Hawaiian culture and history" (Nogelmeier, 2010, p. xiii). On November 28, 2011, Awaiaulu was begun with over 2,000 volunteers who would transform scanned newspaper pages into word-searchable files; this volunteer project is designed to turn Native Hawaiian-language resources into digital objects for research and access (www.awaiaulu.org). Reliance on English translations compromises research about Indigenous leisure and risks appropriation, globalization, and hegemonic glosses of Indigenous life practices.

Postcolonial Indigenous thought emerges from the inability of Eurocentric theory to deal with the complexities of colonialism and its assumptions (Battiste, 2000, p. xix). It is situated in the relentless challenge to so-called evidence-based biomedical models of research that take for granted and/or obscure the understanding that poverty, alienation, illness, and resistance are legacies of forced state dependency upon Indigenous peoples, and the complicity of the academy with neocolonialism. Decolonizing and postcolonial Indigenous scholarship focus critical attention on

- critical personal narratives that disrupt, disturb, and expose the complexities and contradictions of official histories and theories;
- the essential requirement of partnership and voice in research processes (i.e., Indigenous control and joint decision making); and
- commitments to applying knowledge for social change (praxis-oriented inquiry) (Kovach, 2009; Wilson, 2008).

Maori scholar Brendan Hokowhitu (2009, 2010) argued for an "Indigenous existentialism" that moves beyond the colonized and colonizer dialectic. Postcolonial scholarship and political strategies leave intact the power structure of colonizer and colonized and move Indigenous resistance to a Euro-North American rights discourse. Hokowhitu posited that Indigenous existentialism locates knowledge in the lived experiences and choices of Indigenous people as they live their lives in the present. Recognizing the importance of Indigenous "everyday" experiences opens the dialogue between various disciplines including leisure studies and sciences, cultural studies, and Indigenous studies. Indigenous existentialism also refuses to privilege mind over body, or humans over nonhuman entities, and provides a framework to critique the Euro-North American understanding of Indigenous physicality as "less intelligent."

Indigenous scholars ask researchers and research teams to critically consider continuities between past and present (i.e., the past is present in every moment of every day) and to include Indigenous autonomous control and self-government as integral to research goals. Hypervigilance is needed from the moment questions are formed to the analysis and manuscript preparation if the colonial power inherent in much Euro-North American research is to be undermined and transformative goals are to emerge. Maori nurse leaders in New Zealand (Anderson et al., 2003; Papps & Ramsden, 1996; Ramsden, 2002) argued that *cultural safety* (understanding power imbalances on individual and institutional levels) counters tendencies to create *cultural risk* (when people from a particular group believe they are "demeaned, diminished or disempowered by the actions and the delivery systems of people from another culture" [citing Ramsden & Spoonley, 1993]). Researchers, practitioners, and educators increasingly identify cultural safety and cultural risk as a pragmatic tool for placing abstract postcolonial theorizing into the everyday (Ramsden, 2002) by shifting focus away from Indigenous cultural characteristics to the culture of service providers (Browne et al., 2005)—in this case, leisure and recreation scholars, researchers, and practitioners.

Overwhelmingly, Indigenous and non-Indigenous scholars support collaborative and participatory research methods and attention to and respect for sovereignty and local self-government. Consistently, research has demonstrated that coalition building is essential in order for Indigenous knowledges and practices to challenge and to be integrated into dominant mainstream education, research, and practice (Redwing Saunders & Hill, 2007). However, the record of recruiting and sustaining Indigenous peoples in postsecondary educational programs, including those involving leisure, parks, resource management, and recreation, is abysmal (Baskin, Koleszar-Green, Hendry, Lavallée, & Murrin, 2008; Greenwood, de Leeuw, & Fraser, 2008; Orlowski, 2008). There is a strong need for recreation and leisure studies programs to implement recruitment, engagement, and ongoing support strategies for Indigenous peoples in university and other educational or professional programs. Furthermore, the content and pedagogy need to be reframed and reenvisioned in light of Indigenous ways of being and knowing, as well as cultural and critical theories and postcolonial thought.

Cardinal (2002) argues for a transformational leadership approach that recognizes both Indigenous and non-Indigenous cultures in the development of goals based on common ground. Urion (1991) suggested adapting "two pairs of eyes" (i.e., First Nations and Euro-North American academic) for fostering—not translating—access to multidimensional experiences. According to Indigenous and non-Indigenous scholars, successful postsecondary educational programs include participation by and consensual relationships with Indigenous communities and elders in a holistic context; coalition building within and across institutions committed to antiracism practices, integration of worldviews, and participatory processes; flexibility to meet Indigenous participants' needs; developing community ownership of visionary and decision-making processes; and strong Indigenous research, content, and delivery processes (Heber, 2006; Urion, 1991; Wall, 2008).

Programming and delivering recreation services as well as leisure research and scholarship relevant for Indigenous peoples must include the following:

- Collaborative and participatory consultation processes

- Antiracism and anti-essentialist strategies within consultation, decision making, planning, delivering, and group dynamics

- Reassessment of Euro-North American leisure frameworks and their problematic aspects for Indigenous peoples

- Inclusion of Indigenous worldviews and approaches, such as ceremonial protocols, politically aware place-based knowledges, relationships with elders, and Aboriginal practices associated with Indigenous leisure (Orlowski, 2008; Wall, 2008)

Such changes in cofacilitating recreation experiences and research between Indigenous and non-Indigenous recreation professionals and scholars require negotiating Euro-North American institutional cultures that are contrary, if not hostile, to Indigenous ways of being; modifying leadership and group dynamic processes to support and nurture young people whose resiliency challenges traditional middle-class norms; creating compassionate social service networks grounded in Indigenous ways of being and compassionate principles based on the neurophysiology of the human brain and mind (Gilbert, 2010);[3] and entering into long-term relational commitments that are necessary to create trust, relationships, and recreation formats inclusive of Indigenous worldviews and practices.

CONCLUSION

In the last 20 years, the intersection of leisure and Indigenous peoples has surfaced within leisure scholarship. It is a small beginning within a small field concerned with the plight and needs of Indigenous peoples that deserves more attention given the potential of leisure to sustain culture, nourish health, provide frameworks for expression, negotiate and resist globalized forces, and enhance self-determination and sovereignty issues. This chapter (a) discusses the difficulty in identifying Indigenous peoples and problematic aspects of Eurocentric and Euro-North American

leisure, along with legal, postcolonial, historical, and political issues facing Indigenous groups associated with North America (e.g., First Nations, Métis, Inuit, American Indians, Native Hawaiians, Alaskan Natives, and other Pacific Islanders); (b) acknowledges that the scope of leisure research relevant to Indigenous peoples is emerging and limited; and (c) discusses future needs based on Indigenous critiques for research, curricula, and educational opportunities in recreation and leisure studies. The extant leisure literature addresses various challenges in the management and use of protected lands (i.e., national parks and forests, Crown lands); raises questions about the integration of Indigenous holistic perspectives especially when leisure can contribute to healing processes; explores the relevance of Euro-North American constructs of leisure pursuits especially related to recreation or outdoor adventures that stress White middle-class values and self-development; and sketches the lack of research and programs focused on Indigenous peoples, youth, and cultures in urban areas.

There are three critical areas to be addressed. First, there is a need for more research grounded in community-based, collaborative, participatory research perspectives and methods as well as inclusion of Indigenous worldviews, methodologies, and practices. Second, Eurocentric and Euro-North American leisure frameworks need to be interrogated with critical, poststructuralist, and postcolonial, as well as Indigenous and Indigenous postcolonial or existentialist theories, to illuminate problematic assumptions and practices related to Indigenous peoples. Third, current scholarship and research need to incorporate research from other relevant fields, including Indigenous studies (e.g., the relevance of Maori research by Hokowhitu [2009, 2011] and Thompson's [2011] work) and current Indigenous initiatives such as Ka Welina or urban Aboriginal hip-hop programs. Finally, rethinking and adapting major educational and industrial organizations to support Indigenous peoples in their quest for education in leisure studies or sciences and recreation management will increase the presence of Indigenous peoples.

[3]Gilbert's (2010) work resonates with many traditional Indigenous child rearing and communal ethics while providing strong links to Euro-North American and Eurocentric psychological, neuroscientific, and evolutionary biological perspectives.

CHAPTER 8

Leisure Among Religious Minorities

Paul Heintzman and Monika Stodolska

OVERVIEW

Religious minority groups often overlap with racial and ethnic groups (e.g., Muslims, Jews, Amish, the Black church), and thus it is important to include them in this book. The purpose of this chapter is fourfold: to provide background on religion and religion's relationship with leisure; to present information on the current and projected size of the Christian, Muslim, and Jewish minority groups in the United States and Canada; to review the literature on the effects of religious doctrines on leisure behavior of Christians, Muslims, and Jews in the United States and Canada; and finally to assess the current state of empirical research on minority religious groups in North America.

Learning Outcomes

After reading this chapter, readers will be able to

- define religion;
- explain the dimensions of religion;
- outline the different ways in which the relationships between religion and leisure are viewed;
- characterize Christian, Muslim, and Jewish understandings of leisure; and
- identify major characteristics and trends with respect to leisure behavior among members of the Muslim, Jewish, and Christian minority groups in the United States and Canada.

Leisure is the growing time of the human spirit.

Lee (1964, p. 34)

In order to fully appreciate the relationship between religion and leisure, one first needs to have a basic understanding of religion. Etymologically, the word "religion" is related to the Latin word *legare,* which means to connect or to bind (Paloutzian, 1996). Our English word "ligament," which also comes from *legare,* means connection. Therefore, religion has something to do with reconnecting something that has become unconnected, whether it is reconnection to God, a higher power, nature, or other people. The universality of religion seems to indicate that there is a need to repair some form of brokenness in all people. Thus, religion involves a striving for a sense of completeness and wholeness in life.

Religion may be considered at both personal and social levels of analysis (Paloutzian, 1996). At the personal level, religion refers to such things as an individual's sense of meaning, code of conduct, state of feeling free or guilty, and belief system. At the societal level, religion refers to specialized groups that focus on religion, such as synagogues, churches, or other groups, along with their common practices and beliefs.

A distinction can also be made between functional and substantive definitions of religion (Paloutzian, 1996). Functional definitions focus on religion with regard to what it does for an individual or for a society. Substantive definitions of religion focus on the practice, creed, doctrine, or belief system of the specific religion: what is believed or practiced, rather than the function served.

Given all this, religion may be seen as a "generalized, abstract orientation through which people see the world; it defines their reality, provides a sense of significance, and receives their fundamental allegiance and commitment" (Paloutzian, 1996, p. 13). For research purposes, religion may be viewed as a multidimensional variable that includes aspects related to what people believe, do, feel, and know and how they respond to their beliefs. These aspects are called the dimensions of religious commitment, which are briefly explained next.

The religious belief or ideological dimension includes what is believed (e.g., the existence of God), the strength of the belief, the foundation of the intellectual commitment to the belief, and how significant the belief is to a person (Paloutzian, 1996). This dimension refers to the content of belief and is the dimension that tends to differentiate religions. Religious practice or the ritualistic dimension refers to the expected behaviors of an individual who belongs to a specific religion. What are the specific acts of a certain religion? These may include practices such as worship services, prayer, observation of special days, and fasting. The religious feeling or experiential dimension is the internal emotional and mental experience of a person. This dimension focuses on religious experiences. Religious knowledge or the intellectual dimension is the knowledge or information that one has about one's religion, which should not be confused with one's belief. For example, religious knowledge would include the origin and history of a religion, although this knowledge is not essential for the practice of the religion and not all the followers of this religion may have this knowledge. The religious effects or consequential dimension refers to the effect that a person's religion has on the rest of the individual's life. For example, if an alcoholic stops drinking after a religious conversion, the nondrinking behavior would be considered a religious effect. These five dimensions illustrate the pervasiveness of religion in people's lives in that most people exhibit at least one of these dimensions (Paloutzian).

The relationship between religion and leisure has been viewed in different ways. Kelly (1987) outlined at least four approaches. First, religion may be viewed as leisure in terms of an activity or time that is chosen from among other free-time activities due to the anticipation of specific positive outcomes. In this approach, religious groups are seen as voluntary organizations that people decide to join. Second, religion may be viewed as private rather than social, and thus as a form of leisure through freely-chosen activities such as contemplation. Third, religion may be viewed in opposition to leisure in that certain forms of recreation activities may be prohibited by religious groups. However, religious groups may provide alternative forms of leisure for their members (e.g., social activities, camps), and Freysinger and Kelly (2004) noted that the primary conflict is not between religion and leisure but between asceticism and expression. Cases exist to illustrate that religious groups have supported both asceticism and expression. History demonstrates that in addition to conflict, accommodation, reconciliation, and cooperation between religion and leisure have also existed (Freysinger & Kelly, 2004). Many religious groups offer recreation activities and programs to recruit members and to promote community. Fourth, religion may offer a prophetic voice by reevaluating the status quo with regard to leisure and provide a new alternative. While these approaches have been identified, there is a need for empirical research on the relationship between religion and leisure, as asserted by Stodolska and Livengood (2006):

> We believe that the strong need exists to focus more on the effects of religion on leisure behavior. In-depth studies are needed in order to further our understanding of how different groups of Christians and Jews as well as followers of other religions spend their leisure time and how religious doctrine affects their leisure behavior. (p. 317)

The following sections review what empirical research exists on the leisure of Christian, Muslim, and Jewish minority groups in North America.

LEISURE AMONG CHRISTIANS

This section begins with a discussion of biblical perspectives on leisure, which is followed by an examination of historical and current Christian understandings of leisure. While in general there is little empirical research on the leisure of Christians, the section summarizes the few studies on leisure among smaller Christian groups, including the Old Order Mennonites and Amish, evangelical theologians, the Assemblies of God denomination, New Paradigm Christians, and the Black church.

Biblical Perspectives on Leisure

Although the word "leisure" (*scholē*) arose in Greek culture, "there are antecedents to the concept of leisure under other names that share similar traits with the Greek concept of leisure" (Crabtree, 1982, p. 14). In the Christian scriptures composed of the Old and New Testaments, words related to *scholē* are not prominent. One of the few occurrences is in the Septuagint (i.e., the ancient Greek translation of the Hebrew scriptures) rendition of Psalm 46:10, where the Hebrew word is translated with the Greek word *scholē* so that in English the verse reads "Have leisure and know that I am God." This translation of Psalm 46:10 is often quoted in leisure literature (e.g., Bregha, 1991). Hermeneutical research suggests that the verse concerns the spiritual attitude regarding a person's basic posture in relation to God and, therefore, fits with a spiritual understanding of leisure (e.g., Pieper, 1963). Although words related to leisure are not prominent in the Christian tradition, various modern-day writers have identified a number of biblical elements that may be used to develop a Christian understanding of leisure: the creation model (Lehman, 1974), creativity in the Old Testament (Spence, 1973), the principle of Sabbath rest (Heintzman, 2006a; Johnston, 1983; Ryken, 1995), the image of God in play (Holmes, 1983), the advice of Qoheleth in the book of Ecclesiastes (Johnston, 1983), the Hebraic way of life (Johnston, 1983), the quality of life of Jesus (Dahl, 1972), and the Kingdom of God (Holmes, 1983).

Most books outlining a Christian view of leisure draw on the biblical teaching and practice of Sabbath to articulate and explain leisure (e.g., Doohan, 1990; Johnston, 1983; Ryken, 1995). Today, the practice of Sabbath is increasingly popular as a means to cope with consumerism, stress, and the permeation of work into all areas of life (Diddams, Surdyk, & Daniels, 2004). The question that arises is whether the Sabbath may be seen as a type of leisure. Heintzman (1986,

2006a) suggested that the biblical concepts of Sabbath and rest cannot be equated with leisure but that they provide insights for developing a philosophy of leisure that encompasses both quantitative and qualitative dimensions. First, the Sabbath teaches a rhythm to life including periods of work and periods of nonwork (i.e., the quantitative dimension). Second, in terms of the qualitative dimension, the Sabbath inculcates a spiritual attitude regarding a person's basic position in relation to God through rest, joy, freedom, and celebration in God and the gift of God's creation (Heschel, 1951). This qualitative dimension can also be seen in the biblical concept of rest that ranges from a pleasant, secure, and blessed life in the land to a peace and contentment of body, soul, and mind in God.

Historical and Current Christian Understandings of Leisure

The early Christian notion of *otium sanctum,* or holy leisure, was a "sense of balance in life, an ability to be at peace through the activities of the day, an ability to rest and take time to enjoy beauty, an ability to pace ourselves" (Foster, 1978, pp. 20-21). As Christian theology developed, Christian understandings of leisure were influenced by the Greek concept of *scholē.* Augustine (354-430 CE) identified three types of life: the active, the contemplative, and the mixed life of action and contemplation (Neville, 2004). His contemplative life of holy leisure that involved the investigation of truth was not only influenced by Greek thought but was also based on the tranquility of active rest in Christ (Heintzman, 1986; Neville, 2004). Thomas Aquinas (1225-1274 CE), who devoted his life to the reconciliation of Aristotle's thought and Christian faith, located Aristotle's notion of leisure and contemplation in the blessed vision of God. The medieval monastic theme of *otium* was of biblical origin but was also influenced by the Greek notion of *scholē.* This thread of *scholē* continues with Pieper (1963), whose philosophy and theology were heavily influenced by the writings of Thomas Aquinas. Although Pieper has received much attention within leisure studies, his view of leisure is typical of that of many Roman Catholic theologians and scholars (e.g., Doohan, 1990):

Leisure, it must be clearly understood, is a mental and spiritual attitude. . . . It is in the first place, an attitude of mind, a condition of the soul. . . . For leisure is a receptive attitude of mind, a contemplative attitude, and it is not only the occasion but also the capacity for steeping oneself in the whole of creation. (Pieper, pp. 40-41)

Although Christian versions of classical leisure as expressed by Pieper (1963) continue to this day in the Roman Catholic Church, with the Reformation and the development of Protestant theology there was a move away from classical understandings of leisure to activity understandings. A contemporary Christian expression of the activity view was put forward by the Protestant scholar Ryken (1995), who included a quote from Lee, author of an earlier book titled *Religion and Leisure in America: A Study in Four Dimensions:*

Its [leisure's] purpose is to bring us back to physical, mental, and emotional strength and wholeness. . . . The purpose of leisure is to re-create a person, to restore him or her to an earlier condition. . . . Leisure . . . is 'the growing time of the human spirit' and a time 'for rest and restoration, for rediscovering life in its entirety'. . . . Leisure is, in the best sense of the word, an escape. . . . Relaxation is one of the inherent qualities of leisure. (pp. 236, 261)

Christian understandings of leisure are not restricted to classical and activity views. Neville (2004) defined leisure as time: "Anything that might be called a theology of leisure must be a particular aspect of theology of freedom, because leisure, on any definition, is time freed from external constraints, at work or in social duties" (p. 100). More recently a number of Christian authors (Dahl, 2006; Heintzman, 1986, 1994; Joblin, 2009) have articulated a holistic understanding of leisure. For example, Dahl (2006) wrote,

Work and leisure are not distinct; they lie on a continuum. . . . Leisure is being able to combine work, worship, and recreation in a free and loving, holistic way which integrates these three elements as much as possible. Although a person goes to different places to perform different functions, leisure lies in integrating these three aspects in order to experience wholeness in one's life, family, and community. (p. 95)

From this brief review of Christian understandings of leisure, it is clear that there is no one Christian understanding of leisure; multiple Christian views of leisure exist.

Empirical Research on Christian Minorities and Leisure

While Christian authors have developed theologies or understandings of leisure, within leisure studies and other academic disciplines there is very little empirical research on Christianity and leisure. As far as the authors know, no study in North America is similar to Schulz and Auld's (2009) Australian study of Christianity and leisure meanings, including differences between Christian subgroups. This section of the chapter reviews empirical studies, mostly qualitative ones, on smaller subgroups of Christians within North America. Given that this book's focus is on racial and ethnic minorities, the discussion here does not include the very few studies that involved larger Christian groups such as mainline Protestants and Catholics (17% and 38%, respectively, of the Canadian population [Bibby, 2011] and 18.1% and 23.9% of the U.S. population [Lugo et al., 2008]).

Old Order Mennonite and Amish Groups

The Old Order Mennonites and Amish are a religiously, ethnically, and culturally distinct minority population group that has decided to follow a different and unique way of living within Western culture (Fretz, 1989; Wenger, 2003). Both groups are Anabaptist Protestants who originally emigrated from Europe. While the two groups have cultural and historical differences in terms of when they immigrated, where they settled, types of clothing, and types of worship places, they are similar as to their beliefs and way of life. Both groups are "cultural conservationists"

in that they accept change only if it is consistent with their existing moral order and contributes to, rather than modifies, their traditional ways.

The Amish live in some 20 states in the United States, the Canadian province of Ontario, and South America. In 2010 there were approximately 241,356 Amish in the United States (Association of Religious Data Archives, 2012b), and it is estimated that there are 10,000 Amish in Canada (Kraybill, Nolt, & Weaver-Zercher, 2010). A significantly smaller population (Wenger, 2003), the Old Order Mennonites, numbered slightly over 21,000 in the United States in 2000 (Association of Religious Data Archives, 2012a), while in Canada the Kitchener–Waterloo region of Ontario has a large concentration of approximately 4,000 Old Order Mennonites (Vogeler, 2005).

In an ethnographic study that involved participant observation, Anderson and Autry (2011) explored the leisure behavior of the Old Order Amish. People in this group do not typically use modern technologies such as cars, televisions, computers, or phones and intentionally separate themselves from mainstream society so that they do not give in to modernization. Anderson and Autry found that religion influenced every aspect of Amish life. The Amish viewed leisure as free time that provides the opportunity to help others and serve the church. This is consistent with their belief that leisure time is wasted if someone is not being helped. Leisure time is filled with helping the community with activities such as barn raisings, visiting relatives and the sick, eating meals with friends, and attending weddings. Thus leisure is not a recreational activity, but a means to altruistically assist one another. Furthermore, Amish life is not compartmentalized into one's job and the remaining leisure time. Most forms of entertainment, travel, and popular culture are banned, as they are viewed as having the potential to corrupt. Leisure tends to be family oriented, as families are tight-knit and typically do everything together. While the Amish have a strong work ethic, they refrain from all unnecessary work on the Sunday Sabbath, a day devoted to worship, relaxation, family, and friends.

On the basis of symbolic interactionism theory, Anderson and Autry (2011) concluded that the Amish construct meanings in their social interactions whereby they shape their culture and their culture shapes them. Their beliefs are grounded in their particular interpretation of the Bible and are influenced by their social interaction with their church. They shape their church community, and their church community influences their leisure behavior. Religion is their lifestyle, influencing all aspects of their lives including leisure. Thus, they express themselves as a religious community. The researchers observed that the Amish are very satisfied and happy people who experience joy in all dimensions of their lives, including leisure, work, education, and religion. There was no sense that religion constrained the Amish in their leisure.

Noting that Shaw (1985) identified the factors of enjoyment, relaxation, freedom to choose one's activity, and intrinsic motivation as characteristic of leisure, Wenger (2003) observed that while the first three factors characterize both the Amish and Old Order Mennonites, the notion of engaging in an activity entirely for personal satisfaction does not fit well with Old Order beliefs. Wenger stated that work and leisure may be intertwined, as activities such as caring for elders or babies, singing, and Sunday visiting are focused on creating something useful for the family or community, strengthening social connections, developing one's relationship with God, or a combination of these. While the lack of attention on self may seem unusual in contemporary Western society, Wenger claimed that this view can be understood only within the community- and biblically-oriented reality of the Amish and Old Order Mennonites. Furthermore, this understanding of leisure is influenced by the rhythm of farm life, in which evenings and weekends are free of work and extended vacations are not possible.

While the Old Order groups consider hard work a virtue, there are also opportunities for personal renewal, fulfillment, and friendships with others in one's work and chores (Wenger, 2003). Religious holidays, auctions, times of singing, barn raisings, quiltings, funerals, and weddings all offer time for socializing and leisure, while Sundays are days of rest and worship (Wenger). The following quote illustrates this sense of leisure in life and work:

Many of their work bees and ways of making a self-sustaining living are actually very enjoyable get-togethers with friends, family and relatives. . . . Recreational facilities and leisure time activities are more numerous and varied than outsiders realize: checkers, crokinole, jigsaw puzzles, quiltings, apple schnitzing (paring and slicing to dry), Sunday evening singings followed by folk games, farm sales, wood carving, knitting, skating, and swimming in season at local creeks, repair work around the house and barn, barn raisings and reunions, weddings and funerals must all be considered as meaningful and pleasant leisure-time activities for old and young. (Fretz, 1989, p. 220)

These types of leisure are often practical, functional, and without financial cost (Wenger, 2003). For example, quilting can provide warm blankets for the home, supply relief organizations, and give women the opportunity to visit each other. Likewise, children's activities focus on outdoor pursuits such as skating, swimming, or hunting rather than technological products.

Evangelical Theologians

In a qualitative research study, Hothem (1983; cf. Trunfio, 1991) interviewed 10 evangelical theologians, who taught at an evangelical Protestant seminary, on the relationship between their Christian faith and leisure. Evangelicals composed 16.2% of the population in the United States in 2010 (Association of Religious Data Archives, 2012b) and 10% of Canada's population in 2009 (Bibby, 2011); however, evangelical theologians would compose a much smaller subset of the total number of evangelicals. Evangelical theologians tend to be more highly educated than evangelicals and tend to have higher levels of religious knowledge (the intellectual dimension of religion) as explained earlier. Hothem found that the participants had multiple experiences related to leisure and multiple definitions and perceptions of leisure. These theologians did not view work and leisure as totally opposite; rather, they viewed leisure as integrated with work, family, and other roles. Leisure for these participants often had a utilitarian role, although not necessarily with regard to work. Rather, the functions of leisure were related to reward, exercise, family obligations, and change of activity. Although leisure was a priority, it had to be scheduled, or else it would not happen. When the participants were questioned directly about the relationship between their Christian faith and leisure, the common theme was that the purpose of all life experiences was to glorify God. Several of the participants referred to biblical principles that influenced their leisure, including the principles of stewardship and rest. They also noted that leisure should be used for altruistic purposes and not just self-gratification. Perceptions of leisure were shaped by personal emotions, motives, beliefs, and attitudes as much as by external factors of role requirements, social groups, and social structure. The participants explained that their Christian faith is what integrates their lives while their "calling" provides a sense of holism in life. For most, leisure was not viewed in the classical sense of leisure as an end in itself but rather was seen as beneficial because of its utilitarian value.

Assemblies of God

The Assemblies of God are a Christian denomination that had more than 2.9 million adherents in the United States in 2010, which is equivalent to slightly less than 1% of the country's population (Association of Religious Data Archives, 2012b). In Canada, there are 20 member churches with approximately 3,300 members and adherents (D. Cianflone, personal communication, June 7, 2012). Livengood (2004) conducted a qualitative study with Assemblies of God Christians to investigate the roles of leisure within this denomination and how religious beliefs affected the leisure behavior of its members. In-depth interviews were held with 13 Assemblies of God Christians. The study yielded six themes: (1) Some participants viewed weekly Sunday services, prayer meetings, and small group meetings as leisure; (2) church facilities and resources were used to organize leisure activities; (3) leisure and recreational programs were used to introduce non-Christians to Christianity; (4) social networks and close friendships were established and maintained through the

church's leisure activities; (5) the leisure behavior of the participants was influenced by Christian teachings in that biblical passages were used to promote leisure and recreational participation as well as the types of leisure that should be engaged in; and (6) participants attempted to make sense of biblical teaching and apply it to their lives, including their leisure. Livengood concluded that there was an intricate relationship between the Christian faith of Assemblies of God Christians and their leisure behavior.

New Paradigm Christians

New Paradigm churches are a current expression of Christianity focused on worship services for non-Christians that communicate the Christian message through contemporary music, technical presentation formats, casual dress, relational messages customized to the current culture, and comfort for newcomers (Livengood, 2009). As New Paradigm churches span a variety of denominations, it is difficult to determine the number of North Americans who attend these churches. Livengood (2009) used an ethnographic approach that included both participant observations at two New Paradigm churches and in-depth interviews with 17 New Paradigm Christians to explore whether the leisure experiences of these Christians were related to their spirituality. The majority of participants explained that their leisure and their spiritual experiences were related; only one participant claimed that leisure was not related to his spirituality. The relationship between leisure and spirituality was explained by three processes. First, leisure activities engaged in alone such as music playing, knitting, and walking were considered spiritual by most participants. Likewise, leisure allowed participants to quiet themselves, thereby creating the conditions necessary to focus on God. Second, leisure with both Christians and non-Christians was viewed as spiritual. In particular, leisure provided the opportunity for participants to relate to and have fellowship with other Christians. Third, leisure in natural settings was considered an opportunity to experience God in creation. Livengood concluded that leisure played an important role in the spirituality of New Paradigm Christians as it provided them with opportunities to understand their spirituality and their church culture.

The Black Church

Historically, the Black church refers to eight Black denominations: African Methodist Episcopal, Africa Methodist Episcopal Zion, Christian Methodist Episcopal, Church of God in Christ, National Baptist Convention USA Inc., National Baptist Convention of America, National Missionary Baptist Convention, and the Progressive Baptist Convention (Waller, 2010). In 2010 in the United States, close to 4.9 million adherents, which was 1.6% of the country's population, belonged to these eight denominations; however this is an incomplete account (Association of Religious Data Archives, 2012b). According to a survey conducted in 2007 by the Pew Forum on Religion and Public Life (Lugo et al., 2008), in which more than these eight denominations were identified with the Black church, 6.9% of the U.S. population was affiliated with historical Black churches. In the 21st century, African American congregations affiliated with Roman Catholicism and the United Church of Christ have also been included as part of the Black church (Waller, 2010).

The Black church has historically used recreation and leisure to develop community and solidarity among African Americans (Waller, 2010) (also see chapter 4 on leisure among African Americans). These churches have also provided a place of safe haven for fellowship and fun during difficult times. Thus, constructive leisure offered by the Black church has facilitated resilience at the individual, family, and community levels. Furthermore, these churches played a significant role in influencing leisure attitudes and behaviors.

The Black church has been important for cultural as well as spiritual purposes, as it has been the African American community's heart (Waller, 2010). Not only did it work against injustices faced by African Americans; it was also a sanctuary where African Americans could seek comfort, freely express themselves, and find cultural unity in terms of beliefs and practices (Waller). Through its history, tradition, doctrine, and moral teachings, the Black church continues to foster eco-

nomic, political, social, and moral self-help among Black congregations and communities (Waller).

Leisure has been a focus of Black congregational life as a context for individual and communal worship, refreshment from the toil of work, conveying and maintaining native African culture, and developing a sense of community (Waller, 2010). Fellowship and cultural and arts activities, as well as social groups in contemporary Black churches, can be traced back 200 years to the early days of the Black church.

Based on scripture or the church's moral teaching, the Black church encouraged avoidance of morally questionable leisure activities such as drinking, gambling, dancing, smoking, secular music, card playing, and sexual promiscuity (Waller, 2010). Thus, the Black church influenced the leisure attitudes of African American Christians. An example of the influence of a Black church's teaching on morally questionable leisure activities is seen in a case study by Waller (2009), who used a questionnaire survey to investigate the association between religious doctrine and leisure activities in a predominantly African American church in southern Ohio. Waller found a significant association between the belief that specific leisure pastimes are sinful and the source of belief (religious doctrine, scripture, personal belief). First, he discovered that religious doctrine influenced beliefs about the morality of leisure activities at both the congregational and individual level. Religious socialization, which involved both the recitation of doctrinal statements and teaching and encouragement to live within lifestyle boundaries of the faith tradition, had a significant influence on congregational and individual beliefs about the sinfulness of specific leisure activities. Second, personal beliefs, rather than scripture or doctrine, had the greatest influence on whether leisure activities were considered sinful or not. While the church members were knowledgeable about the scriptural and doctrinal foundations for beliefs, ultimately the beliefs resided within the individuals. Third, beliefs about leisure were influenced by the length of congregational membership. In general, the longer a person had been a member, the more doctrinal beliefs were internalized and the more religious socialization took

Recreation at a church picnic provides leisure as refreshment from the work of daily living and service to the church.

place. Waller concluded that in this congregation, religious belief systems influenced leisure choices and behaviors.

Waller (2010) suggested that within the Black church as a whole, teaching about leisure has primarily taken the form of negative admonishments denouncing certain leisure activities while there has been less teaching on the positive aspects of leisure. Waller explained that in the late 20th century, a more theologically balanced view of leisure was presented, in which leisure is seen as a complement to work that is needed for a balanced, godly life. Black clergy today are more aware of the need to encourage the constructive use of leisure as refreshment from the work of daily living and service to the church. Waller summarized this more positive view of leisure as follows:

In the life of the Black church, leisure provides opportunities for spiritual and physical renewal (Mk 6:31); fellowship (Ps 133:1); and in some cases reconciliation of individuals to God and each other (2 Cor 5:18). Increas-

ingly, African American clergy are acknowledging that leisure teaches the value of rest (Gen 2:2-3); godly pleasure and enjoyment (Eccl 8:15); and the beauty of the wise stewardship of leisure (Phil 4:18). (p. 37)

In a study of Black churches, Lincoln and Mamiya (1990) discovered that Black churches that were more progressive provided fellowship halls, gyms, and outdoor basketball courts, as well as social recreation and athletic programs for their congregations.

Summary on Christianity and Leisure

Although this section of the chapter has provided some insights into the leisure of minority Christian groups, it must be noted that all the studies reviewed except for Waller's (2009) study of an African American church were qualitative investigations and relied on small samples. Moreover, groups or denominations were painted with broad strokes; and, for example, differences among the various denominations within the "Black church" and within other groups were not examined in detail. In addition, little information was provided on the historical context of the samples. Therefore, the findings of these studies cannot be generalized. Definitely, more research, particularly investigations employing quantitative methodologies, is needed to provide an understanding of the leisure practices of Christians within specific denominations. Nevertheless, the studies reviewed appear to suggest that Christian faith has an influence on leisure behavior.

LEISURE AMONG MUSLIMS

This discussion of leisure among Muslims begins with an overview of the history of immigration and the demographic background of Muslims in North America. It then covers the basic tenets of Islamic faith and the ways in which they shape leisure behavior among followers. The final topic is the leisure behavior of Muslims in North America, including constraints on leisure that they experience.

Muslims Around the World and in North America

Islam, one of the three major faiths along with Judaism and Christianity (Maqsood, 1994), has approximately 1.6 billion followers worldwide (Bell, 2012). Islam is also reportedly one of the world's fastest-growing religions and is the majority religion in some 46 countries (Martin & Mason, 2004). The number of followers of Islam is predicted to grow to 8.3 billion by 2030, and Muslims are expected to constitute more than 26% of the world's population (Grim & Karim, 2011). Currently, more than 60% of Muslims reside in the Asia Pacific region, followed by the Middle East and North Africa (19.9%) and Sub-Saharan Africa (15.5%) (Grim & Karim).

The first Muslims came to the United States during the period from 1530 to 1851 through the slave trade from Africa (Hasan, 2001). Of the millions of Africans who were brought to the United States from the area of present-day Ghana, Ivory Coast, Burkina Faso, Niger, and Algeria, about 20% to 30% were Muslim (Hasan). Most of them later converted to Christianity. More Muslims began coming to the United States in the late 19th century (1870s) and early 20th century, mainly from Lebanon, Syria, and other countries of the Ottoman Empire (Haddad, 2011; Haddad & Smith, 1994). During the 1960s and 1970s, a third major immigration wave began. It included more educated Muslims, many of whom held professional degrees and who came with the intention of enrolling at American universities (Haddad & Smith). The revocation in 1965 of the provisions of the Immigration Act of 1924 that used national origin quotas to restrict the number of immigrants from certain countries who were allowed to enter the United States dramatically changed the Muslim migration flows to the United States. Since the 1924 Johnson-Reed Act lead to a de-facto complete exclusion of immigrants from Asia, lifting of these restrictions marked the beginning of immigration from diverse Arab and Muslim countries, including those in South Asia and North Africa (Haddad). A majority of foreign-born Muslims (61%) arrived in the U.S. in the decades of the 1990s and 2000s (Pew Research Center, 2007). Today's Muslim American population can be described as a mosaic of ethnic, linguistic, ideological, social, and economic groups (Haddad, 2011). In terms of religious devotion, Muslims range from highly orthodox to moderate and even secular.

According to the Council on American-Islamic Relations (CAIR, 2013), there are 6-7 million Muslims in the United States. The CIA World Factbook (2010) estimates this number at 1.8 million (0.6%) in the U.S. population, and the Pew Research Center (2007) at 2.5 million (0.8%). According to the Pew Research Center, 65% of American Muslims are first-generation immigrants, 39% of whom arrived in the United States between 1990 and 2007. More than one third of foreign-born Muslims (37%) originate from Arab countries of the Middle East and North Africa, and 27% from South Asia (Pakistan, India, Bangladesh, and Afghanistan). Although the majority of American Muslims are immigrants, the Muslim community in the United States is not limited to immigrants. Native-born American Muslims are mainly African Americans, making up about a quarter of the total Muslim population. It is estimated that there are between 10,000 and 100,000 African American members of the Nation of Islam, often referred to as Black Muslims (Hasan). Muslims in the United States reside mainly in 10 states: California, New York, Illinois, New Jersey, Indiana, Michigan, Virginia, Texas, Ohio, and Maryland (Hasan, 2001).

Muslims in the United States have a relatively high socioeconomic status, with education and income levels exceeding those of the U.S. general population. Many are employed in professional and technical occupations, as doctors, scientists, lawyers, engineers, financial analysts, informational technology specialists, and entrepreneurs. Twenty-four percent of all Muslims and 29% of immigrant Muslims have college degrees, 45% of immigrant Muslims have annual household incomes of $50,000 or above and 19% of $100,000 and higher (Pew Research Center, 2007).

Muslim Life and Values[1]

The word Muslim means "the one who submits." Islam is based on two principles: the belief that Muslims must submit and must believe in one God, Allah; and the belief that Muhammad is God's last and greatest prophet, who revealed His final and complete revelations (Esposito, 2004). Islamic laws that were recorded in the Holy book Qur'an were revealed to the Prophet Muhammad over a 23-year period starting in 610 CE. Although Muhammad delivered this last message, Muslims believe in the truth of all messengers of God including Moses and Christ. Arabic is considered the true language in which God revealed the Qur'an (Maqsood, 1994).

Islam has two main sects, Sunnism and Shi'ism. The Sunni sect accounts for the majority of Muslims, while the Shi'ites make up about 10% to 16% of the American and world Muslim population (Hasan, 2001). These two main sects do not disagree on the major tenets of Islam; the difference is in whom the group looks to as their leader (Hasan). Sunni Muslims follow the teachings of the Qur'an and Muhammad only, while Shi'ites follow the traditions of Muhammad and his son-in-law Ali (Hasan).

The Qur'an instructs Muslims to perform five pillars of faith: Faith and bearing witness, Prayers, Fasting, Charity, and Pilgrimage (Esposito, 2004).

Faith is the belief and the declaration that there is only one God and that Muhammad is his last Prophet. The second pillar, Prayer, is the belief that Muslims are to remember God and communicate with Him in the form of a prayer five times a day. Fasting prohibits Muslims from consuming food or drink from sunrise to sunset during the holy month of Ramadan. Charity, the fourth pillar, is the duty of Muslims to donate 1/40 of all their possessions annually to those who are less fortunate. The final pillar, the Pilgrimage, is a requirement for all Muslims to travel to Mecca, the holiest shrine of Islam, at least once in their lifetime (Esposito).

Muslims are not a homogenous group of believers. According to Walseth and Fasting (2003), there are four major ideological tendencies in Islam, differing in how Muslims interpret Islam and in the role Islam should play in society. Secularists consider religion a private, individual matter, while fundamentalists believe that Islamic rules should govern society. Traditionalists use traditional detailed rules and the writings of past scholars to interpret Islam, while modernists believe that Islamic values and principles should inspire laws and rules of behavior. Islam has followers all over the world who speak different languages (Esposito, 2004). Due to the impact of local traditions and socioeconomic conditions among various strata of the population, there are differences in how Islam is practiced in different countries. However, members of the Ummah (the worldwide family of believers) share many similarities and mix well in most aspects of life (Maqsood, 1994). Islam is not a religion of one race or class but a doctrine and a culture of all who desire to follow this faith.

Regardless of the ideological divisions within the Islamic faith and cultural influences on the lifestyles of Muslims, most scholars believe that Islam is a way of life that includes all aspects of living, social behavior, and conduct (Sfeir, 1985). Muslims are collectivistic; they stress the primary role of family in their life and the need to respect the elders, teach the children, and set forth time when families can be together (Hasan, 2001). Islam requires segregation of the sexes in

---

[1]Jennifer Livengood contributed to writing this section.

most aspects of life. Since men and women are not allowed to mingle, marriage partners have traditionally been chosen by the parents of the bride and groom (Maqsood, 1994; Renard, 2002). Muslim men are allowed to have more than one wife; however, this is not encouraged. Men who have more than one wife are expected to treat the wives equally. Islam prohibits consumption of alcohol or drugs, promotes self-control, and requires its followers to pray five times a day (Hasan, 2001).

The majority of Muslim women veil themselves in accordance with their country's or family's interpretation of the Qur'an's command of modesty (Renard, 2002). The Qur'an does not specify that women should veil, but it does say that women should dress modestly at all times (Renard). The various types of head or full-body coverings include hijab (a veil that covers only the hair), krimar (a veil that covers hair and breasts), nikab (face veil used in addition to krimar), and burqa (full-body and face covering) (Walseth & Fasting, 2003).

A Muslim Understanding of Leisure[2]

According to Ibrahim (1982), Islam does not have an official stance on leisure, although religious texts such as the Hadith and the Qur'an suggest a favorable attitude toward free-time activities. Interestingly, unlike Hebrew scripture, the Qur'an does not seem to mention the seventh day that is to be devoted to rest. Martin and Mason (2004) quoted Surah 32, which states, "Allah it is Who created the heavens and the earth, and that which is between them, in six Days. Then He mounted the throne" (p. 6). However, three activities, namely swimming, shooting, and horseback riding, are specifically mentioned in the Hadith. Moreover, Muhammad is reported in religious texts to have raced with his wife. These verses have inspired many Muslims to participate in similar sporting activities (Ibrahim; Walseth & Fasting, 2003). In contemporary times, however, hunting has lost its popularity to sports such as

soccer, basketball, tennis, handball, and horse racing (Ibrahim).

The Qur'an also makes special references to health and instructs Muslims to take special care of their bodies. One of the Hadiths states, "Your body has certain needs that you have to fulfill" (Walseth & Fasting, p. 52). This statement has been interpreted by some Muslims as direct encouragement to take part in leisure and active physical recreation. In addition, in another Hadith, the Prophet is recorded as saying, "There is a time for this [serious endeavors] and a time for that [play and leisure pursuits]" (Walseth & Fasting, p. 53) and "Recreate your hearts hour after hour for the tired hearts go blind" (Ibrahim, p. 200). Martin and Mason (2004) also quoted Qur'anic references to travel and, in particular, to the fact that Muslims are encouraged to travel to appreciate the greatness of God and that pilgrimage should be not only a religious but also a cultural encounter. However, importantly, Martin and Mason also emphasized that while the Qur'an mentions many leisure and sport activities in a positive light (halal), others, such as drinking and gambling, are considered unacceptable (haram). Moreover, some of the generally halal (acceptable) leisure and sport activities may be unacceptable for women if they cause them to violate recommendations related to modesty in dress and behavior. In most Islamic countries, women who wear appropriately modest attire are encouraged to participate in sporting activities.

Islam also emphasizes the importance of maintaining good physical condition in preparation for war. In fact, one sura (verse) in the Qur'an states, "Against them make ready all your strength to the outmost of your power"; and in a Hadith, the Prophet Muhammad says, "A strong Muslim is better and more beloved by God than a weak one, but both are good" (Walseth & Fasting, 2003, p. 53). Sites for recreation are also specifically mentioned in the Qur'an and Hadith where the Paradise is compared to a garden. Gardens, however, have been available only to the wealthy in Muslim countries, as very few parks, gardens, and open spaces have been established in major

[2]Jennifer Livengood contributed to writing this section.

urban centers due to space-related constraints (Ibrahim, 1982).

According to Ibrahim (1982), there are different times and holidays during which Muslims can recreate. Friday, as the holy day in the Muslim calendar, dictates a distinctive pattern of Muslim weekend that usually starts on Thursday afternoon (Martin & Mason, 2004). Before Friday prayers, Muslims often gather to eat, attend movies, and drink coffee. Additionally, the time following Friday prayers is often set aside for playing games and socializing (Ibrahim). Holidays also provide a means for observances as well as recreation. Feasts and socializing accompany regular observances during holidays such as Eid al Fitr, which marks the end of the Ramadan, and Eid al Adha (Feast of the Sacrifice), which takes place at the time of the Hajj. According to

Participation in sporting activities by Muslim women is encouraged and acceptable as long as recommendations for modest attire are followed.

Chai v.d. Laage/Imago/Icon SMI

Ibrahim, a particular lifestyle accompanies the entire month of Ramadan, when people do not work the full day and gather at cafés to socialize and watch TV in the evening. Martin and Mason also noted the importance of celebrations that involve socialization, music, and dancing and that accompany rites of passage such as birth, circumcision, and marriage.

The Leisure of Muslims in North America

In comparison to the scholarship on other ethnic and racial minority groups in the United States and Canada, the literature on leisure behavior of Muslims is rather scarce. One source is a series of longitudinal studies on second-generation South Asian teens and young adults in Canada conducted by Tirone (1999), Tirone and Shaw (1997), Tirone and Pedlar (2000), and Tirone and Goodberry (2011). Tirone and her colleagues observed that although leisure of South Asian teens resembled leisure behavior of their peers from dominant cultural groups, immigrant adolescents spent much of their free time with parents and siblings and stressed the central role of family in other aspects of life. According to Tirone (1999), membership in South Asian social clubs was central to the continuity of religious traditions and provided activities for children and teens such as sports, dances, and festivals. Parents encouraged their children to participate in activities organized by ethnic clubs, which constituted an appropriate social environment for teens to meet people of similar religious and cultural backgrounds and thus lowered chances that teens would develop friendships outside of the ethnic community. The third phase of Tirone and Goodberry's study confirmed that family and ethnic traditions remained central in the lives of South Asian young adults. The participants were closely connected to their parents, siblings, and extended family members and were appreciative of these connections. Participation in ethnic leisure facilitated young adults' ability to maintain ties to their heritage and their cultural group, as well as to develop bicultural or multicultural Indo-Canadian identity. However, belonging to an ethnic group often meant that young South Asian Canadians were obligated to participate in certain activities, and those obligations led to conflict in their lives.

Stodolska and Livengood (2006) examined the effects of religious beliefs on the leisure behavior of immigrant Muslims from Israel, Jordan, Lebanon, Iraq, Egypt, Tunisia, Algeria, Turkey, Pakistan, India, Mexico, and Korea. Their findings showed that the effects of Islam on leisure behavior manifested themselves through the emphasis on strong family ties and on family-oriented leisure, the need to teach and supervise children, and the need to pass traditional moral values on to subsequent generations. Muslims interviewed in their study also commented on the requirement of modesty in dress, speech, and everyday behavior, as well as the restrictions on mixed-gender interactions, dating, food, and alcohol. The study confirmed that the community under study was collectivistic, that Muslim families were united by strong ties, and that the majority of leisure engagements occurred in the family context. This and other studies on the topic have corroborated the family-oriented character of leisure engagements among Muslims and the fact that much of the general socializing takes place in gender-segregated groups (Martin & Mason, 2004). Parents also reported scrutinizing their children's peers, monitoring their free time, encouraging them to stay at home, blocking inappropriate TV channels, and arranging for chaperones to accompany teenagers during mixed-gender meetings. Some Muslim parents also intentionally used leisure to limit their children's interactions with their mainstream friends to protect them from unwanted influences of American culture. Parents would make sure that the free time of children was occupied, preferably with participation in leisure- and sport-oriented clubs organized by local mosques and secular Islamic organizations. Thus, the findings confirmed concerns of not only immigrant Muslim parents, but also of parents of children residing in Islamic countries, about the impacts of the global media on traditional behavior patterns and the possible undermining of traditional teachings of Islam (Martin & Mason).

Studies have also shown that when Arab Muslims emigrate to the United States and Canada, their leisure behavior undergoes certain important changes. For instance, watching television and other sedentary activities become more prominent in Arab lives after immigration, and their rates of participation in exercise decrease (Abu-Laban & Abu-Laban, 1999; Hassoun, 1999). Abu-Laban and Abu-Laban (1999) found that the most popular form of recreation among Arab Canadian youth was watching television. Constant exposure to the American mass media made immigrant teenagers aware of the negative stereotypes of the Arab culture deeply embedded in Western societies.

The Arab culture is collectivistic and centered around the father in a patrilineal line of hierarchy (Abu-Laban & Abu-Laban, 1999). According to Triandis (1995), in collectivistic cultures such as the one shared by Arabs, group needs have priority over individual needs; people define themselves in terms of their group and focus on norms and appropriate behaviors pertaining to that specific group. This collectivistic culture of Arab immigrants is exposed to significant pressures when confronted with the more individualistic and independent family organization typical of American society (Abu-Laban et al.). Despite these differences, however, Arab Muslim families have been shown to maintain collectivistic and family-centered relationships over successive generations.

Constraints on Leisure of Muslims

A number of studies highlighted constraints on leisure faced by Muslim minority members. The results of studies by Carrington and colleagues (1987), Glyptis (1985), and Taylor and Hegarty (1985) suggested that South Asian immigrant girls in the United Kingdom were significantly constrained in many of their leisure pursuits. In particular, their participation in out-of-home activities and sports was restricted due to the lack of parental approval, strict dress codes, inadequate availability of single-sex facilities, and their religious beliefs. Results of a longitudinal study by Tirone (1999; Tirone & Goodberry, 2011) also suggested that due to pressures from parents to remain at home and to conform to traditional cultural practices, Muslim students in Canada experienced more challenges than youth of other religious backgrounds (S. Tirone, personal communication, February 15, 2003). The Hindu, Sikh, and Christian students had more freedom to pursue their desired education than Muslim teens; moreover, their families seemed to be more tolerant of their desire to make decisions regarding friends and marriage partners.

Livengood and Stodolska (2004) identified a number of factors that affected the leisure of Muslim Americans. Their leisure activities had to be modest; they could not involve violence, foul language, or nudity. Moreover, Muslims were prohibited from frequenting establishments that served alcohol and were not allowed to eat certain foods (haram). The necessity to obey husbands and restrictions on mixed-gender interactions, including those related to sport participation and dating, also significantly influenced their leisure behavior. The restrictions on dating and mixed-gender interactions appeared to pose the most problems for Muslims who immigrated at a younger age and who were immersed in the American high school culture that involved dating and attending parties. Islam also imposed certain restrictions on the travel of women, as they were not allowed to travel without a male relative. However, many Muslim women interviewed in this study did not seem to perceive these restrictions as constraints; instead they saw the deeper moral value behind the choices that their religion obliged them to make. As a result, Stodolska and Livengood cautioned against labeling certain restrictions as "constraints" in cross-cultural research.

Experiences with discrimination have also been identified in a number of studies. For instance, Tirone's (1997, 1999; Tirone & Goodberry, 2011) research provided many examples of racism endured by Muslim adolescents in settings such as schools, recreation programs, YMCAs, summer camps, and competitive sport activities. Discriminatory acts were particularly prevalent against Muslim girls who were ridiculed for wearing traditional Muslim clothing and whose religion prevented them from wearing shorts

as required during physical education classes. Problems encountered during sport participation, such as lack of sensitivity on the part of coaches to the fact that Muslim students were required to fast during the month of Ramadan, caused some teenagers to withdraw from sporting competitions. Tirone and Goodberry, however, showed an evolution of views on racism and discrimination among the young adults in their study. The discourse among young Muslim women regarding racism was cautious, and they actively sought ways to engage people in resolving intercultural conflicts rather than resorting to accusations of discrimination.

Similarly to Tirone's studies, Dagkas and Benn's (2006) research touched on the issue of discrimination and other constraints to physical education participation among Muslim immigrants. These studies showed certain differences in how Muslim women experienced physical education classes in Great Britain and Greece. Dagkas and Benn found that Muslim girls in the British school system felt more constrained in their physical education participation than their counterparts in the Greek school system. The authors attributed this, at least in part, to differences in school policies and practice; "the meeting of religious requirements was more problematic in the British [system] than the Greek [system]" (p. 32). In particular, they focused on the influence of teachers whose attitudes toward Islam and Muslims contributed to different experiences of Greek and British female Muslim physical education students.

Contrary to earlier studies by Tirone (1999; Tirone & Goodberry, 2011) and by Dagkas and Benn (2006), Doherty and Taylor's (2007) research on Canadian teens showed that they did not experience any significant constraints on physical education participation and that their teachers and coaches were quite understanding when it came to their religious observances and dress codes. In a study of sport and physical recreation's role in the process of "fitting in" of young immigrants to Canada, female Muslim students did not indicate that their cultural background or religion had imposed any constraints on their ability to take part in sport and physical recreation (Doherty & Taylor). They did not feel particularly constrained by their clothing requirements or by any limits on participation in co-ed groups. The authors attributed this to the fact that the students' schools were accommodating of cultural and religious practices and that, for example, teachers and coaches provided alternative activities when Muslim youth were fasting.

The issue of discrimination as a constraint on leisure was also examined by Livengood and Stodolska (2004). Their results showed that in the wake of the September 11 attacks, discrimination affected leisure of Muslim immigrants in the United States by restricting the range of available leisure options and coparticipants; by affecting their willingness to participate in leisure; and by restricting freedom of movement, travel, timing, and location of activities. Most of the discrimination experienced by Muslim Americans was nonviolent; it included unfriendly looks, verbal abuse, and social isolation. Muslim women experienced more hostility than men since their visibly different dress style and head covering made their religion and ethnic background known to outsiders. Muslims employed a number of negotiation strategies to deal with discrimination, including being vigilant and conscious of their surroundings, walking in groups, attempting to blend in, restricting air travel, and modifying travel patterns.

Cultural differences and discrimination seem to be related to the neighborhoods in which American and Canadian Muslim immigrants reside. For instance, Cainkar's (1999) study on the Muslim Arab community in Chicago suggested that the majority of Arab immigrants negatively perceived overall conditions in their neighborhood. They complained about the lack of security and feared harassment on the part of the general public and local police. Crime, gang activity, and prevalence of drugs also contributed to the negative perception of the neighborhood. Since the neighborhood was seen as a hostile environment, parents demanded that their children, especially girls, stay close to home. At the same time, some Arab immigrants felt that their lack of language skills, cultural barriers, and experiences of outright hostility kept them from frequenting establishments beyond the borders of their ethnic

enclave. According to Georgeski (1987), Arab immigrants felt that they were not fully accepted by the mainstream American society and that they were forced to consolidate their efforts to help the local Arab community.

LEISURE AMONG JEWS

The discussion of leisure among Jews begins with demographic information about Jews around the world and in North America, then proceeds to explore a Jewish understanding of leisure. Next, empirical research is presented on various facets of Jewish leisure in North America: Sabbath; leisure attitudes and preferences, travel, sport, and community recreation.

Jews Around the World and in North America

The world's Jewish population is estimated to be around 13.5 million people, including 7.7 million from the Diaspora living outside of the state of Israel (DellaPergola, 2010). This *core* Jewish population includes all persons who identify themselves as Jewish and do not have another monotheistic religion. It does not, however, include "persons of Jewish ancestry who profess another monotheistic religion, other non-Jews of Jewish ancestry, and other non-Jews who may be interested in Jewish matters" (DellaPergola, p. 5).

Two countries, Israel and the United States, account for about 82% of the world's Jewish population. The remaining 18% is dispersed in countries such as France, Canada, United Kingdom, and the Russian Federation. The world's Jewish population is overwhelmingly urban. In fact, more than half of Jews live in only five metropolitan areas, including Tel Aviv, New York, Jerusalem, Los Angeles, and Haifa. Other major metropolitan centers with large concentrations of Jewish population include the greater Miami area (Miami–Dade, Broward, and Palm Beach counties), Be'er Sheva, San Francisco, Paris, Chicago, and Philadelphia (DellaPergola, 2010).

Jews who reside in the United States include American citizens of the Jewish faith or Jewish ethnicity. The U.S. Census Bureau (2009a) estimated the population of Americans who adhere to Judaism at 5.13 million, or 1.7% of the total population. If those who identify themselves culturally as Jewish but do not follow the Jewish faith were included, this number would increase to 6.49 million (U.S. Census Bureau, 2009b). Sheskin and Dashevsky (2011) estimated the size of the American Jewish community at 6.59 million in 2011. These numbers roughly align with those of the U.S. Religious Landscape Survey conducted by the Pew Research Center (2007), which estimates that people of Jewish faith constitute 1.7% of the adult American population and are divided into Reform (0.7%), Conservative (0.5%), Orthodox (less than 0.3%), and Other (less than 0.3%). In 2006 in Canada, 315,000 Census respondents declared Jewish ethnicity (DellaPergola, 2010); and in 2011, a total of 329,500 declared Jewish religion (Statistics Canada, 2013).

The history of Jewish migration to the United States dates back to the 17th century when a small number of Sephardic Jews of Spanish and Portuguese ancestry arrived in the country. Larger-scale immigration did not start until the mid-19th century and particularly during the 1880s, when large numbers of Ashkenazi Jews from present-day Germany, the Russian Federation, Belarus, Poland, Ukraine, Lithuania, Czech Republic, and Hungary immigrated to the United States (Hertzberg, 1997; Sachar, 1993). These immigrants were mainly Yiddish-speaking, rural residents who were escaping religious persecutions and economic hardships in East Central Europe. Between the late 19th century and 1924, when the Immigration Act of 1924 restricted immigration, some 2 million Jews arrived in the United States.

Today, the American Jewish community comprises mainly Ashkenazi Jews who immigrated from Central and Eastern Europe before World War II and their descendants. Jews of other origins, including Ashkenazi and Sephardic immigrants from Israel and other countries, are also present. Overall, the American Jewish community is quite diverse and includes people of various traditions and types of religious observance. According to DellaPergola (2010), 41% of U.S. Jews live in the Northeast, 26% in the South, 21% in the West, and 12% in the Midwest. More than half (51%) of the Jewish population is over 50 years old, and 95% are white non-Hispanic. The Jewish American population in general has a very high socioeconomic status: 46% have incomes over $100,000, 35% have postgraduate degrees, and 24% have college degrees. Interestingly, 72% of Jews in the United States have no children living with them in the same household (as compared to 61% of Catholics and 53% of Muslims) (DellaPergola). It is generally estimated that the size of the Jewish American population is stagnant or decreasing.

A Jewish Understanding of Leisure

Rabbi Norman Lamm (n.d.) suggested that "one cannot speak of the Jewish view of leisure," (n.p.) but that it is possible to sketch a rough outline of a Jewish leisure ethic. According to Lamm, Jews should balance work and leisure, in the right proportion, as an act of imitating God, who both worked and rested. Work, understood as creative changes to nature, is viewed as a necessity rather than a blessing. Work is not an autonomous virtue, and other activities, such as the study of Torah, are of higher value than work.

As the Sabbath scriptures command the Jewish people not to work on the Sabbath, a central point of Sabbath is refraining from work. However, a corollary of abstaining from work is rest, which was created on the seventh day and is the culmination of creation. Thus, in addition to the pattern of six days of work and a seventh-day Sabbath, the concept of "menucha" or "Sabbath rest" is "paradigmatic for leisure in general, and . . . may serve as model for an ethic of leisure" (Lamm, n.d.). The Jewish understanding is that the six days were created for the Sabbath—not the Sabbath for the other six days. The other six days are a preparation for the Sabbath, which is the purpose of the entire week. On the Sabbath, the creative energies that were focused on changing nature during the rest of the week are now focused on oneself, intellectually and spiritually. Thus, menucha is a model of leisure, defined as "creativity turned in on oneself," and the ideal use of leisure is for the study of Torah (Lamm, n.d.). This turning in on oneself is further explained by Waskow (1995):

It is clear that Shabbat, and the Jewish way of resting is not just a matter of pushing the off switch. Something deeper happens. . . . We get to reflect—to turn back and look at ourselves in the mirror of a time of quiet. (p. 377)

This turning and reflecting makes Jewish time a spiral rather than a straight line or a circle, as each period of turning and reflecting is a turn on the spiral, a turn inward or outward or upward or forward.

Shivers (1977) suggested that the commandment to work six days and rest on the seventh day ensures a twofold sanctification of leisure for every Jew: there is leisure to rest from tiresome work and leisure to worship, pray, and contemplate. Likewise, Heintzman (2006a) documented how the biblical concept of Sabbath provides insights for both quantitative and qualitative dimensions of leisure. First, the Sabbath teaches a rhythm to life, including periods of work and periods of nonwork (i.e., a quantitative dimension similar to the free-time concept of leisure—time free from work). Second, in terms of the qualitative dimension, the Sabbath inculcates a spiritual attitude regarding a person's basic position in relation to God through rest, joy, freedom, and celebration in God and the gift of God's creation. Thus, the Sabbath is a time of no work but also a time of celebration, "not a date but an atmosphere" (Heschel, 1951, p. 21). Therefore, the Jewish view goes beyond a quantitative free-time understanding of leisure to include a qualitative dimension (Heintzman, 2006a).

While it is often suggested that the roots of the Western concept of leisure are in ancient Greek society, some argue that the concept is equally rooted in the ancient Jewish tradition of the Sabbath with its organization of life into seven days and a valuing of leisure (Crabtree, 1982; Trafton, 1985; cf. Heintzman, 2006b). Trafton (1985) noted that the concept of leisure grew from roots in ancient Hebrew, Greek, and Roman civilizations, going so far as to say that leisure "is primarily Hebrew and Christian" (p. 28). Trafton's argument was based on the Genesis account of God's rest on the seventh day of the Judeo–Christian account of creation, life in the Garden of Eden, and the

Sabbath commandment to do no work on the seventh day. He claimed that these ancient traditions have contributed to the organization of life into seven days and a valuing of leisure. For Gordis (1982), Sabbath not only was the cornerstone and capstone of Jewish life but also provided a more democratic form of leisure than in Greek society. Aristotle's leisure was based on the ancient Greek institution of slavery, whereas the Jewish Torah declared that everyone, including male and female servants, had an inalienable right to Sabbath. Similarly, Shivers (1977) noted that historically only the Jewish culture declared the necessity of universal leisure. As Waskow (1995) has noted, the biblical tradition of the Jewish people has two strands of thinking about Sabbath: one related to cosmic rhythms of time based on the process of creation, and the other as an expression of human dignity, equality, justice, and freedom. These two strands are complementary and intertwined rather than contradictory.

Crabtree (1982) documented that the ideal concept of rest in ancient Israel supported a holistic view of leisure that involved components of time, activity, place, attitude, and state of being. The time component included several periods of time observed by the Israelites (i.e., Sabbath day, Sabbath year, Year of Jubilee). Activities included Israel's seven feasts (e.g., Passover), national holidays and festivals that focused on Israel's relationship with God, and associated rest. In terms of geographical place, rest was associated with the experience of settlement, peaceful respite from war, and the presence of God in the Promised Land. The experiences of time, activity, and place gave rise to an attitude of faith and reverence for God that enhanced a physical and spiritual rest or "state of being" manifested at the individual, family, and societal levels. Crabtree observed that this rest was a utopian ideal, which although attainable, was not always actualized, especially at the family and societal levels.

The Leisure of Jews in North America

In a 1977 essay on the contemporary Jewish attitude toward leisure, Shivers suggested that the Jewish population in United States is heterogeneous as a consequence of numerous factors, such as social, political, vocational, economic, educational, age, ethnic heritage, and regional differences, and thus "there can be no statement about the contemporary Jewish attitude to leisure. There can only be a collection of attitudes about leisure" (p. 69). Nevertheless, Shivers claimed that for contemporary American Jews, leisure is almost universally viewed favorably as a time of opportunity, an undeniable good, and a reward rather than a distasteful necessity or a punishment. Thus, there is an attitude of anticipation and positive acceptance with regard to leisure.

Sabbath

Using the Jewish Sabbath as an alternative leisure paradigm, Bundt (1981) investigated the leisure of American Jews using a two-stage research methodology. First, a modified form of Flanagan's critical incident analysis technique was used to identify Sabbath activities and emotional states. Second, a survey questionnaire was used with a stratified random sample of Jews to explore whether Sabbath was a paradigm for leisure. The results suggested that the Jewish Sabbath seemed to be an alternative leisure paradigm in that it presented a pattern or model of leisure focused on the calendar rather than a person's perceived need to rest.

Semantic differential profiles of the words "Sabbath," "leisure," and "work" showed that

- in general, "Sabbath" and "leisure" were described similarly,
- the descriptions of "Sabbath" and "leisure" were more precise than the descriptions of "work," and
- definitions of the three concepts were more on a continuum than antithetical.

Observance of the Sabbath was influenced by the following:

1. the religiosity of the participant's home,
2. the degree of Sabbath observance in the home where the participant grew up,
3. the Jewish education the participant received as an adult,

4. the participant's perception of a positive relationship between Sabbath and leisure, and
5. the participant's awareness of the moral guidance in leisure.

Observance of the Sabbath was not correlated with age, but Jewish childhood education had a slight negative correlation with adult observance of the Sabbath. Bundt (1981) concluded that the Sabbath was the Jewish manifestation of leisure and that leisure, along with sociability and a "joy of celebration," was an important component in the promotion of the Sabbath. The Sabbath presented a paradigm that emphasized the equal value of leisure and work; and as both leisure and work could include any activity, it was necessary for work to be self-defined so that participants knew what they were resting from. This paradigm documented a leisure pattern based on the calendar instead of a participant's perception of his need to rest. The Sabbath was a complete 24-hour time period that balanced individual, family, and community activities.

Recently the importance of the Sabbath for coping with stress has been noted in both therapeutic and psychology literature. Goldberg (1986) argued that the Sabbath themes of balance between work and rest, individual and community, masculine and feminine, and doing and being are very relevant to promoting and maintaining mental and psychological health. Empirical studies are beginning to appear on the benefits of Sabbath keeping. Based on the assumption that the Sabbath's cyclical rhythm of activity and rest helps fulfill the human need for spiritual renewal, Earickson (2004) concluded that Sabbath keeping promoted spiritual well-being and psychological health. Anahalt (1987) investigated the relationship between stress and the Jewish Sabbath. Participants were categorized as observant or nonobservant with regard to Sabbath keeping. The two groups had similar levels of overall stress, weekday stress, and Sunday stress. However, the Sabbath-keeping group had significantly lower Saturday (Sabbath) stress as compared to their weekday stress, and also significantly decreased Saturday stress compared to the Saturday stress level of the nonobservant group.

Anahalt concluded that the Sabbath-keeping group experienced lower Saturday stress but that this decrease in stress did not influence weekday or Sunday stress levels. Research has also been conducted on the influence of Sabbath keeping on human relationships and functioning. Stern (2005) conducted a qualitative study on the meaning and nature of involvement in Jewish Sabbath religious ritual activities for persons with mild to moderate dementia, their family members, and the staff involved in their care. The results showed that meaningful Sabbath ritual activities rooted in retained long-term memories play a facilitative role in enabling meaningful engagements and sustaining personhood.

Leisure Attitudes and Preferences

Dravich (1980) investigated and compared the leisure attitudes of 153 Jewish and non-Jewish elderly individuals living in the Portland, Oregon, area. No statistically significant differences were discovered in attitudes toward spiritual, physical, mass media, intellectual, civic, and aesthetic activities, while differences were observed in attitudes toward touristic and social activities. For example, the Jewish participants disagreed with the statement "Every neighborhood does not need a community center" to a significantly greater extent than the non-Jewish participants. Jewish participants also showed greater agreement with the statement "Young and old people need more opportunities to mix with each other," while the non-Jewish participants disagreed with "Traveling is an upper-class pastime" to a significantly greater degree than the Jewish participants. As 39.6% of the Jewish participants were foreign born, in comparison to 5% of the non-Jewish population, a substudy compared American-born Jews with East European–born Jews. Significant differences between American-born and East European–born Jews were found for five of the 32 leisure attitude items.

Differences between American-born and East European–born elderly Jews were also discovered by Guttmann (1973) in a study of leisure-time activity interests of members of the Baltimore Jewish Community Center. American-born Jews were more interested in activities that expressed and emphasized their individuality, whereas East European–born Jews preferred activities characterized by belongingness to the group. Also, twice as many East European–born Jews (65%) as American-born Jews (32.5%) were interested in Hebrew and Yiddish cultural programs related to traditional Jewish life. Furthermore, while both groups were interested in celebrating Jewish holidays at the center, East European Jews had a much stronger interest (70%) in celebrating all religious holidays at the center than did the American-born Jews (35%), who preferred to celebrate only major holidays such as Purim and Passover at the center. These findings were relevant given the trend at the time toward an increase in American-born Jews and a decline in East European–born Jews.

Religious and Cultural Travel in the Jewish Culture

Even if born in the United States, many Jews travel to their ancestral homelands. In an investigation of the travel patterns of American Jews, Ioannides and Cohen Ioannides (2004) concluded that both orthodox and secular Jews in the United States exhibit a strong desire "to reaffirm their cultural identity" (p. 107) despite increasing assimilation into the larger population (e.g., suburbanization, intermarriage) and secularization. As Judaism devotes much attention to historical events and remembrance rather than to special meanings of specific holy sites, it does not have major holy spaces beyond Jerusalem. Therefore, much of the travel by American Jews may be considered "modern-day pilgrimages," characterized by a nostalgia toward places associated with Jewish culture rather than a traditional religious form of visiting and praying at sacred sites. Their travel behavior, in terms of where to go and what to do, appears to be determined by a persistent search by Jews for their past and cultural roots (Ioannides & Cohen Ioannides). As Jews have settled and resettled numerous times in different places, they have more than one homeland to return to; this situation is different than that for most other American ethnic groups (e.g., Italian, Greek). Whether in Israel, Europe, North America, or elsewhere, every place that has been associated with Judaism has the potential to be a destination for Jewish travelers: museums exhibiting religious or secular Jewish artifacts, the death camps of the Holocaust, Jerusalem, synagogues and graveyards, homes of famous Jewish personalities, old Jewish neighborhoods, and the countries their ancestors came from (Ioannides & Cohen Ioannides). For example, 100,000 American and Israeli Jews annually visit Poland, viewing the wartime ghetto and Nazi death camps (Green, as cited in Ioannides & Cohen Ioannides). Travel to such places brings American Jews closer in a cultural sense, not necessarily a spiritual–religious sense, "to what it means to be Jewish" (Ioannides & Cohen Ioannides, p. 108).

Sport

Another component of Jewish leisure is sport. Throughout the 20th century, baseball was not only a feature of Jewish American popular culture but a cultural love story (Solomon, 1994, 2007). Solomon suggested five reasons for American Jews' strong interest in baseball. First, baseball offered immigrants an excellent means of acculturation and assimilation. Second, baseball, with its statistical and historical records, appealed to "the argumentative, dialectical Jewish intellect, trained in close reading of historical texts, past influencing present" (Solomon, 2007, p. 2). Third, since Jewish parents objected to their sons' playing professional baseball, the sons, while entering professional occupations, "often turned to popular cultural substitutions for becoming players to artistically re-creating baseball's beauties, conflicts, and narratives, combining nostalgia (memoir) and characters (fictions)" (Solomon, 2007, p. 2). Fourth, baseball had become an urban game, and many Jewish youth associated their city life with their baseball allegiances. Fifth, the game was very American yet similar to many cultural memories of Jewish European history—"rich in folklore, deep in mythology, full of anecdotes, Kabbalistic in its numerology, quasi-religious in its gods ('immortals' in a Hall of Fame)" (Solomon, 2007, pp. 2-3). Thus, baseball provided a way into American ceremony, rituals, traditions, history, society, culture, and secular religion, as well as a community and rituals such as crosstown rivalries, the World Series, and Opening Day (Solomon, 1994). The game also gave a focal point to Jewish immigrants, who came to the United States more prepared to adapt to the American way of life than Italian Catholics, who intended to return home, or British Protestants, who discovered little need to change. As Solomon (1994) wrote,

> . . . baseball was a substitute for the *shtetl*—a center of perception and community with strong cultural traditions, psychological sanctions, and emotional commitments—and the *shul,* a center of belief and ritual. Thus to know and love baseball was to know and love America. (p. 78)

Community Recreation

Sport is only one leisure activity of Jewish people; other activities are provided by Jewish organizations. The Jewish Community Center Association (JCAA) is the coordinating organization for the Jewish Community Center (JCC) movement that includes more than 350 Jewish Community Centers, Young Men's and Young Women's Hebrew Associations (YMWAs and YWHAs), and camps throughout North America (JCCA, n.d.). The association "offers a wide range of services and resources to help its affiliates to provide educational, cultural, social, Jewish identity building, and recreational programs for people of all ages and backgrounds" (JCAA, n.d.). The first YMHA was opened in 1854 in Baltimore to offer support to Jewish immigrants, to facilitate Jewish continuity, and to create a space for celebration. Subsequently, other associations in the form of settlement houses, cultural centers, and libraries were established. In the late 19th century, JCCs and YMHAs assisted Jewish immigrants in adapting to their new life by providing English instruction, helping with acculturation to unfamiliar mores and customs, and enabling them to fully participate in civic opportunities and duties. These acculturation activities continued into the 20th century under the direction of the Jewish Welfare Federation (JWF), which was the national association of JCCs and YMHAs and YWHAs. A good example is in Indianapolis, where, beginning in 1920, the JWF offered "a series of carefully managed recreational and educational activities that emphasized proper public behavior and self-reliance and attempted to ease the city's most recent Jewish immigrants into the urban culture of Indianapolis" (Moss, 2007, p. 40). The JWF leaders were fearful, on the one hand, of the old-country ways and cultural isolation of immigrant Jews that made them feel out of place in the United States and, on the other hand, of the dangers of uncontrolled Americanization. The provision of leisure in JWF spaces introduced Jewish immigrants to American culture on the JWF's terms (Moss).

In response to increased prosperity, with more disposable income and leisure time as well as a movement of Jews to the suburbs in the 1950s and 1960s, the JCCs built large, modern facilities in suburban locations to provide recreational opportunities and other new programs such as informal education, programs for seniors, sports and athletics, nursery schools, performing and fine arts, teen travel camps, and day camps. JCCs have also facilitated Jewish cultural events and celebrations, including communal Hanukkah parties, film festivals, and book fairs. The JCC movement strives to support Jewish education, community, and culture as well as enabling and encouraging Jews of all backgrounds and ages to participate in the joys of Jewish living (JCCA).

CONCLUSION

As this overview of research on leisure among Christian, Muslim, and Jewish minorities in the United States and Canada shows, contemporary minority religious populations in these countries are very heterogeneous in terms of their socioeconomic, ethnic, and cultural backgrounds, as well as their types of religious observance—although specific religious groups often overlap with ethnic, cultural, and racial groups (e.g., the Black church). Despite these significant differences, certain important similarities can be noted with regard to attitudes toward leisure and recreation behavior patterns.

First, scriptural references to the act of creation and rest impose a distinct pattern on leisure behavior of Christians, Muslims, and Jews (e.g., rest, relaxation, and religious observance on Friday, Saturday, or Sunday). Moreover, followers of these faiths participate in numerous leisure activities associated with celebration of major religious holidays. Leisure is also almost universally viewed favorably by the followers of Christianity, Islam, and Judaism as an opportunity for rejuvenation, self-improvement, meditation, and connection with the divine. The extant research shows that religion is closely tied to the preservation of culture and traditional ways of life among religious minority groups in the United States and Canada. Strong family and community orientation among minority Christians, Muslims, and Jews is also apparent. The differences among these populations stem from their immigration status (first-generation immigrants vs. people who have resided in the host country for generations), their level of integration into the mainstream American and Canadian societies, and attitudes on the part of the mainstream toward the outward signs of observance of their faith and culture.

Unfortunately, the review also indicates the significant underdevelopment of research on leisure behavior among minority religious groups in the United States and Canada. The existing studies are few and far between; many of them are dated, and offer an incomplete understanding of the effects of faith and religious practice on leisure behavior of religious groups. However, this scarcity of research also offers a great opportunity for future scholars of leisure, religion, and ethnicity. It is the authors' hope that more researchers will examine both historical and contemporary intersections between religious faith and observance and leisure attitudes and behaviors among minority groups in the United States and Canada, and that religious beliefs will be incorporated into future examinations of leisure experiences of ethnic minorities.

PART III

Topics and Issues in Leisure Behavior

This part of the book examines specific topics and issues related to leisure behavior of ethnic and racial minorities, including leisure needs and motivations, leisure constraints, and discrimination in leisure contexts. Chapter 9 provides a comprehensive review of research on racial and ethnic similarities and differences in needs and motivations, as well as identifying specific leisure research areas and topics in need of further study. Chapter 10 provides an overview of the types of leisure constraints and the theoretical frameworks used to examine constraints. Further, it examines leisure constraints that are particularly relevant to racial and ethnic minorities and applies a constraints framework to management issues related to serving racially and ethnically diverse groups. Chapter 11 examines how discrimination operates in leisure contexts and analyzes the roles of discrimination in shaping the leisure experiences of racial and ethnic minorities.

CHAPTER 9

Leisure Needs and Motivations

Gordon J. Walker

OVERVIEW

Researchers have uncovered much about needs and motivations in general—what "pushes" people to do what they do—but far less is known about the needs and motives underlying leisure participation in particular. This chapter begins by discussing needs (e.g., autonomy, competence, relatedness) and motivations (e.g., intrinsic, extrinsic), and then explains how the two are related (e.g., self-determination theory; Deci & Ryan, 1985; Neulinger, 1981). Next is a comprehensive review of research on racial and ethnic similarities and differences in needs, motivations, and explanatory frameworks. A final section identifies specific leisure research areas or topics that are in need of further study.

Learning Outcomes

After reading this chapter, readers will be able to

- define what needs and motivations are, describe how they are linked to each other, and identify their effects on leisure participation;
- examine how needs and motivations may be similar and different across racial and ethnic groups; and
- explain how self-construal, as an intervening variable between race and ethnicity and needs and motivations, may affect leisure participation.

> *There is much to be gained from examining a wider range of dependent variables. In recent years there has been progress on this front. Researchers are beginning to consider ethnic variation in . . . motivations.*
>
> *Floyd, 1998 (p. 16)*

Many of this book's chapters pay considerable attention to how race and ethnicity affect leisure participation. After reading about this topic numerous times, one might ask "But *why* do people participate in leisure activities?" One way researchers have tried to answer this question is by identifying the various needs and motivations that "push" people to engage in such behaviors. To explain why leisure activities sometimes vary across (and even within) groups, an appreciation of what needs and motives entail and an understanding of the different types of each are necessary. Also necessary is an awareness of what Markus and Kitayama (1991) called self-construal—a concept that focuses on how a person perceives himself in relation to other people—and how this perception may differ across groups. Once this base has been built, a fuller understanding of how race and ethnicity affect self-construal, how self-construal affects needs and motivations, and how needs and motivations affect leisure participation is possible.[1]

NEEDS

As Kleiber, Walker, and Mannell (2011) noted, needs are commonly divided into those that have their basis in people's inherited biological nature (i.e., physiological needs, such as rest, thirst, and hunger) and those that people learn through interaction with the social environment (i.e., psychological needs). Early researchers often tried to identify all psychological needs, with Murray (1938), for example, listing, among others, achievement, affiliation, aggression, autonomy, deference, dominance, harm avoidance, nurturance, order, play, sex, and understanding. In con-

trast, later researchers often tried to ascertain the most important psychological needs (e.g., Fiske, 2003, 2004; Deci & Ryan, 1985, 2000) or, going one step further, also arrange them into some sort of framework (e.g., Kenrick, Griskevicius, Neuberg, & Schaller, 2010; Maslow, 1968; Schutte & Ciarlante, 1998). The remainder of this section focuses on social psychological research on core needs and needs hierarchies and related leisure research.

Core Needs

Not surprisingly, there is considerable debate among social psychologists about which needs are fundamental. Fiske (2003, 2004), for instance, believed there were five core needs: belonging, understanding, controlling, enhancing self, and trusting others. Deci and Ryan (1985, 2000) were even more succinct, holding that there are only three core needs: *autonomy* (which involves freedom to initiate one's behavior, typically through personal choice and control); *competence* (which involves effective functioning and, in turn, the desire to seek out and conquer ever bigger challenges); and *interpersonal relatedness* (which involves being loved by, understood by, and connected to others, as well as meaningfully involved with the broader social world) (Deci & Ryan, 1991). Ryan and Deci (2000) called this brief catalogue "basic needs theory."

Although the social psychologists mentioned up to this point considered core needs equally important across racial, ethnic, and cultural groups, there has been little research on this topic. An exception is a study (Sheldon, Elliot, Kim, & Kasser, 2001) that had American and South

---

[1]Some of the material in this chapter is based on, or builds on, the author's earlier work in Kleiber, Walker, and Mannell's (2011) *A Social Psychology of Leisure, Second Edition*. The reader is referred to that text for a more detailed discussion of needs and motivations; self-construal; and cross-ethnic, cross-racial, and cross-cultural similarities and differences in leisure.

Korean college students rate 10 theorized core needs. With the American students, self-esteem was rated highest, followed by interpersonal relatedness, autonomy, and competence (tied for second place), followed by pleasure/stimulation, physical thriving, self-actualization/meaning, security, and popularity/influence (tied for fifth place), with luxury coming in last. Although self-esteem's first-place rating initially appears to conflict with Deci and Ryan's (1985, 2000) proposition that autonomy, competence, and interpersonal relatedness are core psychological needs, Sheldon and colleagues observed that self-esteem is sometimes considered a component of competence. More importantly in this context, however, self-esteem was not identified as the most important need for the South Korean students. Rather, interpersonal relatedness was rated highest, followed by self-esteem in second place, with autonomy, competence, and pleasure/stimulation tied for third place.

These results suggest that even though autonomy, competence, and interpersonal relatedness (and possibly self-esteem) may in fact be core needs, the "push" to satisfy each—through leisure participation, for example—may differ across racial, ethnic, and cultural groups. Unfortunately, no studies have been conducted in the recreation and leisure field regarding this possibility. On the other hand, Walker and Wang (2009) had 35 Chinese Canadians respond to a watch alarm that was programmed to ring seven times a day for 12 days. When the alarm rang, participants reported what activity they were doing, whether it was work, leisure, both, or neither (Shaw, 1984), and how well their needs for autonomy, competence, and interpersonal relatedness were being satisfied. The researchers found that when people were alone, autonomy was satisfied the most during leisure and the least during neither work nor leisure (e.g., doing household chores, driving to work), whereas competence was satisfied the most during work and the least during neither work nor leisure. In contrast, when people were with others, autonomy and competence were satisfied the most during leisure and the least during work. These findings indicate that even though ethnic, racial, and cultural differences may exist, leisure still appears to play a key role in satisfying these needs.

Needs Hierarchies

Abraham Maslow (1968) famously espoused the idea that needs vary in importance. Maslow theorized that everyone strives to satisfy five need categories arranged in a hierarchy. At the lowest level are physiological needs, followed in order by safety and security needs, belongingness and love needs, ego and esteem needs, and self-actualization. Moreover, the levels of the needs hierarchy are not rigidly separated but overlap to some extent and once lower-level needs are satisfied, needs at the next highest level emerge and influence behavior. Maslow speculated that an average adult in the Western world had about 85% of her physiological needs satisfied, 70% of her safety needs, 50% of her social needs, 40% of her self-esteem needs, and 10% of her self-actualization needs. Though Maslow's framework is widely known, many social psychologists now view his "pyramid as a quaint visual artifact without much contemporary theoretical importance" (Kenrick et al., 2010, p. 292).

One reason for this perceptual change is that Maslow's (1968) ultimate need—self-actualization—reflects a very individualistic view of the world (Kenrick et al., 2010). Schutte and Ciarlante (1998), for example, suggested that a different hierarchy of needs may make more sense for more "collectivistic" people. According to these investigators, while physiological and safety and security needs are indeed innate, Maslow's other needs are more relevant for Westerners (e.g., people in the United States, Canada, Europe, Australia, and New Zealand) than for Asians (e.g., people in China, Japan, and Korea). Thus, the researchers proposed that Asians' top three needs are, from third to highest, affiliation, admiration, and status. Status, Schutte and Ciarlante contended, replaces self-actualization because it is socially directed whereas self-actualization is personally directed. This modification is consistent with some social psychologists' (Markus & Kitayama, 1991; Triandis, 1995) proposition that while the individual is primary in Western cultures, the group (e.g., immediate family, fellow employees) is primary in Asian cultures—an important point and one that the upcoming section on self-construal will address.

Unfortunately, as with Maslow's (1968) hierarchy, leisure research using Schutte and Ciarlante's (1998) framework is rare. A study of spa goers in Hong Kong is one exception, with Mak, Wong, and Chang (2009) identifying five underlying reasons Asian travelers visited these leisure facilities. Most important was "relaxation and relief," which the researchers interpreted in terms of satisfying Maslow's physiological need, a necessary condition before higher-level needs could be satisfied (Maslow, 1968). The second and third most important reasons were "escape" and "self-reward and indulgence," neither of which Mak and colleagues explained with regard to either needs hierarchy. They did, however, explicate their participants' fourth most important reason—"health and beauty"—in terms of satisfying both Maslow's physiological and Schutte and Ciarlante's admiration needs. In contrast, they did not mention either hierarchy when explaining their participants' fifth most important reason—

"friendship and kinship"—which is surprising given that this explanation appears consistent with both Maslow's belonging and Schutte and Ciarlante's affiliation needs. In summary, leisure research on needs hierarchies is scant, and this is especially true with regard to racial, ethnic, and cultural leisure research.

Needs and Leisure

One reason for this limited research is that, around the same time social psychologists were identifying basic needs and developing needs hierarchies, researchers in the recreation and leisure field were focusing on leisure-based needs. Two main inventories were created based on the idea that leisure activities can satisfy Deci and Ryan's (1985, 2000) three core psychological needs (i.e., autonomy, competence, and interpersonal relatedness), as well as a number of other often "expressed" needs. First, Tinsley and Kass (1978) proposed that the 44 needs they identified could

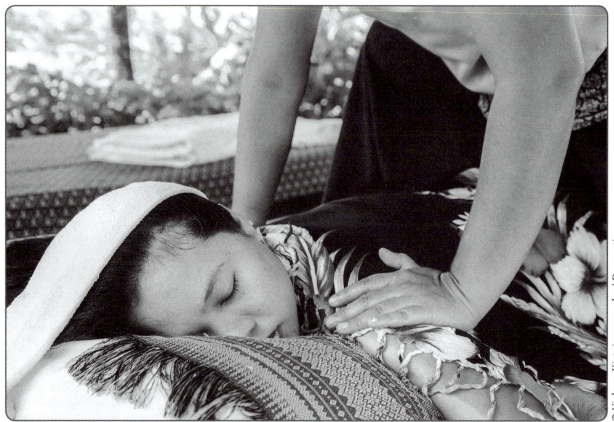

© Vichaya Kiatying-angsulee | Dreamstime.com

In a 2009 study, participants' "health and beauty" reason satisfied both Maslow's physiological and Schutte and Ciarlante's admiration needs.

be reduced to eight subtypes (i.e., self-expression, companionship, power, compensation, security, service, intellectual aestheticism, and solitude). Second, Driver (1976)—whose early research examined expressed needs before he both broadened his scope and began calling them recreation experience preferences (REP)—proposed 19 categories, including exploration, escaping role overload, general nature experience, introspection, exercise, being with similar people, seeking exhilaration, and escaping physical stressors (Manfredo, Driver, & Tarrant, 1996).

Unfortunately, there is little leisure research on how these core and expressed needs might vary across racial, ethnic, and cultural groups. In fact, only one study of core need satisfaction during leisure engagement was uncovered, and that examined White, Asian, and Black British exercisers (Edmunds, Duda, & Ntoumanis, 2010). Visual examination of the results indicated that Whites placed less importance on autonomy than members of the other two groups, whereas Asians placed greater importance on interpersonal relatedness than did Whites, with Blacks in between (competence was not measured). Caution regarding these findings is necessary, however, as statistical tests were not conducted to determine if these differences were indeed significant.

In comparison, four studies that examined expressed need satisfaction during leisure were identified. The first such study examined Anglo and Hispanic American anglers using REP (Hunt & Ditton, 2001). These researchers found, as they had hypothesized, that Anglo Americans placed greater importance on escaping individual stressors and being in a natural environment; but, contrary to their expectations, Hispanic Americans placed greater importance on achievement. A second study (Shaull & Gramann, 1998), also focused on Anglo and Hispanic Americans, and used REP to measure family cohesiveness and nature interaction. What is interesting about this investigation is that the researchers divided the Hispanic American group, based on "language acculturation," into three subgroups (i.e., least and most acculturated, with bicultural in between) before comparing them to an Anglo American group. They found that although there were no differences in nature interaction, bicultural

Hispanic Americans did rate the family variable higher than Anglo Americans. Winter, Jeong, and Godbey (2004) examined differences among Asian Americans (i.e., Chinese, Filipino, Japanese, and Korean Americans). Results of their study, again using REP, showed that the nature-based category was rated higher by Chinese Americans than by those in the other three groups, and the consumptive use and social interaction categories were rated higher by Chinese and Filipino Americans than by those in the other two groups. Finally, Walker, Deng, and Dieser (2001) not only measured four psychological needs using Driver's REP scales but also developed five new "social interdependence" (SI) scales based on Markus and Kitayama's (1991) need-related propositions. Walker and colleagues found, as expected, that Anglo North Americans rated REP autonomy/independence higher than Chinese North Americans whereas Chinese North Americans rated group membership and humility/modesty higher than Anglo North Americans.

It is also possible that certain needs may be construed differently by racial, ethnic, and cultural group members. In the case of control, for example, Weisz, Rothbaum, and Blackburn (1984) contended that there are actually two types of control: primary and secondary. Primary control occurs when individuals enhance their rewards by *influencing* existing realities. In contrast, secondary control occurs when individuals enhance their rewards by *accommodating* to existing realities. From a leisure perspective, Scherl's (1989) work provides nice examples of each. Specifically, in the case of primary control, some wilderness visitors want to demonstrate their power over nature (e.g., by cutting down trees to build a lean-to) whereas in the case of secondary control, other visitors prefer adjusting to nature (e.g., by covering their sleeping bags with fallen leaves).

Importantly, Weisz and colleagues (1984) also proposed that primary control is more common in Western industrialized countries whereas secondary control is more common in Asian, African, and Latin American countries. From a leisure perspective, this proposition suggests that racial, ethnic, and cultural groups might participate in the same activity but that their reasons for doing so might differ depending on which type of control is relevant for them. In a study of aerobics class participants, for example, Morling (2000) found that

> Americans were more likely to report that they choose classes based on convenience and that they change moves in class that are too difficult, a pattern that suggests primary control. Japanese were more likely to report that they choose classes based on their ability level, work harder when moves are too difficult and attribute mistakes to a lack of fit between their own ability and the level of the class, a pattern that suggests more secondary control. (p. 73)

In summary, in the same way that racial, ethnic, and cultural groups may do the same leisure activities differently depending on whether primary or secondary control is foremost, it also seems possible that they might participate in different activities for the same reason.

MOTIVATIONS

Although the terms needs and motivations are sometimes used interchangeably (e.g., Kenrick et al., 2010), Deci and Ryan's (1985, 2000) *self-determination theory* (SDT) makes clear that the two are not equivalent. SDT encompasses several mini-theories, including *basic needs theory* (which, as already discussed, holds that autonomy, competence, and interpersonal relatedness are core needs) and *organismic integration theory* (OIT). Organismic integration theory concerns how different motivations are organized with respect to one another.

According to OIT, individuals attempt to transform socially prescribed norms or standards into personally endorsed values or "self-regulations" (Deci & Ryan, 2000). This process, called internalization, is not a matter of either/or but rather is variable in degree, and how well people internalize something depends on how well their core needs are fulfilled. Competence and interpersonal relatedness are the most easily satisfied. In the case of competence, this is because before a norm can be internalized, a person has to be able to recognize and comprehend it. In the case of interpersonal relatedness, norms are typi-

cally learned from significant others, so a sense of closeness likely already exists. Thus, satisfying the need for autonomy is essential, and the extent to which an activity involves "a full sense of volition and choice" (Deci & Ryan, 2000, p. 237) largely determines whether it is autonomous or "self-determined."

Deci and Ryan (1985) held that motivations could be arranged along a continuum depending on the extent to which a motive was either externally or internally regulated. *External* motivation is the most other-determined motivation. This motivation is enacted to obtain external rewards (so others will feel good about you or privilege you in some way) or to avoid external punishments (e.g., so others will not feel ashamed of you or deprive you in some way). Next and somewhat external is *introjected* motivation. This motive is enacted to obtain internal rewards (e.g., so you will feel good about yourself) or avoid internal punishments (e.g., so you will not feel bad about yourself). *Identified* motivation is somewhat internal and involves valuing a goal as personally important. *Integrated* motivation is internal and involves assimilating an activity or behavior into the self. However, because integration is still instrumental, *intrinsic* motivation, which involves interest, enjoyment, and engagement in activities for their own sake, is considered the most internally regulated (or self-determined) motivation. The opposite of intrinsic motivation is *amotivation*, in which you either do not know why you are doing an activity or are doing it only because there is nothing else to do.

Noteworthy here is that some researchers (e.g., Walker & Wang, 2008) have proposed a modified version of the SDT continuum that divides (1) introjected motivation into separate "reward" or "approach" (e.g., "I would feel prideful") and "punishment" or "avoidance" (e.g., "I would feel guilty") dimensions and (2) external motivation into separate reward or approach (e.g., "Others will think more positively about me") and punishment or avoidance (e.g., "Others would be ashamed of me") dimensions. This modification, as shown in the next section, could prove important because researchers (Hamamura, Meijer, Heine, Kamaya, & Hori, 2009) have found that approach is more important for Euro-Americans whereas avoidance is more important for Asians and Asian Americans.

To date, few studies have examined how race and ethnicity could affect motivations for leisure (Chen & Pang, 2012). Caldwell and Li (2006), for example, examined the leisure motivations of adolescents in seven cultural and regional groups (i.e., Columbia, Germany, Ireland, Nigeria, South Africa, and rural and urban America) using SDT. They found that Nigerian and South African youth reported the highest levels of extrinsic motivation whereas German, Irish, and rural U.S. youth reported the highest levels of intrinsic motivation. Caldwell and Li added that further research was necessary to determine why these differences existed. In another study, Walker and Wang (2008) asked Canadian and Chinese university students to report their motivations for leisure using the modified version of SDT. The researchers correctly hypothesized that Canadian and Chinese students would not rate intrinsic motivation differently because interest and enjoyment, integral aspects of this motive (Deci & Ryan, 1985), are basic emotions (Izard, 1977) that are beneficial across all cultures (Sheldon et al., 2004). They also expected—again correctly—that intrinsic motivation would be the highest-rated SDT motive. Additionally, Walker and Wang hypothesized that Canadian university students would rate the (1) identified motivation higher because it involves "conscious valuing of a behavioral goal" (Ryan & Deci, 2000, p. 72), and research has shown that Chinese people generally view leisure less positively than Westerners (Walker, Deng, & Chapman, 2007); and (2) introjected reward and punishment motivations higher because Canadians are generally more driven by individualistic promises of rewards (e.g., pride) and threats of punishment (e.g., guilt). Statistical analyses supported both these hypotheses. Finally, Walker and Wang (2008) proposed that another concept—self-construal (Markus & Kitayama, 1991; Triandis, 1995)—located between culture and leisure motivations could potentially help explain these similarities and differences. The following section discusses what is meant by self-construal and ways in which this concept could improve understanding of how needs and motives affect leisure participation.

SELF-CONSTRUAL

Self-construal refers to how a person thinks about herself in relation to others. According to Markus and Kitayama (1991), the majority of people in the United States, Canada, Western Europe, and Australia and New Zealand have *independent (or individualistic) self-construals* and thus endorse being unique, asserting oneself, expressing one's inner attributes, and promoting one's own goals. In contrast, the majority of people in Asia, Africa, and Southern Europe have *interdependent (or collectivistic) self-construals* and so they endorse belonging, fitting in, maintaining harmony, restraining oneself, and promoting others' goals. Markus and Kitayama hold that these two types of self-construal "are among the most general and overarching schemata of the individual's self-system" (p. 230).

Triandis (1995) expanded Markus and Kitayama's (1991) framework by developing a self-construal model that included equality and hierarchy as well as individualism and collectivism. Equality stresses that people should be similar on most attributes, especially status, whereas hierarchy stresses inequality and accepts that rank has its privileges. A two-by-two matrix results, composed of (a) vertical collectivism (i.e., hierarchy and interdependence); (b) horizontal collectivism (i.e., equality and interdependence); (c) horizontal individualism (i.e., equality and independence); and (d) vertical individualism (i.e., hierarchy and independence).

One method that Triandis (1995) used to measure self-construal was scenarios, and the following example may help readers better understand similarities and differences among the four types: *If you had to describe yourself to another person, which of the following descriptions would you choose? (1) Dutiful, (2) cooperative, (3) unique, or (4) achievement oriented* (p. 47). "Dutiful" exemplifies vertical collectivism because social cohesion is primary, and cohesion occurs when people (e.g., family members, employees) fulfill the roles of their rank and the related tasks. "Cooperative" typifies horizontal collectivism because social cohesion is primary, and cohesion occurs when people are equal. "Unique" exemplifies horizontal individualism because it suggests that personal, but not status, differences exist. "Achievement oriented" typifies vertical individualism because it reflects personal and status differences, with competitive success leading to moving "up the ranks."

In spite of these conceptual differences, Markus and Kitayama (1991) and Triandis (1995) agreed on three important points concerning self-construal. First, although an individual is multidimensional, one dimension (or more) will be predominant over the other(s) (e.g., though a person is both independent and interdependent, she will also be more independent than interdependent or vice versa). Second, although the ethnic, racial, or cultural group that encompasses an individual is multidimensional, one self-construal dimension (or more) will be predominant within the group over the other dimensions (see also Chick, 2006, 2009; Li, Chick, Zinn, Absher, & Graefe, 2007). For example, a review of self-construal studies (Oyserman, Coon, & Kemmelmeier, 2002) found that African Americans were more individualistic than Latino or European Americans, whereas Latino Americans were more collectivistic than African or European Americans. Interestingly, however, an earlier study with the same first author (Oyserman, Gant, & Ager, 1995) had shown that African Americans were more collectivistic than European Americans. A reason for this conflict between findings could be that so few self-construal studies have involved African Americans (or, for that matter, Latino Americans) to date; but the conflicting findings also suggest that important within-group differences may exist (cf. Hunter & Joseph, 2010). In this case, for instance, both high levels of individualism and collectivism could exist, thus reflecting two different ways African Americans deal with systemic discrimination (cf. Jones, 1997). The third point that Markus and Kitayama and Triandis agreed on was that the type of self-construal a person has affects his needs and motivations. This proposition is important for the recreation and leisure field because

- needs, which are often satisfied through leisure, could differ by self-construal;
- motivations, which help predict leisure participation, could vary by self-construal; and

- need satisfaction facilitates motivation (Deci & Ryan, 2000), and self-construal could affect this process.

Self-Construal, Needs, and Leisure

With respect to self-construal and needs, Walker, Deng, and Dieser (2001) examined the effect self-construal had on the expressed leisure needs of Chinese Canadian and Euro-North American outdoor recreationists. Because, as outlined earlier, the researchers believed that the commonly used REP scales did not fully reflect the expressed needs of people with interdependent self-construals, they also developed five new social interdependence scales. Study findings indicated that, as expected, Euro-North Americans had more independent, and Chinese Canadians had more interdependent, self-construals. In addition, rather than ethnicity *directly* affecting the perceived importance of most expressed needs, it generally did so *indirectly* in one of three ways:

1. Either ethnicity affected independence, which in turn influenced a need's importance; or
2. Ethnicity affected interdependence, which in turn influenced a need's importance; or
3. Ethnicity affected both types of self-construal, and both in turn influenced a need's importance.

More interdependent selves, for example, rated social security, group autonomy, group membership, humility/modesty, attention to others, and respect for/sensitivity to others as more important than did less interdependent selves.

Interestingly, both more independent and more interdependent selves rated nature/tranquility as more important than, respectively, did less independent and less interdependent selves. On the basis of Markus and Kitayama's (1991) contention that, while "on the surface, such actions could look remarkably similar . . . the exact source, or etiology . . . may be powerfully different" (p. 231), Walker and colleagues (2001) proposed that natural environments might be valued by outdoor recreationists with independent self-construals because they facilitate personal expression and self-realization, whereas these same environments might be valued by outdoor recreationists with interdependent self-construals because they facilitate social cohesion and group realization.

Conversely, Cross, Hardin, and Gercek-Swing (2011) have recently noted that although East Asians and Latin Americans are both generally more interdependent, the former emphasize emotional control whereas the latter are expressive and emotive. Thus, it may also be that—to transpose Markus and Kitayama's (1991) earlier contention—while "on the surface, such actions could look remarkably *different* . . . the exact source, or etiology . . . may be strikingly *similar*." It would not be surprising to find therefore that social leisure is often quite different across racial, ethnic, and cultural groups even though members of these groups share the same type of self-construal.

Self-Construal, Motivations, and Leisure

Markus and Kitayama (1991) and Triandis (1995) also held that self-construal affected motivations, and this could hold true for leisure motives as well. Building on his earlier work (Walker & Wang, 2008), Walker (2009) examined Canadian and Chinese university students' self-construals and motivations for leisure. Results showed that while some SDT-based (Deci & Ryan, 1985, 2000) leisure motives did differ by culture, culture's overall effect was relatively small compared with that of self-construal. Moreover, while neither vertical individualism (e.g., being achievement oriented) nor vertical collectivism (e.g., being dutiful) predicted any of the most self-determined motivations, horizontal individualism (e.g., being unique) predicted three (i.e., integrated, identified, and introjected reward), and horizontal collectivism (e.g., being cooperative) predicted all four (i.e., intrinsic, integrated, identified, and introjected reward) of these motives. This finding suggests that people who are predominantly "horizontal" (i.e., those who emphasize equality over hierarchy) may enjoy, value, and benefit from leisure more than people who are predominantly "vertical" (i.e., those who emphasize hierarchy over equality). By extension, this finding also suggests that racial, ethnic, and cultural groups that emphasize "horizontalism" may enjoy, value,

and benefit from leisure more than racial, ethnic, and cultural groups that emphasize "verticalism."

Self-Construal, Needs, Intrinsic Motivation, and Leisure

Although Walker (2009) did not measure whether his participants' core needs were satisfied during leisure, he did refer to this occurrence when explaining why different types of selves might be motivated differently during leisure. As outlined earlier, OIT proposes that people attempt to transform socially prescribed norms or standards into personally endorsed values or "self-regulations" (Deci & Ryan, 2000). This internalization process is variable in degree; and how well people internalize something depends on how well their needs for autonomy, competence, and interpersonal relatedness are satisfied. Satisfying the need for autonomy, Deci and Ryan (2008) held, is particularly important; and how much an activity involves "a full sense of volition and choice" (p. 14) largely determines how autonomous or "self-determined" someone feels. Additionally, Deci and Ryan (2008) proposed that the "gold standard" for self-determined activity is intrinsic motivation. Given the importance of this need and this motive in the social psychology of leisure (Kleiber et al., 2011), one can now see how self-construal could affect whether satisfaction of the need for autonomy facilitates, inhibits, or has no effect on intrinsic motivation. Moreover, one can also recognize how self-construal could affect whether satisfaction of the other core needs (i.e., competence, interpersonal relatedness) influences intrinsic motivation.

Iyengar and Lepper (1999), for example, found that while Anglo American children were intrinsically motivated the most when they personally chose aspects of a puzzle experiment, Asian American children were intrinsically motivated the most when they were told that an in-group member (their mothers) had chosen for them. These findings led the researchers to conclude that "the provision of individual choice seems to be more crucial to American independent selves, for whom the act of making a personal choice offers not only an opportunity to express and receive one's personal preference, but also a chance to establish one's unique self-identity" (p. 363).

Other social psychologists have come to the same conclusion, but they often use everyday leisure events as illustrations. Fiske, Kitayama, Markus, and Nisbett (1998), for example, described visiting a coffee house in Western countries:

> will you have caf or decaf? Swiss water process or chemical decaffeination? large, medium, or small? Columbian, Ethiopian, hazelnut, vanilla, chocolate raspberry, or house blend? organic or regular? espresso, French roast, or light? cinnamon, chocolate, or nutmeg on top? cream, milk, or nondairy whitener? brown sugar, refined sugar, aspartame, or saccharin? for here or to go? plastic or paper bag? cash, debit card, or charge? Choosing involves knowing, communicating, and realizing one's own preferences or attitudes; consequently, choice allows people to manifest their individuality, to express

themselves, and to be active agents who control their own destinies. (p. 921)

Markus and Kitayama (1991) depicted a similar leisure event, but they compared and contrasted how it would look for independent and interdependent selves. For example, "Imagine that one has a friend over for lunch and has decided to make a sandwich for him. If both people have independent selves the conversation might be: 'Hey, Tom, what do you want in your sandwich? I have turkey, salami, and cheese.' Tom responds, 'Oh, I like turkey.' Note that the friend is given a choice because the host assumes that the friend has a right, if not a duty, to make a choice reflecting his inner attributes, such as preferences or desires. And the friend makes his choice exactly because of the belief in the same assumption" (p. 229). Here, as with the Anglo American children in Iyengar and Lepper's study (1999), the core need is autonomy, and it is satisfied through being

Zuma Press/Icon SMI

A coffee shop allows the individual a seemingly endless array of choices giving the customer the opportunity to express and establish his own identity.

able to make personal choices. However, if both people have interdependent selves, the conversation might be "'Hey, Tomio, I made you a turkey sandwich because I remember that last week you said you like turkey more than beef.' And Tomio will respond, 'Oh, thank you, I really like turkey'" (p. 229). In this case, it is the responsibility of the host to be able to "read" the mind of the friend and offer what the host perceives to be the best for the friend. And the duty of the guest, on the other hand, is to receive the favor with grace and to be prepared to return the favor in the near future, if not right at the next moment (Markus & Kitayama, p. 229). Here, as with the Asian American children in Iyengar and Lepper's study, the core need is interpersonal relatedness, and it is satisfied through fulfilling one's responsibilities and "taking the role of the other" (Mead, 1934).

Culture and self-construal may influence not only the need for interpersonal relatedness but also the need for competence. For example, Heine, Kitayama, Lehman, Takata, and Ide (as cited in Heine, Lehman, Markus, & Kitayama, 1999) found that while Canadians (i.e., independent selves) persisted significantly longer on a second creativity test after having been told they had successfully completed an earlier test, Japanese (i.e., interdependent selves) persisted significantly longer on the second test after they had been told that they had *failed* the first test. In interpreting these results, Heine and associates stated that in interdependent cultures such as Japan's, "the individual has neither the liberty nor the inclination to inflate his or her perceptions of competence . . . [because] doing so likely would only serve to alienate the individual from others" (p. 771). Thus, for interdependent selves, "being" good is less important than the process of "becoming" better (Heine et al.), because it is the latter that is most likely to satisfy the need for interpersonal relatedness (see also Triandis, 1995).

In summary, while Fiske and colleagues (1998) and Markus and Kitayama (1991) provided leisure examples of how self-construal could affect intrinsic motivation through the satisfaction of core needs, most of the research (Heine et al., 1999; Iyengar & Lepper, 1999) on this topic has been conducted in classrooms or laboratories. Though some social scientists have argued that still more

lab-based research should be performed, others have concluded that a more naturalistic approach is preferable. Waterman and colleagues (2003), for example, stated that "the trade-off for being able to control relevant variables has been the use of activities of limited personal importance or salience in the lives of research participants" (p. 1447). As it happens, only one study of ethnicity, self-construal, need satisfaction, and intrinsic motivation has been conducted in leisure studies to date, and it used the experience sampling method.

As noted earlier, Walker and Wang (2009) asked Chinese Canadians to respond to watch alarms programmed to ring seven times a day for 12 days. Using this same data set, Walker (2010) examined how participants' self-construal interacted with their needs for autonomy and competence, and how this in turn affected their intrinsic motivation during leisure activities. Results indicated that none of the four types of self-construal interacted with competence and subsequently affected intrinsic motivation. However, Chinese Canadians who were more horizontal individualistic and who experienced high levels of autonomy reported higher levels of intrinsic motivation overall. On the other hand, Chinese Canadians who were more vertical collectivistic and who experienced high levels of autonomy reported lower levels of intrinsic motivation overall, as did Chinese Canadians who were more vertical individualistic. These results suggest that while it is important to understand how the interactions between individualism and collectivism and autonomy affect intrinsic motivation, equally important is how the interactions between horizontalism and verticalism and autonomy influence this process. For instance, for horizontal individualists, it appears that equality and independence may have an additive effect such that autonomy strongly fosters intrinsic motivation. In contrast, for vertical individualists, it appears that independence may regulate hierarchy slightly such that autonomy inhibits intrinsic motivation, whereas for vertical collectivists it seems that hierarchy and interdependence may have an additive effect such that autonomy inhibits intrinsic motivation. One potential reason for this last finding is that people who are vertical are more likely to have an external locus of control (Chen, Fok, Bond, & Matsumoto, 2006). This discovery, in conjunction with Asian people's penchant for less active leisure activities (Tsai, 2007), seems congruent with Mannell and Bradley's (1986) finding that "externals" in a low setting structure who had more free choice were also less psychologically involved (i.e., intrinsically motivated) in a puzzle game.

In summary, self-construal appears to be an important intervening variable between race, ethnicity, and culture and the needs and motivations that operate during leisure participation. Moreover, given the limited amount of research on such variables (Hutchison, 2000), as well as the potential contribution this concept could make to both leisure theory and leisure practice (Walker, Deng, & Dieser, 2005), the lack of research on self-construal in the recreation and leisure field—especially among non-Whites and non-Asians—is lamentable.

CONCLUSION

The chapter overview noted that readers might come to ask, "But *why* do people participate in leisure activities?" Hopefully, having reached this point, readers can now not only answer this question but also explain how various needs and motivations "push" people to seek certain leisure activities, as well as how these same needs and motives can vary by race, ethnicity, and culture depending, in part, on the type of self-construal a group member embodies.

By this point readers are also likely aware of the limited research on how needs, motivations, and self-construal affect the leisure participation of racial and ethnic group members. Based on these perceived gaps, the following recommendations are put forth:

1. Research is needed on which core needs people most want to satisfy during their leisure, and how this varies across ethnic and racial groups. Importantly, before this issue is addressed, a better understanding of whether core needs themselves vary—in terms of both importance (e.g., autonomy vs. interpersonal relatedness) and composition (e.g., primary vs. secondary control)—across these groups is required.

2. Research is needed on which motivations are most important during leisure and how this varies across ethnic and racial groups. Once again, before this issue is addressed, a better understanding of whether motives themselves vary (e.g., in terms of reward or approach vs. punishment or avoidance) across these groups is required.

3. Research is needed on how self-construal affects core needs and motivations during leisure, and whether these effects vary across ethnic and racial groups.

4. Research on how to best put into practice the type of information in this chapter, along with what is learned once the aforementioned research gaps are addressed, is critical. As Walker and colleagues (2005) stated, and Lo (2011) recently reiterated, understanding how race, ethnicity, and culture influence leisure needs and motivations, especially in terms of the intervening variable of self-construal, could make the difference between providing a recreation program that is highly beneficial and one that is highly detrimental.

Finally, rather than answering the question "But why do people participate in leisure activities?" in terms of needs and motivations, it is possible to do so in terms of constraints that limit or prohibit people from participating. This opposing yet complementary approach is examined in detail in the next chapter.

CHAPTER 10

Leisure Constraints

Ingrid E. Schneider, Kimberly J. Shinew, and Mariela Fernandez

OVERVIEW

Most people probably wish they could engage more in recreation, leisure, and tourism. The leisure experiences people have are highly valued and often fondly remembered. However, a number of things constrain people from realizing all the leisure they would like to have: not enough money, not enough time, and maybe a lack of skills. Since the 1980s, an impressive amount of research has been devoted to understanding constraints to leisure and recreation, including their accommodation and negotiation. The same period has seen a number of studies on racial and ethnic influences on leisure participation. The purpose of this chapter is to connect the research in these important areas to provide a greater understanding of the constraints and negotiation processes most relevant to racially and ethnically diverse groups.

Learning Outcomes

After reading this chapter, readers will be able to

- identify and differentiate types of constraints and ways to address them,
- recognize constraints that are particularly relevant to racially and ethnically diverse groups, and
- apply a constraints framework to understand and manage recreational behavior among racially and ethnically diverse constituent groups.

We feel the disregard of culture as an independent variable in the study of leisure constraints is itself highly constraining.

Chick and Dong (2005, p. 179)

A number of things constrain people from realizing all the leisure they would like to have: not enough money, not enough time, and maybe a lack of skills. While some constraints are commonly experienced, others may be unique to or experienced more intensely based on an individual's race and ethnicity. For example, it is likely that all people wish they had more time to pursue their leisure interests while not all perceive discrimination in recreation settings. The purpose of this chapter is to identify constraints to recreation and leisure and the constraints most relevant to racially and ethnically diverse groups, as well as the processes used to negotiate them.

CONSTRAINTS AND NEGOTIATION STRATEGIES DEFINED AND MODELED

What do you like to do in your leisure time and why? Do you get as many of these experiences as you would like and with the people you want? Why or why not? Your answers to these last two questions are the foundation of leisure constraints research. The idea of constraints is fairly straightforward; they are factors that limit and shape the development of leisure interests and preferences as well as the ability to actually participate (Henderson, Stalnaker, & Taylor, 1988).

Three types of constraints have been historically identified in the leisure literature: intrapersonal, interpersonal, and structural (Jackson, 2005). What you like to do is influenced by intrapersonal constraints. For example, if you are anxious about heights, you are not likely to start rock climbing. Similarly, if you think rock climbing would be interesting but do not have the skills to climb, you are less likely to prefer that activity as opposed to one that you do have the skills for, like walking or biking. These personal characteristics and self-perceptions make up the

intrapersonal constraints that influence your leisure preferences. Interpersonal constraints have to do with coordinating personal resources to engage in recreation and leisure. So, if you want to rock climb, you either find others who enjoy it and can participate with you, or you do not. If you do not, you experience interpersonal constraints. Finally, if you know what you would like to do and have someone to do it with but simply cannot get where you need to go due to a lack of time, money, or transportation, you are experiencing structural constraints.

Since 2005, structural constraints have been further differentiated into four subcategories: natural environmental, social environmental, territorial, and institutional (Walker & Virden, 2005). Examples of natural environmental constraints include weather, topography, and landscapes; these affect recreation participation primarily. Social environmental structural constraints include anything that interferes between preference and participation, such as crowding and conflict. Territorial constraints involve situations in which access may be prevented and may be perceived differently depending on race, ethnicity, or socioeconomic class. Institutional constraints emanate from the managing organization and may be intentional, such as closures, or unintentional, such as lack of information in a native language. The last two categories may be particularly relevant to racial and ethnic groups.

As you reflect on your own leisure and recreation experiences, it may not surprise you to learn that research demonstrates that people find ways to participate in and enjoy leisure despite constraints (Kay & Jackson, 1991; Scott, 1991). The "negotiation thesis" (Jackson, Crawford, & Godbey, 1993) spells out how people try to ameliorate or alleviate the effects of constraints (Jackson & Rucks, 1995; Walker & Virden, 2005). Jackson and colleagues (1993) suggested that negotiation strategies are divided into cognitive strategies (i.e., changing leisure aspirations) and behavior strategies (i.e., modifying the use of time and acquiring skills). For example, if you are hiking in the wilderness but see more people than you would like or had expected, you might change your definition of the experience to a more developed or social hike rather than a wilderness hike. Alternatively, if you change the location of your hike because of the number of people, you are exhibiting a behavior strategy. In 2001, these negotiation strategies were further differentiated by Hubbard and Mannell to include time management, skill acquisition, financial strategies, and interpersonal coordination. More recently, Schneider and Wilhelm Stanis (2007) suggested a reconceptualization of these strategies into problem- and emotion-focused coping strategies, similar to those in stress research (Lazarus & Folkman, 1984; Pearlin & Schooler, 1978; Pruitt & Rubin, 1986). Emotion-focused strategies include cognitive responses such as regulation of emotions, product shift (i.e., changing the definition of the experience), rationalization (e.g., reevaluating the situation more favorably), and psychological avoidance. Problem-focused strategies are behavioral responses in which individuals take direct actions such as management of the environment, substitution (e.g., time, resource, activity), or displacement.

While constraints seem fairly straightforward, understanding both the factors that influence them and what they influence can be complex.

Conceptual models to understand constraints emerged in the 1990s. Crawford and colleagues (1991) proposed that the three types of constraints were hierarchical; intrapersonal constraints were the most proximal and structural constraints the most distal to shaping leisure preferences (figure 10.1). Initial research on these constraints supported the idea that they were hierarchical (Raymore, Godbey, & Crawford, 1994; Raymore, Godbey, Crawford, & von Eye, 1993). However, later in the 1990s, it was recognized that the constraints hierarchy was not a comprehensive understanding of constraints (Hawkins, Peng, Hsieh, & Eklund, 1999; Gilbert & Hudson, 2000) and that constraints influence more than just participation (Jackson & Scott, 1999).

At the start of the 21st century, motivations were more explicitly added to the constraints models as a way to provide insight into the relationship between constraints and negotiation. Hubbard and Mannell (2001) explored four different models of constraints, negotiation, and motivation:

1. An independence model, in which constraints, negotiation, and motivation independently affect participation
2. A negotiation–buffer model, in which negotiation moderates the effect of constraints on participation, and motivation has both a direct effect on participation and an effect on negotiation

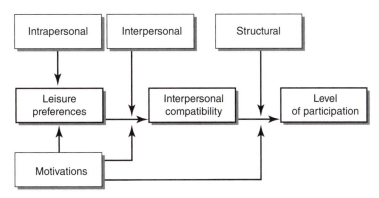

Figure 10.1 The hierarchical model of constraints.

Reprinted from D.W. Crawford, E.L. Jackson, and G. Godbey, 1991, "A hierarchical model of leisure constraints," *Leisure Sciences* 13(4): 309-320. Reprinted by permission from Taylor & Francis Ltd., www.tandf.co.uk/journals.

3. A constraints–effects–mitigation model, in which negotiation partially mediates the constraint–participation and motivation–participation relationships

4. A perceived constraints–reduction model, in which negotiation partially mediates the motivation–participation relationship and constraints partially mediate the negotiation–participation relationship

In the end, the constraints–effects–mitigation model was supported, and it suggested that constraints negatively influence participation yet trigger negotiation strategies that in turn mitigate some of the negative effects of participation constraints (figure 10.2). To date, four studies have tested and modified Hubbard and Mannell's (2001) constraints–effects–mitigation model. Support for the full model has been found (Loucks-Atkinson & Mannell, 2007; Wilhelm Stanis, Schneider, & Russell, 2009), but a reduced model with no relationship between constraints and negotiation has better predicted participation (Covelli, Graefe, & Burns, 2007; Son, Mowen, & Kerstetter, 2008). Also, within this body of work, negotiation efficacy has been introduced and found to positively influence motivation and negotiation efforts but to have no effect on perceived constraints (Loucks-Atkinson & Mannell, 2007). Additional model testing is called for to better understand the role of motivation in constraints and negotiation.

Although still at the conceptual level, a more complex constraints and negotiation model was proposed in 2005 by Walker and Virden (figure 10.3). In this model, micro-level factors, macro-level factors, and characteristics associated with the setting are included as factors that affect leisure preferences, motivations, and constraints. Micro-level factors are individually oriented and include personality traits, human needs, attitudes and beliefs, experience use history, and self-construal. In contrast, and as the name implies, macro-level factors are socially oriented and include race, ethnicity, gender, cultural or national forces, and socioeconomic forces. As another addition to the model, Walker and Virden included the idea that constraints can influence the decision to participate as well as postparticipation evaluation of the experience.

Looking beyond individuals, Crawford and Stodolska (2008) suggested hierarchical levels of constraints that consider the influence of societal issues. This model starts with the basic and individual constraints such as equipment, costs, and transportation as most proximate and more easily negotiated (figure 10.4). The next layer of constraints includes intermediate constraints that are embedded in society and more difficult to negotiate, such as economic structures and legislation. Finally, fundamental constraints such as cultural attitudes are the most distant from an individual and least likely to be effectively negotiated or

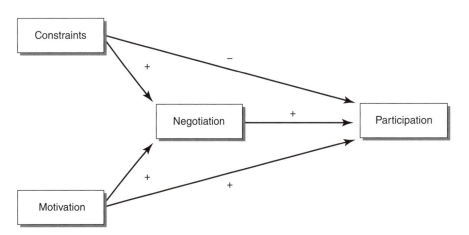

Figure 10.2 Constraints–effects–mitigation model.

Reprinted from J. Hubbard and R.C. Mannell, 2001, "Testing competing models of the leisure constraint negotiation process in a corporate employee recreation setting," *Leisure Sciences* 23(3): 145-163. Reprinted by permission from Taylor & Francis Ltd., www.tandf.co.uk/journals.

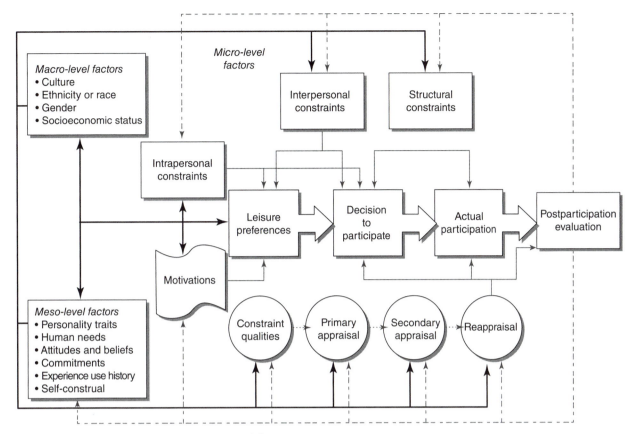

Figure 10.3 Constraints–negotiation model.

Reprinted from G.J. Walker and R.J. Virden, 2005, Constraints on outdoor recreation. In *Constraints to leisure,* edited by E. L. Jackson (State College, PA: Venture).

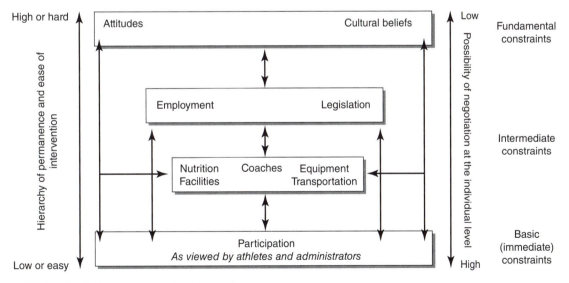

Figure 10.4 Social issues as constraints.

Reprinted, by permission, from J. Crawford and M. Stodolska, 2008, "Constraints experienced by elite athletes with disabilities in Kenya, with implications for the development of a new hierarchical model of constraints at the societal level," *Journal of Leisure Research* 40: 128-155.

subjected to intervention. Although additional empirical testing is needed, the model extends the understanding of constraints to a societal level and has applications to a variety of groups, including those of varied races and ethnicities.

These models and theories have been helpful for understanding the constraints people face in their leisure and recreation, as well as the ways in which people may accommodate or negotiate constraints. Some of the constraints and strategies are especially relevant to racially and ethnically diverse groups. The next section discusses constraints research that has been conducted specifically on racial and ethnic groups to gain a better understanding of their leisure and recreation behavior.

RESEARCH ON CONSTRAINTS AMONG RACIALLY AND ETHNICALLY DIVERSE GROUPS

Although some leisure constraints, such as time and money, seem to be applicable to the general population (Shores, Scott, & Floyd, 2007), others appear to be mediated by racial and ethnic group status. Leisure constraints that are particularly relevant to racially and ethnically diverse groups include access to resources, immigration factors, and discrimination issues (see chapters 5 and 11). Less is known about the strategies these groups use to accommodate constraints; few studies explicitly identify leisure coping and negotiation strategies used by racially or ethnically diverse groups (see, for example, Livengood & Stodolska, 2004; Stodolska, Acevedo, & Shinew, 2009). However, when possible, the following discussion includes research on constraints and the ways in which racially and ethnically diverse groups address these constraints.

Access to Resources

Although racially and ethnically diverse groups have displayed advances in income levels, educational status, and employment since the 1960s, serious disparities remain that often lead to differentiated access to resources (see chapter 3 on practice). With regard to leisure research, Shinew and Floyd (2005) acknowledged that the

field has yet to "understand the complex nature and multifaceted impact of constraints associated with racial stratification" (p. 40). Limited access to resources is a commonly cited constraint among racially and ethnically diverse groups (see chapter 5 on Latino Americans). Access manifests itself through financial resources, transportation, and physical access. Hunt and Ditton (2002) examined the relationship between race and ethnicity and freshwater fishing experiences (i.e., age of first fishing experience) in the state of Texas. They concluded that White males engaged in licensed recreational fishing more often than any other race–gender–ethnic group. One possible explanation was that racially and ethnically diverse groups lacked the financial resources to participate in the activity; census findings showed that minorities had lower income levels compared to Whites in Texas. Additionally, the authors noted that racially and ethnically diverse group members tend to live in urban areas; since fishing generally occurs in nonurban areas, this can also limit their access to fishing opportunities. Dunn and colleagues (2002) found that transportation was a constraint for Hispanics trying to visit lakes in the state of Oklahoma, especially lakes in rural settings. Hispanic families also expressed lack of awareness that these resources existed. Richter and colleagues (2002) found that lack of resources restricted some African American women living in South Carolina from participating in physical activities when resources included the ability to pay the membership fees for exercise facilities and the ability to pay for transportation to the location. Similarly, Henderson and Ainsworth (2000) found that limited monetary resources, lack of transportation, and lack of community infrastructure (i.e., sidewalks) affected older African American and American Indian women's participation in physical activities.

Scholars have noted that racial and ethnically diverse neighborhoods in low-income areas often have less access to attractive and well-maintained community infrastructure, including city parks, sidewalks, and open spaces (Floyd, Taylor, & Whitt-Glover, 2009; Stodolska & Shinew, 2010). In Stodolska and Shinew's study on constraints that affect Latinos' participation in recreation and physical activity, residents commented that their poorly maintained parks had "jogging trails full of potholes, dilapidated playground equipment, trash, lack of water fountains and unsanitary restrooms" (p. 321). Residents noted that lack of access to well-maintained parks affected their recreation participation. Powell, Slater, and Chaloupka's (2004) examination of the association of race, ethnicity, and socioeconomic status with community-level recreation and physical activity settings (i.e., sport areas, green spaces, bike paths) showed that African Americans and individuals of "other" races were less likely to have access to community recreation resources. However, this was not necessarily the case for communities with large populations of Hispanics, which actually had higher levels of access to the recreation settings examined. Indeed, other researchers have acknowledged that not all low-income neighborhoods with highly racially and ethnically diverse populations lack quality recreation resources (Macintyre, 2007; Powell et al.). Unfortunately, in some of these neighborhoods, issues of crime and safety can limit recreation participation (Franzini et al., 2010; Stodolska, Acevedo, & Shinew, 2009; Stodolska, Shinew, Acevedo, & Roman, 2013). However, as demonstrated in Stodolska and Shinew's study, some Latino individuals attempt to overcome the safety constraints restricting their participation. For example, one resident reported that she no longer visited parks due to safety concerns but instead used indoor recreation facilities. Similarly, another female resident reported that she transported her children to a different park that she perceived to be safer to engage in recreation and play. Of course, other families were unable to afford the fees associated with indoor facilities or lacked the transportation to go to another site.

Immigration Factors

Several factors related to immigration may also constrain leisure participation. With regard to immigrants, Stodolska (2000) stated that upon arrival to the country, individuals are faced with "initial transitional shock, imperfect language skills, separation from family and friends, need to regain economic stability, and lack of familiarity with basic institutions of the host country" (p. 65).

Although some immigrant families do comparably better economically in the United States than in their homeland, some have a hard time adjusting to life in the United States. Bengston and Schermann (2008) noted several critical issues and challenges specific to outdoor recreation participation among recent immigrants, including low literacy rates, lack of knowledge regarding laws and regulations governing outdoor recreation, and having a set of norms related to outdoor recreation that can conflict with White mainstream norms and traditions.

Determining what leisure activities can be continued and developing new leisure interests can be a source of stress for new immigrants. Stodolska (2000) studied the postmigration changes that occurred in Polish immigrants in Canada and grouped the leisure participants according to Jackson and Dunn's (1988) classification scheme of four categories: "quitters," "replacers," "adders," and "continuers" (p. 43). Stodolska found that several immigrants in the study "ceased participating in at least one leisure activity" without replacing it with another leisure activity (quitters), whereas many were able to replace their old leisure activities with new ones after migrating to Canada (replacers). Some participants incorporated new leisure activities into their regular activities (adders), while many of the Polish immigrants continued their regular leisure activities (continuers). Upon arriving to Canada, some immigrants noted that certain leisure activities were not feasible as they were "no longer available," "turned out to be too expensive," "were perceived to be too dangerous," or "were too time-consuming."

Lack of language skills can also affect participation. Dunn and colleagues (2002) held two focus groups with Hispanic stakeholders to improve services at lakes in Oklahoma, and stakeholders expressed concern about language barriers. In some situations, the participants felt that the language barrier could pose a potential safety hazard during emergency situations if rangers and Hispanic visitors were not able to communicate with each other. Rublee and Shaw (1991) found that Latin American women who had immigrated to the United States took part primarily in child-related activities because the language barrier deterred them from participating in other leisure activities. Stodolska (2000) documented the "post arrival depression" Polish immigrants experienced after moving to Canada and noted that lack of English proficiency was one of the contributing factors.

Related to language, level of acculturation and assimilation (Gordon, 1964) (see chapter 1 on theoretical frameworks) can also constrain participation. Dunn and colleagues (2002) noted that immigrants often wished to participate in activities in a traditional Mexican way. The authors stated, "They will attempt to reproduce in their new environment the culturally expressive recreational behaviors they grew up with. Unacculturated Hispanics will not usually imitate the recreational behavior of the established White (Anglo) society" (p. 19). Floyd and Gramann (1995) examined the effects of acculturation and structural assimilation on Mexican Americans' outdoor recreation patterns. They found that unacculturated Mexican Americans participated in fewer activities than did Whites and that the least assimilated Mexican Americans were less likely to visit some of the recreation areas, whereas the "highly assimilated Mexican Americans" displayed usage patterns similar to those of Whites.

Both intra- and interpersonal constraints related to immigration have been identified in the literature. Li and Stodolska (2007) examined leisure constraints and negotiation practices in international Chinese graduate students. The findings suggested that the students were limited in their leisure due to a "lack of time, language barrier and cultural differences, lack of friends, and feelings of lack of entitlement to pursue leisure" (p. 115). Li and Stodolska reported that students used a variety of approaches to address these constraints, including turning to their home culture and to friends from their home country during their leisure, expressing feelings of isolation, and contacting family and friends back home through the use of technology. Feelings of isolation and lack of leisure companions were also mentioned by respondents in Tsai and Coleman's (1999) study of Chinese immigrants residing in Australia, who reported that since family and friends were left behind, they had fewer companions for their leisure activities. Tsai and Coleman suggested that

interpersonal factors constrained their leisure since they were "in the process of establishing new friendship networks in a new socio-cultural environment" (p. 256). The specific impact of culture on constraints has also been examined. Hudson, Hinch, Walker, and Simpson (2010) concluded that culture influenced Chinese Canadians' participation in downhill skiing. Chinese Canadians perceived more intrapersonal constraints (many related to their culture) whereas Anglo Canadians' constraints were primarily structural. The authors also noted that people from Asia were more likely to have interdependent self-construals (e.g., sense of belonging, maintaining harmony, promoting the goals of others); thus the Chinese Canadian respondents would often participate "if only to fit in with the Canadian lifestyle. They were also constrained by parental barriers, supporting the theory that conforming to role expectations was highly valued" (p. 82).

Discrimination Issues

Discrimination issues have also constrained the leisure behavior of racially and ethnically diverse groups (see chapter 11 for a detailed discussion of the topic). In 1998, Floyd suggested that the marginality and ethnicity perspectives (Washburne, 1978) (see chapter 1 on theoretical frameworks) were unable to fully explain the complexities behind racial and ethnic minorities' leisure behavior. Thus, Floyd directed attention to discrimination as well as historical occurrences to help explain contemporary leisure behavior. For example, scholars have documented that the White mainstream view of the great outdoors has evolved over time and is often linked to images of spirituality and peacefulness (Johnson & Bowker, 2004). However, for racially and ethnically diverse groups, this is not necessarily the case, and discrimination continues to constrain current use patterns.

Several scholars have reported on the land disenfranchisement experienced by some groups, particularly Hispanics and American Indians, due to the creation of national parks (McAvoy, 2002; Raish, 2000; Schelhas, 2002; Takaki, 2008). In the case of Hispanics in New Mexico, subsistence farmers lost their land when the 1848 Treaty of

Guadalupe Hidalgo went into effect (Schelhas, 2002). The majority of these lands eventually became part of the U.S. Forest Service. At first the U.S. Forest Service took into consideration the interests of its Hispanic stakeholders. However, in time, this relationship deteriorated, and the Forest Service eventually banned grazing of cattle on federal land, which had a major impact on Hispanics' farming and ranching (Schelhas). Tensions from such decisions plagued the relationship between Hispanics and the U.S. Forest Service; and even in the 21st century, many Hispanics still harbor negative feelings about what they perceive as stealing of their land and a disregard for "their needs, interests, and landscape" (Schelhas, 2002, p. 732; Raish, 2000). Studies have linked the overtaking of land and banning of grazing to present-day poverty rates in the Hispanic community (Schelhas; Raish, 2000; Rural Sociological Society Task Force on Persistent Rural Poverty, 1993).

American Indians have also experienced land confiscation (see chapter 7 on Alaskan Natives, American Indians, First Nations, Inuit, Métis, Native Hawaiians, and other Pacific Islanders). In the United States, American Indians have tribal rights to the land managed by federal agencies (Dustin, Schneider, McAvoy, & Frakt, 2002; McAvoy, 2002), but conflicts remain. The example of Devils Tower National Monument and recreational use is one of the most prominent cases. June is typically the month when the American Indian tribes hold their religious celebrations "during the summer solstice" at the monument (Dustin et al., 2002, p. 81). However, June is also prime rock climbing and recreation visit season. The site received its official designation in 1906, but after it was featured in a 1977 film, *Close Encounters of the Third Kind,* Devils Tower Monument experienced an increase in the number of rock climbers. According to Dustin and colleagues, over time the two groups grew to resent each other. American Indians came to resent both the social and the environmental impacts of climbing that interfered with their sacred ceremonies, while climbers grew to resent American Indian prayer bundles being left at various places around the base of the tower and American Indian claims of special privilege as the monument's First People (p. 81). Members of

the Indian tribes requested that rock climbing be limited during the month of June, and this request met resistance by rock climbers, who argued that such restrictions favored the religion of American Indians. McAvoy (2002) found that rock climbers described their climbing experiences as vital to their identity, and some even compared their climbing to a spiritual experience. The conflict resulted in the passage of a voluntary restriction during the month of June, which according to Dustin and associates had been respected by the majority of the rock climbers.

In addition to Hispanics and American Indians, African Americans have been negatively affected in their use of the outdoors due to past discrimination and negative experiences. For African Americans, natural settings have been linked to slavery and lynching (Erickson, Johnson, & Kivel, 2009; Johnson & Bowker, 2004). According to Johnson and Bowker, although slavery and lynching have not been personally experienced by today's African Americans, "collective memories" keep these images intact. African Americans are plagued by images of slavery and lynching in the woods and backcountry from stories or "memories" that are passed down. In some cases, these memories are enough to constrain their leisure participation in natural environments. Erickson and colleagues (2009) analyzed the historical and cultural factors that affect the experiences of African Americans living in the Denver area with respect to their visitation to Rocky Mountain National Park. Beyond lack of parental introduction, fear was cited as a factor inhibiting park visitation in addition to discomfort in places where the majority of the people are White. The participants also reported that the term "woods" was linked with images of "poverty and lynchings" (p. 539). Erickson and colleagues noted that historically, African Americans have differed from their White counterparts in their travel patterns in that they traditionally traveled to see family and friends. This phenomenon was evident in "The Negro Motorist Green Book," a booklet used by African Americans during the 1930s to 1960s to identify sites where discrimination was less likely to occur. Finally, the authors concluded that park visitation was deemed a "White activity" and not associated with the Black culture.

Racially and ethnically diverse group members also experience discrimination as a leisure constraint. For instance, while conducting focus groups with racially and ethnically diverse college student groups, Blahna and Black (1993) documented various acts of discrimination emanating from both other visitors and staff. Respondents reported on the following incidents: a Ku Klux Klan rally that took place in a park; a White man who threatened to call immigration because a Hispanic student used the tennis courts; a park guard who asked a group to leave by stating, "You know you guys don't belong in this park, they kill Hispanic people here" (p. 113); and general overall preferential treatment of Whites.

In the 21st century, reports of discrimination have continued (see chapter 11 on discrimination in leisure settings). Tirone (1999) discussed South Asian Canadian youths' interactions in leisure settings where study participants reported verbal harassment by other children in the youth programs. Unfortunately, staff members failed to intervene when these incidents occurred. Flood and McAvoy (2007) reported that American Indians faced disrespect from other recreationists in the form of stares, racial slurs, and threats. American Indians also felt that staff members harassed and racially profiled them, which deterred further participation. Gobster (2002) found that African Americans were more likely to encounter discrimination, followed by Latinos and then Asians, in Chicago park settings. Various sources of discrimination were identified, including other park visitors, law enforcement, and staff members. Gobster added that the groups were distributed around the park, with few interactions occurring between them, and that conflicts often arose if group boundaries were crossed. One participant mentioned, "Three weeks ago I was knocked off my bike because seven White guys said I was in the 'wrong area'" (p. 155). Sharaievska and colleagues (2010) also conducted a study in Chicago and found that Latinos experienced discrimination from other recreationists as well as from law enforcement and staff attendants in park settings. The authors noted horizontal discrimination (minority to minority) in their findings, which is counter to the more typical vertical discrimination (management to visitor or nonminority visitor to minority visitor) that is often discussed

in the literature. Similarly, a study of three cities, including Chicago, identified discrimination as a significantly higher constraint among non-White ethnic groups than others (Wilhelm Stanis, Schneider, Chavez, & Shinew, 2009).

Limited research has examined how specific groups contend with discrimination. For example, Livengood and Stodolska (2004) examined the effects of discrimination on the leisure behavior of American Muslims after 9/11 and how these discriminatory experiences were managed. The participants encountered various forms of discrimination, including "racist epithets, unpleasant looks, obscene gestures, and avoidance" (p. 192). The harassment affected their leisure behavior in that American Muslims had "reduced freedom of movement, travel, timing and location of activities" (p. 192). In order to continue participating in leisure, the participants displayed various strategies. For instance, some reported traveling by car instead of air because of the expectation of being subjected to embarrassing searches. The women experienced more acts of discrimination, attributed to wearing of the traditional hijab. In these cases, women opted to wear "Western" clothing in order to draw less attention to themselves. Further, before the 9/11 incidents, they prayed in public places without worrying about being seen; but after 9/11, families found alternative places or times to pray so they would not be seen by others.

Although a variety of constraints may affect the leisure and recreation behavior of racially and ethnically diverse groups, access to resources, immigration status, and discrimination issues are particularly relevant. Given this, it is important to consider the management implications of these constraints and what can be done to mitigate their impact on participation.

IMPLICATIONS FOR MANAGEMENT

The research on constraints and negotiation most relevant to racial and ethnic minority groups indicates both challenges and opportunities for recreation management. In the mid-1990s, James recognized that "human service agencies are expected to provide services that are responsive and sensitive to the diverse needs and expectations of their clients or participants. For today's human service providers this is a formidable challenge" (1996, p. 3). Although progress has been made and some challenges have been overcome, much opportunity remains.

Assessing and improving access to recreation experiences are essential. First, potential visitors need to be aware of the existing recreation opportunities. In order to increase the awareness among ethnic and racial minorities, inclusive and intentional communication is vital. Inclusive communications use inviting and accessible language and place the information using media such that prospective visitors will be able to access, identify, and relate to it. Simple communication opportunities include (1) a review of program and other communication materials to see if and how they reflect a diverse public through their pictures and content and (2) assessment of where and how information is delivered and how this relates to ways in which diverse publics obtain leisure information. Moreover, just as potential visitors must be made aware of the opportunities, it is important to clearly communicate behavioral expectations and regulations (Bengston & Schermann, 2008). Bengston and Schermann suggested that one organizational response may be "liaison positions" that serve as bridges and information conduits to help ensure that information reaches the target group. Once people are aware of the resources available, the ability to get to the site is essential. Although research is mixed about site availability, evidence suggests that a multipronged access audit is a worthwhile step. Certainly assessing if and how proximity to resources differs by race and ethnicity is a start. However, proximity to resources is only one indicator of access. Concerning ability to get to the site, the ability to get to local and close-to-home areas primarily relates to perceived safety and routes to the location; but for more distant sites, affordable transportation is critical. Working with public transit, local nonprofits, and schools is a starting point for coordinating transportation options. Important to coordination is considering the work and life schedules of varying publics. For example, Chavez (2012) found that many Latinos were working six days a week and therefore considerations of a "typical" week must be rethought.

Once people are at the sites, the areas need to be safe and in acceptable condition. Unfortunately,

public spending on many parks and open spaces in low-income communities of color lags behind spending in more affluent areas (Wolch, Wilson, & Fehrenbach, 2005). Beyond access and site quality, an access assessment should include identifying perceived fear and actual crime. In cases in which safety is an issue, it is necessary to work with community leaders and local enforcement to create safer spaces. A variety of actions may be appropriate to improve safety, from community patrols to changes in lighting and site design. In cases in which fear perceptions do not match reality, information campaigns that include sharing the actual number of incidents with community residents may help alleviate safety concerns.

Related to site safety is the issue of discrimination, for if people feel discriminated against, they likely do not feel safe. Certainly for management staff, ongoing diversity training and awareness building are critical components in developing multicultural competence. That said, one-time diversity training is insufficient to significantly advance understanding. Rather, a respect for diversity should be embedded in the organizational culture, and efforts toward an inclusive organization must be ongoing (Allison, 2008). This training must include an awareness and appreciation of the diverse set of norms often associated with the leisure behavior of racially and ethnically diverse groups, including an understanding that these norms may conflict with White mainstream traditions. In addition to the ongoing training, simple ways to increase awareness and staff ability include developing and posting a multicultural customer service resource list, posting a multicultural calendar in the work space, and modeling attendance at diverse cultural events (Aguilar, 2008).

Beyond access and comfort, coordinating social factors is also important. Interpersonal constraints, such as having fewer companions to participate with, can limit participation. A strategy to address this constraint includes offering social programs that help build relationships among community members. This type of programming may be particularly useful to recent immigrants who have limited social networks. However, it should not be expected that residents will seek out these social opportunities, so community outreach efforts are needed. Management staff will need to schedule these social offerings in locations that are close and convenient to the target group.

CONCLUSION

The purposes of this chapter were to identify and differentiate types of constraints and ways to address them, recognize constraints that are particularly relevant to racially and ethnically diverse groups, and apply a constraints framework to management issues related to serving racially and ethnically diverse constituent groups. The chapter reviews the three types of constraints that have historically been included in the leisure literature (intrapersonal, interpersonal, and structural constraints) and examines models of constraints, negotiation, and motivation. Constraints that are particularly relevant to racially and ethnically diverse groups such as access to resources, immigration factors, and discrimination issues were discussed.

It is clear that racially and ethnically diverse groups typically face more constraints than the mainstream population. Given the importance of recreation and leisure to overall quality of life, it is essential to understand factors that can limit or shape leisure interests, preferences, and participation. Ultimately, the hope is that such understanding will result in management strategies that can be used to offset some of the constraints that impede satisfying leisure experiences for racially and ethnically diverse populations.

CHAPTER 11

Discrimination in Leisure Contexts

Iryna Sharaievska, Monika Stodolska, and Myron F. Floyd

OVERVIEW

Although overt discrimination is against contemporary social norms, discrimination in more subtle forms—what Justice Felix Frankfurter called "sophisticated" versus "simple-minded modes of discrimination" (Bartlett, 1968)—profoundly affects the well-being of minorities and their experience of leisure. It can create the impression among minority groups that certain leisure options or recreation spaces are not really available to them, which may dampen their desire to engage in leisure in the first place. In this chapter the authors have sought to examine how discrimination operates in leisure contexts and to analyze the role of discrimination in shaping leisure experiences of racial and ethnic minorities. Other aims are to assess the treatment of discrimination as a scholarly topic in leisure studies and to discuss changing social, cultural, and demographic contexts that shape discrimination experiences.

Learning Outcomes

After reading this chapter, readers will be able to

- describe the development of racial and ethnic discrimination research in leisure studies,
- define different types of discrimination that can occur in leisure settings,
- describe how discrimination experiences can affect leisure choices and behavior, and
- identify critical research related to racial and ethnic discrimination.

Ignorance and prejudice are the handmaidens of propaganda. Our mission, therefore, is to confront ignorance with knowledge, bigotry with tolerance, and isolation with the outstretched hand of generosity. Racism can, will, and must be defeated.

Kofi Annan

The moment a little boy is concerned with which is a jay and which is a sparrow, he can no longer see the birds or hear them sing.

Eric Berne, psychiatrist

Despite the ideological aspiration of equality expressed in the Declaration of Independence and the preamble to the U.S. Constitution, White racism and discrimination have been tightly woven into the fabric of U.S. society (Feagin & Vera, 1995). From the inception of African slavery in 1620 to the near genocide of Native Americans in the late 19th century to Japanese internment during World War II, the fortunes of people of color in the United States have been determined largely by a rigid system of racial subordination and discrimination. Undergirding this system was widespread belief in the cultural and intellectual inferiority of Blacks and other people of color (Aguirre & Turner, 1998). According to Feagin and Vera, most Whites in America from the 1600s to the 1990s held anti-Black attitudes. For example, opinion polls from 1942 showed that only 47% of Whites believed that Whites and Blacks were equally intelligent (Schuman, 1997, cited in Quillian, 2006). A 1991 poll found that 55% of Whites thought Blacks were less intelligent (Associated Press, 1991). This legacy continues to weigh on contemporary society.

Although blatant, overt discrimination is typically no longer practiced as public policy (Pager & Shepherd, 2008), substantial research indicates that discrimination is still a significant factor that favors Whites and disadvantages people of color. According to Reskin (2012), "thousands of scholarly studies have documented disparities that favor Whites over Blacks across every major subsystem in American society" (p. 19). For example, both African Americans and Latinos experience higher rates of unemployment and lower wages compared to Whites (Pager & Shepherd, 2008) (see Foreword). In one of the more highly publicized studies on hiring discrimination (Bertrand & Mullainathan, 2004), researchers mailed resumes to prospective employers in Boston and Chicago. Resumes were equivalent in all respects except that they had been randomly assigned a "distinctively African American" (e.g., Ebony or Darnell) or a "distinctively White" name (e.g., Brad or Allison).[1] The study showed that White names generated 50% more callbacks for interviews than did African American names. Resume quality (e.g., more work experience) also generated more callbacks for White names than African American names.

Residential segregation by race and ethnicity continues to be a prominent feature of America cities (Rugh & Massey, 2010). Although residential segregation throughout the United States has declined since the 1960s, cities with large African American populations show minimal or no decline in residential segregation (Iceland, Weinberg, & Steinmetz, 2002). An analysis of panel data covering three decades (1977-2005) (Crowder, Pais, & South, 2012) found that despite the increase of multiethnic neighborhoods, Blacks and Whites continue to live in neighborhoods with high concentrations of their own race. In addition, when they move, Black and White householders are significantly more likely to move to neighborhoods of their own race. Other research attributes residential segregation to historical "redlining" (Massey & Denton, 1993) and other forms of

[1] Readers are encouraged to consult Bertrand and Mullainathan (2004) for details related to the methods.

housing and mortgage discrimination (Rugh & Massey, 2010). Now illegal, redlining refers to the practice among banks and other mortgage lenders of refusing or limiting loans to poor and minority residents. Reskin (2012) argues that residential segregation is what links together many other forms of racial discrimination. She maintains that the concentration of African Americans in neighborhoods with poor schools, lack of access to health care, environmental hazards, punitive policing, and so on creates a system in which racial disparities are "causally" interdependent and reinforcing (p. 23), giving rise to emergent or *meta*-discrimination. Proposing a systems approach to analyzing discrimination, Reskin stated that "emergent discrimination profoundly helps to maintain racial disparities by suffusing the world we occupy, automatically affecting our beliefs and values about color and worthiness and shaping the distribution of resources" (p. 19).

Against this historical backdrop, the remainder of the chapter provides an overview of key concepts in the discrimination literature, describes the range and types of discrimination examined in leisure research, and analyzes how they affect leisure experiences. It concludes with a discussion of key concerns for future research and policy.

DEFINITION OF TERMS

To examine issues of racial discrimination in leisure contexts, it is first necessary to define the main terms used in the literature. *Racism* is an ideology based on the assumption that "intellectual, moral, or cultural superiority" may be associated with physical characteristics of a person (e.g., skin color, facial features) (Henry, Tator, Mattis, & Rees, 1995, p. 4). It is a collective belief system within a given society that sustains racist attitudes and behaviors of individuals, as well as practices and policies of institutions. Moreover, as Sasidharan (2002) suggested, even an ideology that consciously or unconsciously supports the idea that "people can be categorized into a distinct number of discrete races and ethnic groups based on physical and biological criteria" may be called racism (as cited in Arai & Kivel, 2009). Racism is related to power distribution in society; however, it is not reserved only for the mainstream population—White Americans and White Canadians

(Omi & Winant, 1994). Recent societal changes made it possible for certain members of minority groups to obtain enough power to engage in racist and prejudicial treatment of other minorities or even members of the mainstream population (Omi & Winant). It is important to acknowledge the existence of horizontal racism or prejudice of one minority group against another (Johnson & Oliver, 1989; Mindiola, Niemann, & Rodriguez, 2002; Sharaievska, Stodolska, Shinew, & Kim, 2010). However, the majority of White members of American and Canadian societies still enjoy privileges associated with their dominant position. Thus, the main issues of prejudice and inequality in power distribution are still discussed in terms of a White–non-White dichotomy (Arai & Kivel, 2009; Henry et al.).

Hegemonic Whiteness and White privilege have received increased attention in recent years (see chapter 4 on leisure among African Americans and chapter 14 on race, ethnicity, and sport) (Floyd, 1998; Kivel, Johnson, & Scraton, 2009). Researchers have stressed the need to focus on privileges and advantages enjoyed by members of the "White mainstream" and on what is considered "normal" rather than what is thought to be "irregular" or "deviant" (e.g., culture of Blacks and other minorities) (Arai & Kivel, 2009; McDonald, 2009; Mowatt, 2009a; Roberts, 2009). Increased attention to issues of White privilege coincides with and is likely to be intensified by changes in the form and intensity of discrimination documented in recent years (Bonilla-Silva, 2002; Brief et al., 1997; Dovidio & Gaertner, 2000; Gaertner, Dovidio, Nier, Hodson, & Houlette, 2005; Omi & Winant, 1994). According to these studies, the number of incidents of blatant discrimination decreased during the last several decades. However, less overt forms of oppression related to symbolic, aversive, and color-blind racism (see the following discussion) are still common in today's society. Due to these changes it has become harder to identify and confront issues associated with racism and discrimination, which can make discrimination even more dangerous and damaging.

As explained by Brief and colleagues (1997), *symbolic racism* is practiced when people openly support principles of equal opportunity but disapprove of policies and programs that are specifically directed at providing such equal opportunities to all racial and ethnic groups. People engaged in symbolic racism believe that governments and society have already done everything to increase social mobility and equality of minority populations. They explain the disadvantaged position of minorities as owing to their lack of persistence, lack of self-motivation, and laziness.

Dovidio and Gaertner (2000) and Gaertner and colleagues (2005) discussed a similar concept, called *aversive racism*. According to the latter authors, aversive racism is a "conflict between the denial of personal prejudice and unconscious negative feelings and beliefs" (p. 377). While a person might believe and present himself as nonprejudiced, he might also hold negative feelings about people of different race. However, he acts on those feelings only when his judgment can be justified by other factors, such as a person's qualifications for a job. This type of racism becomes very hard to recognize and battle because it is not explicit. Bonilla-Silva (2003) claimed that it is rare for White people in the United States or Canada today to openly admit that they are racist; most Whites assert that they "don't see any color, just people." Bonilla-Silva called such denial of the relevance of race-related issues in modern society *color-blind racism*—new racism practices that are subtle, institutional, and apparently nonracial. Henry and colleagues (1995) also discussed *democratic racism,* defined as a set of beliefs and arguments that "reduces the conflict between maintaining a commitment to both egalitarian and nonegalitarian values" (p. 13) and that is expressed through many covert practices, including blaming the victim, color-blindness, "we–they" polarization, and multicultural programs and policies that perpetuate inequality. Malhi and Boon (2007) wrote that democratic racism is "deeply embedded within Canadian society" (p. 127).

Racism, as opposed to discrimination, is a much broader concept that represents an ideology based on inequality in power distribution. *Discrimination,* on the other hand, was defined by the United Nations as:

> any distinction, exclusion, restriction or preference based on race, color, descent, or national or ethnic origin which has the purpose or effect of nullifying or impair-

ing the recognition, enjoyment or exercise, on an equal footing, of human rights and fundamental freedoms in the political, economic, social, cultural or any other field of public life. (International Convention on the Elimination of All Forms of Racial Discrimination, pt. I, art. 1, par. 1)

Similarly to racism, discrimination may be enacted at the interpersonal, group, or institutional level (Feagin & Eckberg, 1980). Feagin and Eckberg defined discrimination as "the practices and actions of dominant race-ethnic groups that have a differential and negative impact on subordinate race-ethnic groups" (p. 9). Tumin (1973) saw discrimination as a "translation of prejudicial beliefs into consequential behavior" (p. 418), while Allport (1954) suggested that discrimination occurs "when the object of prejudice is placed at some disadvantage not merited by his own misconduct" (p. 10).

Discrimination has been classified in a number of ways based on the intentionality and the level at which it is executed. Feagin and Eckberg (1980) identified isolate, small-group, direct institutionalized, and indirect institutionalized discrimination. *Isolate discrimination* was defined as an intentionally harmful activity, not associated with the functioning of any organization, performed by a member of a dominant group against a member or members of a marginalized group (Feagin & Eckberg). *Small-group discrimination* was characterized as a harmful activity against a member or members of marginalized groups by a small group of members of a dominant group who are not associated or supported by any organization or institution (Feagin & Eckberg). By *direct institutionalized discrimination,* Feagin and Eckberg meant "organizationally or community prescribed actions that by intention have a differential and negative impact on members of a subordinate group" (p. 12). *Indirect institutionalized discrimination* was defined as "organizationally or community prescribed practices, motivated by neither prejudice nor intent to harm, that nevertheless have a negative and differential impact on members of a subordinate group" (p. 12). The authors suggested that people who belong to an organization involved in indirect institutionalized discrimination may not even realize the harm they cause, or may realize and disagree with it but still go along for fear of breaking organizational rules and regulations.

When discussing prejudice, discrimination, and racism, one should remember that these terms are rather fluid and evolve over time because of social and cultural changes in society (Arai & Kivel, 2009; Henry et al., 1995). One should also consider that the terms *racism* and *discrimination* and the terms *race* and *ethnicity* are not interchangeable, despite their often inconsistent use. While Floyd (1998) and Henry and colleagues (1995) cautioned that *race, culture,* and *ethnicity* are distinct concepts, studies in the field of leisure often continue to use these terms interchangeably.

DISCRIMINATION IN LEISURE CONTEXTS

Dating back to the 1970s, several studies acknowledged the role of historical discrimination in influencing the leisure behavior of African Americans (e.g., Craig, 1972; Lindsay & Ogle, 1972; Washburne, 1978; Woodard, 1988). For example, Craig's (1972) study attributed Black recreation patterns to "rigid segregation policies, low income, and lack of leisure time" (p. 114). Discrimination was reflected in the development of Lindsay and Ogle's (1972) opportunity theory. This theory held that outdoor recreation participation rates vary directly in relation to cost and physical availability of a resource to a population. It assumed that "groups long denied opportunities, not only by virtue of their residence, but because of their poverty, ignorance or segregation, might become participants in available opportunities if these barriers are removed" (p. 20). Washburne's (1978) marginality hypotheses suggested that African American "underparticipation" in outdoor recreation was due to "various consequences of socioeconomic discrimination" (p. 176), which in turn was a function of historical racial discrimination.

As Gómez (2002) pointed out, more than a decade passed between the time Washburne (1978) put forth his propositions and the time an empirical study of discrimination appeared in the leisure studies literature. Despite references to the effect of discrimination on recreation and leisure behavior, no direct tests of the discrimination hypothesis were undertaken until West's (1989) seminal article. West explored the constraints on the use of city and regional parks by African American residents of Detroit and found that underuse of regional parks among Detroit's Black minority was primarily attributable to their fears of discrimination. West established that African Americans were more likely than Whites to use Detroit city parks but less likely to visit regional parks. Lack of transportation and feeling unwelcome or feeling uneasy were cited as the most important reasons for lower visitation rates to suburban parks. Since West's paper, several studies have documented that racial and ethnic minority groups experience discrimination in a range of leisure settings including parks, campgrounds, recreation areas, pools, beaches, golf courses, and forests (Blahna & Black, 1993; Chavez, 1993; Floyd, Gramann, & Saenz, 1993; Gobster, 1998a, 2002; Gobster & Delgado, 1993; Livengood & Stodolska, 2004). Discrimination during leisure affects the quality of the recreation experience, as well as recreation site choices, and can force members of minority groups to isolate themselves during their leisure engagements (Blahna & Black, 1993; Gobster, 1998a; Johnson, Bowker, English, & Worthen, 1998; Stodolska & Jackson, 1998). Philipp (1999) also argued that "many, if not most, leisure activities have embedded racial 'information' associated with them in some way" (p. 397). In other words, racial minorities are forced to consider physical settings where their presence is likely to be resisted or accepted and the activities in which they are expected to participate. Gramann (1996) suggested that discrimination experiences among minority groups may lead to avoidance, displacement, or other coping behaviors (e.g., withdrawal from activities or settings).

Despite the increased number of studies that address discrimination, the social and environmental conditions that lead to perceptions of discrimination and how these factors affect the leisure experience are largely unknown. Researchers will be challenged to study a behavior that is often hidden from view and illegal (Quillian, 2006), particularly in governmental agencies. It is also clear from the literature that only recently have studies considered institutional or structural forms of discrimination (e.g., Erickson, Johnson, & Kivel, 2009; Glover, 2007). Proponents of critical theory perspectives have emphasized the importance of understanding racial discrimination within "theoretical frameworks which enable broader discussions of social and structural inequalities, power, ideology and white hegemony" (Arai & Kivel, 2009, p. 464). A more complete understanding of discrimination in leisure contexts will certainly require social–psychological and structural approaches. The next two sections focus on the types of discrimination that have been found to exist in leisure contexts and on minorities' responses to discriminatory treatment.

Types of Discrimination Experienced in Leisure

The typology introduced by Blahna and Black (1993) classified discrimination[2] in leisure based on the sources of discriminatory treatment. The typology includes six categories: discrimination from other recreationists, discrimination from professional staff, differential upkeep and management of leisure settings, potential discrimination, historical racism, and effects of past economic discrimination. The following subsections employ Blahna and Black's classification to provide an overview of studies that have examined discrimination in the context of leisure.

Discrimination by Other Recreationists

In a 1999 study, Philipp compared how welcome middle-class African Americans and Whites felt while participating in 20 leisure activities and found significant differences in the perceptions of welcomeness for 16 of them. The authors concluded that "both racial groups share a very similar basic understanding of where African Americans will find the most racial acceptance during their leisure time" (p. 397). Participation in activities perceived as inappropriate to members of a given racial or ethnic group, or as

"trespassing" on a territory controlled by another group, may result in discriminatory treatment (Sharaievska et al., 2010). These hostile acts may be perpetrated by members of a dominant group (Fernandez & Witt, 2013) or by members of the same group who may want to "punish" their in-group for taking part in activities deemed not suitable for a person of a certain ethnic–racial origin. For instance, cases of African Americans experiencing mistreatment from other African Americans due to their desire to participate in "White" activities have been reported (Washburne & Wall, 1980; West, 1989).

Discrimination by other recreationists is among the most often reported types of mistreatment (Doherty & Taylor, 2007; Feagin, 1991; Hibbler & Shinew, 2002; Livengood & Stodolska, 2004; Stodolska & Jackson, 1998; Flood & McAvoy, 2007; Tirone, 1999). Discriminatory acts discussed in the literature range from frequent hostile stares to threats and even physical attacks against minority recreationists. For instance, in the study by Feagin, a 10-year-old girl reported that she had been called racist names in the swimming pool, while Polish immigrants in Canada spoke of being frequently ridiculed and spoken to in a patronizing manner (Stodolska & Jackson, 1998). Tirone (1999) described incidents of blatant discrimination encountered by South Asian Canadian teens, and Doherty and Taylor (2007) discussed unpleasant experiences of recent immigrant youth during physical education classes in Canada. Even simple stares may spoil leisure experience, as was reported by interracial couples in Hibbler and Shinew's (2002) study and by Livengood and Stodolska's (2004) Muslim interviewees.

The incidents of discrimination are not always limited to unpleasant words or gazes. Two African American young men in Blahna and Black's (1993) study reported being chased out of a beach in a White Chicago neighborhood by a group of Caucasian boys wielding baseball bats. In Sharaievska and colleagues' (2010) study, African Americans were seen as trespassers in "Hispanic parks," and physical altercations between African American

---

[2]Blahna and Black (1993) used the terms "racism" and "discrimination" interchangeably.

and Latino parents were reported. On the other hand, Fernandez and Witt (2013) reported that Latino children were bullied by their African American peers in a recreation center described as "historically Black." Such blatant cases of discrimination, however, may happen even if minorities are not recreating in areas perceived to "belong" to a different racial or ethnic group. Flood and McAvoy (2007) reported that Native Americans were threatened with firearms by groups of White visitors on their own reservation land (Kootenai National Forest). Similar stories were recounted by Native Americans in McDonald and McAvoy's (1997) study.

The frequency and strength of discrimination can fluctuate depending on the political, social, and economic situation of the country (Livengood & Stodolska, 2004; Stodolska & Walker, 2007). For instance, Livengood and Stodolska showed that in the post-9/11 period, discriminatory acts against American Muslims increased significantly. Members of this group were called racist names and experienced hostile looks and gestures in parks, in libraries, and on the streets. Other reasons for discriminatory treatment against minority residents were discussed by Stephenson and Hughes (2005), Neal (2002), and Neal and Agyeman (2006) in their studies of the English countryside. They described rural areas of the United Kingdom as unwelcoming to minority populations and explained racially charged actions of the White local residents by their worries about the loss of traditional values and customs. Furthermore, marketers of rural tourism often perpetuate images of romantic, idyllic all-White landscapes associated with the English nobility and traditional way of life.

While often more difficult to identify and address, racism may be expressed in ways other than through obvious acts of differential treatment or open hostility. McDonald (2009) argued that the *denial of difference* between the experiences of people from different racial and ethnic groups can also be a form of racism. Even though this may be seen as unbiased, it leads to perceptions of the irrelevance of issues related to discrimination and racism, as well as normalization of Whiteness. The negative consequences of

such normalization are numerous; they include derogation of minority experiences and needs, unequal distribution of funding, and differential treatment by recreation staff (McDonald).

Discrimination on the Part of Professional Staff

Racism expressed by members of professional staff can restrict access to recreation programs and services and lead to feelings of hopelessness and loss of interest in the activity among minority recreationists. In the studies by Doherty and Taylor (2007), Tirone (1999), and Fernandez and Witt (2013), minority youth noted the significant role that professional staff played in their leisure experiences. While South Asian teens already felt unwelcome due to behavior of other recreationists that was less than friendly, the indifference and unwillingness of professional staff to intervene during discriminatory incidents made them feel even more so (Tirone). Similar experiences were described by Fernandez and Witt, who showed how lack of attention from the staff of a recreation center allowed physical attacks and bullying of Latino children to continue. In contrast, the coaches and physical education teachers described by Doherty and Taylor used their leadership skills and position to affect the atmosphere and attitudes among youth. They not only served as role models and created a feeling of welcomeness among recently immigrated adolescents, but also helped them enjoy physical activities without feeling excluded.

While undoubtedly most of the professional staff of recreation organizations adhere to the principles of fairness and equality, frequent cases of tension and confrontation between recreation practitioners and minority populations have been reported. Many of these tensions result from differences in the operational practices of recreation organizations and resistance toward preferred recreation patterns among minorities. For example, Latinos interviewed by Burset and Stodolska (2012) and by Stodolska and Santos (2006) complained about not being allowed to play soccer on the fields operated by some Illinois park districts. Conflict between professionals responsible for maintaining recreation grounds and enforcing organization rules, on the one hand, and Latinos who desire to play soccer without formal league affiliation, on the other hand, have been reported across the United States (for further discussion of this topic see chapter 3 on race, ethnicity, and leisure services). In another study, Flood and McAvoy (2007) found that among the constraints most often reported by Native Americans recreating in national forests were "conflict with official personnel" and the "rules and attitudes of Forest Service" (p. 204). The respondents described their experiences of being closely watched, harassed, profiled, and threatened by forest rangers. Similarly, Latino interviewees in Stodolska and Shinew's (2010) study reported being overly scrutinized by recreation staff and police officers, and commented that staff of the local recreation center failed to market their programs to local Latino residents. The director of the recreation center interviewed by Fernandez and Witt (2013) openly admitted that his organization did not see the need to market its programs to local Latinos, even though they constituted a majority population in the neighborhood. Interracial couples in Hibbler and Shinew's (2002) study also reported cases of poor treatment, substandard service, and even refusal of service experienced in leisure settings.

Differential Upkeep and Management of Leisure Settings as a Form of Institutional Discrimination

Insufficient access to and funding of parks and recreation organizations, poor maintenance of recreation spaces, and other examples of environmental racism are well-documented phenomena (Blahna & Black, 1993; Floyd, Taylor, & Whitt-Glover, 2009; Stodolska & Shinew, 2010; Stodolska, Shinew, Acevedo, & Izenstark, 2011; Wolch, Wilson, & Fehrenbach, 2005). Poorly funded and managed parks, as well as unattractive and insufficiently maintained areas, may lead to lower visitation rates and as a result contribute to secondary outcomes of physical inactivity such as obesity and other health concerns (Floyd et al., 2009). Floyd and colleagues' assertion was confirmed by Stodolska and Shinew (2010), who found that poor maintenance of parks and other

natural environments in Latino neighborhoods dissuaded minority residents from using these spaces for physical activity. Moreover, the study showed that many minorities resided in neighborhoods with little outdoor recreation space and that the environments that were accessible were overrun by gangs and surrounded by an industrial landscape (see chapter 5 on Latino Americans for further discussion of this topic). Crime has been shown to be an important constraint that prevents minorities from visiting parks and in turn leads to further deterioration of recreation spaces (Stodolska, Acevedo, & Shinew, 2009). The respondents in Blahna and Black's (1993) study also complained about the differential upkeep of parks in African American neighborhoods. They noted that the amount of money spent, as well as cleanliness and the general upkeep of parks in their neighborhoods, were subpar as compared to parks in White suburban communities.

Various explanations have been advanced to account for the poor quality of recreation environments in minority neighborhoods. Floyd and Johnson (2002) invoked an environmental justice framework and argued that minorities often lack political clout to mount successful resistance to environmental degradation in their communities. Long and Hylton (2002) and McDonald (2009) suggested that normalization of Whiteness is responsible for the channeling of the majority of resources to recreation areas in affluent, White communities. When leisure settings and activities are assessed as "appropriate," "healthy," and "normal," funding for their construction and maintenance is easier to obtain, and public decision making is streamlined. Conversely, a Latino director of a recreation center interviewed by Stodolska and Shinew (2010) claimed that it was the local residents who engaged in destructive activities such as tagging and littering and who generally "did not care" about the recreation environments, while the park was receiving generous funding from the local park district. High mobility of the local immigrant population, a lack of belief that things could improve in the community, the undocumented status of many residents, and the perception that local parks were "overrun by gangs" were cited as the reasons residents did not seem to care about the upkeep of local recreation spaces.

Potential Discrimination

To be affected by discrimination, one does not have to personally experience discrimination. It may be enough for the individual to simply believe that a particular recreation location is not welcoming for someone of her racial background (Philipp, 2000) or to expect that the discrimination will occur. According to Blahna and Black (1993), perceived, expected, or potential racism exists in "cases where respondents express general fear of discomfort due to potential for, or expectation of, prejudice or discrimination" (p. 114). Such fear or unwillingness to visit certain areas may be formed as a result of previous experiences with discrimination. These feelings may also be the result of a history of encounters with discrimination on the part of a person's acquaintances or family members, of witnessing incidents of discrimination in the media, or of stories passed down through generations and circulating in the ethnic or racial community.

One of the first studies that discussed issues of potential discrimination was conducted by West (1989), who showed how expectation of discrimination and feeling "unwelcome" and "uneasy" prevented African Americans from visiting suburban Detroit parks. Also, in 1988, Woodard found that Blacks were more constrained in their leisure by fear of discrimination and racial prejudice, and Hibbler and Shinew (2002) documented fears of potential discrimination among interracial couples. African Americans in Gobster's (1998a) study explained that they did not feel comfortable on a golf course because they were raised with the idea that golf is a White male game and "knew" that they would be stared at and stereotyped as criminals. Similarly, people of different races interviewed in Chicago's Lincoln Park reported that there were certain areas of the park where they felt most comfortable since they perceived these places to be associated with people of their own race (Gobster, 2002).

Other researchers who have discussed potential discrimination include Gobster (1998a, 1998b), Flood and McAvoy (2007), McDonald and McAvoy (1997), Philipp (1999), Shinew, Mowatt, and Glover (2007), and Stodolska and Jackson (1998), who highlighted the important role it plays in influencing recreation patterns of minority groups. Stephenson and Hughes (2005), Neal (2002), and Neal and Agyeman (2006) showed that potential discrimination influences not only everyday leisure activities of minority populations but also their travel experiences. Asian and Black immigrants in Europe avoided visiting the countryside due to a higher probability of race-related violence.

It should be noted that the perception of discrimination is a dynamic concept that can change over time and with growing assimilation levels. For example, Floyd and Gramann (1995) examined how cultural assimilation, primary structural assimilation, and socioeconomic assimilation affect perceptions of discrimination among Mexican American recreationists. Their findings showed that more acculturated Latinos with higher levels of socioeconomic assimilation perceived a lower incidence of discrimination than those who were less assimilated.

Historical Racism and Effects of Past Economic Discrimination

The history of racism in the United States has left a large shadow that still looms over the leisure experiences of minorities (for additional discussion of this topic see chapter 10 on constraints and chapter 3 on leisure services). Until recently, few studies had directly examined how past discrimination affects contemporary leisure choices of marginalized groups. As discussed by Floyd (1998), discriminatory practices lie at the foundation of the marginality thesis frequently used to explain differences in leisure participation patterns between minority groups and mainstream Whites (Washburne, 1978). Blahna and Black (1993) cited several examples illustrating why African American and Hispanic families saw visitation to natural areas as dangerous and unattractive. One of the African American participants in their study reported that his mother associated "the woods" with a history of lynching and death; and a Latino participant explained that for his parents, natural areas were associated with poverty and inconvenience. Similarly, Johnson, Bowker, English, and Worthen (1998) explained African Americans' lack of preference for visiting wooded areas as owing to the history of violence perpetrated in the South against African American residents. Mowatt's (2009b) study poignantly illustrated how "the woods" have been associated with the history of lynching of African Americans and how lynchings were often considered a "recreation activity" by the local Whites.

Erickson and colleagues (2009) provided many examples of past racist practices that shaped the current leisure behavior of minorities. They discussed *The Negro Motorist Green-Book*, published from 1936 until approximately 1960, which identified leisure places where African American visitors were welcome. In the racially segregated country, "The Green Book" provided alternative places for lodging and eating and shaped the individual behavior of minorities who were channeled toward seeking out these alternatives. Although much has changed since that era, African Americans are still aware of this history and, as interview data provided by Erickson and colleagues (2009) illustrate, their memories and knowledge of past segregation and historical racism affect their intentions and interest related to Rocky Mountain National Park. Another example of past inequalities that have affected the current leisure behavior of minorities is insufficient funding of public recreation facilities such as swimming pools, playgrounds, parks, camps, and libraries located in minority communities. Erickson and colleagues also described how subpar economic resources (including lack of money to purchase camping gear, car, and gas), which often represented a legacy of past racism and economic discrimination, affected the ability to develop attachments to natural areas. Moreover, forests and national parks were referred to by some African American participants as "woods" and "country" and had a negative connotation due to past experiences of poverty, hard manual labor, and lynching.

In addition to discrimination from other recreationists, along with discrimination from professional staff, differential upkeep and management of leisure settings, potential discrimination,

historical racism, and effects of past economic discrimination as described by Blahna and Black (1993), several scholars of discrimination and discrimination have identified *institutional discrimination* as negatively affecting life chances of minorities (Feagin & Eckberg, 1980). Institutional discrimination is related to intentional or unintentional harmful actions of a member of the mainstream population who acts on behalf of a particular organization and whose actions are directed against one or more members of a minority group (Feagin & Eckberg). Cases of institutional discrimination in leisure have been documented by Richmond and Johnson (2009), Stephenson and Hughes (2005), and others. Institutional discrimination is discussed in detail in chapter 3 on race, ethnicity, and leisure services.

Behavioral Responses to Discrimination

A number of studies have documented responses to discrimination in leisure settings. Common reactions to perceived or experienced discrimination included verbal or physical confrontation or both, withdrawal, and changes in leisure behavior (additional responses to discriminatory treatment are examined in chapter 16 on research in Australia and New Zealand).

Verbal and Physical Confrontation

Many factors affect how people respond to discriminatory actions, including personal characteristics of the victim, power differential between the victim and the perpetrator, and the type of and location of the encounter. Verbal and physical confrontations are rather time- and energy-consuming and in some cases have unforeseen consequences. They may be also impossible due to the brevity of the interaction and lack of language skills, undocumented status, or shyness on the part of the victim. People may choose to respond to discrimination with a polite suggestion or with sarcastic or even aggressive remarks (Feagin, 1991). Others try to prevent discrimination from happening by being extremely polite, using icebreakers, or even providing others with information about their culture or religion (Livengood &

Stodolska, 2004). According to research, social class is an important factor that affects the way in which people respond to discrimination. For instance, Feagin discussed the case of an African American president of a financial institution who used his power and social networks to respond to a discriminatory encounter in a restaurant by publicizing it in the local press. Unfortunately, few people have the ability and resources to respond actively to discrimination. The majority of victims choose the strategy of withdrawal and resigned acceptance (Feagin).

Withdrawal and Passive Acceptance

Withdrawal is one of the most common and most detrimental reactions to discrimination. Silent acceptance of the situation negatively affects leisure experiences of minorities and can even completely deprive them of participation in leisure activities and visits to recreation spaces. It also affects society as a whole by masking existing problems, by encouraging the perpetrators, and by creating an image of peace and happiness in leisure settings.

The leisure literature provides many examples of withdrawal in response to discrimination. For instance, as reported by Flood and McAvoy (2007), more than 20% of interviewed tribal members who had faced discriminatory attacks chose not to return to specific places in the Kootenay National Forest. A very similar case was reported by African American park users in West's (1989) study. The Latino participants in a study by Sharaievska and colleagues (2010) also quietly accepted instances of discrimination due to their fear of being deported and lack of comfort with the English language. In many cases of perceived discrimination, the result is withdrawal from or avoidance of a specific leisure activity or leisure setting. For example, African American youth in Gobster's (1998a) study avoided riding their bikes next to a golf course due to their fear of stereotyping and stares.

While racism has a detrimental effect on any person who is exposed to it, it may be particularly hard on children and those who are new to the country. Blahna and Black (1993) described a situation in which an African American man had to explain racism to his daughter after she overheard a racist remark for the first time at a local pool. In Tirone's (1999) and Doherty and Taylor's (2007) studies, many adolescent newcomers to Canada stopped participating in sport activities because they felt unwelcome and were being stared at. In general, the response of withdrawal is quite common among immigrants due to their lack of confidence in the new environment, lack of language skills, or often undocumented status (Sharaievska et al., 2010; Stodolska, 2007).

The choice to withdraw or to respond with passive acceptance can be made for various reasons, including personal characteristics of the victim, perception of unequal power distribution, or even doubts as to the true intentions of the perpetrators. For example, in Yi's (2005) study, recent Korean immigrants explained discriminatory treatment they had experienced as connected to their socioeconomic status ("they are not discriminating against me because I'm Asian but because I'm poor") or attributed it to personality flaws on the part of individuals engaged in discrimination. They did not see racism as a systemic problem but rather as a trait typical of a small minority of troubled individuals. Thus, Yi's study confirmed Portes' (1984) claim that more assimilated and affluent minority group members may be more attuned to discriminatory attacks because they are aware of their rights, have often been educated in the American system, and have been exposed to multicultural discourse.

As a result of discriminatory comments made by family members, coworkers, and other recreationists, interracial couples in Hibbler and Shinew's (2002) study were forced to abandon many of their favorite leisure activities. Consequently, their leisure became more home based and their social interactions more limited. Participants in Stephenson and Hughes' (2005) study had little ability to influence discriminatory encounters experienced during their European travels. Many of the Black and Asian tourists found local residents, leisure service providers, and even governmental institutions such as custom control at the airports unwelcoming and prejudiced. As a result, many Black tourists decided to avoid specific countries or regions.

Changes in Leisure Behavior

Besides responding to discrimination verbally or by withdrawing, minority group members may alter their leisure behavior in several ways. These include changing the place and time of participation, altering the activity per se, visiting leisure settings with a group of people, and being more careful about and aware of the surroundings. For example, to decrease the occurrence of racist incidents, Native Americans in Flood and McAvoy's (2007) and McDonald and McAvoy's (1997) studies changed times and places for picnicking, fishing, camping, and picking wild berries in the Kootenai National Forest. They also participated in leisure activities only with members of their families or Native American friends. Similar tactics were employed by Polish, Mexican, and Korean immigrants in the study by Stodolska (2007). The interviewees preferred the more relaxed and less threatening atmosphere of ethnically enclosed settings for their leisure.

Visiting recreation places in large groups was reported by African American and Latino participants in Blahna and Black's (1993) study. Interracial couples interviewed by Hibbler and Shinew (2002) were cautious regarding their surroundings and obtained information about the setting before the visit. They called the place or asked friends for recommendations. Latino participants in the study by Sharaievska and colleagues (2010) changed their behavior in response to discrimination by traveling to the park in groups or having an "insider" with them in order to avoid violence from African American residents of the neighboring community. Delgado (1994) described adjustments in the leisure patterns of Chinese American senior visitors to Lincoln Park, who visited in the morning in order to avoid verbal harassment from African American teenagers (as cited in Gobster, 1998b). The Muslim participants in Livengood and Stodolska's (2004) study reported various changes to their recreation behavior in response to discrimination. Due to the increased level of hostility toward Muslims in post-9/11 America, members of this group often had to adjust places, times, and coparticipants during their leisure activities and use caution while choosing recre-

ation activities and locations. They also preferred ethnically enclosed areas where they could avoid hostile remarks, hate stares, or physical violence.

CONCLUSION

This literature review clearly indicates the detrimental effects of realized and potential discrimination on the well-being of minorities and on their leisure experience. From limiting the range of leisure options to restricting spaces that may be used for recreation to affecting the desire of minorities to engage in leisure, discriminatory actions have a profound effect on shaping the leisure experiences of millions of Americans and Canadians. Racism and discrimination are not new phenomena. In fact, many claim that they are deeply embedded in the U.S. and Canadian societies. However, they are not limited to the United States or Canada but are seen in most countries and communities where interethnic or interracial contact occurs.

While much of the research focuses on discrimination perpetrated by mainstream Whites against African Americans, more recent scholarship clearly indicates that discrimination goes beyond the Black–White context. Minority Whites are discriminated against (Stodolska & Jackson, 1998), and conflict and discrimination among minorities themselves are quite prevalent as well (e.g., Hispanic–African American) (Fernandez & Witt, 2013; Sharaievska et al., 2010). Moreover, discriminatory actions have been documented within minority populations based on their ethnic origin (e.g., African Americans vs. immigrants from Africa or the Caribbean; Waters, 1994), generational tenure, immigration status, and assimilation level (Stodolska & Yi, 2003).

The changing racial and ethnic structure of the United States and realignment of the racial hierarchy (Bonilla-Silva, 2002; Floyd, 2007) are likely to intensify incidents of interethnic conflict and discrimination. The pervasiveness of racism and discrimination may be exacerbated by increasing migration flows, the growing size of minority groups, their cultural distinctiveness, and perceptions that some minorities "are just not assimilating" (for the controversy regarding this matter see the debate surrounding Huntington's [1993,

1996] clash of civilizations thesis). Such trends are well exemplified in Europe, where anti-Muslim sentiments have been documented in many countries, including Sweden, the Netherlands, Denmark, Germany, and France (see chapter 15 on Europe). The debate about illegal immigration in the United States is also clearly indicative of attitudes shared by many Americans. Interracial and interethnic conflict and discrimination may also be exacerbated when minorities are relegated to living in isolated and impoverished communities (a good example is the 2005 riots by youth of African and Maghrebian origin that started in the poor immigrant community of Clichy-sous-Bois and spread to many cities across France). The global recession that began in 2007 across North America and much of the world and the corresponding increase in unemployment rates, as well as the outsourcing of jobs, also contributed to perceptions that minorities are taking jobs that "rightfully belong to Americans." Interethnic conflict and discrimination may also flare up at times of political and military crisis and in connection with tragic events such as the September 11 attacks, which sparked anti-Muslim sentiments in the United States, Canada, and much of Western Europe. Conversely, increasing intermarriage and the mixed racial and ethnic heritage of a large part of the American and Canadian populations may potentially alleviate some of the tensions.

Such trends are indicative of the need to further examine discrimination issues in the context of the changing social, cultural, and demographic makeup of the United States and Canada. These investigations should explore inter- and intraracial dynamics as well as the intersection of class, race, and immigration status. Moreover, while the existing studies have done an excellent job of documenting the incidence of discrimination in leisure settings, little attention has been devoted to exploring minorities' resistance to racism and discrimination (Shinew & Floyd, 2005). One may argue that the existing research is quite deterministic and often portrays minorities as a monolithic group passively enduring discrimination from above. At the same time, however, growing socioeconomic mobility among minorities has led to the emergence of educated, wealthy, progressive, and socially aware middle- and upper-middle-class African Americans, Latinos, and Asians who are at the forefront of the battle to eradicate racism from the public discourse in the United States and Canada. It is the authors' belief that leisure researchers investigating issues of racial and ethnic discrimination should move this research to a new level, should avoid essentializing the experiences of ethnic and racial groups, and should explore the roles of leisure in the empowerment of minorities and in their active resistance against racist discourses.

PART IV

Special Types of Leisure and Leisure Settings

This part of the book examines special types of leisure (physical activity and sport) and leisure settings (wilderness) as they relate to ethnic and racial minorities. Chapter 12 addresses immigrant interaction with wildlands and wilderness by examining the environmental worldviews of Latino and Asian cultures in the United States. Chapter 13 examines culturally based attitudes toward physical activity, provides an overview of conceptual models that have been used in past research on physical activity, and explores leisure-time physical activity patterns among different racial and ethnic groups. Chapter 14 provides a critical analysis of the persistent beliefs about racial superiority in sport. In particular, it examines historical and psychosocial influences on health and physical activity and provides future directions for research on the impacts of ethnicity on sport activity choices.

CHAPTER 12

Wilderness in the U.S. Immigrant Mind

Cassandra Johnson-Gaither

OVERVIEW

The perspective of Latin American and Asian immigrants on nature and wildlands is strikingly different from the view typical of European Americans. The very idea of outdoor recreation may be strange to the cultures from which many of these immigrants originate. This chapter addresses immigrant interaction with wildlands and wilderness by examining the environmental worldviews of Latino and Asian cultures in the United States. The aim is to assess how congruent these various ontologies may be with European American[1] ideals of nature interaction and preservation. Implications for managing wildlands and wilderness are also considered.

Learning Outcomes

After reading this chapter, readers will be able to

- identify potential problems related to immigration and land conservation and management agencies;
- describe views of nature and wildlands associated with European, Latino, and Asian American cultures; and
- suggest possible ways of introducing wildlands and wilderness to immigrant populations.

[1]In this chapter the term European American refers to the cultures, politics, and economies of Anglo and other Northern European–origin peoples.

> *Just who are 'we' who have inherited the wilderness idea? And who are 'our' forebears?*
>
> *Callicott and Nelson (1998, p. 2)*

Individuals representing the U.S. land trust community gathered in the summer of 2008 at a workshop hosted by Yale University to discuss the woeful underrepresentation of people of color in the conservation movement (Newsome & Gentry, 2008). Those convened urged that organizations advocating for nature conservation be diversified along racial, ethnic, and class lines. Participants raised concerns about the future of wildland conservation in the United States, arguing that it might decline considerably if the wider populace does not have direct contact with these lands. Outdoor nature activists and public lands managers also convened in 2009 at Atlanta's "Breaking the Color Barrier" conference with a similar goal of "integrating outdoor nature experiences" along ethnic and racial lines.

These meetings are but two examples of natural resource organizations' and outdoor advocates' attempts both to understand and to respond to the United States' changing sociodemographic makeup. An important element to consider in the diversification of both nature-based recreation and wildland advocacy is immigrant populations. The proportion of immigrants in the U.S. population reached its maximum in the late 1800s and early 1900s when large numbers of southern Europeans immigrated to the United States. From 1880 to 1920, the foreign-born population accounted for between 13% and 15% of the U.S. population (Grieco & Trevelyan, 2010). In 2010, almost 40 million foreign-born persons resided in the United States. This number represented 13% of the 2010 population (Acosta & de la Cruz, 2011). Importantly, between 2000 and 2010, the U.S. foreign-born population increased by 28%; and roughly 61% of this increase was accounted for by

persons from either Mexico or South and East Asia (see Introduction) (Pew Hispanic Center, 2012).

Since the early 1990s, a fair amount of research has focused on the recreation behavior of non-U.S.-born populations (Carr & Williams, 1993; Chavez, 2001; Stodolska & Yi, 2003), but relatively little research has examined this topic in the context of wildlands or wilderness-based recreation[2] (Johnson, Bowker, Bergstrom, & Cordell, 2004; Johnson, Bowker, & Cordell, 2005). This is an important consideration, given charges by some that wildland and wilderness recreation represents elitist or class-based activities relevant primarily to Euro-American cultures (Cronon, 1996; Callicott, 1994/1995; Walker & Kiecolt, 1995). Although the early wilderness champion John Muir was a Scottish-born immigrant, it is argued that the cultural underpinnings informing Muir's appreciation of the wild were different from those that characterize the experiences of contemporary immigrants (Inglehart, 1990, 1995). Increased immigration from Latin American and Asian countries begs questions of whether and to what extent these immigrant groups engage with wildland and wilderness activities after they arrive in the United States. For instance, how relevant is the idea of wilderness, as defined in the 1964 Wilderness Act, to more recent immigrant populations? Might increases in the foreign-born population result in greater wear and tear on wildland and wilderness resources? To what extent do Latino and Asian American immigrants' environmental worldviews determine engagement with wildlands? Can natural resource management agencies expect to receive continued political support for conservation among groups newly arrived to the United States?

---

[2]Wilderness refers to lands that are part of the National Wilderness Preservation System. These lands were established by the 1964 Wilderness Act.

IMMIGRATION AT ODDS WITH CONSERVATION?

Increases in the U.S. population stemming from both domestic births and immigration led one of the nation's premier conservation groups, The Wilderness Society (TWS), to formally adopt a policy in the 1990s encouraging reductions in birth and immigration rates. The policy explicitly refers to the degradation of wildland recreation resources resulting from population increase:

> [S]ince 1940, the U.S. population has doubled, but [national] park visitation has increased sixteen times. Recreational demand on our other public lands—the forests, wildlife refuges, and Bureau of Land Management lands—has also reached record numbers. An increase only one-half as great in the next fifty years would devastate these areas, diminishing the quality of visitors' experience and reducing resources to unsustainable levels. (The Wilderness Society, 1998)

The Sierra Club was criticized from both within and outside of the organization for considering a similar resolution calling for restricted immigration as a means to reduce the U.S. population in the late 1990s (Clarke, 2001). Although the mainstream organization shied away from advocating an immigration reduction policy, some Sierra Club activists formed the organization Support U.S. Population Stabilization (SUSPS) to reverse the club's neutral stance on immigration. The goal is to limit what SUSPS terms "over-immigration" to the United States.

Some in the conservation community make the "overcrowding" argument that the more immigration, the higher the number of people recreating on U.S. wildlands. But this reasoning equates demand for wildland and wilderness recreation with demands for routine or life-sustaining necessities such as food, shelter, or employment. Because wildland and wilderness visitation is influenced to a large extent by cultural values, immigrants' cultural views would act as a sieve through which demand is filtered. Cultural

norms about nature held by groups from Latin America and Asia may constrain these groups' interaction with wildlands and wilderness. European American ideals around conservation and wildland preservation emphasize the separation of humans and nature. This ontology has played out in the formal designation of wilderness, parks, and forest preserves. However, this mode of viewing nature may not resonate with cultures from around the world because many traditional non-Western cultures do not segregate culture and nature (Buijs, Elands, & Langers, 2009; Guha, 1989; Han, 2008; Parajuli, 2001). Indeed, the distinction between society and nature has been roundly criticized when exported to other parts of the globe and has been critiqued in the U.S. context as well. American academics Callicott and Nelson (1998, p. 2) go so far as to state that federally recognized wilderness areas are "ethnocentric, androcentric, phallogocentric, unscientific, unphilosophic, impolitic, outmoded, even genocidal." Diegues (2008, p. 265) called the American model of distinguishing nature and civilization "devastating" for those people and cultures directly dependent upon natural resources.

Dong and Chick (2005) argued for a "cultural constraints" model of outdoor recreation that acknowledges the legitimacy of culture in influencing outdoor recreation behavior. Along similar lines, Lee (1972) argued that an understanding of the culturally based meanings that sociocultural groups attribute to an environment can help explain a group's interaction with that particular milieu or class of milieus. Because of the saliency of culture in immigrant societies, it behooves researchers to examine culturally based meanings and images of nature.

Johnson, Bowker, Bergstrom, and Cordell (2004) examined whether immigrants were less likely than those born in the United States to visit wilderness or to deem it worthy of preservation. Study results showed that immigrants were indeed less likely than native-born respondents to say they had visited wilderness or that they would visit such places in the future. Immigrants were also less likely to indicate agreement with either of these statements: "I enjoy knowing that other people are currently able to visit Wilderness" or "I support protecting wilderness just so they [these areas] will always exist in their natural condition, even if no one were to ever visit or otherwise benefit from them." Further, Johnson, Bowker, and Cordell (2005) examined the role of nature-based recreation in the acculturation of Mexican and Chinese immigrants to American society. The study made explicit the role of acculturation in influencing nature-based or wildland recreation participation. Findings showed that Mexican immigrants were less likely than U.S.-born Whites to say they had done either birding, developed or primitive camping, or mountain biking. Similarly, Chinese immigrants were less likely to do all activities except birding. Interestingly, higher acculturation levels increased the probability of developed camping but decreased the likelihood of primitive camping.

The following section presents an overview of the various ontologies or human–nature paradigms found in European American, Asian, and Latin American cultures. This explication should aid the reader in better understanding immigrant interactions with and perceptions of wildland-based nature in America. Note that the various "Americas" referenced in this chapter are not monolithic. Latin America includes an array of cultures, climates, and economic systems. The intent in this chapter is not to summarize a single "Latin American" view of the wild but rather to discuss some of the fundamental differences between views of the topic in European-dominated America and Latin countries of the Americas. Similarly, the following discussion of wild nature in the European and Asian imagination should be understood with the caveat that country-specific variations exist.

© Jeff Greenberg/age fotostock

Wildland and wilderness visitation is influenced to a large extent by cultural values; therefore, it is important to understand the environmental worldviews of Latino and Asian cultures in the United States.

EUROPEAN AMERICAN CULTURE AND NATURE-BASED RECREATION

The underpinnings for wilderness and other wild nature preservation in the United States can be traced to the mid- to late 1800s and the influence of American icons such as Ralph Waldo Emerson in New England and John Muir, who eventually found his way to the American West. Both men espoused transcendentalism, a philosophy that included the belief that the natural world—wild, natural places—could help redeem humanity from the denaturalization caused by industrial society. Important in this worldview are clear distinctions between the natural world and civilization.

No doubt influenced by this culture–nature dichotomy, early ecologist Charles C. Adams presaged the 1964 Wilderness Act's intent of clearly demarcating wilderness from society by stressing that wild places are reservations "set aside . . . *to allow nature to take her own course, with as little interference by man as is possible*" (original emphasis, in Adams, 1929, p. 57). That federally designated wilderness lands are viewed as sanctified or set apart from pedestrian human habitat is also evident in the writings and musings of early preservationists such as Emerson, Henry David Thoreau, and Muir. This central theme is taken up again in Sanders' (2008) discussion of "Wilderness as Sabbath," which likens wilderness to the ancient Judeo–Christian avocation of resting the mind, body, soul—in the case of wilderness, a recognition of the limits to human growth and exploitation (Sanders, 2008).

Inglehart (1990, 1995) would also argue that the interest in and protection of wildland and wilderness in Anglo-dominated North America have been aided by the comparative wealth of large North American countries. Inglehart's (1990, 1995) postmaterialist thesis suggests that lack of material need in Western countries affords individuals in those countries the luxury of adopting egalitarian attitudes and actions more inclusive of others in society. Because basic needs have been attended to in the West, a greater number of people are freer to concentrate on issues and concerns besides those that are most fundamental, such as racial and gender equality; animal rights; and environmental protection, including wildland and wilderness preservation.

NATURE PERCEIVED IN LATIN AMERICA

Latin American perspectives on wildland and wilderness offer an interesting contrast to those of European Americans (see chapter 5 on leisure among Latino Americans). Although the Judeo–Christian influence pervades both of the Americas, Latin countries have a decidedly different conceptualization of the wild. This view appears more consistent with Inglehart's postmaterialism. Price (1994, p. 42) commented that "environmental conservation is not widely embraced by Latin Americans." Citing the Latin American terror and tumult of the 1970s and 1980s, she wrote that more pressing concerns revolving around political instability and unemployment took precedence over concern for environmental quality during this time. Price (1994) and Diegues (2008), however, stressed that conservation, environmentalism, and overall concern for the environment were increasing in Latin America through the efforts of nongovernmental organizations (NGOs), but that the environmentalism of Latin American NGOs differed from that of their European American counterparts; the former included a broader base of support across political and class spectra. DeLuca's (1999) charge, for instance, that wilderness preservation is dominated by elite White males in America would carry much less weight in the Latin American context given that their NGOs employ a model more akin to the United States' environmental justice movement, which emphasizes both economic justice and environmental integrity in the nonwild places that people inhabit. Price (1994) remarked, "Combining the goal of environmental stewardship with economic needs of the poor, these NGOs are more likely to promote extractive reserves than parklands free of human inhabitants" (p. 44).

To suppose that nature-based or wildland and wilderness recreation would resonate with newly arrived or even more acculturated Latino and Asian immigrants may be presumptuous given that the very concept of outdoor *recreation* (as opposed to nature contact for sustenance) may be wholly unfamiliar to native cultures from which many of these groups stem. Cowell (1991), for instance, quoted in Gómez-Pompa and Kaus (2008), remarked that South American Indians in tropical forests approach natural resources from a sustainable albeit utilitarian perspective: "There are saplings for making bows, and jatoba for making canoes . . . but there are never trees noticeable for self-conscious reasons—beauty, terror, wonder" (p. 297). Lynch (1993) also asserted that people of Latin American descent in the United States hold a contrasting view of nature, relative to Whites. Unlike the traditional American view of nature as separate from the individual and community, Latinos perceive humans to be intimately connected with their natural surroundings (see chapter 5 on Latino Americans). In support of these claims, Schultz, Unipan, and Gamba (2000) found that less acculturated foreign-born Latinos in southern California were more likely than acculturated Latinos to agree with the New Ecological Paradigm worldview of "people in harmony with nature." Schultz and colleagues (2000) attributed the differences to two possible sources. One relates to the argument presented here, that Latin American collectivism encourages a harmonious relationship between humans and nature. The second explanation is that more acculturated Latinos have been in the United States longer than recent immigrants and perceive less environmental degradation because its level in the United States is comparatively lower. Schultz and colleagues (2000) remarked that the first explanation seems an oversimplification given the gross exploitation of material resources throughout Latin America. However, in explaining Latin American concern for the wild, both Price (1994) and Gómez-Pompa and Kaus (2008) highlighted stark class differences within Latin America. Price (1994) argued that folk understandings of nature remain throughout the region but that wild places have been degraded via the actions of economic and political urban elites, both from within the region and from the United States and Canada.

WILD NATURE IN ASIAN THOUGHT

In China, scenic and historic interest areas are included in the country's national park system (Han, 2008). The designation of these areas, however, has not been without controversy because their establishment follows the Western or American model of culture–nature schism, which demands that anthropocentric features be removed. As Han (pp. 252-253) wrote, "These policies are strongly opposed by local communities and local governments because local people are uprooted and traditional lifeways [sic] and subsistence economies are ruined . . . such policies are not consistent with the traditional Chinese attitudes toward and values regarding nature." Hung (2003) noted the increases in land set aside for conservation in China since the 1970s but questioned whether the Chinese have actually embraced wilderness and conservation values. In stark contrast to the Western idea of wilderness as cathartic, spiritual cleanser, in the Chinese mind, wildlands are perceived as anathema to humans. Rather, valued nature includes carefully cultivated landscapes arranged with intention. Han (2008, p. 254) identified several characteristics that distinguish traditional Chinese and Western ideas about nature. For the Chinese, nature is

- humanistic rather than religious;
- aesthetic rather than scientific;
- consistent with human culture;
- an extension of home, an enjoyable and inspiring place; and
- managed to imitate art because art is more beautiful than uncultured nature.

Importantly, the aim of traveling is to be companionable instead of solitary and physically daunted.

Along similar lines, Yu and Berryman (1996) cited four cultural factors that distinguish Chinese and American outdoor recreation (also see chapter 6 on Asian North Americans). Two of these are relevant for the present discussion: (1) Chinese people view recreation as relaxing, passive engagement rather than as strenuous activity, in contrast to forms of wildland- and wilderness-based recreation that require much effort; and (2) *outdoor* recreation generally is not viewed positively by Chinese families.

Han (2008) argued that contemporary Chinese views of nature are rooted in Confucianism and Taoism, which includes significant elements of humanism and, again, a human culture in situ with nature. The Chinese also place much greater value on designed garden spaces than on wild nature. Hung (2003), for instance, wrote that the manicured gardens in Chinese mountain monasteries are examples of cultural distinctiveness for the Chinese and are analogous to the national park ideal for North Americans.

In traditional Chinese society, engaging in outdoor woodland activities is closely aligned with class—primarily with peasants, who are most connected to wild nature because they must eke out a subsistence from the land. As a result, modern, more Westernized Chinese distance themselves from wild, undeveloped settings. The difference in wildland engagement as described by Hung and the symbiosis espoused in the Taoist and Buddhist traditions seem to be a difference between a contemporary, secularized relationship to nature and a more philosophic stance. Also important in China is that communism contributed greatly to the former perspective by attempting to supplant centuries-old views of nature with more self-centered modern ideas that emphasize mastery over nature (Sodowsky, Maguire, Johnson, Ngumba, & Kohles, 1994).

Writing from the perspective of a "sympathetic outsider" to deep ecology,[3] the Indian ecologist Ramachandra Guha (1989) criticized the lens through which deep ecologists and other Western writers have constructed East and South Asia's relationship with nature. Guha (1989) wrote that the "complex and internally differentiated religious traditions—Hinduism, Buddhism, and Taoism—are lumped together as holding a view of nature believed to be quintessentially biocentric" (p. 76). Guha argued, to the contrary, that ordinary Easterners have continually altered their surrounding environment, sometimes with lasting and devastating results. Guha too emphasized that wilderness designation and protection is a uniquely American concept that has little resonance in India among the common folk. Rather, when rural Indian peasants engage in environmental activism, they are not seeking to shelve or restrict access to pristine nature but are seeking rights to lands so that they might be used *sustainably* to support traditional livelihoods.

Importantly, Sodowsky and colleagues (1994) suggested that East Asian immigrants to the United States may not adhere to traditional Taoist views of holism but adapt to a more material culture that has as its basis unsustainable resource depletion. The so-called BRIC nations, Brazil, Russia, India, and China (so named for their emergent economies), are quickly adding to the amount of human-produced carbon emissions worldwide (Chousa, Tamazian, & Chaitanya, 2008). Indeed, China's economic expansion, which is consuming natural resources at accelerating rates both within the country and abroad, bears scant resemblance to the holism discussed here and detailed by Altman and Chemers (1980) or Goodman (1980). The contradictions that appear in Latin America regarding environmental stewardship and economic realities are also evident in the Asian interpretation of nature. Traditional conceptualizations of nature are necessarily tempered by contemporary realities of globalism and strivings of emergent economies for wealth maximization.

FUTURE DIRECTIONS

Returning to the issues that the land managers and agency heads raised at the land trust and outdoor recreation conferences mentioned earlier, the present author thinks that a key to engaging these communities is to emphasize conservation and outdoor recreation activities in and near respective immigrant communities. While wildland restoration may be ideal for mainstream U.S. conservation and land management organizations,

[3]The term "deep ecology" was penned by Arne Naess in the 1960s. Deep ecology is an ecological philosophy that advocates for the interconnectedness of all living organisms, a philosophy that sees humans as part of a larger biotic structure rather than at the pinnacle of that structure (Harding, n.d.).

immigrants from places in the world where there is little contact with wild nature would best be introduced to conservation practices and wildland protection in the United States by first engaging with these resources where they live. In many instances, these are urban areas.

Viewing urban and immigrant populations as legitimate constituencies of land management organizations would help to direct attention to the potential for support in these communities. Some of these initiatives have already taken place. The Trust for Public Land founded the Parks for People program in six urban areas, and the Sierra Club is actively engaged with environmental justice efforts (Lanfer & Taylor, n.d.). The U.S. Forest Service also supports urban greening, but outside of the Northeast, these programs are not well known or established. The southern United States is ripe for such programming given the dramatic increases in immigrant migration and immigration to the South over the past 30 years (Johnson-Gaither, 2011).

Land management and conservation agencies should look into ways of highlighting the "wild" nature that exists near immigrant communities. Traditional interpretations of wildlands and wilderness do not include tree-adorned urban parks or commons; however, these resources may be as close to the Great Outdoors as some people may be able to or desire to come. In an effort to help engage urban communities with the nature that exists in cities, Harnik (2010) and Campbell and Wiesen (2009) suggested that municipalities encourage the planting of community gardens in permissible areas around homes and in abandoned lots. Neighborhood gardens have been successful in urban areas in the Northeast. Campbell and Wiesen documented a number of cases in some of New York City's high-crime areas, such as the South Bronx, where the planting of gardens helped to reestablish community. Latinos of Caribbean descent were highlighted in this research. The gardens are cultural expressions brought with Latino immigrants from their native countries or passed on by their immigrant parents. Public parks and community gardens may provide immigrants a venue for establishing meaning and attachment to their new environs while remaining connected through nature to their culture of origin.

CONCLUSION

The environmental worldviews held by immigrants from Latin America and Asia may be useful for understanding these immigrants' likely demand for wilderness in the United States. The complexity of these attitudes and beliefs is not easily deciphered, however, because of the various, often contradictory, interpretations of nature. Still, the literature presented in this chapter does not suggest high demand for wildland and wilderness activities among Latino and Asian immigrants. Thus, concerns in the conservation community that the rise in immigrant populations may overload the carrying capacity of wild nature may be unwarranted. Latino and Asian interest in nature-based activities may depend on whether these involve physically demanding activities in remote settings or activities in developed settings. For instance, Chavez's[4] research in and around national forests in California shows relatively high visitation by Latinos in that part of the country; but again, these impacts are concentrated in day-use, developed areas and do not indicate system-wide Latino visitation increases. In fact, Chavez and others (Roberts, Chavez, Lara, & Sheffield, 2009) decry the lack of cultural diversity in publicly managed forests and parks in California. Garnering political support for these preserves may be an especially difficult task given that research shows that political activism for environmental concerns among immigrants is usually low (Pfeffer & Stycos, 2002). The U.S. land trust community clearly understands that protection of wildlands and wilderness will depend, to a great extent, on the continued popular political support of all Americans and the varied perspectives they hold about the land. Yet, as immigrant populations grow, their support of wilderness values will be crucial as well.

---

[4]Chavez (2001, 2005) documented decades of Latino recreation in urban proximate national forests in Southern California.

CHAPTER 13

Race, Ethnicity, and Physical Activity

Kindal A. Shores and Kimberly J. Shinew

OVERVIEW

The purpose of this chapter is to provide a greater understanding of the current health status and physical activity patterns of racial and ethnic minority groups. The World Health Organization asserts that health encompasses physical, mental, and social well-being; physical activity is one of the key components of this holistic health definition. Although physical inactivity has reached epidemic proportions across all demographic categories, it tends to be most prevalent among certain ethnic and racial groups. The negative health effects of physical inactivity, such as obesity and chronic disease, also tend to be higher among these minority groups. The chapter explores these patterns and relationships and presents strategies for combating these issues.

Learning Outcomes

After reading this chapter, readers will be able to

- identify the roles of physical activity in leisure service provision and research;
- contrast the leisure-time physical activity (LTPA) for people of different races and ethnicities;
- evaluate theoretical approaches to the study of racial and ethnic minority groups' LTPA and ways in which an individual's race is considered in each theoretical approach;
- compare current knowledge with what remains to be understood about the intersection of race, ethnicity, and LTPA; and
- support LTPA among racial and ethnic minorities.

Social determinants of health inequity themselves are not causes of social injustice and inequity. They reflect deeper social divisions which generate multiple social risks, reproduced over time.

Hofrichter and Bhatia (2010, p. 15)

Physical activity is defined as any bodily movement that is produced by skeletal muscle contraction and is also characterized by an increase in energy expenditure (U.S. Department of Health and Human Services, 1996). Regular physical activity can reduce the risk of obesity and can help people live longer, healthier lives (Ogden, Carroll, McDowell, & Flegal, 2007).

Due, in part, to either a lack of or inadequate physical inactivity, obesity in the United States has reached epidemic proportions across age, race–ethnic, and socioeconomic groups. As a result of chronic health conditions associated with obesity, health care costs continue to increase in the United States. According to National Health Accounts, $147 billion in medical spending was attributed to obesity in 2008 (Finkelstein, Trogdon, Cohen, & Dietz, 2009).

Achieving an increase in physical activity is one of the most important public health issues in the United States and internationally because of the contribution of physical activity to decreasing premature mortality rates and lowering health care costs (Brownson, Hoehneer, Day, Forsyth, & Sallis, 2009). In line with this goal is the need to reduce the physical activity disparity between people of different races and ethnicities. Both overall health and physical activity prevalence are lower among racial and ethnic minorities compared to Whites (Hofrichter & Bhatia, 2010). These differences persist even within similar income categories and among insured individuals (Agency for Healthcare Research and Quality, 2005; Crespo, Smit, Carter-Pokras, & Ainsworth, 2000; Seo & Torabi, 2007). One mechanism to increase physical activity is to facilitate active living. Active living is the integration of physical activity within everyday lives (Gobster, 2005).

Leisure and recreation programs and settings have a long history of helping people become more physically active. For example, during the industrial revolution, reformers "focused on the ability of non-work activity to improve the health, education, social adjustment, and life chances of the masses" (Godbey, Caldwell, Floyd, & Payne, 2005, p. 150). Physical activity was incorporated into this model as many organizations, such as the YMCA, provided opportunities for people to be physically active. In the 1950s, Morris and colleagues (1953) conducted the first empirical investigation of what was termed the "exercise hypothesis"—the idea that physical activity reduces the occurrence of coronary heart disease. The study focused exclusively on work activity, but later Morris and colleagues (1973) showed that physical activity in leisure time can be "cardioprotective." Vendien and Nixon (1968) stated that "general fitness and obesity" were public concerns that warranted support for physical activity. Harris (1973) addressed the "somatopsychic" reasons for physical activity. She stated that those who engage in sport and physical activity must do so for reasons beyond simply getting fit and referred to the fulfillment that comes from engaging in active pursuits. Additionally, she specifically addressed how a lack of physical activity promotes obesity. She noted findings indicating that youth who were overweight or obese did not necessarily eat more than their thinner counterparts; rather, overweight and obese youth engaged in less physical activity. Harris concluded that "physical activity involvement should be a consideration along the entire continuum of human existence . . . and may serve to add life to years instead of only years to life" (p. 9).

Given the potential health benefits of physical activity, there has been an increased volume of new research in this area in the last 10 years. A review of five major North American peer-review research journals in recreation and leisure studies identified a significant upward trend in physical activity research. Between 1995 and 2011, a total of 128 articles related to physical activity were published. As shown in figure 13.1, most of this writing occurred after 2005. This coincides with national attention to physical activity promotion at interdisciplinary conferences (e.g., the National Recreation and Park Association Active Living Research Workshop [2005] and the Cooper Institute Conference on Parks, Recreation, and Public Health: Collaborative Frameworks for Promoting Physical Activity [2006]), as well as funding made available from major foundations such as the Robert Wood Johnson Foundation. Given the national and international spotlight on the importance of regular physical activity, this research trend is expected to continue.

Many stakeholders are invested in increasing leisure-time physical activity. Professionals in exercise and sport science, public health, education, transportation and design, medicine, health promotion, and other disciplines have identified the unique contribution that they can each make to promote physical activity. For example, teachers may integrate activity breaks into classroom learning exercises. Urban planners may advocate for bike lanes in their communities. Similarly, leisure service providers have identified the unique attributes of leisure, parks, and recreation that lend themselves to physical activity promotion.

The provision of leisure services has natural connections to physical activity. First, park and recreation agencies are the primary agencies responsible for the provision of parks, trails, and aquatic, sport, and recreation facilities in most communities in the United States and Canada. These facilities provide opportunities for active participation. A recent study showed that children living within a half-mile of a park or playground were five times more likely to be at a healthy weight than children who did not have a park with a playground nearby (Potwarka, Kaczynski, & Flack, 2008). Second, leisure service providers offer youth and adult programs that facilitate active recreation, such as sport leagues, tournaments, recreation programs, summer camps, and after-school programs and fitness classes. Third, although no one definition of leisure exists, a leisure experience is often characterized by perceived freedom and enjoyment (Mannell & Kleiber, 1997). To this end, recreation providers work to design physical activity experiences that are rewarding and enjoyable. If physical activity can be "leisure-like," then individuals are more likely to regularly engage in such activity (Henderson & Ainsworth, 2002).

Finally, as our nation became more developed, natural links between physical activity and labor were lost for much of the population (Cross, 1990). Instead, physical activity is often a purposive activity undertaken during nonwork time. This nonwork or "free" time is often equated with leisure time. In fact, participation in physical activity is so closely linked to free time and leisure in modern and postmodern society that the term *leisure-time physical activity* has been adopted across disciplines to refer to nonoccupational physical activities. The notion of leisure-time physical activity (LTPA) is so ubiquitous that the Centers for Disease Control and Prevention's annual surveillance of health behaviors includes data on LTPA. However, it should be noted that for some racial and ethnic groups, work activities still include a fair amount of physical activity, causing them to select more sedentary activities in their free time. For example, Crespo (2000) suggested that the differences between LTPA participation rates among Mexican Americans and members of other ethnic groups might be attributable to the fact that Latinos are overrepresented in highly physically active jobs, which in turn may limit their desire and ability to participate in LTPA.

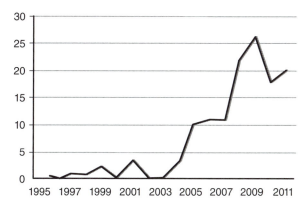

Figure 13.1   Peer-review publications related to physical activity in five major leisure journals.

RELATIONSHIP BETWEEN RACE AND ETHNICITY AND PHYSICAL ACTIVITY

National data sets help us understand the relationships between race and ethnicity and physical activity. Based on the 2008 Physical Activity Guidelines for Americans, *adults should aim for 150 minutes of moderate physical activity weekly and engage in strength exercises two days per week.* According to Behavioral Risk Factor Surveillance System (BRFSS) data, fewer than half of adults report that they achieve the recommended amount of regular physical activity on a weekly basis (Centers for Disease Control and Prevention [CDC], 2009). In addition, 25% of all adults are completely sedentary. These figures are even lower among racial and ethnic minorities. The most recent prevalence data for U.S. citizens indicate that 22.2% of Whites report no LTPA weekly. This compares to 31.9% of Blacks and 34.6% of Hispanics who report no LTPA. Furthermore, whereas 50.3% of non-Hispanic Whites reported meeting national recommendations for physical activity in 2005 (CDC, 2007), fewer Black, Asian, and Hispanic respondents met these recommendations (41.1%, 40.2%, and 42.7%, respectively). When the more than 350,000 Americans in this sample were asked if they had exercised in the last month, Hispanic and Black respondents were significantly more likely than all others (non-Hispanic White, multiracial, other race) to report no leisure-time physical activity (CDC, 2009).

Similar trends are evident among youth. According to 2005 Youth Risk Behavior Survey data for high school–aged boys and girls, White non-Hispanic students reported significantly greater participation in moderate physical activity than African American and Hispanic students (CDC, 2004). The ramifications of this inactivity are evident in obesity rates. Among high school age youth, non-Hispanic Blacks have the highest rate of obesity (18.2%), compared with Hispanic (14.1%) and non-Hispanic Whites (11.5%) (Eaton et al., 2012). These trends continue into adulthood; age-adjusted rates of adult obesity are highest for non-Hispanic Blacks (49.5%), compared with all Hispanics (39.1%) and non-Hispanic Whites

(34.3%) (Flegal, Carroll, Kit, & Ogden, 2012). These trends continue into adulthood; 77.3% of Mexican men, 74.4% of Mexican women, 72% of African American men, and 80.5% of African American women are either overweight or obese.

It is important to note, however, that increases in the prevalence of regular physical activity have been observed for some racial and ethnic groups. As of 2007, gains in physical activity ranging from 11.6% to 15% were observed among non-Hispanic Black women, non-Hispanic Black men, Hispanic women, and women of other races. However, among men and women, non-Hispanic Whites still had the highest prevalence of regular physical activity (CDC, 2007). In general, racial and ethnic minorities' limited physical activity participation rates remain troubling. Many explanations have been suggested, but these differences have persisted even in models that adjusted for variations in health problems, body mass index, marital status, employment status, smoking, and social class (Crespo et al., 2000; Seo & Torabi, 2007).

Assessing attitudes toward physical activity may help one understand why some people are more likely than others to engage in physical activity (Thompson, 2010). Further, it is important to explore how these attitudes are mediated by racial or cultural background. For example, appearance and body image have influenced racial groups' perceptions toward physical activity. Thompson noted that adolescent girls often have a negative attitude toward physical activity due to its immediate impacts on appearance. Similarly, Boyinton and colleagues' (2008) study of 12 overweight African American girls revealed that the girls hesitated to engage in physical activity due to "beauty costs," typically characterized by "sweating" and disheveled hair. Further, Juarbe, Lipson, and Turok (2003), in a study of 51 Mexican immigrant women, reported that their families viewed exercise as conducive to a slim and "sexy" body, which was inappropriate for married women and was considered a sign of promiscuity and trying to "act White."

Although many women express positive views toward physical activity, they are often restricted because of the expectation that as females they are the caretakers of the family. For instance, Im and Choe's (2001) study on Korean immigrant women revealed that despite their positive attitudes toward physical activity, hectic schedules and lack of child care services left little time available for exercise. Latino and African American women also appear to be restricted because of family and household duties (Henderson, & Ainsworth, 2002; Richter, Wilcox, Greaney, Henderson, & Ainsworth, 2002; Skowron, Stodolska, & Shinew, 2008; Young, He, Harris, & Mabry, 2002). Many of the women view family responsibilities such as taking care of children or aging parents as uppermost in importance. This type of attitude led a participant in Im and Choe's study to conclude that physical activity was nonessential, or a "waste of time." Although understanding attitudes toward physical activity provides insight into behavioral ramifications, it is important to apply this insight to conceptual models that take a broader perspective.

CONCEPTUAL MODELS

Conceptual models have been devised to organize the study of LTPA. The most prevalent framework in LTPA research is the social ecological model (Powell, Slater, Chaloupka, & Harper, 2006; Sallis & Owen, 1997; Trost et al., 1997). The relationship between parks and physical activity (Bedimo-Rung, Mowen, & Cohen, 2005) and the concept of environmental justice have also been used as guiding frameworks in the study of LTPA.

Briefly, the social ecological model proposes that layered factors affect whether a person will engage in a health behavior such as physical activity. These levels are labeled intrapersonal, interpersonal, institutional, community, and public policy factors and are arranged in a hierarchy that expands outward from individual to higher-order concerns (figure 13.2). *Intrapersonal* factors include an individual's knowledge, skills, attitudes, behaviors, and sociodemographic characteristics that are expected to influence that person's physical activity. *Interpersonal* factors include relationships and coparticipation with family members, friends, coworkers, neighbors, and others. *Institutional* factors are the places where we learn, live, worship, work, and play. These organizations provide the context for what individuals are and are not able to do each day.

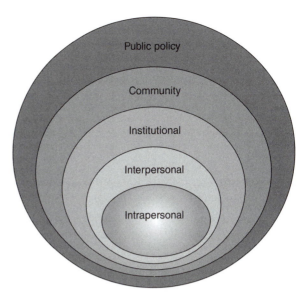

Figure 13.2 The social ecological model.

Community factors are also important influences on many health behaviors, including physical activity. Neighborhood design, city zoning, and park locations are important community factors with respect to physical activity behavior. The outermost level of influence includes *public policy* related to health behavior. This level of the social ecological model recognizes that laws and rules can encourage or discourage physical activity.

The social ecological model recognizes that an individual's physical activity behavior is a complex act that is best understood as the outcome of multiple layers of influence. Each factor in the social ecological model should be considered, as should the interactions between levels of influence.

Race and ethnicity are not a major focus of the social ecological model. Instead, this model treats race and ethnicity as two of many relevant factors at the intrapersonal level. When researchers adopt this framework to guide their research, race and ethnicity are often included as demographic characteristics (intrapersonal factors). In addition, since residential location and religious faith are often tied to race and ethnicity in modern American society (Anderson & Massey, 2001), race and ethnicity bear heavily on results at the community level of the social ecological model. For example, Powell, Slater, Chaloupka, and Harper (2006) examined the association of race, ethnicity, and socioeconomic status with community-level physical activity settings (i.e., sport areas, green spaces, bike paths) and found that African Americans and individuals of "other" races were less likely to have access to physical activity–related amenities.

Much of the research on LTPA has relied on the social ecological model (see Powell et al., 2006; Sallis & Owen, 1997; Trost et al., 1997). However, some studies that specifically describe the role of parks in active living have used a model presented by Bedimo-Rung, Mowen, and Cohen (2005) named the Relationship between Parks and Physical Activity model. The model characterizes the potential relationships among park environmental characteristics, park visitation, physical activity within parks, and the different outcomes individuals and communities may experience in parks. As shown in figure 13.3, the lower part of the model identifies personal characteristics and environmental components thought to influence the use or nonuse of parks. The middle section of the model addresses on-site park behavior. The uppermost section enumerates possible outcomes resulting from parks and park usage. The authors' conceptualization of positive outcomes stemming from park visitation and physical activity provides the conceptual foundation for studies of park environments and LTPA (see Rung, Mowen, Broyles, & Gustat, 2011; Shores & West, 2008a;

Stodolska, Shinew, Acevedo, & Izenstark, 2011). As in the social ecological model, concepts of race and ethnicity are not highlighted in this conceptualization. Instead, race and ethnicity are again embedded in the intrapersonal antecedents to park use.

Stodolska and colleagues (2011) provided an expanded version of Bedimo-Rung and colleagues' model (2005) that focuses attention on racial and ethnic minorities. Although the authors used the Relationship between Parks and Physical Activity framework as a starting point to ground their research, results from four focus groups with urban Mexican American participants led the authors to expand the model to capture themes related to race, ethnicity, and variables such as culture and neighborhood that often are confounded with race. This expanded model (see figure 13.4) recognizes that park visitation and the potential for visitation outcomes (e.g., physical activity, socialization) result from the quality of the park itself, as well as the traits of other park users (e.g., cultural background, socioeconomic status) and the safety and composition of the proximate neighborhood. This framework differs from others in the physical activity and park visitation literature in that it explicitly addresses minority park visitation. The model includes immigrant status, cultural background, and acculturation level as individual user characteristics, and integrates

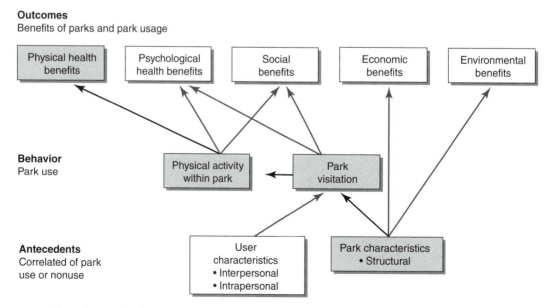

Figure 13.3 The relationship between parks and physical activity.

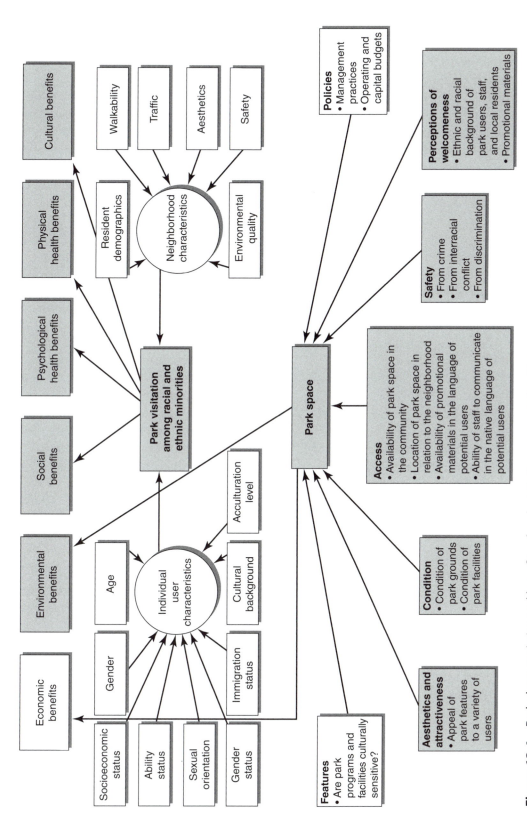

Figure 13.4 Park characteristics and benefits of park visitation among minorities.

Reprinted from M. Stodolska et al., 2011, "Perceptions of urban parks as havens and contested terrains by Mexican-Americans in Chicago neighborhoods," *Leisure Sciences* 33(1): 103. Reprinted by permission from Taylor & Francis Ltd., www.tandf.co.uk/journals.

social and physical attributes of a park space as indicators of racial and ethnic minorities' park visitation.

Another avenue for LTPA investigations is to adopt environmental justice as a conceptual foundation for research. Although less commonly used, its relevance to race-ethnicity and physical activity is clear. The term environmental justice refers to efforts to address the disproportionate exposure to and burden of harmful environmental conditions experienced by low-income and racial and ethnic populations (Taylor, Floyd, Whitt-Glover, & Brooks, 2007). As a framework for LTPA research, environmental justice directs attention to low-income and racial and ethnic minority populations and the substantial environmental challenges they must overcome to be physically active (Taylor et al.). Studies of active recreation facility access, quality, and site distribution have relied on the environmental justice framework (e.g., Dachmann, Wolch, Joassart-Marcelli, Reynolds, & Jerrett, 2010; Joassart-Marcelli, 2010).

Although race and ethnicity are included as variables of interest in the social ecological model and the conceptual description of park use and health benefits, only Stodolska and colleagues' (2011) model and the environmental justice approach explicitly direct researchers to the role of race and ethnicity in LTPA. Despite this strength in these approaches, most LTPA research, even racial and ethnic disparity research, has not used these frameworks. The result is that many studies linking LTPA to race or ethnicity have simply treated these factors as independent variables of interest among many others (Henderson, 2009).

RESEARCH CONNECTING RACE, ETHNICITY, AND LTPA

Floyd (2007) noted that race–ethnicity research has progressed through stages of increasing complexity. This pattern occurs when researchers move from assumptions of racial sameness to recognizing and documenting racial inequalities. From this step, analyses of group differences often emerge. Studies at the intersection of race-ethnicity and other topical issues like LTPA typically follow this understanding of differences.

This same pattern can be observed in the subset of studies describing connections between race, ethnicity, and LTPA. Much of the research linking concepts of race, ethnicity, and LTPA falls into one of three types of investigations: (1) documentation of inequalities, (2) analyses of group differences, and (3) theoretical analysis of factors associated with LTPA for minority populations. A few studies stand out among these as pushing forward to understand the meaning of physical activity across cultures. This section summarizes the current research connecting race, ethnicity, and LTPA, focusing specifically on African American, Latino, and Asian populations.

African American Populations and LTPA

The prevalence of physical activity and inactivity among racial and ethnic minorities is a primary focus for race–ethnic research related to physical activity. This research lays the groundwork for more complex studies by demonstrating the breadth of physical activity disparity between majority White populations in the United States and racial and ethnic minorities. Many of these data are derived from national surveillance initiatives including the Behavioral Risk Factor Surveillance System and the National Health and Nutrition Examination Survey. Results characterize the racial and ethnic groups broadly and also pinpoint subgroups (i.e., Crespo et al., 2000; CDC, 2004, 2007, 2009).

Among racial and ethnic minorities in the United States, perhaps the most research attention has been devoted to African Americans and LTPA. Crespo and colleagues (2000) presented national data on LTPA in an African American population that effectively teased out the impacts of race. Using a national sample of more than 18,000 U.S. adults, the authors concluded that current indicators of social class are unable to explain the observed higher levels of physical inactivity among African American and Mexican American adults compared to their Caucasian counterparts. Patterson and colleagues (2004) observed that inactivity is exacerbated among rural Southern Blacks. In one of the most comprehensive assessments of Blacks' physical activity,

Whitt-Glover and colleagues (2007) summarized data from three national assessments: the 2003 Behavioral Risk Factor Surveillance System, the 2004 National Health Interview Survey, and the 1999 to 2004 National Health and Nutrition Examination Survey. Results indicated that the proportion of Black adults reporting regular physical activity ranged from 24% to 36% depending on the surveillance system used. Overall, older Black adults and those with lower incomes and educational attainment were at the greatest risk for inactive lifestyles.

In addition to reporting the prevalence of African Americans' physical inactivity, studies often compare LTPA between Blacks and Whites. In the mid- to late 1980s, the question of Black–White differences was examined using surveillance data (Washburn, Kline, Lackland, & Wheeler, 1992). Findings indicated that African Americans engaged in less physical activity than did Whites. Folsom and colleagues (1991) compared Black and White men's and women's physical activity in Minneapolis-St. Paul, Minnesota. Black men and women reported greater occupational physical activity but less LTPA and significantly less overall physical activity each week. Kimm and colleagues (2002) compared the relative decline of Black and White girls' physical activity during adolescence. Although the study was designed to examine self-report and objective measures of physical activity, the authors observed precipitous declines in both White and Black girls' physical activity from ages 9 and 10 to ages 18 and 19. Black adolescents, however, had a significantly steeper rate of decline in LTPA than did Whites.

Consistent with the development of race and ethnicity research in general, studies of group differences in LTPA have been augmented with examinations of factors associated with LTPA for minority subpopulations. Since the social ecological model has heavily influenced the study of LTPA, researchers often examine the relative importance of intrapersonal, interpersonal, and community or environmental factors for African Americans' LTPA. For example, data drawn from a sample of 240 volunteers in a Midwestern city allowed Sargent (2001) to examine the extent to which social support of family and friends and self-efficacy for specific LTPAs affected Afri-

can American women's LTPA. Self-efficacy and social support from friends accounted for 25% of the variance in the women's LTPA, although by and large, the women engaged in little physical activity ($M = 9$-14 minutes a day). Twelve African American informants aided Cherubini (2008) in a qualitative identification of individual, social, and environmental factors that impeded their LTPA. The author identified social interpersonal factors as most salient for African Americans' decision to participate in LTPA.

Finally, researchers profile the LTPA that African Americans do undertake with the hope of learning how to facilitate LTPA for the majority population who are less active. To this end, Shores and West (2008b) described park use rates across rural and urban park sites and found that African Americans engaged in park-based physical activity in greater proportion than Whites; they also visited parks with the greatest density of facilities more often than they did larger, less dense parks. Floyd and colleagues (2008) reported environmental and social correlates of physical activity in urban parks. More than 9,000 visits were observed in 28 parks in Tampa, Florida, and in Chicago, Illinois. In Tampa parks, visitors observed in Hispanic neighborhoods were more likely than park users in White and African American park neighborhoods to engage in the physical activity of walking. In Chicago, visitors to parks in African American neighborhoods were significantly more likely to engage in walking and vigorous activity than visitors to parks in White or Hispanic neighborhoods.

Important work aimed at intervening and increasing LTPA among African Americans is under way. For example, Rogers (1997) described a walking club and a self-directed activity program that was effective in increasing moderate-intensity LTPA among African American women. Other studies have stressed the importance of church-based physical activity (Young & Stewart, 2006) and have tried to integrate physical activity into cultural identity (Airhihenbuwa, Kumanyika, TenHave, & Morssink, 2000). Since the efficacy and effect size of interventions undertaken to date have been problematic, experts have focused their recommendations on improving the visibility of and participation in interventions instead of

Photo courtesy of Myron F. Floyd.

Race–ethnic research related to physical activity primarily focuses on the prevalence of physical activity and inactivity among racial and ethnic minorities.

endorsing a particular technique or curriculum to increase physical activity (Yancey et al., 2004).

Latino Populations and LTPA

The literature on physical activity participation among Latinos has significantly increased in recent years. Many studies (Ahmed et al., 2005; Neighbors, Marquez, & Marcus, 2008; Pichon et al., 2007; Ransdell & Wells, 1998) have reported that Latinos are significantly less likely to engage in LTPA than all other groups, and some have indicated that these higher rates of inactivity span age categories. According to Crespo (2000) and Jamieson and colleagues (2005), while physical activity tends to decrease with age for many groups, Latino Americans are less active across the entire life span, including childhood and adolescence. For example, neighbors and colleagues compared LTPA between Hispanic and non-Hispanic Whites and found that all Hispanic subgroups were less active than were non-Hispanic Whites; however, significant diversity was evident among Hispanic

respondents. When sociodemographic variables were included in the analysis, the disparity between Hispanic and non-Hispanic Whites was attenuated. However, disparities between Hispanic and non-Hispanic women persisted despite the inclusion of sociodemographic factors.

In recognition of the diverse heritage and immigration history of Latinos in the United States, researchers often examine the role of acculturation in their LTPA behavior (e.g., Berrigan, Dodd, Trojano, Reeve, & Ballard-Barbash, 2006; Crespo, Smit, Carter-Pokras, & Andersen, 2001; Evenson, Sarmiento, & Ayala, 2004; Liu, Probst, Harun, Bennett, & Torres, 2009). Liu and associates examined the association of acculturation with LTPA and obesity among Hispanic adolescents. Using data from the 2003 National Survey of Children's Health, the authors concluded that children in first-generation immigrant families and those who did not speak English at home had significantly higher odds of not obtaining recommended levels of physical activity compared to third-generation Hispanic adolescents. Using data from the Third National Health and Nutrition Examination Survey, Crespo and colleagues reported that Mexican American men and women who were less acculturated (e.g., spoke Spanish vs. English and had lived in the United States for less than five years) were less likely to be physically active than more acculturated Mexican Americans after age and socioeconomic status were controlled for. In contrast, Pichon and colleagues (2007) examined U.S. Latinas and concluded that acculturation to the U.S. mainstream culture was positively associated with moderate and vigorous physical activity, but was not related to walking behavior. In their study of first-generation Latina immigrants living in North Carolina, Evenson and colleagues observed that Latinas with higher language acculturation or those who had arrived in the United States when they were younger than 25 years were more likely to be physically active than women who had arrived later in life or who had lower language acculturation. Time living in the United States was not independently related to physical activity participation. Marquez and McAuley (2006) included both men and women in their study of physical activity and acculturation. Their findings suggested that acculturation was linked to occupational physical activity but not significantly related to recreational physical activity among Latinos.

In keeping with the levels of influence described in the social ecological model, a host of other personal, social, and institutional factors have been examined as correlates of Latinos' LTPA. Across multiple studies, social support has been a significant correlate of LTPA. In their review of correlates and outcomes of physical activity among Latinos, Marquez, McAuley, and Overman (2004) observed that the majority of studies with Latino participants examined constructs similar to those studied in the general population, namely, self-efficacy, social support, and perceived constraints. In this vein, Marquez and McAuley (2006) examined the relationship between LTPA, exercise self-efficacy, and exercise social support. Results from 153 respondents revealed a significant positive relationship between having social support for exercise from friends and achieving more LTPA. In another examination of social and ecological correlates, Morgan and colleagues

(2003) discussed the centrality of demographic, psychological, social, and environmental correlates among Mexican American youth. Mexican American boys and girls (average age of 12.1 years) had lower levels of social support and poorer physical self-perceptions than their European American counterparts. However, social factors did not predict engagement in LTPA for European American or Mexican American children. Instead, enjoyment of physical activity, physical self-perception, and opportunity to join sport teams were significantly related to children's LTPA. Mexican American girls reported the lowest scores for each of these correlates and had the lowest physical activity. Further, Mexican American girls in the sample reported significantly less opportunity to join sport teams than did Mexican American boys. European American boys reported the most opportunity to join sport teams.

In a study of attitudes, social support, and constraints affecting physical activity among Latina women, Skowron and colleagues (2008) found that despite low LTPA participation among the women, their attitudes toward and social support for LTPA were high. What limited their LTPA was instead structural constraints such as a lack of child care and insufficient time. Conversely, Voorhees and Young (2003) reported that personal factors were not significant correlates in their study of urban Latinas' physical activity. Using a sample of 285 women, they found that social factors were significantly related to physical activity in this group. In contrast to findings suggesting that women's social relationships often encourage physical activity, engagement in social clubs and religious services was negatively related to physical activity. Women were significantly less likely to be active if they reported knowing people who exercise, if they belonged to community groups, or if they attended religious services.

The impact of the environment on LTPA has also been explored. Stodolska and Shinew (2010) examined the importance of environmental constraints on LTPA in two communities of low-income urban Latinos. Focus groups and in-depth interviews elicited the following constraints: lack of access to natural environments that support LTPA, poor maintenance of parks, general safety of the outdoors, and racial tensions and discrimination. The issue of safety was explored in greater depth in two other papers that dealt with how gangs operate in recreation spaces in Latino neighborhoods (Stodolska, Acevedo, & Shinew, 2009; Stodolska, Shinew, Acevedo, & Roman, 2013). Focus group participants indicated that gang members were typically in the parks, which constrained the use of these open spaces for LTPA.

In addition to studies of LTPA correlates, a handful of studies have described the leisure-time activities of Latinos in the United States and have examined which environments are most condu-cive to physical activity. On-site questionnaire data were gathered from 917 Latino visitors to three park environments in the greater Chicago area. Broadly, the researchers concluded that women were more likely to be involved in passive leisure or walking, whereas men were more likely to be involved in other types of LTPA (Stodolska, Shinew, & Li, 2010). It should be noted, however, that Latino immigrants in the United States might not be representative of Latinos in their home country. The LTPA levels among middle- and upper-class Latinos in their home countries often resemble rates among non-Hispanic Whites in the United States. Thus, investigators might be observing social class differences on top of the cultural ones.

Asian Populations and LTPA

Scholarship linking Asian populations and LTPA is not well developed. This may be attributed, in part, to the less frequent incidence of obesity among Asian populations. According to 2005 Behavioral Risk Factor Surveillance System sta-tistics, a significantly smaller percentage of the Asian American population compared to non-Hispanic Whites reports meeting physical activity guidelines. Despite this, only 36% of the Asian American population is at risk of being overweight or obese whereas 60% of non-Hispanic Whites are at risk (CDC, 2007). However, research indicates that physical activity acts as a protective health factor irrespective of an individual's weight status (Welk, Blair, & President's Council on Physical Fitness and Sports, 2000). Therefore, examina-tions of leisure-time energy expenditure are also critical for this population.

Similar to other racial and ethnic groups, examination of Asian populations' LTPA is complex. Asians have immigrated to the United States from many countries and under varying political and social circumstances. Thus, stud-ies of "Asian" LTPA are likely to mask important regional and ethnic differences. For example, Wai and colleagues (2008) compared Taiwanese adults living in Taiwan and in the United States. Using data from the Taiwan National Health Interview Survey conducted in 2001 and commensurate U.S. data, the authors found that half of Taiwanese adults reported having engaged in no LTPA in the last week. When LTPA efforts were converted to calories of energy expenditure, the results showed that only one-seventh of the more than 15,000 respondents burned over 1,000 calories in a week compared to one-third of the U.S. population. In a study of Taiwanese Americans, prevalence data from nearly 30,000 people across four years led the authors to conclude that approximately 14% of Taiwanese adults met national physical activity recommendations (Ku, Fox, McKenna, & Peng, 2006). Kandula and Lauderdale (2005) analyzed results from the 2001 California Health Interview Survey and observed that Asian Americans were much less likely to meet recommended levels of LTPA than non-Asian U.S. residents. Moreover, Asian immigrants' risk of heart disease, diabe-tes, and obesity increased with their duration of residence in the United States. Mehta, Sharma, and Bernard (2009-2010) probed the paradox of diet and physical activity further and collected data from a sample of 200 middle-aged Asian Indian women residing in Chicago. The authors had hypothesized that the women's expectations, self-control, and self-efficacy (components of social cognitive theory) accounted for variance in observed dietary and LTPA behaviors. Results indicated that women's expectations for LTPA were related to their physical activity behaviors; but in contrast to findings from other studies, self-efficacy for exercise was not related to LTPA in this sample.

Finally, a study examining needs and attitudes of Korean immigrant women living in the United States reported that Korean women expressed a broader definition of physical activity than Anglo Americans. Their conceptualization of physical activity included housework, child care, and even social engagements (Im & Choe, 2001). These qualitative results echo the quantitative findings of Khaing Nang and colleagues (2010), who observed the importance of occupational and household work to daily physical activity achievement. The Korean women included in the Im and Choe study described exercise as enjoyable but often unattainable type of physical activity that was available only if all familial and household duties were completed. Interestingly, similar results were obtained by Tortolero and colleagues (1999) in their study of Latina women.

IMPLICATIONS FOR PRACTICE AND FURTHER RESEARCH

As mentioned earlier, surveillance data systems are in place to monitor the LTPA disparity between racial and ethnic groups in the United States. Although the items on these instruments are continuously being refined and expanded (Active Living Research, 2010), trend data on physical inactivity are readily available to researchers and leisure service providers. These data sets are publicly available through the websites of the Centers for Disease Control and Prevention and can be used by local health officials and park and recreation planners to gauge baseline physical activity patterns in their city and region. Data demonstrate physical activity disparity and can be a starting point for interventions to improve physical activity among regionally specific populations. Accessing and understanding the physical activity disparity in one's region is a critical starting point for acquiring the external funds often needed to launch an LTPA intervention.

The body of evidence describing correlates of LTPA for residents of different races and ethnicities has not elicited consensus. This also offers avenues for future research. The diversity of samples selected, the geographic and social context of the research, and the use of divergent measures have allowed knowledge to expand but not yet coalesce. Thus, under the umbrella of social ecological correlates research, there is still much uncertainty. With regard to specific populations, basic research on Asian, biracial, multiracial,

and people of other races LTPA and the effects of personal, interpersonal, institutional, community, and policy factors on LTPA is needed. Research on the LTPA of Latinos in the United States should continue with focused attention on potentially significant differences by country of origin, geographic location, and level of acculturation. Similarly, studies of African Americans' LTPA need to be differentiated to recognize geographic and rural–urban differences and to examine the centrality of African American identity to LTPA behaviors. Across all races, less is known about rural minorities than about urban minority racial and ethnic groups. This remains a ripe area for inquiry.

Of even greater importance, however, is the need for a dramatic shift in how researchers and practitioners examine LTPA, race, and ethnicity. National trend data notwithstanding, the research described in this chapter is predominately descriptive and cross sectional. With a few exceptions, intervention efficacy studies, advocacy research, and community-based participatory research are absent.

Meaningful change to racial disparity in LTPA is not likely to occur unless these more labor-intensive approaches are employed by researchers and service providers. In a review of 14 studies addressing physical activity in high-need populations, common components of ethnic minority group interventions included advisory panels, needs assessments, and interventions delivered by community members (Taylor, Baranowski, & Young, 1998). According to Lee (2005), participatory research may prove to be one of the most significant contributions to understanding of physical activity in minority populations. Involving members of the minority population when one is conducting needs assessments and subsequent physical activity interventions has shown the most promising results, particularly among African American populations. With respect to the interventions, the best approaches include culturally tailored messages and role models (Lee). Reliance on community health advisors (e.g., pastors, community leaders, health workers and promoters) has also been shown to be effective in lifestyle and behavior change programs with minority populations (Yancey et al.,

2004). As these examples indicate, this type of work draws on the expertise of residents, service providers, faith-based leaders, and researchers. The development of local physical activity and nutrition working groups is a first step to bring these partners together.

In addition to community-based participatory research, macro-level policy changes can have an immediate impact on targeted populations. At the macro level, a disparity exists in access to LTPA sites (Active Living Research, 2010). This is problematic since current research indicates that park access, proximity to parks or trails, and density of recreation resources are associated with greater participation in LTPA (Moore, Diez Roux, Evenson, McGinn, & Brines, 2008; Kaczynski & Henderson, 2007; Powell et al., 2006). Thus, the capacity of parks and recreation agencies to increase physical activity has not been fully realized (Active Living Research). Equity models used to allocate parks and trail sites need to be evaluated. While most communities rely on market or equality approaches for resource allocation (West & Crompton, 2008), adoption of a compensatory equity model may serve the greater good in communities. Compensatory equity policies can provide community leaders with a formalized approach to systematically allocate relatively low-cost park and recreation resources to racial and ethnic minority neighborhoods. In turn, larger health care costs and reduced quality of life may be partially mitigated.

Of course, there are explanations as to why this type of research is lacking. First, as noted throughout this chapter, studies at the intersection of race, ethnicity, and LTPA are relatively new. Second, as scholars have noted across the last two decades, studies of race are complicated (Henderson & Ainsworth, 2001; Gobster, 1998; Philipp, 1995). Race is a socially constructed categorization that is rife with meaning, history, and the interaction of multiple identities. Third, community-based participatory research is necessarily a site-specific, labor-intensive approach to research, and temporal and financial resources are required. Fourth, understanding of best practices in physical activity interventions is still emerging. In particular, most studies of interventions to increase physical activity have not been designed with or targeted for specific ethnic minority populations (Kahn et al., 2002). However, as has been mentioned by others (e.g., Allison, 2000; Floyd, 2007; Henderson, 2009; Henderson & Ainsworth, 2001; Philipp, 2000; Stodolska, 2000; Taylor, 2000), these difficult issues of race, ethnicity, and resources must be addressed if behavior changes are to be realized.

CONCLUSION

In summary, the purposes of this chapter were to identify the roles of physical activity in leisure service provision and research; compare the LTPA of people of different races and ethnicities; evaluate theoretical approaches used to understand this phenomenon; and compare current knowledge with what remains to be understood about the intersection of race, ethnicity, and LTPA. Due, in part, to either a lack of or inadequate physical inactivity, obesity in the United States has reached epidemic proportions and is particularly problematic among some racial and ethnic populations. Thus, understanding the physical activity patterns of racial and ethnic minority groups is a fertile area of research that requires attention. Moreover, applying the knowledge gained from this research to recreation and leisure service programs and policies is vital to increasing the LTPA participation rates of racial and ethnic groups. As noted earlier, the provision of leisure services has natural connections to physical activity. Park and recreation agencies are responsible for the provision of parks, trails, and aquatic, sport, and recreation facilities in most communities. Additionally, leisure service providers offer youth and adult programs that facilitate active recreation, and they work to design physical activity experiences that are rewarding and enjoyable. The literature demonstrates that if physical activity can be more "leisure-like," individuals will be more likely to regularly engage in it. Finally, assessing attitudes toward physical activity may advance understanding of why some people are more likely to engage in physical activity than others, and it is important to explore how these attitudes are mediated by racial or cultural background. Given the importance of physical activity to overall health and well-being, racial and ethnic physical activity disparities will remain relevant for many years.

CHAPTER 14

Race, Ethnicity, and Sport

Louis Harrison Jr. and Albert Y. Bimper Jr.

OVERVIEW

Since the election of the first Black president of the United States, some suggest that we live in a postracial society. But nowhere is this suggestion challenged more than in the realm of sport. While few venture to verbalize beliefs of superiority or inferiority by race, research suggests that when it comes to sport, *race matters*. The aim of this chapter is to provide a critical analysis of persistent beliefs of racial superiority in sport. Historical and psychosocial influence of race on the selection, persistence in, and performance of particular sport activities are examined, as well as their influence on health and physical activity. Future directions for research are suggested to help advance understanding of the impact of race and ethnicity on choices in sport activities.

Learning Outcomes

After reading this chapter, readers will be able to

- demonstrate awareness of the disparity in sport participation of racial and ethnic groups by citing the approximate percentages of ethnic groups participating in the most popular sports,
- list at least three historical explanations of differential sport performance by race and ethnicity and the corresponding counterarguments,
- define stereotypes and articulate the influence of stereotyping on sport participation and performance,
- cite specific emerging research on the impact of racial and ethnic identity on sport participation, and
- explain the social influences and environmental contexts affecting sport participation.

> *. . . athletics will continue to occupy a central place in African American life simply because it is one of the few places where an African American man can be a man.*
>
> Harrison, Harrison, and Moore (2002)

While it has become politically incorrect in many circles to espouse the idea of racial or ethnic inferiority or superiority, these beliefs still persist. Particularly in the realm of sport, the idea of the naturally gifted athlete draws the immediate suggestion that if the sport is American football, basketball, or track, the athlete is Black. Casual observation of professional and collegiate football, basketball, and track and field events reveals an obvious racial disparity. While African Americans are a minority in the U.S. population, 12.6% according to a very recent figure (Rastogi, Johnston, Hoeffel, & Drewery, 2011), they are a clear majority in professional football at 67% and basketball at 77% (Lapchick, 2009). Though much literature and recent research call these ideas into question, the prevailing thought remains the same.

It is difficult to argue with someone who regularly views ESPN or other sport channels that this idea of superiority or inferiority is not valid. The exponential increase in exposure of African Americans in media coverage of sporting events reinforces the ideology of racial–ethnic superiority in particular sport activities. Apart from a few exceptions such as Tiger Woods and the Williams sisters in golf and tennis, respectively, sport observers are fed a steady diet of racial disparity in sport that supports the established dogma of dominance in certain sports. This chapter is designed to fuel more critical analysis of this phenomenon, challenge prevalent beliefs, and suggest alternate explanations of racial–ethnic disparity in sport participation. Another aim is to endeavor to stimulate research from other theoretical perspectives that may provide alternate explanations for the observed disparity in particular sports. Hopefully, other epistemological orientations will seek to give voice to those being studied, namely, athletes from racial–ethnic groups. These alternatives can enlighten readers and potentially inform all sport stakeholders of the implications, both positive and negative, of the racial–ethnic disparities.

While it is not the authors' intent to disparage or diminish the experiences of female athletes, this chapter focuses primarily on the experiences of and issues regarding male athletes of color. There has been relatively little research on women of color in sport (Greene & Green, 2007). Though a body of literature on females of color in sport and physical activity (e.g., Bruening, 2005; Bruening, Armstrong, & Pastore, 2005; Carter & Hart, 2010) has evolved recently, the majority of this research conflates race and gender. Most of the research on the various concerns centered on race and sport focuses on male athletes.

Race and ethnicity are sensitive topics. Thus, conversations about perceived racial differences are often difficult. Nonetheless, these conversations, along with critical analyses of the racial–ethnic issues, are important to any understanding of the topic. Because of the difficulty in discussing racial issues, many find it easier to adopt a color-blind point of view that claims to ignore racial differences (Burden, Hodge, O'Bryant, & Harrison, 2004). But no matter how much one may desire to disregard the issue, researchers from numerous fields have come to the same conclusion: "Race matters," particularly when one is considering sport (e.g., Coakley, 2004, pp. 283-323; Eitzen & Sage, 2003, pp. 285-306). Jackson (1989) suggested,

> [R]acial and ethnic experiences may affect the very nature of social and psychological processes of interest . . . the roles of these factors in influencing an individual's basic psychological processes of perception, cognition, intellectual functioning, value acquisition, personality development and expression, and social interaction. Based

upon this view, psychological theories . . . that claim universality should include integral components [of] how the nature of race and ethnicity may influence these basic psychological processes. (p. 1)

What is curiously missing from this debate is an examination of Whiteness in sport; that is, White culture and the normality, privileges, and advantages taken for granted by White people in the United States rarely enter the discussion. Much of the conversation in the race–sport domain focuses on African American athletes and their superior ability (Johal, 2001). This one-sided discussion privileges Whiteness as the norm to which other groups are compared (Carrington & McDonald, 2001). Investigation of the meaning and influence of Whiteness has been overwhelmingly ignored by researchers, thereby escaping critical analysis (Kusz, 2001; Long & Hylton, 2002). This perspective inflates the perceived prowess of African American athletes by normalizing White

athletes as a comparison group (see chapter 11 on discrimination in leisure contexts). This, as in many other philosophical outlooks, colors the evaluation of sport performances and racializes the lens through which people view sport.

RACIAL–ETHNIC PARTICIPATION PATTERNS IN SPORT: OVERVIEW

Lapchick (2009) provided the most comprehensive and detailed view of racial and gender participation in professional and collegiate sport in his annual Racial and Gender Report Card. He examined variables such as player opportunities, diversity initiatives, hiring practices, coaches, and administrative diversity by race and gender. The Report Card covers Major League Baseball (MLB), the National Basketball Association (NBA), the National Football League (NFL), Major League Soccer (MLS), the Women's National Basketball League (WNBA), and college sport. Variables are weighted, and a grade is calculated based on the

AP Photo/Margaret Bowles

Racial–ethnic participation varies by sport. In the NFL, African Americans make up a large portion of the player population but a smaller portion of other team roles.

number of individuals in these various roles by race and gender.

The NFL provides an interesting example in that African Americans make up 67% of the player population compared to only about 12.6% of the U.S. population (Rastogi et al., 2011). Yet African Americans compose only 34% of assistant coaches, 19% of head coaches, 17% of head trainers, 16% of general managers, 14% of senior administrators, 14% of radio and television announcers, 11% of the professional team administrators, 8.6% of the league office, 8% of vice presidents, 5% of physicians, 0% of CEOs or presidents, and 0% of majority owners. This disparity in authority prevails even on the field. Although there are a few high-profile African American quarterbacks, they make up only 17% of NFL quarterbacks compared to 67% of the player population (Lapchick, 2009).

Extant research on racial influences in sport preferences and participation suggests that perceptions vary regarding the appropriateness of particular sports for different racial–ethnic groups (Ainsworth, Berry, Schnyder, & Vickers, 1992; Bungum, Pate, Dowda, & Vincent, 1999; Goldsmith, 2003; Harrison, 1999; Harrison, Lee, & Belcher, 1999b). In general, sports such as football, basketball, and track sprinting are regarded as more appropriate for African Americans while sports such as golf and hockey are deemed more appropriate for Whites. The X-Games and the "alternative" activities within them are quickly becoming White sport venues. Examples that have been researched are windsurfing and skateboarding (Wheaton & Beal, 2003). Again it is notable that where concerns regarding race-ethnicity and sport exist, African Americans have been the focus of most of the research and theoretical postulating. As Johal (2001) stated, "In popular and academic debates focused around sport and race . . . the term race is reduced to, or conflated with being black" (p. 155). The focus on African Americans' "natural" sporting ability (Entine, 2000) has privileged European Americans as the norm and the point of comparison (Carrington & McDonald, 2001). Therefore, Whiteness escapes substantive interrogation (Kusz, 2001; Long & Hylton, 2002). This makes African American athletes hypervisible, and Whites become some-

what invisible (Gallagher, 2003). As Tate (2003) postulated,

> The fact that 'whiteness' has gone unexamined for so long is a function of the power of paradigmatic thinking in the social sciences. The predominant viewpoint in the social sciences has been that people of color lack many of the characteristics associated with being white, thus the focus of scholarship has been on documenting these differences or examining interventions designed to remedy these so-called deficiencies. (p. 121)

THEORETICAL FRAMEWORKS AND HISTORICAL EXPLANATIONS

While much of the research suggesting the biological or genetic superiority of racial groups in sport has been found wanting (Coakley, 2004; Miller, 1998; Wiggins, 1997), some still contend that African American overrepresentation in particular sports is a consequence of biological determinism (Entine, 2000). Though such a viewpoint may be construed as politically incorrect, many in contemporary society still harbor stereotypical views that position African American athletes as genetically gifted performers (Harrison, 2001; Hodge, Kozub, Dixson, Moore, & Kambon, 2008).

Attempts to explain racial disparity in sport performance and participation patterns are based on anthropometric (Meredith & Spurgeon, 1980), physiological, biological (Ama, Lagasse, Bouchard, & Simoneau, 1990; Entine, 2000), sociological (Coakley, 2004), and psychosocial explanations (Goldsmith, 2003; Harrison et al., 1999a, 1999b) and identity formation (Harrison & Moore, 2007; Harrison, Sailes, Rotich, & Bimper, 2011). Anthropometric, biological, and physiological theories are thought to be largely unsubstantiated (Hunter, 1998); none of these studies provide a clear genetic or scientific definition of race, nor do they include a method of racial determination of the participants other than self-report. Wiggins' (1997) historical review pointed out that theoretical explanations for African American sport superiority included genetic, physiological, psychological, anatomical, motivational, evolutional, and sociological reasons. He also noted that relatively little research has focused on other racial or ethnic groups or their overrepresentation in particular sports. Sport sociologist Jay Coakley stated,

> Skiers from Austria and Switzerland, countries that together are half the geographical size of the state of Colorado, white populations that together are one twentieth the size of the U.S. population, have won many more World Cup championships than U.S. skiers. Even though this occurs year after year, people do not look to race-based genetic ancestry to discover why Austrians and Swiss are such good skiers. Dominant racial ideology has not led to studies looking for race-related genetic explanations for success of athletes packaged in white skin, even when the shades of white and genetic histories vary among so-called Caucasians around the world. (Coakley, 2004, pp. 290-291)

The distinctions between races are blurry at best; and while they have social, political, and psychological implications, the labels have little if any genetic meaning. Even those in the field of genomics argue against the use of race, noting that the vast majority of genetic variation occurs within, not between, continental populations (Cooper, Kaufman, & Ward, 2003). The aim of a recent effort is again to turn to racial categories in medical genetics through the suggestion that race can be a tool for classifying a specific population's risk for disease. Regarding this effort, Copper, Kaufman, and Ward concluded that race has proven useful in providing genetic information regarding drug response or diagnosis or causes of diseases. One glaring example, regarding height, is that sub-Saharan Africa is inhabited by both the tallest and the shortest groups of people in the world.

Terms such as biracial and multiracial have been used recently as demographic indicators that give an even foggier glimpse of the racial self-identity of an individual. Ascribing genetic and biological labels to racial groups has been considered futile, as these designations involve "loose and leaky" categorizations that resist logic and are not objective (Dole, 1995). The fact is that the majority of our population could be classified as bi- or multiracial if a precise family tree investigation were possible. Therefore, to imply that performance differences in sport are explained by genetically determined racial categories would be illogical.

Even in view of all of this, the idea that an individual will perform better in a particular sport because of her perceived racial affiliation still pervades our society. It is the view of the present authors and others (Coakley, 2004; LaVeist, 1996) that race is more accurately viewed as a social category reflective of a common social, political, and psychological history. Individuals within different racial designations perceive the world differently, are afforded different opportunities, and develop different identities and behavioral styles. There are also powerful external influences that shape racial identities and profoundly affect people in different racial categories. That is, being a member of a racial group in the United States, in particular, depends more on social and psychologically shared experiences than on shared genetic material. This leads to an endorsement of a psychosocial framework that takes into account the interaction of the social realities and the psychological consequences of living in a racialized society.

Participation in a racialized society often makes it challenging for White people to see themselves in racial terms. In the United States, a predominantly White culture, Whiteness has been normalized. In sport, as in other realms, the subtle assumption is that Whiteness is the norm and that any variation from the norm is problematic and warrants scientific study. Thus, Scandinavian skiers' domination of that sport in the Olympic Games does not stimulate a rush of research as has African American overrepresentation in basketball. This kind of race logic kindles a view of sport performances along racialized lines. It leads to labeling of people's sport success or failure in terms of skin color (Coakley, 2004, pp. 290-291). On this logic rest theoretical underpinnings for many of the genetic, biological, and physiological studies in the realm of race and sport. More recently, some have acknowledged the potent influences of psychological and sociological catalysts that give rise to the racial overrepresentation and disparities observed in sport. These include the influence of stereotypes and accompanying self-fulfilling prophecies, self-stereotyping, and stereotype threat. The following discussion examines these influences; the psychosocial concepts of self-schemata and racial and athletic identity; and social and environmental factors, along with the role of modeling and physical activity choice in health.

The Influence of Stereotypes in Sport

Stereotyping is a means of reducing cognitive processing by categorizing information or, in this case, people, based on their perceived group membership (Fiske & Neuberg, 1990; Oakes, Haslam, & Turner, 1994). It is an attempt to simplify the vast amount of information people encounter, thereby allowing them to operate efficiently in the cognitive realm. Stereotypes are developed subconsciously and retrieved automatically, making it extremely difficult to develop awareness of their use (Devine, 1989). When these cognitive categorizations are based on a wealth of knowledge and not used to make inferences about individuals, they are generally harmless. But when stereotypes are based on inaccurate and misleading information or are used to ascribe traits to individuals, they become problematic.

Sport provides ample opportunities for the development, deployment, and maintenance of stereotypes, particularly by gender, race, or ethnicity. The social nature of sport is a breeding ground for emergent ideas about the perceived abilities of people of different races, ethnicities, or both. Stereotypes regarding the abilities of African Americans are rooted historically in a plethora of often contradicting theories (Miller, 1998; Wiggins, 1997); and after years of dissemination with little challenge, these theories have shaped the beliefs of entire populations (Hoberman, 1997). Though some perceive stereotypical views regarding the "natural abilities" of African American athletes as politically incorrect or unfair to individuals, these notions remain prevalent in our society (Harrison, 2001; Hodge et al., 2008; Sheldon, Jayaratne, & Petty, 2007).

The Self-Fulfilling Prophecy

Stereotyping is foundational to the development of self-fulfilling prophecies (Merton, 1948). Self-fulfilling prophecy exists when behavioral expectations are confirmed by the individual who is being stereotyped (Hamilton & Trolier, 1986; Myers, 1993). Developing potent stereotypes can very easily lead to self-fulfilling prophecies. Since stereotypes can be developed subconsciously and retrieved automatically (Devine, 1989), it is feasible that one can create a self-fulfilling prophecy without being aware (Hamilton & Trolier, 1986).

Self-fulfilling prophecies may be partly responsible for both the overrepresentation of African Americans and other ethnicities in particular sports and the lack of participation of these same groups in coaching and administration. If a coach harbors strong stereotypes regarding the abilities of African American athletes in basketball, an African American athlete may be afforded more attention, feedback, and opportunities to perform. This would give the athlete more opportunities to improve skills and thus fulfill the coach's prophecy. Additionally, Horn and Lox (1993) suggested that coaches established higher expectations for African American athletes than for other players and disparaged those African American athletes who did not perform well. This indicates that African American athletes may be held to a higher standard. These and other researchers confirm the influence that physical activity teachers and coaches have on individuals under their authority (Martinek, 1981; Trouilloud, Sarrazin, Martinek, & Guillet, 2002).

The data presented in the Racial and Gender Report Card (Lapchick, 2009) also provide hints of the self-fulfilling prophecy at work. In 2008, 27% of MLB players were Latino; only 13% were managers, 3% were directors of player personnel, 5% were vice presidents, and 8% were senior administrators. If those in decision-making positions hold negative stereotypical conceptions about the administrative abilities of people of color, they could conceivably communicate those lowered expectations, seek evidence to confirm the expectations, and negatively affect the responses of interviewees so that they are unacceptable, thus completing the self-fulfilling prophecy.

Self-Stereotyping

Members of racial–ethnic groups frequently recognize shared stereotype information and experience similar social interaction patterns (Haslam, Oakes, Reynolds, & Turner, 1999). This often leads to group members developing shared perceptions of themselves, that is, to self-stereotyping (Oakes et al., 1994). This does not indicate a loss of individuality, but it does include the tendency to identify with a group that the individual shares salient characteristics. Haslam and colleagues (1999) indicated that self-stereotyping is revealed in agreement on social issues and stereotypes of the self and others. Self-stereotyping is especially potent when the attributes of a group are perceived as exceptional and advantageous to the development of positive affect (Biernat, Vescio, & Green, 1996). Thus, in the case of African Americans or other minority groups, being endorsed as a "natural athlete" would be viewed positively and the label may be worn proudly. Considering the research on the positive influence of self-efficacy (Bandura, 1982), the efficacious impact of self-stereotyping in African Americans with respect to athletic performance may be a significant factor in their success.

Some have suggested that this seemingly positive label carries with it the hidden presumption of intellectual inferiority (Davis & Harris, 1998; Edwards, 1972; Harrison, 1998). However, it has been found that self-stereotyping selectively reinforces group self-esteem while rejecting negative self-stereotypes (Biernat et al., 1996). Thus, it is easy to see how African American and other minority athletes can embrace the superior athletic stereotype while refusing to accept the inferior intellectual stereotype.

Stereotype Threat

Stereotype threat refers to the depression of performance due to the impact of negative stereotypes. Research evidence shows that the anxiety produced by cognizance of prevailing stereotypes significantly impairs performance in a stereotyped task (Stone, Lynch, Sjomeling, & Darley, 1999; Stone, Perry, & Darley, 1997). While self-stereotyping of desirable traits may positively influence performance, negative stereotypes, when made salient, have been found to depress performance in sport (Beilock & McConnell, 2004; Stone et al., 1997, 1999) and intellectual test performance (Steele & Aronson, 1995).

In particular sports, being White may pose a stereotype threat, thus depressing performance, while being African American may act as a positive self-stereotype and thereby increase self-efficacy and improve performance. These advantages and disadvantages may reverse themselves in an academic setting. Both may exert plausible influence on the overrepresentation of particular groups in certain sports.

Self-Schemata

Recently researchers have proposed a psychosocial conceptualization for the disparity in participation and performance in particular sports by race-ethnicity. Coakley (2004) suggested that a historic racial orientation accentuating innate physical abilities has a history of segregation and discrimination by race. While this notion restricts some opportunities, it emphasizes opportunities and motivation to develop skills in a limited range of sports. This can steer one to the notion of natural and cultural fate to excel in these sports. Group members are nudged to acquire the abilities needed to live up to their destiny and are provided with the necessary motives and opportunities to develop requisite sport skills. Thus, those possessing the required physical characteristics are likely to become superior athletes in these sports. It is easy to apply this theory to African Americans in sports such as basketball, football, and track (p. 293).

Coakley's construct coincides with the psychosocial concept of self-schemata. Self-schemata are perceptions of the self-stemming from previous experiences. They are theorized as cognitive structures produced by efforts to explicate one's conduct in specific spheres, in this case sport. Self-schemata form from repeated analyses of one's own behavior and also originate from others. They involve the perception and processing of incoming information that explains previous conduct and guides future behavior (Markus, 1977). In the arena of sport, it is plausible to envision how environment, expectations, stereotypes, and other factors can combine to influence the development of narrowly defined sport self-schemata that lead those with similar traits to perceive themselves as relegated to a very narrow range of sport activities (Harrison, 1995). There are indications that the forces molding self-schemata are present and active early in life (Harrison et al., 1999b). Harrison and colleagues suggested that differing expectations for sport engagement and performance, as well as pervasive stereotypes and self-stereotypes, are present and potent in the lives of young people of color.

Identity in Sport

Sport participation has become a fixture in the lives of many Americans. From an early age, many people are engaged in or connected to various sporting activities in some fashion. Sport participation crosses many racial and ethnic boundaries; however, one's identity may lead to an increased participation in particular sports. Because of the strong ethnic labels applied to certain sports, ethnicity may lead people to develop an identity that focuses on participation in a particular sport viewed as self-defining (Harrison et al., 1999b).

This self-defining role ascribed to sport, termed athletic identity (Brewer, Van Raalte, & Linder, 1993), has historical roots, especially when it comes to African Americans in sport. The integration of Black participants in sport in America was a catalyst for a significant amount of sport research focused on race and sport. As mentioned previously, early stages of research on the relationship between race and sport tended to rely on genetic, biological, and anthropometric assumptions that have produced unreliable explanations. However, the phenomenon of the overrepresentation of Black sport participants, especially in a limited range of sports, led sport scholars to question the meanings created by Black sport participants. Based on the historical contexts of race relations between ethnic groups, people's self-conceptualizations that they are part of a particular racial–ethnic group may contribute vital meanings for them.

Racial and Ethnic Identity Development

The exploration of identity may have important implications for understanding connections to behavior and choice decisions in sport. Research

on the racial identity development of Blacks has a long history (see Cokley & Chapman, 2008). A seminal model of racial identity development stemming from this line of research is Cross' (1971) model of *Nigrescence*. The Nigrescence model may be applicable across various arenas because it affords researchers the opportunity to examine psychological changes in Blacks' identification with being Black (Cross, 1995).

In lieu of various adaptations and changes to the model of Nigrescence since its inception, the current four-stage model includes the following stages: pre-encounter, encounter, immersion-emersion, and internalization. In the stage of *pre-encounter*, a Black person embraces a White worldview ranging from an absence of Black perspective to an anti-Black perspective. The range of these perspectives encompasses three attitudes illustrated as being assimilated, being mis-educated, and having self-hatred (Cross & Vandiver, 2001). An athlete with an assimilationist attitude does not see his race identity as salient in comparison to being an American while likely viewing race as a problem or stigma (Harrison, Harrison, & Moore, 2002). Mis-educated athletes are accepting of racialized, misinformed, and negative stereotypic depictions of Blacks that are often congruent with dominant racist beliefs. Anti-Black attitudes are embraced by those who espouse a self-hatred derived from seeing Blackness as a burden and as associated with a hindrance. The valorization of a White worldview, along with a sense of entitlement derived from athletic achievement, can serve as a crutch for individual identity beliefs in this pre-encounter stage.

The second stage, *encounter*, is not characterized in the same way as the other stages of the model. Rather, this "stage" comprises an event or series of experiences that pilot a transformational change in the person's worldview and personal identity. Interpretation of this event or series of experiences associated with the person's race is troubling, resulting in an exploration of a new identity with regard to race and group identity. The stage for encounter incidents is often set when minority athletes participate at elite levels on college campuses and in predominantly White communities. However, an important point in relation to the Nigrescence model and Black athletes is that those encapsulated in sport culture may be shielded from experiences perceived as an encounter (Harrison et al., 2002).

In the third stage, *immersion-emersion,* individuals become immersed in Black culture. Harrison and colleagues (2002) characterize this stage as one in which the previous identity beliefs are deconstructed while a new Afrocentric identity is idealized and developed. In this stage a person creates a new conceptualization about the meaning of Blackness.

The maturation of one's racial identity beliefs is characterized by a final stage, *internalization.* In this stage the individual comes to a realization about the strengths and weaknesses associated with Black and White cultures. The person's identification with her racial identity is not created in opposition to what is considered White culture. Participation in sports or physical activities is not based on their significance or lack of significance in Black culture but rather on the motivation to remain fit or to participate in an enjoyable physical activity (Harrison et al., 2002).

Another frequently used framework for understanding racial identity is Sellers and colleagues' (1998) Multidimensional Model of Racial Identity (MMRI). Unlike Cross' stage model, the MMRI conceptualizes racial identity in terms of salience, centrality, regard, and ideological dimensions. The MMRI concedes, based on identity theory (see Stryker, 1968, 2007), that racial identity is one of many hierarchically ordered identities. Operationalized using the Multidimensional Inventory of Black Identity (MIBI), the MMRI measures racial centrality, public and private regard of race, four ideological dimensions of race (i.e., assimilationist, humanist, oppressed minority, and nationalist), and the qualitative interpretation of racial salience.

Athletic Identity

A growing strand of research in the domain of sport has focused on sport participants' identity perceptions. One of the most obvious assertions that athletes are likely to make about themselves is that being an athlete has a lot to do with their self-concept. This said, how important is being an athlete to individuals? What effect does an athletic identity have on other identities as a part of one's self-conceptualization? Brewer, Van Raalte, and Linder (1993) defined athletic identity as the degree to which an individual identifies with the role of being an athlete. Identification with the athlete role is explained by the strength and exclusivity of that identity (Good, Brewer, Petitpas, Van Raalte, & Mahar, 1993). As athletes begin to participate in sport at an early age, their athletic identity presumably strengthens over time. The links between athletic identity salience and other self-perceptions and behavior have been extensively investigated (Beamon & Bell, 2006; Brewer et al., 1993; Griffith & Johnson, 2002; Miller & Kerr, 2003; Mignano, Brewer, Winter, & Van Raalte, 2006; Webb, Nasco, Riley, & Headrick, 1998). However, many of these studies have included limited measures beyond demographic information to account in any significant way for the diverse populations that participate in sport.

Race and Athletic Identity Convergence

Identity research interests have centered on the relationship between racial identity development and athletic identity. In a study on the relationships of athletic and racial identity with aggression in first-year student-athletes, Jackson and colleagues (2002) empirically tested the hypothesis that racial identity salience and racial discrimination perceptions were minimized by higher athletic identities. Their results showed that Black student-athletes with higher athletic identity were prone to saying that their self-image had little to do with their racial–ethnic group membership.

Brown and colleagues (2003) examined the degree of athletic identity and its association with perception of racial discrimination. They found that Black student-athletes, in contrast to their White counterparts, showed an inverse relationship between high athletic identity and perceptions that racial and ethnic discrimination was a problem in the United States. Brown and colleagues postulated that Black participants' responses regarding racial and ethnic discrimination (i.e., its nonexistence) were potentially a product of their "pedestaled" (p. 177) status as athletes and an acculturation into sport that positioned their athletic identity as salient in relation to other identities.

In a recent study, Steinfeldt, Reed, and Steinfeldt (2010), using the MIBI, investigated the relationship between student-athletes' racial and athletic identity and college adjustment and attachment perceptions. The findings from their sample of participants, consisting of Black student-athletes at both historically Black colleges and universities (HBCUs) and predominantly White institutions (PWIs), showed that participants' year in school, perceptions of public regard of Blacks, and a nationalist ideology were partial predictors of institutional attachment. This study adds to knowledge about the relationship between racial and athletic identity by showing the presence of varied racial ideologies in the sample and ways in which the racial identity and centrality of Black student-athletes can manifest in sport culture. Also interesting in this study was evidence that the age of Black student-athletes explained changes in aspects of racial identity such as the athletes' perception of others' view of them.

Socialization Into Sport

According to Coakley (2004), sport participation is mediated by several factors, including the individual's abilities and characteristics, influences of others, and accessibility and opportunities for involvement. It is easy to ascertain that race and ethnicity influence each of these factors and how each factor influences the others. Individual characteristics such as race-ethnicity and gender likely are early and powerful determinants of sport choice (Harrison et al., 1999b). To use the example of a young African American male, it is plausible to suggest that he will be stereotyped by others, as well as by himself, to engage in basketball, football, or track and field. The same stereotypes were likely at work with his parents, whose expectations will shape his aspirations and provide opportunities early in life. If he is reared in an urban environment, accessibility and opportunities may also be limited to these

Photodisc/Getty Images

An African American male can be stereotyped by others and himself to participate in certain sports, such as basketball, football, or track and field.

sports. Additionally, his perceived choices are influenced by media, peers, and the community in which he lives.

Peers are an integral part of the socialization process during adolescence because this is a crucial time of identity formation. The socialization process is particularly potent in students of color as peer interaction and peer group formation are often based on social factors that influence group dynamics (Payne & Isaacs, 2005). For many, the peer group is determined by sport participation. During adolescence, youth begin to ask "Who am I?"; in addition, race-ethnicity becomes more salient to them and to those in their environment (Tatum, 1997, p. 53). Research indicates that African Americans are more committed to their racial identity than Whites, suggesting that race is a more powerful socializing agent for African Americans (Spencer & Markstrom-Adams, 1990).

Though this impact can be easily seen in African American males, evidence suggests that these influences may function very differently in White adolescents. There are some indications that many potential White athletes are steered away from ardent sport participation (Harrison, Azzarito, & Burden, 2004). Though the influences are varied, the impact of parents may be especially potent. An incident recalled by *Washington Post* writer Michael Wilbon (2002) exemplifies this point:

> Fifteen years ago when I was still playing pickup basketball, a White kid in upper Northwest was the best ball handling guard in the neighborhood. He probably was one of the best in the city, and he was 13. Suddenly and inexplicably, he stopped showing up to play. I ran into his parents one evening at the grocery store and asked why he had stopped coming to the playground. And the father said, 'He's just a skinny White kid. Why should he waste his time playing against all those Black players?'

During adolescence, however, youth are also increasingly exposed to values and norms outside of the family sphere of influence. Parental authority gradually subsides, giving way to a peer-dominated realm (Payne & Isaacs, 2005). For males, particularly African American males,

participation in sport and development of athletic ability elevate social acceptability while providing access to privileged social groups. Payne and Isaacs further suggested not only that athletic ability facilitates group membership, but also that athletic skills are developed and motivation is provided to improve these skills to attain and maintain peer approval. Because this occurs during adolescence, it coincides with a time of rapid growth, development, and acquisition of knowledge, which are parameters required for noteworthy sport performance.

Though it may appear that others outside of the athlete's racial–ethnic group do not significantly influence this process, nothing could be farther from the truth. African American youth who may often feel marginalized and unwelcomed by the dominant culture in environments outside the home and community are welcomed and applauded in the sport arena. While an African American athlete who scores 98 on a math test may find that the teacher and peers are surprised, indifferent, or even suspicious, scoring a touchdown or dunking a basketball brings praise and adulation from all. Sport is one of the few arenas where the African American youth is lauded. Majors (1990) suggested that African Americans cope with marginalization by focusing their efforts on creating distinctive demonstrations of sport skills that set them apart from the dominant culture and define their identities.

Environmental Influences

Those who study the social aspects of sport attest to the potent influence of the home and community environment on determining sport choices. Coakley (2004) listed features of the community, accessibility, and opportunities as factors in sport choice. Though the United States and other countries have made progress in overcoming racism and discrimination, neighborhoods and schools retain a substantial degree of segregation (Saporito & Sohoni, 2006).

The salient characteristics of race and ethnicity have been shown to significantly influence sport choices (Goldsmith, 2003; Harrison et al., 1999b). Because many neighborhoods and communities are still segregated to a substantial degree, youth from comparable areas likely have similar accessibility, opportunities, and limitations regarding sport selection. Additionally, if these individuals experience similar media, peer, family, and community influences, the perceived array of sport choices will likely be consistent. Carlston (1983) provided a compelling illustration of how urban and suburban environments can shape participation patterns in basketball and the way in which the game is played.

Modeling

The saying "A picture is worth a thousand words" typifies findings on modeling. Magill (2004) suggested that the recent increase in research on the role of vision in the acquisition of sport skills often involves the observation of skilled performance by a model. Bandura's (1977) social learning theory indicates that self-efficacy is based on self-confidence in one's ability to perform in specific contexts. Self-confidence increases when one observes someone succeed in performing similar actions. Magill (2004) contended that some individuals in a social group are given more attention than others and thus are more influential than others who lack attractive attributes. Research confirms that social factors influence the modeling process (Gould & Roberts, 1981). Increases in performance occur when models and observers are similar on salient characteristics such as age, gender, ability level, and race-ethnicity (Meaney, Griffin, & Hart, 2005; McCullagh, 1986; Rotich, 2009). Schunk (1987) further suggested that the greater the similarity between model and observer, the greater the probability that modeled actions will be emulated and the more socially appropriate those actions will be regarded. Evidence of this comes from Andersen and Cavallaro (2002), who indicated that Black and White children more often chose models similar to themselves versus different from themselves.

The results of these and other studies suggest that preferences for particular sport and physical activities may be strongly influenced by the highly visible and readily available (via television) plethora of sport models. Since particular sports are overrepresented by Black athletes, the preferences, participation patterns, persistence, and career aspirations of Black youth are disproportionately geared toward these sports.

Sport Activity Choices and Health

Consideration of the race–ethnicity differences in sport choices seldom takes health aspects into account. Though sport choice is not likely a major factor in an individual's health, it may very well be an indirect contributing factor. It has been argued that sport participation varies by race-ethnicity, however the sports identified as African American are mainly vigorous team sports. Middle-aged and older adults find it difficult to participate in these sports. If people have a strong identification with these activities and their physical abilities diminish later in life, they may have a perception that viable options do not exist. African Americans who cease participation in these sports and do not develop skills in other sustainable physical activities are more likely to resort to a sedentary lifestyle (Harrison, 1995). Kumanyika and Adams-Campbell (1991) suggested that this could be a factor contributing to the elevated incidence of diabetes, hypertension, and coronary artery disease in the African American population. The authors also indicated that body fat percentages are lower in African American males up to age 35, when the pattern reverses. It is around the beginning of middle age that participation in vigorous team sports becomes a less viable choice. Choosing and identifying with vigorous team sports, coupled with avoidance and lack of development of skills and appreciation of lifetime activities, may exacerbate health disparities between individuals of color and those of the dominant culture. Placing racial labels on certain sports may be a key issue in developing a better understanding of health disparities between people of color and the dominant culture. Of course the influence of heredity and diet is crucial, but sport choice during early life may be a contributing factor in the elevated levels of obesity and chronic diseases linked to physical inactivity.

FUTURE RESEARCH

A determined effort is required to ignore racial influences in any discussion of major sports. Racial–ethnic overrepresentation and underrepresentation in particular sports are evident, but explaining this clearly observable fact presents a difficult and sensitive challenge. Historical explanations of racial–ethnic influences in sport performance differences have been premised on, and diluted with, untenable evidence to support such phenomena. The aim in this chapter was to advance critical analysis of racial and ethnic disparities in contemporary sport and illuminate psychosocial factors that affect sport participation and performance. Recent literature has signaled the significant impact of stereotypes and stereotype threat, pertinent identities, socialization, and environmental ecologies on sport participation and performance. These psychosocial factors and conditions more suitably account for racial–ethnic disparities in sport participation than do blurred socially constructed racial and ethnic categories or biological assertions of difference.

Those who endeavor to understand and explain these differences risk being labeled racist or being accused of hypersensitivity, but ignoring the issue fosters continued ignorance and perpetuation of detrimental stereotypes and myths. A better understanding of racial–ethnic differences in sport is important to an increasingly multicultural society. More research is needed to improve understanding of the potency and extent of racial–ethnic influences and precisely how they affect sport choice, participation patterns, persistence, and identity. Future directions for this research include, but are not limited to, (1) conducting studies that examine the complexity and fluidity of sport participants' racial–ethnic identity development in relation to other self-perceptions and personal development; (2) investigating ways to encourage racial–ethnic sport participation in a broader range of sports and physical activities; (3) examining how stereotypes limit or restrict sport participation and activity levels of racial–ethnic minorities over the life span; and (4) exploring whether racial–ethnic ascriptions to specific sports are associated with or even predictive of health issues (e.g., obesity, heart disease, type 2 diabetes) by race and ethnicity of sport participants.

With the growing number of individuals from racially, ethnically, and culturally blended families, it is important to assess the impact of such family backgrounds on sport participation. Further research on the complex relationships between race, ethnicity, and sport will yield important implications for understanding the culture of sport worldwide. Developing enhanced knowledge of these issues will increase understanding in the recreation and leisure field, aid in planning, and inform the rendering of recreational and leisure services in an increasingly culturally diverse society.

CONCLUSION

The landscape of sport has become increasingly complex with regard to the racial and ethnic backgrounds of participants. This chapter showcased ways in which race and ethnicity continue to play a significant role in the sport industry. Continuing critical analysis of the bidirectional impacts between race and ethnicity and sport will enable greater knowledge of the influence of these factors on current and future sport participation patterns, as well as the beliefs and perceptions of persons from racial and ethnic groups.

Lack of progress on understanding of the impact of race and ethnicity on sport participation has been diminished by lack of attention to their centrality within the dialogue about sport and sport participation. Further research is needed regarding the connections between race and ethnicity and sport. There is still much to learn in terms of understanding the experiences of group members overrepresented and underrepresented in various sports. The vitality of a critical consideration of these issues in sport may depend heavily on multidisciplinary and multicultural approaches that use relevant theoretical lenses to appropriately and effectively illuminate the complex intersection among race, ethnicity, and sport.

PART V

International Perspectives

This part of the book examines the scholarship on racial and ethnic minorities in Europe, Australia and New Zealand, and East Asia. Chapter 15 provides an overview of the history of migration to Europe and the current status of ethnic and racial minority groups in the Netherlands, France, Great Britain, Germany, Sweden, and Denmark. It then presents a comprehensive overview of research on leisure behavior of ethnic minority populations, including, but not limited to, West Indians, Indians, Pakistanis, Algerians, and Turks. Chapter 16 examines settlement histories and ethnic policies in Australia and New Zealand and critically reviews research and projects related to leisure of Indigenous peoples and migrants in these two countries. It discusses leisure and sport participation patterns of Indigenous peoples and migrants, as well as the meanings and roles of traditional Indigenous games and the functions and meanings of contemporary leisure and sport for ethnic minorities. Chapter 17 provides an overview of the history of migration to East Asia and the current status of ethnic groups in mainland China, Japan, and Korea. It then reviews research on leisure behavior of ethnic minority populations, including Chinese Koreans, Korean Chinese, Korean Japanese, and Chinese Japanese, as well as other ethnic groups in the region.

CHAPTER 15

Research in Europe

Karin Peters

OVERVIEW

The face of Europe has changed dramatically over the last half century, with European countries becoming much more multiethnic than in the past. This chapter begins by presenting information about Europe as a continent of immigration and the changes in composition of Western European countries over the past century. Next, this chapter discusses the position of non-Western immigrants in Europe, specifically the socioeconomic, sociocultural, and spatial distribution of these groups. This chapter also examines studies of leisure participation and behavior among minorities in the United Kingdom, Germany, the Netherlands, and the Scandinavian countries. A final section offers some recommendations for future research and practice related to recreation among minority populations in Europe.

Learning Outcomes

After reading this chapter, readers will be able to

- identify major trends with respect to the size and characteristics of selected minority groups in Western Europe,
- explain how Western European countries became more multiethnic and which ethnic minorities are present in today's societies,
- analyze current leisure participation and the extent to which ethnic minority groups are underrepresented in certain leisure activities, and
- explain issues that affect leisure participation of ethnic minorities in Western Europe.

I note the obvious differences between each sort and type, but we are more alike, my friends, than we are unalike.

Maya Angelou

In the second half of the 20th century, Europe underwent a major transformation. What had once been an area of emigration toward the New World became an area of immigration. Until then, many European countries had never seen themselves as countries of immigration (Bade, 2003). As a result of immigration, these societies became multiethnic. Decolonization, a temporary but massive need for low-skilled and unskilled workers, wars and political suppression, the end of the Cold War, and the reunification of Germany led to a variety of migration movements both toward and within Europe (Muus, 2001). In response, workers from countries such as India, Pakistan, Morocco, Tunisia, and Turkey were invited to Western Europe. Many people, mainly Africans and Asians, set off for Europe or the United States in search of better places to live. For years, many European governments considered the presence of these "guest workers" a temporary solution to labor shortages. So, too, did the immigrants. They left their families behind, intending to return to their home countries after a few years. However, the "temporary" solution became permanent, which led to a new stream of immigrants arriving in Europe in order to unify their families or form new ones (Van Amersfoort, 1986). Multicultural societies were born. In particular, Western cities have become multicultural and cosmopolitan "chowder pots" (Bhabha, 1994).

Related to this development, issues of multiculturalism and integration have become hotly debated political topics throughout Europe. The tone of the debate on integration and multiculturalism has sharpened since the 9/11 terrorist attacks and tends to focus on issues related to religious minorities and, in particular, on the perceived differences in norms and values between Muslims and non-Muslims. This is reflected in discussions regarding the refusal of some Muslims to shake hands or the prohibition against wearing headscarves at public functions or in schools. The discussion about headscarves is part of a wider debate about multiculturalism in Europe and reflects people's differing opinions on the topic of assimilation or integration of ethnic and religious minorities. France was the first country in Europe to publicly ban a form of dress whose wearing is regarded as a religious duty among some Muslims. In Belgium, a law banning the full-face veil went into effect in July 2011. In the Netherlands, a ban on wearing the full Islamic veil is part of a government program enacted to form a political coalition. However, as of this writing, no legislation had yet been passed. In the United Kingdom in the beginning of 2012, the issue of banning veils was discussed in Parliament, with the aim of making it an offense to wear a face covering in certain public and private venues.

This chapter discusses multicultural societies in relation to various aspects of leisure, with the aim of increasing the reader's awareness and knowledge of the situation regarding leisure and ethnicity in various Western European countries. Readers are introduced to relevant concepts and factors that influence the relation between leisure participation and the meaning of leisure for various ethnic groups in Western Europe. One purpose of the chapter is to provide an overview of the history of immigration to Western Europe and the current status of ethnic and racial groups in countries such as the Netherlands, Great Britain, Germany, Sweden, Denmark, Finland, and Norway. Second, by reviewing research on leisure behavior of ethnic minority populations, such as Indians, Pakistanis, Moroccans, Algerians, and Turks, the chapter provides an overview of the leisure participation, motivations, and constraints of various ethnic minorities in the Western European context. People with different ethnic backgrounds have different leisure patterns. Some activities are more popular among immigrants than among nonimmigrants and vice versa, while other activities are equally popular among all residents. Research shows that these differences can be explained by people's socioeconomic characteristics and ethno-cultural backgrounds, with issues of immigration, religion, and gender also taken into account. Although Western Europe has become more diverse, the amount of scholarship on issues of ethnicity, race, immigration, and leisure in the context of Europe differs between countries. While in some countries, such as the United Kingdom, more studies have been conducted, overall this area of research is still underdeveloped. The chapter overviews the studies on issues of leisure of ethnic minority populations in Western Europe.

EUROPE: A CONTINENT OF IMMIGRATION

International migration is part of the process of globalization that is reshaping economic, political, and cultural systems. It is commonly believed that the current flows of migrants, mainly related to labor, are fundamentally different from earlier forms of mass migration (Munck, 2009). For a long time, as already noted, many European countries did not see themselves as countries of immigration. This changed during the last decades of the 20th century (Burgers & Van der Lugt, 2005). However, it is important to realize that until the end of the 1960s, Europe still was a continent of emigration (Bade, 2003), described by Muus (2001, p. 31) as "a mosaic of migration movements and of resident immigrant populations, and a mosaic with a view to type and history of migration, country of origin, size of the migration flows and immigrant populations." At the beginning of the 21st century, the debate in Europe concerning migration centers on the need for the inflow of people because of the aging and declining populations in many European countries, but also on the misuse of the asylum system and the trafficking of migrants (Muus). At the same time, fears related to the perceived increase of religious extremism or religious fundamentalism drive much of the debate in Europe regarding ethnic and racial minority issues.

Demographics

On January 1, 2009 (Eurostat, 2010), 31.9 million foreign citizens[1] lived in the EU27 Member States,[2] of whom 11.9 million were citizens of another EU27 Member State. The remaining were citizens of countries outside the EU27, in particular from other European countries (7.2 million), Africa (4.9 million), Asia (4.0 million), and the American continent (3.3 million). Foreign citizens accounted for 6.4% of the total EU27 population. In 2009, the largest numbers of foreign citizens were recorded in Germany (7.2 million people, 8.8% of the total population), Spain (5.7 million, 12.2%), the United Kingdom (4.0 million in 2008, 6.5%), Italy (3.9 million, 6.5%), and France (3.7 million, 5.7%). More than 75% of the foreign citizens in the EU27 lived in these member states. Among the citizens of countries outside the EU27, the largest groups were from Turkey (2.4 million or 8% of the total number of foreign citizens in the EU27), Morocco (1.8 million or 6%), and Albania (1.0 million or 3%). However, the statistics on nationality do not tell the whole story about the presence of immigrants and their descendants in a country or about ethnic minorities in general. Some immigrants, like those from former colonies, may already possess the nationality of the host country (Muus, 2001). Furthermore, naturalization by definition has an impact on the size of the nonnational population as well (Clarke, van Dam, & Gooster, 1998).

In the various European countries, immigrants or members of ethnic minority groups are defined differently, for example as Black and minority ethnic groups (BME) in the United Kingdom,

---

[1]Foreign citizens are persons who are not citizens of the country in which they reside. They also include persons of unknown citizenship and stateless persons.

[2]Austria, Belgium, Bulgaria, Cyprus, Czech Republic, Denmark, Estonia, Finland, France, Germany, Greece, Hungary, Ireland, Italy, Latvia, Lithuania, Luxembourg, Malta, Netherlands, Poland, Portugal, Romania, Slovakia, Slovenia, Spain, Sweden, United Kingdom.

autochtones (native Dutch) and allochtones (non-native Dutch) in the Netherlands, or people with or without a migration background in Germany. Moreover, different countries have attracted a variety of ethnic minorities. France has received large numbers of immigrants from Algeria and other North African countries whereas in the United Kingdom, the two major groups include Blacks and immigrants from India, Pakistan, and Bangladesh. In the Netherlands, guest workers from Turkey and Morocco and immigrants from former colonies in the Caribbean are dominant. In Belgium, Moroccans are an important group; in Germany, mainly Turks and, to a lesser extent, immigrants from the former Yugoslavia are present. In Scandinavia, the minority population is very diverse and includes immigrants from Yugoslavia, Iran, Iraq, Somalia, Ethiopia, and Chile (Musterd, 2005). The various definitions used in different European countries to refer to ethnic and racial minority populations can be confusing and lead to much debate about the use of appropriate terms. This chapter uses the term ethnic minority groups to refer to all persons with an ethnic or migration background, that is, immigrants, their descendants, or members of ethnic minorities.

Ethnic Minority Group Incorporation

Throughout Western Europe, governments took different stances toward the incorporation of ethnic minority groups into host societies. Two important concepts dealing with the incorporation of immigrants need to be discussed—citizenship and integration. The Netherlands was the first European country to introduce citizenship trajectories for (non-EU) immigrant newcomers. These trajectories included language lessons and a number of introductory courses on the institutions and practices of the Dutch society. The Dutch integration program, demanding a considerable amount of acculturation, is currently the strictest in Europe. Other European nation states have followed this policy. Flanders, a region in Belgium, more or less adopted the original Dutch citizenship trajectories in the beginning of the 21st century. The Dutch program also served as a model for the German *Integrationskurse.*

The United Kingdom introduced a citizenship test, which includes a language test and a test of knowledge about life in the United Kingdom, as a qualification for British citizenship. France introduced *Contrats d'acceuil et de l'intégration,* and Austria put forth *Integrationsvereinbarungen.* Both have become necessary intermediary steps toward entitlement to a long-term residence permit. Estonia launched an Estonian language and citizenship test that its sizable Russian-speaking minority must take to obtain Estonian nationality. Poland, Hungary, and Spain are contemplating special integration programs for newcomers as well. Non-EU member Switzerland is also debating the introduction of *contrats d'intégration* involving obligatory language and civic courses in its cantons. Scandinavian countries including Denmark, Sweden, and Finland have integration programs whose origins predate the Dutch experience.

The second important concept related to immigrant incorporation is integration. The first country to put an integration policy in place, in the mid-1970s, was Sweden. Shortly thereafter, in the beginning of the 1980s, the Netherlands designed an ethnic minority policy in the form of a welfare state policy that was intended to stimulate equality and equity of vulnerable groups in society (Bruquetas-Callejo, Garcés-Mascareñas, Penninx, & Scholten, 2007). The programs at that time had a strong focus on the real or alleged ethnocultural features of "ethnic minorities"; and in line with this thinking, group-specific measures were popular up to the early 1980s (Rath, 1993). In the United Kingdom, the intent of the integration policy is to foster and facilitate integration by preventing racial discrimination and eliminating it from society. The basis for the policy is the Race Relations Act (1976). The integration policy is directed at eliminating racial discrimination and does not emphasize different ethnic or religious identities or socioeconomic integration. As in many countries, in France the integration policy could be defined as "symbolic politics" instead of a coping approach to problems (Favell, 1998). With respect to more concrete policies concerning integration, several positions can be distinguished. Britain, Finland, and Belgium can be characterized as having relatively heterogeneous populations with evidence of multicultural policy approaches that emphasize the acknowledgement of diversity. Societies must change in order to accommodate all ethnic and cultural groups that form a part of the given society (Parekh, 1996; Taylor, 1994). France, Germany, Luxemburg, the Netherlands, Austria, and Spain, on the other hand, could be identified as heterogeneous but with a generally assimilationist tendency evident in policies that aim at full adjustment of minorities to the culture of the majority (Amara, Aquilina, & Henry, with PMP Consultants, 2004). As of 2011, several European governments have pronounced multiculturalism a "failure" and opted for more aggressive means of integrating immigrants into their societies (Triadafilopoulos, 2011; see also Joppke, 2004). In general, European countries established a renewed commitment to policy approaches aimed at promoting ethnic desegregation, common values, stability, and national unity (Philips, 2010).

EUROPE TODAY: SOCIOECONOMIC, SOCIOCULTURAL, AND SPATIAL ASPECTS OF ETHNIC MINORITIES IN EUROPE

European countries differ considerably not only in the composition of ethnic minority groups; intragroup differences are always present and have to be taken into account in the study of individuals with an ethnic minority background. This section takes a closer look at the socioeconomic, sociocultural, and spatial aspects of ethnic minorities in Europe.

Socioeconomic Position

A number of studies have been aimed at gaining insight into the socioeconomic position of ethnic minorities in Europe. It is difficult to make comparisons among these studies because of problems related to incongruence of data. In 2009, Ward and colleagues attempted an overall European analysis but encountered problems with national data

that do not differentiate between immigrants and people born into immigrant families (unless they live in the same household); a notable exception is the United Kingdom, which keeps records of such characteristics as ethnicity.

Despite these problems, Ward and colleagues (2009) concluded that people with immigrant backgrounds in all age groups tend to have lower levels of income and are at higher risk of poverty than those born locally throughout most of the EU, or at least in those countries for which the data are reasonably reliable (EU15).[3] For those of working age, this cannot easily be attributed to lower levels of education, since there does not appear to be a significant difference in education levels between the immigrants and the rest of the population, especially with regard to the proportion of people with tertiary, or university-level, education. On the other hand, there appear to be marked differences in the rates of employment, types of employment, and earnings of immigrants—even in the case of those with tertiary-level qualifications. For instance, in the EU15 (except for the Netherlands), the unemployment rate for men with tertiary education born in a developing country is over 11%, compared to less than 3% for men born in one of the EU15 countries. Furthermore, 65% of men (age 25-64) with a tertiary education born in developing countries are employed in high-level jobs as managers, professionals, or technicians, compared with 81% of men with a similar level of education but born in the EU15. Additionally, 8% of men with high education who were born in a developing country were employed in elementary occupations (i.e., doing low-skilled manual jobs), in contrast to only just over 1% of men born in the EU15. Such differences in employment are especially obvious for immigrant women, whose employment rate in most EU15 countries is much lower than that among their locally born counterparts and who tend to disproportionately be employed in low-level jobs. According to Ward and colleagues, the employment rate for women with tertiary education and born in the EU15 averaged just over 83%, compared to only over 71% for women from

[3]Belgium, Denmark, Germany, Ireland, Greece, Spain, France, Italy, Luxembourg, the Netherlands, Austria, Portugal, Finland, Sweden, and the United Kingdom.

developing countries. With regard to the types of jobs, 62% of women born in developing countries had high-level jobs compared to 78% of women born in EU15.

Findings from the United Kingdom indicate that ethnic background is an important factor in assessing inequalities in income distribution and the risk of poverty among different ethnic groups. While only 16% of White British were below the poverty line, the poverty rates among the Bangladeshi and the Pakistani were at 57% and 49%, respectively, followed by Black Africans, Black Caribbeans, and Indians, whose rates of poverty were at 29%, 25%, and 24%. This indicates the need for an analysis that would include wider, cultural factors to provide a better understanding of the problems that lead toward social inclusion or exclusion among minority populations (Ward et al.).

Sociocultural Position

Whether or not diversity is promoted, three main points can be noted regarding differences in cultural background and religious affiliation between ethnic minorities and the majority population in Europe. First, ethnic minorities in Europe are assumed to have a different cultural background; one of the most often mentioned differences between the majority population and the non-Western ethnic minorities relates to what has been called by Hofstede (2003) the individualistic versus collectivistic spectrum. In particular, certain minority ethnic groups, such as people originating from Morocco and Turkey, are perceived as emphasizing collective values more than individual values. Second, shared language usage is an important factor that enables intercultural communication. According to Masso (2009),

> [M]any European countries face a situation where different forms of intercultural communication such as foreign language expertise and intercultural contacts have turned out to be basic but extremely necessary proficiencies. These communication skills are crucial in assuring the legitimacy of common laws and institutions and the sustainability of supranational structures political, economic and cultural and thereby

help in the search for opportunities to create a common public sphere. (pp. 251-252)

Third, religious distinctions seem to play a role. In particular, since many of the immigrants to Western Europe come from countries dominated by Islam (Gundelach, 2010), a significant and growing portion of the ethnic minority population in Western Europe perceives itself as Muslim. In some European countries, this leads to tensions between the Muslim and non-Muslim populations. Moreover, in EU countries such as France, Germany, and the Netherlands, high levels of Muslim spatial segregation are of particular concern (EUMC, 2006).

Spatial Distribution

In European cities, residential segregation by ethnicity and race exists, although segregation levels are lower than in most U.S. urban areas (Musterd, 2005). In addition, even the more segregated neighborhoods tend not to be dominated by one ethnic minority group but instead consist of people of several ethnic backgrounds. Overall, even though the term "integration" is widely used both in the national political discourse of Northern and Western European countries and in policy statements related to housing and settlement, what exactly is meant by integration is often unclear. What is clear, however, is that minority ethnic neighborhoods are often seen as "problem areas," and there seems to be a growing consensus in policy circles that residential segregation of ethnic groups is undesirable (Bolt, Özüekren, & Phillips, 2009). The segregation is often related to issues of social deprivation and poverty, and, in the end, to the exclusion of ethnic minority groups. Much less attention is paid to the added value of ethnic concentrations in terms of social capital for the residents. The literature suggests that immigrants have tended to settle within close proximity of people with similar ethnic backgrounds, for reasons of mutual support and security against hostility from the majority ethnic population and also because of the availability of cheap and accessible accommodation (Johnston, Forrest, & Poulsen, 2002). Urban and housing policies have also played an important role in determining the supply of housing in certain parts of the cities. In the United Kingdom, the most deprived households in some cities are concentrated in the social rented sector. In the Netherlands, the large numbers of social renting dwellings are concentrated in specific areas (Lee & Murie, 1999; Van Kempen & Murie, 2009; Van Kempen & Van Weesep, 1998). Due to high rental costs, many immigrants have little "choice" when it comes to housing options (Department for Communities and Local Government, 2006).

Only recently has more attention been paid to the establishment of attractive ethnic enclaves in connection with tourism. As Landry and Bianchini (1995) stated, newly settled immigrants contribute to the creative as well as the economic life of European cities. For example, Chinatowns are now firmly established in many European cities. In Berlin, instead of having an image of deprivation, the Kreuzberg neighborhood has become known as "Little Turkey"; it is now associated with multicultural attractiveness and called a "bohemian quarter" (Shaw, Bagwell, & Karmowska, 2004, p. 1984). As some claim, however, in many other European cities, ethnic diversity has been commodified (Rath, 2007). This development, in which the presence of cultural others is used for commercial purposes, is increasingly visible in Europe where lifestyle and consumption patterns of urban citizens reflect a distinctive taste for cultural products offered by ethnic minorities (Rath). Many examples can be found across Europe, including immigrant-initiated events such as Chinese Lunar New Year, Tropical Carnivals (Notting Hill, Berlin; Rotterdam, The Netherlands), and the Bollywood Film Festival (The Hague, The Netherlands).

LEISURE RESEARCH: OVERVIEW OF PAST AND PRESENT RESEARCH ON THE LEISURE OF MINORITIES IN EUROPE

Although in Europe as compared to the United States, research on leisure, recreation, and ethnicity does not have a long tradition, a number of studies have been conducted in Western European countries on participation rates, as well as attitudes, constraints, and behaviors of people belonging to different ethnic groups (e.g., Jokovi,

2000, 2001; Ward, 2000). Most of the research conducted outside of the United Kingdom involves case studies based on populations in specific cities or regions whereas in the United Kingdom, more national studies have been done. The following sections discuss the leisure behavior of ethnic minority groups. The review focuses on research carried out in the United Kingdom, the Netherlands, Germany, Finland, Denmark, Sweden, and Norway. These countries have been chosen because together they provide a broad overview of different immigration histories and, equally importantly, a substantial amount of research on issues of minority leisure has been conducted.

Leisure Behavior of Immigrants in the United Kingdom: Participation, Motivations, and Constraints

The presence of immigrants from Asia and Africa in the United Kingdom dates back to the 16th century (Fryer, 1984). However, only in the early 21st century did truly polyethnic towns and cities emerge (Department for Communities and Local Government, 2006). The majority of today's minority ethnic populations, especially South Asians, have their roots in the migration flows of the decades immediately following World War II (Ratcliffe, 2004). In the United Kingdom, almost 8% of the population belongs to an ethnic minority group. The major groups include Asians of Indian, Pakistani, and Bangladeshi origin; Chinese; Black Caribbeans; Black Africans; and persons of mixed race. Nearly 45% of ethnic minority members live in London, and 13% live in the West Midlands. The rights of ethnic minority populations in the United Kingdom are protected by Equality Act 2010, which brings together all previous equality legislations, including the Race Relations (Amendment) Act of 2000, and is aimed at protecting people of different age, gender, religion and belief, sexual orientation, and race. As a result of the preexisting acts and the new Equality Act, improving equality of access to natural spaces has become an increasingly important consideration for nature and green space policy and management in the United Kingdom.

In the United Kingdom, a range of qualitative and quantitative research has examined motivations for leisure and recreation among ethnic and racial minorities. For instance, Ward Thompson and colleagues (2008) found that motivations for informal recreation among various ethnic groups in the United Kingdom were quite general and included seeking fresh air, exercise, and relaxation. It also appeared that social and family gatherings were particularly important to ethnic minorities. In Hindu culture, people have a significant attachment to trees, and many religious festivals celebrate and honor trees. Cultural events help people celebrate their local identity and natural amenities (Bell et al., 2004).

Visiting the countryside is a popular leisure activity in the United Kingdom. In 2002, residents made 167.3 million trips within the United Kingdom, spending more than £26.5 billion in total. Walking is the most popular reason for visiting the countryside, next to participation in other leisure activities such as cycling, riding, and water-based sports. However, research shows that visitors to the countryside are mostly White, usually 35 to 54 years of age, with relatively high incomes (Uzzell, Kelay, & Leach, 2005). Minority ethnic groups are underrepresented in countryside recreation. However similarly, when visiting the countryside, non-White ethnic minority groups are most likely to engage in walking (91%) (Countryside Council for Wales, 2005). Young people of Asian and African Caribbean backgrounds also enjoy outdoor adventure activities, while their parents and grandparents take pleasure mainly in walking and landscape views (Askins, 2004). Research for the Forestry Commission (O'Brien & Morris, 2009) showed that while 80% of White British and people from any other White background had visited woodlands in the previous 12 months, only 64% of people of mixed ethnic origin, 50% of Asians or Asian British, 44% of Black origin or Black British, and 62% of Chinese or other origin had done so. Similarly, a study done by Natural England (2010) found that levels of participation in nature visits were significantly lower for the BME (Black and minority ethnic) population, and visits were mostly to green spaces in towns and cities rather than to the countryside (83% and 13%, respectively). Twenty percent of those who had never visited the natural environment were from BME groups. In line with this preference for urban green spaces, Ravenscroft and Markwell (2000) found that ethnic minority young people were not underrepresented in local parks. They were even more willing than Whites to visit urban parks where certain sport facilities were present. Although this could be interpreted as an inclusive leisure activity, the authors saw the overrepresentation as an apparent "confining" of ethnic youth to parks with poorer facilities, which results in lower user satisfaction and thus exacerbates social divides. These authors' results indicate that Asian and White youths tend to be more satisfied with their use of the parks than are Black youths.

Research on constraints to participation in leisure activities shows that fear of verbal or physical attacks is a problem for ethnic minority groups, who consider themselves much more vulnerable in the countryside than in towns (OPENspace, 2006). Other constraints to participation identified in the study ranged from lack of knowledge about the English countryside, as well as lack of information on how to get access, to the costs. Cultural issues such as the absence of a cultural tradition of visiting the countryside also seemed to act as constraints. Some ethnic communities did not think visiting a national park was a leisure activity, suggesting that their nonparticipation should be considered underrepresentation and not exclusion (Askins, 2004; OPENspace). Worries about intimidation and feelings of being threatened, as well as lack of culturally appropriate provisions such as appropriate dietary options and praying facilities, have also been identified (see Askins; Ethnos Research and Consultancy, 2005; Green, Bowker, Johnson, Cordell, & Wang, 2007; OPENspace). Fears of racial attacks, fears of being alone in an unfamiliar environment, and worries regarding dangerous flora and fauna all contributed to a sense of unease in the countryside and other natural open spaces (Morris, 2003). Ward Thompson and colleagues (2008) argued that fear of unknown places should not be underestimated, as ethnic minority members may feel unsure about what is appropriate behavior. To stimulate visits to the countryside, a national park awareness campaign could be beneficial. Moreover, one may attempt to influence attitudes of staff in rural locations through diversity awareness training (Askins; Ethnos). Since in some urban areas minority ethnic groups are also underrepresented, Madge (1997) suggested that a "park watch" scheme with more wardens would be helpful in that it might decrease fear.

A focus on ethnic minority sport participation is evident in the research commissioned by Sport England (2000) and Sport Scotland (Scott Porter Research & Marketing Ltd., 2000) and in the development of a system of good practice guidelines for national sport governing bodies by Sporting Equals (2000; Amara et al., 2004). The results of the 2002 General Household Survey showed that the overall participation rates in sport[4] among BBME were lower than for the population as a whole, at 40% compared with 46%. Among BME communities, this figure fell to as low as 18% for the Pakistani and Bangladeshi groups. Black Caribbean (39%) and Indian (39%) populations also had rates of participation in sport below the national average (46%). Only the "Black Other" group (60%) had participation rates higher than in the general population. The participation rates in sport among BME men were 49%, compared with a national average for men of 54%; for BME women, they were 32% compared with a national average for all women of 39%. The gap between men's and women's participation in sport was greater among some ethnic minority groups than in the population as a whole. The gender gap between all men and women nationally was 15 percentage points, whereas for the Black Other ethnic group it was 35 points, for Bangladeshis 27 points, for Black Africans 26 points, and for Pakistanis 20 points.

Many differences exist in participation rates of ethnic and racial minorities in various physically active pastimes. Levels of participation in walking among ethnic minorities in the United Kingdom were found to be significantly below those for the population as a whole (Amara et al., 2004). Only 19% of the Bangladeshi population took long walks regularly, compared with 44% of the population as a whole. For all ethnic groups, apart from the Bangladeshi, keeping fit/aerobics/yoga featured as the second most popular activity, while swimming ranked lower in participation. Keeping fit was by far the most popular activity after walking for women from all ethnic groups. Participation in football (soccer) among males from ethnic minority groups, and especially among Black males, was relatively high, with participation rates as high as 31% among the Black Other ethnic group—three times the national average for males (10%). Cricket was very popular among Pakistani (10%), Black Other (8%), and Indian (6%) men (average for all men of 2%). A large proportion of individuals from all ethnic groups said that they would like to take up a new sport. A number of possible constraints may decrease the rates of participation in sport. For instance, some studies estimated that 57% of people from BME backgrounds are socially excluded from sport on grounds of poverty (Amara et al.). Moreover, in general, men are more likely than women to say that they have had a negative experience in sport due to their ethnicity; but this may partly reflect the fact, as seen earlier, that more men take part in sport than women. On the other hand, a study by Kelaher and colleagues (2008) found that African Caribbean and Indian and Pakistani adults with more than secondary school education reported experiencing fewer acts of discrimination during sports and leisure (5.1% and 3.6%, respectively) than, for example, at school (11.9% and 12.7%, respectively), at work (28.8% and 18.2%, respectively), or on the street (23.7% and 30.9%, respectively).

The studies reviewed show that, in general, the BME population in the United Kingdom is underrepresented in leisure activities such as visiting the countryside and participating in various sports. Discrimination and socioeconomic disadvantage have been mentioned as the main reasons for this underrepresentation.

Leisure Behavior of Former Labor Immigrants in the Netherlands and Germany: Participation, Motivations, and Constraints

Both in Germany and in the Netherlands, a large part of the nonnative population comprises former labor immigrants from Turkey and Morocco. In Germany, people of Turkish descent are the biggest

---

[4]The measure used for participation in sport was "at least one occasion in the previous four weeks, excluding walking."

ethnic minority group (2.4 million people or 2.9% of the total population). Many of them settled in Berlin, where, since the beginning of the 1990s, "Turkish" cafes, bars, clubs, and discos have multiplied and are immensely popular among Turkish youth. "Turkish" places are located both in Berlin's "Turkish quarters" and in "nonethnic" neighborhoods in other major cities. The four main immigrant groups in the Netherlands are Turks, Moroccans, and people originating from Suriname and the Dutch Antilles, who together comprise 10% of the total population. In the Netherlands, immigrants are concentrated in the largest cities, particularly in Amsterdam, The Hague, Rotterdam, and Utrecht, where almost half of all ethnic minorities reside. Recent immigration has been dominated by people from Africa, the Caribbean, and Asia rather than from European countries (Martinez & Vreeswijk, 2002; Uunk, 2002).

Research aimed at gaining insights into leisure participation and behavior of ethnic minorities in the Netherlands and Germany has mostly focused on these larger groups (Fertig, 2004). Studies of the differences in leisure behavior between natives and nonnatives in Germany have shown that native Germans have significantly higher rates of attendance at cultural events (e.g., theater, concerts, presentations) and participation in sport. Moreover, native Germans are significantly more likely than nonnative Germans to hold official positions in clubs, associations, or social services (Fertig). On the other hand, nonnative Germans have a higher probability of socializing with friends or neighbors and being involved in religious activities. Sauer's (2009) research in Nordrhein-Westfalen showed that the main leisure activities of Turkish immigrants took place in private environments and included listening to music, visiting friends and family, and reading. Leisure activities in public spaces were less popular. In general, the differences between the first-generation immigrants and Germans born in Germany have been found to be much more pronounced than those between natives and the second generation (Fertig). All immigrant groups in Germany participate in various dimensions of social life, and second-generation immigrants seem to be more assimilated than their parents to the activities of native Germans (Fertig).

Research in the Netherlands shows that members of ethnic minorities have a much smaller repertoire of leisure activities than the native Dutch citizens (Jokovi, 2000; Van de Broek & Keuzenkamp, 2008). This applies in particular to Turks and Moroccans, while Surinamese and Antilleans occupy a middle position. These differences can be traced back largely, although not entirely, to differences in personal characteristics of group members such as education level, income, and command of the Dutch language. Turks spend more of their leisure time than others with family and fellow neighborhood residents. Te Kloeze (2001) found that Turkish Dutch families, even second generation, were still strongly oriented toward their original cultural traditions, values, and ways of life. Furthermore, he revealed that the lives of Turkish Dutch families could be characterized by unequal gender power relations. The mosques and cafes are popular places for leisure for Turkish Dutch men but not for women. In addition, the notion that married women have the right to free time is not strong among some Turkish women (Te Kloeze). Surinamese and Antilleans have the most interethnic contacts, both within and outside of the home. At the same time, they spend more time at home alone than other groups. Native Dutch citizens receive the fewest visitors at home and maintain the fewest interethnic leisure contacts, both within and outside of the home.

The majority of members of ethnic minorities read Dutch newspapers, watch Dutch-language television programs, and use the Internet. However, they do so less often than the native population, although the Surinamese and Antilleans closely resemble the native Dutch in this regard. Media consumption by Turks differs most from that among the native Dutch, due to their fairly strong preference for newspapers and television programs from their country of origin. Ethnic minorities, Turks and Moroccans in particular, also participate less in leisure-time pursuits outside of the home, such as visiting bars and restaurants and engaging in cultural activities, than the native Dutch population (Van den Broek & Keuzenkamp, 2008).

Regarding outdoor recreation, some similarities and differences between ethnic minority groups and the majority population have been found; these relate to the activities and the motives for recreation. Two findings came from Dutch studies (Buijs, Langers, & De Vries, 2006; Peters, 2010; Peters, Elands, & Buijs, 2010) of outdoor recreation among people of Moroccan, Turkish, Surinamese, or Antillean descent. First, these ethnic minority groups use nature as a space for social gatherings, both to visit with friends or family and to meet new people. Second, among these groups, the most popular activities in the natural environment revolve around food; these include barbecuing, picnicking, and picking fruits in forests. The social function of outdoor recreation and the importance of food were also identified in a German study among immigrants from Turkey and the Balkan countries and Russian Germans (Jay & Schraml, 2009).

De Haan and Breedveld (2000) showed that the rates of participation in sport among Surinamese and Antilleans were lower than among the native Dutch but higher than among Turks and Moroccans. Differences were found by generation, with higher participation rates in sport activities among the second generation. Even after education, occupation, sex, and age were controlled for, differences in sport participation between groups did not disappear. Differences in membership in recreational associations, however, disappeared when these explanatory variables were included, suggesting that there are no significant differences in membership in sport clubs between native and nonnative Dutch (De Haan & Breedveld).

Volunteer work in sport clubs and recreational associations is clearly less common for immigrants as compared to the native Dutch population (Klaver, Tromp, & Oude Ophuis, 2005). The same holds for political participation (Fennema et al., 2000). Similar trends seem to be observable in Germany; Breuer and Wicker (2008) concluded in their research on German sport clubs that 10% of the members had an immigrant background. This

© K.B.M. Peters.

A group of ethnic minorities and native Dutch having a picnic in one of Nijmegen's parks. This group likes to use nature as a space for social gatherings, especially picnics and barbecues.

indicates a clear underrepresentation (overall, the immigrant population in Germany is almost 20%). Moreover, only 2.6% of all volunteers in sport clubs are immigrants. The participation of immigrant girls and women as club members and volunteers seems to be especially low.

Despite the fact that, in general, sport participation rates among most immigrants are lower than among the native Dutch and Germans, there are some sports in both countries in which minority ethnic groups are overrepresented. For instance, in the Netherlands, 12% of non-Western ethnic minorities participate in football (soccer), as compared to 6% of the native Dutch (Breedveld, Kamphuis, & Tiessen-Raaphorst, 2008). In Germany, a large study conducted in the Mannheim region pointed to the overrepresentation of some age cohorts of immigrant players (born between 1971 and 1980) in football. Older players (born before 1966) tended to be underrepresented, especially in the higher amateur leagues.

In both countries, much attention has been paid to the social character of leisure activities. Studies have investigated the extent to which leisure stimulates interethnic interactions and, as a result, social integration. Research in Nordrhein-Westfalen, Germany, showed that 40% of the nonnative German respondents had frequent (meaning at least once a week) interactions with Germans during leisure activities; 17% met native Germans only a couple of times a year, and 15% did not interact with native Germans at all (Sauer, 2009). Research in the Netherlands has shown that of the minority ethnic groups, Turkish Dutch people are the most ethnically enclosed. Moroccan Dutch have more contact with the native Dutch but less than Surinamese and Antilleans, who have the most contact with native Dutch people in their leisure time. Still, one out of three Turkish or Moroccan Dutch does not have any contact with native Dutch people during leisure activities. Figures for the 1994 to 2006 time period show

© K.B.M. Peters.

A group of ethnic minorities and native Dutch playing soccer in a Nijmegen park. There are some sports, such as soccer, in which these minority ethnic groups are overrepresented.

that little changed in the degree to which non-Western immigrants and native Dutch citizens engaged in informal social contacts with each other. In fact, some findings suggest that social contacts between some non-Western groups such as Turkish Dutch and the native Dutch actually declined during this period (Gijsberts & Dagevos, 2010). Members of the second generation in all immigrant groups have more contact with the native Dutch in their leisure time than do the first-generation immigrants. On the other hand, in the same time period, an increase was seen in the percentage of second-generation immigrants of Turkish and Moroccan origin as to the amount of social contact they had with members of their own group. This trend is most marked among second-generation immigrants of Turkish origin (Gijsberts & Dagevos).

From research done in Nijmegen (Peters, 2010), a middle-sized city in the Netherlands, it became clear that although not many interactions among ethnic groups occurred in public spaces, and although most people (both native and non-native Dutch) tended to describe their visits as leisure and as a time to be with family and friends rather than focusing on interactions with others, the chats and encounters that did occur were viewed positively. Furthermore, the very fact that people from various ethnic backgrounds saw each other in the parks is important. Far from a passive activity, people-watching provides a flow of information about one's fellow citizens—who they are, what they are doing, and what they look like. In the parks in Nijmegen, people enjoyed watching each other because of the diversity of ethnic groups. People from different ethnic backgrounds were present in the two parks studied, and they seemed familiar and comfortable in this atmosphere.

Little research has been done on perceived discrimination in Germany and the Netherlands. Research conducted in pubs and discos in the Netherlands (Geldrop & van Heewaarden, 2003; Komen, 2004) showed that some younger members of ethnic groups felt they were unable to enter all the clubs and discos they wanted. Komen found that discrimination affected leisure participation of immigrant youth; especially Moroccan Dutch and Turkish Dutch boys stated that they were refused entry to certain places. Other studies (Bruin, 2006; Yücesoy, 2006) showed that nonnatives use more spaces of their own in order to be in control of their events. Ethnic minority members organize ethnic parties, soccer events, and other activities and decide on the rules for them—for example, no alcohol, no mixing of genders, and starting early so that the women can return home at an appropriate hour. Research by Sijtsma (2011) on Muslim women in the Netherlands showed that veiled Muslim women experienced a range of nonviolent discriminatory actions while engaging in outdoor leisure activities. The discrimination included unpleasant looks, prejudice, disapproval, behaviors that made people feel unwelcome, and negative remarks. Yet the women rarely perceived discrimination as a factor that affected their leisure behavior. Although mostly nonviolent, even relatively small incidents of discrimination can reduce the level of enjoyment Muslim women derive from outdoor leisure activities. The Dutch Anti-Discrimination Agency registered 385 complaints in the category sport and recreation in the period from 2003 to 2007 (FRA, 2010). In Germany, racism, xenophobia, and anti-Semitism in sport are predominantly perceived as problems in football (soccer). With few exceptions, the racist incidents in sport were reported in men's and (to a lesser degree) youth football (Peucker, 2009).

In short, findings demonstrate that minority ethnic groups in the Netherlands and Germany are to some extent underrepresented in various leisure activities. However, there are some exceptions, and some sports and pastimes seem more popular among minority groups than among the native Dutch and Germans. Furthermore, it has become clear that in Germany, as well as the Netherlands, leisure is seen as an important way to stimulate integration.

Leisure Behavior of Immigrants in Scandinavia: Participation, Motivations, and Constraints

Scandinavia consists of four countries: Denmark, Sweden, Finland, and Norway. Few ethnic minorities lived in Denmark until the 1960s. However, in the late 1960s, immigrants from Pakistan and

Turkey started to settle there and have continued to do so. They were followed by people from the former Yugoslavia. All these immigrants were called guest workers. In the middle of the 1980s, refugees from Iran, Somalia, and Vietnam entered the country (Gundelach, 2010). In 2006, immigrants constituted almost 10% of the Danish population of 5.5 million (Statistics Denmark, 2009). More than half of them had their origins elsewhere in Europe, while the rest originated from Southwest Asia, especially Turkey.

The first immigrants in Sweden came from other Nordic countries and from neighboring countries such as Estonia and Latvia. Then labor immigration took place, and people from Italy, Finland, Greece, and Yugoslavia entered the country in the 1950s and 1960s. In the early 1970s, non-European immigrants, particularly from Turkey, Lebanon, Ethiopia, Somalia, and Chile, started arriving in Sweden (Andersson, 2007). In 2008, the foreign-born Swedish population (15%) consisted mainly of Europeans (57%), particularly those from other Scandinavian countries (21%), while Asians accounted for 28.2%, Africans for 7.1%, and South Americans for 4.8% of the foreign-born Swedish population.

Until the 1980s, Finland was a country of emigration. From the beginning of the 1980s, immigrants to this country mainly consisted of people from the Soviet Union and Finns who returned to Finland. Only in the beginning of the 1990s did ethnic diversity increase with the immigration of people from the former Yugoslavia and Somalia. Later, Kurds, Vietnamese, and Iraqis began to settle in Finland. Nowadays, immigrants to Finland arrive mainly from Russia, Estonia, Sweden, and Somalia. In total, less than 5% of the total Finish population of 5.2 million consists of nonnative Finns.

Of the total population of Norway (4.9 million), about 11% are of foreign origin. Most immigrants (34%) come from other European countries, primarily from Poland and Sweden. Other large immigrant groups are Pakistani, Iraqi, and Somali (together approximately 25%).

Relatively little research has been conducted on the leisure behavior of nonnative Scandinavians. The few studies published in English focus on the non-European immigrants in these countries.

In Sweden, Lindström and colleagues (Axén & Lindström, 2002; Lindström, 2005; Lindström & Sundquist, 2001) examined the extent to which Arabic people (e.g., persons born in Turkey) and people born in other countries such as Chile, Vietnam, and those in Sub-Saharan Africa participated in social and physical activities. These studies showed that men and women born in Arabic countries, as well as other immigrants, were underrepresented in social activities; this was particularly pronounced among women from Arabic countries. Social leisure examined in these studies was quite eclectic; it consisted of organizational activities (union and other meetings, study circles at work or elsewhere), cultural activities (theater and cinema, arts exhibitions), church visits, sport events, writing articles and editorials for newspapers or journals, participation in demonstrations, night club entertainment, and participation in large gatherings of relatives or in private parties (Lindström, 2005). The author suggested that ethnic differences in social participation could possibly be explained by differences in culture and the process of acculturation (partly dependent on the length of time spent in Sweden). Low participation was defined as involvement in less than three activities during the last year. People from Arabic-speaking countries had the lowest participation, followed by people from Poland and the former Yugoslavia.

Results have also shown that participation rates in leisure-time physical activity are lower among immigrants than among native Swedes. For instance, Dawson and colleagues (2006) found that low levels of physical activity were significantly more likely to be found among men from "all other countries" and among women born in Southern Europe, Eastern Europe, and all other countries compared with men and women born in Sweden. Participation in physical activity among immigrant women had increased with longer stays in the host country, but no relationship was observed for men (Dawson et al.).

In Norway, Walseth (2006) conducted an interesting study on sport participation among female Pakistanis. The author suggested that being a young Muslim woman and participating in sport challenges the boundaries of one's ethnic identities. Young Pakistanis who did not participate in sport claimed that they were not interested in participation, while those who were involved in sport activities often experienced sanctioning by people who were guarding the ethnic boundaries of the community. Young female participants who mainly identified themselves as Muslim tended to focus more on health and physical activity since these were seen as important to Islam. Moreover, women engaged in sport in accordance with Islam; that is, they adhered to certain restrictions relating to clothing and the presence of men.

Also in the context of Norway, Friberg (2006) found that young people from ethnic minorities participated less often in leisure activities such as sport clubs and hobby clubs than young people with ethnic Norwegian backgrounds. Ethnic minority girls in particular had low levels of participation. While 58% of students with ethnic Norwegian backgrounds were active members of one or more organizations or teams, this was true for only 12% of Pakistani girls. Moreover, a large majority of the "hobby clubs" Pakistani girls were involved in were in fact religious organizations. In the case of minority boys, a somewhat lower level of participation in sport clubs was offset by the fact that they participated to a greater extent in unorganized sport activities. The same, however, was not true for minority girls. Youth with lower levels of participation in organized leisure activities also had less contact with friends during their leisure time. Friberg found that young people with ethnic minority backgrounds evaluated the positive and the negative aspects of participation in organizations in the same way as their mainstream peers. Although at least 93% of Pakistani girls wanted to participate in an organized leisure activity, they encountered constraints such as lack of financial resources or culturally linked factors. More than one-third of the Pakistani girls stated, for example, that they spent their leisure time doing housework at home every single day. How inclusive and open the organizations are is also questionable. Youth who were least likely to participate in organized leisure activities claimed that the main reasons for nonparticipation were their belief that they would not fit in with other

participants, that they did not know anyone who took part in the activities, and that no one had asked them.

In Denmark, Schipperijn and colleagues (2010) examined the use of green spaces for leisure and concluded that individuals with non-Western ethnic backgrounds visited parks, forests, and lakes less often than individuals with a Danish background. A number of municipal-level studies focused on youth participation in Denmark (FRA, 2010). In 2007, 68% of students in grade 5 with parents born in Denmark were members of sport associations. Students with immigrant parents were underrepresented, with a membership rate of 49%. In grade 9 the gap was smaller; 41% of students with Danish parents were members of sport clubs compared to 39% with immigrant parents. The main result of another comparative study in four Danish municipalities was the "remarkable differences related to gender, age and ethnicity concerning children's choice of sport"; while ethnic minority girls tended to be underrepresented, ethnic minority boys "participate[d] in football, martial arts and basketball to the same degree as ethnic majority boys, whereas there [were] few children and young people from an ethnic minority background participating in what is called 'traditional Danish sports' such as handball, dance and riding" (FRA, 2010, p. 46).

The structural societal position of minorities is clearly less favorable than that of native Danes. The rate of employment, as well as the level of education and income, is considerably lower among immigrants than among second-generation ethnics (Gundelach, 2010), which may account for their lower participation rates in certain leisure and sport pursuits. Private projects have been undertaken to help minority children from underprivileged family backgrounds participate in sports clubs. They provided financial assistance to foster the youths' membership in sport clubs in hopes of broadening their networks and creating social capital useful for improving employment possibilities (Amara et al., 2004).

In Finland[5] and Sweden, Muslim women and girls were affected by discriminatory treatment;

---

[5]No other English-language research regarding leisure of immigrants in Finland was found.

specifically, they were denied access to sport services such as fitness clubs, swimming pools, and karate clubs. In all these cases, the prohibition on headscarves or "burqinis" was used to legitimate discriminatory rejection (FRA, 2010).

From this review one may conclude that although few studies have examined sport among ethnic minority members in Scandinavian countries, the existing evidence points to underrepresentation of non-Western immigrants in sport activities in these countries. Although the available information on leisure participation of ethnic minority people is not sufficient to provide a definitive assessment, the existing research tends to indicate that participation of ethnic and racial minorities in organized leisure activities is lower than among the general population in the Scandinavian countries. More importantly, discussion of whether this is problematic is warranted. If it is problematic, it would be useful to find out why, since understanding the reasons will provide a better appreciation of possible constraints such as discrimination or socioeconomic factors.

CONCLUSION

This chapter provides an overview of the studies on the leisure behavior of non-Western immigrants in various Western European countries. It is clear that apart from studies in the United Kingdom, and to a lesser extent in the Netherlands, limited research has been published on the leisure behavior and participation of ethnic minorities, at least in English. European scholarship differs markedly from that in the United States in that this field of research originated in the United States in the 1960s, but in Europe, the first studies did not appear until the early 1990s. Sport is one leisure activity that has attracted the attention of researchers in Western Europe. Studies in Germany and the Netherlands show that leisure is seen as a way to deal with issues related to the integration of non-Western minorities and as a strategy to stimulate interethnic contacts. In the United Kingdom, more attention has been paid to discrimination and other constraints that negatively affect par-

ticipation in certain leisure and sport activities among non-Western immigrants. The author of this chapter believes that more research is needed in countries other than the United Kingdom to determine the extent to which discrimination and other constraints negatively affect leisure behavior among ethnic minority groups.

Another important issue to address is that much of the research conducted in Europe views ethnic minority groups as homogenous entities and in so doing neglects intragroup variations. This emphasis on differences between minority groups and the mainstream can lead to the development of stigmatized images of minorities. Moreover, discussions of trends in leisure and sport have tended to downplay issues of discrimination and exclusion as reasons for nonparticipation. The question of why non-Western immigrants are underrepresented in certain leisure pursuits has not been answered sufficiently, and more research in this area is needed.

Related to practice, it is important to acknowledge that multiethnic societies demand culturally sensitive policies and practices. For example, in management of natural areas, it is vital to acknowledge culturally specific wishes of minority visitors. The same should apply to the provision of sport activities. However, the extent to which specific wishes and demands of minority members with respect to provision of single-sex recreation opportunities should be accommodated requires broader discussion. Such dialogue is very much related to the sensitive nature of political discussions taking place in many European countries regarding integration of ethnic minority groups. More dialogue and information are needed on how to involve all citizens in these debates and to form a basis for creating societies in which all can participate in leisure and sport activities as they choose. Overall, it is clear that expanding the body of knowledge related to leisure and ethnicity in Europe is necessary. Focusing on perceived discrimination and intragroup differences in leisure behavior can foster better understanding of the meanings of leisure for people with various ethnic backgrounds.

CHAPTER 16

Research in Australia and New Zealand

Eva Hiu-Lun Tsai, Grant Cushman, Bob Gidlow, and Michael Toohey

OVERVIEW

This chapter critically reviews research related to the leisure of Indigenous peoples and migrants in Australia and New Zealand—countries known for their love of sport and outdoor recreation. First, it presents the settlement histories, including changes in the ethnic populations of the two countries and their subsequent ethnic policies, which provide a foundation for understanding the ethnic leisure issues. The discussion then turns to leisure and sport participation patterns of Indigenous peoples and migrants, as well as the meanings and roles of traditional Indigenous games and the functions and meanings of contemporary leisure and sport for ethnic minorities. This is followed by an exploration of the relationships between cultural adaptation, leisure participation, and leisure constraints experienced by ethnic minorities. The chapter also discusses the pervasive influence of historical and contemporary ethnocentrism and racial discrimination on leisure opportunities of ethnic minorities. The review leads to recommendations for improving current practices to meet challenges in the management of leisure in multicultural communities. It also identifies gaps and limitations in Australian and New Zealand ethnic leisure research.

Learning Outcomes

After reading this chapter, readers will be able to

- describe how the different circumstances of British colonization in Australia and New Zealand led to different cultural ideologies and ethnic policies that affected the leisure of ethnic minorities,

- explain some of the main underlying causes of the different patterns of participation of various Australian and New Zealand cultural groups in popular mainstream and Indigenous leisure and cultural activities,

- compare the cultural and racial challenges and leisure constraints experienced by Indigenous peoples and migrants in Australia and New Zealand,

- evaluate current inadequacies and future challenges in the development and management of leisure of Indigenous peoples and migrants in Australia and New Zealand, and

- identify gaps and limitations in current research and advocate future leisure research directions in Australia and New Zealand.

We have devoted so much energy to exploring the existence of life forms on other planets. Yet we have committed so little effort to understanding challenges that arise from diverse human cultures on earth and to embracing and to capitalizing on cultural differences. How has leisure enhanced and worsened our cultural understanding and interethnic relationships? What lessons have we learnt from the past research in Australia and New Zealand? It is time to take a new path for leisure research in our multicultural societies, think anew and act anew.

Eva Hiu-Lun Tsai

On the opposite sides of the Tasman Sea in the Southwest Pacific Ocean are two young nations, Australia and New Zealand, that have developed from former British colonies to contemporary multiethnic societies along somewhat similar pathways. Woven into the multicultural fabric of these populations are descendants of the countries' Indigenous peoples, Aborigines and Torres Strait Islanders in Australia and Maori in New Zealand. The diverse cultures and leisure heritages of the Indigenous peoples and immigrants have enriched the ways of life of Australian and New Zealand people. However, cultural and racial differences have also led to challenges for Indigenous, immigrant, and mainstream cultures in these two countries.

The common Anglo–Celtic heritage and geographic proximity of Australia and New Zealand have facilitated the formation and maintenance of a strong bond between the two countries, as reflected in the similarity of their flags; their British parliamentary democracy; their love of the outdoors; and their passion for competitive sport, particularly rugby and cricket, with much friendly cross-Tasman rivalry. Nevertheless, Australia and New Zealand have as many differences as similarities. Their differing cultural ideologies and policies, multiculturalism in Australia and biculturalism in New Zealand, contribute to the shaping of the relations between the governments and the Indigenous peoples and ethnic minorities of the two countries.

Over the past 30 years, Australian governments have been struggling to promote multiculturalism and to educate people and public agencies to accept cultural differences, appreciate cultural diversity, and provide inclusive services for ethnic minorities. However, many Indigenous Australians feel uncomfortable being considered just another ethnic group under the umbrella of multiculturalism (Curthoys & Moore, 1995; Dunn, Kamp, Shaw, Forrest, & Paradies, 2010) because this ignores their position as the first inhabitants; their continued connection to their land; and in particular their different experiences, including their history of dispossession and genocide (Curthoys, 2000). On the other hand, New Zealand has made concerted efforts to implement its bicultural policies, acknowledging British and Maori cultures as the two founding cultures, signifying the legal recognition of Maori governance and their social institutions and, to an extent, the sharing of power between two peoples (Curthoys; Sibley & Liu, 2004). At the opening of sport and leisure events, the New Zealand teams or delegations often proudly perform Maori rituals such as the *haka* or welcome guests with a *powhiri*, whereas the Australian teams merely sing Australia's national anthem. These distinctive displays are more than theater—they reflect the strong cultural and political positions of Indigenous peoples in New Zealand but less so in Australia. These differing cultural policies have implications for the leisure of ethnic minorities in the two countries.

Although ethnic immigrants and Indigenous peoples have various common racial and cultural experiences, challenges, and concerns, their receptiveness toward the dominant cultures is different in many ways. Indigenous peoples have been resisting the cultural assimilation policy that, until recent decades, was imposed on them by the "colonizers." On the other hand, immigration is largely self-determined. Immigrants willingly make considerable efforts to emigrate to Australia or New Zealand, primarily because they are attracted to aspects of the lifestyles, the social systems, the political stability, the economic development of the countries, or some combination of these.

LEISURE OF INDIGENOUS PEOPLES AND IMMIGRANTS IN AUSTRALIA

To understand the leisure experiences of Indigenous peoples and immigrants in contemporary Australia and New Zealand, the cultural and political power structures of the countries and the ways in which the past underlies and imbues the present day need to be taken into account. An understanding of ethnic leisure in Australia also requires the recognition that concerns about Indigenous cultures and Indigenous land ownership in Australia are a recent phenomenon. As well, Australia's progression from a White Australia to a multicultural Australia started just four decades ago after adherence to an ethnocentric ideology for almost two centuries.

Indigenous Australians

Before British annexation, the Australian continent was populated by over 500 clans of Aboriginal and Torres Strait Islanders who had their own territories, histories, cultures, and more than 200 distinct languages (Pascoe, 2008). Archaeological evidence suggests that Aboriginal peoples inhabited Australia from at least 60,000 years ago and that Torres Strait Islander people, whose cultural origins were in nearby Melanesia, lived on their islands for more than 10,000 years. An estimated minimum of 315,000 Aboriginal people lived on the continent before British colonization (Australian Bureau of Statistics [ABS], 2008b).

Early Aborigines were seminomadic, with tribes hunting and gathering their food within recognized areas of land that they called their "country." In Australian Aboriginal culture, people did not own their land; instead, their country owned its people. When Captain James Cook claimed the East Coast of Australia for the British Empire in 1770, colonists failed to appreciate this unique relationship between Aborigines and their country; neither could they recognize the complex political order of these peoples. Consequently, the British government occupied Aboriginal and Islander land without negotiations or treaties, justifying the seizure by declaring Aboriginal and Torres Strait Islander land *terra nullius*—land without owners. Despite the tragic loss of their land and aggressive marginalization by British colonizers, Indigenous Australians have been struggling hard to retain their cultures. In the present day, those living in remote areas are generally more able to retain their traditional lifestyles and cultures whereas those living in urban and regional areas are likely to experience pressure to assimilate into Western cultures.

Australian Settlement History

In 1788, Australia was established as a British penal colony. About 160,000 convicts were brought to Australia before penal transportation ended in 1868 (Department of Immigration and Multicultural Affairs [DIMA], 2001). The convicts were accompanied by officials and colonial gentry from Great Britain and later on were joined by free immigrants, mostly from the United Kingdom. The unilateral claiming of Indigenous land was the beginning of the desecration and marginalization of the Indigenous peoples. For example, in 1804, colonizers in Tasmania were authorized to kill Aborigines, leading to the almost complete extermination of local Aborigines. In addition to murders and massacres, smallpox and other diseases brought to Australia by the colonizers decimated Aboriginal populations (DIMA).

From the last decades of the 19th century, reserves, settlements, and missions were established by Australian governments and church organizations to "protect" Indigenous Australians and to enable the "civilizing" and Christianizing processes (Human Rights and Equal Opportunity Commission [HREOC], 1997). In practice, these institutions were tools used for segregation and control of Indigenous Australians. Indigenous people who lived in these institutionalized settings lost basic human rights such as freedom of movement and control over personal property, work, leisure, and family lives. Governments had regulatory powers over most aspects of Indigenous people's lives. During this time, many Indigenous children were forcibly removed from their families and placed in government- or church-run institutions, adopted out to White parents, or fostered in White families (HREOC). These people became known as the "stolen generations." The main purpose of forced removal was to cut the children off from their culture and to raise them to think and act "White." In the 2008 National Aboriginal and Torres Strait Islander Social Survey, 8.2% of the respondents reported that they had been removed from their natural families (ABS, 2009b). Only after 1965 were Indigenous people around Australia given the same voting rights as other Australians. A successful referendum in 1967 allowed Indigenous people to be counted for the first time in the 1971 Census (ABS, 1986). During the 1970s, government control over Indigenous life was gradually removed, and Indigenous Australians became free to live wherever they wished. However, the traumatic experiences of genocide, dispossession, disempowerment, and institutionalization have ongoing effects on many aspects of the lives and cultures of Indigenous peoples. Today, Indigenous Australians remain one of the most disadvantaged groups in the world.

Social Demographics of Indigenous Australians

The Indigenous population of Australia, estimated at 517,200 in the 2006 Census, constitutes about 2.5% of the total Australian population (Australian Institute of Health and Welfare [AIHW] & ABS, 2008). Approximately 90% of the Indigenous population is of Aboriginal origin; 6% is of Torres Strait Islander origin, and 4% is of both Aboriginal and Torres Strait Islander origin. Almost one-third (32%) of the Indigenous population resides in major cities; 43% lives in rural areas, while 26% lives in remote areas of Australia. As of 2009, only 27% of Indigenous people living in remote areas could not speak an Indigenous language, compared with 68% of those living in major cities (ABS, 2009b). Although many Indigenous Australians, in particular those living in the cities, have lost their Indigenous languages, the majority identify themselves as Indigenous and engage in some traditional Indigenous activities. More

than 80% of remote-dwelling Indigenous people and 55% of city dwellers identify themselves as belonging to a tribal or language group (ABS). This suggests that many Indigenous Australians demonstrate continuing allegiance to some core Indigenous cultural values.

The Australian Indigenous population is relatively young (median age of 21 years) compared with the non-Indigenous population (37 years). According to data from 2005 to 2007, the life expectancy of Indigenous Australians was estimated to be 67.2 years for males and 72.9 years for females. In other words, Indigenous males on average die 11.5 years earlier and females 9.7 years earlier than their non-Indigenous counterparts (ABS, 2010b). Indigenous Australians, in comparison with non-Indigenous Australians, also endure high rates of unemployment and incarceration; low income and education; substandard housing; a high burden of ill health; high rates of risk factors such as smoking, substance misuse, and exposure to violence; lack of exercise; and obesity (AIHW & ABS, 2008). Historical and contemporary discrimination against Indigenous Australians have significantly reduced their opportunities to access the societal resources that affect their well-being and many aspects of their lives, including leisure.

Meanings and Roles of Indigenous Leisure and Sport

Australian Indigenous cultures are diverse and complex, but most Indigenous communities have a culture that is recognizably different from that of the mainstream Euro-Australians. In contrast to the individualistic culture of Euro-Australians, Indigenous Australians tend to be collectivistic; meaningful lives are sought through the quality of human relationships rather than individual achievement and work success (Australia Department of Sport, Recreation and Tourism [ADSRT], 1986). Thus maintenance and promotion of relationships with others, observing reciprocal obligations, conforming to the expectations of kinship rules, and being loyal to family and clan are highly valued in Indigenous communities (ADSRT; Atkinson, 1991). According to Atkinson, an Aboriginal scholar, family and community leisure play important roles in the maintenance of Indigenous well-being.

The Indigenous Australians well-being framework developed by ABS in conjunction with its stakeholders (ABS, 2010a) not only provides a conceptual map for measuring Indigenous well-being; it also articulates the potential contribution of leisure programs and community events and highlights the importance of community ownership, control of culture, and the need for maintaining and sharing of traditional knowledge for Indigenous well-being. The framework also emphasizes the importance of Indigenous rights and self-determination and censures the damage caused by racism and discrimination. These values, traditions, and concerns permeate many aspects of Indigenous leisure and sport, shaping people's leisure meanings, preferences, and motivations.

Leisure in Traditional Indigenous Societies

Early explorers, anthropologists, historians, and scholars have written a substantial collection of literature about traditional games and play practices of Indigenous Australians living in tribal or semitribal environments. These documents provide detailed descriptions and classifications of Indigenous pastimes, games, playthings, and toys (e.g., Edwards, 2009; Haagen, 1994; Oates, 1979; Robertson, 1975; Roth, 1902). Although these accounts were obtained by non-Indigenous people mainly through their observations and interpretation of the daily lives of Indigenous people, they provide insights into the nature and roles of leisure and games in traditional Indigenous communities.

In traditional Indigenous lives, "leisure" did not exist as a separate time or experience. Leisure was often embedded in the social, cultural, and economic practices, integrated into and inseparable from daily life and rituals (Atkinson, 1991). Children's play and adult games were also a context for learning and improving skills that were needed for more serious purposes.

> For example, a group of women on a gathering excursion (an economic pursuit) could also be teaching the younger members of the group, giving instruction and passing on skills necessary for survival (education).

> At the same time, such activities can be very much recreational, as women laugh and talk, enjoying each others' company. (Atkinson, 1991, p. 1)

These multifunctional leisure-like economic activities also contributed to strengthening family and community bonds. Veal and Lynch (2001) referred to this leisure style, characterized by unclear dividing lines between leisure and activities necessary to sustain life, as "eco-leisure." The variety of leisure functions in traditional Indigenous societies has been discussed extensively by Salter (1967). On the basis of secondary data, Salter analyzed the nature and functions of 93 traditional Indigenous games and pastimes in traditional life. He concluded that the games and pastimes served six vital functions in traditional life: economic activities, political activities, domestic aspects, ceremonial rites, cultural identification, and social interaction.

Indigenous Australians had a rich repertoire of traditional games and pastimes. Popular traditional pastimes included singing, dancing, storytelling, and "theater" in which all participants were simultaneously performers, orchestra, and audience (Atkinson, 1991). Making arts (e.g., sand pictures, wooden engravings, rock paintings)

Photo courtesy of Glen Fam.

Indigenous Australians playing a traditional wind instrument, the didgeridoo, and clapsticks, with non-Indigenous spectators appreciating the performance. Playing of traditional instruments is an important component in Indigenous ceremonial dancing and singing.

and crafts (e.g., body decorations with armlets, anklets, and feather and opossum string necklaces and headbands) was also a popular recreational pursuit. Fundamental to these creative activities and the resulting objects were spiritual enrichment and caring for their country (Atkinson). Physical games (e.g., wrestling, spear throwing, sham fights, football using possum skin, spinning discs, and stick games) had important economic functions, as adults needed to be athletic and skillful to hunt and find food for their families (Robertson, 1975; Salter, 1967). Cultural events such as corroborees (Aboriginal ceremonies that involved dancing and singing) facilitated the transfer of cultural knowledge, reinforcement of Indigenous cultures, and promotion of interpersonal relationships (Atkinson). Although traditional Indigenous activities are practiced today to a lesser extent, they still play important roles in preserving the unique cultural identity of many Indigenous Australians.

The majority of traditional games and pastimes of Indigenous Australians were based on dexterity and learned through imitation (Edwards, 2009). Because of their oral tradition (no written languages), having keen observation skills, strong experiential memories, and ability to replicate was necessary for effective transference of information and skills in traditional societies. These learning qualities seem to have been maintained in modern times. When teaching athletic activities at Indulkana, Robertson (1975), a physical education academic, found that Aboriginal children and youths had developed enhanced abilities to closely observe complex movements and successfully duplicate them; and their body awareness and kinesthetic senses were superior to those of their European counterparts. There is still a wide belief among Australians that Indigenous athletes possess "black magic," generally enjoying superior physical abilities and sporting talents.

In contrast to the predominant ethic of serious competition and winning in Western sporting activities, Indigenous games tended to be cooperative, played in groups rather than in competing teams, and played more casually. Moreover, participation was largely motivated by intrinsic enjoyment and skill development (Robertson, 1975; Salter, 1967). This cooperative orienta-

tion has, to an extent, been sustained up to the present time in some Indigenous communities. For example, Robertson observed an interesting Indigenous version of the hide-and-seek game of Pitjantjatjara people:

> For example, in games like 'hide-and-seek,' after counting to 'ninety-nine' (or other numbers), in the Western context, the seeker would go looking for the group. However, aboriginal way of playing the game is different – it is the group members that cooperate in looking for one or two individuals 'lost' in the bush. (Robertson, p. 7)

Robertson also found that in running foot races, some Indigenous children who were winning deliberately slowed down to enjoy crossing the finish line with their friends.

Indigenous Heritage Leisure in Contemporary Australia

With the disruption of Indigenous cultures, many traditional activities have disappeared or changed, and Western sports and leisure activities have been taken up by Indigenous Australians (Tatz, 1987). However, some traditional activities have retained their popularity among Indigenous communities. Traditional arts and crafts, music, theater, and dance are still favorite leisure pursuits among Indigenous Australians. Social surveys conducted in 2002 indicated that 27% of Indigenous Australians aged 15 years or over had participated in at least one of a selected set of Indigenous creative arts activities (ABS, 2006a). The activity with highest participation was making Indigenous arts or crafts (16%), followed by writing or telling Indigenous stories (13%) and performing Indigenous music, dance, or theater (8%, including paid and unpaid; figure 16.1). However, the extent to which Indigenous people participate in creating non-Indigenous arts is unclear. Participation in Indigenous arts, crafts, music, dance, or theater did not vary greatly across broad age groups or across remote and nonremote groups; but the writing or telling of Indigenous stories, as expected, increased with age (ABS). More Indigenous females participated in Indigenous creative arts activities (30%) than males (25%), but there were no substantial gender

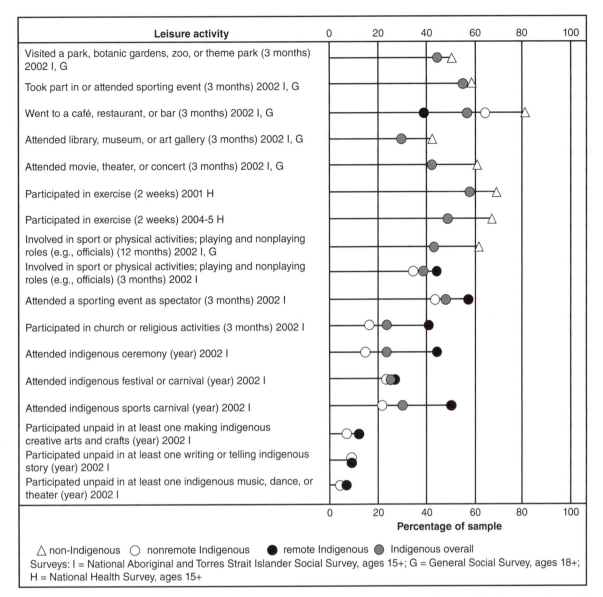

Figure 16.1   Participation in selected leisure activities by non-Indigenous Australians and Indigenous Australians living in remote and nonremote areas.

Note: The data in the chart are from "Aboriginal and Torres Strait Islander Peoples: Aspects of Sport and Recreation," by Australian Bureau of Statistics (ABS), 2004; and "Aboriginal and Torres Strait Islander Australians: Involvement in Arts and Culture," by ABS, 2006. As data in the chart come from various surveys and some used different reference periods and survey methods, one should take care when comparing and interpreting the sample percentages.

differences in participation in other cultural activities (ABS). Through Indigenous arts and crafts and theater, Indigenous Australians are able to express and preserve the cultures they value while non-Indigenous Australians are starting to appreciate their work.

According to Atkinson's (1991) study, apart from creative pursuits, some Indigenous Australians were keen to learn other traditional skills (e.g., bush activities and traditional sports); con-

duct research to record family and community histories; and exchange visits between groups to share culture, knowledge, skills, and enjoyment. On the other hand, some young Indigenous Australians rejected involvement in these activities in the belief that engaging in traditional activities contributed to the stereotyping of Indigenous people.

Large intercommunity activities (e.g., Yuendumu Sports Weekend, the Barrunga Sports

Festival, and the All Blacks Carnivals) and cultural celebrations (e.g., Cape York Dance Festival) have important meanings for Indigenous Australians. For example, the Yuendumu Sports Festival began in 1963 when three communities came together at Yuendumu to play Australian football (Atkinson, 1991). Over the years to the present day, the event has expanded to include more communities and a wider variety of activities, for example spear throwing, boomerang throwing, tug-of-war, fire making, basketball, softball, athletics, corroboree, rock and roll, country and western music concerts, and rap-dancing competitions (Kelly, 2012; Tatz, 1987). The social and cultural exchanges between and within the participating communities provide support to a pan-Aboriginal culture (Atkinson). At the same time, through Indigenous ownership of the festivals and celebration of Aboriginality, Indigenous identities are strengthened, traditional cultures are sustained, communities are interconnected, and Indigenous well-being may be enhanced (Atkinson).

Indigenous Australians and Western Leisure

The Australian government's involvement in the delivery of public recreation began in 1939 following the formation of the National Fitness Movement. However, little consideration had been given to the different leisure needs of its minority populations. In 1992, the Royal Commission into Aboriginal Deaths in Custody recommended that sport and recreation be taken up as a positive alternative to antisocial behavior and as a community development tool (Cairnduff, 2001). Consequently, the Indigenous Sport Program (ISP) and the Indigenous Sport and Recreation Program (ISRP) were developed, aimed at providing sporting and physical recreation opportunities for Indigenous Australians and reducing social disadvantages. Much of the ISP effort has been directed toward engaging sporting organizations to deliver mainstream sport and develop programs for Indigenous people. ISRP, on the other hand, focuses more on promoting community health through community sport and physical activities. However, in the broader government policy agenda, recreation and sport are generally less of a priority than other initiatives such as

health, employment, and social order in Indigenous communities. Thus, the ISP and ISRP are often used by authorities as a means to achieve these nonrecreation objectives. Consequently, the inherent personal and social values of recreation and sport tend to be neglected (Small Candle Consulting, 2009).

Since 2000, ABS has conducted surveys that measure Indigenous Australians' (non)participation in several broad categories of mainstream leisure activities, usually over a 3- or 12-month period. This chapter presents the results from various surveys side by side to facilitate understanding of leisure activity participation rates among remote- and nonremote-living Indigenous Australians and non-Indigenous Australians (ABS, 2004, 2006a; see figure 16.1). The surveys indicate that generally, Indigenous Australians have lower levels of participation in mainstream leisure activities, including social, physical, cultural, and outdoor pursuits. Similarly, a study that focused on children and teenagers in remote communities in the Torres Strait indicated that Indigenous youth had lower levels of physical activity compared with general national levels, and Indigenous high school girls were the least active (Abbott et al., 2008). Many factors could have led to this consistently low involvement in these mainstream activities, but only two structural factors have been considered in an ABS survey—unemployment and lack of transportation (ABS, 2004). Other potential factors—social, cultural, or racial—have not been explored.

Interestingly, despite limited access to leisure and sport resources (e.g., facilities) among remote-dwelling Indigenous Australians, they were more likely than their nonremote counterparts to engage not only in heritage activities (e.g., attending Indigenous ceremonies or sport carnivals, making Indigenous arts and crafts), but also in some Western activities (e.g., sport and physical recreation, sporting events, church or religious activities; ABS, 2006a). One speculative explanation for this is that there are fewer competing leisure opportunities in remote areas.

Australian government recreation initiatives have been oriented toward organized mainstream sports, which are competitive and often emphasize individual achievements. However, these are not the preferred forms of leisure for many Indigenous Australians, particularly women, young children, and older adults. Although some recreation professionals have raised the issue of the young male focus in program provision and suggested increasing support for traditional, cultural, and family-oriented activities and fun sports (e.g., ADSRT, 1986; Atkinson, 1991), improvement in addressing the problems has been slow. The ISP evaluation report acknowledged that, although the sporting circumstances and needs of Indigenous peoples have changed significantly over the years, there has been little change in the way the ISP has been administered and delivered.

Leisure Challenges Facing Indigenous Australians

Indigenous leisure needs and constraints, and in particular, ways to help fulfill these needs and to negotiate these constraints are relatively untouched areas within the Australian research literature. A few studies have considered sport or recreation participation difficulties experienced by Indigenous Australians. For example, Hunt, Marshall, and Jenkins' (2008) study suggested that the perception of unfriendly social environments—the feeling of "being judged" in public spaces—has inhibited physical activity engagement of some urban Indigenous Australians. Hunt and colleagues' reporting of the feelings of interpersonal discrimination by an Indigenous male demonstrates the pervasive influence of racial constraints on physical activities:

> We walk down the street and people are watching us and we don't like that, you know, we are all human beings. . . . That is why I don't like street walking because people all of a sudden they are judging me and watching me and thinking: is he going to steal my car or something? That is the perception you get all the time you are walking around. I don't bother walking on the streets. (p. 105)

The perception of racism among Indigenous Australians has been high—reportedly experienced by 58% to 79% of Indigenous people (Paradies, Harris, & Anderson, 2008). Numerous examples of racial discrimination against Indig-

enous Australians in sporting contexts, such as vilification, nonselection for teams, and name calling, have been recorded (e.g., Tatz, 1987; Tynan, 2007). The experiences of historical racism (e.g., loss of traditional lands, breakdown of traditional cultures and social order, separation of children from their families) and contemporary racism (e.g., lack of access to social resources, interpersonal discrimination) have significant impacts on the self-concepts and cultural identities of Indigenous Australians. In the absence of appropriate remedies, deep-seated sorrow and stress have led to psychological and emotional distress, and many Indigenous Australians have resorted to engaging in deviant activities such as marijuana use and alcohol consumption as temporary escape strategies (Zubrick et al., 2005).

Leisure boredom and aimlessness are common problems in Indigenous communities with high unemployment (Musharbash, 2007). With too much free time and a lack of culturally meaningful opportunities including leisure, many young Indigenous people resort to petrol sniffing, drug use, excessive alcohol consumption, vandalism, and gambling. Even when Indigenous programs are developed, non-Indigenous demands tend to be fulfilled first. For example, a recreation outreach program was to be established in Arnhem Land for the Yolngu people to help address alcohol misuse. However, since the concern of the non-Indigenous communities was to curb the resulting antisocial behavior and a litter problem, employment of Yolngu to collect litter became the core activity of the program and very few resources were put into recreation (Wearne, Chesters, & Whyte, 2005). Unclear program objectives and a lack of program evaluation and public accountability have been common problems of Australian Indigenous programs and services. An unpublished Indigenous Spending Report of the Australia Finance Department, obtained by Australia's Seven Network (television) under freedom of information in August 2011, suggested that many Indigenous programs had poorly articulated objectives (Grattan, 2011). The report concluded that the history of Commonwealth policy for Indigenous Australians over the past 40 years was largely a story of good intentions, flawed policies, unrealistic assumptions, poor implementation, unintended consequences, and dashed hopes. Moreover, strong policy commitments and large investments of government funding have too often produced outcomes that have been disappointing at best and appalling at worst (Grattan).

Public Accountability

Australian governments and their agents have expressed high expectations for sport and physical recreation to deliver social benefits for Indigenous communities. A recent statement from the Australian Government Independent Sport Panel (2009) summarized these expectations:

> . . . sport should be given the same importance as housing and education in Indigenous communities given the "flow on" benefits to improved health, education, social integration and disengagement from the justice system. There could also be economic benefits from professional careers through jobs associated with the sport sector. (p. 194)

However, convincing evidence that current recreation and sport programs could deliver the expected benefits to the Indigenous communities is lacking. An important reason is that program evaluation is usually not undertaken or is conducted only on an ad hoc basis, typically relying on anecdotal evidence. Although Cunningham and Beneforti undertook a project on behalf of the Australian Sports Commission and identified components and indicators of successful recreation programs in Indigenous communities (Beneforti & Cunningham, 2002; Cunningham & Beneforti, 2005), a lack of funding hindered further application and testing of the indicators (J. Cunningham, personal communication, October 18, 2010). Surprisingly, when Small Candle Consulting, also on behalf of Australian Sports Commission, conducted an evaluation of ISP in 2009, the indicators proposed in the Cunningham and Beneforti study were not considered or even mentioned. The current lack of coordinated effort between public agencies and researchers, as well as a lack of systematic evaluation of program quality and objectives and programming processes, reflects a general need to improve public accountabilities in Indigenous recreation development. Moreover, a lack of representation and

of direct involvement of Indigenous Australians in the management processes is likely to weaken the programs. Only 0.7% of Australian sport and recreation managers were of Indigenous origin, according to the 2001 Census (ABS, 2004).

As contemporary forms of systemic racism are often covert, these internalized, taken-for-granted deprivations tend to elicit less resistance from Indigenous Australians and also lead to less resolution (Paradies et al., 2008). Research, public policies, and management practices need to strive *actively* toward systematically redressing leisure disadvantages of Indigenous peoples.

Australian Immigrants

Australia, since its federation, has been a nation of immigrants. According to the 2006 Census, about one in four Australian people were born overseas. Because of the country's changing cultural ideologies and immigration policies, its ethnic mix has gone through a series of significant changes over the years.

Building a Multicultural Australia

As in New Zealand, the 19th century saw multiracial migration contributing to Australian population growth, particularly during the gold rushes in the later part of the 19th century. However, racial antagonisms surfaced as a result of competition in the gold fields, labor disputes, and Australian nationalism. Continuing antiracial attitudes led to the adoption by the Australian parliament of the Immigration Restriction Act 1901 that formalized the White Australia policy (DIMA, 2001). The act intentionally restricted non-White immigration to Australia in the belief that non-White immigrants not only were less likely to assimilate into the Australian society but also would pose a threat to Australia's Anglo–Celtic culture.

After World War II, the Australian government began to actively recruit immigrants from the United Kingdom and Ireland to maintain its workforce and sustain economic growth. However, a shortage of willing British immigrants forced the government to also recruit people from Eastern and Central Europe. In the mid-1960s, Australia extended assisted immigration passages to people from Southern Europe (e.g., Italians, Greeks, and Maltese). Gradually, the White Australia policies that drove this selective recruitment were dismantled, and the Whitlam Labor government reforms of the early 1970s contributed to the formal abolition of the White Australia policies in 1973. Following its election in 1975, the Fraser Liberal-National government publicly supported multiculturalism. For example, the government-funded multilingual radio and television network, the Special Broadcasting Service (SBS), was established (SBS, 2011). However, Australia's multiculturalism tends to focus on cultural practices and expression such as festivals, cuisines, sports, and arts at a relatively superficial level. Earle (1995) rightly pointed out that Australian multiculturalism does not address the power and political relationship between ethnic minorities and majorities as have the New Zealand bicultural policies.

Over the past 50 years, patterns of immigration have changed toward increased diversity of immigrant sources. The United Kingdom remains the largest source country, but the proportion of immigrants from the United Kingdom decreased from 52% of the overseas-born population in 1954 to 23% in 2006 (ABS, 2008a). The older European immigrant streams (e.g., Italy, Greece, and the Netherlands) have also been in steady decline. Italian-born immigrants have dropped from the second to the third largest immigrant group, making up 4% of the overseas-born in 2006 (ABS). In contrast, since the 1980s, together with the steadily increasing New Zealand–born population, Asian immigrants have become the fastest-growing immigrant sector in Australia. The New Zealand–born population has nearly doubled over the past 25 years and is now the second largest immigrant group, making up 10% of the overseas-born population, while the China-born population has become the fourth largest. Today, Australia has one of the most diverse populations in the world. The number of overseas-born Australians reached 5 million in 2006, representing almost a quarter (24%) of the total population and accounting for 46% of the population growth (ABS).

Leisure Patterns and Participation of Immigrants

Immigrants to Australia have brought with them their widely differing heritages of arts, leisure,

sport, and cuisine, many of which have become popular among mainstream Australians. However, the current understanding of leisure participation patterns and preferences of Australian immigrants is rather limited. Some surveys conducted by ABS (2007a, 2007b, 2007c, 2007e) measured Australian immigrants' rates of (non)participation in some popular mainstream leisure and sporting activities. In these studies, immigrants were mainly classified into two groups according to whether they had been born in a main English-speaking country (MESC; i.e., United Kingdom and Ireland, New Zealand, Canada, United States, South Africa) or in a country where English is not the main language (other than main English-speaking country, OMESC). Participation rates in popular mainstream leisure activities obtained from these surveys are presented together in figure 16.2 to show patterns of participation differences between MESC, OMESC, and Australian-born populations.

Compared with immigrants from MESC, people from OMESC have lower rates of participation in almost all types of popular mainstream Australian leisure activities (except church or religious activities), including social, cultural, physical, and outdoor pursuits (see figure 16.2). The ABS (2006b) survey also indicated that immigrants with very high proficiency in spoken English had a higher rate of participation (63.0%) in sport and physical recreation than those who did not speak English well (36.9%) or did not speak English at all (17.4%). The systematic differences suggest that English-language experience has a significant impact on immigrants' participation in mainstream leisure. However, it is also likely that people whose primary language is English share certain cultural backgrounds and exposure to activities that are similar to those in Australia. This familiarity may also shape their preferences for certain mainstream Australian leisure and facilitate their access to them.

Within the MESC and the OMESC immigrant categories, there have been significant variations in the extent of sport and physical recreation participation between immigrants from different countries. For example, people from the North-Western Europe subgroup, an OMESC group, had the highest participation rate (67.4%) in these activities, whereas those born in North African

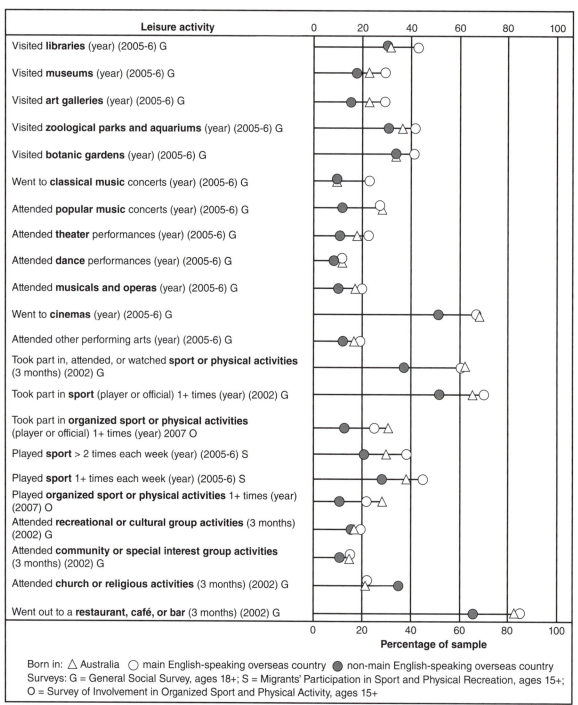

Figure 16.2 Participation in selected leisure activities by people born in Australia and overseas in main English-speaking countries and non-main English-speaking countries.

Note: The data in the chart are from "Attendance at Selected Cultural Venues and Events, Australia, 2005–06," by Australian Bureau of Statistics (ABS), 2007; "Migrants, General Social Survey, Australia, 2002," by ABS, 2007; "Migrants, Participation in Sports and Physical Recreation, Australia, 2005–06," by ABS, 2007; "Survey of Involvement in Organised Sport and Physical Activity," by ABS, 2007. As data in the chart come from various surveys and some used different reference periods and survey methods, one should take care when comparing and interpreting the sample percentages.

or Middle Eastern countries, also OMESCs, had the lowest participation rate (31.2%; ABS, 2006b). Therefore, dichotomizing immigrants into English and non-English-speaking groups has essentially masked the large variations within the groups. Furthermore, when the activity structure was taken into account, people from the North African or the Middle Eastern group actually had very high participation rates in *nonorganized* sport or physical recreation activities (88%) but the lowest participation rates in those *organized* activities (17%). Thus, the activity format or social environment of sport and recreation clubs or certain cultural factors seem to influence immigrants' recreation participation decisions.

Interestingly, compared with people born in Australia, immigrants from MESC tended to have higher rates of participation in most of the leisure activities surveyed except for playing organized sport (see figure 16.2). Since language could not account for these differences, other factors or processes (e.g., cultural preferences and migration–settlement processes) might contribute to the differences. For instance, immigrants' leisure culture and practices in their home countries might interact with the excitement and challenges of living in a new country to heighten leisure involvement of immigrants from the main English-speaking countries.

Roles of Leisure and Sport for Immigrants

The value of sport in the lives of Australian immigrants has been widely acknowledged (e.g., Australian Government Independent Sport Panel, 2009; Cairnduff, 2001; Mosely, 1997). However, the importance of leisure has received much less attention from researchers and leisure professionals. Some studies indicate that leisure and sport contribute to the maintenance of ethnic identity, heritage, and practices of Australian immigrants, as well as strengthening of social networks within ethnic communities (Centre for Multicultural Youth Issues [CMYI], 2007b; Huang, 2009; Taylor, 2001). These studies also suggest that leisure plays significant roles in immigrants' settlement and integration processes. For example, some immigrants would participate in mainstream

leisure and sport activities, groups, and clubs to broaden their social networks outside their ethnic communities and to learn English. On the other hand, racial conflicts in sport, leisure sites, and public settings have continually concerned Australian sporting organizations and governments; examples are ethnic soccer club fan violence and the Cronulla Beach visitor altercations (Taylor, Lock, & Darcy, 2009; Vamplew, 1994; Wearing, Goodall, Byrne, & Kijas, 2008). In December 2005, an incident of verbal and physical conflict between four Lebanese youth and three Caucasian lifeguards at Cronulla Beach in Sydney was distorted and widely commented on in racist and inappropriate ways in Sydney media, which prompted a series of racially motivated violent confrontations. Some Lebanese Australians were distressed over the riot and stopped going to Cronulla Beach (Kabir, 2007).

Although leisure and sport have the potential to deliver many social and individual benefits, with inadequate planning and orchestration they may fail to play a constructive role or even turn destructive. At present, little research seeks to explain the leisure processes or factors that lead to positive or negative leisure and sport outcomes, or factors that shape different leisure preferences of Australian immigrants.

Leisure Constraints of Immigrants in Australia

A few studies in Australia have aimed at understanding the leisure challenges of specific ethnic groups. Toohey and Taylor's (1997) study of ethnic women (59% overseas-born) from seven ethnic groups (Chinese, Croatian, Greek, Italian, Lebanese, Serbian, and Vietnamese) indicated that their most common constraints to sport participation were time limitations (49%), nobody to go with (42%), family responsibilities (38%), and lack of information (36%). In a study of leisure constraints of first-generation adult Chinese immigrants in Australia, Tsai and Coleman (1999) obtained similar results. Of the six leisure constraint factors derived using factor analysis, resources constraints (time and money related) and interpersonal constraints (lack of leisure companions) were perceived as most detrimental to leisure participation. These constraints tended to inhibit the Chinese immigrants' desire to take part in new leisure activities, hinder them from starting new activities, and lead to reduction in levels of leisure participation. The high levels of perceived resources constraints and interpersonal constraints among Chinese immigrants and ethnic women possibly reflect the fact that many ethnic immigrants prioritize work, care for their family, learning English, or other activities that facilitate their settlement (Keogh, 2002). Moreover, finding leisure companions with whom to engage in enjoyable activities can be difficult for new immigrants, as the building of social networks takes time.

Differing conclusions regarding immigrants' leisure constraints were reached in a study of Korean immigrants in Australia. Contrary to their expectations, Tcha and Lobo (2003) found that Korean immigrants in their study had low levels of perceived constraints to leisure. The researchers speculated that the immigrants might not have actually attempted to engage in mainstream leisure and therefore had not detected strong constraints to leisure. Examining how immigrants' leisure expectations and satisfaction with opportunities for ethnic leisure intertwine with a lack of interest in mainstream leisure, and how these processes could buffer their perception of leisure constraints, might shed more light on the leisure meanings and constraint perceptions of ethnic immigrants.

In the 2005-2006 Multi-Purpose Household Survey in Australia, respondents were asked to state the reasons for (non)participation in sport or physical recreation. The most frequently reported constraints of immigrants from OMESC were insufficient time due to work/study (23%), age (22%), and not being interested (19%; ABS, 2007d). However, English proficiency, which has been considered the key constraint of immigrants from OMESC in other ABS studies, was not included in their list of constraints. This probably reflects the fact that without prompting and the ability to clarify responses to open-ended questions, people tend to provide intuitive responses with little serious thinking, or just state their excuses for not engaging in socially desirable behaviors.

Acculturation and Marginality of Immigrants to Australia

An Australian study explored the impact of acculturation and marginality on Chinese immigrants' perception of leisure constraints by adopting a multidimensional acculturation framework (Tsai, 2000). Acculturation was measured using three indices—English proficiency, use of English and Chinese languages, and cultural orientation. Tsai's study indicated that, irrespective of the immigrants' level of education and financial status, those who were less acculturated tended to be more susceptible to sociocultural constraints, interpersonal constraints, and access constraints. In other words, less acculturated Chinese immigrants tended to feel more uncomfortable and insecure in public leisure settings than those who were more acculturated; they also had more difficulty fitting into these public settings. Similarly, other studies suggested that some immigrant parents were fearful for the safety of themselves and their children and were therefore reluctant to allow their children to be involved in mainstream leisure activities with which they were unfamiliar (CMYI, 2007a; Taylor, 2001). Greater understanding of these insecure feelings may lead to ways to negotiate the feelings and to improve the social atmosphere and exchanges between cultural groups.

Tsai and Coleman (1999) found that both marginality and acculturation contributed to perception of leisure constraints of Chinese immigrants. Higher levels of education were associated with lower levels of access constraints, affective constraints (perceived lack of appealing and meaningful leisure opportunities), and social–cultural constraints of the Chinese immigrants; but financial conditions had an insignificant impact. Ang, Brand, Noble, and Sternberg's (2006) study of Australian multiculturalism indicated that education can facilitate intercultural mixing of immigrants from OMESC. Thus, education seems to play important roles in immigrants' cultural understanding and appreciation of and access to mainstream leisure.

Tcha and Lobo (2003) found that acculturation was not associated with perceived leisure constraints of Korean immigrants. The authors measured acculturation with a single item that gauged ethnic identification, which is only one component of acculturation and one that explains limited variance of acculturation (Sabnani & Ponterotto, 1992). Ang and colleagues' (2006) study showed that very few immigrants from OMESC (less than 10%) identified themselves as Australian. A lack of variance in ethnic identification or perceived constraints (as discussed in the preceding section) could contribute to a nonsignificant relationship between acculturation and perceived constraints.

A longer period of living in Australia does not automatically lead to lower levels of perceived constraints to leisure (Tsai, 2000). Rather, it is the actual cultural adaptation that contributes to reducing leisure constraints of immigrants. An excellent tool for facilitating cultural adaptation and integration is inclusive leisure. However, many immigrants prefer to recreate with people from the same cultural or language background or within their small ethnic communities, as this allows them to escape from cultural pressures and racial discrimination (Oliver, 2006; Stodolska, 2000a, 2007; Taylor, 2003). Moreover, the extent to which immigrants can or want to integrate or to engage in leisure activities outside their ethnic communities varies over a wide spectrum (Taylor; Tsai). It is important to understand the heterogeneity of immigrants' leisure needs and preferences and to respect their choices.

Racism and Marginalization of Leisure of Immigrants to Australia

In the Human Rights and Equal Opportunity Commission's study of racism in Australian sport (Oliver, 2006), all sporting organizations surveyed reported having member protection polices and codes for addressing discrimination-related concerns and complaints. However, many of them have not developed initiatives for promoting inclusive environments, or they implement some procedures only on an ad hoc basis (Oliver). Other studies showed that most sport or recreation clubs lacked specific policies and management strategies to encourage cultural diversity—or did not see a need or were unable or reluctant

to provide inclusive opportunities for ethnic minorities (Hanlon & Coleman, 2006; Taylor, 2003). Some sport and recreation managers' intentions to improve inclusion procedures have been inhibited by the belief that a closed-group membership would result in minimum risks and a lower potential for social conflicts (Hanlon & Coleman; Keogh, 2002; Taylor). In Hanlon and Coleman's study, some sport managers revealed that antagonistic responses from existing members regarding provision of inclusionary services to ethnic minorities have inhibited recruitment of ethnic minorities. Narratives of ethnic women in Taylor's (2001) study also contained stories of exclusionary incidents.

Although discrimination laws and policy can deter overt discriminatory behaviors, they are not effective in reducing prejudice or systematic discrimination. Reduction of discriminatory attitudes requires an enhanced understanding and appreciation of other cultures. Inadequate cultural understanding and sensitivity among recreation, sport, and parks professionals could hinder the development of equitable leisure opportunities for ethnic minorities. For example, most sport providers in Toohey and Taylor's (1997) study assumed that the low level of sport participation among ethnic women was due to cultural constraints. However, these women attributed their low participation mainly to noninclusionary practices of providers. Similar kinds of misunderstandings also exist in urban park management in Australia. Wearing and colleagues (2008) found striking differences between park managers' understanding of local urban park use and ethnic communities' actual use of parkland and the values they attached to it.

In fact, the number of informational resources assisting inclusion and cultural understanding has increased in Australia over the decade (e.g., CMYI, 2003; Keogh, 2002; Western Australia Department of Sport and Recreation, n.d.). However, mere information provision is insufficient for improving the *affective* aspect of attitudes (Pate, 1995; Wright, Aron, McLaughlin-Volpe, & Ropp, 1997). From his extensive review of the effects of interventions aimed at reducing prejudice, Pate concluded that the use of information in conjunction with provision of direct social contact between people is most effective. However, *favorable* interaction conditions (mutual benefits, equal status between groups, frequent contacts with opportunities for mutually satisfying personal interactions between members, and opportunities for making cooperative efforts) need to be present to achieve positive outcomes (Allport, 1954; Pettigrew & Tropp, 2006). Without adequate preparation, social contacts may further entrench negative stereotyping. At present, stereotyping and racial and cultural discrimination are still prevalent in the Australian recreation and sport scene (Oliver, 2006; Victorian Health Promotion Foundation, 2007).

Leisure and sport are ideal media to bring people from different cultural backgrounds together to enjoy their common interests, achieve common goals, and develop friendships. However, careful planning and facilitation are necessary in using leisure and sport as a tool for reducing racial prejudice or increasing cultural understanding. Sport in particular is inherently competitive and can easily create further alienation or even hatred of opposition group members as has happened frequently in ethnic soccer. Even in recreational soccer, ethnic group boundaries could be reinforced and interethnic tensions could be magnified (Walker & Deng, 2011). Emphasis on skill development, sportsmanship, social aspects of the games, and fun rather than on winning will help make the activities more effective for social integration and reduction of prejudice.

Recommendations for Research in Australia

At present, analysis of leisure of ethnic minorities in Australia is sparse and fragmented and tends to be atheoretical. The application of current leisure theories in conjunction with other conceptual models and theoretical frameworks such as post-colonialism (Macdonald, Abbott, Knez, & Nelson, 2009; Nelson, 2009) and social ecological models (Nelson, Abbott, & Macdonald, 2010; Sallis & Owen, 1997), which take into account historical context and environmental, cultural, social, and individual levels of influences, is expected to provide a better understanding of leisure in multicultural societies.

The current understanding of leisure and sport concepts and behaviors is based primarily on Western male-centered perspectives. The application of critical race theory (Macdonald et al., 2009; Nelson, 2009) and the exploration of intersections of race, ethnicity, gender, class (Arai & Kivel, 2009), and acculturation, in conjunction with critiques of Whiteness in studies of leisure, could enhance understanding of the leisure of ethnic minorities in Australia. Consideration of the discourse of Whiteness and the social justice paradigm (Roberts, 2009) may expand understanding of the ways in which the benefits of racism and privilege for White Australian-born and White English-speaking overseas-born Australians lead to leisure advantages for these people but disadvantages for others.

The Indigenous and immigrant leisure and sport surveys conducted by the Australian government mainly describe proportions of people participating and not participating in broad categories of leisure activities and some structural constraints to sport and physical recreation participation. Although these studies help increase understanding of the current state of (non)participation in popular mainstream leisure, they provide limited understanding of ethnic leisure needs, constraints, and behaviors. Future studies need to go beyond *describing* leisure participation rates and seek *explanations* of factors that influence leisure preferences, leisure processes, and outcomes of participation. Research should also seek to explain *how* racial, cultural, social, and personal factors influence the leisure practices and experiences of ethnic minorities (see Floyd, 1998, for more on this issue). Understanding of leisure needs, meanings, and the processes of negotiating leisure constraints of ethnic minorities, as well as how these minorities resist and come to terms with the dominant discourse, needs to be expanded through research. Phenomenological research approaches such as ethnographies that seek understandings of ethnic minority issues from their point of view, and action research that seeks to bring about positive social change to the study participants and community, lend themselves to this area of research (see chapter 2 on methods).

Many of the leisure-related social issues of Indigenous Australians, such as alcohol and drug abuse and petrol sniffing, as well as the lower levels of participation of immigrants from OMESC in mainstream leisure activities, appear to be symptoms of much deeper problems associated with social inequality and historic and contemporary racism. However, leisure and sport professionals often adopt a "victim-blaming" discourse, seeing the people who experience these problems as deficient or inferior, or as having cultural limitations regarding leisure, rather than considering the problem as a consequence of systemic racism. Much research is needed to expand understanding of the ways in which systematic, interpersonal, and internalized racism restricts Indigenous Australians' and immigrants' access to resources that are essential to effective participation in the society, including their leisure and sport.

As racism and Whiteness are evident within Australian public policies and managerial practices, policy analysis, and study of managerial practices, incorporating both the cultural majorities' and minorities' perspectives may help explain how specific ideologies and practices produce advantages and disadvantages in leisure opportunities and experiences and reinforce inequitable social relationships (Mowatt, 2009).

Researchers, policy makers, and practitioners from the mainstream and minority cultures should jointly and regularly discuss leisure development, generate research agendas, and share findings in this field. Synergies of Western and Indigenous knowledge and knowledge from other ethnic minorities are expected to provide fresh perspectives and enhance leisure knowledge (Fox, 2007; Nelson et al., 2010), for example, by exploring ways to capitalize on leisure assets of diverse cultures to achieve social and individual benefits.

When engaging in a multicultural partnership, those involved should understand each other's histories, cultural values and practices, and worldviews; deconstruct the familiar ideological knowledge patterns (Brislin, Lonner, & Thorndike, 1973); and place the knowledge and standpoints of the ethnic minorities at least on equal footing (Schinke et al., 2008). Minority groups are sometimes invited to participate in the development of research questions, refinement of questionnaire items, data collection, or data analysis; but very seldom are they invited to contribute to the writing of research reports (Schinke et al.). This is an important part of the development of knowledge that facilitates synthesis of understandings from their perspectives and allows minority voices to be heard firsthand.

Moving beyond integration to inclusion implies that people should seek to embrace the diverse cultures of other people; and public policies, services, and programs should be able to cater to people from different cultures. However, achieving these aims has been less than successful in Australia, as the issues have largely been dealt with through top-down political processes. A substantial increase in the direct involvement of the ethnic stakeholders is necessary if Australian Indigenous and ethnic leisure is to be better appreciated and managed. Development of Indigenous and ethnic leisure is expected to be more effective if it moves away from the political processes toward social and legal processes.

LEISURE OF INDIGENOUS PEOPLES AND IMMIGRANTS IN NEW ZEALAND

Superficially, settlement patterns in New Zealand resembled those in Australia in that in both cases, White settler colonization was imposed upon Indigenous peoples—Aborigines in the case of Australia and Maori in New Zealand. In reality, however, the timing and the circumstances under which these respective colonizations took place, together with the subsequent history of immigration in the two countries, require a much more discriminating analysis.

New Zealand Settlement History and Immigration Policy

Circa 1350 CE, the ancestors of the estimated 663,900 New Zealanders who now identify themselves as Maori (Indigenous New Zealanders) arrived from East Polynesia by voyaging canoe. By the late 18th century, when the first Pakeha (non-Maori), of mainly Anglo–Celtic descent, began settling New Zealand, its Maori population had grown to an estimated 100,000.

Unlike what occurred in Australia, Pakeha settlement of New Zealand predated its British annexation by approximately 40 years. Formalized by the signing of the Treaty of Waitangi in 1840,[1] the annexation has traditionally been portrayed in New Zealand's historiography as an act designed to protect Maori rights and interests from the depredations of avaricious settlers and unscrupulous "foreigners." Central to the treaty was a clause meant to protect Indigenous property rights by making the Crown the only entity able to legally purchase land from Maori. One should not lose sight, however, of the fact that Britain's annexation of New Zealand was an "act of state" that seized new territory for the British government, rather than a consensual acquisition grounded in benevolent protection of Indigenous interests (Hill, 2009). Moreover, although the treaty is now viewed as New Zealand's founding document, it was never ratified by the Crown and was largely ignored by both the legislative and judicial arms of government until the Treaty of Waitangi Act 1975. Land acquisition was effected by both purchase and confiscation; and although the outcome of the New Zealand wars (1860-1872) was not a resounding British military success, it nevertheless paved the way for outright confiscation of Maori land. The experience of Indigenous New Zealanders over the ensuing 150 years has been one of political, social, and economic marginalization in the face of British colonization. By 1896, New Zealand's Maori population fell to a nadir of 43,000.

Although it has become fashionable to describe New Zealand as an "immigrant nation," New Zealand governments in the past, like their Australian federal and state counterparts, in fact, "always preferred immigrants to be of British Stock or, failing these, of northern European" (Wilson, 1966, p. 628). This remained the case until the 1960s, when Pasifika peoples—those indigenous to the three major subregions of Oceania (Polynesia, Melanesia, and Micronesia)—were targeted as potential workers to ease a drastic labor shortage.

Before the Polynesian diaspora, non-White ethnic minorities were identified by the New Zealand government as "race aliens." In 1881, the New Zealand government, following a lead set by California and Victoria, Australia, enacted

an "anti-Chinese poll tax." Although this was New Zealand's most notorious piece of immigration legislation, it is the Immigration Restriction Amendment Act of 1920 that can be pinpointed as the foundation of an explicit White New Zealand policy, a policy similar to that followed at the time in Australia. Speaking in the Parliamentary debates which preceded the legislation, Prime Minister William Massey claimed the Act's sweeping powers were "the result of a deep seated sentiment on the part of a huge majority of the people of this country that this Dominion shall be what is often called a 'white' New Zealand" (Beaglehole, 2012, p. 3).

In the mid-1970s, an economic downturn brought a swift end to official encouragement of Polynesian migration. Dawn raids by police and immigration officers racially profiled potential work permit "overstayers" as Polynesian, reinforcing the impression that New Zealand remained a country for White migrants only (see Pearson, 2005).

Changes in Patterns of Immigration

The *Immigration Acts* of 1987 and 2010 sought to move New Zealand farther away from the use of predominantly ascriptive migrant selection criteria—nation of origin and ethnicity—to achievement criteria, recognizing the abilities of would-be immigrants and the way these matched specific needs of New Zealand society, particularly the skills needed in the economy. The acts established the three-stream framework that has guided New Zealand immigration policy through to the present day and that successive governments have fine-tuned but not replaced. The three streams of the New Zealand Residence Programme for permanent migrants are Skilled/Business, accounting for 60% of permanent migrants; Family Sponsored (30%); and International/Humanitarian (10%).

The number and proportions of people born overseas but now living in New Zealand are increasing. At the time of the 2006 Census, almost 23% of New Zealand residents had been born overseas; close to one-third of these had been

[1]This treaty (Te Tiriti) of the bicultural relationship between the tangata whenua (the first peoples) and the English Crown was signed between a number of Maori chiefs and representatives of the Crown in February, 1840, at Waitangi, in New Zealand's North Island. It was subsequently circulated among other chiefs who were unable or reluctant to attend with a view to extracting pantribal recognition.

born in Asia,[2] equaling the proportion born in the United Kingdom and Ireland. (Corresponding figures for the 2001 and 1996 Censuses are 19.5% and 17.5%, respectively.) The People's Republic of China moved from fourth to second place, after England, as the most common overseas birthplace. By 2021, if current projections hold, Asian ethnic groups, which include second and third generations, will account for almost 15% of the New Zealand population (Dixon, Tse, Rossen, & Sobrun-Maharaj, 2010). In 2006, European ethnic groupings constituted 67.7% of the population, Maori 14.6%, Other 11.2%, Asian 9.2%, and Pasifika peoples 6.9%. Those who identified with Middle Eastern, Latin American, and African groups constituted 0.9% of the resident population (Statistics New Zealand, 2010).[3] Between the 2001 and 2006 Censuses, the Asian ethnic grouping increased by almost 50% and the Pasifika peoples by 14.7%. Auckland was the most ethnically diverse region in New Zealand and the home of most Pasifika peoples (Statistics New Zealand).

A discussion of immigration is not complete without mention of those who come to New Zealand as refugees. The New Zealand government established a formal annual quota in 1987, one that was followed by successive governments, of approximately 750 places annually. Over the past 15 years, more than 10,000 refugees have settled in New Zealand under this refugee quota scheme (Statistics New Zealand, 2010).

Some Maori are dismayed that the screening process applied to would-be immigrants does not require an investigation of their attitudes toward racial equality or their bicultural awareness. As reported in one of the major national Sunday newspapers, Dr. Margaret Mutu, an academic at Auckland University—and not one to shy away from controversy—stated that "White" immigrants "bring with them, as much as they deny it, an attitude of white supremacy destructive to Maori" (Hill, 2011, p. 4). On this basis, Dr. Mutu called for the placement of restrictions on White immigration to New Zealand, a suggestion that led the Race Relations Commissioner Joris de Bres

(who is a Dutch immigrant) to claim that Dr. Mutu was herself demonstrating "racism" in the way she denigrated certain immigrant groups on the basis of their skin color and ethnic origin. This "spat" demonstrates the complexity of interethnic relations but also strongly suggests that the wider implications, including those related to leisure, of an increasingly multicultural New Zealand must be considered in the context of the Crown's prior and ongoing commitment to biculturalism.

Significance of Biculturalism

Before the late 1980s, the New Zealand government pursued a policy of assimilation rather than biculturalism or multiculturalism. By the late 19th century, "the complacent assumption among White New Zealanders" was that Maori would soon become culturally and ethnically unidentifiable as a separate race; they would either "die out" completely or be assimilated into the Anglo–Celtic majority (Stafford & Williams, 2006, p. 111). The assumption that Maori could be assimilated rested on their status among some settlers as "intelligent savages," able to adapt and transition into modernity if given sufficient chance. In the 1970s, a generation of young, educated, politically aware, and urbanized Maori looked toward self-determination and restoration of tribal land as a way of improving Maori lives. In addition to demanding that the Treaty of Waitangi be ratified and Maori sovereignty formally recognized, this new generation sought to reestablish the primacy of Maori culture and language. This strengthened a dichotomous cultural landscape of Maori and Pakeha rather than a heterogeneous, polytribal, and multiethnic landscape.

The *Treaty of Waitangi Act 1975* offered the first formal recognition of the treaty in New Zealand law by establishing the Waitangi Tribunal to investigate and advise government on contemporary (post-1975) potential breaches of treaty guarantees. In 1985, the Fourth Labor government extended the tribunal's investigative abilities by allowing it to hear historical claims and grievances. Although unable to settle claims, the

---

[2]The seven largest ethnic groups within the Asian grouping at the 2006 Census were Chinese, Indian, Korean, Filipino, Japanese, Sri Lankan, and Cambodian, with the Chinese constituting 41.6% and Indians 29.5% of this grouping.

[3]People could choose to identify with more than one ethnic group. At the 2006 Census, 10.4% of people did so.

Waitangi Tribunal makes recommendations to government on how individual claims should be settled. These can be brought before the tribunal by individuals, but settlements are made on a tribal basis, reaffirming the role of iwi (tribes) as the principal political and social unit in Maori society. Despite this, pantribal institutions continue to play an important organizational and political role. In 2004, for example, the Maori Party was formed as a response to the Labor government's Foreshore and Seabed Act 2004, which vested "the full legal and beneficial ownership of the public foreshore and seabed in the Crown" ("Foreshore and Seabed Act 2004," n.d.). In contrast, the Maori Party claimed that since the Treaty of Waitangi had not specifically mentioned New Zealand's foreshore or seabed, ownership of these resources remained in Maori hands.

Before the passing of the *Foreshore and Seabed Act 2004*, the National Party organized the "Beaches for All" petition (English, 2003). Use of the word "Beach" in the petition's title suggests that public access to the foreshore for recreation was an important issue in the debate, a link made more explicit by a further petition, sponsored by Public Access New Zealand (PANZ). Claiming that "'The beach' is New Zealand's most popular outdoor recreation setting—it is very much part of the national psyche," PANZ requested

> [t]hat the House of Representatives pass legislation that clearly establishes inalienable, sole Crown title, ownership, and authority over New Zealand's beaches, foreshore and seabed and guarantees secure rights of recreation for all New Zealanders. (Public Access New Zealand, 2003)

In 2011, the Fifth National government, in coalition with the Maori Party, repealed the Foreshore and Seabed Act via Section 5 of the Marine and Coastal Area (Takutai Moana) Act 2011. The new act restored Maori access to the courts to claim customary marine title while simultaneously guaranteeing right of public access to all "common marine coastal areas" by relinquishing the Crown's own title to those areas.

In announcing the act's passage, Attorney General Chris Finlayson said "all New Zealanders will always be able to walk, swim, fish, sail, dive, surf, picnic or play at the beach. The Bill guarantees public access, fishing, navigation, and existing use rights" ("New Foreshore Bill Passed," 2011). While debate over the foreshore and seabed—as a common marine coastal area—had sometimes concentrated on economic issues such as oil, gas, and mineral exploration or coastal shipping, a dominant story in the public and political arena remained the right (and, perhaps, rite) of access to beaches as recreation venues.

For immigrant minorities, acceptance of such public leisure rites was a key component of assimilation, but the foreshore and seabed debate brought the "bicultural" versus "multicultural" allegiances of New Zealand society into prominence via an issue that was, to the greater public, predominantly a recreational one.

New Zealand Research on Indigenous and Immigrant Leisure

Research on Indigenous and immigrant leisure in New Zealand is not as extensive as in Australia and some other countries. Nevertheless, sufficient information is available from historical inquiries, from leisure participation surveys of New Zealanders (including immigrants), and from studies focusing specifically on more recent leisure experiences of immigrants and immigrant communities to allow interesting comparisons with Australia and elsewhere.

Historical Research on Ethnic Minority and Immigrant Leisure

Explicit historical research on ethnic minority and immigrant leisure in New Zealand is limited. Initially, much research was heavily influenced and limited by trends in the disciplines of history and anthropology, which exhibited a primary interest in "ancient" or precontact societies. Attempts by early New Zealand ethnographers such as Best (1925) to identify traditional leisure were confounded by a missionary-led suppression of Indigenous culture, particularly of those aspects construed as not "civilized" or "industrious" according to Protestant strictures (Howe, 1984). That "games connected Maori directly and powerfully to their spiritual beliefs and wairua [spirit or soul]" must have further strengthened missionary resolve to "eradicate" Indigenous pastimes (Brown, 2008, p. 9). While it is sometimes difficult to find a positive note in missionaries' attempts at cultural reprogramming, McLean (1996) noted that the "Maori practices they strove to eradicate included cannibalism, infanticide, polygamy, slavery and warfare, together with associated customs and beliefs" (pp. 270-271). Given the interconnectedness between games, song, dance, decorative arts, warfare, death, and spirituality in daily Maori life, missionary suppression of Indigenous cultural practices may be better understood if, retrospectively, not fully endorsed.

One gains an impression of the richness and complexity of precontact Maori leisure from the fact that, working primarily with one central North Island tribe approximately 100 years after the missionary suppression of traditional Maori leisure practices began, Best (1925) recorded over a hundred separate Indigenous pastimes. Adopting a Eurocentric framework that had already divided workers' time into periods of work and play, Best largely ignored the interconnectedness of Maori leisure; yet his categories of Maori games provide insight into the importance of play as a method of physical and mental training:

- Games and exercises viewed as useful elementary training for boys
- Aquatic games and pastimes
- Games requiring manual dexterity and agility
- Games requiring calculation, mental alertness, or memorizing powers
- Games and pastimes for children (p. 128)

While acknowledging Best's pioneering contribution to the current understanding of Maori leisure activities, Brown (2008), a Maori scholar, explicitly highlighted the ethnographer's tendency to ignore conceptually and technologically complicated artifacts and to refuse to acknowledge sexualized games. Best had been openly critical of missionary practices and beliefs, but he was also reluctant to explore the inherent relationship between Maori spirituality and Indigenous games. In contrast, Brown saw "Connection to the Gods" as an overarching belief system governing games

and pastimes. Like Best, however, Brown also recognized a utilitarian purpose in Indigenous games, which influenced physical and mental as well as spiritual well-being.

More broadly, and in contemporary New Zealand, aspects of leisure and sport are central to popular and academic observations of the nature of New Zealand society. The place of leisure in New Zealanders' social history can be gauged from the title of the essay "Of Verandahs and Fish and Chips and Footie on Saturday Afternoon: Reflections on 100 Years of New Zealand Historiography" (Phillips, 1990). "Footie" refers to rugby union, which, although a socially elite sport in England, is widely seen as New Zealand's national game, played and followed by a broad social spectrum of people, including many Pakeha, Maori, and Pasifika. It played an increasingly important social and cultural role throughout the 20th century, becoming commonly recognized and referred to as New Zealand's "unofficial religion" (Brown, Guthrie, & Growden, 2007). Daley (2009) referred to a "Rugby as Nation" myth and attempted to redress its gendered and culturally myopic tendencies with a more inclusive and nuanced historical perspective on "Modernity, Consumption and Leisure." Another first step toward unpacking the heterogeneity of New Zealand leisure was provided by Clarke (2007), who identified discrete regional and ethnic holiday celebrations imported from Britain and Ireland by immigrants to form the basis of religious and secular celebrations in New Zealand. By and large, however, historical research on the relationship between leisure and ethnicity in New Zealand is largely confined to descriptive passages in more general ethnic histories or theories that centralize rugby union in the development of a single and singular male-centric New Zealand culture. Leisure as footie and as holiday celebrations certainly fails to account for or analyze the role of leisure in New Zealand's ethnic minority communities.

Leisure Participation Research

National-level surveys are a major source of information about New Zealanders' (including immigrants') involvement in leisure, but specifically with respect to time use and two forms of leisure: "active" leisure, in keeping with the mandate of

Sport and Recreation New Zealand (SPARC), and "artistic" leisure, consistent with the mission of Creative New Zealand.

With regard to time use, the findings of the 1998-1999 and recently released 2009-2010 time-use surveys (TUS; Statistics New Zealand, 2001, 2011) included free time and leisure as elements in the day-to-day lives of New Zealanders. The data from the 2009-2010 TUS indicate that between 5 and 6 hours in an average day can be classified as "free," based on an analysis of "primary" activities. However, as identified by Walker, Donn, and Laidler (2005), "In reality, people often engage in more than one activity at a time and when these are aggregated, free-time activity virtually doubles" (p. 179). The category *free time* comprises 30 activities clustered in groups to include sports and hobbies, religious/cultural/civic participation, social entertainment, and mass media activities. The question of how much of this free time is leisure cannot be answered without further analysis of the disaggregated data (Walker et al.), but as free time is potential time available for leisure, it provides an important context for leisure activity choices made by different ethnic groups. The data show that the proportion of free time varies across ethnic groups; on average, Asian New Zealanders had less free time daily available for leisure in both the 1998-1999 and 2009-2010 surveys (5.05 and 5.00 hours) compared to Maori (5.50 and 5.35 hours), Pasifika (5.26 and 5.37 hours), and European (5.31 and 5.39 hours) New Zealanders. The 2009-2010 TUS offers the potential for a much closer look at the way New Zealanders of different ethnic backgrounds spend their leisure time. However, as the analysis was yet to be carried out and as the release of the survey was so close to the completion of this chapter, surveys commissioned by sport and arts agencies were left as the main sources of leisure-as-activity information.

In relation to active leisure, the 2007-2008 Active New Zealand Survey (SPARC, 2009) provides some descriptive sport, recreation, and physical activity participation data for New Zealand European, Maori, Pasifika, Asian, and Other ethnic groups. While the homogeneity implied in the self-assigned Asian, Other, and (arguably) Pasifika categories may hide more than it reveals, the data from this participation survey provide a wide-angle-lens "snapshot" of adult sport and physical recreation activities by broad ethnic category. The most notable finding was that a much higher proportion of Asian adults were physically inactive (21.0%) compared to the general New Zealand population (12.7%) and did not meet the 30 minutes of five physical activity (defined as recreational and nonrecreational physical activity) sessions per week recommended in the New Zealand Physical Activity Guidelines. In contrast, a lower proportion of Maori (11.8%) and Pasifika adults (10.9%) were in the inactive group and a higher proportion met the recommended guidelines compared to the overall New Zealand population. A more in-depth look at the data reveals that activities popular with Maori were touch (a variant of rugby) and rugby; Pasifika adults participated frequently in volleyball, rugby, touch, and basketball. Popular activities for Asian adults were Pilates/yoga, badminton, and basketball; and football was popular with adults belonging to Other ethnicities. Popular activities across all ethnic groups included walking, swimming, gardening, and equipment-based exercise.

These data, along with comparable data from the 2002-2003 and 2006-2007 New Zealand Health Surveys, which measured the proportion of the population aged 15 years and over who met physical activity guidelines and which produced similar findings, provide a limited longitudinal snapshot of adult physical activity participation. Asians aged 15 years and over were significantly less likely than the general population in that age group to have met physical activity guidelines in the previous week. In 2006 to 2007, the age-standardized rate for Asians was 40%, while the rate for all New Zealanders aged 15 years and over was 51%. In each ethnic group other than Pasifika, males were significantly more likely than females to have met physical activity guidelines. These patterns were similar in 2002 to 2003.

Between 2002-2003 and 2006-2007, for all ethnic groups, there were no significant increases in the rates at which the population 15 years and over met physical activity guidelines (figure 16.3).

In terms of the arts, the New Zealanders and the Arts survey (Creative New Zealand, 2008) gives a picture of arts participation similar to that for sport participation among New Zealand's ethnic groups. Active participation rates in the arts for minority ethnic groups (Maori, 68.0%; Other ethnicities, 58.0%; Pasifika people, 54.0%) were higher than the national average (48.0%) except among Asians (44.0%). While both attendance and participation rates were lower than average for Asian people, 76% had attended at least one arts event in the past 12 months (figure 16.4).

There were also ethnic differences in attitudes toward the arts. For Maori, the arts appeared to be strongly tied to identity. Maori were more likely on average to agree with the statement "The arts help define who we are as New Zealanders" (87.0%

vs. 79.0% on average) and "The availability of arts activities and events is an important reason why I like living where I do" (58.0% agreed vs. 49.0% on average). Pasifika people were as supportive of the arts as other New Zealanders, and were particularly likely to agree that "The arts are strong in New Zealand" (86.0% agreed vs. 76.0% on average). Attitudinally, Asian New Zealanders were also supportive of the arts and also tied the arts to their sense of national identity. Asian New Zealanders saw opportunities for the arts to be strengthened in New Zealand, particularly in comparison with the arts in other countries.

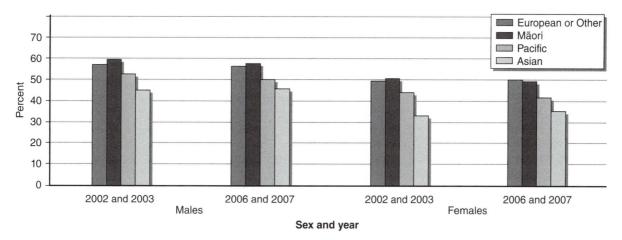

Figure 16.3   Proportion of the New Zealand population aged 15 years and over who met physical activity guidelines by ethnic group and sex, 2002-2003 and 2006-2007.

From Ministry of Health, 2004, *New Zealand Health Survey, 2002/2003* and from Ministry of Health, 2008, *New Zealand Health Survey, 2006/2007* (Wellington, NZ: Ministry of Health).

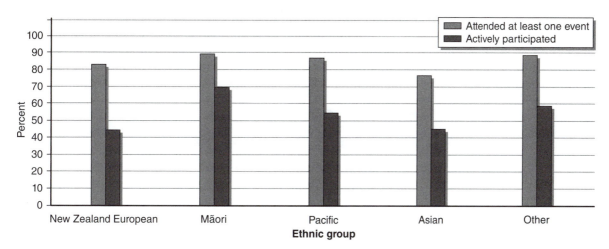

Figure 16.4   Proportion of the New Zealand population aged 15 years and over who attended arts events or participated in the arts, by ethnic group, 2008.

From Creative New Zealand, 2008, *New Zealanders and the Arts: Attitudes, Attendance and Participation* (Wellington, NZ: Creative New Zealand).

Asian people were less likely than the average population to agree that "The arts are strong in New Zealand" (67.0% agreed vs. 76.0%) and were more likely to agree with the statement "The arts in New Zealand aren't as good as in some overseas countries" (47.0% agreed vs. 37.0%).

Ideas about what the arts include tended to be broader among Maori, Pasifika, and Asian peoples compared with Other New Zealanders. These ethnic groups were more likely to view crafts, cultural events, and expressions or interpretations of ideas, feelings, and beliefs as part of the arts. For example, maintaining or passing on tradition was a significant reason for Maori participation in Maori arts activities. This was reflected in participation in the Maori cultural activities of *karakia, waiata, te reo, kapa haka,* and *poi* (see table 16.1 for an explanation of these activities).

Together, the findings of these national surveys are consistent as to ethnic participation in recreational sport and recreational art. Higher proportions of Asian New Zealanders are inactive or do not participate in either form of recreation compared to the total or average New Zealand population. In contrast, a higher proportion of Maori and Pasifika people actively participate in sport and art in comparison to the overall New Zealand population. In the case of sport, whereas the Indigenous cultures of Maori and Pasifika people are strongly represented in recreational sport, the cultures of more recent immigrants from Asia may not place equivalent value on active, and in particular, physical contact sport,

which is arguably a core value in New Zealand culture.

The appeal of Pilates, yoga, badminton, and basketball to people of Asian descent or the (ethnic) social networks within which these activities are pursued may support Floyd and Gramann's (1993) argument that leisure behavior may be a means by which minorities maintain their ethnic distinctiveness, because leisure is less dictated by majority culture norms. In the case of Maori and Pasifika people, ethnic distinctiveness may be met in other, nonsporting ways, because they have histories and cultures in which recreational sport, and particularly traditional New Zealand physical contact sport (e.g., rugby union and rugby league), are already widely accepted.[4] Their relatively higher levels of participation in sport are consistent with New Zealand's having a tradition as a very sporting and active nation— a nation in which physical recreation and sport have been assumed to be central to the leisure phenomenon, leading to legislation and policies designed to address low levels of involvement in certain forms of vigorous activity (Laidler & Cushman, 1993).

Clearly, in offering these interpretations, the present authors are "stepping beyond" the data. The data reflect the fact that much New Zealand research on Indigenous and immigrant leisure is purely descriptive, and there is an urgent need to undertake theoretically informed research in this area. A later section of the chapter will return to this point.

Table 16.1 Participation in Maori Cultural Activities by Adult (Age 18+) New Zealand Maori and General Population

Maori cultural activities	PARTICIPATION RATES (%)	
	Maori	General population
Karakia (prayer-chant)	24	5
Waiata (singing)	23	5
Te reo (Maori language)	22	4
Kapa haka (performance involving song, dance, and martial arts)	11	2
Poi (ball attached to string manipulated to a rhythmic beat)	8	1

From Hillary Commission 1997, 1999; Creative New Zealand 1999.

[4]Many Asian cultures also have their own national contact sports, for example Thai boxing, Korean karate, Japanese judo, and Chinese martial arts. These contact sports are less popular in New Zealand and Australia than the British ones, but they are gaining in popularity.

In the case of arts participation, an examination of definitions of art forms and stereotypes associated with national identity may also be appropriate. In the New Zealanders and the Arts survey (Creative New Zealand, 2008), it may not be a coincidence that Maori and Pasifika people have relatively high participation in the arts and a strong association between the arts and their own and New Zealand's identity (with much lower figures for Asian people), given the way this survey and Creative New Zealand define the various art forms: visual arts, performing arts, literature (or written arts), Maori arts, and Pasifika arts. In part at least, this may be a case in which the priorities of the commissioning agency—in this case Creative New Zealand—limit the current understanding of participation patterns of wider ethnic groups beyond ethnicities central to its mission. Stodolska and Alexandris (2004) allude to a more general reservation regarding the use and interpretation of these recreational sport and arts participation data in the context of ethnicity:

> . . . we may argue that the *types of activities* in which immigrants participate can be interpreted to be an imperfect indicator of their acculturation level. It appears that not the activities themselves, but rather the *context of participation* defines the role of leisure in the lives of immigrants and in the internal dynamics of immigrant communities. (pp. 407-408)

Immigrant Leisure Research

This section reviews a number of specific New Zealand studies of contemporary immigrant leisure, beginning with those by Lovelock, Lovelock, Jellum, and Thompson (2010a, 2010b, 2011), who examined recent immigrants' experiences of nature-based recreation. Their findings are broadly in line with findings of research conducted in the context of the United States, summarized by Juniu (2000) when she says "ethnic minorities tend to recreate closer to home, use city parks, be more family oriented, and utilize local facilities rather than national, state or regional sites" (p. 358). Lovelock and colleagues (2010a) provided data on the frequency of participation in nature-based recreation, social interactions, motivations, and destination preferences, and these data were cross-tabulated with sociodemographic information for the self-assigned ethnic categories of New Zealand European, European, Chinese, and Other.[5] *New migrants* (those who had been in New Zealand for up to five years) engaged in more activities, more often, than *settled migrants* (those who had resided in New Zealand for at least five years). The authors' sociodemographic data showed that settled migrants were older, and therefore age differences confounded any attempt to assess whether, for example, new immigrants are in an "exploratory" phase of settlement and more motivated to socialize and make friends within and outside their own ethnic groups. Respondents named a total of 17 nature-based recreational activities in which they had participated in the previous year, with members of the Chinese ethnic category indicating the lowest mean number of activities. These data supported the interpretation that the individualistic character of Western nature-based recreation (Johnson, Bowker, & Cordell, 2005) may be at odds with the collective values of some immigrant cultures, whose members feel more comfortable when recreating as families or groups in approachable urban parks and "front country" locations of state and national parks. Lovelock and coauthors (2010a) extended this point, noting that some immigrants have very different understandings of what is "natural," "wild," and "beautiful" and that, despite the close geographical proximity of wild places to New Zealand urban centers, they may find them unfamiliar and challenging. Such data led Lovelock and colleagues (2010b) to the following conclusion:

> While overall the study reinforced our understandings of how minority groups recreate (e.g., larger groups, more socially-oriented, greater use of park facilities), the differences observed are just as important.

---

[5]Other consisted of all ethnicities other than the three categories specified, and included multiple identities. Forty-two such identities in total were recorded.

Collectively they suggest that the research setting—physically, ecologically, socially and economically—may play a more important role in shaping the 'away' nature-based recreation practices and preferences of migrants and ethnic minorities than has previously been considered. (pp. 37-38)

A point of comparison with Lovelock and colleagues' (2010a, 2010b) New Zealand study is the work of Johnson and coauthors (2005) in the United States. These authors found that U.S.-born Chinese, as well as Chinese immigrants, demonstrated low involvement in a number of nature-based activities—"developed" camping, "primitive" camping, and mountain biking—compared with Whites. While Lovelock and colleagues' (2010a, 2010b, 2011) sample included New Zealand–born as well as new and settled immigrants, however, only one New Zealand–born Chinese respondent was included in the study, and it is not apparent from which ethnic groups the 19 respondents in the New Zealand–born "Other" category were drawn. Given the small size of the samples, it is thus not possible to comment on the extent to which involvement in nature-based recreation is a cultural as distinct from a "relocation" issue.

On behalf of the Auckland Regional Physical Activity and Sport Strategy (ARPASS), Spoonley and Taiapa (2009) completed a report designed to help sporting bodies and local authorities in the Auckland area address the needs of the increasingly diverse immigrant communities in their midst. In their introduction, Spoonley and Taiapa made a point that reinforces data from the national leisure participation surveys (see previous section): Pasifika peoples are strongly represented in sport in New Zealand, particularly in physical contact sport, while other immigrant groups are less so. Immigration from the South Pacific to New Zealand has an extensive history, and prowess in sport is a source of pride among these communities. The cultures of some new immigrants from East and South Asia, as noted earlier, do not place equivalent value on sporting success—and in cases in which sports are valued, they are typically not "mainstream" ones.

Spoonley and Taiapa's (2009) results display a bimodal distribution in the extent to which regional sport organizations in the Auckland area have been affected by and have responded to the sporting interests of immigrant groups. The formation of ethnic sporting organizations is proving important in encouraging and disseminating sports such as table tennis that are different from those in the Anglo–Celtic mainstream. Ethnic sporting organizations often emphasize participation—socializing with people who share one's culture and ethnic history—rather than competition. The presence of organizations representing the interests of particular ethnic communities, according to Spoonley and Taiapa, divides regional sport organizations and administrators. Some see this as encouraging and condoning separatism, while others see it as an appropriate step or bridge toward later inclusiveness. Sports that "migrated" with particular ethnic groups were more likely to see continuing participation on the part of members of those groups following settlement (Spoonley & Taiapa). Overall, Spoonley and Taiapa concluded that local authorities have done more than sport organizations to address the needs of immigrants and ethnic minorities.

Government-Based Research on Immigration and Resettlement

Turning to the contribution of government and quasi-government agencies in New Zealand, this section briefly considers the content of those reports on immigration and resettlement that contain references to "leisure," broadly conceived.

A report for the Families Commission (Dixon et al., 2010) examined the settlement experiences of Asian immigrant families in New Zealand. The report was based on focus group discussions and interviews with Chinese, Korean, and Indian families and families from Asia or Southeast Asia with refugee histories. When coping with "stress" was raised during the focus groups, none of the stress reduction strategies mentioned by participants involved leisure, recreation, hobbies, or sport. In family interviews, the only mentions of leisure, recreation, or sport as stress reduction measures related to "hobbies" (Dixon et al.). The report noted that family interviews raised the issue of intergenerational conflict, which was seen to be increasing, but that only the refugee families discussed this at length (Dixon et al.).

In a pilot survey for the Department of Labour's longitudinal immigration survey, 691 immigrants were interviewed six months after taking up permanent residency, and 546 were interviewed again after 18 months (Dunstan, Boyd, & Crichton, 2004). The sample was defined by those who were excluded: persons who did not speak one of the pilot study languages (English, Tongan, Samoan, Mandarin, Cantonese) and those who did not live in the pilot study areas (Christchurch, Wellington, the Waikato, Auckland). The resulting sample was composed of English speakers (North American, South African, English) and North Asian, Pacific, and Other Asian respondents. Between the interview periods, the proportion of respondents who indicated that they belonged to clubs and groups increased from 48% to 57%. Immigrants from North Asia (People's Republic of China, Taiwan, and Korea) were least likely to join a club or group at either time period. Overall, twice as many respondents at each time period indicated that they were members of religious groups compared with sport clubs or groups, but there were marked differences between North Asian and Other Asian respondents; the former were markedly less likely to be involved in religious groups at either time period.[6] In a subsequent report based on data gathered from the entire sample of more than 7,000 respondents after the first six months of residency (Masgoret, Merwood, & Tausi, 2009), almost half of the immigrants indicated that they belonged to clubs and groups, most commonly religious groups, sport groups, and job-related groups (22%, 20%, and 11%, respectively). Those from South Africa and the Pacific were more likely to be members of religious groups, and those from the United Kingdom and the Irish Republic were more likely to be members of sport clubs (Masgoret et al.).

In another report for the Family Commission, Stuart, Jose, and Ward (2009) used interviews with immigrants from Africa, the Middle East, and Asia to examine relationships between parents and their adolescent children in the settlement process. Thirty-nine interviews, matching parents and adolescent sons or daughters, were conducted with respondents who had been residents in New Zealand for up to seven years. Overall, Stuart and colleagues found a high level of respect between parents and their adolescent children and agreement about the importance of education and maintaining traditional cultural values and religious beliefs among all respondents. Among sources of disagreement were adolescents' use of the media (playing video games, watching TV, and using the Internet), (inappropriate) clothing, (declining) manners, and time devoted to housework. Perhaps surprisingly, there were few disagreements over smoking, drinking, and drugs; both generations saw these as unhealthy for individuals and families. The major disagreements, in terms of cultural adaptation, were generational differences in values regarding rights of adolescent children to have privacy, rights to be trusted in their actions without intrusive "policing" by parents and other adult relatives, and the practice of dating and forming intimate relationships. It is of course entirely possible that these sites of conflict are typical of relationships between today's young people and their parents and not specifically a cultural adaptation issue.

Research conducted by the New Zealand Immigration Service (NZIS, 2004) investigated the experiences of 398 recently arrived (interviewed at 6 months and 24 months) and established (resident for approximately five years) refugees. Respondents included those who entered New Zealand under the aforementioned Refugee Quota; those who came as individuals, claimed asylum, and were subsequently given refugee status ("Convention" refugees); and those who entered New Zealand through the family-sponsored immigration policy (NZIS). Respondents were concentrated in major urban centers, particularly in Auckland. Among these immigrants, recently arrived teenagers identified the opportunity to play sports and take part in leisure activities such as going to the beach as an aspect of what they liked about "being teenagers in New Zealand" (NZIS, pp. 285-286). Involvement in sport and recreational activities such as going to the movies, parks, and beaches, also figured in the responses of established teenage refugees.

---

[6]Differences between ethnic groups in their membership in various clubs and groups are noted in the report.

Among all respondents in the NZIS (2004) study, English-language difficulties were given as a factor with regard to resisting joining groups or clubs, including sport clubs, but joining clubs was not a high priority for most respondents. The study also noted that some respondents came from countries where such clubs were associated with the political and cultural elite, while others interpreted a question about club membership as referring to night clubs. *Friends, relatives and neighbors,* and *school/other study* figured prominently among both recently arrived and established refugees as ways of meeting people outside of their own ethnic group. Sporting and other clubs barely rated in this context. In cases in which respondents joined groups, these were most likely to be clubs with an ethnic or religious base (or both); for established refugees, sport clubs were third in terms of the proportions belonging to clubs and groups. With respect to how respondents maintained their cultures, in the case of both recently arrived and established refugees, speaking their own language, eating traditional foods, and practicing their religion were key, and mixing with their ethnic communities was also important. "Religious observance was central to ethnic communities getting together, with many people saying they met with members of their ethnic group for religious occasions" (NZIS, p. 328). Overall, the findings were surprising with respect to the similarities between recently arrived and settled refugees on issues of concern to them and their settlement experiences.

Recommendations for Research in New Zealand

The research reviewed and the government documents examined suggest that research on the roles of leisure among immigrant groups and ethnic minorities in New Zealand is of recent origin; sparse in quantity (Spoonley & Taiapa, 2009); mostly based on cross-sectional (one point in time) survey techniques; focused on participation and activity data; and inclined to use collective ethnic labels, notably "Asian," which possibly conceals important "intralabel" differences. These foci reflect the priorities of the agencies most responsible for commissioning the research, notably SPARC and Creative New Zealand. Furthermore, the research tends to be descriptive or atheoretical (or both) as befits the "practical" purposes for which the data have been gathered, such as assessment by local authorities of current and future community demand for swimming pools and recreation centers. With the possible exception of the Families Commission report on family resilience (Dixon et al., 2010), New Zealand research has not been driven by, or designed in terms of, hypotheses or questions arising from the theoretical perspectives current in the overseas literature that are reviewed in other chapters of this book. Thus, in making analytical sense of the data, reviewers must frequently resort to ex post facto interpretations. It is the authors' hope that this chapter, and the book to which it contributes, will encourage more theoretically grounded research—research nearer to the "pure" than to the "applied" end of a continuum.

The existing data are also marked by methodological shortcomings. For example, Spoonley and Taiapa (2009) interviewed just four representatives of immigrant groups or ethnic minorities in their study of Auckland sport organizations' responsiveness to the needs of immigrant communities. In the research leading to the Families Commission's report on the settlement experiences of Asian immigrant families, the researchers failed to persuade families to allow individual family members to be interviewed (Dixon et al., 2010). Lovelock and colleagues' (2010a, 2010b, 2011) self-completed questionnaire returned an overall response rate of 26%, which raises questions about the representativeness of their data. Given resource constraints, their study focused on two North Island urban areas, and their questionnaire was available in only two languages—English and Chinese.[7]

---

[7]In fairness, many of the overseas studies also display methodological deficiencies. For example, Juniu's (2000) study, in part designed to evaluate which of two current theories best explained the experiences of South American immigrants to the United States (the marginality thesis and the ethnicity thesis), was based on interviews with 17 respondents. In the view of the present authors, this is an example of data stretching—requiring data to carry more interpretive freight than it can handle.

On the basis of the review in this chapter of New Zealand research planning and methods related to immigrant leisure, the authors suggest the following priorities (see also chapter 2 on methods):

1. Methodologically, (a) greater use of longitudinal studies of ethnic minority and immigrant leisure in response to policy initiatives to increase participation and, in the case of immigrant communities, following resettlement; and (b) participant observation and case study techniques to engage with the social worlds of different ethnic and immigrant groups.

2. Theoretically, developing research designs capable of differentiating between a number of possible explanations of immigrant experiences and behavior associated with leisure, such as whether household tensions between parents and teenagers in immigrant families (Stuart et al., 2009) reflect acculturation differences, suggest different perceptions of leisure constraints, or are part of the "normal" teenage "individuation" processes.

3. With respect to leisure policy–related research, extending government surveys on leisure participation to include a more specific focus on ethnic leisure is desirable. Consistent with the recommendations for such research in Australia presented earlier in the chapter, this means going beyond solely describing leisure participation patterns to seek explanations of factors that influence leisure, leisure processes, and consequences of participation on the part of ethnic groups. If policy making is to be responsive in relation to leisure provision for ethnic groups, such surveys need to catch more than a few glancing images of ethnic leisure within a vast, moving picture of New Zealanders at leisure.

4. Adopting a broader disciplinary perspective that integrates leisure research on ethnic and immigrant groups into the wider theoretical frameworks of ethnicity and minorities rather than focusing on mini-theories relating to "narrowly defined leisure problems whose applicability is limited to specific groups and specific situations" (Stodolska, 2000b, p. 158), may prove to be a productive strategy. However, a macroscopic view of leisure participation in New Zealand needs to be supplemented with a microscopic perspective on ethnic leisure. If leisure policy making is to be equitable, it will be important to recognize and examine the tendency of certain values, experiences, and preferences to predominate in leisure provision in New Zealand. As indicated earlier, typically these dominating values are based on a Western, male, Pakeha perspective, in which leisure is perceived to be physically "active" and culturally prescribed (typically Eurocentric) and "serious" (Stebbins, 2006). These values and leisure preferences are usually of greater interest to the shapers and providers of leisure services in both the public and private sectors, as opposed to the more passive and culturally "immersed," "popular," leisure of ethnic minorities. Consistent with this approach, research is also needed that involves researchers, policy makers, and practitioners from Maori and other ethnic cultures in its conceptualization and implementation. Their roles should include participating as investigators and authors and in the development of research strategies or agendas that focus on the leisure research needs and interests of ethnic and immigrant groups (Annear, Cushman, Espiner, Gidlow, & Toohey, 2010).

RECOMMENDATIONS FOR PRACTICE IN AUSTRALIA AND NEW ZEALAND

To fulfill their consistent pledges to provide equitable leisure opportunities, all levels of Australian and New Zealand government agencies are encouraged to review their recreation planning processes and resource allocations and to direct more effort toward improving leisure opportunities for Indigenous peoples and ethnic immigrants, especially for women, older adults, those living in the remote and rural communities, and new arrivals. This includes stabilizing funding support at adequate levels to provide quality leisure opportunities for Indigenous people and immigrant groups.

Australian and New Zealand public agencies may also address the current imbalance that favors sport by allocating more resources to other recreation initiatives, especially those that are popular with Indigenous peoples and ethnic immigrants. Recreation program providers have an obligation to ensure that the fundamental leisure focus of recreation or sport initiatives is not subjugated to other social policy agendas (e.g., addressing unemployment in Indigenous communities).

If the diverse needs of ethnic minorities are to be sufficiently fulfilled, increasing the current support for both ethno-specific leisure and inclusive leisure strategies in the wider communities is necessary. A systematic, coordinated, and long-term set of plans for Indigenous and ethnic recreation, guided by inclusive service delivery frameworks, could be developed in both countries. Governments might consider providing incentives toward inclusive leisure in their recreation funding policies (e.g., linking some funding support to inclusion-promoting initiatives and practices). As well, more training toward improving inclusive management knowledge and skills of recreation professionals is necessary.

The importance of maintaining traditional cultural practices and values for Indigenous peoples and for ethnic minorities is widely recognized (e.g., Atkinson, 1991; Lovelock et al., 2010b; Salmond, 1975). For many Indigenous Australians and New Zealanders, connection with kinfolk, customs, and land, as indicated earlier, can also be a source of personal strength. Leisure providers and managers need to be more responsive to the cultural values and leisure priorities of Indigenous and ethnic Australians and New Zealanders. Minority groups have called for strengthened support for cultural and nonphysical recreation that are family or group oriented and are social or noncompetitive. For Indigenous communities, an approach based on activities for all members of the community, not just targeted groups, is expected to be more effective when recreation is applied to solve social problems (Cunningham & Beneforti, 2005).

Community involvement and consultation are necessary for developing meaningful leisure schemes and generating community acceptance. Empowerment of cultural minorities through community involvement and ownership of programs is expected to contribute to their social and individual well-being. To this end, increased support and training directed at developing skills present within ethnic communities and fostering leisure leadership would be necessary. Cultural sensitivity training may enhance the confidence of recreation practitioners in the provision of sport and recreation programs for diverse cultural groups.

At present, strategic levels of sport and recreation management and their advisory bodies lack ethnic representation. Increasing the involvement of Indigenous peoples and ethnic immigrants in both management and service delivery would enhance cultural relevancy of the services and programs, create more inviting social environments, and increase sense of security of ethnic minorities.

Clearer understandings of social justice principles will help recreation practitioners recognize current problems of individual, institutional, and internalized racism that continue to infect sport and recreation. Vigilance and appropriate responsiveness to the existence of racism in sport and recreation in the wider community are continually needed. Many cultural minorities, such as Indigenous and Asian people in New Zealand and Australia, tend to cope with prejudice and discrimination by putting them out of mind (thus minimizing the negative impact) or just suffering the discriminatory treatment (which may have long-term negative consequences on their psychological well-being) rather than confronting them and seeking to change the situation (Dunn, Forrest, Pe-Pua, Hynes, & Maeder-Han, 2009; Girling, Liu, & Ward, 2010; Paradies et al., 2008). Ethnic minorities need not only to be attuned to subtle and less subtle experiences of racism but also to be proactive in making changes while learning appropriate responses to incidents.

Acculturation and inclusion are two-way processes. Although leisure and sport have been used as tools for integrating ethnic minorities into the wider society, less consideration has been given to their potential in the opposite direction—to help the cultural majority learn minority cultures. Within many ethnic activities and events are cultural philosophies, practices, and skills that offer unique experiences and enjoyment. With effective leisure programming and inclusion management, ethnic events and pastimes have great potential for increasing cross-cultural understandings and mutual respect, as well as for broadening the leisure repertoires of Australian and New Zealand communities—including those of White Australians and Pakeha New Zealanders.

CONCLUSION

Leisure of Indigenous peoples and immigrants has been a low priority in the Australian and New Zealand research and public policy agendas. Research on leisure of ethnic minorities in the two countries is at a developmental stage and is fragmented and spasmodic. Much prioritized research needs to be conducted to fill the knowledge gaps and provide a sound foundation for policy making.

The divergent colonization backgrounds and the ensuing cultural policies of Australia and New Zealand have led to different levels of cultural respect and social disadvantage of Indigenous peoples and other ethnic minorities in the two countries. Cross-national comparative research, seeking to understand how different cultural and social policies of Australia and New Zealand and different degrees of systematic discrimination and ethnocentrism toward Indigenous peoples and immigrants contribute to the shaping of leisure and other aspects of lives of ethnic minorities, may assist in enhancing leisure provision and facilitation for the cultural minorities in the two countries. The authors suggest a comprehensive review of the cultural wealth to capitalize on Indigenous, Western, and non-Western cultures to enhance the quality of life of Australian and New Zealand people through leisure.

While the cultures and leisure heritages of Indigenous peoples and immigrants have enriched the leisure lives of Australians and New Zealanders, racial and cultural challenges continue to be a part of daily life and constrain the leisure of many Indigenous peoples and ethnic immigrants. With more people learning to treasure the "riches" of cultural diversity, and with changes in moral maturity associated with such diversity, adherence to social equity principles applied to the leisure of Indigenous peoples and immigrant groups will hopefully become the norm.

CHAPTER 17

Research in East Asia

Erwei Dong, Monica Li, and Junhyoung Kim

OVERVIEW

Over the past three decades, a large number of studies on racial and ethnic groups' leisure have been conducted in North America. However, the leisure behaviors of ethnic minority populations within East Asia have received little attention from researchers. The purpose of this chapter is to provide an overview of the leisure behavior patterns of ethnic minority groups in Mainland China, Japan, and Korea. To provide a deeper understanding of leisure behavior patterns, the chapter also reviews the history of migration to East Asia, differentiates among meanings of leisure in the East Asian ethnic community, and analyzes major ethnic minority groups in the region.

Learning Outcomes

After reading this chapter, readers will be able to

- describe the history of migration to East Asia and differentiate meanings of leisure in the East Asian ethnic community;
- identify leisure patterns, aspects of leisure involvement, and the impact of leisure in the East Asian ethnic community; and
- discuss the future of leisure research and practice in the East Asian ethnic community.

We do not know a nation until we know its pleasures of life just like we do not know a man until we know how he spends his leisure.

Lin Yutang (1962, p. 304)

In the preface to Erwei Dong's 2010 book, *Korean Leisure From Tradition to Modernity,* American anthropologist Garry Chick states that "all people from every corner of the world have some free time and try to devote a part of it to activities done largely for recreation and pleasure" (p. xi). Although Chick's claim is largely true, and while the study of leisure in North America dates back to 1899, it is also clear that cross-cultural leisure research within East Asia has received little attention from either Western or Eastern scholars. The purpose of this chapter, therefore, is to provide an overview of the leisure behaviors of ethnic groups in China, Korea, and Japan.

Korea and Japan have been influenced by Chinese culture dating back to ancient times, yet each of these countries is unique with respect to the factors that influence leisure involvement, leisure preferences, and leisure motivations among the minority populations. While China is traditionally viewed as a multicultural country, Korea and Japan are often considered ethnically homogenous nations. Fifty-six ethnic minority groups reside in China, while the main minority groups in Korea are Chinese Koreans and new immigrant workers from China, Mongolia, and Southeast Asia. In Japan, the major ethnic groups include Okinawans, Ainu people, Koreans (translated as "*zainichi* Koreans" in the Japanese language), Chinese (translated as "*zainichi* Chinese" in the Japanese language), and new immigrants. In addition, Chinese, Korean, and Japanese understand leisure differently, and leisure has different meanings in their languages. An overview of research on leisure behavior of these groups allows for future cross-cultural comparisons in the context of East Asia.

MEANINGS OF LEISURE IN CHINA, KOREA, AND JAPAN

Although China, Korea, and Japan are located in the same geographical region, Chinese, Koreans, and Japanese understand the concept of leisure differently. In particular, Chinese use only Chinese characters to denote "leisure," whereas both Koreans and Japanese use their own languages and phonetic translations of English to refer to leisure. The following sections discuss the meanings of leisure in China, Korea, and Japan. The leisure of minorities and migrants in the region has never been examined cross-culturally. Since comparing words and concepts cross-linguistically and cross-culturally is difficult (Chick, 1998), this section does not examine the concept of leisure in each cultural group. However, examining the meanings of leisure among the mainstream Chinese, Koreans, and Japanese should lead to a better understanding of how minorities' and migrants' leisure is influenced by the mainstream society.

Meanings of Leisure in China

Leisure is often translated into Chinese as *xiu xian* (i.e., "休闲" in Chinese). The Chinese character "休" (*xiu*) began as a portrait of a person leaning on a tree, symbolizing physical relaxation. The character evolved to include psychological good feelings, and over time included the "fine" qualities of people and objects. The second Chinese character, "闲" (*xian*), symbolizes a physical opening or space, or an interlude in time (i.e., a period of free time occurring between two periods of occupied time). The primary meaning of this character is "free and unoccupied" (Liu, Yeh, Chick, & Zinn, 2008) (see also chapter 6 on leisure among Asian North Americans). Chinese people's perception of *xiu xian* and Chinese ways of spending free, unoccupied time are deeply rooted in Chinese culture and ancient philosophy (see chapter 6).

Self-cultivation has a long history in China and provides guidance for the Chinese art of living. For instance, Confucianism and Taoism, two major schools of ancient thought in China, were both developed around the same time as the classical period of ancient Greece in the fifth and fourth centuries BCE and have had major impacts on traditional Chinese ideas and ideals of leisure. Under the influence of Confucianism, Chinese people are work oriented and usually hold a negative attitude toward leisure. Conventionally, leisure activities, such as traveling or festival celebrations, are often family oriented and typically involve visiting families and friends and showing respect for parents and elders.

To Chinese people, learning is an important motivation and a necessary justification for involvement in leisure activities. Leisure is not necessarily for pure pleasure or fun for Chinese people who believe in Confucianism. Taoism, on the other hand, considers leisure more a state of mind, or an individual's experience. Influenced by Taoism, Chinese people cultivate a love for nature and a longing for a peaceful leisure life. For Chinese people, leisure is a means for both pursuing the tranquility of a peaceful leisure life and appreciating the beauty of the natural world (Wang & Stringer, 2000). Through this type of leisure, people can experience true rest and relaxation and comprehend the harmony between the spirit and the objective world (Gong, 1998). This partly explains the characteristics of leisure in traditional Chinese society, including the preference for quiet, passive activities rather than strenuous physical exertion; for spectating rather than participating; and for solitary rather than collective leisure activities (Yu & Berryman, 1996).

The remarkable political and economic changes that have occurred in China in recent decades have in part provided the conditions for the current social and cultural transformations. One example of the manifestation of such changes is the increasing awareness of Western leisure lifestyles among Chinese people (Wang, 2001). Due to exposure to a much wider collection of cultural experiences as a result of globalization, the interest of Chinese people has turned toward mass popular entertainment (Weber, 2002). Endowed with more discretionary income and free time, a significant number of Chinese people, especially the urban population, have expressed their interest in increasing expenditures on leisure, recreation, and tourism (Du, Li, Qin, & Li, 2002).

Leisure has increasingly constituted a special form of culture, as well as an important public realm of everyday life, in Chinese urban centers. Under the rule of Mao Tse Tung until 1977, "plea-sure seeking" was viewed not only as frivolous but also as a dangerous waste of time. Recently, however, people have begun to dedicate themselves to "fun." The growing leisure phenomenon in urban centers is closely related to the changing particularities of people's economic situation, education, knowledge, and abilities, as well as their inclinations, attitudes, interests, and behaviors under the influence of globalization. The emerging new public sphere of life facilitates an optimal environment for gaining new experiences, knowledge, skills, attitudes, values, and identities, yet at the same time it presents the challenge of balancing the need to change and the need to maintain stability (Wang, 2001).

On one hand, the new concept of leisure promises a good life and fulfills people's hedonistic needs. For many, leisure associated with "pleasure" and "fun" is the equivalent of liberation. Such needs are promoted and facilitated by more leisure-oriented social policies. These policies have not only transformed the work week to allow more time for leisure, but have also supported the creation of leisure infrastructure and social structures and systems. On the other hand, the nature of the new avenues for self-understanding in the transition setting is contradictory. The exciting new opportunities and, at the same time, terrifying new pressures of a global market economy, as well as the models of aspiration conveyed by global popular culture, are all looming large in urban society (Link, Madsen, & Pickowicz, 2002). The kind of contemporary popular culture that is steeped in consumerism has profoundly changed the areas of private life and social life in China. Consumerist pop culture has also greatly affected economic and political formations. The lines between global and local, old and new, East and West, and socialist and capitalist are blurred, and the causes of happiness and unhappiness have become deeper and more complex (Chen, Clark, Gottschang, & Jeffery, 2001; Wang, 2001; Weber, 2002).

Meanings of Leisure in Korea

The Korean language does not have a word that directly translates the English word "leisure." Both Chinese characters "餘" (*yeo*) "暇" (*ga*) and the phonetic translation "레져" are used to express "leisure" in Korean society. In Korea, leisure researchers have applied the meaning of leisure derived from Western cultures, which is characterized as discretionary time, activity, and a state of mind (Lee, 2005). They generally incorporate these characteristics to determine the meaning of leisure and adjust it to Korean society. As a consequence, leisure researchers in Korea often have different interpretations of the meaning of leisure. For example, Choi (2002) mentioned that the meaning of leisure in Korea has been developed and diversified because of cultural complexity in that society. He summarized the definition of leisure as meaningful activities resulting from freedom of choice and intrinsic motivation, which contribute to life satisfaction and self-actualization. Lee described leisure as certain activities or kinds of activities, such as games, play, volunteerism, sports, expressive activities (e.g., art and music), travel and tourism, and certain religious activities. The challenge inherent in this approach is that, in Korea, leisure is not distinguished from recreation (Lee).

For some researchers in Korea, leisure has the meaning "leisure sports" (Kim, 2004; Lee, 2007). In Western cultures, the concept of leisure sports may be unfamiliar or may not even exist. However, in Korea (as well as in China), leisure may mean any activity related to sport participation, such as sport activities per se or art creation activities, domestic and international tourism, hobbies, and recreational activities that involve sport in some way. Leisure sports include a variety of activities (e.g., hobbies, recreation activities, school-based extracurricular activities, and community-based activities) that people engage in voluntarily. Leisure in this sense refers to leisure-time sport participation (Her, 1999).

Meanings of Leisure in Japan

As with the Korean language, the Japanese language does not have an exact equivalent for the English word "leisure." The Japanese use "レジャー" (rejaa), which is a phonetic translation intended to "imitate the sound of leisure with an attempt to convey the meaning of leisure-like pursuits" (Iwasaki, Nishino, Onda, & Bowling, 2007, p.

114). In the Japanese language, "レジャー" (rejaa) often refers to consumptive leisure activities (e.g., going on a vacation or visiting a theme park) rather than more culturally contextualized activities (e.g., going to see kabuki theater). In addition, Japanese language has a similar word for leisure, "ユトリ" (yutori), meaning something to spare; latitude; leeway, elbow room, or breathing space (Iwasaki et al.). Yoka ("余暇") is used to refer to free time and is interchangeable with "レジャー" (leisure). The *White Paper of Leisure of Japan* has been published by the Japan Productivity Center since 1977. This is a comprehensive market report regarding the Japanese leisure industry, leisure patterns, and leisure activities. "レジャー" (leisure) and yoka ("余暇") are used interchangeably in this publication.

ETHNIC MINORITY GROUPS IN EAST ASIA

Many people erroneously believe that East Asia is an ethnically homogeneous region. In fact, China is composed of 56 distinct ethnic groups. Although Korea and Japan are not as diverse as China, neither of these countries are homogenous. For example, Chinese Koreans have lived in Korea for more than a century, whereas Okinawans and Ainu people are native to Okinawa and Hokkaido (in Japan), respectively. The following section introduces the ethnic minority groups within each country.

Ethnic Minority Groups in China

Although Han Chinese account for 91.5% of the overall Chinese population, the other 55 ethnic groups make up the remaining 8.5%.[1] The multiethnic character of China is a result of many centuries of migration, expansion, and modern consolidation of territories incorporated into the Qing Dynasty, whose emperors were Manchu and not members of the Han majority. Currently, the degree of integration of ethnic minorities with the national mainstream community varies widely from group to group. Within some groups, such as the Tibetans and Uyghurs, there is some resent-

[1]For more information, please see www.stats.gov.cn/tjsj/ndsj/2012/indexeh.htm.

Photo courtesy of Erwei Dong.

Ethnic women at a celebration in Yunnan, China.

ment against the majority. Other groups, such as the Zhuang and Manchu, are well integrated into the national community.

Ethnic minority groups in China differ greatly in the size of their populations. Eighteen groups are composed of over 1 million people. Zhuang is the largest minority group, with a total of more than 15 million people. Some minority groups have a population of less than 10,000 people, for example the Monba, Oroqen, and Tartars. These officially designated ethnicities play a vital role in China, and ethnic status is stated on every citizen's official identity card; it is also used for school, legal, and official records (Gustafsson & Sai, 2006). Although the Chinese government emphasizes equity for each ethnic group, similarly to the U.S. affirmative action policy, people belonging to minority groups can also benefit from some specific governmental policies, such as special college entrance examinations and

exemption from the one-child population growth control policy.

Geographically, ethnic minority groups are mostly concentrated in the more sparsely populated northwest, north, northeast, south, southwest, and central interior areas. Many of these group members have traditionally established their villages in the mountainous and pastoral areas, on high plateaus, or in deep forests, where economic development has been disadvantaged partly due to the physically unfavorable conditions. The vicissitudes of time, war, migration, and seizure of lands throughout history have produced frequent shifts of ethnic inhabitants in these areas. Some ethnic groups intermingle, while other groups live as exclusive communities.[2]

Economically, ethnic minorities in China, especially those living in the central and western areas, tend to perceive themselves as the most disadvantaged groups in the country (Shan,

[2]For more information, please see www.china.org.cn/e-groups/shaoshu/mix.htm.

2009). In comparison with the Han majority, the minority groups are worse off economically, less satisfied with their lives, and less interested in politics (Knight & Gunatilaka, 2010). Culturally, the ethnic groups of China are distinguished by their different traditions and customs in marriage, childbirth, funerals, food, housing, and costume, as well as festivals and recreational activities. Many enjoy music and traditional dancing and have a fine artistic tradition. Their unique social, cultural, and historical backgrounds represent an important part of China's culture and history.

On the other hand, the massive internal population migrations, especially the migration from rural to urban areas, has been a part of the tremendous economic and social transformations in China over the past three decades. These internal temporary migrants become new urban minorities in China. Statistics show that currently more than 15% of the country's population live in places other than their home villages, towns, or cities, and the momentum of migration in China is increasing quickly (Sun & Fan, 2011). People seeking higher incomes continue to move from rural areas with a large labor surplus to urban areas. The urban–rural income gap is quite large and has remained so for many years (Gustafsson & Sai, 2006). According to survey results released by the National Bureau of Statistics of China in 2012, the total number of migrants who moved from their rural residence to urban areas was 145,330,000. Of these migrants, 43.6% chose the eastern coastal area[3] as their destination.[4] This rural-to-urban migration flow has had consequences for almost every social, economic, and political issue in China. Migrants have been described both as agents of change at their places of origin and as essential contributors to economic

Photo courtesy of Erwei Dong.

An ethnic dance performed in the China Folk Culture Village.

[3]This refers to Beijing, Tianjin, Hebei, Liaoning, Shanghai, Jiangsu, Zhejiang, Fujian, Shandong, Guangdong, and Hainan.

[4]For more information, please see www.stats.gov.cn/tjfx/fxbg/t20100319_402628281.htm.

growth in destination areas (Gao & Smyth, 2010; Garcia, 2004).

A unique feature of migration in China is a two-track system consisting of permanent migration and temporary migration (Gu, 1992). In permanent migration, people have changed their registration to their place of residence; in temporary migration, people's place of residence differs from their place of registration. Much of the rural-to-urban migration is temporary, partly because of how difficult it is for people without urban registration to find housing and social services for themselves and their families. The registration (*hukou*), functioning as a sort of "internal passport," acts as the main barrier among temporary migrants to enjoying the same institutional, economic, and social statuses as permanent and urban migrants (Sun & Fan, 2011). Excluded from urban citizenship, rural urban migrants rely heavily on social networks to identify prospective destinations, find jobs at the destination, facilitate migration, and ease adjustment (Zhao, 1999). They mainly rely on kinship and hometown connections for mutual assistance and community formation at destination areas. However, their condition is similar to that of a noncitizen in a foreign country, as they are not considered full members of the mainstream society (Garcia, 2004), and their presence is regarded as temporary and "floating" (Gao & Smyth, 2010).

Ethnic Minority Groups in Korea

Although Korea has sometimes been considered one of the most homogeneous nations, Chinese people have a relatively long history of living in this country. Moreover, because of the growing number of international marriages, in conjunction with the growing number of immigrants, Korea is becoming increasingly ethnically and culturally diverse.

The Overseas Chinese Affairs Office of the State Council in China reported that more than 95% of early Chinese migrants to Korea came from Shandong Province on the East Coast of China. Most chose to live in the city of Incheon because of its close proximity to Shandong Province. Like the Chinese in Japan, the Chinese in Korea can be divided into "old-timer" and "newcomer" groups. The old-timer group comprises those who

immigrated to Korea more than 100 years ago and who currently live in Incheon, which has the only "Chinatown" in Korea. Compared to "Chinatowns" in other nations (e.g., in New York, Vancouver, London, and Paris), Incheon's Chinatown is relatively small. However, it is noteworthy that one of the "national foods" of South Korea, *jajangmyeon* (i.e., white wheat noodles topped with a thick sauce made of a salty black soybean paste and cucumbers), was created by Chinese migrants residing in Incheon's Chinatown. Although the history of Chinese immigration to Korea is over a century long, more than 90% of these immigrants have not been naturalized. The low naturalization rate of Chinese immigrants is a result of (1) nationalism, (2) strong connections with Mainland China, and (3) little sense of loyalty to Korea (Yang & Yang, 2005). Furthermore, 43% of Chinese immigrant families use the Chinese language as their "family language." All of Korea's modern historic events, including the Sino-Japanese Wars (1937-1945), the Japanese colonial period (1910-1945), Korean Independence (1946-1949), and the Korean War (1950-1953), contributed to Chinese immigration to Korea (Beauchamp, 2007). China did not establish formal diplomatic relations with South Korea until after the Korean War, and Chinese stopped immigrating to Korea until after formal Sino-Korea diplomatic relations were reestablished in 1992.

With respect to other immigrants, according to the Korea Ministry of Public Administration and Security (2012), there are 1.4 million foreigners living in Korea. This accounts for 2.8% of the population of Korea. Since 2006, the number of foreigners in Korea has been increasing. While Chinese and Vietnamese constitute a majority (67%), five percent (68,648 people) of foreigners are from the U.S. More specifically, the total number of foreign residents staying in Korea for more than 90 days numbered 1,261,415; long-term foreign residents numbered 1,002,742; short-term foreign residents numbered 258,673; and illegal immigrants numbered 168,515 (Statistics of Korea, 2010). In Seoul itself, according to e-Seoul Statistics (2009), the number of foreign residents reached 255,000. Of this total, 192,618 (75.5%) were from China, followed by the United States with 12,821 (5%), Taiwan with 8,818 (3.5%), and

Japan with 6,840 (2.7%). The legal status of the foreigners in Korea ranged from workers (149,000 or 58.5%) to international marriage immigrants (29,560 or 11.6%) to students (19,869 or 7.8%) to professional employees (10,503 or 4.1%). According to the Ministry of Justice of Korea (2005), the majority of ethnic Korean migrant workers are from China (62,420), followed by Korean Chinese (59,101), people from Vietnam (31,805), those from the Philippines (30,092), and those from Thailand (27,488). Finally, the number of international marriage immigrants has also increased. A total of 43,121 international marriages were reported in 2007, representing 13.6% of the total population (Korea National Statistical Office, 2005). Of these, 9.8% involved a foreign wife and 3.8% involved a foreign husband. The reason for this rise has to do with the rapid pace of industrialization in Korea that began in the 1960s. Many rural young men found it difficult to get married because so many rural young Korean women had migrated to urban areas (Seol & Lee, 2011). Consequently, migration to Korea from other countries (especially those in Southeast Asia) for the purpose of marriage has rapidly expanded (Seol, 2007).

Ethnic Minority Groups in Japan

In his 2005 book chapter, "Political and Cultural Perspectives on 'Insider' Minorities," American anthropologist Joshua Hotaka Roth divided Japanese ethnic minorities into "insiders" and "outsiders." Insider minority groups include Okinawans, Ainu, and Nikkeijin (i.e., overseas Japanese who have returned to Japan); outsider minority groups include Korean, Chinese, and foreign residents from Brazil, Chile, the Philippines, and other countries. Insider minorities do not "deny their Japanese-ness in the eyes of other Japanese" (p. 73), whereas the term outsider minorities, until recently, "referred predominantly to Koreans who came to Japan during the colonial period (1910-45)" (p. 90). The latter include foreign residents, who have increased to an average rate of over 60,000 newcomers a year. While zainichi Koreans and Chinese live everywhere in Japan, the major-

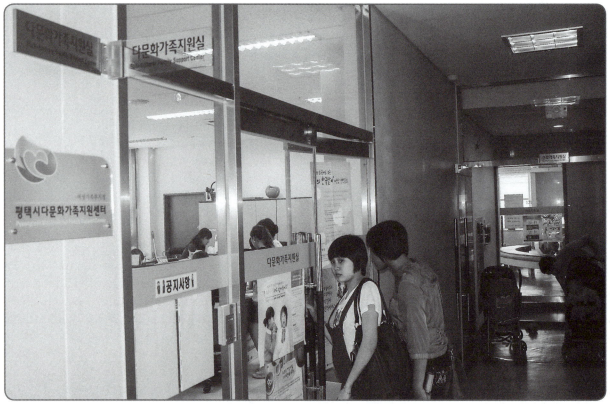

Photo courtesy of Erwei Dong.

New immigrants from Southeast Asian countries seeking social supports in a multicultural family support center located in Pyeongtaek City Community Center in southern Seoul, Korea.

ity of Ainu live in Hokkaido, and Okinawans live in Okinawa. Due to the paucity of leisure research on Nikkeijin and foreign residents from Brazil, Chile, and the Philippines, this chapter focuses only on Okinawans, Ainu, zainichi Koreans, and Chinese.

Okinawans live in the Ryukyu archipelago, located between Kyushu and Taiwan. The Indigenous people of the Ryukyu archipelago are ethnically distinct from the Japanese who live on the mainland. Japanese researchers believe that Okinawans are direct descendants of the prehistoric Jomon people who were conquered, eliminated, or assimilated by the ancestors of the modern Japanese people (Taira, 1997). Okinawa is one of 47 subnational jurisdictions in Japan with a population of approximately 1.3 million people. As of 2009, nearly 9,000 foreigners live in Okinawa, with American (24%), Chinese (24.1%), and Filipinos (18.3%) accounting for more than 65% of the foreigner population (Exchange Promotion Division of Okinawa, n.d.).

Even though the United Nations has requested that the Japanese government conduct an Ainu population survey, it has not yet complied (Ainu Association of Hokkaido, 2010). Although the actual number of Ainu people in Japan remains unknown, census data for the Ainu population can be found in the Survey on the Hokkaido Ainu Living Conditions conducted by the Hokkaido government since 1972. According to the 2006 survey, a total of 23,782 Ainu people lived in the Hokkaido area. The most recent census data for the Ainu people who live outside of Hokkaido is a survey conducted in the Tokyo Metropolitan Area in 1988. Tokyo is the only city outside of Hokkaido that was included in this survey, and it resulted in a total of 2,700 Ainu people being identified that year.

For historical and political reasons, Koreans in Japan cannot be simply referred to as Korean Japanese. Instead, they are called "diaspora," which means "without homeland" (Ryang, 2009). The majority of these individuals are first-generation

Photo courtesy of Erwei Dong.

Okinawa is one of 47 subnational jurisdictions in Japan and Okinawans were believed to be direct descendants of the prehistoric Jomon people (Taira, 1997).

colonial immigrants who arrived from the Korean peninsula between 1910 and 1945 or are descendants of these immigrants. Koreans cannot become Japanese nationals because Japanese nationality law is based on "bloodline." Instead, Koreans in Japan "hold the special permanent residence status available only to colonial immigrants and their descendants" (Ryang, p. 3). Thus, Korean Japanese should be considered residents of Korea or Koreans in Japan (also called "zainichi Korean" in the Japanese language). By the early 1970s, more than 75% of zainichi Koreans had been born in Japan, and more than 50% of them were married to mainstream Japanese people (Lie, 2008). The largest zainichi Korean community is located in Osaka, with a population of 200,000 people. Zainichi Koreans in this city accounted for 22% of the Korean population in Japan (Portal Site of Official Statistics of Japan, 2013). Similar to the Ainu in Japan, zainichi Koreans are not included in any national survey conducted by the Ministry of Internal Affairs and Communications of Japan (MIACJ).

According to *Statistics of Foreign Nationals* (2011) published by the Japanese Ministry of Justice, Chinese people are the most predominant, with a total of 674,871 residents, accounting for 32.5% of all foreign nationals. However, those who have already been naturalized as Japanese nationals are excluded from this number. Chinese in Japan can be divided into "old-timer" and "newcomer" groups (Yin, 2005). The old-timer group comprises those who immigrated to Japan before 1949 and currently live in the Yokohama, Kobe, and Nagasaki "Chinatowns." The newcomer group comprises those who initially studied in Japanese educational institutions after 1978 and remained in Japan after their studies (Yin, 2005). Nearly 38% of the Chinese newcomer group live in the Kando area, which includes the Tokyo metropolitan area, Saitama Prefecture, Chiba Prefecture, and Kanagawa Prefecture.

OVERVIEW OF LEISURE RESEARCH ON ETHNIC MINORITY GROUPS IN EAST ASIA

Leisure research was originally established and developed in North America. Later, leisure research spread to other English-speaking countries such as the United Kingdom, Australia, and New Zealand. In East Asia, leisure research began approximately two decades ago. To date, leisure research on ethnic minority groups in East Asia has largely focused on tourism, dance, ritual, festival, and sport.

China

This section discusses the leisure behaviors of native ethnic minorities and Chinese migrant workers in China.

Leisure Behaviors of Native Ethnic Minorities in China

Because relatively little research has been conducted to date on native ethnic minorities in China, this section is largely descriptive rather than explanatory. Minority groups in China usually reside in remote rural areas, where public leisure space, leisure facilities, and leisure service provisions are limited. The lack of quality leisure infrastructure constrains leisure and recreation participation, especially among those in lower income groups (Li, 2008). When compared with the Han majority, especially those living in the cities, rural ethnic groups have considerably fewer opportunities to participate in leisure. Minority groups tend to participate in low-cost recreational sports and leisure activities. Modern recreation that requires organization and facilities, such as table tennis, golf, and billiards, is therefore not popular among many ethnic minority groups (Li). Within the ethnic minority communities, there are imbalances in leisure participation due to ethnic and gender differences. Some religions and value systems, for example, impose certain regulations and restrictions on women's leisure in public places.

Despite these cultural constraints, ethnic groups develop and maintain their own forms of leisure; these are deeply rooted in their distinctive cultural and religious traditions and manifested in their rituals and ceremonies, their everyday work and leisure life, and indigenous arts. For instance, many minorities have rich traditions of festivals such as the Shoton (Yogurt) Festival of the Tibetan people, the Knife-ladder-Climbing Festival of the Lisu people, the Naadam Fair of the Mongolian people, the Water Sprinkling Festival of the Dai people, and the Torch Festival of the Yi people.[5] These festivals have become an important leisure "carrier" in terms of the cultural and spiritual life of these minorities (Zhou, 2003). For example, the Knife-ladder-Climbing Festival of the Lisu ethnic group is a traditional festival of the Lisu and Yi people in Lushui County of Nujiang Lisu Nationality Autonomous Prefecture in China's Yunnan Province. It is held on the 15th day of the first month of every lunar year. Local people put on holiday dress and gather in groups for this celebratory event. For the traditional and customary main performance, "climbing the knife-ladder and jumping into the sea of fire represents the arduous struggle in one's life and the spirit of tramping over the hills and dales of their hill nation."[6]

Ethnic groups often excel in their athletic skills and have great enthusiasm for sport activities such as wrestling, running, and shooting and other traditional leisure activities (Li, 2008). Various entertaining and competitive sport activities are maintained and developed in the country's minority-inhabited areas. The traditional sport activities of ethnic minorities are rooted in the history of the ethnic groups, embedded in the local folk customs, and mostly performed during traditional festivals. Examples of such activities are wrestling and horsemanship among Mongols, Uyghurs, and Kazaks; Tibetan yak racing; ethnic Korean "seesaw jumping"; crossbow archery among the Miao; and dragon-boat racing among the Dai ethnic minority. In August of every year, the Mongolians hold the Naadam Fair, a gala meeting in which ethnic sports including Mongolian-style wrestling and horse racing are performed. The special skills that are required in sport leisure activities make it hard for outsiders

Photo courtesy of Erwei Dong.

Wrestling at Naadam Fair, Mongolia.

[5]For more information please see www.globaltimes.cn/content/472770.shtml.

[6]Information retrieved on May 25, 2012, from http://traditions.cultural-china.com/en/115Traditions3548.html.

to participate, which partly explains the exclusive and self-contained nature of some ethnic leisure forms (Li, 2008).

The content and form of daily leisure life of the Chinese minority groups have gradually changed during the past three decades as a consequence of the country's democratic and economic reforms, as well as continuing local economic, social, and cultural development. Today, traditional festivals represent a more vibrant form of entertainment and the number of recreational activities at the festivals has increased considerably. For example, the province of Guizhou alone holds more than 1,000 festival gatherings in a given year (Zhou, 2003). At the annual Naadam Fair, the traditional horse racing, wrestling, archery, and other sport activities are accompanied by new forms of modern entertainment, such as large-scale theatrical performances and movies.

Furthermore, ethnic minorities have become important to China's tourist industry in recent years. For instance, located in China's tropical southwest, the villages of the Dai people are famous for a traditional annual recreational event, the water-splashing festival. As Wong (2010) argued, the Dai park is just one example of an increasingly popular form of entertainment in China—the ethnically themed playground. The implications of such commercial practices for the protection of traditional culture and ways of life for the minorities have generated controversial debates. Some scholars have argued that with such practices, minority communities attain new opportunities to display their ethnic identities, to reinvent cultures that may otherwise die out, and to reconstruct the ways in which they operate as unique societies (Zong, 2006). Others, however, argue that through such processes, permanent and damaging alterations are made to traditional ways of life (Peng & Zheng, 2008).

Leisure Behaviors of Chinese Migrant Workers

Migrant workers from rural provinces (also called peasant workers) primarily work in the industrial and commerce sectors, and are typically employed in jobs often described as "3D – Difficult, Dirty, and Dangerous" (Ma & Biao, 1998, p. 547). These 3D jobs are not desired by the urban popula-

tion because they are too hard or demeaning. Typically, migrant workers work longer than the legally enforced 8-hour workday. Many work six days per week, as opposed to the normal five-day work week. In a study conducted by Ma (2010) on migrant workers in the Dongcheng and Xuanwu districts in Beijing, 64% worked over 8 hours per day, and 55% had only one day off each week. As some scholars indicate, to a large extent the migrant workers are deprived of time for their physical and leisure needs (Ma; Yan, 2007). Moreover, migrant workers work most of the year in cities with only one long vacation every year: the Chinese Lunar New Year holiday.

The ebb and flow between work time and work space in the cities and leisure time and leisure space in the home communities result in the "time–space separation" aspect of migrant workers' leisure. This leads to a conflict between their desire for modern urban life and their pursuit of greater self-development, as they are not entitled to enough leisure time or opportunities either to truly relax, enjoy, and experience urban life or to improve themselves (Xia, 2006). In fact, when they do have some free time, they participate more frequently in passive forms of entertainment and noncommercial leisure activities, such as watching TV, listening to the radio, reading the newspaper, window shopping, chatting, sleeping, surfing the Internet, drinking, and gambling, than in active and commercial leisure activities (e.g., physical exercise; going to the cinema, dance halls, or night clubs; karaoke; learning; and tourism) (Ma, 2010; Xia). Studies of migrant workers in China have also shown that the majority have encountered obstacles to their participation in leisure activities. Among the constraints observed in their daily life, the most prominent are limited free time, high cost of facilities and services, and strenuous labor (which are closely related to longer working hours, low wages, and inadequate availability of leisure resources) (Ma; Xia; Yan, 2007).

Korea

This section discusses the leisure behaviors of minority group members in Korea. However, it is worth noting that although the Chinese old-timer group who originate from Shandong Province has been living in Korea for more than a century and therefore may have become highly acculturated, no research on these individuals' leisure has been undertaken to date. Therefore, the following section examines the leisure behaviors of other minority groups.

Leisure Behaviors of Ethnic Minorities in Korea

In spite of Korea's increasing ethnic and cultural diversity, the body of research on leisure behavior of minority populations in this country is limited. The existing research shows that recent immigrants face numerous challenges associated with leisure participation. These issues often have to do with adaptation processes and include communication barriers, limited social networks, cultural and ethnic differences, and lack of social support. For example, Lee and Kim (2010) found that immigrants in Korea faced constraints to participation in various festivals and events because of limited leisure resources and communication problems. In 2008, the Ministry of Culture, Sports, and Tourism conducted a study to explore the leisure behaviors (e.g., leisure desires and leisure constraints) of immigrants in Korea. The findings were similar to those of Lee and Kim: The main barriers to leisure participation were lack of time (39.6%) and money (28.8%). When participants had sufficient time and money, 78.5% reported being willing to take part in travel, followed by social activities (34.3%), self-exploration through leisure (30.3%), and hobbies (27.4%).

Women in Korea who are immigrants based on marriage are especially likely to struggle to adapt to a new society because of limited social interaction, communication barriers, and ethnic differences. According to a study by Seol (2007), 31% of these women reported being verbally abused by their husbands, 10% to 14% reported being physically abused, and over 40% reported being sexually abused. Unfortunately, 40% of women immigrants also reported that there was no one to turn to for help or counseling. It can thus be argued that women who have immigrated based on marriage receive limited social support from family and friends, which may in turn restrict their leisure participation. In a related study, Kwon and Ko (2011) suggested that there is a posi-

tive relationship between the level of acculturation and leisure participation among married Korean Chinese immigrants. The study showed that the more immigrants were acculturated, the more they engaged in leisure activities for psychological reasons.

An analysis of the Korean labor market (Seol, 2006) showed that immigrant foreign workers were often engaged in construction (27.6%) and service industries (22.2%). Because of a difficult work environment and a heavy workload, ethnic Korean migrant workers have limited time to engage in leisure and recreation activities. Baek and Lee (2006) found, for example, that most foreign workers engaged in passive leisure activities such as watching television, Internet use, and talking on the phone with their family; on weekends, they participated in religious activities. Additionally, people mentioned that they experienced some constraints to leisure participation, including lack of time and money, language barriers, and cultural and ethnic differences. Hong (1995) suggested that the Korean government should provide programs that address life challenges and constraints faced by foreign workers to allow them to enhance their quality of life.

Japan

The most comprehensive market report on the Japanese leisure industry is the *White Paper of Leisure of Japan* which has been published by the Japan Productivity Center since 1977. However, the publication covers only mainstream Japanese society, including Okinawa Prefecture (one of 47 prefectures in Japan). Because leisure research on the Ainu people and other ethnic groups is not included in this report, in the following section we will discuss the leisure behavior of Okinawan, Ainu, zainichi Korean, and zainichi Chinese based on information obtained from other sources.

Leisure Behaviors of Okinawans Minority Members

Okinawa is geographically isolated from mainland Japan and is the poorest prefecture in the country. Surprisingly, however, the area is also known as the world's longest-living region based on its residents' long life expectancy and low risk for major age-related chronic diseases (Willcox, Willcox,

He, Wang, & Suzuki, 2008). In 2000, according to the Japan Ministry of Health and Welfare Life, Okinawa had surpassed Japan, Sweden, and the United States to become the longest-living region, with an average age of 81.2. Although it is currently unknown whether active leisure is more beneficial for reducing stress than passive activities, a healthy diet and less stress in daily life contribute to Okinawans' health. Research has shown that especially family-oriented leisure activities and strong patterns of kinship relations associated with ancestor worship may reduce stress in daily life among Okinawans (Cockerham & Yamori, 2001). For example, it is very common for family members to attend gatherings such as *Umachi* (in Okinawan language) festival that involves feasting, drinking, and ceremonies honoring ancestors.

Although there is currently little research on Okinawans' leisure in either English or Japanese language, every five years since 1976 the Ministry of Internal Affairs and Communications of Japan (MIACJ) has conducted the National Survey on Time Use and Leisure Activities. This survey provides comprehensive data on time use and the leisure activities of 1,400 Okinawan households, which were randomly selected by enumerators. The MIACJ surveys divide daily activities into three types: (1) primary activities, (2) secondary activities, and (3) tertiary activities. Primary activities are physically required activities, such

as sleeping and eating. Secondary activities are activities obligatory for citizens, such as work and housework. Tertiary activities are activities that people do during their free time other than primary activities and secondary activities. Based on the MIACJ's activity categorization, leisure activities are considered tertiary and are further categorized as (1) Internet use, (2) volunteer activities, (3) travel and excursion, (4) studies, research and sports, and (5) hobbies and amusements ("Leisure Activities," n.d.). Interestingly, although studies and research are not normally considered leisure in the leisure literature, they are listed as such in this survey. "Studies and research" particularly refers to "club activities at school, but exclude[s] worker training at the workplace and study and research activities performed by children, pupils or students as schoolwork, such as study in class, preparation for class and review of lessons" (p. 6).

Table 17.1 summarizes the MIACJ's six leisure activity categories for the 2001 survey. As shown, Okinawans participated in sport activities the most, followed by travel and excursions. Additionally, when compared with data from the 1999 survey, participation in hobbies and amusements had decreased slightly.

The 2011 Survey on Social Life (n.d.) compared the six main leisure activity categories between Okinawa and 46 other subnational jurisdictions, with the following interesting results. (1) The

Table 17.1 Number of Participants and Participation Rates for the Main Leisure Activities* of Okinawan People

Main leisure activities	Number of participants	Participation rate (%)	Compared to 1996	Activity with highest participation (participation rate)
Internet	421,000	37.3	Not available	Building or updating websites, blogging, bulletin board system, online chatting, and so on (31.1%)
Volunteer activities	293,000	26.0	+3.8%	Community service activities (12.3%)
Travel and excursions	680,000	60.3	+1.9%	One-day trips (44.8%)
Studies and research	347,000	30.8	+5.3%	Computer use (13.4%)
Sports	831,000	73.7	−1.4%	Walking or light physical exercise (42.0%)
Hobbies and amusements	921,000	81.7	−2.8%	Karaoke (42.2%)

*Main leisure activities: a group of leisure activities categorized by MIACJ.

Internet participation rate was below the average of all of the 47 subnational jurisdictions in Japan. Reservations, purchases, and payments for goods or services were ranked last in Okinawa among the 47 subnational jurisdictions. (2) The volunteering participation rate was below the average for all subnational jurisdictions. Although Okinawans live on an island, their participation rate in conservation or environmental activities was the second lowest among the subnational jurisdictions. (3) The participation rate for travel and excursions was 20% below the national average. Only 4.7% of Okinawans experienced overseas travel; this was the second lowest participation rate among the subnational jurisdictions. Income level, age, and geographic location may be factors responsible for the low travel rate (Katsuura, 2010). (4) The participation rate in "studies and research" was below the average rate across the subnational jurisdictions. However, nearly 10% of Okinawans participated in learning a foreign language. (5) The participation rates in sport in Okinawa were above the national average. Among all sports, the most people (30.1%) participated in bowling, 17% in jogging or running, and 13.3% in baseball. For all three sport activities, Okinawans had the highest participation rates among all the subnational jurisdictions. Similar to National Collegiate Athletic Association football in America, high school baseball tournaments enjoy widespread popularity in Japan. Konan High School, located in Okinawa, won the 2010 National Championship, which could be a factor contributing to the popularity of this sport in the area. (6) Finally, the participation rate in hobbies and amusements was lower than the average of all subnational jurisdictions. Karaoke, however, was a popular leisure activity in Okinawa, with 42.2% of Okinawans reporting participation.

Leisure Behavior of Ainu Minority Members

Ainu means "human" in the Ainu language, and the Ainu are truly the Indigenous people of northern Japan (i.e., the Hokkaido area where Ainu primarily reside). Unfortunately, the existence of the Ainu is largely ignored by Japanese society because mainstream Japanese (or *Wajin*) consider Japan a monoethnic country (Hiwasaki, 2000). Similar to other "Fourth World" popula-

tions, including Native Americans, Australian Aborigines, Inuit, Maori, and Sami, the Ainu were subordinated and dispossessed of their ancestral lands and resources by the expansion of a vigorous colonial state. According to the Office of Ainu Policy administered by Hollaido Prefecture, Wajin (Japanese from Mainland Japan) began to move to Hokkaido in 1443. Thereafter, waves of immigrants from *Hodo* (i.e., mainland Japan) resulted in the disappearance of the traditional lifestyle among the Ainu (e.g., hunting and fishing) (Siddle, 1997).

Ainu lifestyle items have not been included in the MIACJ surveys on time use and leisure activities. Similar to the other Indigenous people (e.g., Maori, Hawaiians), hunting, fishing, collecting shellfish, and cultivating crops constituted the primary way of life among the Ainu. In 1970, more than one-third of the Ainu people made their living through agriculture. Since the early 1990s, the Ainu have started to manage various businesses, including the ethnic tourism industry developed in the Ainu community in Hokkaido. The Ainu were distracted from their tradition of agriculture by the boom in the new tourism industry, such that only 7.6% were involved in agriculture in 2006 (Nakamura, 2008). It is not surprising that the Ainu are involved in the tourism industry because the connection they have with nature fits perfectly with tourism promotion (Hiwasaki, 2000). Tourism promotion has generated a significant number of visitors to Ainu communities. For example, Akan, located in the eastern part of Hokkaido, attracts approximately 1.6 million tourists annually. The Ainu people who are involved in tourism also benefit from the ethnic tourism industry. The Ainu culture is preserved, revived, and developed in the area. This revitalization resulted in the establishment of the Shiraoi Institute for the Preservation of Ainu Culture in 1976 and the first annual Ainu Cultural Festival in 1989.

Since Ainu tourism opportunities are heavily promoted by the Japan National Tourism Organization, tourism-related documents, travel agencies, and websites contain more information about the Ainu than do academic articles. According to the Japan National Tourism Organization (2013), current aspects of Ainu life, including clothing, food, education, work, and leisure, are quite similar to those of the mainstream Japanese culture. Only a small proportion of the Ainu in Hokkaido remain involved in native cultural leisure activities such as dances and ceremonies (Stevens, 2008).

Leisure Behavior of Korean Minority Members

Pachinko, the Japanese adaptation of pinball, is played by nearly 17 million people each year in Japan (Association of Gaming Industry of Japan, 2009). Among a total of 12,323 pachinko parlors, more than 90% are owned by zainichi Koreans—which in turn influences their own leisure (Kaji, 2007). Golf, overseas travel, attending the theater, and computer-related leisure activities have also become very popular among zainichi Koreans.

Zainichi Koreans typically do not celebrate Japan's national holidays unless they are attempting to integrate into the mainstream culture. Nevertheless, Japan's public holidays have greatly influenced the daily lives of zainichi Koreans.

Zainichi Korean–owned businesses and schools are normally closed for public holidays. Although the younger generations of zainichi Koreans show little interest in politics, "celebration of national holidays of North Korea and South Korea . . . used to reveal a clear-cut political division in the community" (Ryang, 2005, p. 979). Research suggests that there are few differences between the Japanese mainstream and zainichi Koreans with regard to leisure participation (Ryang).

Leisure Behavior of Chinese Minority Members

Leisure is used by Chinese in Japan to build ethnic identity, create networks, and recover individual identity potentially lost through the migration process. Traditional Chinese leisure activities have been well preserved by the old-timer group in Japan. For example, the lion dance is a traditional dance in which performers mimic a lion's movements while wearing a two-person lion costume. The lion dance was started by Cantonese

Photo courtesy of Erwei Dong.

Pachinko is a Japanese adaptation of pinball and is played by almost 17 million people in Japan each year (Association of Gaming Industry of Japan, 2009). Most pachinko parlors are owned by zainichi Koreans.

immigrants living in southern China as a way to worship the Chinese deity Guandi, who protects people from evil. While there are no statistics on the rate of participation in the lion dance in the community, it is regarded as one of the most popular leisure activities in Japanese Chinatowns. The lion dance is typically performed during Chinese traditional holidays, the birthday of Guandi, festivals, wedding ceremonies, and construction ceremonies. The dance has a broader meaning related to ethnic identity among the old-timer group. Through this dance, the old-timer groups demonstrate both their local identity in Chinatowns, which means they were born in these traditional neighborhoods, and their global identity, which means they have contributed to the overseas Chinese culture (Zhang, 2003).

The old-timer group is integrated into Japanese mainstream society. In particular, Chinatowns in Japan are accepted by the mainstream society. Approximately 20 million people visited Yokohama Chinatown (Yokohama China Town, 2011). On the other hand, the integration of the newcomer group into the mainstream society has not been as complete, and the members face some unique constraints to leisure. Similar to other new immigrant groups, the newcomers struggle with inadequate Japanese language skills, lack of general knowledge about Japan, social isolation, and cultural differences (Liu-Farrer, 2004). Leisure spaces (e.g., social dance halls) are used by the newcomers to "adopt individual strategies to maintain a continuity and consistency of personal identity and individual purpose" (p. 672).

Traditionally, the old-timer group was concentrated in the Chinatowns of Japan. However, most modern Chinese are residentially integrated into Japanese society. For example, in 2002, only 26.9% of Chinese people residing in Yokohama City lived in that city's Chinatown. The newcomers tend to move to the suburban areas of Tokyo because they are looking for more living space, better air quality, and lower apartment rental fees. Therefore, public housing complexes have become the Chinese newcomers' main settlement areas instead of Chinatowns.

Sports are more popular among the newcomer group than other leisure activities because they often use sport participation to develop social networks. They form badminton, table tennis, and other sport clubs, for example, and play these sports in local community centers and recreation centers. The sport clubs also attract local Japanese participants. Internet-based mailing lists have become a communication tool among the newcomer groups for leisure, education, and other informational exchanges. Influenced by Japanese culture, summer festivals including dance, games, and sports are also held in immigrant communities (Jiang & Yamashita, 2005).

FUTURE DIRECTIONS

In the East Asia region, leisure research has been largely descriptive and atheoretical, and the role of leisure among ethnic minority groups in the region is unclear. Although physical activity and health research are predominant in North America, the impacts of leisure (both active and passive) have not been studied cross-culturally. This section presents recommendations about future leisure research and leisure practice.

Recommendations for Leisure Research

Because it has been strongly influenced by North American leisure research, research on leisure in East Asia has focused heavily on leisure involvement, leisure participation, and festivals. However, how applicable this research is to East Asia is open to debate (Iwasaki et al., 2007). For example, in the United States and the United Kingdom, the social gradient theory of life expectancy has often been used to understand the relationship between people's longevity and their social rank. People in higher social classes typically have longer life expectancies and lower mortality rates than those who belong to the lower social classes. However, the social gradient theory of life expectancy may not be applicable in East Asia in general and in Okinawa in particular. Life expectancy in Okinawa, which is Japan's poorest prefecture, exceeds that of Japan as a whole. Cockerham and Yamori (2001) have suggested that Okinawans' unique leisure lifestyles (e.g., family gatherings including feasting, drinking, and ceremonies honoring ancestors) are more important for longevity than the sense of social hierarchy. Therefore, as Mannell (2007) suggested, the cross-cultural applicability of principles, theories, and findings related to the effects of leisure should be examined in future research. (See also chapter 1 on theory and chapter 2 on methods.)

With the increasing ethnic and cultural diversity in East Asia, researchers also need to focus on developing positive intergroup interactions and ameliorating intergroup tensions. Research has demonstrated that immigration itself may create undesirable or traumatic life experiences that result from language barriers, isolation from society, lack of social networks, and cultural conflicts (Mio, Barker-Hackett, & Tumambing, 2008; Stodolska, 1998). These studies indicate that immigrant groups in East Asia may also face numerous challenges while experiencing intergroup contact with individuals from the host culture. Unfortunately, limited information exists regarding intergroup relations among individuals with different ethnic or cultural backgrounds in East Asia. Therefore, future studies are needed to explore the phenomenon of intergroup contacts from the immigrants' perspective and to examine how immigrant groups interact with other racial groups in East Asia.

Recommendations for Leisure Practice

From a practical perspective, the present authors recommend that two key topics be addressed with regard to leisure in East Asia. First, leisure is increasingly viewed as a domain that is important to people's health. Thus, leisure services should understand that the degree of leisure consonance (i.e., adaptive leisure) in minority communities is critical in explaining adaptive health outcomes such as quality of life, stress, and wellness (Chick, 1995). In addition, leisure services should develop practical strategies to close the leisure consonance gap across different types of ethnic and immigrant communities. Second, immigrants may face numerous challenges (i.e., language barriers, limited social networks, lack of transportation, cultural differences) that can limit their knowledge of leisure resources. Immigrants in East Asia can benefit from learning to identify leisure opportunities as encompassing situations that promote social connectedness rather than simply a list of activities traditionally engaged in for fun. Therefore, leisure education can be

a process through which immigrants can learn more about themselves as well as their abilities, talents, and interests.

The authors suggest three major goals of leisure education for immigrants in East Asia. First, leisure education programs should be designed to teach immigrants to access leisure resources (e.g., senior centers, traditional activity centers, hobby clubs) in their communities, gain leisure skills, and increase social skills that are valuable for developing social connections within their communities. Despite various leisure resources offered by leisure service providers, immigrants may not fully use these resources because they lack knowledge, are unfamiliar with leisure resources, or experience some other leisure constraints. Second, leisure education programs can enhance the self-esteem of immigrants by addressing boredom and anxiety. Through leisure education, immigrants can identify personal motives and desired social factors related to their leisure participation, which may lead to greater social acceptance and inclusion in the community. Third, leisure education can enable immigrants to establish new networks of friends, which are regarded as the foundation of social inclusion. In summary, leisure education programs could be highly beneficial for immigrants. Skills and knowledge acquired through such programs may assist immigrants in pursuing optimal leisure involvement, foster social interactions, and enhance self-esteem, which could result in psychological and social well-being.

CONCLUSION

Leisure remains an integral part of East Asian daily life, as it has since ancient times. Studying leisure in East Asia offers a fresh perspective on human development, modernity, and diversity. Although East Asian ethnic studies have been conducted under the rubrics of religion, folklore, music, art, games, and sport, to date there has been relatively little such research within the leisure studies field. Thus, an aim of this chapter was to address this research gap by providing an overview of the relationships among leisure, language, history, culture, economy, and politics within the East Asian ethnic community.

CONCLUSIONS

Emerging Issues

Myron F. Floyd, Gordon J. Walker, Monika Stodolska, and Kimberly J. Shinew

OVERVIEW

This concluding chapter presents reflections on key trends and themes in the preceding chapters. In light of the knowledge gained from the survey of literature in this volume, we also assess limitations and gaps in the literature as well as potential opportunities that can advance future leisure research and practice.

Learning Outcomes

After reading this chapter, readers will be able to

- identify key themes and trends in the current literature related to race, ethnicity, and leisure; and
- identify research needs related to theory development and management of leisure services.

Lu chang er dao yuan/There is a long way to go.

Gao, Ting-Toomey, and Gudykunst (1996, p. 293)

With reference to the topic of race, ethnicity, and leisure, all four of the editors have at one time or another made a comment similar to the quote (e.g., Floyd, Bocarro, & Thompson, 2008; Shinew et al., 2006; Walker & Deng, 2003/2004). In one way, this book speaks to how far the field has come, and thus we want to summarize what has been learned. However, at the same time, the book speaks to how far we have yet to go in understanding the manifold ways race and ethnicity affect leisure experiences. Therefore, we also want to identify some of the research and practice issues, needs, and opportunities that exist. This last chapter summarizes what we've learned from the contributors to this book and outlines several directions for the future.

WHAT HAVE WE LEARNED?

The chapters in this book survey the breadth of the leisure studies literature focused on race, ethnicity, and leisure. The contributors demonstrate how this research has increased current knowledge of the ways race, ethnicity, and culture interact with leisure in a range of contexts (e.g., sport, urban parks, wilderness recreation). The literature has expanded to encompass studies of participation, motives and benefits, constraints, discrimination, physical activity, and sport, among others. In these studies, researchers have applied a great variety of theoretical and methodological approaches to study leisure among a broad array of racial and ethnic groups from many parts of the world. Thus, contributions from scholars throughout the world are increasing. In this section, we draw from the wide range of literature covered in the preceding chapters to offer several broad themes with the aim of summarizing what we have learned.

The Importance of Context

Leisure patterns related to race and ethnicity should be understood within the appropriate his-

torical, social, and cultural contexts. In addition to empirical research, leisure services management and practice should be guided by what is known about the history associated with minority groups. As Tsai and colleagues (chapter 16) state, "The ways in which the past underlies and imbues the present day need to be taken in account." The philosophy, values, and ideologies underlying leisure service provision reflect mainstream and dominant groups, and the significance of this is echoed throughout the text (e.g., Scott, chapter 3; Floyd & Mowatt, chapter 4; Fox et al., chapter 7; Johnson-Gaither, chapter 12). Management and practice can be guided by a number of factors, including research, legal mandates, agency policy, and available resources, but professional judgment is also required (Manning, 2011). In providing leisure services to diverse populations, practitioners need to reflect on whether programs and policies serve to increase access and promote freedom of choice or continue to maintain and reproduce inequalities and stereotypes.

Diversity in Concepts and Theories

Theories and concepts used to explain and understand racial and ethnic patterns in leisure are becoming more diverse and comprehensive (Floyd & Stodolska, chapter 1). The Ethnicity and Public Recreation Participation Model (Gómez, 2002) and the multiple stratification hierarchy perspective are examples of models that integrate different concepts known or hypothesized to affect leisure participation among minority groups. Theorizing at both micro and macro levels is also evident. At the micro level, for example, Walker and colleagues (e.g., Walker, Deng & Dieser, 2001; Walker & Virden, 2005) sought to understand leisure needs and motivations of Chinese Canadians in terms of self-construal or how individuals perceive themselves in relation to others. On the other hand, the application of critical theory approaches has brought more attention to the significance of societal-level historical and structural forces in limiting opportunities for minority groups. Given the increased number of racial and ethnic groups being studied, the various topics under consideration, and the variety of contexts, the development of a broader range of relevant concepts and theories is a sign of progress.

Diversity in Methodological Tools

Similarly, application of a variety of methodological approaches is evident in the literature. Along with improvements in theory and concepts, use of a greater variety of methodological tools is also a sign of progress in this research. Historically, quantitative methods have been the dominant form of data collection and analysis in studies of leisure among racial and ethnic minority groups. As discussed by Henderson and Walker (chapter 2), quantitative methods offer several strengths in research, such as the ability to use large samples, to generalize results more broadly, and to use more sophisticated statistical techniques. More recently, a greater number of studies have used qualitative methods as well as mixed methods. This has allowed researchers to penetrate and engage "localized and contextualized aspects of leisure" (Henderson & Walker, chapter 2) in ways quantitative methods cannot. It is important to consider choice of methods in view of the main research questions and the perspective that a set of methods provides for a particular ethnic group and context. It is wise to sidestep the "either/or" quantitative versus quantitative debate. Rather, strengths and limitations of approaches should be evaluated by their potential to improve our knowledge of race and ethnicity in relation to leisure.

Commonality of Constraints

Minority groups continue to experience a variety of constraints to leisure. Research from various world regions indicates that minority groups are more likely than others to have less access to recreation opportunities or are restricted to certain types of leisure experiences. For example, Scott (chapter 3), Floyd and Mowatt (chapter 4), Stodolska and Shinew (chapter 5), Schneider and coauthors (chapter 10), and Fox and colleagues (chapter 7) document historical and contemporary problems of unequal access to leisure opportunities experienced by African Americans, Latinos,

and Native Americans. Unequal access or limited leisure opportunities have also been documented for minority groups in Europe, particularly in the United Kingdom, where more empirical studies have been conducted (Peters, chapter 15). Discrimination remains a salient factor for minority groups in the United States and Canada, as well as in Europe, Australia, and New Zealand.

Leisure and Immigration Experiences

Leisure patterns are influenced by immigration experiences. Leisure can play a role in adaptation and cultural integration of immigrants in host countries. Research on Latino Americans in the United States (Stodolska & Shinew, chapter 5), Asians in North America (Walker & Deng, chapter 6), and religious minority groups (Heintzman & Stodolska, chapter 8) indicates that immigration experiences significantly influence, and often constrain, leisure patterns. On the other hand, leisure can be a vehicle for coping with the stress of immigration and can facilitate integration into host communities (Tsai et al., chapter 16).

Diversity Within Ethnic and Racial Groups

Substantial diversity exists *within* racial and ethnic groups. Diversity within groups is related to nationality, immigration histories, language usage and preference, socioeconomic differences, and discrimination experiences. For example, among U.S. Latinos are the native born and those originating from Mexico and Central and South America (Stodolska & Shinew, chapter 5). Diversity among Indigenous populations is found in their geographic distribution, tribal communities, and political status (Fox et al., chapter 7). From the limited research that exists on East Asia, Dong and coauthors (chapter 17) discuss the significant population heterogeneity of some East Asian countries (e.g., China). At a more fundamental level, the concept of leisure is not monolithic in how it is defined and understood across or within ethnic groups. As pointed out by Fox and coauthors (chapter 7), few Indigenous languages have a word for leisure or recreation. Similarly, work and leisure are not treated as separate life domains (Fox et al.). Walker and Deng (chapter 6) and Johnson-Gaither (chapter 12) show that leisure meanings vary significantly among Chinese ethnic groups. In research and practice, treating racial and ethnic groups as monolithic entities obscures important variations, which limits more complete understanding of leisure behavior among minority populations. Regarding practice, misreading or not recognizing within-group differences means that leisure service providers may fail to offer the services that meet the needs of particular populations.

Some observations can be made about how the themes from the chapters compare with key themes identified by Floyd, Bocarro, and Thompson (2008) in their review of race and ethnicity research in five major journals (*Journal of Leisure Research, Leisure Sciences, Leisure Studies, Journal of Park and Recreation Administration, and Loisir et Société*). First, these authors found that literature reviews and conceptual discussions were the types of article most frequently published through 2005. This led them to suggest that researchers were responding to criticisms about limitations of current conceptual approaches. This issue is also evident within the contributions to this book, given the level of conceptual development and application of diverse theoretical perspectives. Second, generally, there is substantial overlap between themes identified by Floyd and colleagues (2008) and topics addressed by contributors in this volume (e.g., topics such as activity participation, constraints, discrimination and interracial relations, gender and race, and forest- and park-based recreation). Third, we also found that immigration experiences were more prominent in the chapters and less represented in the review by Floyd and colleagues (2008), who described immigration as an underdeveloped area of research. Floyd and coauthors identified only 12 studies with an immigration theme. Although immigration is not treated as a stand-alone topic in this text, it receives significant attention in a majority of the chapters describing research in the United States, Europe, Asia, Australia, and New Zealand. This discrepancy between the findings of Floyd and colleagues (2008) and the attention given to immigration issues in this book might be explained by the fact that a large portion of

minorities in the United States, Canada, Australia, and New Zealand are immigrants. Thus, even articles not identified by Floyd and colleagues as having an "immigration theme" that focused on ethnic minorities (e.g., Irwin, Gartner, & Phelps, 1990; Stodolska & Livengood, 2006) in reality examined mostly immigrants. Fourth and finally, regarding methods, Henderson and Walker's overview of quantitative and qualitative methods (chapter 2) reflects increased use of a variety of methodologies, particularly qualitative methods, in race and ethnicity research. However, results of the review of methods reported by Floyd and colleagues (2008) showed that telephone and mail surveys (quantitative approaches) were dominant.

In drawing inferences about how themes and topics of this book compare to those covered by Floyd and colleagues (2008), it is important to note that the latter were limited to a review of five major journals. In contrast, the authors contributing to this book drew upon a broad array of literature sources (e.g., books, conference proceedings, journal articles). Moreover, the chapters represent more authors and research from different parts of the world. However, we should point out that while the book overviews research from several world regions (North America, Europe, East Asia, Australia and New Zealand), it does not include a chapter on leisure in Latin America. This is particularly important given that Latin America is the largest source region of immigration for the United States and that Latinos are predicted to constitute almost 30% of the U.S. population by 2050. This omission is indicative of the limited state of this research and of how much work related to this region needs to be done.

FUTURE DIRECTIONS

Each chapter presents a number of opportunities for further research on race, ethnicity, and leisure. In this closing chapter, we highlight some of the key directions future research and practice might take.

Societal- and Global-Level Factors

Future race, ethnicity, and leisure research must begin to attend to macro processes at the societal and global levels. As Kivel, Johnson, and Scraton (2009) stated, "In terms of understanding and explaining leisure experiences vis-à-vis 'race,' the bulk of work [has focused] on identifying and examining 'differences' without regard to macro social issues" (p. 479). Several recommendations are offered in this regard. First, research needs to pay more attention to globalization issues and to the mobility of minority populations. Economic, social, and cultural trends *in the source countries* of immigration should be noted, as many migrants are exposed to Western culture before they embark on their trips to the West. Research also needs to take into account that many of these traditional immigrant-sending countries are undergoing rapid and significant economic and cultural changes (e.g., China, India, Mexico). Therefore, those who emigrate from these countries may be doing so for different reasons (e.g., economic, political) and may have considerably different experiences (e.g., transnationalism) than earlier arrivals from the same region. Conversely, the effects of economic trends *in destination countries* (e.g., the United States, Canada, Western Europe, Australia, and New Zealand) must also be taken into account, as this could have consequences for current immigrants (e.g., because of heightened unemployment among some minority groups), as well as for future immigrants (i.e., because of changes in immigration policy).

Finally, and probably most importantly, the growing minority population in the United States, Canada, Australia, and New Zealand will lead to major realignment of the ethnic hierarchies in these countries—and this will have significant implications for leisure studies generally; for race, ethnicity, and leisure research specifically; and for the provision of leisure programs and services to racial and ethnic groups especially.

Trajectories of Success, Advancement, and Resistance

More focus is needed on issues of resistance and trajectories of success and advancement, both within racial and ethnic groups (e.g., middle-class African Americans and Latinos) and with respect to racial and ethnic groups that have traditionally

tended to fare better than others (e.g., Japanese and Korean immigrants). One can claim that extant research has been somewhat deterministic and that leisure studies have consequently too often portrayed minority populations as underprivileged, homogenous entities. Shinew and Floyd (2005) outlined several possible forms of resistance in leisure. For example, they characterized parallel activities as a form of intentional resistance in which members of minority groups are able to create and control their own "sphere of influence and control" (p. 45). Examples include Black ski clubs or scuba diving clubs among affluent, middle-class African Americans. As discussed by Floyd and Mowatt (chapter 4), parallel leisure organizations were important sources of leisure opportunities for affluent Blacks in the decades following slavery and during the era of legal segregation. Given the growing number of middle-class African Americans and Latinos, the question of how parallel leisure serves their needs should be explored in more detail. Participation in parallel activities is also likely to be linked to the issue of ethnic enclosure in leisure, whose positive and negative consequences have been explored in the past (Stodolska, 2007). How ethnic enclosure in leisure relates to acculturation and transmission of cultural traits needs to be investigated in future research. Unique material, relational, symbolic, and option resources that are at the disposal of minorities and that might be helpful in mounting resistance (Shinew & Floyd, 2005) would also constitute an important topic of inquiry.

Race, Ethnicity, and the Life Span: Experiences of Minority Youth and Older Adults

In their comprehensive review of the extant race, ethnicity, and leisure literature, Floyd et al. (2008) suggested that one of the underdeveloped areas future researchers should emphasize was children and youth. In this book, the continuing need for such studies is reemphasized by, among others, Floyd and Mowatt (chapter 4), Stodolska and Shinew (chapter 5), Fox, McAvoy, Wang, and Henhawk (chapter 7), and Shores and Shinew (chapter 13). Furthermore, examination of the youthful age

structure of the U.S. African American and Latino populations suggests a greater need in the future for leisure services demanded by youth and young families. These issues are likely to be particularly salient among some immigrant populations that have an increasing number of children and teenagers. Immigrant youth accounted for one-fourth of the 75 million children in the United States in 2009, and this number is projected to increase to one-third by 2050 (Tienda & Haskins, 2011). Hispanic children constitute a majority of this population. Such increases in the proportion of immigrant and minority youth have been seen in certain areas of the United States for the last two decades. Problems common to immigrant families, such as high rates of youth poverty (particularly among children of undocumented parents), unstable living arrangements, fear of deportation, language barrier, and discrimination are likely to have a significant effect on their leisure patterns and thus should be investigated in future leisure research.

Many of the previously mentioned chapters, as well as others (e.g., Floyd & Stodolska's chapter 1, Walker & Deng's chapter 6), also recommend that future researchers attend to the experiences of minority older adults. Part of the reason is that "among immigrant groups, older adults are the most vulnerable to mental health problems, with the exception of victims of warfare and torture" (American Psychological Association [APA], Presidential Task Force on Immigration, 2012, p. 46). The APA report adds that while the rate of depression among older Filipino immigrants is roughly the same as that of the general U.S. adult population (15%, and 15% to 20%, respectively), it is much higher for older Asian immigrants from other ethnic groups (e.g., Chinese, 46%; East Indian, 50%; Vietnamese, 64%; Japanese, 76%). The APA report also mentions that older immigrants access formal health care services at an even lower rate than the already low rate of the general immigrant population. This suggests that greater access to leisure services, and in particular leisure education programs (see chapter 6 for more on this point), could prove especially beneficial. Thus, we strongly recommend that future research also attend to the emerging issue of leisure experiences of minority older adults.

Role of the Arts, Music, and Youth Culture

In their chapter, Floyd and Mowatt (chapter 4) observe that the rise of the hip-hop and house music genres and the associated youth culture have largely escaped the notice of leisure research. Hip-hop and house music have helped to define a generation as rock and roll did in a previous era. Among Black and Native youth, in particular, hip-hop has provided a means for identifying with peers and an extended culture through music, dance styles, clothes, and media (e.g., radio, TV, videos) (Kitwana, 2002; Fox et al., chapter 7). Studying minority youth leisure through expressive arts such as hip-hop presents a number of opportunities. As Lashua and Fox (2006) have shown, there are opportunities for participatory research (as described by Henderson & Walker, chapter 2) in which insights from the youth perspective can be gained more directly and more intimately. Second, it is surprising that urban hip-hop culture is not reflected in the youth development literature in leisure studies. Third, given the global reach of the art form, there are also opportunities to explore similarities and differences in how hip-hop contributes to youth and leisure identity across nations. Research in these areas also presents additional opportunities for leisure studies to bridge with other disciplines such as cultural studies, media, arts, and education (Gibson & Anderson, 2008).

Perceived Benefits and Related Outcomes

In 1998, Floyd recommended that race, ethnicity, and leisure researchers examine perceived benefits as a dependent variable. In some respects this did happen (e.g., Gómez, 2002; Hunt & Ditton, 2001; Tinsley, Tinsley, & Croskeys, 2002); but with the exception of health and physical activity (see chapter 13), this work has been very limited and largely independent of what has been done in origin and cognate fields. For example, despite tremendous growth in the area of positive psychology over the past few years, comparable research on happiness, life satisfaction, and subjective well-being is largely lacking in the leisure studies field generally and in the race, ethnicity, and leisure studies subfield specifically (one of the few exceptions is the work of Spiers & Walker, 2009). These gaps are especially disconcerting given the number of quality life-focused studies conducted by early leisure researchers (e.g., Brown & Frankel, 1993; Philipp, 1997), as well as recognition by leading positive psychologists that free time plays an important role in people's quality of life (e.g., Ryan, Bernstein, & Brown, 2010). Thus, we recommend that future research on race, ethnicity, and leisure move beyond the factors that affect participation and begin considering the outcomes (objective *and* subjective, positive *and* negative) that result from participation.

Similarly, Floyd (1998) recommended that race, ethnicity, and leisure researchers examine a wider range of dependent variables, including motivations for and constraints to leisure. As evidenced in the chapters by Walker (chapter 9) and Schneider, Shinew, and Fernandez (chapter 10), considerable research has since been conducted on both variables, as well as (in terms of motives) on the related constructs of needs and (in terms of constraints) on negotiation. Still, this area of research has a long way to go before it exhibits substantial conceptual development and accumulation of findings. Walker provides a detailed list of recommendations for future research, and Schneider and coauthors provide a thorough discussion of implications for practice (chapters 9 and 10, respectively).

Homogeneity Within and Heterogeneity Across Ethnic Groups

Henderson and Walker (chapter 2) note that past race, ethnicity, and leisure research has often suffered from the fallacy of monolithic identity *within* racial and ethnic groups as well as the failure to acknowledge appreciable similarities *across* racial and ethnic populations. In the case of the former, for example, Chinese, Japanese, and Korean American recreationists have often been lumped together to form an "Asian" comparison group; the consequence is that important cultural

and acculturative differences were overlooked. In the latter case, for example, a researcher may focus too much on racial and ethnic differences and too little on similarities (i.e., beyond what the data actually indicate), possibly because of his ideological stance, lack of statistical expertise, or not necessarily erroneous belief that a more compelling answer to reviewers' "So what?" question will result. Homogenizing within and heterogenizing across racial and ethnic groups are equally deleterious, and leisure researchers must ensure that they are aware of and alleviate both problems in the future.

Intersectionality

As Henderson and Walker note (chapter 2), "The reality of the world is that all people have multiple identities, and to understand a behavior such as leisure requires that more than one dimension be examined . . . a monolithic identity is simply not a reality of any racial or ethnic group's experience." Because of this intersectionality, it is important that future research acknowledge and embrace people's multiple identities, including those associated not only with their race or ethnicity but also with their age, gender, social class, socioeconomic status, ability status, and sexual orientation. Moreover, because the salience of ethnic and racial identity can vary across situations (e.g., when one is with others belonging to the same group vs. when one is with others all of whom belong to a different group), this too must be taken into account. Additionally, for some people, other identities (e.g., gender, ability status, sexual orientation) may be more salient and have a more powerful influence on their leisure behavior than race or ethnicity. Given all this, researchers must begin to recognize the complexity inherent in studying racial and ethnic identity and the need to contextualize racial and ethnic identity with regard to the many different identities a person holds. Having said this, we are also cognizant that research on the leisure experiences of those belonging to "multiple minority" groups (e.g., African American women with lower socioeconomic status, Latino children who are overweight, Asian immigrant women with disabilities) is especially lacking.

Theory

Theory development remains a significant need in the study of race, ethnicity, and leisure as identified by several authors (e.g., Allison, 1988; Arai et al., 2009; Floyd, 1998; Floyd & Stodolska, chapter 1). At the same time, the development of models such as Gómez's (2002) Ethnicity and Public Recreation Participation Model and the application of intersection theory, critical race theory, and other theories from the broader social sciences demonstrate that the field has moved far beyond Washburne's (1978) initial articulation of the marginality and ethnicity hypotheses. However, despite the criticism that the marginality–ethnicity perspective has received, it served as a much-needed influential "research paradigm" providing direction for predictions, measurement, analysis, and interpretation. Recent work shows greater appreciation for a diversity of perspectives, particularly qualitative and postpositivist perspectives (Floyd et al., 2008; Henderson & Walker, chapter 2). This is a positive development, but complementary work representing more quantitative and deductive strategies is falling behind. In making this recommendation, we emphasize that researchers building new theory should provide clear, precise, and logical arguments that facilitate empirical testing and refinements (Markovsky, 2008; Sell, Knottnerus, & Adcock-Azbill, 2012).

Additionally, there have been increasing calls in our field for less "theory shyness" (Kruglanski, 2001) and more theoretical integration (Crawford & Jackson, 2005; Kleiber, Walker, & Mannell, 2011). Crawford and Jackson, in fact, after stating that the potential for integration was a sign of "good" theory (Popper, 1959), added that leisure constraint researchers

[m]ay ultimately come to the realization that one of the major issues this line of work faces is not that it has been too brazen, but that it may not have been adventurous enough. Why not be daring and speculate imaginatively now, at this relatively early stage? (p. 165)

We concur with these researchers' comments and believe that race, ethnicity, and leisure research must be equally bold and theoretically integrative in the future.

Diversity of Methods

Calls for the use of more diverse research methods are common throughout this book (e.g., chapters 4, 7, and 16), with Henderson and Walker (chapter 2) providing a list of alternatives for both qualitative (e.g., participatory inquiry, creative analytical practice, critical race ethnography) and quantitative (e.g., longitudinal, secondary data, experience sampling) researchers. However, these authors also recommend that race, ethnicity, and leisure scholars not necessarily limit themselves to one or the other but also consider employing mixed-methods approaches. Regardless of the type of research—qualitative, quantitative, or mixed—it is equally important that methodological range *and* methodological rigor be suitably demonstrated. Arguably, the latter did not always occur in earlier studies in the area; and this may have meant that differences between or among ethnic and racial group members went unnoticed or, equally detrimental, that similarities between or among ethnic and racial group members went unreported. Giving attention to similarities could present opportunities for developing and using common measures in intergroup comparisons. Use of common measures could also enable comparisons through meta-analysis across groups, times, and settings (Henderson & Walker, chapter 2; Vaske & Manning, 2008).

Translating Research for Practice

Scott (chapter 3) makes a strong case for his proposal that "inequity in service delivery has been perpetuated over time by established practices and beliefs that are firmly embedded in the normal, everyday functioning of society and how agencies do business." Floyd and Mowatt's (chapter 4) account of African Americans' leisure lends credence to Scott's proposition; and together, these discussions suggest that the first step in trying to better understand the relationship between race, ethnicity, and leisure practice may be to review the historical documents that detail how we got to where we are today.

If the first step is to look back, the second step is to plot how best to move forward. Walker and Deng (chapter 6) hold that because many leisure scholars, including themselves, "often find it difficult to translate abstract results into concrete policies, programs, and services," future race, ethnicity, and leisure studies should "include either a practice-proficient researcher or a research-conversant practitioner . . . as part of their team." Moreover, because research in race, ethnicity, and leisure now requires not only more efficient knowledge transfer but also greater theoretical sophistication, as well as increased methodological diversity and rigor, the era of solo or duo researchers has likely begun to pass, soon to be replaced by large, multitalented investigative teams. This trend also reflects increasing demands by research sponsors for dissemination and knowledge transfer products for practitioner use (e.g., policy briefs, research summaries). As the literature on race, ethnicity, and leisure continues to expand, how to best translate and disseminate research findings in systematic ways should be a priority. Designing and evaluating evidence-based programs and interventions focused on diverse groups could be one approach to thinking more deeply about how to translate and apply our findings.

SUMMARY

In the Foreword to this book, Murdock notes that in the coming decades, rapid racial and ethnic diversification in North America and abroad will create a very dynamic environment for providing leisure services and for conducting research on race, ethnicity, and leisure. In this concluding chapter, we have described a number of themes common to diverse world regions, populations, and leisure settings that illustrate advances in this area of leisure scholarship. Both the quantity and qualitative content (i.e., breadth of topics) of studies focused on racial and ethnic minority groups have markedly increased. We noted the shift toward more diverse and sophisticated theoretical and methodological approaches used to understand leisure experiences of minority groups. However, the progress made in these areas is tempered by limitations associated with the current state of conceptual development and lack of standardized methodological approaches (qualitative or quantitative or mixed methods). As we move into the future that Murdock describes, the field will be challenged to respond. Thus, the recommendation to think more deeply about research translation and dissemination is just as critical as recommendations focused on theory and methods.

REFERENCES

FOREWORD

DeNavas-Walt, C., Proctor, B. D., & Smith, J. C. (2010). *Income, poverty, and health insurance coverage in the United States.* U.S. Census Bureau, Current Population Reports, P60-238. Washington, DC: U.S. Government Printing Office.

Pew Hispanic Center. (2002). *National survey of Latinos, 2002.* Washington, DC: Pew Hispanic Center.

U.S. Census Bureau. (2012). *Projections of the population of the United State by age, sex, race and ethnicity, 2012-2060.* Washington, DC: U.S. Census Bureau.

U.S. Department of the Interior, U.S. Fish and Wildlife Service, & U.S. Department of Commerce, U.S. Census Bureau. (2012). *2011 National survey of fishing, hunting, and wildlife-associated recreation.* Washington, DC.

U.S. Forest Service (2004). *National survey on recreation and the environment.* Washington, DC: National Forest Service, United States Department of Agriculture.

INTRODUCTION

Allison, M. T., & Schneider, I. E. (2000, 2008). *Diversity and the recreation profession. Organizational perspectives.* State College, PA: Venture.

Anderson, A. B., & Frideres, J. S. (1981). *Ethnicity in Canada. Theoretical perspectives.* Toronto: Butterworths.

Berry, B. (1958). *Race and ethnic relations.* Boston: Houghton Mifflin.

Bonilla-Silva, E. (1987). Rethinking racism: Toward a structural interpretation. *American Sociological Review, 62,* 465-480.

Floyd, M. F. (1998). Getting beyond marginality and ethnicity: The challenge for race and ethnic studies in leisure research. *Journal of Leisure Research, 30,* 3-22.

Floyd, M. F., Bocarro, J. N., & Thompson, T. D. (2008). Research on race and ethnicity in leisure studies: A review of five major journals. *Journal of Leisure Research, 40,* 1-22.

Humes, K. R., Jones, N. A., & Ramirez, R. R. (2011). Overview of race and Hispanic origin: 2010. 2010 Census Briefs. www.census.gov/prod/cen2010/briefs/c2010br-02.pdf.

Hutchison, R. (1988). A critique of race, ethnicity, and social class in recent leisure-recreation research. *Journal of Leisure Research, 20,* 10-30.

Jackson, E. L. (2005). *Constraints to leisure.* State College, PA: Venture.

Jackson, E. L., & Burton, T. L. (1999). *Leisure studies: Prospects for the twenty-first century.* State College, PA: Venture.

Kaplan, M. (1975). *Leisure: Theory and policy* (pp. 18-29, 44-51). New York: Wiley.

Kivel, B., Johnson, C., & Scraton, S. (2009). (Re)Theorizing leisure, experience, and race. *Journal of Leisure Research, 41*(4), 473-493.

Kleiber, D. A., Walker, G. J., & Mannell, R. C. (2011). *A social psychology of leisure* (2nd ed.). State College, PA: Venture.

Passel, J. S., & Cohn, D. (2008). U.S. population projections: 2005-2050. Pew Research Center Social & Demographic Trends. http://pewsocialtrends.org/files/2010/10/85.pdf.

Passel, J. S., Livingston, G., & Cohn, D. (2012). Explaining why minority births now outnumber white births. Pew Research Center Social & Demographic Trends. www.pewsocialtrends.org/2012/05/17/explaining-why-minority-births-now-outnumber-white-births/?src=hispanic-footer.

Pew Research Center. (2010). Statistical portrait of the foreign-born population in the United States, 2010. www.pewhispanic.org/files/2012/02/PHC-2010-FB-Profile-Final_APR-3.pdf.

Statistics Canada. (2001). Visible minorities in Canada. Canadian Centre for Justice Statistics Profile Series. http://publications.gc.ca/Collection/Statcan/85F0033M/85F0033MIE2001009.pdf.

Statistics Canada. (2010). Projections of the diversity of the Canadian population, 2006 to 2031. www.statcan.gc.ca/pub/91-551-x/91-551-x2010001-eng.htm.

Statistics Canada. (2013). Immigration and ethnocultural diversity in Canada. www12.statcan.gc.ca/nhs-enm/2011/as-sa/99-010-x/99-010-x2011001-eng.cfm.

U.S. Census Bureau. (2010). Table 229. Educational attainment by race and Hispanic origin 1970 to 2010. www.census.gov/compendia/statab/2012/tables/12s0229.pdf.

U.S. Office of Management and Budget. (n.d.). Revisions to the standards for the classification of federal data on race and ethnicity. www.whitehouse.gov/omb/fedreg_1997standards.

CHAPTER 1

Aguirre, B. E., Saenz, R., & Hwang, S. (1989). Discrimination and the assimilation and ethnic competition perspectives. *Social Science Quarterly, 70*(3), 594-606.

Ajzen, I. (1991). The theory of planned behavior. *Organisational Behavior and Human Decision Process, 50,* 179-211.

Alba, R. D., & Nee, V. (1997). Rethinking assimilation theory for a new era of immigration. *International Migration Review, 31,* 826-874.

Allison, M. T. (1988). Breaking boundaries and barriers: Future directions in cross-cultural research. *Leisure Sciences, 10*(4), 247-259.

Arai, S., & Kivel, B. D. (2009). Critical race theory and social justice perspectives on whiteness, difference(s) and (anti)racism: A fourth wave of race research in leisure studies. *Journal of Leisure Research, 41*(4), 459-472.

Arnold, M., & Shinew, K. J. (1998). The role of gender, race, and income on park use constraints. *Journal of Park and Recreation Administration, 16*(4), 39-56.

Barth, F. (1969). *Ethnic groups and boundaries: The social organization of culture.* London, UK: Allen and Unwin.

Blahna, D., & Black, K. S. (1992). Racism: A concern for recreation resource managers?: In-park user survey findings. In P. Gobster (Ed.), *Managing urban and high-use recreation settings,* Gen. Tech. Rep. NC-163 (pp. 111-118). St. Paul, MN: USDA Forest Service, North Central Forest Experiment Station.

Blanchard, C. M., Kupperman, J., Sparling, P., Nehl, E., Rhodes, R. E., Courneya, K., et al. (2007). Ethnicity as a moderator of the theory of planned behavior and physical activity in college students. *Research Quarterly for Exercise and Sport, 78*(5), 531-541.

Blanchard, C., Nehl, E., Rhodes, R., Baker, F., Annesi, J., Courneya, K., & Spence, J. (2004). Does ethnicity moderate the associations between the theory of planned behavior and physical activity? *International Journal of Cancer Prevention, 1,* 89-97.

Bogardus, E. S. (1933). A social distance scale. *Sociology and Social Research, 17,* 265-271.

Bourdieu, P. (1986). *The forms of capital.* New York: Greenwood.

Carr, D. S., & Williams, D. R. (1993). Understanding the role of ethnicity in outdoor recreation experiences. *Journal of Leisure Research, 25*(1), 22-38.

Chavez, D. J. (1993). *Visitor perceptions of crowding and discrimination at two national forests in southern California.* Berkeley, CA: Pacific Southwest Research Station.

Coon, H., & Kemmelmeier, M. (2001). Cultural orientations in the United States: (Re)Examining differences among ethnic groups. *Journal of Cross-Cultural Psychology, 32,* 348-364.

Crawford, D. W., & Jackson, E. L. (2005). Leisure constraints theory: Dimensions, directions, and dilemmas. In E. L. Jackson (Ed.), *Constraints to leisure* (pp. 153-167). State College, PA: Venture.

Crawford, D. W., Jackson, E. L., & Godbey, G. (1991). A hierarchical model of leisure constraints. *Leisure Sciences, 13,* 309-320.

Cutler Riddick, C., & Stewart, D. G. (1994). An examination of the life satisfaction and importance of leisure in the lives of older female retirees: A comparison of blacks and whites. *Journal of Leisure Research, 26*(1), 75-87.

Erickson, B., Johnson, C. W., & Kivel, B. D. (2009). Rocky Mountain National Park history and culture as factors in African-American park visitation. *Journal of Leisure Research, 41*(4), 529-545.

Floyd, M. F. (1995). Perceptions of discrimination in a recreation context. *Journal of Leisure Research, 27*(2), 192-199.

Floyd, M. F. (1998). Getting beyond marginality and ethnicity: The challenge for race and ethnic studies in leisure research. *Journal of Leisure Research, 301*(1), 3-22.

Floyd, M. F. (1999). Race, ethnicity and use of the National Park System. *Social Science Research Review, 1*(2), 1-23.

Floyd, M. F., & Gramann, J. H. (1993). Effects of acculturation and structural assimilation in resource-based recreation: The case of Mexican Americans. *Journal of Leisure Research, 25,* 6-21.

Floyd, M. F., & Gramann, J. H. (1995). Perceptions of discrimination in a recreation context. *Journal of Leisure Research, 27,* 192-199.

Floyd, M. F., Gramann, J. H., & Saenz, R. (1993). Ethnic factors and the use of public outdoor recreation areas: The case of Mexican Americans. *Leisure Sciences, 15,* 83-98.

Floyd, M. F., Nicholas, L., Lee, I., Lee, J., & Scott, D. (2006). Social stratification in recreational fishing participation: Research and policy implications. *Leisure Sciences, 28*(4), 351-368.

Floyd, M. F., Shinew, K. J., McGuire, F. A., & Noe, F. P. (1994). Race, class, and leisure activity preferences: Marginality and ethnicity revisited. *Journal of Leisure Research, 26*(2), 158-173.

Freeberg, A., & Stein, C. (1996). Felt obligation towards parents in Mexican-American and Anglo-American young adults. *Journal of Social and Personal Relationships, 13,* 457-471.

Glover, T. D. (2004). Social capital in the lived experiences of community gardeners, *Leisure Sciences, 26* (2), 1-20.

Glover, T. D. (2007). Ugly on the diamonds: An examination of white privilege in youth baseball. *Leisure Sciences, 29*(2), 195-208.

Gobster, P. H. (1998). Explanations for minority "underparticipation" in outdoor recreation: A look at golf. *Journal of Park and Recreation Administration, 16*(1), 46-64.

Gobster, P. H., & Delgado, A. (1993). Ethnicity and recreation use in Chicago's Lincoln Park: In-park user survey findings. In P. Gobster (Ed.), *Managing urban and high-use recreation settings,* Gen. Tech. Rep. NC-163 (pp. 75-81). St. Paul, MN: USDA Forest Service, North Central Forest Experiment Station.

Gómez, E. (2002). The Ethnicity and Public Recreation Participation Model. *Leisure Sciences, 24*(2), 123-142.

Gómez, E. (2006). The Ethnicity and Public Recreation Participation (EPRP) Model: An assessment of unidimensionality and overall fit. *Leisure Sciences, 28*(3), 245-265.

Gómez, E., & Malega, R. (2007). Residential attributes, park use, and perceived benefits: An exploration of individuals and neighbourhood characteristics. *Leisure/Loisir, 31*(1), 77-104.

Gordon, M. M. (1964). *Assimilation in American life.* New York: Oxford University Press.

Gramann, J. H., & Allison, M. T. (1999). Ethnicity, race, and leisure. In E. Jackson & T. Burton (Eds.), *Leisure studies: Prospects for the twenty first century* (pp. 283-297). State College, PA: Venture Publishing.

Gramann, J. H., Floyd, M. F., & Saenz, R. (1993). Outdoor recreation and Mexican American ethnicity: A benefits perspective. In A. W. Ewert, D. J. Chavez, & A. W. Magill (Eds.), *Culture, conflict, and communication in the wildland-urban interface* (pp. 69-84). Boulder, CO: Westview Press.

Hudson, S., Walker, G. J., Simpson, B., & Hinch, T. (2013). The influence of ethnicity and self-construal on leisure constraints. *Leisure Sciences, 35,* 145-166.

Hunter, C., & Joseph, N. (2010). Racial group identification and its relations to individualism/interdependence and race-related stress in African Americans. *Journal of Black Psychology, 36*, 483-511.

Hutchison, R. (1988). A critique of race, ethnicity, and social class in recent leisure-recreation research. *Journal of Leisure Research, 20*(1), 10-30.

Hylton, K. (2005). "Race," sport and leisure: Lessons from critical race theory. *Leisure Studies, 24*(1), 81-98.

Johnson, C. Y., Bowker, J., English, D. B. K., & Worthen, D. (1998). Wildland recreation in the rural South: An examination of marginality and ethnicity theory. *Journal of Leisure Research, 30*(1), 101-120.

Keefe, S. E., & Padilla, A. M. (1987). *Chicano ethnicity*. Albuquerque, NM: University of New Mexico Press.

Kelly, J. R. (1987). *Freedom to be: A new sociology of leisure*. New York: Macmillan.

Kivel, B. D., Johnson, C. W., & Scraton, S. J. (2009). (Re) Theorizing leisure experience and race. *Journal of Leisure Research, 41*(4), 473-494.

Kleiber, D. A., Walker, G. J., & Mannell, R. C. (2011). *A social psychology of leisure* (2nd ed.). State College, PA: Venture.

Lee, J.-H., Scott, D., & Floyd, M. F. (2001). Structural inequalities in outdoor recreation participation: A multiple hierarchy stratification perspective. *Journal of Leisure Research, 33*(4), 427-449.

Lee, K. J., & Scott, D. (2011). Participation in wildlife watching: A multiple hierarchy perspective. *Human Dimensions of Wildlife, 16*(5), 330-344.

Li, M. Z., & Stodolska, M. (2006). Transnationalism, leisure, and Chinese graduate students in the United States. *Leisure Sciences, 28*, 39-55.

Lin, N. (2002). *Social capital: A theory of social structure and action*. New York: Cambridge University Press.

Livengood, J., & Stodolska, M. (2004). The effects of discrimination and constraints negotiation on leisure behavior of American Muslims in the post-September 11 America. *Journal of Leisure Research, 36*(2), 183-208.

Markides, K., Liang, J., & Jackson, J. (1990). Race, ethnicity, and aging: Conceptual and methodological issues. In R. H. Binstock & L. K. George, (Eds.), *Handbook of aging and the social sciences* (pp. 112-129). San Diego, CA: Academic Press.

Markus, H., & Kitayama, S. (1991). Culture and the self: Implications for cognition, emotion, and motivation. *Psychological Review, 98*, 224-253.

Meeker, J. W., Woods, W. K., & Lucas, W. (1973). Red, white, and black in the national parks. *North American Review, 258*(3), 3-7.

Murphy, J. F. (1972). *Egalitarianism and separatism: A history of public recreation and leisure service for Blacks, 1906-1972*. Corvallis, OR: Oregon State University.

Nigg, C. R., Lippke, S., & Maddock, J. E. (2009). Factorial invariance of the theory of planned behavior applied to physical activity across gender, age, and ethnic groups. *Psychology of Sport and Exercise, 10*(2), 219-225.

Omi, M., & Winant, H. (1994). *Racial formation in the U.S.: From the 1960s to the 1990s*. New York: Routledge.

Philipp, S. F. (1995). Race and leisure constraints. *Leisure Sciences, 19*, 109-120.

Philipp, S. F. (1997). Race, gender, and leisure benefits. *Leisure Sciences, 19*(3), 191-207.

Portes, A. (1984). The rise of ethnicity: Determinants of ethnic perceptions among Cuban exiles in Miami. *American Sociological Review, 49*(3), 383-397.

Portes, A. (1998). Social capital: Its origin and applications in modern sociology. *Annual Review of Sociology, 24*, 1-24.

Portes, A., & Rumbaut, R. G. (1996). *Immigrant America: A portrait*. Berkeley, CA: University of California Press.

Portes, A., & Zhou, M. (1993). The second new generation: Segmented assimilation and its variants. *Annals of the American Academy of Political and Social Science, 530*, 74-96.

Putnam, R. (2000). Thinking about social change in America. In *Bowling alone: The collapse and revival of American community* (pp. 15-28). New York: Simon & Schuster.

Sharaievska, I., Stodolska, M., Shinew, K. J., & Kim, J. (2010). Perceived discrimination in leisure settings in Latino urban communities. *Leisure/Loisir, 34*, 295-326.

Shaull, S. L., & Gramann, J. H. (1998). The effect of cultural assimilation and the importance of family-related and nature-related recreation among Hispanic Americans. *Journal of Leisure Research, 30*(1), 47-63.

Shinew, K. J., Floyd, M. F., McGuire, F. A., & Noe, F. P. (1995). Gender, race and subjective social class and their association with leisure preference. *Leisure Sciences, 17*(2), 75-89.

Shinew, K. J., Glover, T. D., & Parry, D. C. (2004). Leisure spaces as potential sites for interracial interaction: Community gardens in a segregated urban area. *Journal of Leisure Research, 36*(3), 336-355.

Shores, K. A., Scott, D., & Floyd, M. F. (2007). Constraints to outdoor recreation: A multiple hierarchy stratification perspective. *Leisure Sciences, 29*(3), 227-246.

Stodolska, M. (1998). Assimilation and leisure constraints: Dynamics of constraints on leisure in immigrant populations. *Journal of Leisure Research, 30*, 521-551.

Stodolska, M. (2005). A Conditioned Attitude Model of Individual Discriminatory Behavior. *Leisure Sciences, 27*(1), 1-20.

Stodolska, M. (2007). Ethnic enclosure, social networks, and leisure behaviour of immigrants from Korea, Mexico, and Poland. *Leisure/Loisir, 31*, 277-324.

Stodolska, M., & Alexandris, K. (2004). The role of recreational sport in the adaptation of first generation immigrants in the United States. *Journal of Leisure Research, 36*(3), 379-413.

Stodolska, M., & Jackson, E. L. (1998). Discrimination in leisure and work experienced by a white ethnic minority group. *Journal of Leisure Research, 30*(1), 23-46.

Stodolska, M., & Santos, C. A. (2006). Transnationalism and leisure: Mexican temporary migrants in the United States. *Journal of Leisure Research, 38*, 143-167.

Su, C., & Hynie, M. (2011). Effects of life stress, social support, and cultural norms on parenting styles among Mainland Chinese, European Canadian, and Chinese

Canadian immigrant mothers. *Journal of Cross-Cultural Psychology, 42,* 944-962.

Taylor, D. E. (1989). Blacks and the environment: Toward an explanation of the concern and action gap between blacks and whites. *Environment and Behavior, 21*(2), 175-205.

Triandis, H. (1995). *Individualism & collectivism.* Boulder, CO: Westview Press.

Turner, J. H. (1986). *The structure of sociological theory.* Chicago: Dorsey Press.

Walker, G. J., Courneya, K. S., & Deng, J. (2006). Ethnicity, gender, and the theory of planned behavior: The case of playing the lottery. *Journal of Leisure Research, 38,* 224-248.

Walker, G. J., Deng, J., & Dieser, R. (2001). Ethnicity, acculturation, self-construal, and motivations for outdoor recreation. *Leisure Sciences, 23,* 263-283.

Walker, G. J., Jackson, E. L., & Deng, J. (2008). The role of self-construal as an intervening variable between culture and leisure constraints: A comparison of Canadian and Mainland Chinese university students. *Journal of Leisure Research, 40,* 90-109.

Walker, G. J., & Virden, R. J. (2005). Constraints on outdoor recreation. In E. L. Jackson (Ed.), *Constraints to leisure* (pp. 201-219). State College, PA: Venture.

Washburne, R. F. (1978). Black underparticipation in wildland recreation: Alternative explanations. *Leisure Sciences, 1*(2), 175-189.

Washburne, R.F., & Wall, P. (1980). *Black-White ethnic differences in outdoor recreation* (Res. Pap. INT-249). Ogden UT: U.S. Department of Agriculture, Forest Service, Intermountain Forest and Range Experiment Station.

West, P. C. (1989). Urban region parks and black minorities: Subculture, marginality, and interracial relations in park use in the Detroit metropolitan area. *Leisure Sciences, 11*(1), 11-28.

Woodward, C. V. (1974). *The strange career of Jim Crow.* New York: Oxford University Press.

CHAPTER 2

Ajzen, I. (1991). The theory of planned behavior. *Organizational Behavior and Human Decision Process, 50,* 179-211.

Allison, M. T. (1988). Breaking boundaries and barriers: Future directions in cross-cultural research. *Leisure Sciences, 10,* 247-259.

American Psychological Association. (2009). *Publication manual of the American Psychological Association* (6th ed.). Washington, DC: APA.

Ammerman, A., Corbie-Smith, G., St. George, D., Washington, C., Weathers, B., & Jackson-Christian, B. (2003). Research expectations among African American church leaders in the PRAISE! project: A randomized trial guided by community-based participatory research. *American Journal of Public Health, 93*(10), 1720-1727.

Arai, S., & Kivel, B. (2009). Critical race theory and social justice perspectives on whiteness, difference(s) and (anti)racism: A fourth wave of race research in leisure studies. *Journal of Leisure Research, 41*(4), 459-470.

Arai, S., & Pedlar, A. M. (1997). Building communities through leisure: Citizenship participation in a healthy communities initiative. *Journal of Leisure Research, 29*(2), 167-183.

Babbie, E. (2003). *The practice of social research* (6th ed.). Belmont, CA: Wadsworth.

Bachman, J., & O'Malley, P. (1984). Yea-saying, nay-saying, and going to extremes: Black-white differences in response styles. *Public Opinion Quarterly,* 491-509.

Banks-Wallace, J., & Conn, V. (2002). Interventions to promote physical activity among African American women. *Public Health Nursing, 19*(5), 321-335.

Barnett, L. (2005). Measuring the ABCs of leisure experience: Awareness, boredom, challenge, distress. *Leisure Sciences, 27,* 131-155.

Beatty, L. A., Wheeler, D., & Gaiter, J. (2004). HIV prevention research for African Americans: Current and future directions. *Journal of Black Psychology, 30,* 40-58.

Brewer, M. (2000). Research design and issues of validity. In H. Reis & C. Judd (Eds.), *Handbook of research methods in social and personality psychology* (pp. 3-39). Cambridge: Cambridge University Press.

Bullock, C. C. (1983). Qualitative research in therapeutic recreation. *Therapeutic Recreation Journal, 17*(4), 36-43.

Chen, C., Lee, S.-Y., & Stevenson, H. (1995). Response style and cross-cultural comparisons of rating scales among East Asian and North American students. *Psychological Science, 6,* 170-175.

Cohen, J. (1992). A power primer. *Psychological Bulletin, 112,* 155-159.

Cole, E. R. (2009). Intersectionality and research in psychology. *American Psychologist, 61*(3), 170-180.

Creswell, J. W. (1998). *Qualitative inquiry and research design: Choosing among five traditions.* Thousand Oaks, CA: Sage.

Davis, W. (1983). China, the Confucian ideal, and the European age of enlightenment. *Journal of the History of Ideas, 44,* 523-548.

Deci, E., & Ryan, R. (1985). *Intrinsic motivation and self-determination in human behavior.* New York: Plenum Press.

Denzin, N. K. (1978). *The research act.* New York: McGraw-Hill.

Dillman, D., Reips, U.-D., & Matzat, U. (2010). Advice in surveying the general public over the internet. *International Journal of Internet Science, 5,* 1-4.

Driver, B. (1977). *Item pool for scales designed to quantify the psychological outcomes desired and expected from recreation participation.* Fort Collins, CO: USDA Forest Service, Rocky Mountain Forest and Range Experiment Station.

Ellis, G., Voekl, J., & Morris, C. (1994). Measurement and data analysis issues with explanation of variance in daily experience using the flow model. *Journal of Leisure Research, 26,* 337-356.

Floyd, M. F. (1998). Getting beyond marginality and ethnicity: The challenge for race and ethnic studies in leisure research. *Journal of Leisure Research, 30*(1), 3-22.

Floyd, M. F. (2007). Research on race and ethnicity in leisure: Anticipating the fourth wave. *Leisure/Loisir, 3*(1), 245-254.

Floyd, M. F., Bocarro, J., & Thompson, T. (2008). Research on race and ethnicity in leisure studies: A review of five major journals. *Journal of Leisure Research, 40*(1), 1-22.

Gibson, P., & Abrams, L. (2003). Racial difference in engaging, recruiting, and interviewing African American women in qualitative research. *Qualitative Social Work, 2,* 457-476.

Glover, T. D. (2007). Ugly on the diamonds: An examination of white privilege in youth baseball. *Leisure Sciences, 29*(2), 195-208.

Gobster, P. (2002). Managing urban parks for a racially and ethnically diverse clientele. *Leisure Sciences, 24,* 143-159.

Gómez, E. (2002). The Ethnicity and Public Recreation Participation (EPRP) Model. *Leisure Sciences, 24,* 123-142.

Gómez, E. (2006). The Ethnicity and Public Recreation Participation (EPRP) Model: An assessment of unidimensionality and overall fit. *Leisure Sciences, 28,* 245-265.

Gravlee, C., Kennedy, D., Godoy, R., & Leonard, W. (2009). Methods for collecting panel data: What can cultural anthropology learn from other disciplines? *Journal of Anthropological Research, 65,* 453-483.

Gregoire, T., & Driver, B. (1987). Type II errors in leisure research. *Journal of Leisure Research, 19,* 261-272.

Henderson, K. A. (2006). *Dimensions of choice: Qualitative approaches to research in parks, recreation, tourism, sport and leisure.* State College, PA: Venture.

Henderson, K. A. (2007). Just research and physical activity: Diversity is more than an independent variable. *Leisure Sciences, 31,* 100-105.

Henderson, K. A. (2011). Post-positivism and the pragmatics of leisure research. *Leisure Sciences, 33*(4), 341-346.

Higgins, J. W., & Rickert, T. (2005). A taste of healthy living: A recreational opportunity for people at risk of developing Type II diabetes. *Leisure Sciences, 27,* 439-458.

Hofstede, G. (1980). *Culture's consequences: International differences in work-related values.* Beverly Hills, CA: Sage.

Hoshino-Browne, E., Zanna, A., Spencer, S., & Zanna, M. (2004). Investigating attitudes cross-culturally: A case of cognitive dissonance among East Asians and North Americans. In G. Haddock & G. Maio (Eds.), *Contemporary perspectives on the psychology of attitudes* (pp. 375-397). New York: Psychology Press.

Huang, H., & Coker, A. D. (2010). Examining issues affecting African American participation in research studies. *Journal of Black Studies 40,* 619-636.

Hutchison, R. (2000). Race and ethnicity in leisure studies. In W. Gartner & D. Lime (Eds.), *Trends in outdoor recreation, leisure and tourism* (pp. 63-71). New York: CABI.

Ito, E., & Walker, G. J. (in press). Similarities and differences in leisure conceptualizations in leisure conceptualizations between Japan and Canada and between two Japanese leisure-like terms. *Leisure/Loisir.*

Iwasaki, Y., Nishino, H., Onda, T., & Bowling, C. (2007). Leisure research in a global world: Time to reverse the Western domination in leisure research? *Leisure Sciences, 29,* 113-117.

Johnson, B., & Eagly, A. (2000). Quantitative synthesis of social psychological research. In H. Reis & C. Judd (Eds.), *Handbook of research methods in social and personality psychology* (pp. 496-528). Cambridge: Cambridge University Press.

Johnson, C., Bowker, J., English, D., & Worthen, D. (1998). Wildland recreation in the rural south: An examination of marginality and ethnicity research. *Journal of Leisure Research, 30,* 101-120.

Johnson, T., Shavitt, S., & Holbrook, A. (2011). Survey response styles across cultures. In D. Matsumoto & F. Van de Vijver (Eds.), *Cross-cultural research methods in psychology* (pp. 130-175). Cambridge: Cambridge University Press.

Kim, H. (2002). We talk, therefore we think? A cultural analysis of the effect of talking on thinking. *Journal of Personality and Social Psychology, 83,* 828-842.

Kirk, R. (1996). Practical significance: A concept whose time has come. *Educational and Psychological Measurement, 56,* 746-759.

Kivel, B., Johnson, C., & Scraton, S. (2009). (Re)Theorizing leisure, experience, and race. *Journal of Leisure Research, 41*(4), 473-493.

Kleiber, D. A., Walker, G. J., & Mannell, R. C. (2011). *A social psychology of leisure* (2nd ed.). State College, PA: Venture.

Lashua, B. D., & Fox, K. (2007). Defining the groove: From remix to research in *The Beat of Boyle Street. Leisure Sciences, 29,* 143-158.

Li, C.-L., Chick, G., Zinn, H., Absher, J., & Graefe, A. (2007). Ethnicity as a variable in leisure research. *Journal of Leisure Research, 39,* 514-545.

Liu, H., Yeh, C.-K., Chick, G., & Zinn, H. (2008). An exploration of meanings of leisure: A Chinese perspective. *Leisure Sciences, 30,* 482-488.

Mannell, R. (2005). Evolution of cross-cultural analysis in the study of leisure: Commentary on "Culture, self-construal, and leisure theory and practice." *Journal of Leisure Research, 37,* 100-105.

Marin, G., & Marin, B. V. (1991). *Research with Hispanic populations.* Applied Social Research Methods Series, Vol. 23. Newbury Park, NJ: Sage.

Markus, H., & Kitayama, S. (1991). Culture and the self: Implications for cognition, emotion, and motivation. *Psychological Review, 98,* 224-253.

Matsumoto, D., Kim, J., Grissom, R., & Dinnel, D. (2011). Effect sizes in cross-cultural research. In D. Matsumoto & F. Van de Vijver (Eds.), *Cross-cultural research methods in psychology* (pp. 244-272). Cambridge: Cambridge University Press.

McAvoy, L. M., Winter, P. L., Outley, C. W., McDonald, D., & Chavez, D. J. (2000). Conducting research with communities of color. *Society and Natural Resources, 13,* 479-488.

McClelland, G. H., & Judd, C. M. (1993). Statistical difficulties of detecting interactions and moderator effects. *Psychological Bulletin, 114,* 376-390.

McCormack, G. R., Rock, M., Toohey, A. M., & Hignell, D. (2010). Characteristics of urban parks associated with park use and physical activity: A review of qualitative research. *Health & Place, 16,* 712-726.

McDonald, M. G. (2009). Dialogues on whiteness, leisure, and (anti)racism. *Journal of Leisure Research, 41,* 5-28.

Nezlek, J. (2011). Multilevel modeling and cross-cultural research. In D. Matsumoto & F. Van de Vijver (Eds.), *Cross-cultural research methods in psychology* (pp. 299-345). Cambridge: Cambridge University Press.

Oh, C.-O., & Ditton, R. (2009). Toward an understanding of racial and ethnic differences in conservation attitudes among recreation participants. *Leisure Sciences, 31,* 53-67.

Parker, L., & Lynn, M. (2002). What's race got to do with it? Critical race theory's conflicts with and connections to qualitative research methodology and epistemology. *Qualitative Inquiry, 8,* 7-22.

Parry, D. C., & Johnson, C. W. (2007). Contextualizing leisure research to encompass complexity in lived leisure experience. The need for creative analytic practice. *Leisure Sciences, 29,* 119-130.

Parry, D. C., Johnson, C. W., & Stewart, W. (2013). Leisure research for social justice: A response to Henderson. *Leisure Sciences, 35,* 81-87.

Pew Internet & American Life Project. (2010). Internet, broadband, and cell phone statistics. www.pewinternet.org/Reports/2010/Internet-broadband-and-cell-phone-statistics.aspx.

Reis, H., & Gable, S. (2000). Event-sampling and other methods for studying everyday experience. In H. Reis & C. Judd (Eds.), *Handbook of research methods in social and personality psychology* (pp. 190-222). Cambridge: Cambridge University Press.

Roberts, N. S. (2009). Crossing the color line with a different perspective on whiteness and (anti)racism: A response to Mary McDonald. *Journal of Leisure Research, 41,* 495-509.

Ryan, A. B. (2006). Post-positivist approaches to research. In M. Antonesa, H. Fallon, A. B. Ryan, A. Ryan, & T. Walsh, with L. Borys, *Researching and writing your thesis: A guide for postgraduate students* (pp. 12-28). Maynooth: MACE.

Sasidharan, V. (2002). Special issue introduction: Understanding recreation and the environment within the context of culture. *Leisure Sciences, 24,* 1-11.

Shinew, K., Stodolska, M., Floyd, M., Hibbler, D., Allison, M., Johnson, C., & Santos, C. (2006). Race and ethnicity in leisure behavior: Where have we been and where do we need to go? *Leisure Sciences, 28,* 403-408.

Shores, K. A., Scott, D., & Floyd, M. F. (2007). Constraints to outdoor recreation: A multiple hierarchy stratification perspective. *Leisure Sciences, 29,* 227-246.

Smale, B. (1996). The improbability of less than .05 probability: Over-reliance on statistical testing in leisure research. *Abstracts from the 1996 Symposium on Leisure Research* (p. 76). Arlington, VA: NRPA.

Stansfield II, J. H., & Dennis, R. M. (1993). *Race and ethnicity in research methods.* Newbury Park, CA: Sage.

van de Vijver, F., & Leung, K. (1997). *Methods and data analysis for cross-cultural research.* Thousand Oaks, CA: Sage.

Visser, P., Krosnick, J., & Lavrakas, P. (2000). Survey research. In H. Reis & C. Judd (Eds.), *Handbook of research methods in social and personality psychology* (pp. 223-252). Cambridge: Cambridge University Press.

Walker, G. J. (2008). Motivation in everyday life: The case of Chinese/Canadians. *World Leisure Journal, 50,* 116-126.

Walker, G. J. (2010). The effects of personal, contextual, and situational factors on the facilitation of intrinsic motivation: The case of Chinese/Canadians. *Journal of Leisure Research, 42,* 43-66.

Walker, G. J., Courneya, K. S., & Deng, J. (2006). Ethnicity, gender, and the theory of planned behavior: The case of playing the lottery. *Journal of Leisure Research, 38,* 224-248.

Walker, G. J., Deng, J., & Dieser, R. (2001). Ethnicity, acculturation, self-construal, and motivations for outdoor recreation. *Leisure Sciences, 23,* 263-283.

Walker, G. J., Deng, J., & Dieser, R. (2005). Culture, self-construal, and leisure theory and practice. *Journal of Leisure Research, 37,* 77-99.

Walker, G. J., Dieser, R., & Deng, J. (2005). "Whoa versus go!" A rejoinder to Mannell and Caldwell. *Journal of Leisure Research, 37,* 117-127.

Walker, G. J., Jackson, E. L., & Deng, J. (2008). The role of self-construal as an intervening variable between culture and leisure constraints: A comparison of Canadian and Mainland Chinese university students. *Journal of Leisure Research, 40,* 90-109.

Walker, G. J., & Wang, X. (2008). A cross-cultural comparison of Canadian and Mainland Chinese university students' leisure motivations. *Leisure Sciences, 30,* 179-197.

Walker, G. J., & Wang, X. (2009). The meaning of leisure for Chinese/Canadians. *Leisure Sciences, 31,* 1-18.

Washburne, R. G. (1978). Black under-representation in wildlife recreation: Alternative explanations. *Leisure Sciences, 1,* 175-189.

White, R., & Arzi, H. (2005). Longitudinal studies: Validity, practicality, and value. *Research in Science Education, 35,* 137-149.

Whyte, W. F. (1995). Encounters with participatory action research. *Qualitative Sociology, 18*(3), 289-300.

Wilkinson, L., & Task Force on Statistical Inference. (1999). Statistical methods in psychology journals: Guidelines and explanations. *American Psychologist, 54,* 594-604.

Wu, H.-C., & Van Egeren, L. (2010). Voluntary participation and parents' reasons for enrollment in after-school programs: Contributions of race/ethnicity, program quality, and program policies. *Journal of Leisure Research, 42,* 591-620.

CHAPTER 3

Allison, M. T. (1999). Organizational barriers to diversity in the workplace. *Journal of Leisure Research, 31,* 78-101.

Allison, M. T. (2000). Leisure, diversity and social justice. *Journal of Leisure Research, 32,* 2-6.

Allison, M. T., & Hibbler, D. K. (2004). Organizational barriers to inclusion: Perspectives from the recreation professional. *Leisure Sciences, 26,* 261-280.

Aron, C. S. (1999). *Working at play: A history of vacations in the United States.* New York: Oxford University Press.

Austin, R. (1997-1998). "Not just for the fun of it!" Governmental restraints on black leisure, social inequality, and the privatization of public space. *Southern California Law Review, 71,* 667-714.

Baron, H. M. (1969). The web of urban racism. In L. K. Knowles & K. Prewitt (Eds.), *Institutional racism in America* (pp. 134-176). Englewood Cliffs, NJ: Prentice-Hall.

Boone, C. G., Buckley, G. L., Grove, J. M., & Sister, C. (2009). Parks and people: An environmental justice inquiry in Baltimore, MD. *Annals of the Association of American Geographers, 99,* 767-787.

Bowker, J. M., & Leeworthy, V. R. (1998). Accounting for ethnicity in recreation demand: A flexible count data approach. *Journal of Leisure Research, 30,* 64-78.

Butler, G. D. (1949). *Introduction to community recreation.* New York: McGraw-Hill.

Byrne, J., & Wolch, J. (2009). Nature, race, and parks: Past research and future directions for geographic research. *Progress in Human Geography, 33,* 743-765.

Caro, R. (1974). *The power broker: Robert Moses and the fall of New York.* New York: Vintage Books.

Carter, P. L. (2008). Coloured places and pigmented holidays: Racialized leisure travel. *Tourism Geographies, 10,* 265-284.

Cavallo, D. (1981). *Muscles and morals: Organized playgrounds in urban reform, 1980-1920.* Philadelphia: University of Pennsylvania Press.

Cavin, D. A. (2008). *Understanding the experiences of African American outdoor enthusiasts.* Unpublished doctoral dissertation, Texas A&M University, College Station.

Creighton, M. S. (2005). *The colors of courage: Gettysburg's forgotten history.* New York: Basic Books.

Crompton, J. L. (1999). *Financing and acquiring park and recreation resources.* Champaign, IL: Human Kinetics.

Crompton, J., & Kaczynski., A. T. (2004, July). Repositioning for resources. *Parks & Recreation, 26,* 28-33.

Dagkas, S., & Benn, T. (2006). Young Muslim women's experiences of Islam and physical education in Greece and Britain: A comparative study. *Sport, Education and Society, 11,* 21-38.

Dahl, R. (1993). Principles for effective cross-cultural communication. In A. W. Ewert, D. J. Chavez, & A. W. Magil (Eds.), *Culture, conflict, and communication in the wildland-urban interface* (pp. 147-160). Boulder, CO: Westview Press.

Diliberto, G. (1999). *A useful woman: The early life of Jane Addams.* New York: Scribner's.

Dollard, J. (1937). *Caste and class in a southern town.* New Haven, CT: Yale University Press.

Edwards, M. B., Jilcott, S. B., Floyd, M. F., & Moore, J. B. (2011). County-level disparities in access to recreational resources and associations with obesity. *Journal of Park and Recreation Administration, 29*(2), 39-54.

Erickson, B., Johnson, C. W., & Kivel, B. D. (2009). Rocky Mountain National Park: History and culture as factors in African-American park visitation. *Journal of Leisure Research, 41,* 529-545.

Estabrooks, P. A., Lee, R. E., & Gyurcsik, N. C. (2003). Resources for physical activity participation: Does availability and accessibility differ by neighborhood socioeconomic status? *Annals of Behavioral Medicine, 25,* 100-104.

Falk, J. H. (1995). Factors influencing African Americans leisure time utilization of museums. *Journal of Leisure Research, 27,* 41-60.

Feagin, J. R. (1991). The continuing significance of race: Antiblack discrimination in public places. *American Sociological Review, 56,* 101-116.

Feagin, J. R. (2006). *Systemic racism: A theory of oppression.* New York: Routledge.

Feagin, J. R., & Feagin, C. B. (1986). *Discrimination American style: Institutional racism and sexism* (2nd ed.). Malabar, FL: Robert E. Krieger.

Frazier, E. F. (1940). *Recreation and amusements among American Negroes: A research memorandum.* New York: Carnegie-Myrdal Study of the Negro in America.

Gobster, P. H. (1998). Urban parks as green walls or green magnets? Interracial relations in neighborhood boundary parks. *Landscape and Urban Planning, 41,* 43-55.

Godbey, G. C., Caldwell, L. L., Floyd, M., & Payne, L. L. (2005). Contributions of leisure studies and recreation and park management research to the active living agenda. *American Journal of Preventive Medicine, 28*(2S2), 150-158.

Godbey, G., Graefe, A., & James, S. (1992). *The benefits of local recreation and park services: A nationwide study of the perceptions of the American public.* Unpublished manuscript.

Harnik, P. (2010, August). Secrets of the private sector. *Parks & Recreation,* 32-35.

Harris, E. L. (1997, December). Solo faces. *Outside,* 106-110, 177, 178.

Henderson, K. A. (1997). A critique of constraints theory: A response. *Journal of Leisure Research, 29,* 453-457.

Holland, J. W. (2002). *Black recreation: A historical perspective.* Chicago: Burnham.

Hose, S. L. (1983). *Jane Addams and the provision of public recreation: A study of Jane Addams' ideas on recreation and their relationship to urban reform, 1889-1913.* Unpublished master's thesis, Texas A&M University, College Station.

Hunt, K. S., Scott, D., & Richardson, S. (2003). Positioning public recreation and park offerings using importance-performance analysis. *Journal of Park and Recreation Administration, 21*(3), 1-21.

Hutchison, I. (1983). Recreation and racial minorities. In T. A. Stein, & H. D. Sessoms (Eds.), *Recreation and special populations* (pp. 325-358). Boston: Allyn & Bacon.

Jones, W. H. (1927). *Recreation and amusement among Negroes in Washington, D.C.* Washington, DC: Howard University Press.

Kelly, T. (2008). *2007 Minnesota state parks research summary report.* Unpublished manuscript.

Kraus, R. (1968). *Public recreation and the negro: A study of participant and administrative practices*. New York: Center for Urban Education.

Lee, I., Floyd, M. F., & Shinew, K. J. (2002). The relationship between information use and park awareness: A study of urban park users. *Journal of Park and Recreation Administration, 20*(1), 22-41.

Lee, J. H., Scott, D., & Floyd, M. F. (2001). Structural inequalities in outdoor recreation participation: A multiple hierarchy stratification perspective. *Journal of Leisure Research, 33*, 427-449.

Low, S. M., Taplin, D., & Scheld, S. (2005). *Rethinking urban parks: Public space and cultural diversity*. Austin, TX: University of Texas Press.

Massey, D. S. (2007). *Categorically unequal: The American stratification system*. New York: Russell Sage Foundation.

Massey, D. S., & Denton, N. A. (1993). *American apartheid: Segregation and the making of the under-class*. Cambridge, MA: Harvard University Press.

McKenna, D. (2009, April 17). Pickup soccer gets fenced out by the National Park Service. *Washington City Paper*. www.washingtoncitypaper.com/articles/37087/barrier-grief.

Meyer, H. D., & Brightbill, C. K. (1948). *Community recreation: A guide to its organization and administration*. Boston: Heath.

Meyer, H. D., & Brightbill, C. K. (1956). *Community recreation: A guide to its organization* (2nd ed.). Englewood Cliffs, NJ: Prentice-Hall.

Meyer, H. D., & Brightbill, C. K. (1964). *Community recreation: A guide to its organization* (3rd ed.). Englewood Cliffs, NJ: Prentice-Hall.

Meyer, H. D., Brightbill, C. K., & Sessoms, H. D. (1969). *Community recreation: A guide to its organization and administration* (4th ed.). Englewood Cliffs, NJ: Prentice-Hall.

Mladenka, K. R. (1980). The urban bureaucracy and the Chicago political machine: Who gets what and the limits to political clout. *American Political Science Review, 74*, 991-998.

Mowen, A. J., & Baker, B. L. (2009). Park, recreation, fitness and sport recommendations for a more physically active America: A white paper for the United States National Physical Activity Plan. *Journal of Physical Activity and Health, 6*(Suppl 2), S236-S244.

Mowen, A. J., Kerstetter, D., Graefe, A. R., & Miles, J. (2006). *A concession program evaluation for Pennsylvania state parks*. Unpublished manuscript.

Murphy, J. F. (1972). *Egalitarianism and separatism: A history of approaches in the provision of public recreation and leisure service for blacks, 1906-1972*. Unpublished doctoral dissertation, Oregon State University, Corvallis.

Myrdal, G. (1944). *An American dilemma: The Negro problem and modern democracy*. New York: Harper & Brothers.

Nasaw, D. (1993). *Going out: The rise and fall of public amusements*. New York: Basic Books.

National League of Cities. (1968). *Recreation in the nation's cities: Problems and approaches*. Washington, DC: Author.

Nesbitt, J. A., Brown, P. D., & Murphy, J. F. (Eds.). (1970). *Recreation and leisure service for the disadvantaged*. Philadelphia: Lea & Febiger.

Nicholls, S., & Shafer, C. S. (2001). Measuring accessibility and equity in a local park system: The utility of geospatial technologies to park and recreation professionals. *Journal of Park and Recreation Administration, 19*(4), 102-124.

Noonan, D. S. (2005). Neighbours, barriers and urban environments: Are things "different on the other side of the tracks"? *Urban Studies, 42*, 1817-1835.

Patterson, P. D., Moore, C. G., Probst, J. C., & Shinogle, J. A. (2004). Obesity and physical activity in rural America. *Journal of Rural Health, 20*, 151-156.

Phillip, S. (2000). Race and the pursuit of happiness. *Journal of Leisure Research, 32*, 121-124.

Price, M., & Whitworth, C. (2004). Soccer and Latino cultural space: Metropolitan Washington *fútbol* leagues. In D. D. Arreola (Ed.), *Hispanic spaces, Latino places* (pp. 167-186). Austin, TX: University of Texas Press.

Public Broadcasting Service. (2009). The national parks: America's best idea. www.pbs.org/nationalparks/.

Rosenzweig, R., & Blackmar, E. (1992). *The park and the people: A history of Central Park*. Ithaca, NY: Cornell University Press.

Rugh, S. S. (2008). *Are we there yet? The golden age of American family vacations*. Lawrence, KS: University of Kansas Press.

Scott, D. (2000). Tic, toc, the game is locked and nobody else can play! *Journal of Leisure Research, 32*, 133-137.

Scott, D. (2005). The relevance of constraints research to leisure service delivery. In E. L. Jackson (Ed.), *Constraints to leisure* (pp. 279-293). State College, PA: Venture.

Scott, D., & Munson, W. W. (1994). Constraints to park usage among persons who are economically disadvantaged. *Journal of Park and Recreation Administration, 12*(4), 79-96.

Selin, S. W., Howard, D. R., Udd, E., & Cable, T. T. (1988). An analysis of consumer loyalty to municipal recreation programs. *Leisure Sciences, 10*(3), 217-223.

Sessoms, D. H., Meyer, H. D., & Brightbill, C. K. (1975). *Leisure services: The organized recreation and park system* (5th ed.). Englewood Cliffs, NJ: Prentice-Hall.

Settle, T. S. (1916). Recreation for Negroes in Memphis. *Recreation, 9*, 441-444.

Shimoda, J. (1988). My National Park Service experience. *Trends, 25*(1), 18-22.

Shinew, K. J., & Hibbler, D. K. (2002). African-Americans' perceptions of workplace equity: A starting point. *Journal of Park and Recreation Administration, 20*(1), 42-60.

Shores, K. A., Scott, D., & Floyd, M. K. (2007). Constraints to outdoor recreation: A multiple hierarchy stratification perspective. *Leisure Sciences, 29*, 227-246.

Solop, F. I., Hagen, K. K., & Ostergren, D. (2003). *Racial and ethnic diversity of national park system visitors and non-visitors*. Tech. Rep. Flagstaff, AZ: Northern Arizona University, Social Research Laboratory.

Stodolska, M., & Livengood, J. (2006). The influence of religion on the leisure behavior of immigrant Muslims in the United States. *Journal of Leisure Research, 38*, 293-320.

Taylor, D. E. (1999). Central Park as a model for social control: Urban parks, social class and leisure behavior in nineteenth-century America. *Journal of Leisure Research, 31*, 420-477.

Taylor, D. E. (2000). Meeting the challenge of wild land recreation management: Demographic shifts and social inequality. *Journal of Leisure Research, 32*, 171-179.

Thapa, B., Graefe, A. R., & Absher, J. D. (2002). Information needs and search behaviors: A comparative study of ethnic groups in the Angeles and San Bernardino National Forests, California. *Leisure Sciences, 24*, 89-107.

Tierney, P. T., Dahl, R., & Chavez, D. (2001). Cultural diversity in use of undeveloped natural areas by Los Angeles county residents. *Tourism Management, 22*, 271-277.

Tye, L. (2009). *Satchel: The life and times of an American legend.* New York: Random House.

Verbrugge, M. H. (2010). Recreation and racial politics in the Young Women's Christian Association of the United States, 1920s-1950s. *International Journal of the History of Sport, 27*, 1191-1218.

West, P. C. (1989). Urban region parks and black minorities: Subculture, marginality, and interracial relations in park use in the Detroit metropolitan area. *Leisure Sciences, 11*, 11-28.

Wicks, B. E., Backman, K. F., Allen, J., & Van Blaricom, D. (1993). Geographic information systems (GIS): A tool for marketing, managing and planning municipal park systems. *Journal of Park and Recreation Administration, 11*(1), 9-23.

Williams, J. (1985). Redefining institutional racism. *Ethnic and Racial Studies, 9*, 323-348.

Williams, J. (1987). *Eyes on the prize: America's civil rights years, 1954-1965.* New York: Viking Penguin.

Wiltse, J. (2007). *Contested waters: A social history of swimming pools in America.* Chapel Hill, NC: University of North Carolina Press.

Wolch, J., Wilson, J. P., & Fehrenbach. (2005). Parks and park funding in Los Angeles: An equity-mapping analysis. *Urban Geography, 26*, 4-35.

Wolcott, V. W. (2006). Recreation and race in the postwar city: Buffalo's 1956 Crystal Beach Riot. *Journal of American History, 6*, 63-90.

Woodard, C. V. (1966). *The strange career of Jim Crow* (2nd ed.). New York: Oxford University Press.

Woofter, T. J. Jr. (1928). *Negro problems in cities.* New York: Negro Universities Press.

Zueblin, C. (1896). Municipal playgrounds in Chicago. *American Journal of Sociology, 4*, 146-158.

CHAPTER 4

Aguirre, A. Jr., & Turner, J. H. (1998). *American ethnicity: The dynamics and consequences of discrimination* (2nd ed.). Boston: McGraw-Hill.

Allen, W. F., Ware, C. P., & Garrison, L. M. (1996). *Slave songs of the United States.* Bedford, MA: Applewood Books.

Arai, S., & Kivel, B. D. (2009). Critical race theory and social justice perspectives on whiteness, difference(s) and (anti) racism: A fourth wave of race research in leisure studies. *Journal of Leisure Research, 41*(4), 459-472.

Arnold, M., & Shinew, K. J. (1998). The role of gender, race, and income on park use constraints. *Journal of Park and Recreation Administration, 16*(4), 39-56.

Asante, M. K. (1998). *Afrocentric idea.* Philadelphia: Temple University Press.

Asante, M. K. (2002). *100 greatest African Americans: A biographical encyclopedia.* Amherst, New York. Prometheus Books.

Austin, R. (2004). Back to basics: Returning to the matter of black inferiority and white supremacy in the post-Brown era. *Journal of Appellate Practice and Process, 6*(1), 79-99.

Azar, D., Naughton, G. A., & Joseph, C. W. (2009). Physical activity and social connectedness in single-parent families. *Leisure Studies, 28*(3), 349-358.

Baker, B. E. (2007). *What Reconstruction meant? Historical memory in the American South.* Charlottesville; VA: University of Virginia Press.

Behrendt, S. (1999). Transatlantic Slave Trade. In K. A. Appiah & H. L. Gates (Eds.), *Africana: The encyclopedia of the African and African American experience* (pp. 1865-1966). New York: Basic Civitas Books.

Bell, D. A. (1995). Who's afraid of critical race theory? *University of Illinois Law Review*, 893-910.

Berlin, I. (2003). *Generations of captivity: A history of African-American slaves.* Cambridge, MA: Belknap Press of Harvard University Press.

Bialeschki, M. D., & Walbert, K. L. (1998). "You have to have some fun to go along with your work": The interplay of race, class, gender, and leisure in the industrial New South. *Journal of Leisure Research, 30*(1), 79-100.

Blahna, D., & Black, K. (1993). Racism: A concern for recreation resource managers? In P. Gobster (Ed.), *Managing Urban and High-Use Recreation Settings: Selected Papers from the 4th North American Symposium on Society and Natural Resource Management* (pp. 111-118). St. Paul, MN: USDA Forest Service GTR NC-163. USDA Forest Service North Central Forest Experiment Station.

Blassingame, J. W. (1979). *The slave community: Plantation life in the Antebellum South.* Oxford: Oxford University Press.

Bourdieu, P. (1977). *Outline of a theory of practice.* New York: Cambridge University Press.

Brooks, S., & Conroy, T. (2011). Hip-hop culture in a global context: Interdisciplinary and cross-categorical investigation. *American Behavioral Scientist, 55*(1), 3-8.

Brown, V. B. (2004). *The education of Jane Addams.* Philadelphia: University of Pennsylvania Press.

Bryant, B. (1995). *Environmental justice: Issues, policies, and solutions.* Washington, DC: Island Press.

Buzinde, C. N., & Santos, C. A. (2008). Representations of slavery. *Annals of Tourism Research, 35*(2), 468-488.

Carter, P. (2008). Coloured places and pigmented holidays: Racialized leisure travel. *Tourism Geographies, 10,* 265-284.

Centers, R. (1949). *The psychology of social classes.* Princeton, NJ: Princeton University Press.

Clark, K.B., & Clark, M.P. (1947). Racial identification and preference in Negro children. In T.M. Newcomb & E.L. Hartley, (Eds.), *Readings in social psychology* (pp. 169-178). New York: Holt, Rinehart & Winston.

Cloke, P. (2004). Rurality and racialized others: Out of place in the countryside? In N. Chakroborti & J. Garland, *Rural racism* (pp. 17-35). Portland, OR: Willan Publishing.

Colby, I. C. (1985). The Freedmen's Bureau: From social welfare to segregation. *Phylon, 46,* 219-230.

Conrad, C., Whitehead, J., Mason, P., & Stewart, J. (Eds.). (2005). *African Americans in the U.S. economy.* Lanham, MD: Rowman & Littlefield.

Craig, W. (1972). Recreational activity patterns in a small negro urban community: The role of the cultural base. *Economic Geography, 48*(1), 107-115.

DeNavas-Walt, C., Proctor, B. D., & Smith, J. C. (2011). *Income, poverty, and health insurance coverage in the United States: 2010.* Washington, DC: U.S. Department of Commerce, U.S. Census Bureau.

DeSantis, V. P. (1982). Rutherford B. Hayes and the removal of the troops and the end of reconstruction. In M. Kousser & J. McPherson (Eds.), *Region, race and reconstruction: Essays in honor of C. Vann Woodward* (pp. 417-450). London: Oxford University Press.

Douglass, F. (2001). *The narrative of the life of Frederick Douglass, an American slave: Written by himself.* New Haven, CT: Yale Nota Bene.

Dray, P. (2002). *At the hands of persons unknown: The lynching of Black America.* New York: Random House.

DuBois, W. E. B. (1899). *The Philadelphia Negro: A social study.* Philadelphia: University of Pennsylvania Press.

DuBois, W. E. B., & Lewis, D. L. (1998). *Black Reconstruction in America, 1860-1880.* New York: Free Press.

Durant, T. J., & Knottnerus, J. D. (Eds.). (1999). *Plantation society and race relations: The origins of inequality.* Westport, CT: Praeger.

Edwards, P. K. (1981). Race, residence, and leisure style: Some policy implications. *Leisure Sciences, 4*(2), 95-112.

Ennis, S. R., Rios-Vargas, M., & Albert, N. G. (2011). *The Hispanic population: 2010,* Vol. C2010BR-04. Washington, DC: U.S. Department of Commerce, U.S. Census Bureau.

Erickson, B., Johnson, C. W., & Kivel, B. D. (2009). Rocky Mountain National Park history and culture as factors in African-American park visitation. *Journal of Leisure Research, 41*(4), 529-545.

Farley, W. R., & Allen, W. R. (1989). *The color line and the quality of life in America.* New York: Oxford University Press.

Feagin, J. R. (1991). The continuing significance of race: Antiblack discrimination in public places. *American Sociological Review, 56,* 101.

Feagin, J. R., & Vera, H. (1995). *White racism.* New York: Routledge.

Fields, B. (1982). Ideology and race in American history. In K. Morgan & J. McPherson (Eds.), *Region, race, and reconstruction: Essays in honor of C. Vann Woodward* (pp. 143-177). London: Oxford University Press.

Floyd, M. F. (2002). Deconstructing diversity in leisure studies. In D. K. Hibbler (Ed.), *Unsilencing the dialogue: Voices of minority faculty* (pp. 75-83). Miami: Florida International University Center for Urban Education and Innovation.

Floyd, M. F. (2007). Research on race and ethnicity in leisure: Anticipating the fourth wave. *Leisure/Loisir, 31*(1), 245-254.

Floyd, M. F., Gramann, J. H., & Saenz, R. (1993). Ethnic factors and the use of public outdoor recreation areas: The case of Mexican Americans. *Leisure Sciences, 15*(2), 83-98.

Floyd, M. F., Nicholas, L., Lee, I., Lee, J., & Scott, D. (2006). Social stratification in recreational fishing participation: Research and policy implications. *Leisure Sciences, 28*(4), 351-368.

Floyd, M. F., & Shinew, K. J. (1999). Convergence and divergence in leisure style among Whites and African Americans: Toward an interracial contact hypothesis. *Journal of Leisure Research, 31*(4), 359-384.

Floyd, M. F., Shinew, K. J., McGuire, F. A., & Noe, F. P. (1994). Race, class, and leisure activity preferences: Marginality and ethnicity revisited. *Journal of Leisure Research, 26*(2), 158-173.

Foner, E. (1987). Rights and the Constitution in black life during the Civil War and Reconstruction. *Journal of American History, 74*(3), 863-883.

Foster, M. S. (1999). In the face of "Jim Crow": Prosperous Blacks and vacations, travel and outdoor leisure, 1890-1945. *Journal of Negro History, 84*(2), 130-149.

Frazier, E. F. (1963). *The Negro church in America.* New York: Schocken Books.

Glover, T. D. (2007). Ugly on the diamonds: An examination of White privilege in youth baseball. *Leisure Sciences, 29*(2), 195-208.

Godbey, G. C., Caldwell, L. L., Floyd, M., & Payne, L. L. (2005). Contributions of leisure studies and recreation and park management research to the active living agenda. *American Journal of Preventive Medicine, 28*(2S2), 150-158.

Gómez, E. (2002). The Ethnicity and Public Recreation Participation Model. *Leisure Sciences, 24*(2), 123-142.

Gordon-Larsen, P., Nelson, M. C., Page, P., & Popkin, B. M. (2006). Inequality in the built environment underlies key health disparities in physical activity and obesity. *Pediatrics, 117*(2), 417-424.

Grieco, E. M., Acosta, Y. D., de la Cruz, G. P., Gambino, C., Gryn, T., Larsen, L., et al. (2012). *The foreign-born population in the United States: 2010.* Washington, DC: U.S. Department of Commerce, U.S. Census Bureau.

Guelzo, A. C. (2004). *Lincoln's Emancipation Proclamation: The end of slavery in America.* New York: Simon & Schuster.

Gunning, S. (1996). *Race, rape, and lynching: The red record of American literature, 1890-1912.* London: Oxford University Press.

Hahn, S. (2003). *A nation under our feet.* Cambridge, MA: Belknap Press of Harvard University Press.

Hauser, P. (1962). *Demographic and ecological changes as factors in outdoor recreation* (pp. 27-59). Washington: Government Printing Office, ORRC Report 22.

Hine, D. C. (2003). Black professionals and race consciousness: Origins of the Civil Rights movement, 1890–1950. *Journal of American History, 89*(4), 1279-1294.

Hunt, K. M., Floyd, M. F., & Ditton, R. B. (2007). African-American and Anglo anglers' attitudes toward the catch-related aspects of fishing. *Human Dimensions of Wildlife, 12*(4), 227-239.

Hutchison, R. (1987). Ethnicity and urban recreation: Whites, blacks, and Hispanics in Chicago's public parks. *Journal of Leisure Research, 19*(3), 205-222.

Ifill, S. A. (2007). *On the courthouse lawn: Confronting the legacy of lynching in the twenty-first century.* Boston: Beacon Press.

Jackman, M. R., & Jackman, R. W. (1983). *Class awareness in the United States.* Berkeley, CA: University of California Press.

Jackson, E. L., Crawford, D. W., & Godbey, G. (1993). Negotiation of leisure constraints. *Leisure Sciences, 15*(1), 1-11.

Johnson, B. R., Jang, S. J., Li, S. D., & Larson, D. (2000). The "invisible institution" and Black youth crime: The church as an agency of local social control. *Journal of Youth and Adolescence, 29*(4), 479-498.

Johnson, C.S. (1934). *Shadow of the plantation.* Chicago: University of Chicago Press.

Johnson, C. Y., & Bowker, J. M. (1999). On-site wildland activity choices among African Americans and White Americans in the rural South: Implications for management. *Journal of Park and Recreation Administration, 17*(1), 21-39.

Johnson, C. Y., Bowker, J. M., & Cordell, H. K. (2001). Outdoor recreation constraints: An examination of race, gender, and rural dwelling. *Southern Rural Sociology, 17,* 111-133.

Johnson, C. Y., Bowker, J. M., English, D. B. K., & Worthen, D. (1997). *Theoretical perspectives of ethnicity and outdoor recreation: A review and synthesis of African-American and European-American participation.* Gen. Tech. Rep. SRS-11. Asheville, NC: U.S. Department of Agriculture, Forest Service.

Johnson, C. Y., Bowker, J., English, D. B. K., & Worthen, D. (1998). Wildland recreation in the rural South: An examination of marginality and ethnicity theory. *Journal of Leisure Research, 30*(1), 101-120.

Johnson, C. Y., Horan, P. M., & Pepper, W. (1997). Race, rural residence, and wildland visitation: Examining the influence of sociocultural meaning. *Rural Sociology, 62*(1), 89-110.

Johnson, H. B. (1998). *Black Wall Street: From riot to renaissance in Tulsa's historic Greenwood district.* Austin, TX: Eakin Press.

Joseph, P. E. (2006). *Waiting 'til the midnight hour: A narrative history of Black Power in America.* New York: Henry Holt.

Kivel, B. D., Johnson, C. W., & Scraton, S. J. (2009). (Re) Theorizing leisure experience and race. *Journal of Leisure Research, 41*(4), 473-494.

Knight, L. W. (2005). *Citizen: Jane Addams and the struggle for democracy.* Chicago: University of Chicago Press.

Landry, B., & Marsh, K. (2011). The evolution of the new Black middle class. *Annual Review of Sociology, 37,* 373-394.

Larson, R., Dworkin, J., & Gillman, S. (2001). Facilitating adolescents' constructive use of time in one-parent families. *Applied Developmental Science, 5*(3), 143-157.

Lashua, B., & Fox, K. (2006). Rec needs a new rhythm cuz rap is where we're livin'. *Leisure Sciences, 28*(3), 207-283.

Lee, J.-H., Scott, D., & Floyd, M. F. (2001). Structural inequalities in outdoor recreation participation: A multiple hierarchy stratification perspective. *Journal of Leisure Research, 33*(4), 427-449.

Lee, K. J., & Scott, D. (2011). Participation in wildlife watching: A multiple hierarchy perspective. *Human Dimensions of Wildlife, 16*(5), 330-344.

Lovejoy, P. (1989). The impact of the Atlantic slave trade on Africa: A review of the literature. *Journal of African History, 30*(3), 365-394.

Madigan, T. (2001). *The burning: Massacre, destruction, and the Tulsa race riot of 1921.* New York: St. Martin's Griffin Press.

Mahar, W. J. (1998). *Behind the burnt cork mask: Early blackface minstrelsy and antebellum American popular culture.* Champaign, IL: University of Illinois Press.

Manning, R. E. (2011). *Studies in outdoor recreation: Search and research for satisfaction.* Corvallis, OR: Oregon State University Press.

Martin, D. C. (2004). Apartheid in the great outdoors: American advertising and the reproduction of a racialized outdoor leisure activity. *Journal of Leisure Research, 36*(4), 513-535.

McDonald, M. G. (2009). Dialogues on Whiteness, leisure, and (anti)racism. *Journal of Leisure Research, 41*(1), 5-21.

McEwen, B. S. (2003). Mood disorders and allostatic load. *Society of Biological Psychiatry, 54,* 200-207.

McMillian, L. K. (1958, April). Anthony Bowen and the YMCA. *Negro History Bulletin,* p. 159.

Mitchell, T. W. (2001). From reconstruction to deconstruction: Undermining black landownership, political dependence, and community through partition sales of tenancies in common. *Northwestern University Law Review, 95*(2), 505-580.

Mowatt, R. (2008). The king of the damned: Reading lynching as leisure. *Policy Futures in Education, 7*(2), 185-199.

Mowatt, R. A. (2012). Lynching as leisure: Broadening notions of a field. *American Behavioral Scientist, 56*(10), 1361-1387.

Mueller, E., & Gurin, G. (1962). Participation in outdoor recreation: Factors affecting demand among American adults. *Report to the Outdoor Recreation Resources Review Commission, ORRRC Study Report 20.* Washington, DC: U.S. Government Printing Office.

Murdock, S. H. (1995). *An America challenged: Population change and the future of the United States.* Boulder, CO: Westview Press.

Murphy, J. F. (1972). *Egalitarianism and separatism: A history of public recreation and leisure service for Blacks, 1906-1972.* Doctoral dissertation, Oregon State University, Corvallis.

National Advisory Commission of Civil Disorders. (1967). Report of the National Advisory Commission on Civil Disorders: Summary of report. United States, Government Printing Office.

Negro League Baseball Players Association. (2012). Negro league history. Retrieved May 11, 2012, from www.nlbpa.com/history.html.

Nunn, N. (2008). The long-term effects of Africa's slave trades. *Quarterly Journal of Economics, 123*(1), 139-176.

Ogunwole, S. U., Drewery, M. P. Jr., & Rios-Vargas, M. (2012). *The population with a bachelor's degree or higher by race and Hispanic origin: 2006-2010.* ACSBR/10-19. Washington, DC: U.S. Department of Commerce, U.S. Census Bureau. www.census.gov/prod/2012pubs/acsbr10-19.pdf.

Outley, C. W., & Floyd, M. F. (2002). The home they live in: Inner city children's views on the influence of parenting strategies on their leisure behavior. *Leisure Sciences, 24*(2), 161-179.

Pattillo-McCoy, M. (2000). *Black picket fences.* Chicago: University of Chicago Press.

Payne, L. L., Mowen, A. J., & Orsega-Smith, E. (2002). An examination of park preferences and behaviors among urban residents: The role of residential location, race, and age. *Leisure Sciences, 24,* 181-198.

Perry, F. E. (2009). Kidnapping: An underreported aspect of African agency during the Slave Trade (1440-1886). *Ufahamu: A Journal of African Studies, 35*(2). Retrieved November 20, 2010, from http://escholarship.org/uc/item/8kf4m24x.

Philipp, S. F. (1995). Race and leisure constraints. *Leisure Sciences, 17,* 109-120.

Philipp, S. F. (1997). Race, gender, and leisure benefits. *Leisure Sciences, 19*(3), 191-207.

Philipp, S. F. (1999). Are we welcome? African American racial acceptance in leisure activities and the importance given to children's leisure. *Journal of Leisure Research, 31*(4), 385-403.

Philipp, S. F. (2000). Race and the pursuit of happiness. *Journal of Leisure Research, 32*(1), 121-124.

Powell, L. M., Slater, S., & Chaloupka, F. J. (2004). The relationship between community physical activity settings and race, ethnicity and socioeconomic status. *Evidence-Based Preventive Medicine, 1*(2), 135-144.

Quarmby, T., & Dagkas, S. (2010). Children's engagement in leisure time physical activity: Exploring family structure as a determinant. *Leisure Studies, 29*(1), 53-66.

Quillian, L. (2006). New approaches to understanding racial prejudice and discrimination. *Annual Review of Sociology, 32*(1), 299-328.

Raper, A. F. (1933). *The tragedy of lynching.* Chapel Hill, NC: University of North Carolina Press.

Rastogi, S., Johnston, T. D., Hoeffel, E. M., & Drewery, M. P. Jr. (2011). *The black population: 2010.* Washington, DC: U.S. Department of Commerce, U.S. Census Bureau.

Roberts, N. S. (2009). Crossing the color line with a different perspective on whiteness and (anti) racism: A response to Mary McDonald. *Journal of Leisure Research, 41*(4), 563-578.

Rodney, W. (1982). *How Europe underdeveloped Africa.* Washington, DC: Howard University Press.

Ruef, M., & Fletcher, B. (2003). Legacies of American slavery: Status attainment among southern Blacks after emancipation. *Social Forces, 82*(2), 445-480.

Russell, R. V. (2009). *Pastimes: The context of contemporary leisure* (4th ed.). Champaign, IL: Sagamore.

Samdahl, D. M. (2011). What can "American Beach" teach us? Complicity in race, class, and power. In K. Paisley & D. Dustin (Eds.), *Speaking up and speaking out: Working for social and environmental justice through parks, recreation, and leisure* (pp. 83-93). Champaign, IL: Sagamore Publishing.

Santos, C. A., & Rozier, S. (2007). Intercultural communication competence and conflict negotiation strategies: Perceptions of park staff and diverse park users. *Journal of Park and Recreation Administration, 25*(1), 22-49.

Sawyer, P., Major, B., Casad, B. J., Townsend, S. S. M., & Mendes, W. B. (2012). Discrimination and the stress response: Psychological and physiological consequences of anticipating prejudice in interracial interaction. *American Journal of Public Health, 102,* 1020-1026.

Segal, R. (1995). *The Black Diaspora: Five centuries of the black experience outside Africa.* New York: Farrar, Straus & Giroux.

Shinew, K. J., Floyd, M. F., McGuire, F. A., & Noe, F. P. (1995). Gender, race and subjective social class and their association with leisure preference. *Leisure Sciences, 17*(2), 75-89.

Shinew, K. J., Floyd, M. F., McGuire, F. A., & Noe, F. P. (1996). Class polarization and leisure activity preferences of African Americans: Intragroup comparisons. *Journal of Leisure Research, 28*(4), 219-232.

Shinew, K. J., Floyd, M. F., & Parry, D. (2004). Understanding the relationship between race and leisure activities and constraints: Exploring an alternative framework. *Leisure Sciences, 26*(2), 181-199.

Shinew, K. J., Mowatt, R., & Glover, T. (2007). An African American community recreation center: Participants' and volunteers' perceptions of racism and racial identity. *Journal of Park and Recreation Administration, 25*(2), 84-106.

Shores, K. A., Moore, J. B., & Yin, Z. (2010). An examination of triple jeopardy in rural youth physical activity participation. *Journal of Rural Health, 26*(4), 352-360.

Shores, K. A., Scott, D., & Floyd, M. F. (2007). Constraints to outdoor recreation: A multiple hierarchy stratification perspective. *Leisure Sciences, 29*(3), 227-246.

Silver, D. M. (1998). *Lincoln's Supreme Court*. Urbana, IL: University of Illinois Press.

Stamps, S. M., & Stamps, M. B. (1985). Race, class, and leisure activities of urban residents. *Journal of Leisure Research, 17*(1), 40-56.

Taylor, H. (2009). *The origin and growth of the American Constitution*. Ithaca, NY: Cornell University Press.

Taylor, W. C., Floyd, M. F., Whitt-Glover, M. C., & Brooks, J. (2007). Environmental justice: A framework for collaboration between the public health and parks and recreation fields to study disparities in physical activity. *Journal of Physical Activity and Health, 4*(Suppl. 1), S50-S63.

The Civil War Home Page. (2000). Results from the 1860 Census. www.civil-war.net/pages/1860_census.html.

Thoreau, H. D. (2007). *On the duty of civil disobedience*. Minneapolis: Filiquarian.

Tinsley, H. E. A., Tinsley, D. J., & Croskeys, C. E. (2002). Park usage, social milieu, and psychosocial benefits of park use reported by older urban park users from four ethnic groups. *Leisure Sciences, 24*(2), 199-218.

Tolnay, S. E., & Beck, E. M. (1995). *A festival of violence: An analysis of Southern lynchings, 1882-1930*. Urbana: University of Illinois Press.

Toth, J. F., & Brown, R. B. (1997). Racial and gender meanings of why people participate in fishing. *Leisure Sciences, 19*(2), 129-146.

Ture, K., & Hamilton, C. V. (1992). *Black power: The politics of liberation*. New York: Vintage Books.

Tuttle, W. M. (1996). *Race riot: Chicago in the red summer of 1919*. Urbana, IL: University of Illinois Press.

Tyson, T., & Cecelski, D. S. (Eds.). (1998). *Democracy betrayed: The Wilmington race riot of 1898 and its legacy*. Chapel Hill, NC: University of North Carolina Press.

U.S. Census Bureau. (2012). Annual estimates of the white alone resident population by sex and age for the United States: April 1, 2000 to July 1, 2009 (NC-EST2009-04-WA). www.census.gov/popest/data/historical/2000s/vintage_2009/index.html.

Van DeBurg, W. L. (1992). *New day in Babylon: The Black power movement and American culture, 1965-1975*. Chicago: University of Chicago Press.

Wagner, F. W., & Donahue, T. R. (1976). The impact of inflation and recession on urban leisure in New Orleans. *Journal of Leisure Research, 4*(4), 300-306.

Waller, S. N. (2010). Leisure in the life of the 21st century Black church: Re-thinking the gift. *Journal of the Christian Society for Kinesiology and Leisure Studies, 1*(1), 33-47.

Washburne, R. F. (1978). Black underparticipation in wildland recreation: Alternative explanations. *Leisure Sciences, 1*(2), 175-189.

Washburne, R. F., & Wall, P. (1980). *Black-White ethnic differences in outdoor recreation*. Research Paper INT-249. Ogden, UT: Intermountain Forest and Range Experiment Station, U.S. Department of Agriculture Forest Service.

Washington, H. A. (2006). *Medical apartheid: The dark history of medical experimentation on Black Americans from Colonial times to the present*. New York: Doubleday.

West, P. C. (1989). Urban region parks and black minorities: Subculture, marginality, and interracial relations in park use in the Detroit metropolitan area. *Leisure Sciences, 11*(1), 11-28.

White, W. F. (1921, June 29). The eruption of Tulsa: An NAACP official investigates the Tulsa race riot of 1921. *Nation, 112,* 909-910.

White, W. (1992). *Rope and faggot: A biography of Judge Lynch*. Notre Dame, IN: University of Notre Dame Press.

Will, T. E. (1999). Weddings on contested grounds: Slave marriage in the antebellum South. *Historian, 62*(1), 99-117.

Wilson, B. C. (1981). Idlewild: A black eden in Michigan. *Michigan History, 65*(5), 33-37.

Wilson, J. J., & Wallace, R. (2004). *Black Wallstreet*. Long Island City, NY: Seaburn.

Wolch, J., & Zhang, J. (2004). Beach recreation, cultural diversity and attitudes toward nature. *Journal of Leisure Research, 36*(3), 414-443.

Woodard, M. D. (1988). Class, regionality, and leisure among urban black Americans: The post-Civil Rights era. *Journal of Leisure Research, 20*(2), 87-105.

Woodward, C. V. (1974). *The strange career of Jim Crow*. New York: Oxford University Press.

Young, I. M. (1990). *Justice and the politics of difference*. Princeton, NJ: Princeton University Press.

CHAPTER 5

Acevedo, J. C. (2009). *A cross-cultural study of leisure among Mexicans in the state of Guerrero, Mexico, and Mexican immigrants from Guerrero in the United States*. Unpublished MS thesis, University of Illinois at Urbana-Champaign.

Acevedo, J. C. (2010, October). *Cross-cultural examination of leisure among Mexicans in Guerrero and Midwest*. Paper presented at the NRPA Leisure Research Symposium, Minneapolis.

Acosta-Belén, E. (2005). Puerto Ricans on the mainland. In S. Oboler & D. J. Gonzales (Eds.), *The Oxford encyclopedia of Latinos and Latinas in the United States*. Oxford, New York: Oxford University Press.

Anzaldua, G. (1999). *Borderlands/La frontera: The new Mestiza*. San Francisco: Aunt Lute Books.

Barnett, L. (2006). Accounting for leisure preferences from within: The relative contributions of gender, race or ethnicity, personality, affective style, and motivational orientation. *Journal of Leisure Research, 38,* 445-474.

Burgess, E. W., Locke, H. J., & Thomes, M. M. (1963). *The family: From institution to companionship* (3rd ed.). New York: American Book.

Carr, D. S., & Williams, D. R. (1993). Understanding the role of ethnicity in outdoor recreation experiences. *Journal of Leisure Research, 25,* 2238.

Castillo, A. (1995). *Massacre of the dreamers: Essays on Xixanism.* Plume.

Cave, D. (2012). American children, now struggling to adjust to life in Mexico. *New York Times,* June 19, 2012. www.nytimes.com/2012/06/19/world/americas/american-born-children-struggle-to-adjust-in-mexico.html?pagewanted=all.

Cerrutti, M., & Massey, D. S. (2004). Trends in Mexican migration to the United States, 1965-1995. In J. Durand & D. S. Massey (Eds.), *Crossing the border: Research from the Mexican migration project* (pp. 17-44). New York: Russell Sage Foundation.

Chavez, D. J. (1991). Crowding and discrimination: Unwelcome guests in wildland recreation. *Proceedings of the 1991 Society of American Foresters National Convention* (pp. 425-430). San Francisco.

Chavez, D. J. (1993). Visitor perceptions of crowding and discrimination at two national forests in southern California. *USDA Forest Service Research Paper PSW-RP-216.* Albany, CA: Pacific Southwest Research Station, Forest Service, U.S. Department of Agriculture.

Chavez, D. J., Larson, J., & Winter, P. L. (1995). To be or not to be a park: That is the question. In *Proceedings of the Second Symposium on Social Aspects and Recreation Research.* General Tech. Rep. PSW-156. Albany, CA: USDA Forest Service, Pacific Southwest Research Station.

Chick, G. (1991). Acculturation and community recreation in rural Mexico. *Play and Culture, 4*(2), 185-193.

Christenson, O. D., Zabriskie, R. B., Eggett, D. L., & Freeman, P. A. (2006). Family acculturation, family leisure involvement, and family functioning among Mexican-Americans. *Journal of Leisure Research, 38,* 475-495.

Comas-Diaz, L. (1987). Feminist therapy with mainland Puerto-Rican women. *Psychology of Women Quarterly, 11,* 461-474.

Crespo, C. J. (2000). Encouraging physical activity in minorities. *Physician and SportsMedicine, 28,* 36-51.

Cromwell, R. E., & Ruiz, R. A. (1979). The myth of macho dominance in decision making within Mexican and Chicano families. *Hispanic Journal of Behavioral Sciences, 1,* 355-373.

Cronan, M. K., Shinew, K. J., & Stodolska, M. (2008). Trail use among Latinos: Recognizing diverse uses among a specific population. *Journal of Park and Recreation Administration, 26,* 62-86.

Davison, C., Frankel, S., & Smith, G. D. (1992). The limits of lifestyle: Reassessing fatalism in the popular culture of illness prevention. *Social Science & Medicine, 34,* 675-685.

Dunn, R. A. (1999). *Hispanic American recreation at two Corps lakes in Texas and California: A preliminary assessment.* Natural Resources Technical Notes Collection (TN REC-11). Vicksburg, MS: U.S. Army Engineer Research and Development Center.

Durand, J., Massey, D. S., & Capoferro, C. (2005). The new geography of Mexican migration. In V. Zúñiga & R. Hernández-León (Eds.), *New destinations: Mexican immigration in the United States* (pp. 1-20). New York: Russell Sage Foundation.

Edwards, M. B., & Matarrita-Cascante, D. (2011). Rurality in leisure research: A review of four major journals. *Journal of Leisure Research, 43,* 447-474.

Ennis, S. B., Rios-Vargas, M., & Albert, N. G. (2011). The Hispanic population: 2010. 2010 Census Briefs. www.census.gov/prod/cen2010/briefs/c2010br-04.pdf.

Floyd, M. F., Bocarro, J. N., & Thompson, T. D. (2008). Research on race and ethnicity in leisure studies: A review of five major journals. *Journal of Leisure Research, 40,* 1-22.

Floyd, M. F., & Gramann, J. H. (1992). Perceived benefits of outdoor recreation participation: A comparison of AngloAmericans and Mexican Americans. *Proceedings of the 1992 NRPA Leisure Research Symposium.* Cincinnati, OH: National Recreation and Park Association.

Floyd, M. F., & Gramann, J. H. (1993). Effects of acculturation and structural assimilation in resource-based recreation: The case of Mexican Americans. *Journal of Leisure Research, 5,* 621.

Floyd, M. F., & Johnson, C. Y. (2002). Coming to terms with environmental justice in outdoor recreation: A conceptual discussion with research implications. *Leisure Sciences, 24,* 59-77.

Floyd, M. F., Taylor, W., & Whitt-Glover, M. (2009). Measurement of park and recreation environments that support physical activity in low-income communities of color. *American Journal of Preventive Medicine, 36,* 156-160.

Fuentes-Rohwer, L. (2005). Puerto Rico. In I. Stavans & H. Augenbraum (Eds.), *Encyclopedia Latina. History, culture, and society in the United States* (pp. 431-437). Danbury, CT: Scholastic Library.

Gil, R. M., & Vazquez, C. I. (1996). *The Maria paradox: How Latinas can merge old world traditions with new world self-esteem.* New York: Putnam's.

Gobster, P. H. (1992). Urban park trail use: An observational approach. In G. Vander Stoep (Ed.), *Proceedings, 1991 Northeastern Recreation Research Symposium* (Gen. Tech. Rep. NE-160, pp. 215-221). Radnor, PA: USDA Forest Service, Northeastern Forest Experiment Station.

Gobster, P. (2002). Managing urban parks for a racially and ethnically diverse clientele. *Leisure Sciences, 24,* 143-159.

Gómez, E., & Malega, R. (2007). Residential attributes, park use, and perceived benefits: An exploration of individual and neighborhood characteristics. *Leisure/Loisir, 31,* 77-104.

Gonzalez, J. (2011). *Harvest of empire: A history of Latinos in America.* New York: Penguin Books.

Gordon, M. M. (1964). *Assimilation in American life. The role of race, religion, and national origins.* New York: Oxford University Press.

Gordon-Larsen, P., McMurray, R. G., & Popkin, B. M. (2000). Determinants of adolescent physical activity and inactivity patterns. *Pediatrics, 105,* E83.

Gramann, J. H. (1996). *Ethnicity, race, and outdoor recreation: A review of trends, policy, and research.* Miscellaneous Paper R-96-1. Vicksburg, MS: U.S. Army Engineer Waterways Experiment Station.

Gramann, J. H., Floyd., M. F., & Saenz, R. (1993). Outdoor recreation and Mexican American ethnicity: A benefits perspective. In A. W. Ewert., D. J. Chavez, & A. W. Magill (Eds.), *Culture, conflict, and communication in the wildland-urban interface* (pp. 69-85). Boulder, CO: Westview Press.

Grieco, E. M., & Cassidy, R. C. (2000). Overview of race and Hispanic origin. Census 2000 Brief. Retrieved February 9, 2011, from www.census.gov/prod/2001pubs/cenbr01-1.pdf.

Herrera-Sobek, M. (2006). *Chicano folklore: A handbook.* Westport, CT: Greenwood Press.

Hutchison, R. (1987). Ethnicity and urban recreation: Whites, Blacks, and Hispanics in Chicago's public parks. *Journal of Leisure Research, 19,* 205-222.

Hutchison, R., & Fidel, K. (1984). Mexican-American recreation activities: A reply to McMillen. *Journal of Leisure Research, 16,* 344-349.

Irwin, P. N., Gartner, W. C., & Phelps, C. C. (1990). Mexican-American/Anglo cultural differences as recreation style determinants. *Leisure Sciences, 12,* 335348.

Juniu, S. (2000). The impact of immigration: Leisure experience in the lives of South Americans immigrants. *Journal of Leisure Research, 32*(3), 358-381.

Kirschner, L. A. (2005). Machismo. In I. Stavans & H. Augenbraum (Eds.), *Encyclopedia Latina. History, culture, and society in the United States.* Danbury, CT: Scholastic Library.

Lynch, B. D. (1983). The garden and the sea: U.S. Latino environmental discourse and mainstream environmentalism. *Social Problems, 40,* 108-124.

Massey, D. S., Durand, J., & Malone, N. J. (2003). *Beyond smoke and mirrors: Mexican immigration in an era of economic integration.* New York: Russell Sage Foundation.

McCarthy, M. C., Ruiz, E., Gale, B., Karam, C., & Moore, N. (2004). The meaning of health: Perspectives of Anglo and Latino older women. *Health Care for Women International, 25,* 950-969.

McMillen, J. (1983). The social organization of leisure among Mexican-Americans. *Journal of Leisure Research, 15,* 164-173.

Moore, L. V., Roux, A. V., Evenson, K. R., McGinn, A. P., & Brines, S. J. (2008). Availability of recreational resources in minority and low socioeconomic status areas. *American Journal of Preventive Medicine, 34,* 16-22.

Niemeyer, A. E., Wong, M. M., & Westerhaus, K. J. (2009). Parental involvement, familismo, and academic performance in Hispanic and Caucasian adolescents. *North American Journal of Psychology, 11,* 613-631.

Noe, F. P., & Snow, R. (1990). Hispanic cultural influence on environmental concern. *Journal of Environmental Education, 21,* 27-34.

Oh, C., & Ditton, R. B. (2009). Toward an understanding of racial and ethnic differences in conservation attitudes among recreation participants. *Leisure Sciences, 31,* 53-67.

O'Reilly Herrera, A. (2007). *Cuba: Idea of a nation displaced.* Albany, NY: State University of New York Press.

Paris, M. L. (2002). *Embracing America: A Cuban exile comes of age.* Gainesville, FL: University Press of Florida.

Passel, J. S., Livingston, G., & Cohn, D. (2012). Explaining why minority births now outnumber white births. PEW Research Center Social & Demographic Trends. www.pewsocialtrends.org/2012/05/17/explaining-why-minority-births-now-outnumber-white-births/?src=hispanic-footer.

Perez, R. (2005). Cuban Americans. In I. Stavans & H. Augenbraum (Eds.), *Encyclopedia Latina. History, culture, and society in the United States.* Danbury, CT: Scholastic Library.

Pew Hispanic Center. (2009). Mexican immigrants: How many come? How many leave? A report by Jeffrey Passel and D'Vera Cohn. Retrieved January 7, 2011, from http://pewhispanic.org/reports/report.php?ReportID=112.

Pfister, R. E., & Ewert, A. (1993). Ethnicity and environmental concerns of forest visitors. *Proceedings of the 1993 NRPA Leisure Research Symposium.* San Jose, CA, National Recreation and Park Association.

Poyo, G. E. (2005). Cuban Americans. In S. Oboler & D. J. Gonzales (Eds.), *The Oxford encyclopedia of Latinos and Latinas in the United States.* Oxford, New York: Oxford University Press.

Purnell, L. D., & Paulanka, B. J. (2003). *Transcultural health care: A culturally competent approach* (2nd ed.). Philadelphia: Davis.

Ruiz, V. L., & Sanchez, V. (2006). *Latinas in the United States: A historical encyclopedia.* Bloomington, IN: Indiana University Press.

Sabogal, F., Marín, G., Otero-Sabogal, R., Marín, B., & Perez-Stable, E. J. (1987). Hispanic familism and acculturation: What changes and what doesn't? *Hispanic Journal of Behavioral Sciences, 9,* 397-412.

Saenz, R. (1991). Intergenerational migration patterns of Chicanos: The core, periphery, and frontier. *Social Science Quarterly, 72,* 135-148.

Santiago-Rivera, A. (2005). Marianismo. In I. Stavans & H. Augenbraum (Eds.), *Encyclopedia Latina. History, culture, and society in the United States.* Danbury, CT: Scholastic Library.

Schultz, P. W., Unipan, J. B., & Gamba, R. J. (2000). Acculturation and ecological worldview among Latino Americans. *Journal of Environmental Education, 31,* 22-27.

Shaull, S. L. (1993). *Family-related and nature-related recreation benefits among Anglo Americans and Hispanic Americans: A study of acculturation and primary structural assimilation*. Unpublished MS thesis, Texas A&M University, Department of Recreation, Park and Tourism Sciences, College Station.

Shaull, S. L., & Gramann, J. H. (1998). The effect of cultural assimilation on the importance of family-related and nature-related recreation among Hispanic Americans. *Journal of Leisure Research, 30*, 47-63.

Steidel, A. G., & Contreras, J. M. (2003). A new familism scale for use with Latino populations. *Hispanic Journal of Behavioral Sciences, 25*, 312-330.

Stodolska, M., Acevedo, J. C., & Shinew, K. J. (2009). Gangs of Chicago: Perceptions of crime and its effect on the recreation behavior of Latino residents in urban communities. *Leisure Sciences, 31*, 466-482.

Stodolska, M., & Santos, C. A. (2006a). "You must think of *familia*": The everyday life of Mexican migrants in destination communities. *Social and Cultural Geography, 7*, 627-647.

Stodolska, M., & Santos, C. A. (2006b). Transnationalism and leisure: Mexican temporary migrants in the United States. *Journal of Leisure Research, 38*, 143-167.

Stodolska, M., & Shinew, K. J. (2010). Environmental constraints on leisure time physical activity among Latino urban residents. *Qualitative Research in Sport and Exercise, 2*, 313-335.

Stodolska, M., Shinew, K. J., Acevedo, J. C., & Izenstark, D. (2011). Perceptions of urban parks as havens and contested terrains by Mexican-Americans in Chicago neighborhoods. *Leisure Sciences, 33*, 103-126.

Stodolska, M., Shinew, K. J., Acevedo, J. C., & Roman, C. G. (2013). "I was born in the hood": Fear of crime, outdoor recreation and physical activity among Mexican-American urban adolescents. *Leisure Sciences, 35*, 1-15.

Stodolska, M., Shinew, K. J., & Li., M. Z. (2010). Recreation participation patterns and physical activity among Latino visitors to three urban outdoor recreation environments. *Journal of Park and Recreation Administration, 28*, 36-56.

Tann, S. S. (2005). Implications for quality of life research on Latino populations. *Journal of Transcultural Nursing, 16*(2), 136-141.

Taylor, W. C., & Lou, D. (2011). Do all children have places to be active? Disparities in access to physical activity environments in racial and ethnic minority and lower-income communities. Research Synthesis, Active Living Research. www.casaferoutestoschool.org/wp-content/uploads/2011/05/Synthesis_Taylor-Lou_Disparities_Nov2011.pdf.

Thapa, B., Graefe, A. R., & Absher, J. D. (2002). Information needs and search behaviors: A comparative study of ethnic groups in the Angeles and San Bernardino National Forests, California. *Leisure Sciences, 24*, 89-107.

Tinsley, H. E. A., Tinsley, D. J., & Croskeys, C. E. (2002). Park usage, social milieu, and psychological benefits of park use reported by older urban park users from four ethnic groups. *Leisure Sciences, 24*, 199-218.

Triandis, H. D. (1989). Cross-cultural studies of individualism and collectivism. *Nebraska Symposium on Motivation, 37*, 41-133.

Vazquez-Nuttall, E., Romero-Garcia, I., & de Leon, B. (1987). Sex roles and perceptions of femininity and masculinity of Hispanic women. *Psychology of Women Quarterly, 11*, 409-425.

Vigil, J. D. (1998). *From Indians to Chicanos: The dynamics of Mexican-American culture*. Long Grove, IL: Waveland Press.

Walker, G., & Wirden, R. J. (1992). Ethnic group membership, value orientations and leisure participation patterns. *Proceedings of the 1992 NRPA Leisure Research Symposium*. Cincinnati, OH: National Recreation and Park Association.

Welch, S., Comer, J., & Steinman, M. (1973). Some social and attitudinal correlates of health care among Mexican Americans. *Journal of Health and Social Behavior, 14*, 205.

Wolch, J., Wilson, J. P., & Fehrenbach, J. (2005). Parks and parks funding in Los Angeles: An equity mapping analysis. *Urban Geography, 26*, 4-35.

Zinn, M. B. (1982). Familism among Chicanos: A theoretical review. *Humboldt Journal of Social Relations, 10*, 224-238.

CHAPTER 6

Afable-Munsuz, A., Ponce, N. A., Rodriguez, M., & Perez-Stable, E. J. (2010). Immigrant generation and physical activity among Mexican, Chinese & Filipino adults in the U.S. *Social Science & Medicine, 70*(12), 1997-2005.

Ajzen, I. (1991). The theory of planned behavior. *Organizational Behavior and Human Decision Process, 50*, 179-211.

Allison, M. T., & Geiger, C. W. (1993). Nature of leisure activities among the Chinese-American elderly. *Leisure Sciences, 15*(4), 309-319.

Ap, J. (2002). *Inter-cultural behavior: Some glimpses of leisure from an Asian perspective*. Invited paper presented at the Leisure Futures Conference, April 11-13, 2002, Innsbruck, Austria.

Bengston, D. N., & Schermann, M. (2008). Hmong Americans: Issues and strategies related to outdoor recreation. In M. T. Allison & I. E. Schneider (Eds.), *Diversity and the recreation profession: Organizational perspectives* (pp. 19-24). State College, PA: Venture.

Berry, J. W., Poortinga, Y. H., Segall, M. H., & Dasen, P. R. (2002). *Cross-cultural psychology: Research and application* (2nd ed.). Cambridge: Cambridge University Press.

Bowring, P. (1987, February). What is "Asia"? *Far Eastern Economic Review, 135*(7). http://afe.easia.columbia.edu/geography/geo_whatis.html.

Burgess, J. S. (1909). *A study of the characteristics of the Cantonese merchants in Chinatown, New York, as shown by their use of leisure time*. Unpublished master's dissertation, Columbia University, New York.

Cheng, D. T. (1948). *Acculturation of the Chinese in the United States: A Philadelphia study*. Unpublished doctoral dissertation, University of Pennsylvania, Philadelphia.

Cities of Migration. (n.d.). Hockey night in Canada – In Punjabi! http://citiesofmigration.ca/good_idea/hockey-night-in-canada-in-punjabi/.

Crawford, D., Jackson, E. L., & Godbey, G. (1991). A hierarchical model of leisure constraints. *Leisure Sciences, 13,* 309-320.

Csikszentmihalyi, M. (1975). *Beyond boredom and anxiety.* San Francisco: Jossey-Bass.

Deci, L., & Ryan, M. (2000). The "what" and "why" of goal pursuits: Human needs and the self-determination of behaviour. *Psychological Inquiry, 11*(4), 227-268.

Deng, J., Walker, G. J., & Swinnerton, G. (2005). Leisure attitudes: A comparison between Anglo-Canadians and Chinese in Canada. *Leisure/Loisir, 29*(2), 239-273.

Dong, E., & Yi-Kook, J. (Eds.). (2010). *Korean leisure from tradition to modernity.* Jaipur, India: Rawat.

Emery, L. (1984, March-April). *Games and sport of Southern California's Chinese-Americans.* Paper presented at the annual convention of the American Alliance for Health, Physical Education, Recreation and Dance, Anaheim, CA.

Emmerson, D. K. (1984). "Southeast Asia": What's in a name? *Journal of Southeast Asian Studies, 15*(1), 1-21.

Friesen, J., & Perreaux, L. (2010, May 21). New Canadians find common ground on the ice. *The Globe and Mail,* A1, A10.

Fuligni, A., & Masten, C. L. (2010). Daily family interactions among young adults in the United States from Latin American, Filipino, East Asian, and European backgrounds. *International Journal of Behavioural Development, 34*(6), 491-499.

Gao, G., Ting-Toomey, S., & Gudykunst, W. B. (1996). Chinese communication processes. In M. H. Bond (Ed.), *The handbook of Chinese psychology* (pp. 280-293). Hong Kong: Oxford University Press.

Gregory, S. (2009, December 31). Harvard's hoops star is Asian. Why's that a problem? *Time.* www.time.com/time/printout/0,8816,1951044,00.html.

Hall, M. H., & Rhyne, D. (1989). *Leisure behavior and recreation needs of Ontario's ethnocultural populations.* Toronto: Ministry of Tourism and Recreation.

Heo, J., & Lee, Y. (2007). "I don't want to feel like a stranger": Korean students who play basketball seriously. *Leisure/Loisir, 31*(1), 133-154.

Hirschman, E. (1982). Ethnic variation in hedonic consumption. *Journal of Social Psychology, 118*(2), 225-234.

Ho, C., & Card, J. A. (2001). Older Chinese women immigrants and their leisure experiences: Before and after emigration to the United States. In S. Todd (Ed.), *Proceedings of the 2001 Northeastern Recreation Research Symposium* (pp. 291-297). New York: State University of New York.

Hung, K. (2003). *Achieving cultural diversity in wilderness recreation: A study of the Chinese in Vancouver.* Unpublished master's thesis, University of Waterloo, Waterloo, ON.

Iso-Ahola, S. (1999). Motivational foundations of leisure. In E. Jackson & T. Burton (Eds.), *Leisure studies: Prospects for the twenty-first century* (pp. 35-51). State College, PA: Venture.

Kang, D. S., & Davenport, L. (2009). Strategic communication in multicultural markets: Korean and American cultural differences toward leisure. *International Journal of Strategic Communication, 3,* 249-267.

Kim, E., Kleiber, D. A., & Kropf, N. (2001). Leisure activity, ethnic preservation, and cultural integration of older Korean Americans. *Journal of Gerontological Social Work, 36*(1/2), 107-129.

Kim, J. (2012). Exploring the experience of intergroup contact and the value of recreation activities in facilitating positive intergroup interactions of immigrants. *Leisure Sciences, 34,* 72-87.

Kleiber, D., Walker, G. J., & Mannell, R. (2011). *A social psychology of leisure* (2nd ed.). State College, PA: Venture.

Kwong, P. (1987). *The new Chinatown.* American Century Series. New York: Noonday Press.

Lee, J., Oh, S. S., & Shim, J. M. (2000). The meaning of leisure: Conceptual differences between Americans and Koreans. *Proceedings of the 2000 Northeastern Recreation Research Symposium.* Gen. Tech. Rep. NE-276 (pp. 145-149). Newtown Square, PA: USDA Forest Service, Northeastern Research Station.

Lee, M. K. (2005). Pre- and post-retirement leisure in South Korea and the implications for life satisfaction. *World Leisure, 4,* 23-31.

Lewin, K. (1951). *Field theory in social science: Selected theoretical papers.* New York: Harper & Row.

Li, H., & Chick, G. (2007). A comparison of the leisure lifestyles of Chinese and American graduate students at the Pennsylvania State University. *Proceedings of the 2006 Northeastern Recreation Research Symposium.* Gen. Tech. Rep. NRS-P-14 (pp. 442-446). Newtown Square, PA: USDA Forest Service, Northern Research Station.

Li, M. Z., & Stodolska, M. (2006). Transnationalism, leisure, and Chinese graduate students in the United States. *Leisure Sciences, 28,* 39-55.

Li, P. S. (1998). *The Chinese in Canada* (2nd ed.). Toronto: Oxford University Press.

Lin, Y. (2010). *Predicting Chinese Canadians' visitation to local and distant parks.* Unpublished master's thesis, University of Alberta, Edmonton.

Liu, H., Yeh, C. K., Chick, G. E., & Zinn, H. C. (2008). An exploration of meanings of leisure: A Chinese perspective. *Leisure Sciences, 30*(5), 482-488.

Manfredo, M. J., Driver, B. L., & Tarrant, M. A. (1996). Measuring leisure motivation: A meta-analysis of the recreation experience preference scale. *Journal of Leisure Research, 28,* 188-213.

Muller, C. (2005). *The analects of Confucius.* www.acmuller.net/con-dao/analects.html.

Neulinger, J. (1974). *The psychology of leisure.* Springfield, IL: Charles C Thomas.

Pew Research Center. (2012, June 19). *The rise of Asian Americans. Pew Social & Demographic Trends.* Washington, DC. www.pewsocialtrends.org/2012/06/19/the-rise-of-asian-americans/.

Qin, D. B., Way, N., & Rana, M. (2008). The "model minority" and their discontent: Examining peer discrimination and harassment of Chinese American immigrant youth. In H. Yoshikawa & N. Way (Eds.), Beyond the family: Contexts of immigrant children's development. *New Directions for Child and Adolescent Development, 121,* 27-42.

Sasidharan, V., Willits, F., & Godbey, G. (2005). Cultural differences in urban recreation patterns: An examination of park usage and activity participation across six population subgroups. *Managing Leisure, 10,* 19-38.

Shaw, S. (1984). The measurement of leisure: A quality of life issue. *Loisir et Société/Society and Leisure, 7,* 91-107.

Spiers, A., & Walker, G. J. (2009). The effects of ethnicity and leisure satisfaction on happiness, peacefulness, and quality of life. *Leisure Sciences, 31,* 84-99.

Stack, J. A. C., & Iwasaki, Y. (2009). The role of leisure pursuits in adaptation processes among Afghan refugees who have immigrated to Winnipeg, Canada. *Leisure Studies, 28*(3), 239-259.

Statistics Canada. (2006). 2006 Census dictionary (Cat. No. 92-566-X). www12.statcan.gc.ca/census-recensement/2006/ref/dict/pdf/92-566-eng.pdf.

Statistics Canada. (2010). Projections of the diversity of the Canadian population, 2006 to 2031 (Cat. No. 91-551-X). www.statcan.gc.ca/pub/91-551-x/91-551-x2010001-eng.pdf.

Statistics Canada. (2013). 2011 National household survey: Data tables: Visible minority. www12.statcan.gc.ca/nhs-enm/2011/dp-pd/dt-td/Rp-eng.cfm?LANG=E&APATH=3&DETAIL=0&DIM=0&FL=A&FREE=0&GC=0&GID=0&GK=0&GRP=1&PID=105392&PRID=0&PTYPE=105277&S=0&SHOWALL=0&SUB=0&Temporal=2013&THEME=95&VID=0&VNAMEE=&VNAMEF=.

Stebbins, R. A. (1992). *Amateurs, professionals, and serious leisure.* Montreal: McGill-Queen's University Press.

Stodolska, M. (2008). Adaptation challenges among adolescent immigrants from Korea, Mexico, and Poland. *Journal of Immigrant and Refugee Studies, 6*(2), 197-229.

Stodolska, M. (2010). Korean leisure and leisure constraints. In E. Dong & J. Yi-Kook (Eds.), *Korean leisure from tradition to modernity* (pp. 231-252). Jaipur, India: Rawat.

Stodolska, M., & Alexandris, K. (2004). The role of recreational sport in the adaptation of first generation immigrants in the United States. *Journal of Leisure Research, 36*(3), 379-413.

Stodolska, M., & Walker, G. J. (2007). Ethnicity and leisure: Historical development, current status, and future directions. *Leisure/Loisir, 31,* 3-26.

Stodolska, M., & Yi, J. (2003). Impacts of immigration on ethnic identity and leisure behavior of adolescent immigrants from Korea, Mexico, and Poland. *Journal of Leisure Research, 35*(1), 49-79.

Tafarodi, R., Lo, C., Yamaguchi, S., Lee, W., & Katsura, H. (2004). The inner self in three countries. *Journal of Cross-Cultural Psychology, 35,* 97-117.

Tirone, S. (2000). Racism, indifference, and the leisure experience of South Asian Canadian teens. *Leisure/Loisir, 24,* 89-114.

Tirone, S., & Goodberry, A. (2011). Leisure, biculturalism, and second-generation Canadians. *Journal of Leisure Research, 43,* 427-444.

Tirone, S. C., & Shaw, S. M. (1997). At the center of their lives: Indo Canadian women, their families and leisure. *Journal of Leisure Research, 29*(2), 225-244.

Tsai, E. H. (2000). The influence of acculturation on perception of leisure constraints of Chinese immigrants. *World Leisure, 42*(4), 33-42.

Tsai, J., Knutson, B., & Fung, H. (2006). Cultural variation in affect valuation. *Journal of Personality and Social Psychology, 90,* 288-307.

United Nations. (2013). *Composition of macro geographical (continental) regions, geographical sub-regions, and selected economic and other groupings.* http://unstats.un.org/unsd/methods/m49/m49regin.htm.

U.S. Census Bureau. (2001). *The white population: 2000.* www.census.gov/prod/2001pubs/c2kbr01-4.pdf.

U.S. Census Bureau. (2007). *The American community—Asians: 2004.* www.census.gov/prod/2007pubs/acs-05.pdf.

U.S. Census Bureau. (2008). *An older and more diverse nation by midcentury.* www.census.gov/newsroom/releases/archives/population/cb08-123.html.

U.S. Census Bureau. (2011). *Profile America: Facts for features: Asian/Pacific American Heritage Month: May 2011.* www.census.gov/newsroom/releases/archives/facts_for_features_special_editions/cb11-ff06.html.

Walker, G. (2008). The effects of ethnicity and gender on facilitating intrinsic motivation during leisure with a close friend. *Journal of Leisure Research, 40*(2), 200-311.

Walker, G. J., & Deng, J. (2003/2004). Comparing leisure as a subjective experience with the Chinese experience of *rùmí. Leisure/Loisir, 28*(3-4), 245-276.

Walker, G. J., Deng, J., & Dieser, R. B. (2001). Ethnicity, acculturation, self-construal, and motivations for outdoor recreation. *Leisure Sciences, 23*(4), 263-283.

Walker, G. J., Halpenny, E., & Deng, J. (2011). Leisure satisfaction and acculturative stress: The case of Chinese-Canadian immigrants. *Journal of Leisure Research, 43,* 226-245.

Walker, G. J., & Wang, X. (2009). The meaning of leisure for Chinese/Canadians. *Leisure Sciences, 31,* 1-18.

Wang, J., & Stringer, L. A. (2000). The impact of Taoism on Chinese leisure. *World Leisure, 42*(3), 33-41.

Winter, P. L., Jeong, W. C., & Godbey, G. C. (2004). Outdoor recreation among Asian Americans: A case study of San Francisco Bay area residents. *Journal of Park and Recreation Administration, 22*(3), 114-136.

Wong, M. (2006). Chinese Americans. In P. G. Min (Ed.), *Asian Americans: Contemporary trends and issues* (2nd ed., pp. 110-145). Thousand Oaks, CA: Pine Forge.

Xiao, H. (1997). Tourism and leisure in China: A tale of two cities. *Annals of Tourism Research, 24*(2), 357-370.

Yu, P., & Berryman, D. L. (1996). The relationship among self-esteem, acculturation, and recreation participation of recently arrived Chinese immigrant adolescents. *Journal of Leisure Research, 28*(4), 251-273.

Zhang, T., & Gobster, P. H. (1998). Leisure preferences and open space needs in an urban Chinese-American community. *Journal of Architectural Planning and Research, 15*(4), 338-355.

CHAPTER 7

Ackerman, W. V. (2009). Indian gaming in South Dakota: Conflict in public policy. *American Indian Quarterly, 33*(2), 253-279.

Aikenhead, G. (2011). *Bridging cultures: Scientific and Indigenous ways of knowing nature.* Toronto: Pearson Canada.

Alvord, L. A. (1999). *The scalpel and the silver bear: The first Navajo woman surgeon combines western medicine and traditional healing.* New York: Bantam Books.

Anderson, J., Perry, J., Blue, C., Browne, A., Henderson, A., Khan, K. B., Kirkham, S. R., Lynam, J., Semeniuk, P., & Smye, V. (2003). Rewriting cultural safety within the postcolonial and postnational feminist project: Toward new epistemologies of healing. *Advances in Nursing Science, 26*(3), 196-214.

Andrews, T. J., & Olney, J. (2007). Potlatch and powwow: Dynamics of culture through lives lived dancing. *American Indian Culture and Research Journal, 31*(1), 63-108.

Anzaldua, G. E. (1999). *Borderlands/La Frontera: The New Mestiza.* San Francisco: Aunt Lute Books.

Balsdon, J. P. V. D. (2002). *Life and leisure in ancient Rome.* London: Phoenix Press.

Barnhardt, R. (2008). Indigenous knowledge systems and higher education: Preparing Alaska Native PhDs for leadership roles in research. *Canadian Journal of Native Education, 31*(2), 154-174.

Barnhardt, R., & Kawagley, A. O. (2005). Indigenous knowledge systems/Alaska Native ways of knowing. *Anthropology and Education Quarterly, 36*(1), 8-23. www.ankn.uaf.edu//curriculum//Articles//BarnhardtKawagley//Indigenous_Knowledge.html.

Bartlett, J., Iwasaki, Y., Gottlieb, B., Hall, D., & Mannell, R. (2007). Framework for Aboriginal guided decolonizing research involving Metis and First Nations persons with diabetes. *Social Science & Medicine, 65,* 2371-2382.

Baskin, C., Koleszar-Green, R., Hendry, J., Lavallée, L., & Murrin, J. (2008). We pass the talking stick to you: Forming alliances and identities in the academy. *Canadian Journal of Native Education, 31*(1), 89-106.

Bates, L., Bean, R., Ching, K., Dieser, R., Eads, L., Fox, K., Kahakalau, K., Kakalia, M., Lindsey, L., Puhi, A., Puhi, K., & Rundle, K. (2002). Native Hawaiian ways of knowing, project-approach learning, and leisure education. In N. McIntyre (Ed.), *Proceedings from the Pacific-Rim Education Conference* (CD). Presented at Tokai University, Tokyo, Japan, and at the University of Waikato, New Zealand.

Battiste, M. (1998). Enabling the autumn seed: Toward a decolonized approach to Aboriginal knowledge, language, and education. *Canadian Journal of Native Education, 22*(1), 16-27.

Battiste, M. (2000). *Protecting Indigenous knowledge and heritage: A global challenge.* Saskatoon, SK: Purich.

Benoit, C., Carroll, D., & Chaudhry, M. (2003). In search of a healing place: Aboriginal women in Vancouver's downtown eastside. *Social Science & Medicine, 56,* 821-833.

Brant, C. C. (1990). Native ethics and rules of behaviour. *Canadian Journal of Psychiatry, 35*(6), 534-439.

Briggs, J., & Sharp, J. (2004). Indigenous knowledges and development: A postcolonial caution. *Third World Quarterly,* 661-676.

Brown, J. E. (1976). The roots of renewal. In W. Capps (Ed.), *Seeing with a Native eye* (pp. 25-34). Salt Lake City: University of Utah Press.

Browne, A. J., Smye, V. L., & Varcoe, C. (2005). The relevance of postcolonial theoretical perspectives to research in Aboriginal health. *Canadian Journal of Nursing Research, 37*(4), 16-37.

Burnham, P. (2000). *Indian country, God's country: Native Americans and the national parks.* Washington, DC: Island Press.

Butler, R., & Hinch, T. (Eds.). (2007). *Tourism and Indigenous peoples: Issues and implications.* Oxford, UK: Butterworth-Heinemann.

Cajete, G. (2000). *Native science: Natural laws of interdependence.* Santa Fe, NM: Clear Light.

Cajete, G. (2005). *Spirit of the game: An indigenous wellspring.* Albuquerque, NM: Kivaki Press.

Cardinal, L. (2002, October). *Applied Aboriginal/Indigenous perspectives on leadership and community decision making.* Paper presented at the Alberta Parks and Recreation annual conference, Red Deer, AB.

Chick, G. (1998). Leisure and culture: Issues for an anthropology of leisure. *Journal of Leisure Sciences, 20*(3), 111-121.

Coffman, T. (2009). *Nation within: The history of the American occupation of Hawai'i* (Rev. ed.). Kihei, HI: Koa Books.

Cohen, K. (2002). A mutually comprehensible world? Native Americans, Europeans, and play in eighteenth-century America. *American Indian Quarterly, 26*(1), 67-93.

Colchester, M. (2004). Conservation policy and Indigenous peoples. *Cultural Survival Quarterly, 28,* 17-22.

Cordell, K. H. (1999). *Outdoor recreation in American life: A national assessment of demand and supply trends.* Champaign, IL: Sagamore.

Cronon, W. (1996). The trouble with wilderness; or, getting back to the wrong Nature. *Environmental History, 1*(1), 7-55.

Culin, S. (1898). American Indian games. *Journal of American Folklore,* 245-252.

Culin, S. (1899). Hawaiian games. *American Anthropologist, 1*(2), 643-656.

Culin, S. (1903). American Indian games. *American Anthropologist, 5,* 58-64.

Culin, S. (1907). *24th annual report of the Bureau of American Ethnology: Games of North American Indians.* Washington, DC: U.S. Government Printing Office. (Rev. ed. 1975 by Dover; Rev. ed. 1994 by University of Nebraska Press.)

Cushing, F. H. (1896). *Outlines of Zuñi creation myths. Report of the Bureau of American Ethnology for the years 1891-1892,* No. 13. Washington, DC: Smithsonian Institution.

Davis, L. (2009). The high stakes of protecting Indigenous homelands: Coastal First Nation turning point initiative and environmental groups on the B.C. coast. *International Journal of Canadian Studies, 39*(4), 137-159.

Dell, C. A., Chalmers, D., Dell, D., Sauve, E., & MacKinnon, T. (2008). Horse as healer: An examination of equine assisted learning in the healing of First Nations youth from solvent abuse. *Pimatisiwin: A Journal of Aboriginal and Indigenous Community Health, 6*(1), 81-106.

Deloria, V. (1992). Prospects for restoration of tribal lands. *Restoration and Management Notes, 10,* 48-58.

Deloria, V. (2003). *God is red* (Rev. ed.). Golden, CO: Fulcrum.

Denevan, W. M. (1992). The pristine myth: The landscape of the Americas in 1492. *Annals of the Association of American Geographers, 82,* 369-385.

Denzin, N. K., Lincoln, Y. S., & Smith, L. T. (2008). *Handbook of critical and indigenous methodologies.* Los Angeles: Sage.

DeRenne, C., Maeda, J. K., Chai, D. X., Ho, K., Kaluhio-kalani, N., & Braun, K. L. (2008). Afterschool physical activity program to reduce obesity-related cancer risk: A feasibility study. *Journal of Cancer Education 23*(4), 230-234.

Deyhle, D. (1998). From break dancing to heavy metal: Navajo youth, resistance, and identity. *Youth & Society, 30*(1), 3-31.

Dimitriadis, G. (2001a). Coming clean at the hyphen: Ethics and dialogue at a local community center. *Qualitative Inquiry, 7*(5), 578-597.

Dimitriadis, G. (2001b). "In the clique": Popular culture, constructions of place, and the everyday lives of urban youth. *Anthropology and Education Quarterly, 32*(1), 29-51.

Dowsley, M. (2009). Inuit-organised polar bear sport hunting in Nunavut territory, Canada. *Journal of Ecotourism, 8*(2), 161-175.

Dustin, D., Schneider, I., McAvoy, L., & Frakt, A. (2002). Cross-cultural claims on Devils Tower National Monument: A case study. *Leisure Sciences, 24,* 79-88.

Feeser, A. (2001). Real-time and digital communication in and about contested Hawaii: The public art project Historic Waikiki. http://english.chass.ncsu.edu/jouvert/v5i3/feeser.htm.

Fennell, D. A. (2008). Ecotourism and the myth of Indigenous stewardship. *Journal of Sustainable Tourism, 16*(2), 129-149.

Flood, J. P., & McAvoy, L. H. (2007a). Use of forests by North American tribal members: Traditional recreation vs. a legacy of cultural values. *Leisure/Loisir, 31*(1), 191-216.

Flood, J. P., & McAvoy, L. H. (2007b). Voices of my ancestors, their bones talk to me: How to balance US Forest Service rules and regulations with traditional values and culture of American Indians. *Human Ecology Review, 14*(1), 76-89.

Forsyth, J. (2007). Aboriginal leisure in Canada. In R. McCarville & K. MacKay (Eds.), *Leisure for Canadians* (pp. 157-163). State College, PA: Venture.

Fox, K. M. (2001). Manawa Nanea: Native Hawaiian perspectives on leisure. *2000 Symposium on Leisure Research: Book of abstracts.* Ashburn, VA: National Recreation and Park Association.

Fox, K. (2006a). Leisure and Indigenous peoples. *Leisure Studies, 25*(4), 403-409.

Fox, K. M. (2006b). Leisure and Indigenous peoples. In E. L. Jackson (Ed.), *Leisure and the quality of life: Impacts on social, economic and cultural development Hangzhou consensus* (pp. 179-190). Hangzhou, China: Zhejiang University Press.

Fox, K. (2007). Aboriginal peoples in North America and Euro-North American leisure. *Leisure/Loisir, 31*(1), 217-243.

Fox, K. (2010). Can you hear the music? Toward a polyphonic leisure scholarship. In K. Paisley & D. Dustin (Eds.), *Speaking up/speaking out: Addressing social and environmental injustice in the leisure services profession* (pp. 181-192). Champaign, IL: Sagamore.

Fox, K., & Klaiber, E. (2006). Listening for a leisure remix. *Leisure Sciences, 28*(5), 411-430.

Fox, K. M., & Lashua, B. D. (2010/2011). Hold gently people who create space on the margins: Urban Aboriginal-Canadian young people and hip-hop rhythms of "leisures." In H. Mair, S. M. Arai, & D. G. Reid (Eds.), *Decentering work: Critical perspectives on leisure, social policy, and human development* (pp. 229-250). Calgary, AB: University of Calgary Press.

Fox, K. M., & Lashua, B. D. (2011). Where're ya going, where ya been? Alternative leisures and Indigenous peoples. In J. Dodd & V. Sharma (Eds.), *Leisure and tourism: Cultural paradigms* (pp. 50-65). Jaipur, India: Rawat.

Friesen, J. W., & Friesen, V. L. (2008). *Western Canadian Native destiny: Complex questions on the cultural maze.* Calgary, AB: Detselig Enterprises.

Gabriel, K. (1996). *Gambler way: Indian gaming in mythology, history and archaeology in North America.* Boulder, CO: Johnson Books.

Gilbert, P. (2010). *The compassionate mind: A new approach to life's challenges.* Oakland, CA: New Harbinger.

Giles, A. R. (2004). Kevlar, Crisco, and menstruation: "Tradition" and Dene games. *Sociology of Sport Journal, 21,* 18-35.

Giles, A. R. (2008). Beyond "add women and stir": Politics, feminist development, and Dene games. *Leisure/Loisir, 32*(2), 489-512.

Giles, A. R., & Forsyth, J. (2007). On common ground: Power, knowledge and practice in the study of Aboriginal sport and recreation. *Journal of Sport and Leisure, 1*(1), 1-20.

Gladden, J. N. (1999). Bioregionalism as an Arctic wilderness idea. *Worldviews: Environment, Culture, Religion, 3*(1), 51-67.

Grande, S. (2004). *Red pedagogy: Native American social and political thought.* Lanham, MD: Rowman & Littlefield.

Greenwood, M., de Leeuw, S., & Fraser, T. N. (2008). When the politics of inclusivity become exploitative: A reflective commentary on Indigenous peoples, Indigeneity, and the academy. *Canadian Journal of Native Education, 31*(1), 198-207.

Grossman, Z. (2005). Unlikely alliances: Treaty conflicts and environmental cooperation between Native American and rural white communities. *American Indian Culture and Research Journal, 29*(4), 21-43.

Hawaiian Kingdom. (2010). The Hawaiian Kingdom. http://hawaiiankingdom.org.

Heber, R. W. (2006). Aboriginal post-secondary education: Taiwan and Canada. Aboriginal planet. Foreign Affairs and International Trade Canada. Retrieved December 28, 2010, from www.dfait-maeci.gc.ca/foreign_policy/aboriginal/resource/canada/documents/rewesley-en.asp. (page discontinued).

Heffeman, C., Herbert, C., Grams, G. D., Grzybowski, S., Wilson, M. A., Calam, B., & Brown, D. (1999). The Haida Gwaii diabetes project: Planned response activity outcomes. *Health and Social Care in the Community, 7*(6), 379-386.

Henhawk, D. A. (2009). *Aboriginal participation in sport: Critical issues of race, culture, and power.* Unpublished master's thesis, University of Waterloo, Waterloo, ON.

Henhawk, D. A. (May 19, 2010). Critical Reflections blog. https://henhawk78.wordpress.com.

Hokowhitu, B. (2009). Indigenous existentialism and the body. *Cultural Studies Review, 15*(2), 101-118.

Hokowhitu, B. (2010). A genealogy of Indigenous resistance. In B. Hokowhitu, N. Kermoal, C. Anderson, A. Petersen, M. Reilly, I. Altamirano-Jimenez, & P. Rewi (Eds.), *Indigenous identity and resistance: Researching the diversity of knowledge* (pp. 207-225). Dunedin, NZ: Otago University Press.

Hollands, R. (2004). 'Rappin' on the reservation: Canadian Mohawk youth's hybrid cultural identities. *Sociological Research Online, 9*(3). www.socresonline.org.uk/9/3/hollands.html.

Howard, J. H. (1955). The pan-Indian culture of Oklahoma. *Southwest Journal of Anthropology, 8*(5), 215-220.

Howard, J. H. (1976). The Plains gourd dance as a revitalization movement. *American Ethnologist, 3*(2), 243-259.

Hunter, L. M., Logan, J., Goulet, J. G., & Barton, S. (2006). Aboriginal healing: Regaining balance and culture. *Journal of Transcultural Nursing, 17*, 13-21.

Ingold, T. (2000). *The perception of the environment: Essays in livelihood, dwelling and skill.* London, UK: Routledge.

Ingold, T. (2005). Epilogue: Towards a politics of dwelling. *Conservation and Society, 3*(2), 501-508.

Iwasaki, Y., & Bartlett, J. G. (2006). Culturally meaningful leisure as a way of coping with stress among Aboriginal individuals with diabetes. *Journal of Leisure Research, 38*(3), 321-338.

Iwasaki, Y., Bartlett, J. G., Gottlieb, B., & Hall, D. (2009). Leisure-like pursuits as an expression of Aboriginal cultural strengths and living actions. *Leisure Sciences, 31*(2), 158-173.

Jaramillo, N., & McLaren, P. (2008). Rethinking critical pedagogy: Socialismo Nepantla and the specter of Che. In N. K. Denzen, Y. S. Lincoln, & L. T. Smith (Eds.), *Handbook of critical and Indigenous methodologies* (pp. 191-208). Oakland, CA: Sage.

Johnston, R., Hixon, K., & Anton, V. (2009). The never-ending circle of life: Native American hoop dancing from its origin to the present day. *Journal of Physical Education, Recreation and Dance, 80*(6), 21-30.

Kauanui, J. K. (2008). Colonialism in equality: Hawaiian sovereignty and the question of U.S. civil rights. *South Atlantic Quarterly, 107*(4), 635-650.

Keller, R., & Turek, M. (1998). *American Indians and national parks.* Tucson, AZ: University of Arizona Press.

Kidani, L. (2006). *Native Hawaiian legal research guide.* Honolulu: William S. Richardson School of Law, Center for Excellence in Native Hawaiian Law.

Kirk, A., & De Feo, P. (2007). Strategies to enhance compliance to physical activity for patients with insulin resistance. *Applied Physiology, Nutrition, and Metabolism, 32*(3), 549-556.

Kovach, M. (2009). *Indigenous methodologies: Characteristics, conversations, and contexts.* Toronto: University of Toronto Press.

Kwaku. (1999). A global look at Indigenous hip-hop. *Billboard, 46*, 27-28.

Lai, D. (2005). Aiwaworld. *Communication Arts, 47*(5), 128-129.

Lashua, B. D. (2005). *Making music, re-making leisure in The Beat of Boyle Street.* Unpublished doctoral dissertation, University of Alberta, Edmonton, AB.

Lashua, B. (2006a). "Just another Native"? Soundscapes, chorasters, and borderlands in Edmonton, Alberta, Canada. *Cultural Studies <=> Critical Methodologies, 6*(3), 391-410.

Lashua, B. (2006b). The arts of the remix: Ethnography and rap. *Anthropology Matters, 8*(2). www.anthropologymatters.com/journal/2006-2/lashua_2006_the.htm.

Lashua, B. (2010). (Re)percussions: Addressing social injustice through popular music and youth leisure. In K. Paisley & D. Dustin (Eds.), *Speaking up/speaking out: Addressing social and environmental injustice in the leisure services profession* (pp. 73-82). Champaign, IL: Sagamore.

Lashua, B., & Fox, K. (2006). Rec needs a new rhythm cuz rap is where we're livin'. *Leisure Sciences, 28*(3), 267-283.

Lashua, B., & Fox, K. (2007). Defining the groove: From remix to research in The Beat of Boyle Street. *Leisure Sciences, 29*(2), 143-158.

Lashua, B., & Kelly, J. R. (2008). Rhythms in the concrete: Re-imagining the relationships between space, race, and mediated urban youth cultures. *Leisure/Loisir 32*(2), 461-488.

Lavallée, L. F. (2007). Physical activity and healing through the Medicine Wheel. *Pimatisiwin: A Journal of Aboriginal and Indigenous Community Health 5*(1), 127-153.

Ledogar, R. J., & Fleming, J. (2008). Social capital and resilience: A review of concepts and selected literature relevant to Aboriginal youth resilience research. *Pimatisiwin: A Journal of Aboriginal and Indigenous Community Health, 6*(2), 25-46.

Lemelin, R., & Bennett, N. (2010). The proposed Pimachiwoin Aki world heritage site project: Management and protection of Indigenous world heritage sites in a Canadian context. *Leisure/Loisir, 34*(2), 169-187.

Limerick, P. N. (1987). *The legacy of conquest.* New York: Norton.

Lowan, G. (2009). Exploring place from an Aboriginal perspective: Considerations for outdoor and environmental education. *Canadian Journal of Environmental Education, 14*, 42-58.

Mann, C. C. (2006). *1491: New revelations of the Americas before Columbus.* New York: Vintage Books.

Mason, C. C. (2004). Sound and meaning in Aboriginal tourism. *Annals of Tourism Research, 34*(4), 837-854.

Mau, M. K., Glanz, K., Severino, R., Grove, J. S., Johnson, B., & Curb, J. D. (2001). Mediators of lifestyle behavior change in Native Hawaiians. *Diabetes Care, 24*(20), 1770-1775.

McAvoy, L. (2002). American Indians, place meanings and the old/new west. *Journal of Leisure Research, 34*(4), 383-396.

McAvoy, L., McDonald, D., & Carlson, M. (2003). American Indian/First Nation place attachment to park lands: The case of the Nuu-chah-nulth of British Columbia. *Journal of Park and Recreation Administration, 21*(2), 84-104.

McAvoy, L., Shirilla, P., & Flood, J. (2004). American Indian gathering and recreation uses of national forests. In K. Bricker (Comp., Ed.), *Proceedings of the 2004 Northeastern Recreation Research Symposium.* Gen. Tech. Rep. NE-326 (pp. 81-87). Newtown Square, PA: USDA Forest Service, Northeastern Research Station.

McDonald, D., & McAvoy, L. (1997a). Native Americans and leisure: State of the research and future directions. *Journal of Leisure Research, 29*(2), 145-166.

McDonald, D., & McAvoy, L. (1997b). *Racism, recreation and Native Americans.* Paper presented at the meeting of the National Recreation and Park Association Leisure Research Symposium, Salt Lake City.

McDonald, D., McDonald, T., & McAvoy, L. (2000). Tribal wilderness research needs and issues in the United States and Canada. In D. N. Cole & S. F. McCool, *Proceedings: Wilderness science in a time of change* (pp. 290-294). Proc. RMRS-P-000. Ogden, UT: USDA Forest Service, Rocky Mountain Research Station.

Meyer, M. (2003). *Ho'oulu: Our time of becoming: Hawaiian epistemology and early writings.* Honolulu: Ai Pohaku Press.

Mihesuah, D. A., & Wilson, A. C. (Eds.). (2004). *Indigenizing the academy: Transforming scholarship and empowering communities.* Lincoln, NE: University of Nebraska Press.

Mitchell, T. (2000). Doin' damage in my native language: The use of "resistance vernaculars" in hip hop in France, Italy, and Aotearoa/New Zealand. *Popular Music and Society, 24*(3), 41-54.

Mokuau, N. (2002). Culturally based interventions for substance use and child abuse among Native Hawaiians. *Public Health Reports, 117*(3, Suppl. 1), S82-87.

Momper, S. L. (2010). Implications of American Indian gambling for social work research and practice. *Social Work, 55*, 139-146.

Mooney, J. (1896). *The Ghost-Dance religion.* Report of the Bureau of American Ethnology, No. 19, 1897-1898. Washington, DC: Smithsonian Institution.

Mooney, J. (1898a). *Calendar history of the Kiowa Indians.* Report of the Bureau of American Ethnology, No. 19, 1897-1898. Washington, DC: Smithsonian Institution.

Mooney, J. (1898b). The Jicarilla Genesis. *American Anthropologist, 11*, 98.

Moss, L. (Ed.). (2003). *Is Canada postcolonial? Unsettling Canadian literature.* Waterloo, ON: Wilfrid Laurier University Press.

Mowforth, M., & Mont, I. (2005). *Tourism and sustainability: Development and new tourism in the Third World.* London, UK: Routledge.

Mullins, P. (2009). Living stories of the landscape: Perception of place through canoeing in Canada's north. *Tourism Geographies, 11*(2), 235-255.

Mullins, P. (2011). *A phenomenological approach to the role of canoe tripping in mediating environmental meaning: The applicability of the dwelling perspective.* Unpublished doctoral dissertation, University of Alberta, Edmonton, AB.

Mullis, A., & Kamper, D. (Eds.). (2000). *Indian gaming: Who wins?* Los Angeles: UCLA American Indian Studies Center.

Nabokov, P. (1981). *Indian running: Native American history and tradition.* Santa Fe, NM: Ancient City Press.

Nadjiwan, S., & Blackstock, C. (2003). Caring across the boundaries: Promoting access to voluntary sector resources for First Nations children and families. First Nations Child and Family Caring Society of Canada. http://philanthropyandaboriginalpeoples.files.wordpress.com/2011/01/vsifinalreportv2-copy.pdf.

Nepal, S. K. (2004). Indigenous ecotourism in British Columbia: The potential for building capacity in the Ti'azt'en Nations territories. *Journal of Ecotourism, 3*(3), 173-194.

Newbold, K. B. (1998). Problems in search of solutions: Health and Canadian Aboriginals. *Journal of Community Health, 23*(1), 59-73.

Nogelmeier, M. P. (2010). *Mai Pa'a I Ka Leo: Historical voice in Hawaiian primary materials, looking forward and listening back.* Honolulu: Bishop Museum Press/Awaiaulu.

Notzke, C. (2004). Indigenous tourism development in Southern Alberta, Canada: Tentative engagement. *Journal of Sustainable Tourism, 12*(1), 29-54.

Oneha, M. F. M. (2002). *Ka mauli O ka 'aina a he mauli kanaka (The life of the land is the life of the people): An ethnographic study from a Hawaiian sense of place.* Doctoral dissertation, University of Colorado Health Sciences Center.

Orlowski, P. (2008). "That would be certainly be spoiling them": Liberal discourses of social studies teachers and concerns about Aboriginal students. *Canadian Journal of Native Education, 31*(2), 110-129.

Pannekoek, F. (2006). Cyber imperialism and the marginalization of Canada's Indigenous peoples. In J. Baillargeon (Ed.), *The handing down of culture, smaller societies and globalization.* Toronto: Grub Street Books.

Papps, E., & Ramsden, I. (1996). Cultural safety in nursing: The New Zealand experience. *International Journal of Qualitative Health Care, 8*(5), 491-497.

Paraschak, V. (2007). Doing race, doing gender: First Nations "sport" and gender relations. In K. Young & P. White (Eds.), *Sport and gender in Canada* (2nd ed., pp. 137-154). Don Mills, ON: Oxford University Press.

Pargee, D., Lara-Albers, E., & Puckett, K. (1999). Building on tradition: Promoting physical activity with American Indian community coalitions. *Journal of Health Education, 30,* S37-43.

Perkins, U. (2007). Pono and the Koru: Toward indigenous theory in Pacific Island literature. *Hulili: Multidisciplinary Research on Hawaiian Well-Being, 4*(1), 59-89.

Perrottet, T. (2003). *Pagan holiday: On the trail of ancient Roman tourists.* New York: Random House.

Raibmon, P. (2005). *Authentic Indians: Episodes of encounter from the late-nineteenth-century Northwest Coast.* Durham, NC: Duke University Press.

Ramsden, I. M. (2002). *Cultural safety and nursing education in Aotearoa and Te Waipounamu.* Unpublished doctoral dissertation, Victoria University of Wellington, NZ.

Redmond, L. (1996). Diverse Native American perspectives on the use of sacred areas on public lands. In B. L. Driver, D. Dustin, T. Baltic, G. Elsner, & G. Petersen (Eds.), *Nature and the human spirit: Toward an expanded land management ethic* (pp. 127-134). State College, PA: Venture.

Redwing Saunders, S. E., & Hill, S. M. (2007). Native education and in-classroom coalition-building: Factors and models in delivering an equitous authentic education. *Canadian Journal of Education, 30*(4), 1015-1045.

Rose, A., & Giles, A. R. (2007). Alberta's Future Leaders Program: A case study of Aboriginal youth and community development. *Canadian Journal of Native Studies, 27*(2), 421-446.

Rowe, S. M. (2008). We dance for knowledge. *Dance Research Journal, 40*(1), 31-44.

Royal Commission on Aboriginal Peoples. (1996). *The report of the Royal Commission on Aboriginal Peoples, Vol. 3, Gathering strength.* Ottawa: Government of Canada. www.aadnc-aandc.gc.ca/eng/1307458586498/130745 8751962.

Rutledge, R., & Vold, T. (1995). Canada's wilderness. *International Journal of Wilderness, 1*(2), 8-13.

Sai, K. (2011). *Ua Mau Ke Ea: Sovereignty endures: An overview of the political and legal history of the Hawaiian Islands.* Honolulu: Pūʻā Foundation.

Said, E. (1979). *Orientalism.* Toronto, CA: Vintage Press.

Said, E. (1994). *Culture and imperialism.* Toronto, CA: Vintage Press.

Salter, M. A. (1972). *Games in ritual: A study of selected North American Indian tribes.* Doctoral dissertation, University of Alberta.

Sanchez, J., Stucky, M. E., & Richard, M. (1998). Distance learning in Indian Country: Becoming the spider on the web. *Journal of American Education, 37*(3), 1-17.

Sanford Kanahele, G. H. (1986). *Ku Kanaka stand tall: A search for Hawaiian values.* Honolulu: University of Hawaii Press.

Schaap, J. I. (2010). The growth of the Native American gaming industry: What has the past provided, and what does the future hold? *American Indian Quarterly, 34*(3), 365-389.

Sibthorp, J. (2011, December 6). *Youth development and adventure-based recreation: Questioning research and practice.* Keynote speech at the Australia and New Zealand Leisure Association Conference 2011, Dunedin, NZ.

Smith, C., & Warke, G. K. (Eds.). (2000). *Indigenous cultures in an interconnected world.* Vancouver: University of British Columbia Press.

Smith, L. T. (1999). *Decolonizing methodologies: Research and Indigenous peoples.* London, UK: Zed Books.

Smith, L. T. (2005). On tricky ground: Researching the native in the age of uncertainty. In N. K. Denzin & Y. S. Lincoln (Eds.), *The Sage handbook of qualitative research* (3rd ed., pp. 85-107). Thousand Oaks, CA: Sage.

Statistics Canada. (2006). Aboriginal identity population by age groups, median age and sex, 2006 counts for both sexes, for Canada, provinces and territories. www12.statcan.ca/census-recensement/2006/dp-pd/hlt/97-558/pages/page.cfm?Lang=E&Geo=PR&Code=01&Table=1 &Data=Count&Sex=1&Age=1&StartRec=1&Sort=2& Display=Page.

Stoffle, R., Halmo, D., & Austin, D. (1998). Cultural landscapes and traditional cultural properties: A Southern Paiute view of the Grand Canyon and the Colorado River. *American Indian Quarterly, 21*(2), 229-247.

Swayze, N. (2009). Engaging Indigenous urban youth in environmental learning: The importance of place revisited. *Canadian Journal of Environmental Education, 14,* 59-73.

Thompson, A., Lovelock, B., & Carvalhedo Reis, A. (2011, December 8). *Maori "voices" and "adventures" in the outdoors.* Presentation at the Australia and New Zealand Leisure Association Conference 2011, Dunedin, NZ.

Torgerson, D. (1999). Images of place in green politics: The cultural mirror of indigenous traditions. In F. Fischer & M. Hajer (Eds.), *Living with nature: Environmental politics as cultural discourse* (pp. 186-203). Oxford: Oxford University Press.

Transken, S. (2005). Meaning making and methodological explorations: Bringing knowledge from British Columbia's First Nations women poets into social work courses. *Cultural Studies <=> Critical Methodologies, 5,* 3-28.

Tyler, M. E. (1993). Spiritual stewardship in aboriginal management systems. *Environments, 22,* 1-8.

Urion, C. (1991). Changing academic discourse about Native education: Using two pairs of eyes. *Canadian Journal of Native Education, 18,* 1-9.

Wall, K. (2008). Reinventing the wheel? Designing an Aboriginal recreation and community development program. *Canadian Journal of Native Education, 31*(2), 70-93.

Warry, W. (2007). *Ending denial: Understanding Aboriginal issues.* Peterborough, ON: Broadview Press.

Wheeler, W. (2002, September 25). *Indigenous knowledge in the academy.* Paper presented at the Indigenous education program seminar, Athabasca University.

Wilkinson, C. (1997). Paradise revised. In W. E. Riebsame (Ed.), *Atlas of the American west: Portrait of a changing region* (pp. 15-45). New York: Norton.

Williams, R. (1980). *Problems in materialism and culture: Selected essays.* London: Verso.

Wilson, K., & Young, T. K. (2008). An overview of Aboriginal health research in the social sciences: Current trends and future directions. *International Journal of Circumpolar Health, 67*(2-3), 179-189.

Wilson, S. (2001). What is an Indigenous research methodology? *Canadian Journal of Education, 25,* 175-179.

Wilson, S. (2008). *Research is ceremony: Indigenous research methods.* Halifax, NS: Fernwood.

Wishart Leard, D., & Lashua, B. (2006). Popular media, critical pedagogy, and inner city youth. *Canadian Journal of Education, 29*(1), 244-264.

Wutzke, J. (1997/1998). Dependent independence: Application of the Nunavut model to Native Hawaiian sovereignty and self-determination claims. *American Indian Law Review, 22*(2), 509-565. http://jstor.org/stable/20068858.

Young, T. K. (2003). Review of research on Aboriginal populations in Canada: Relevance to their health needs. *British Medical Journal, 327,* 419-422.

CHAPTER 8

Abu-Laban, S. M., & Abu-Laban, B. (1999). Teens between: The public and private spheres of Arab-Canadian adolescents. In M. W. Suleiman (Ed.), *Arabs in America: Building a new future* (pp. 113-128). Philadelphia: Temple University Press.

America.gov. (2008). Muslims in America – a statistical portrait. Retrieved May 20, 2012, from www.america.gov/st/peopleplace-english/2008/December/20081222090246jmnamdeirf0.4547083.html.

Anahalt, M. B. (1987). *The relationship between the Jewish Sabbath and stress as a function of personality type.* Unpublished PhD thesis, Hofstra University.

Anderson, S. C., & Autry, C. E. (2011). Research note: Leisure behaviour of the Amish. *World Leisure Journal, 53*(1), 57-66.

Association of Religious Data Archives. (2012a). Old Order Mennonite—number of adherents (2000). Retrieved October 23, 2012, from www.thearda.com/mapsReports/maps/map.asp?variable=326&state=101&variable2=.

Association of Religious Data Archives. (2012b). U.S. membership report: United States: Religious traditions, 2010. Retrieved June 1, 2012, from www.thearda.com/rcms2010/r/u/rcms2010_99_US_name_2010.asp.

Association of Statisticians of American Religious Bodies. (2012). U.S. Religious Census 2010: Summary findings. Retrieved June 1, 2012, from www.rcms2010.org/press_release/ACP%2020120501.pdf.

Bell, J. (2012). The world's Muslims: Unity and diversity. The PEW Forum on Religion & Public Life. Washington, DC. Retrieved February 25, 2013 from www.pewforum.org/uploadedFiles/Topics/Religious_Affiliation/Muslim/the-worlds-muslims-full-report.pdf.

Bibby, R. (2011, September 27). Project Canada Surveys Press Release: The religious situation in Canada. Retrieved June 1, 2012, from www.reginaldbibby.com/images/PCS_Release_The_Religious_Situation_in_Canada.pdf.

Bregha, F. (1991). Leisure and freedom re-examined. In T. L. Goodale & P. A. Witt (Eds.), *Recreation and leisure: Issues in an era of change* (pp. 47-54). State College, PA: Venture.

Bundt, B. A. K. (1981). *Leisure and religion: A contemporary Jewish Sabbath paradigm.* Unpublished PhD thesis, University of Minnesota.

Cainkar, L. (1999). The deteriorating ethnic safety net among Arab immigrants in Chicago. In M. W. Suleiman (Ed.), *Arabs in America: Building a new future* (pp. 192-206). Philadelphia: Temple University Press.

Carrington, B., Chievers, T., & Williams, T. (1987). Gender, leisure and sport: A case study of young people of South Asian descent. *Leisure Studies, 6,* 265-279.

CIA. The world factbook. (2013). Retrieved February 27, 2013, from https://www.cia.gov/library/publications/the-world-factbook/.

Cianflone, D. (2012). Personal communication with Dino Cianflone, General Treasurer of the Canadian Assemblies of God.

Council of American-Islamic Relations (2013). American Muslims. Retrieved February 25, 2013 from www.cair.com/american-muslims/about-islam.html.

Crabtree, R. D. (1982). *Leisure in ancient Israel.* Unpublished PhD thesis, Texas A&M University, College Station.

Dagkas, S., & Benn, T. (2006). Young Muslim women's experiences of Islam and physical education in Greece and Britain: A comparative study. *Sport, Education and Society, 11,* 21-38.

Dahl, G. (1972). *Work, play and worship in a leisure-oriented society.* Minneapolis: Augsburg.

Dahl, G. (2006). Whatever happened to the leisure revolution? In P. Heintzman, G. A. Van Andel, & T. L. Visker (Eds.), *Christianity and leisure: Issues in a pluralistic society* (Rev. ed., pp. 85-97). Sioux Center, IA: Dordt College Press.

DellaPergola, S. (2010). World Jewish population, 2010. *Current Jewish Population Reports, 2.* Berman Institute. Retrieved June 1, 2012, from www.jewishdatabank.org/Reports/World_Jewish_Population_2010.pdf.

Diddams, M., Surdyk, L. K., & Daniels, D. (2004). Rediscovering models of Sabbath keeping: Implications for psychological well-being. *Journal of Psychology and Theology, 32*(1), 3-11.

Doherty, A., & Taylor, T. (2007). Sport and physical recreation in the settlement of immigrant youth. *Leisure/Loisir, 31*(1), 27-55.

Doohan, L. (1990). *Leisure: A spiritual need.* Notre Dame, IN: Ave Maria Press.

Dravitch, R. B. (1980). *A comparison of the leisure attitudes of elderly Jews and elderly non-Jews.* Unpublished DEd thesis, University of Oregon.

Earickson, J. M. (2004). *The religious practice of the Sabbath: A framework for psychological health and spiritual well-being.* Unpublished PhD thesis, Alliant International University, San Diego.

Esposito, J. (2004). *Islam: The straight path.* (3rd ed.). New York: Oxford University Press.

Foster, R. J. (1978). *Celebration of discipline: The path to spiritual growth.* San Francisco: Harper & Row.

Fretz, W. J. (1989). *The Waterloo Mennonites: A community in paradox.* Waterloo, ON: Wilfrid Laurier University Press.

Freysinger, V. J., & Kelly, J. R. (2004). *21st century leisure: Current issues* (2nd ed.). State College, PA: Venture.

Georgeski, J. D. (1987). *Nature and differences in adjustment to and valuing the American culture among refugees from Eastern Europe, the Middle East and African countries.* PhD dissertation, United States International University.

Glyptis, S. (1985). Women as a target group: The views of the staff of Action Sport – West Midlands. *Leisure Studies, 4,* 347-362.

Goldberg, A. D. (1986). The Sabbath as dialectic: Implications for mental health. *Journal of Religion and Health, 25*(3), 237-244.

Gordis, R. (1982, Winter). The Sabbath—cornerstone and capstone of Jewish life. *Judaism, 31,* 6-11.

Grim, B. J., & Karim, M. S. (2011). The future of the global Muslim population. Projections for 2010-2030. PEW Forum on Religion & Public Life. Washington DC., Retrieved February 25, 2013 from www.pewforum.org/uploadedFiles/Topics/Religious_Affiliation/Muslim/FutureGlobalMuslimPopulation-WebPDF-Feb10.pdf.

Guttman, D. (1973). Leisure-time activity interests of Jewish aged. *Gerontologist, 13*(2), 219-223.

Haddad, Y. Y. (2011). *Becoming American?: The forging of Arab and Muslim identity in pluralist America.* Waco, TX: Baylor University Press.

Haddad, Y., & Smith, J. (1994). *Muslim communities in North America.* Albany, NY: State University of New York Press.

Hasan, A. G. (2001). *American Muslims: The new generation.* New York: Continuum International.

Hassoun, R. (1999). Arab-American health and the process of coming to America: Lessons from the metropolitan Detroit area. In M. W. Suleiman (Ed.), *Arabs in America: Building a new future* (pp. 157-176). Philadelphia: Temple University Press.

Heintzman, P. (1986). *A Christian perspective on the philosophy of leisure.* Unpublished master's thesis, Regent College, Vancouver.

Heintzman, P. (1994). *Holistic leisure: A paradigm for leisure in Christian perspective.* Paper presented at HPERD Christianity, Sport, Leisure and Wellness Conference, Grand Rapids, MI.

Heintzman, P. (2006a). Implications for leisure from a review of the biblical concepts of Sabbath and rest. In P. Heintzman, G. A. Van Andel, & T. L. Visker (Eds.), *Christianity and leisure: Issues in a pluralistic society* (Rev. ed., pp. 14-31). Sioux Center, IA: Dordt College Press.

Heintzman, P. (2006b). Listening for a leisure remix in ancient Israel and early Christianity. *Leisure Sciences, 28*(5), 431-435.

Hertzberg, A. (1997). *The Jews in America. Four centuries of an uneasy encounter: A history.* New York: Columbia University Press.

Heschel, A. J. (1951). *The Sabbath.* New York: Farrar, Straus, & Giroux.

Holmes, A. (1983). *Contours of a world view.* Grand Rapids, MI: Eerdmans.

Hothem, M. (1983). *The integration of Christian faith and leisure: A qualitative study.* Unpublished EdD dissertation, Boston University.

Ibrahim, H. (1982). Leisure and Islam. *Leisure Studies, 1,* 197-210.

Ioannides, D., & Cohen Ionannides, M. (2004). Jewish past as a "foreign country": The travel experiences of American Jews. In T. Coles & D. J. Timothy (Eds.), *Tourism, diasporas and space* (pp. 94-110). New York: Routledge.

Jewish Community Centers Association. (n.d.). About JCC Association. Retrieved September 9, 2010, from www.jcca.org/about_us.html.

Joblin, D. (2009). Leisure and spirituality: An engaged and responsible pursuit of freedom in work, play, and worship. *Leisure/Loisir, 33*(1), 95-120.

Johnston, R. K. (1983). *The Christian at play.* Grand Rapids, MI: Eerdmans.

Judaism Online. (2012). World Jewish population. Retrieved June 1, 2012, from www.simpletoremember.com/vitals/world-jewish-population.htm.

Kelly, J. R. (1987). *Freedom to be: A new sociology of religion.* New York: Macmillan.

Kraybill, D. B., Nolt, S. M., & Weaver-Zercher, D. L. (2010). *The Amish way: Patient faith in a perilous world.* San Francisco: Jossey-Bass.

Lamm, N. (n.d.). A Jewish ethic of leisure. Retrieved September 9, 2010, from www.heritage.org.il/innernet/archives/leisure1.htm.

Lee, R. (1964). *Religion and leisure in America: A study in four dimensions.* New York: Abingdon Press.

Lehman, H. (1974). *In praise of leisure.* Kitchener, ON: Herald Press.

Lincoln, C. E., & Mamiya, L. H. (1990). *The Black church in the African American experience.* Durham, NC: Duke University Press.

Livengood, J. (2004). Religion and leisure: An examination of the Assemblies of God Church. In W. T. Borrie & D. Kerstetter (Comps.), *Abstracts of the 2004 Leisure Research Symposium* (p. 23). Ashburn, VA: National Recreation and Park Association.

Livengood, J. (2009). The role of leisure in the spirituality of New Paradigm Christians. *Leisure/Loisir, 33*(1), 389-417.

Livengood, J., & Stodolska, M. (2004). The effects of discrimination and constraints negotiation on leisure behavior of American Muslims in the post-September 11 America. *Journal of Leisure Research, 36*(2), 183-208.

Lugo, L., Stencel, S., Green, J., Smith, G., Cox, D., Pond, A., Miller, T., Podrebarac, E., & Ralstohn, M. (2008). *U.S. religious landscape survey.* Pew Forum on Religion & Public Life. Washington, DC. Retrieved from http://religions.pewforum.org/pdf/report-religious-landscape-study-full.pdf.

Maqsood, R. (1994). *World faiths: Islam.* Lincolnwood, IL: NTC Publishing Group.

Martin, W. M., & Mason, S. (2004). Leisure in an Islamic context. *World Leisure Journal, 46*(1), 4-13.

Moss, R. (2007). Creating a Jewish American identity in Indianapolis: The Jewish Welfare Foundation and the regulation of leisure, 1920-1934. *Indiana Magazine of History, 103*(1), 39-65.

Neville, G. (2004). *Free time: Toward a theology of leisure.* Birmingham, UK: University of Birmingham Press.

Paloutzian, R. F. (1996). *Invitation to the psychology of religion* (pp. 6-23). Boston: Allyn & Bacon.

Pew Research Center. (2007). Muslim Americans: Middle class and mostly mainstream. Retrieved May 20, 2012, from http://pewresearch.org/pubs/483/muslim-americans.

Pew Research Center. (2009). Mapping the global Muslim population: A report on the size and distribution of the world's Muslim population. Retrieved May 20, 2012, from www.pewforum.org/newassets/images/reports/Muslimpopulation/Muslimpopulation.pdf.

Pieper, J. (1963). *Leisure: The basis of culture.* New York: New American Library.

Renard, J. (2002). *101 questions and answers on Islam.* New York: Gramercy Books.

Ryken, L. (1995). *Redeeming the time: A Christian approach to work and leisure.* Grand Rapids, MI: Baker Books.

Sachar, H. M. (1993). *A history of the Jews in America.* New York: Vintage Books.

Schulz, J., & Auld, C. (2009). A social psychological investigation of the relationship between Christianity and contemporary meanings of leisure: An Australian perspective. *Leisure/Loisir, 33*(1), 121-146.

Sfeir, L. (1985). The status of Muslim women in sport: Conflict between cultural tradition and modernization. *International Review for the Sociology of Sport, 20,* 283-305.

Shaw, S. M. (1985). The meaning of leisure in everyday life. *Leisure Sciences, 7*(1), 1-24.

Sheskin, I., & Dashevsky, A. (2011). Jewish population in the United States, 2011. *Current Jewish Population Reports, 4.* Retrieved June 1, 2012, from www.jewishdatabank.org/Reports/Jewish_Population_in_the_United_States_2011.pdf.

Shivers, J. S. (1977). The contemporary Jewish attitude towards leisure. In U. Simri (Ed.), *Physical education and sport in the Jewish history and culture. Proceedings of the Second International Seminar, July 1977* (pp. 63-69). Netanya, Israel: Wingate Institute for Physical Education and Sport.

Solomon, E. (1994). Jews and baseball: A cultural love story. In G. Eisen & D. K. Wiggins (Eds.), *Ethnicity and sport in North American history and culture* (pp. 75-101). Westport, CT: Greenwood Press.

Solomon, E. (2007). Jews, baseball, and American fictions. In P. Buhle (Ed.), *Jews and American popular culture, Vol. 3, Sports, leisure and lifestyle* (pp. 1-13). Westport, CT: Praeger.

Spence, D. (1973). *Towards a theology of leisure with special reference to creativity.* Ottawa, ON: Canadian Parks and Recreation Association.

Statistics Canada. (2013). Immigration and ethnocultural diversity in Canada. National household survey, 2011. Statistics Canada Catalogue no. 99-010-x2011001. Ottawa, ON: Author. Retrieved June 17, 2013, from www12.statcan.gc.ca/nhs-enm/2011/as-sa/99-010-x/99-010-x2011001-eng.pdf.

Stern, B. (2005). *A phenomenological approach towards understanding the nature and meaning of engagement in religious ritual activity: Perspectives from persons with dementia and their caregivers.* Unpublished MSc thesis, University of Toronto, ON.

Stodolska, M., & Livengood, J. S. (2006). The effects of religion on the leisure behavior of American Muslim immigrants. *Journal of Leisure Research, 38,* 293-320.

Taylor, M. J., & Hegarty, S. (1985). *The best of both worlds? A review of research into the education of pupils of South Asian origin.* Windsor, UK: NFER-Nelson.

Tirone, S. (1997). Leisure and centrality of family: Issues of care in the lives of south Asians in Canada. *Leisurability, 24*(3), 23-32.

Tirone, S. (1999). Racism, indifference and the leisure experiences of South Asian Canadian teens. *Leisure: The Journal of the Canadian Association of Leisure Studies, 2,* 89-114.

Tirone, S., & Goodberry, A. (2011). Leisure, biculturalism, and second-generation Canadians. *Journal of Leisure Research, 43,* 427-444.

Tirone, S., & Pedlar, A. (2000). Understanding the leisure experiences of a minority ethnic group: South Asian teens and young adults in Canada. *Loisir et Société/Society and Leisure, 23,* 145-169.

Tirone, S., & Shaw, S. M. (1997). At the center of their lives: Indo Canadian women, their families and leisure. *Journal of Leisure Research, 29,* 225-244.

Trafton, D. (1985). In praise of three traditional ideas of leisure. In B. G. Gunter, J. Stanley, & R. St. Clair (Eds.), *Transitions to leisure: Conceptual and human issues* (pp. 23-31). Lanham, MD: University Press of America.

Triandis, H. C. (1995). *Individualism and collectivism.* Boulder, CO: Westview Press.

Trunfio, M. (1991). A theological perspective on the ethics of leisure. In G. S. Fain (Ed.), *Leisure and ethics: Reflections on the philosophy of leisure* (pp. 151-159). Reston, VA: American Association for Leisure and Recreation in association with the American Alliance for Health, Physical Education, Recreation and Dance.

U.S. Census Bureau Statistical Abstract. (2009a). Table 74. Religious composition of U.S. population: 2007. Retrieved June 1, 2012, from www.census.gov/compendia/statab/2009/tables/09s0074.pdf.

U.S. Census Bureau Statistical Abstract. (2009b). Table 76: Christian church adherents and Jewish population – 2010 states. Retrieved February 27, 2013 from www.census.gov/compendia/statab/2012/tables/12s0077.pdf.

Vogeler, I. (2005). Old Order Mennonites in Ontario, Canada. Retrieved October 23, 2012, from www.uwec.edu/Geography/Ivogeler/w188/utopian/oldorderMennonitesON.htm.

Waller, S. N. (2009). Doctrinal beliefs as a determinant of sin associated with select leisure activities. *Journal of Unconventional Parks, Tourism, and Recreation Research, 2*(1), 7-18.

Waller, S. N. (2010). Leisure in the life of the 21st century Black church: Re-thinking the gift. *Journal of the Christian Society for Kinesiology and Leisure Studies, 1*(1), 33-47.

Walseth, K., & Fasting, K. (2003). Islam's view on physical activity and sport. *International Review for the Sociology of Sport, 38,* 45-60.

Waskow, A. (1995). *Down-to-earth Judaism: Food, money, sex and the rest of life.* New York: William Morrow.

Wenger, L. (2003). *Unser Satt Leit: Our sort of people. Health understandings in the old order Mennonite and Amish community.* Unpublished master's thesis, Recreation and Leisure Studies, University of Waterloo, Waterloo, ON.

Zaman, H. (1997). Islam, well-being and physical activity: Perceptions of Muslim young women. In G. Clark & B. Humberstone (Eds.), *Researching women and sport.* London: Macmillan.

CHAPTER 9

Caldwell, L., & Li, H. (2006). A cross-national comparison of leisure motivation among adolescents. In W. Hendricks & I. Schneider (Comps.), *Abstracts from the 2006 Symposium on Leisure Research* (p. 37; CD). Ashburn, VA: National Recreation and Parks Association.

Chen, M., & Pang, X. (2012). Leisure motivation: An integrative review. *Social Behavior and Personality, 40,* 1075-1082.

Chen, S., Fok, H., Bond, M., & Matsumoto, D. (2006). Personality and beliefs about the world revisited: Expanding the nomological network of social axioms. *Personality and Individual Differences, 41,* 201-211.

Chick, G. (2006). Leisure and cultural identity. In E. L. Jackson (Ed.), *Leisure and the quality of life: Impacts on social, economic, and cultural development: Hangzhou Consensus* (pp. 164-178). Zhejiang, China: Zhejiang University Press.

Chick, G. E. (2009). Culture as a variable in the study of leisure. *Leisure Sciences, 31,* 305-310.

Coon, H., & Kemmelmeier, M. (2001). Cultural orientations in the United States: (Re)Examining differences among ethnic groups. *Journal of Cross-Cultural Psychology, 32,* 348-364.

Cross, S., Hardin, E., & Gercek-Swing, B. (2011). The *what, how, why,* and *where* of self-construal. *Personality and Social Psychology Review, 15,* 142-179.

Deci, E. L., & Ryan, R. M. (1985). *Intrinsic motivation and self-determination in human behavior.* New York: Plenum Press.

Deci, E. L., & Ryan, R. M. (1991). A motivational approach to self: Integration in personality. In R. Dienstbier (Ed.), *Nebraska Symposium on Motivation: Vol. 38. Perspectives on motivation* (pp. 237-288). Lincoln, NE: University of Nebraska Press.

Deci, E., & Ryan, R. M. (2000). The "What" and "Why" of goal pursuits: Human needs and the self-determination of behavior. *Psychological Inquiry, 11,* 227-268.

Deci, E. L., & Ryan, R. M. (2008). Facilitating optimal motivation and psychological well-being across life's domains. *Canadian Psychology, 49,* 14-23.

Driver, B. (1976). Quantification of outdoor recreationists' preferences. In B. van der Smissen (Ed.), *Research, camping, and environmental education* (pp. 165-188). University Park, PA: Penn State University.

Edmonds, J., Duda, J., & Ntoumanis, N. (2010). Psychological needs and the prediction of exercise-related cognitions and affect among an ethnically diverse cohort of adult women. *International Journal of Sport and Exercise Psychology, 8,* 446-463.

Fiske, A., Kitayama, S., Markus, H., & Nisbett, R. (1998). The cultural matrix of social psychology. In D. Gilbert, S. Fiske, & G. Lindzey (Eds.), *The handbook of social psychology, Vol. 2* (4th ed., pp. 915-981). New York: Oxford University Press.

Fiske, S. T. (2003). Five core social motives, plus or minus five. In S. Spencer, S. Fein, M. Zanna, & S. Olson (Eds.), *Motivated social perception* (pp. 233-256). Mahwah, NJ: Erlbaum.

Fiske, S. T. (2004). *Social beings: A core motives approach to social psychology.* New York: Wiley.

Floyd, M. F. (1998). Getting beyond marginality and ethnicity: The challenge for race and ethnic studies in leisure research. *Journal of Leisure Research, 30,* 3-22.

Hamamura, T., Meijer, Z., Heine, S., Kamaya, K., & Hori, I. (2009). Approach-avoidance motivation and information processing: A cross-cultural analysis. *Personality and Social Psychology Bulletin, 35,* 454-462.

Heine, S., Lehman, D., Markus, H., & Kitayama, S. (1999). Is there a universal need for positive self-regard? *Psychological Review, 106,* 766-794.

Heo, J., & Lee, Y. (2007). "I don't want to feel like a stranger": Korean students who play basketball seriously. *Leisure/Loisir, 31,* 133-154.

Hunt, K., & Ditton, R. (2001). Perceived benefits of recreational fishing to Hispanic-American and Anglo anglers. *Human Dimensions of Wildlife, 6,* 153-172.

Hunter, C., & Joseph, N. (2010). Racial group identification and its relation to individualism/interdependence and race-related stress in African Americans. *Journal of Black Psychology, 36,* 483-511.

Hutchison, R. (2000). Race and ethnicity in leisure studies. In W. C. Gartner & D. W. Lime (Eds.), *Trends in outdoor recreation, leisure and tourism* (pp. 63-71). New York: CABI.

Iyengar, S., & Lepper, M. (1999). Rethinking the value of choice: A cultural perspective on intrinsic motivation. *Journal of Personality and Social Psychology, 76,* 349-366.

Izard, C. E. (1977). *Human emotions*. New York: Plenum Press.

Jones, R. (1997). Individualism: Eighteenth century origins—twentieth century consequences. *Western Journal of Black Studies, 21,* 20-33.

Kenrick, D., Griskevicius, V., Neuberg, S., & Schaller, M. (2010). Renovating the pyramid of needs: Contemporary extensions built upon ancient foundations. *Perspectives on Psychological Science, 5,* 292-314.

Kleiber, D. A., Walker, G. J., & Mannell, R. C. (2011). *A social psychology of leisure* (2nd ed.). State College, PA: Venture.

Li, C., Chick, G., Zinn, H., Absher, J., & Graefe, A. (2007). Ethnicity as a variable in leisure research. *Journal of Leisure Research, 39,* 514-545.

Lo, S. (2011). *Adventure education and the acculturation of Chinese Canadians in Vancouver, Canada.* Doctoral dissertation, Lincoln University, Christchurch, NZ. http://researcharchive.lincoln.ac.nz/dspace/bitstream/10182/3918/1/lo_phd.pdf.

Mak, A., Wong, K., & Chang, R. (2009). Health or self-indulgence? The motivations and characteristics of spa-goers. *International Journal of Tourism Research, 11,* 185-199.

Manfredo, M., Driver, B., & Tarrant, M. (1996). Measuring leisure motivation: A meta-analysis of the Recreation Experience Preference scales. *Journal of Leisure Research, 28,* 188-213.

Mannell, R. C., & Bradley, W. (1986). Does greater freedom always lead to greater leisure? Testing a person X environment model of freedom and leisure. *Journal of Leisure Research, 18,* 215-230.

Markus, H. R., & Kitiyama, S. (1991). Culture and the self: Implications for cognition, emotion and motivation. *Psychological Review, 98,* 224-253.

Maslow, A. H. (1968). *Toward a psychology of being* (2nd ed.). Toronto: Van Nostrand Reinhold.

Mead, G. H. (1934). *Mind, self, and society*. Chicago: University of Chicago Press.

Morling, B. (2000). "Taking" an aerobics class in the U.S. and "entering" an aerobics class in Japan: Primary and secondary control in a fitness context. *Asian Journal of Social Psychology, 3,* 73-85.

Murray, H. A. (1938). *Explorations and personality*. New York: Oxford University Press.

Neulinger, J. (1981). *The psychology of leisure* (2nd ed.). Springfield, IL: Charles C. Thomas.

Oyserman, D., Coon, H., & Kemmelmeier, M. (2002). Rethinking individualism and collectivism: Evaluation of theoretical assumptions and meta-analysis. *Psychological Bulletin, 128,* 3-72.

Oyserman, D., Gant, L., & Ager, J. (1995). A socially contextualized model of African American identity: Possible selves and school persistence. *Journal of Personality and Social Psychology, 69,* 1216-1232.

Ryan, R., & Deci, E. (2000). Self-determination theory and the facilitation of intrinsic motivation, social development, and well-being. *American Psychologist, 55,* 68-78.

Scherl, L. (1989). Self in wilderness: Understanding the psychological benefits of individual-wilderness interaction through self-control. *Leisure Sciences, 11,* 123-135.

Schutte, H., & Ciarlante, D. (1998). *An alternative consumer behaviour model for Asia*. London: Creative Print & Design.

Shaull, S., & Gramann, J. (1998). The effect of cultural assimilation on the importance of family-related and nature-related recreation among Hispanic Americans. *Journal of Leisure Research, 30,* 47-63.

Shaw, S. (1984). The measurement of leisure: A quality of life issue. *Loisir et Société/Society and Leisure, 7,* 91-107.

Sheldon, K., Elliot, A., Kim, Y., & Kasser, T. (2001). What is satisfying about satisfying events? Testing 10 candidate psychological needs. *Journal of Personality and Social Psychology, 80,* 325-339.

Sheldon, K., Elliot, A., Ryan, R., Chirkov, V., Kim, Y., Wu, C., Demir, M., & Sun, Z. (2004). Self-concordance and subjective well-being in four cultures. *Journal of Cross-Cultural Psychology, 35,* 209-223.

Stebbins, R. A. (1992). *Amateurs, professionals, and serious leisure*. Montreal: McGill-Queen's University Press.

Tinsley, H. E. A., & Kass, R. A. (1978). Leisure activities and need satisfaction: A replication and extension. *Journal of Leisure Research, 10,* 191-202.

Triandis, H. (1995). *Individualism and collectivism*. Boulder, CO: Westview Press.

Tsai, J. (2007). Ideal affect: Cultural causes and behavioral consequences. *Perspectives on Psychological Sciences, 2,* 242-259.

Walker, G. J. (2009). Culture, self-construal, and leisure motivations. *Leisure Sciences, 31,* 347-363.

Walker, G. J. (2010). The effects of personal, contextual, and situational factors on the facilitation of intrinsic motivation: The case of Chinese/Canadians. *Journal of Leisure Research, 42,* 43-66.

Walker, G. J., Deng, J., & Chapman, R. (2007). Leisure attitudes: A follow-up study comparing Canadians, Chinese in Canada, and Mainland Chinese. *World Leisure Journal, 49,* 207-215.

Walker, G. J., Deng, J., & Dieser, R. (2001). Ethnicity, acculturation, self-construal, and motivations for outdoor recreation. *Leisure Sciences, 23,* 263-283.

Walker, G. J., Deng, J., & Dieser, R. (2005). Culture, self-construal, and leisure theory and practice. *Journal of Leisure Research, 37,* 77-99.

Walker, G. J., & Wang, X. (2008). A cross-cultural comparison of Canadian and Mainland Chinese university students' leisure motivations. *Leisure Sciences, 30,* 179-197.

Walker, G. J., & Wang, X. (2009). The meaning of leisure for Chinese/Canadians. *Leisure Sciences, 31,* 1-18.

Waterman, A., Schwartz, S., Goldbacher, E., Green, H., Miller, C., & Philip, S. (2003). Predicting the subjective experience of intrinsic motivation: The roles of self-determination, the balance of challenge and skills, and self-realization values. *Personality and Social Psychology Bulletin, 29,* 1447-1458.

Weisz, J., Rothbaum, F., & Blackburn, T. (1984). Standing out and standing in: The psychology of control in America and Japan. *American Psychologist, 39,* 955-969.

Winter, P., Jeong, W., & Godbey, G. (2004). Outdoor recreation among Asian Americans: A case study of San Francisco Bay area residents. *Journal of Park and Recreation Administration, 22,* 114-136.

CHAPTER 10

Aguilar, L. (2008). Customer service in a culturally diverse world. In M. T. Allison & I. E. Schneider (Eds.), *Diversity in the recreation profession: Organizational perspectives* (Rev. ed., pp. 213-222). State College, PA: Venture.

Allison, M. T. (2008). Introduction: Diversity in organizational perspective. In M. T. Allison & I. E. Schneider (Eds.), *Diversity in the recreation profession: Organizational perspectives* (Rev. ed., pp. 1-15). State College, PA: Venture.

Bengston, D. A., & Schermann, M. (2008). Hmong American: Issues and strategies related to outdoor recreation. In M. T. Allison & I. E. Schneider (Eds.), *Diversity in the recreation profession: Organizational perspectives* (Rev. ed., pp. 19-24). State College, PA: Venture.

Blahna, D., & Black, K. (1993). Racism: A concern for recreation resource managers. In P. Gobster (Ed.), *Managing urban and high-use recreation settings: Selected papers from the 4th North American Symposium on Society and Natural Resource Management* (GTR NC-163, pp. 111-118). St. Paul, MN: USDA Forest Service.

Chavez, D. (2012). Latinos and outdoor recreation. In H. K. Cordell (Ed.), *Outdoor recreation trends and futures: A technical document supporting the Forest Service 2010 RPA assessment* (GTR SRS-150, pp. 74-77). Asheville, NC: USDA Forest Service, Southern Research Station.

Chick, G., & Dong, E. (2005). Cultural constraints on leisure. In E. L. Jackson (Ed.), *Constraints to leisure* (pp. 169-183). State College, PA: Venture.

Covelli, E. A., Burns, R. C., & Graefe, A. (2007). Perceived constraints by non-traditional users on the Mt. Baker-Snoqualmie National Forest. In R. Burns & K. Robinson (Eds.), *Proceedings of the 2006 Northeastern Recreation Research Symposium* (Vol. GTR-NRS-P-14, pp. 422-429). Newtown Square, PA: USDA Forest Service, Northern Research Station.

Crawford, D. W., Jackson, E. L., & Godbey, G. (1991). A hierarchical model of leisure constraints. *Leisure Sciences, 13,* 309-320.

Crawford, J., & Stodolska, M. (2008). Constraints experienced by elite athletes with disabilities in Kenya, with implications for the development of a new hierarchical model of constraints at the societal level. *Journal of Leisure Research, 40,* 128-155.

Dunn, R. A., Kasul, R. L., & Brown, D. (2002). *Hispanic recreation at Corps of Engineers lakes in the Greater Tulsa area: Results of two Hispanic focus groups* (NRTN REC-13). Vicksburg, MS: Environmental Laboratory.

Dustin, D. L., Schneider, I. E., McAvoy, L. H., & Frakt, A. N. (2002). Cross-cultural claims on Devils Tower National Monument: A case study. *Leisure Sciences, 24,* 79-88.

Erickson, B., Johnson, C. W., & Kivel, B. D. (2009). Rocky Mountain National Park: History and culture as factors in African-American park visitation. *Journal of Leisure Research, 41*(4), 529-545.

Flood, J. P., & McAvoy, L. H. (2007). Use of national forests by Salish-Kootenai Tribal Members: Traditional recreation and a legacy of cultural values. *Leisure/Loisir, 31*(1), 191-216.

Floyd, M. F. (1998). Getting beyond marginality and ethnicity: The challenge for race and ethnic studies in leisure research. *Journal of Leisure Research, 30,* 3-22.

Floyd, M. F., & Gramann, J. H. (1995). Perceptions of discrimination in a recreation context. *Journal of Leisure Research, 27,* 192-199.

Floyd, M. F., Taylor, W. C., & Whitt-Glover, M. C. (2009). Measuring park and recreation environments in low-income communities of color: Highlights of challenges and recommendations. *American Journal of Preventive Medicine, 36*(1), 156-160.

Franzini, L., Taylor, W., Elliott, M. N., Cuccaro, P., Tortolero, S. R., Gilliland, M. J., Grunbaum, J., & Schuster, M. A. (2010). Neighborhood characteristics favorable to outdoor physical activity: Disparities by socioeconomic and racial/ethnic composition. *Health & Place, 16,* 267-274.

Gilbert, D., & Hudson, S. (2000). Tourism demand constraints: A skiing participation. *Annals of Tourism Research, 27*(4), 906-925.

Gobster, P. H. (2002). Managing urban parks for a racially and ethnically diverse clientele. *Leisure Sciences, 24,* 143-159.

Gordon, M. M. (1964). *Assimilation in American life.* New York: Oxford University Press.

Hawkins, B., Peng, J., Hsieh, C., & Eklund, S. L. (1999). Leisure constraints: A replication and extension of construct development. *Leisure Sciences, 21,* 179-192.

Henderson, K. A., & Ainsworth, B. E. (2000). Sociocultural perspectives on physical activity in the lives of older African American and American Indian women: A cross cultural activity participation study. *Women & Health, 31*(1), 1-20.

Henderson, K. A., Stalnaker, D., & Taylor, G. (1988). The relationship between barriers to recreation and gender-role personality traits for women. *Journal of Leisure Research, 20,* 69-80.

Hubbard, J., & Mannell, R. (2001). Testing competing models of the leisure constraint negotiation process in a corporate employee recreation setting. *Leisure Sciences, 23,* 145-163.

Hudson, S., Hinch, T., Walker, G., & Simpson, B. (2010). Constraints to sport tourism: A cross-cultural analysis. *Journal of Sport & Tourism, 15*(1), 71-88.

Hunt, K. M., & Ditton, R. B. (2002). Freshwater fishing participation patterns of racial and ethnic groups in Texas. *North American Journal of Fisheries Management, 22,* 52-65.

Jackson, E. L. (2005). *Constraints to leisure.* State College, PA: Venture.

Jackson, E. L., Crawford, D. W., & Godbey, G. (1993). Negotiation of leisure constraints. *Leisure Sciences, 15,* 1-11.

Jackson, E. L., & Dunn, E. (1988). Integrating ceasing participation with other aspects of leisure behavior. *Journal of Leisure Research, 20,* 31-45.

Jackson, E. L., & Rucks, V. C. (1995). Negotiation of leisure constraints by junior-high and high-school students: An exploratory study. *Journal of Leisure Research, 27,* 85-105.

Jackson, E. L., & Scott, D. (1999). Constraints to leisure. In E. L. Jackson & T. L. Burton (Eds.), *Leisure studies: Prospect for the twenty-first century* (pp. 299-322). State College, PA: Venture.

James, C. (1996). *Perspectives on racism and the human services sector.* Buffalo: University of Toronto Press.

Johnson, C. Y., & Bowker, J. M. (2004). African-American wildland memories. *Environmental Ethics, 26,* 57-75.

Kay, T., & Jackson, E. L. (1991). Leisure despite constraint: The impact of leisure constraints on leisure participation. *Journal of Leisure Research, 23,* 301-313.

Lazarus, R. S., & Folkman, S. (1984). *Stress, appraisal and coping.* New York: Springer.

Li, M. Z., & Stodolska, M. (2007). Working for a dream and living for the future: Leisure constraints and negotiation strategies among Chinese international graduate students. *Leisure/Loisir, 31*(1), 105-132.

Livengood, J. S., & Stodolska, M. (2004). The effects of discrimination and constraints negotiation on leisure behavior of American Muslims in the post-September 11 America. *Journal of Leisure Research, 36*(2), 183-208.

Loucks-Atkinson, A., & Mannell, R. C. (2007). Role of self-efficacy in the constraints negotiation process: The case of individuals with fibromyalgia syndrome. *Leisure Sciences, 29,* 19-36.

Macintyre, S. (2007). Deprivation amplification revisited: Or, is it always true that poorer places have poorer access to resources for healthy diets and physical activity? *International Journal of Behavioral Nutrition and Physical Activity, 4*(32).

McAvoy, L. (2002). American Indians, place meanings and the old/new West. *Journal of Leisure Research, 34*(4), 383-396.

Pearlin, L. I., & Schooler, C. (1978). The structure of coping. *Journal of Health and Social Behavior, 19,* 2-21.

Powell, L. M., Slater, S., & Chaloupka, F. J. (2004). The relationship between community physical activity settings and race, ethnicity and socioeconomic status. *Evidence-Based Preventive Medicine, 1,* 135-144.

Pruitt, D. G., & Rubin, J. Z. (1986). *Social conflict.* New York: Random House.

Raish, C. (2000). Environmentalism, the Forest Service, and the Hispano communities of northern New Mexico. *Society and Natural Resources, 13,* 489-508.

Raymore, L., Godbey, G., & Crawford, D. (1994). Self-esteem, gender and socio-economic status: Their relation to perception of constraint on leisure among adolescents. *Journal of Leisure Research, 26*(2), 99-118.

Raymore, L., Godbey, G., Crawford, D., & von Eye, A. (1993). Nature and process of leisure constraints: An empirical test. *Leisure Sciences, 15,* 99-113.

Richter, D. L., Wilcox, S., Greaney, M. L., Henderson, K. A., & Ainsworth, B. E. (2002). Environmental, policy, and cultural factors related to physical activity in African American women. *Women & Health, 36*(2), 89-107.

Rublee, C. B., & Shaw, S. M. (1991). Constraints on the leisure and community participation of immigrant women: Implications for social integration. *Loisir et Société/ Society and Leisure, 14*(1), 133-150.

Rural Sociological Society Task Force on Persistent Rural Poverty. (1993). *Persistent poverty in rural America.* Rural Studies Series of the Rural Sociological Society. Boulder, CO: Westview Press.

Schelhas, J. (2002). Race, ethnicity, and natural resources in the United States: A review. *Natural Resources Journal, 42*(4), 723-763.

Schneider, I. E., & Wilhelm Stanis, S. (2007). Coping: An alternative conceptualization for constraint negotiation and accommodation. *Leisure Sciences, 29,* 391-401.

Scott, D. (1991). The problematic nature of participation in contract bridge: A qualitative study of group-related constraints. *Leisure Sciences, 13,* 321-336.

Sharaievska, I., Stodolska, M., Shinew, K. J., & Kim, J. (2010). Perceived discrimination in leisure settings in Latino urban communities. *Leisure, 34*(3), 295-326.

Shinew, K., & Floyd, M. F. (2005). Racial inequality and constraints to leisure in the post-Civil Rights era: Toward an alternative framework. In E. L. Jackson (Ed.), *Constraints to leisure* (pp. 35-51). State College, PA: Venture.

Shores, K. A., Scott, D., & Floyd, M. F. (2007). Constraints to outdoor recreation: A multiple hierarchy stratification perspective. *Leisure Sciences, 29*(3), 227-246.

Son, J. S., Mowen, A. J., & Kerstetter, D. L. (2008). Testing alternative leisure constraint negotiation models: An extension of Hubbard and Mannell's study. *Leisure Sciences, 30,* 198-216.

Stodolska, M. (2000). Changes in leisure participation patterns after immigration. *Leisure Sciences, 23,* 39-63.

Stodolska, M., Acevedo, J. C., & Shinew, K. J. (2009). Gangs of Chicago: Perceptions of crime and its effects on the recreation behavior of Latino residents in urban communities. *Leisure Sciences, 31,* 466-482.

Stodolska, M., & Shinew, K. J. (2010). Environmental constraints on leisure time physical activity among Latino urban residents. *Qualitative Research in Sport and Exercise, 2*(3), 313-335.

Stodolska, M., Shinew, K., Acevedo, J., & Roman, C. (2013). "I was born in the hood": Fear of crime, outdoor recreation and physical activity among Mexican-American urban adolescents. *Leisure Sciences, 35,* 1-15.

Takaki, R. (2008). *A different mirror: A history of multicultural America* (Rev. ed.). New York: Little, Brown.

Tirone, S. (1999). Racism and intolerance in recreation and leisure: A Canadian experience. In P. Heintzman (Ed.), *Leisure, politics, and power driving the social agenda into the twenty-first century: Book of abstracts* (pp. 200-203). Wolfville, NS: Acadia University Printing Services.

Tsai, E. H., & Coleman, D. J. (1999). Leisure constraints of Chinese immigrants: An exploratory study. *Loisir et Société/Society and Leisure, 22,* 243-264.

Walker, G. J., & Virden, R. J. (2005). Constraints on outdoor recreation. In E. L. Jackson (Ed.), *Constraints to leisure* (pp. 201-219). State College, PA: Venture.

Washburne, R. (1978). Black under-participation in wildland recreation: Alternate explanations. *Leisure Sciences, 1,* 175-189.

Wilhelm Stanis, S. A., Schneider, I. E., Chavez, D., & Shinew, K. (2009). Visitor constraints to physical activity in park and recreation areas: Differences by race and ethnicity. *Journal of Park and Recreation Administration, 27*(3), 78-95.

Wilhelm Stanis, S. A., Schneider, I. E., & Russell, K. (2009). Leisure time physical activity of park visitors: Retesting constraint models in adoption and maintenance stages. *Leisure Sciences, 31*(3), 287-304.

Wolch, J., Wilson, J. P., & Fehrenbach, J. (2005). Parks and park funding in Los Angeles: An equity mapping analysis. *Urban Geography, 26,* 4-35.

CHAPTER 11

Aguirre, A. Jr., & Turner, J. H. (1998). *American ethnicity: The dynamics and consequences of discrimination* (2nd ed.). Boston: McGraw-Hill.

Allport, G. W. (1954). *Nature of prejudice.* New York: Doubleday.

Arai, S., & Kivel, B. D. (2009). Critical race theory and social justice perspectives on whiteness, difference(s) and (anti)racism: A fourth wave of race research in leisure studies. *Journal of Leisure Research, 41,* 459-473.

Associated Press. (1991, January 10). Poll finds Whites use stereotypes. Retrieved on March 9, 2013 from www.nytimes.com/1991/01/10/us/poll-finds-whites-use-stereotypes.html.

Bartlett, J. (1968). *Familiar quotations* (14th ed., p. 967). Boston: Little, Brown.

Bertrand, M., & Mullainathan, S. (2004). Are Emily and Greg more employable than Lakisha and Jamal? A field experiment on labor market discrimination. *American Economic Review, 94,* 991-1013.

Blahna, D., & Black, K. (1993). Racism: A concern for recreation resource managers. In P. Gobster (Ed.), *Managing urban and high-use recreation settings: Selected papers from the 4th North American Symposium on Society and Natural Resource Management* (GTR NC-163, pp. 111-118). St. Paul, MN: USDA Forest Service.

Bonilla-Silva, E. (2002). We are all Americans!: The Latin Americanization of racial stratification in the USA. *Race and Society, 5,* 3-16.

Bonilla-Silva, E. (2003). *Racism without racists: Color-blind racism and the persistence of racial inequality in the United States.* Lanham, MD: Rowman & Littlefield.

Brief, A. P., Buttram, R. T., Reizenstein, R. M., Pugh, S. D., Callahan, J. D., McCline, R. L., & Vaslow, J. B. (1997). Beyond good intentions: The next steps toward racial equality in the American workplace. *Academy of Management Executive, 11,* 59-72.

Burset, S., & Stodolska, M. (October, 2012). *Constraints on leisure and travel among undocumented Latino immigrants.* Paper presented at the NRPA Leisure Research Symposium, Anaheim, CA.

Chavez, D. J. (1993). *Visitor perceptions of crowding and discrimination at two national forests in southern California.* Gen. Tech. Rep. PSW-216. Riverside, CA: USDA Forest Service, Pacific Southwest Research Station.

Craig, W. (1972). Recreational activity patterns in a small Negro urban community: The role of the cultural case. *Economic Geography, 48,* 107-115.

Crowder, K., Pais, J., & South, S. J. (2012). Neighborhood diversity, metropolitan constraints, and household migration. *American Sociological Review, 77*(3), 325-353.

Delgado, A. (1994). *Recreation preferences of Black/Latinos/Asians: A case study of Chicago's Park District minority planning and policy with focus on Lincoln Park.* PhD dissertation, University of Illinois at Chicago.

Doherty, A., & Taylor, T. (2007). Sport and physical recreation in the settlement of immigrant youth. *Leisure/Loisir, 31,* 27-55.

Dovidio, J. F., & Gaertner, S. L. (2000). Aversive racism and selection decisions: 1989 and 1999. *Psychological Science, 11,* 315-319.

Erickson, B., Johnson, C. W., & Kivel, B. D. (2009). Rocky Mountain National Park: History and culture as factors in African-American park visitation. *Journal of Leisure Research, 41,* 529-545.

Feagin, J. R. (1991). The continuing significance of race: Antiblack discrimination in public places. *American Sociological Review, 56,* 101-116.

Feagin, J. R., & Eckberg, D. L. (1980). Discrimination: Motivation, action, effects, and context. *Annual Review of Sociology, 6,* 1-20.

Feagin, J. R., & Vera, H. (1995). *White racism.* New York: Routledge.

Fernandez, M., & Witt, P. (2013). Attracting Hispanics to a public recreation center: Examining intergroup tension and historical factors. *Journal of Leisure Research, 45,* 423-444.

Flood, J. P., & McAvoy, L. H. (2007). Use of national forests by Salish-Kootenai tribal members: Traditional recreation and a legacy of cultural values. *Leisure/Loisir, 31,* 191-216.

Floyd, M. (1998). Getting beyond marginality and ethnicity: The challenge for race and ethnic studies in leisure research. *Journal of Leisure Research, 30,* 3-22.

Floyd, M. F. (2007). Trends in leisure research on race and ethnicity: Anticipating the fourth wave. *Leisure/Loisir, 31*(1), 245-254.

Floyd, M. F., & Gramann, J. H. (1995). Perceptions of discrimination in a recreation context. *Journal of Leisure Research, 27,* 192-199.

Floyd, M. F., Gramann, J. H., & Saenz, R. (1993). Ethnic factors and the use of public outdoor recreation areas: The case of Mexican Americans. *Leisure Sciences, 15,* 83-98.

Floyd, M. F., & Johnson, C. Y. (2002). Coming to terms with environmental justice in outdoor recreation: A conceptual discussion with research implications. *Leisure Sciences, 24,* 59-77.

Floyd, M. F., Taylor, W., & Whitt-Glover, M. (2009). Measurement of park and recreation environments that support physical activity in low-income communities of color. *American Journal of Preventive Medicine, 36*(Suppl. 4), S156-S160.

Gaertner, S. L., Dovidio, J. F., Nier, J., Hodson, G., & Houlette, M. A. (2005). Aversive racism: Bias without intention. In L. B. Nielsen & R. L. Nelson (Eds.), *Handbook of employment discrimination research* (pp. 377-395). Dordrecht, The Netherlands: Springer.

Glover, T. D. (2007). Ugly on the diamonds: An examination of white privilege in youth baseball. *Leisure Sciences, 29,* 195-208.

Gobster, P. H. (1998a). Explanations for minority "underparticipation" in outdoor recreation: A look at golf. *Journal of Park and Recreation Administration, 16*(1), 46-64.

Gobster, P. H. (1998b). Urban parks as green walls or green magnets? Interracial relations in neighborhood boundary parks. *Landscape and Urban Planning, 41,* 43-55.

Gobster, P. (2002). Managing urban parks for a racially and ethnically diverse clientele. *Leisure Sciences, 24,* 143-159.

Gobster, P. H., & Delgado, A. (1993). Ethnicity and recreation use in Chicago's Lincoln Park: In-park user survey findings. In P. Gobster (Ed.), *Managing urban and high-use recreation settings: Selected papers from the 4th North American Symposium on Society and Natural Resource Management* (GTR NC-163, pp. 75-81). St. Paul, MN: USDA Forest Service.

Gómez, E. (2002). The Ethnicity and Public Recreation Participation Model. *Leisure Sciences, 24*(2), 123-142.

Gramann, J. H. (1996). *Ethnicity, race, and outdoor recreation: A review of trends, policy, and research.* Miscellaneous Paper R-96-1. Vicksburg, MS: U.S. Army Corps of Engineers Waterways Experiment Station.

Henry, F., Tator, C., Mattis, W., & Rees, T. (1995). *The colour of democracy: Racism in Canadian society.* Toronto: Harcourt Brace.

Hibbler, D. K., & Shinew, K. J. (2002). Interracial couples' experience of leisure: A social network approach. *Journal of Leisure Research, 34,* 135-156.

Huntington, S. P. (1993). The clash of civilizations? *Foreign Affairs, 72,* 22-49.

Huntington, S. P. (1996). *The clash of civilizations and the remaking of world order.* New York: Simon & Schuster.

Iceland, J., Weinberg, D. H., & Steinmetz, E. (2002). *Racial and ethnic residential segregation in the United States, 1980–2000.* U.S. Census Bureau, Special Report Series, CENSR-3. Washington, DC: U.S. Government Printing Office. Retrieved March 9, 2013 from www.census.gov/hhes/www/housing/resseg/pdf/front_toc.pdf.

Johnson, C. Y., Bowker, J. M., English, D. B., & Worthen, D. (1998). Wildland recreation in the rural South: An examination of marginality and ethnicity theory. *Journal of Leisure Research, 30,* 101-120.

Johnson, J. H. Jr., & Oliver, M. L. (1989). Interethnic minority conflict in urban America: The effects of economic and social dislocation. *Urban Geography, 10,* 449-463.

Kivel, B. D., Johnson, C. W., & Scraton, S. J. (2009). (Re)Theorizing leisure experience and race. *Journal of Leisure Research, 41*(4), 473-494.

Lindsay, J. J., & Ogle, R. A. (1972). Socioeconomic patterns of outdoor recreation use near urban areas. *Journal of Leisure Research, 4,* 19-24.

Livengood, J. S., & Stodolska, M. (2004). The effects of discrimination and constraints negotiation on leisure behavior of American Muslims in the post-September 11 America. *Journal of Leisure Research, 36,* 183-208.

Long, J., & Hylton, K. (2002). Shades of white: An examination of whiteness in sport. *Leisure Studies, 21,* 87-103.

Malhi, R. L., & Boon, S. P. (2007). Discourses of "democratic racism" in the talk of South Asian Canadian women. *Canadian Ethnic Studies, 39,* 125-149.

Massey, D. S., & Denton, N. A. (1993). *American apartheid: Segregation and the making of the underclass.* Cambridge, MA: Harvard University Press.

McDonald, D., & McAvoy, L. (1997). *Racism, recreation and Native Americans.* Paper presented at the Leisure Research Symposium. Salt Lake City.

McDonald, M. G. (2009). Dialogues on Whiteness, leisure, and (anti)racism. *Journal of Leisure Research, 41,* 5-21.

Mindiola, T. Jr., Niemann, Y. F., & Rodriguez, N. (2002). *Black-Brown relations and stereotypes.* Austin, TX: University of Texas Press.

Mowatt, R. (2009a). The king of the damned: Reading lynching as leisure: The analysis of lynching photography for examples of violent forms of leisure. *Policy Futures in Education, 6*(2), 185-199.

Mowatt, R. A. (2009b). Notes from a leisure son: Expanding and understanding of Whiteness in leisure. *Journal of Leisure Research, 41,* 511-528.

Neal, S. (2002). Rural landscapes, representations and racism: Examining multicultural citizenship and policy-making in the English countryside. *Ethnic and Racial Studies, 25*(3), 442-461.

Neal, S., & Agyeman, J. (2006). *The new countryside? Ethnicity, nation and exclusion in contemporary rural Britain.* Bristol, UK: The Policy Press.

Office of United Nations High Commissioner for Human Rights. (1965). International convention on the elimination of all forms of racial discrimination. Retrieved April 16, 2013, from www.ohchr.org/EN/ProfessionalInterest/Pages/CERD.aspx.

Omi, M., & Winant, H. (1994). *Racial formation in the United States from the 1960s to the 1990s*. New York: Routledge.

Pager, D., & Shepherd, H. (2008). The sociology of discrimination: Racial discrimination in employment, housing, credit, and consumer markets. *Annual Review of Sociology, 34*, 181-209.

Philipp, S. F. (1999). Are we welcome? African American racial acceptance in leisure activities and the importance given to children's leisure. *Journal of Leisure Research, 31*, 385-403.

Philipp, S. F. (2000). Race and the pursuit of happiness. *Journal of Leisure Research, 32*, 121-124.

Portes, A. (1984). The rise of ethnicity: Determinants of ethnic perceptions among Cuban exiles in Miami. *American Sociological Review, 49*, 383-397.

Quillian, L. (2006). New approaches to understanding racial prejudice and discrimination. *Annual Review of Sociology, 32*, 299-328.

Reskin, B. (2012). The race discrimination system. *Annual Review of Sociology, 38*, 17-35.

Richmond, L., & Johnson, C. W. (2009). "It's a race war:" Race and leisure experiences in California State Prison. *Journal of Leisure Research, 41*(4), 565-580.

Roberts, N. S. (2009). Crossing the color line with a different perspective on Whiteness and (anti)racism: A response to Mary McDonald. *Journal of Leisure Research, 41*, 495-509.

Rugh, J. S., & Massey, D. S. (2010). Racial segregation and the American foreclosure crisis. *American Sociological Review, 75*, 629-651.

Sasidharan, V. (2002). Special issue introduction: Understanding recreation and the environment within the context of culture. *Leisure Sciences, 24*(1), 1-11.

Schuman, H., Steeh, C., Bobo, L., & Krysan, M. (1997). *Racial attitudes in America: Trends and interpretations*. Cambridge, MA: Harvard University Press.

Sharaievska, I., Stodolska, M., Shinew, K. J., & Kim, J. (2010). Perceived discrimination in leisure settings in Latino urban communities. *Leisure/Loisir, 34*, 295-326.

Shinew, K. J., & Floyd, M. F. (2005). Racial inequality and constraints to leisure in the post-Civil Rights era: Toward an alternative framework. In E. L. Jackson (Ed.), *Constraints to leisure* (pp. 35-54). State College, PA: Venture.

Shinew, K. J., Mowatt, R., & Glover, T. (2007). An African American community recreation center: An examination of participants' and volunteers' perceptions of racism and racial identity. *Journal of Park and Recreation Administration, 25*, 84-106.

Stephenson, M. L., & Hughes, H. L. (2005). Racialised boundaries in tourism and travel: A case study of the UK Black Caribbean community. *Leisure Studies, 24*, 137-160.

Stodolska, M. (2007). Ethnic enclosure, social networks, and leisure behaviour of immigrants from Korea, Mexico, and Poland. *Leisure/Loisir, 31*, 277-324.

Stodolska, M., Acevedo, J. C., & Shinew, K. J. (2009). Gangs of Chicago: Perceptions of crime and its effect on the recreation behavior of Latino residents in urban communities. *Leisure Sciences, 31*, 466-482.

Stodolska, M., & Jackson, E. L. (1998). Discrimination in leisure and work experienced by a white ethnic minority group. *Journal of Leisure Research, 30*, 23-46.

Stodolska, M., & Santos, C. A. (2006). Transnationalism and leisure: Mexican temporary migrants in the United States. *Journal of Leisure Research, 38*, 143-167.

Stodolska, M., & Shinew, K. J. (2010). Environmental constraints on leisure time physical activity among Latino urban residents. *Qualitative Research in Sport and Exercise, 2*, 313-335.

Stodolska, M., Shinew, K. J., Acevedo, J. C., & Izenstark, D. (2011). Perceptions of urban parks as havens and contested terrains by Mexican-Americans in Chicago neighborhoods. *Leisure Sciences, 33*, 103-126.

Stodolska, M., & Walker, G. J. (2007). Ethnicity and leisure: Historical development, current status, and future directions. *Leisure/Loisir, 31*, 3-26.

Stodolska, M., & Yi, J. (2003). Impacts of immigration on ethnic identity and leisure behavior of adolescent immigrants from Korea, Mexico, and Poland. *Journal of Leisure Research, 35*, 49-79.

Tirone, S. (1999). *Racism and intolerance in recreation and leisure: A Canadian experience*. Paper presented at the Ninth Canadian Congress on Leisure Research, May 1999. Wolfville, Nova Scotia: Acadia University.

Tumin, M. (1973). *Patterns of society*. Boston: Little, Brown.

Washburne, R. F. (1978). Black under-participation in wildland recreation: Alternative explanations. *Leisure Sciences, 1*, 175-189.

Washburne, R., & Wall, P. (1980). *Black-white ethnic differences in outdoor recreation*. Research Paper INT-249. Ogden, UT: USDA Forest Service, Intermountain Forest and Range Experiment Station.

Waters, M. (1994). Ethnic and racial identities of second-generation Black immigrants in New York City. *International Migration Review, 28*, 795-820.

West, P. C. (1989). Urban region parks and black minorities: Subculture, marginality, and interracial relations in park use in the Detroit metropolitan area. *Leisure Sciences, 11*, 11-28.

Wolch, J., Wilson, J. P., & Fehrenbach, J. (2005). Parks and park funding in Los Angeles: An equity-mapping analysis. *Urban Geography, 26*, 4-35.

Woodard, M. D. (1988). Class, regionality, and leisure among urban Black Americans: The post-Civil Rights era. *Journal of Leisure Research, 20*(2), 87-105.

Yi, J. (2005). *The role of leisure in reproduction of race and ethnicity among Korean Americans*. Unpublished doctoral dissertation, University of Illinois at Urbana-Champaign.

CHAPTER 12

Acosta, Y. D., & de la Cruz, G. P. (2011). *The foreign born from Latin America and the Caribbean: 2010*. American Community Survey Briefs. Washington, DC: U.S. Department of Commerce, Economics and Statistics Administration, U.S. Census Bureau.

Adams, C. C. (1929). The importance of preserving wilderness conditions. In M. P. Nelson & J. B. Callicott (Eds.), *The wilderness debate rages on* (pp. 55-66). Athens, GA: University of Georgia Press.

Altman, I., & Chemers, M. (1980). *Culture and environment.* Monterey, CA: Brooks/Cole.

Bowker, J. M., Murphy, D., Cordell, H. K., English, D. B. K., Bergstrom, J. C., Starbuck, C. M., & Green, G. T. (2006). Wilderness and primitive area recreation participation and consumption: An examination of demographic and spatial factors. *Journal of Agricultural and Applied Economics, 38*(2), 317-326.

Buijs, A. E., Elands, B. H. M., & Langers, F. (2009). No wilderness for immigrants: Cultural differences in images of nature and landscape preferences. *Landscape and Urban Planning, 91*(3), 113-123.

Callicott, J. B. (1994/1995). A critique of and an alternative to the wilderness idea. *Wild Earth, 4,* 54-59.

Callicott, J. B., & Nelson, M. P. (1998). Introduction. *The great new wilderness debate* (pp. 1-20). Athens, GA: University of Georgia Press.

Campbell, L., & Wiesen, A. (2009). *Restorative commons: Creating health and well-being through urban landscapes.* Gen. Tech. Rep. NRS-P-39. Newtown Square, PA: USDA Forest Service, Northern Research Station.

Carr, D. S., & Williams, D. R. (1993). Understanding the role of ethnicity in outdoor recreation experiences. *Journal of Leisure Research, 25*(1), 22-38.

Chavez, D. J. (2001). *Managing outdoor recreation in California: Visitor contact studies 1989-1998.* Gen. Tech. Rep. PSW-GTR-180. Albany, CA: USDA Forest Service, Pacific Southwest Research Station.

Chavez, D. J. (2005). Latinos and public lands in California. *California Parks and Recreation, 61*(2), 32-35.

Chousa, J. P., Tamazian, A., & Chaitanya, V. K. (2008). *Rapid economic growth at the cost of environment degradation? Panel data evidence from BRIC economies.* William Davidson Institute working paper 908. Ann Arbor: University of Michigan.

Clarke, A. L. (2001). The Sierra Club and immigration policy: A critique. *Politics and the Life Sciences, 20*(1), 19-28.

Cowell, A. (1991). *The decade of destruction: The crusade to save the Amazon rainforest.* New York: Henry Holt.

Cronon, W. (1996). The trouble with wilderness; or, getting back to the wrong nature. *Environmental History, 1*(1), 7-28.

DeLuca, K. (1999). In the shadow of whiteness: In T. K. Nakayama & J. N. Martin (Eds.), *Whiteness: The communication of social identity* (pp. 217-246). Thousand Oaks, CA: Sage.

Diegues, A. C. (2008). Recycled rain forest myths. In M. P. Nelson & J. B. Callicott (Eds.), *The wilderness debate rages on* (pp. 264-281). Athens, GA: University of Georgia Press.

Dong, E., & Chick, G. (2005). Culture constraints on leisure through cross-cultural research. In T. Delamere, C. Randell, & D. Robinson (Eds.), *Proceedings of the Eleventh Canadian Congress on Leisure Research.* Nanaimo, BC:

Malaspina University-College. Retrieved from http://lin.ca/Uploads/cclr11/CCLR11-30.pdf.

Ehrlich, P. R., & Ehrlich, A. H. (1990). *The population explosion.* London: Frederick Muller Ltd.

Floyd, M. F., & Gramann, J. H. (1993). Effects of acculturation and structural assimilation in resource-based recreation: The case of Mexican Americans. *Journal of Leisure Research, 25*(1), 6-21.

Giradot, N. J., Miller, J., & Xiaogan, L. (2001). *Daoism and ecology: Ways within a cosmic landscape.* Cambridge, MA: Harvard University Press.

Gómez-Pompa, A., & Kaus, A. (2008). Taming the wilderness myth. In J. B. Callicott & M. P. Nelson (Eds.), *The great new wilderness debate* (pp. 293-313). Athens, GA: University of Georgia Press.

Goodman, R. (1980). Taoism and ecology. *Environmental Ethics, 2*(1), 73-80.

Grieco, E. M., & Trevelyan, E. N. (2010). Place of birth of the foreign-born population: 2009. American Community Survey Briefs. www.census.gov/prod/2010pubs/acsbr09-15.pdf.

Guha, R. (1989). Radical American environmentalism and wilderness preservation: A third world critique. *Environmental Ethics, 11*(1), 71-83.

Han, F. (2008). Cross-cultural confusion: Application of world heritage concepts in scenic and historic interest areas in China. In M. P. Nelson & J. B. Callicott (Eds.), *The wilderness debate rages on* (pp. 252-263). Athens, GA: University of Georgia Press.

Harding, S. (n.d.). What is deep ecology? Retrieved March 18, 2013, from www.morning-earth.org/DE6103/Read%20DE/Harding,%20What%20is%20DE.pdf.

Harnik, P. (2010). Urban green: Innovative parks for resurgent cities. Washington, DC: Island Press.

Hartmann, B. (2004). Conserving racism: The greening of hate at home and abroad. Retrieved March 22, 2013 from http://popdev.hampshire.edu/sites/default/files/uploads/u4763/DT%2027%20-%20Hartmann.pdf.

Hung, K. (2003). *Achieving cultural diversity in wilderness recreation: A study of the Chinese in Vancouver.* Unpublished master's thesis, University of Waterloo, Waterloo, ON.

Inglehart, R. (1990). *Culture shift in advanced industrial society.* Princeton, NJ: Princeton University Press.

Inglehart, R. (1995). Public support for environmental protection: Objective problems and subjective values in 43 societies. *PS: Political Science & Politics,* March, 57-72.

Johnson, C. Y., & Bowker, J. M. (2004). African American wildland memories. *Environmental Ethics, 26*(1), 57-75.

Johnson, C. Y., Bowker, J. M., & Cordell, H. K. (2004). Ethnic variation in environmental belief and behavior: An examination of the New Ecological Paradigm in social psychological context. *Environment and Behavior, 36*(2), 157-186.

Johnson, C. Y., Bowker, J. M., & Cordell, H. K. (2005). Acculturation via nature-based outdoor recreation: A comparison of Mexican and Chinese ethnic groups in the U.S. *Environmental Practice, 7,* 257-272.

Johnson, C. Y., Bowker, J. M., Bergstrom, J. C., & Cordell, H. K. (2004). Wilderness values in America: Does immigrant status or ethnicity matter? *Society and Natural Resources, 17*(7), 611-628.

Johnson-Gaither, C. (2011). Latino park access: Examining environmental equity in a "new destination" county in the South. *Journal of Park and Recreation Administration, 29*(4), 37-52.

Lanfer, A. G., & Taylor, M. (n.d.). Immigrant engagement in public open space: Strategies for the new Boston. www.barrfoundation.org/files/Immigrant_Engagement_in_Public_Open_Space.pdf.

Lee, R. G. (1972). The social definition of outdoor recreational places. In W. Burch, N. Cheek Jr., & L. Taylor (Eds.), *Social behavior, natural resources, and the environment* (pp. 68-84). New York: Harper & Row.

Lynch, B. D. (1993). The garden and the sea: U.S. Latino environmental discourses and mainstream environmentalism. *Social Problems, 40*(1), 108-124.

Murota, Y. (1985). Culture and the environment in Japan. *Environmental Management, 9*(2), 105-111.

Nelson, M. P., & Callicott, J. B. (Eds.). (2008). *The wilderness debate rages on.* Athens, GA: University of Georgia Press.

Newsome, D., & Gentry, B. (Eds.). (2008). *Broadening the base through open space: Addressing demographic trends by saving land and serving people.* Yale School of Forestry & Environmental Studies. Retrieved from http://environment.research.yale.edu/publication-series/environmental_politics_and_management/5864.

Parajuli, P. (2001). How can four trees make a jungle? In D. Rothenberg & M. Ulvaeus (Eds.), *The world and the wild: Expanding wilderness beyond its American roots* (pp. 3-20). Tucson, AZ: University of Arizona Press.

Patten, E. (2012). Statistical portrait of the foreign-born population in the United States, 2010. Table 4: Change in the foreign-born population, by region of birth: 2000-2010. www.pewhispanic.org/2012/02/21/statistical-portrait-of-the-foreign-born-population-in-the-united-states-2010.

Pfeffer, M. J., & Stycos, J. M. (2002). Immigrant environmental behaviors in New York City. *Social Science Quarterly, 83*(1), 64-81.

Price, M. (1994). Ecopolitics and environmental nongovernmental organizations in Latin America. *Geographical Review, 84*(1), 42-58.

Roberts, N. S., Chavez, D. J., Lara, B. M., & Sheffield, E. A. (2009). *Serving culturally diverse visitors to forests in California: A resource guide.* Gen. Tech. Rep. PSW-GTR-222. Albany, CA: USDA Forest Service, Pacific Southwest Research Station.

Sanders, S. R. (2008). Wilderness as a sabbath for the land. In M. P. Nelson & J. B. Callicott (Eds.), *The wilderness debate rages on* (pp. 603-610). Athens, GA: University of Georgia Press.

Schultz, P. W., Unipan, J. B., & Gamba, R. J. (2000). Acculturation and ecological worldview among Latino Americans. *Journal of Environmental Education, 31*(2), 22-27.

Sodowsky, G. R., Maguire, K., Johnson, P., Ngumba, W., & Kohles, R. (1994). World views of white American,

mainland Chinese, Taiwanese, and African students: An investigation into between-group differences. *Journal of Cross-Cultural Psychology, 25*(3), 309-324.

Stodolska, M., & Yi, J. (2003). Impacts of immigration on ethnic identity and leisure behavior of adolescent immigrants from Korea, Mexico, and Poland. *Journal of Leisure Research, 35*(1), 49-79.

Walker, G. J., & K. J. Kiecolt. (1995). Social class and wilderness use. *Leisure Sciences, 17*(4), 295-308.

Western, D. (2001). In the dust of Kilimanjaro. In D. Rothenberg & M. Ulvaeus (Eds.), *The world and the wild: Expanding wilderness beyond its American roots* (pp. 65-79). Tucson, AZ: University of Arizona Press.

Wilderness Society, The. (1998). Wilderness Society population policy. www.susps.org/ibq1998/discuss/twspolicy.html.

Yu, P., & Berryman, D. L. (1996). The relationship among self-esteem, acculturation, and recreation participation of recently arrived Chinese immigrant adolescents. *Journal of Leisure Research, 28*(4), 251-273.

CHAPTER 13

Active Living Research. (2010). Research synthesis: Parks, playgrounds and active living. Retrieved December 19, 2010, from www.activelivingresearch.org/files/Synthesis_Mowen_Feb2010_0.pdf.

Agency for Healthcare Research and Quality. (2005). *National healthcare disparities report.* AHRQ Publication No. 06-0017. Rockville, MD: U.S. Department of Health and Human Services.

Ahmed, N., Smith, G., Flores, A., Pamies, R., Mason, H., Woods, K., & Stain, S. (2005). Racial/ethnic disparity and predictors of leisure-time physical activity among U.S. men. *Ethnicity & Disease, 15*(1), 40-52.

Airhihenbuwa, C., Kumanyika, S., TenHave, T., & Morssink, C. (2000). Cultural identity and health lifestyles among African Americans: A new direction for health intervention research? *Ethnicity & Disease, 10*(2), 148-164.

Allison, M. T. (2000). Leisure, diversity and social justice. *Journal of Leisure Research, 22*(1), 39-63.

Anderson, E., & Massey, D. S. (2001). The sociology of race in the United States. In E. Anderson & D. S. Massey (Eds.), *Problem of the century: Racial stratification in the United States* (pp. 3-12). New York: Russell Sage Foundation.

Bedimo-Rung, A. L., Mowen, A. J., & Cohen, D. A. (2005). The significance of parks to physical activity and public health: A conceptual model. *American Journal of Preventive Medicine, 28*(S2), 159-168.

Berrigan, D., Dodd, K., Troiano, R. P., Reeve, B. B., & Ballard-Barbash, R. (2006). Physical activity and acculturation among adult Hispanics in the United States. *Research Quarterly for Exercise and Sport, 77*(2), 147-157.

Boyinton, J. E. A., Carter-Edwards, L., Piehl, M., Hutson, J., Langdon, D., & McManus, S. (2008). Cultural attitudes toward weight, diet, and physical activity among overweight African American girls. *Preventing Chronic Disease, 5*(2), A36. www.ncbi.nlm.nih.gov/pmc/articles/PMC2396970/.

Brownson, R. C., Hoehneer, C. M., Day, K., Forsyth, A., & Sallis, J. F. (2009). Measuring the built environment for physical activity. *American Journal of Preventive Medicine, 36,* S99-123.

Centers for Disease Control and Prevention. (2004). Surveillance summaries. *Morbidity and Mortality Weekly Report, 53*(SS-2), 1-96.

Centers for Disease Control and Prevention. (2007). Prevalence of regular physical activity among adults—United States, 2001 and 2005. *Morbidity and Mortality Weekly Report, 56*(46), 1209-1212.

Centers for Disease Control and Prevention. (2009). Prevalence of no leisure-time physical activity—35 states and the District of Columbia, 1988-2008. *Morbidity and Mortality Weekly Report, 53*(4), 82-86.

Cherubini, J. (2008). Adult African American women's perspective on influences that affect their physical activity involvement. *ICHPER-SD Journal of Research, 3*(1), 84-96.

Crespo, C. J. (2000). Encouraging physical activity in minorities. *Physician and SportsMedicine, 28,* 36-51.

Crespo, C., Smit, E., Andersen, R., Carter-Pokras, O., & Ainsworth, B. (2000). Race/ethnicity, social class and their relation to physical inactivity during leisure time: Results from the Third National Health and Nutrition Examination Survey, 1988-1994. *American Journal of Preventive Medicine, 18*(1), 46-53.

Crespo, C., Smit, E., Carter-Pokras, O., & Andersen, R. (2001). Acculturation and leisure-time physical inactivity in Mexican American adults: Results from the Third National Health and Nutrition Examination Survey, 1988-1994. *American Journal of Public Health, 91*(8), 1254-1257.

Cross, G. (1990). *A social history of leisure since 1600.* State College, PA: Venture.

Dachmann, N., Wolch, J., Joassart-Marcelli, P., Reynolds, K., & Jerrett, M. (2010). The active city? Disparities in urban public recreation resources. *Health & Place, 16*(3), 431-445.

Eaton, D. K., Kann, L., Kinchen, S., Shanklin, S., Flint, K. H., Hawkins, J., Harris, W. A., Lowry, R., McManus, T., Chyen, D., Whittle, L., Lim, C., & Wechsler, H. (2012). Youth risk behavior surveillance—United States, 2011. *MMWR, 61*(SS04), 1-162.

Evenson, K. R., Sarmiento, O. L., & Ayala, G. X. (2004). Acculturation and physical activity among North Carolina Latina immigrants. *Social Science & Medicine, 59,* 2509-2522.

Finkelstein, E., Trogdon, J., Cohen, J., & Dietz, W. (2009). Annual medical spending attributable to obesity: Payer- and service-specific estimates. *Health Affairs (Millwood), 28*(5), w822-w831.

Flegal, K. M., Carroll, M. D., Kit, B. K., & Ogden, C. L. (2012). Prevalence of obesity and trends in the distribution of body mass index among US adults, 1999-2010. *Journal of the American Medical Association, 307*(5), 491-497.

Floyd, M. F. (2007). Research on race and ethnicity in leisure: Anticipating the fourth wave. *Leisure/Loisir, 31*(1), 245-254.

Floyd, M. F., Spengler, J. O., Maddock, J. E., Gobster, P. H., & Suau, L. (2008). Environmental and social correlates of physical activity in neighborhood parks: An observational study in Tampa and Chicago. *Leisure Sciences, 30*(4), 360-375.

Folsom, A., Cook, T., Sprafka, J., Burke, G., Norsted, S., & Jacobs, D. (1991). Differences in leisure-time physical activity levels between blacks and whites in population-based samples: The Minnesota Heart Survey. *Journal of Behavioral Medicine, 14*(1), 1-9.

Gobster, P. H. (1998). Explanations for minority "underparticipation" in outdoor recreation: A look at golf. *Journal of Park and Recreation Administration, 16*(1), 46-64.

Gobster, P. H. (2005). Recreation and leisure research from an active living perspective: Taking a second look at urban trail use data. *Leisure Sciences, 27,* 367-383.

Godbey, G. C., Caldwell, L. L., Floyd, M., & Payne, L. L. (2005). Contributions of leisure studies and recreation and park management research to the active living agenda. *American Journal of Preventive Medicine, 28*(S2), 150-158.

Harris, D. V. (1973). *Involvement in sport: A somatopsychic rationale for physical activity.* Philadelphia: Lea & Febiger.

Henderson, K. A. (2009). Just research and physical activity: Diversity is more than an independent variable. *Leisure Sciences, 31*(1), 100-105.

Henderson, K. A., & Ainsworth, B. E. (2001). Researching leisure and physical activity with women of color: Issues and emerging questions. *Leisure Sciences, 23*(1), 21-34.

Henderson, K. A., & Ainsworth, B. E. (2002). Enjoyment: A link to physical activity, leisure, and health. *Journal of Park and Recreation Administration, 20*(4), 130-146.

Hofrichter, R., & Bhatia, R. (2010). *Tackling health inequities through public health practice: Theory to action* (2nd ed.). New York: Oxford University Press.

Im, E. O., & Choe, M. (2001). Physical activity of Korean immigrant women in the U.S.: Needs and attitudes. *International Journal of Nursing Studies, 38*(5), 567-577.

Jamieson, K. M., Araki, D., Chung, Y. C., Kwon, S. Y., Riggioni, L., & Musalem, V. A. (2005). Mujeres (In)Activas: An exploratory study of physical activity among adolescent Latinas. *Women in Sport and Physical Activity Journal, 14,* 95-105.

Joassart-Marcelli, P. (2010). Leveling the playing field? Urban disparities in funding for local parks and recreation in the Los Angeles region. *Environment and Planning A, 42*(5), 1174-1192.

Juarbe, T. C., Lipson, J. G., & Turok, X. (2003). Physical activity beliefs, behaviors, and cardiovascular fitness of Mexican immigrant women. *Journal of Transcultural Nursing, 14,* 108-116.

Kaczynski, A. T., & Henderson, K. A. (2007). Environmental correlates of physical activity: A review of evidence about parks and recreation. *Leisure Sciences, 29*(4), 315-354.

Kahn, E. B., Ramsey, L. T., Brownson, R. C., Heath, G. W., Howze, E. H., Powell, K. E., & Corso, P. (2002). The effectiveness of interventions to increase physical activity: A systematic review. *American Journal of Preventive Medicine, 22*(S4), 73-106.

Kandula, N. R., & Lauderdale, D. S. (2005). Leisure time, non-leisure time, and occupational physical activity in Asian Americans. *Annals of Epidemiology, 15*(4), 257-265.

Khaing Nang, E., Khoo, E., Salim, A., Tai, E., Lee, J., & Van Dam, R. (2010). Patterns of physical activity in different domains and implications for intervention in a multi-ethnic Asian population: A cross-sectional study. *BMC Public Health, 10,* 644.

Kimm, S., Glynn, N., Kriska, A., Barton, B., Kronsberg, S., Daniels, S., & Liu, K. (2002). Decline in physical activity in black girls and white girls during adolescence. *New England Journal of Medicine, 347*(10), 709-715.

Ku, P., Fox, K. R., McKenna, J., & Peng, T. (2006). Prevalence of leisure-time physical activity in Taiwanese adults: Results of four national surveys, 2000–2004. *Preventive Medicine, 43*(6), 454-457.

Lee, S. M. (2005). Physical activity among minority populations: What health promotion practitioners should know—A commentary. *Health Promotion Practice, 6*(4), 447-452.

Liu, J., Probst, J. C., Harun, N., Bennett, K. J., & Torres, M. E. (2009). Acculturation, physical activity, and obesity among Hispanic adolescents. *Ethnicity & Health, 14*(5), 509-525.

Mannell, R. C., & Kleiber, D. A. (1997). *A social psychology of leisure.* State College, PA: Venture.

Marquez, D. X., & McAuley, E. (2006). Gender and acculturation influences on physical activity in Latino adults. *Annals of Behavioral Medicine, 31*(2), 138-144.

Marquez, D. X., McAuley, E., & Overman, N. (2004). Psychosocial correlates and outcomes of physical activity among Latinos: A review. *Hispanic Journal of Behavioral Sciences, 26*(2), 195-229.

Mehta, P., Sharma, M., & Bernard, A. (2009-2010). Social cognitive theory as a predictor of dietary behavior and leisure time physical activity behavior in middle-aged Asian Indian women residing in United States. *International Quarterly of Community Health Education, 30*(5), 257-269.

Moore, L. V., Diez Roux, A. V., Evenson, K. R., McGinn, A. P., & Brines, S. J. (2008). Availability of recreational resources in minority and low socioeconomic status areas. *American Journal of Preventive Medicine, 34*(1), 16-22.

Morgan, C. F., McKenzie, T. L., Sallis, J. F., Broyles, S. L., Zive, M. M., & Nader, P. R. (2003). Personal, social, and environmental correlates of physical activity in a bi-ethnic sample of adolescents. *Pediatric Exercise Science, 15*(3), 288-301.

Morris, J. N., Chave, S. P. W., Adams, C., Sirey, C., Epstein, L., & Sheehan, D. J. (1973). Vigorous exercise in leisure-time and the incidence of coronary heart-disease. *Lancet, 301,* 333-339.

Morris, J. N., Heady, J. A., Raffle, P. A., Roberts, C. G., & Parks, J. W. (1953). Coronary heart-disease and physical activity of work. *Lancet, 265,* 1111-1120.

Neighbors, C. J., Marquez, D. X., & Marcus, B. H. (2008). Leisure-time physical activity disparities among Hispanic subgroups in the United States. *American Journal of Public Health, 98*(8), 1460-1464.

Ogden, C. L., Carroll, M. D., McDowell, M. A., & Flegal, K. M. (2007). *Obesity among adults in the United States.* NCHS Data Brief No. 1. Hyattsville, MD: National Center for Health Statistics.

Patterson, P., Moore, C., Probst, J., & Shinogle, J. (2004). Obesity and physical inactivity in rural America. *The Journal of Rural Health: Official Journal of the American Rural Health Association and The National Rural Health Care Association, 20*(2), 151-159.

Philipp, S. F. (1995). Race and leisure constraints. *Leisure Sciences, 17*(2), 109-120.

Philipp, S. S. (2000). Race and the pursuit of happiness. *Journal of Leisure Research, 32*(1), 121-124.

Pichon, L. C., Arredondo, E. M., Roesch, S., Sallis, J. F., Ayala, G. X., & Elder, J. P. (2007). The relation of acculturation to Latinas' perceived neighborhood safety and physical activity: A structural equation analysis. *Annals of Behavioral Medicine, 34*(3), 295-303.

Potwarka, L. R., Kaczynski, A. T., & Flack, A. L. (2008). Places to play: Association of park space and facilities with healthy weight status among children. *Journal of Community Health, 33*(5), 344-350.

Powell, L. M., Slater, S., Chaloupka, F. J., & Harper, D. (2006). Availability of physical activity-related facilities and neighborhood demographic and socioeconomic characteristics: A national study. *American Journal of Public Health, 96*(9), 1676-1680.

Ransdell, L. B., & Wells, C. L. (1998). Physical activity in urban White, African-American and Mexican-American women. *Medicine and Science in Sports and Exercise, 30,* 1608-1615.

Richter, D. L., Wilcox, S., Greaney, M. L., Henderson, K. A., & Ainsworth, B. E. (2002). Environmental, policy, and cultural factors related to physical activity in African American women. *Women & Health, 36*(2), 89-107.

Rogers, T. M. (1997). *Effectiveness of a walking club and a self-directed physical activity program in increasing moderate intensity physical activity among African-American females.* Eugene, OR: University of Oregon, Microform Publications.

Rung, A. L., Mowen, A. J., Broyles, S. T., & Gustat, J. (2011). The role of park conditions and features on park visitation and physical activity. *Journal of Physical Activity and Health, 8*(2), S178-S187.

Sallis, J. F., & Owen, N. (1997). Ecological models. In K. Lewis, F. Rimer, & B. Glanz (Eds.), *Health behavior and health education: Theory, research, and practice* (pp. 403-424). San Francisco: Jossey-Bass.

Sargent, L. A. (2001). *The role of social support and self-efficacy in influencing moderate leisure time physical activity among African American women.* Eugene, OR : University of Oregon, Kinesiology Publications.

Seo, D., & Torabi, M. (2007). Differences in vigorous and moderate physical activity by gender, race/ethnicity, age, education, and income among U.S. adults. *American Journal of Health Education, 38*(3), 122-128.

Shores, K. A., & West, S. T. (2008a). The relationship between built park environments and physical activity in four park locations. *Journal of Public Health Management Practice, 14*(3), E1-7.

Shores, K. A., & West, S. T. (2008b). Physical activity outcomes associated with African American park visitation in four community parks. *Journal of Park and Recreation Administration, 26*(3), 75-92.

Skowron, M. A., Stodolska, M., & Shinew, K. J. (2008). Determinants of leisure time physical activity participation among Latina women. *Leisure Sciences, 30*(5), 429-447.

Stodolska, M. (2000). Looking beyond the invisible: Can research on leisure of ethnic and racial minorities contribute to leisure theory? *Journal of Leisure Research, 32*(1), 156-160.

Stodolska, M., Acevedo, J., & Shinew, K. J. (2009). Gangs of Chicago: Perceptions of crime and its effect on the recreation behavior of Latino residents in urban communities. *Leisure Sciences, 31*(5), 466-482.

Stodolska, M., & Shinew, K. J. (2010). Environmental constraints on leisure time physical activity among Latino urban residents. *Qualitative Research in Sport and Exercise, 2*(3), 313-335.

Stodolska, M., Shinew, K. J., Acevedo, J. C., & Izenstark, D. (2011). Perceptions of urban parks as havens and contested terrains by Mexican-Americans in Chicago neighborhoods. *Leisure Sciences, 33*(2), 103-126.

Stodolska, M., Shinew, K. J., Acevedo, J. C., & Roman, C. G. (2013). "I was born in the hood": Fear of crime, outdoor recreation and physical activity among Mexican American urban adolescents. *Leisure Sciences, 35*, 1-15.

Stodolska, M., Shinew, K. J., & Li, M. Z. (2010). Recreation participation patterns and physical activity among Latino visitors to three urban outdoor recreation environments. *Journal of Park and Recreation Administration, 28*(2), 36-56.

Taylor, D. E. (2000). Meeting the challenge of wild land recreation management: Demographic shifts and social inequality. *Journal of Leisure Research, 32*(1), 171-179.

Taylor, W. C., Baranowski, T., & Young, D. (1998). Physical activity interventions in low-income, ethnic minority, and populations with disability. *American Journal of Preventive Medicine, 15*(4), 334-343.

Taylor, W., Floyd, M. F., Whitt-Glover, M., & Brooks, J. (2007). Environmental justice: A framework for collaboration between the public health and recreation and parks fields to study disparities and physical activity. *Journal of Physical Activity and Health, 4*(S1), S20-S29.

Thompson, W. M. (2010). Physical inactivity of Black adolescent girls: Is it all about attitude? *Home Health Care Management and Practice, 23*(3), 186-192.

Tortolero, S., Masse, L., Fulton, J., & Torres, I. (1999). Assessing physical activity among minority women: Focus group results. *Women's Health Issues, 9*, 135-142.

Trost, S. G., Pate, R. R., Saunders, R., Ward, D. S., Dowda, D., & Felton, G. (1997). A prospective study of the deter-minants of physical activity in rural 5th grade children. *Preventive Medicine, 26*, 257-263.

U.S. Department of Health and Human Services. (1996). *Physical activity and health: A report of the surgeon general.* Atlanta: Centers for Disease Control and Prevention, National Center for Chronic Disease Prevention and Health Promotion.

Vendien, D. L., & Nixon, J. E. (1968). *The world today in health, physical education, and recreation.* Englewood Cliffs, NJ: Prentice-Hall.

Voorhees, C. C., & Young, D. (2003). Personal, social, and physical environmental correlates of physical activity levels in urban Latinas. *American Journal of Preventive Medicine, 25*(3), 61-68.

Wai, J. P., Wen, C. P., Chan, H. T., Chiang, P. H., Tsai, M. K., Tsai, S. P., & Chiang, H.Y. (2008). Assessing physical activity in an Asian country: Low energy expenditure and exercise frequency among adults in Taiwan. *Asia Pacific Journal of Clinical Nutrition, 17*(2), 297-308.

Washburn, R., Kline, G., Lackland, D., & Wheeler, F. (1992). Leisure time physical activity: Are there black/white differences? *Preventive Medicine, 21*(1), 127-135.

Welk, G. J., & Blair, S. N. (2000). Physical activity protects against the health risks of obesity. *President's Council on Physical Fitness and Sports Research Digest, 3*(12), 1-5.

West, S. T., & Crompton, J. L. (2008). A comparison of preferences and perceptions of alternate equity operationalizations. *Leisure Sciences, 30*(5), 409-428.

Whitt-Glover, M. C., Taylor, W. C., Heath, G. W., & Macera, C. A. (2007). Self-reported physical activity among Blacks: Estimates from national surveys. *American Journal of Preventive Medicine, 33*(5), 412-417.

Yancey, A., Kumanyika, S., Ponce, N., McCarthy, W., Fielding, J., Leslie, J., & Akbar, J. (2004). Population-based interventions engaging communities of color in healthy eating and active living: A review. *Preventing Chronic Disease, 1*(1), A09.

Young, D. R., He, X., Harris, J., & Mabry, I. (2002). Environmental, policy, and cultural factors related to physical activity in well-educated urban African American women. *Women & Health, 36*(2), 29-41.

Young, D., & Stewart, K. (2006). A church-based physical activity intervention for African American women. *Family & Community Health, 29*, 103-117.

CHAPTER 14

Ainsworth, B. E., Berry, C. B., Schnyder, V. N., & Vickers, S. R. (1992). Leisure-time physical activity and aerobic fitness in African-American young adults. *Journal of Adolescent Health, 13*, 606-611.

Ama, P. F., Lagasse, P., Bouchard, C., & Simoneau, J. A. (1990). Anaerobic performances in black and white subjects. *Medicine and Science in Sports and Exercise, 22*, 508-511.

Andersen, K. J., & Cavallaro, D. (2002). Parents or pop culture? Children's heroes and role models. *Childhood Education, 78*, 161-168.

Bandura, A. (1977). Self-efficacy: Toward a unifying theory of behavioral change. *Psychological Review, 84,* 191-215.

Bandura, A. (1982). Self-efficacy mechanism in human agency. *American Psychologist, 37,* 122-147.

Beamon, K., & Bell, P. A. (2006). Academics versus athletics: An examination of the effects of background and socialization on African American male student athletes. *Social Science Journal, 43,* 393-403.

Beilock, S. L., & McConnell, A. R. (2004). Stereotype threat and sport: Can athletic performance be threatened? *Journal of Sport and Exercise Psychology, 26,* 597-609.

Biernat, M., Vescio, T. K., & Green, M. L. (1996). Selective self-stereotyping. *Journal of Personality and Social Psychology, 71,* 1194-1209.

Brewer, B. W., Van Raalte, J. L., & Linder, D. (1993). Athletic identity: Hercules' muscles or achilles heel? *International Journal of Sport Psychology, 24,* 237-254.

Brown, T. N., Jackson, J. S., Brown, K. T., Sellers, R. M., Keiper, S., & Manuel, W. J. (2003). There's no race on the playing field: Perceptions of racial discrimination among white and black athletes. *Journal of Sport and Social Issues, 27,* 162-183.

Bruening, J. E. (2005). Gender and racial analysis in sport: Are all the women white and all the Blacks men? *Quest, 57,* 330-349.

Bruening, J. E., Armstrong, K. L., & Pastore, D. L. (2005). Listening to the voices: The experiences of African American female student athletes. *Research Quarterly for Exercise and Sport, 76,* 82-100.

Bungum, T., Pate, R., Dowda, M., & Vincent, M. (1996). Correlates of physical activity among African-American and Caucasian female adolescents. *American Journal of Health Behavior, 23,* 25-31.

Burden, J. Jr., Hodge, S. R., O'Bryant, C. P., & Harrison, L. Jr. (2004). From colorblindness to intercultural sensitivity: Infusing diversity training in PETE programs. *Quest, 56,* 173-189.

Carlston, D. E. (1983). An environmental explanation for race differences in basketball performance. *Journal of Sport and Social Issues, 7,* 30-51.

Carrington, B., & McDonald, I. (2001). *Race, sport and British society.* London, UK: Routledge.

Carter, A. R., & Hart, A. (2010). Perspectives of mentoring: The black female student-athlete. *Sport Management Review, 13,* 382-394.

Carter, R. T. (1995). *The influence of race and racial identity in psychotherapy: Toward a racially inclusive model.* New York: Wiley.

Coakley, J. J. (2004). *Sport in society: Issues and controversies.* Boston: McGraw-Hill.

Cokley, K., & Chapman, C. (2008). Racial identity theory: Adults. In H. A. Neville, B. M. Tynes, & S. O. Utsey (Eds.), *Handbook of African American psychology* (pp. 283-297). Thousand Oaks, CA: Sage.

Cooper, R. S., Kaufman, J. S., & Ward, R. (2003). Race and genomics. *New England Journal of Medicine, 348,* 1166-1170.

Cross, W. E. Jr. (1971). The Negro-to-Black conversion experience. *Black World, 20,* 13-27.

Cross, W. E. Jr. (1991). *Shades of Black: Diversity in African-American identity.* Philadelphia: Temple University Press.

Cross, W. E. Jr. (1995). The psychology of Nigrescence: Revising the Cross model. In J. G. Ponterotto, J. M. Casas, L. A. Suzuki, & C. M. Alexander (Eds.), *Handbook of multicultural counseling* (pp. 93-122). Thousand Oaks, CA: Sage.

Cross, W. E., Jr., & Vandiver, B. J. (2001). Nigrescence theory and measurement: Introducing the Cross Racial Identity Scale (CRIS). In J. G. Ponterotto, J. M. Casas, L. A. Suzuki, & C. M. Alexander (Eds.), *Handbook of multicultural counseling* (2nd ed., pp. 371–393). Thousand Oaks, CA: Sage.

Davis, L. R., & Harris, O. (1998). Race and ethnicity in US sports media. In L. A. Wenner (Ed.), *MediaSport* (pp. 154-169). New York: Routledge.

Devine, P. G. (1989). Stereotypes and prejudice: Their automatic and controlled components. *Journal of Personality and Social Psychology, 56,* 5-18.

Dole, A. A. (1995). Why not drop race as a term? *American Psychologist, 50,* 40.

Edwards, H. (1972). The myth of the racially superior athlete. *Intellectual Digest, 44,* 32-38.

Eitzen, D. S., & Sage, G. H. (2003). *Sociology of North American sport.* Boston: McGraw-Hill.

Entine, J. (2000). *Taboo: Why black athletes dominate sports, and why we are afraid to talk about it.* New York: Public Affairs.

Fiske, S. T., & Neuberg, S. L. (1990). A continuum of impression formation, from category based to individuating process: Influences of information and motivation on attention and interpretation. In M. P. Zanna (Ed.), *Advances in experimental social psychology, Vol. 23* (pp. 1-79). New York: Academic Press.

Gallagher, C. A. (2003). Miscounting race: Explaining White's misperception of racial group size. *Sociological Perspectives, 46,* 381-396.

Goldsmith, P. A. (2003). Race relations and racial patterns in school sports participation. *Sociology of Sport Journal, 20,* 147-171.

Good, A. J., Brewer, B. W., Petitpas, A. J., Van Raalte, J. L., & Mahar, M. T. (1993). Identity foreclosure, athletic identity, and college sport participation. *Academic Athletic Journal, 8,* 1-12.

Gould, R. D., & Roberts, C. G. (1981). Modeling and motor skill acquisition. *Quest, 33,* 214-230.

Greene, L. S., & Green, T. S. (2007). Beyond tokenism to empowerment: The black women in sport foundation. In D. Brooks & R. Althouse (Eds.), *Diversity and social justice in college sports* (pp. 313-332). Morgantown, WV: Fitness Information Technology.

Griffith, K. A., & Johnson, K. A. (2002). Athletic identity and life roles of Division I and Division III collegiate athletes. *University of Wisconsin-La Crosse Journal of Undergraduate Research, 5,* 225-231.

Hamilton, D. L., & Trolier, T. K. (1986). Stereotypes and stereotyping: An overview of the cognitive approach. In J. F. Dovidio & S. L. Gaertner (Eds.), *Prejudice, discrimination, and racism* (pp. 127-163). New York: Academic Press.

Harrison, C. K. (1998). Themes that thread through society: Racism and the athletic manifestation in the African American community. *Race Ethnicity and Education, 1,* 63-74.

Harrison, L. (1995). African Americans: Race as a self-schema affecting physical activity choices. *Quest, 47,* 7-18.

Harrison, L. Jr. (1999). *Racial attitudes in sport: A survey of race-sport competence beliefs.* Reston, VA: Ethnic Minorities Council of the American Association for Active Lifestyles and Fitness.

Harrison, L. Jr. (2001). Understanding the influence of stereotypes: Implications for the African American in sport and physical activity. *Quest, 53,* 97-114.

Harrison, L. Jr., Azzarito, L., & Burden, J. Jr. (2004). Perceptions of athletic superiority: A view from the other side. *Race Ethnicity and Education, 7,* 149-166.

Harrison, L. Jr., Harrison, C. K., & Moore, L. (2002). African American racial identity and sport. *Sport, Education and Society, 7,* 121-133.

Harrison, L. Jr., Lee, A., & Belcher, D. (1999a). Race and gender differences in the sources of students' self-schemata for sport and physical activities. *Race Ethnicity and Education, 2,* 219-234.

Harrison, L. Jr., Lee, A., & Belcher, D. (1999b). Self -schemata for specific sports and physical activities: The influence of race and gender. *Journal of Sport and Social Issues, 23,* 287-302.

Harrison, L. Jr., & Moore, L. N. (2007). Who am I? Racial identity, athletic identity and the African American athlete. In D. Brooks & R. Althouse (Eds.), *Diversity and social justice in college sports* (pp. 245-260). Morgantown, WV: Fitness Information Technology.

Harrison, L. Jr., Sailes, G., Rotich, W. K., & Bimper, A. Y. Jr. (2011). Living the dream or awakening from the nightmare: Race and athletic identity. *Race Ethnicity and Education, 14,* 91-103.

Haslam, S. A., Oakes, P. J., Reynolds, K. J., & Turner, J. C. (1999). Social identity salience and the emergence of stereotype consensus. *Personality and Social Psychology Bulletin, 25,* 809-818.

Hoberman, J. (1997). *Darwin's athletes: How sport has damaged Black America and preserved the myth of race.* New York: Houghton Mifflin.

Hodge, S. R., Kozub, F. M., Dixson, A. D., Moore, J. L. III, & Kambon, K. (2008). A comparison of high school students' stereotypic beliefs about intelligence and athleticism. *Educational Foundations, 22,* 99-119.

Horn, T. S., & Lox, C. (1993). The self-fulfilling prophecy theory: When coaches' expectations become reality. In J. M. Williams (Ed.), *Applied sport psychology* (pp. 68-81). Mountain View, CA: Mayfield.

Hunter, D. W. (1998). Race and athletic performance: A physiological review. In G. A. Sailes (Ed.), *African Americans in sport* (pp. 85-101). New Brunswick, NJ: Transaction.

Jackson, J. (1989). Race, ethnicity, and psychological theory and research. *Journal of Gerontology: Psychological Sciences, 44,* 1-2.

Jackson, J. S., Keiper, S., Brown, K. T., Brown, T. N., & Manuel, W. (2002). Athletic identity, racial attitudes, and aggression in first-year black and white intercollegiate athletes. In M. Gatz, M. A. Messner, & S. J. Ball-Rokeach (Eds.), *Paradoxes of youth and sport* (pp. 159-186). Albany, NY: State University of New York Press.

Johal, S. (2001). Playing their own game: A south Asian football experience. In B. Carrington & I. McDonald (Eds.), *"Race," sport and British society* (pp. 153-169). New York: Routledge.

Kumanyika, S., & Adams-Campbell, L. L. (1991). Obesity, diet, and psychosocial factors contributing to cardiovascular disease in blacks. In E. Saunders (Ed.), *Cardiovascular diseases in Blacks* (pp. 47-73). Philadelphia: Davis.

Kusz, K. W. (2001). I want to be the minority! The politics of youthful White masculinities in sport and popular culture in 1990s America. *Journal of Sport and Social Issues, 25,* 390-416.

Lapchick, R. E. (2009). 2009 Racial and gender report card. http://web.bus.ucf.edu/documents/sport/2009_RGRC.pdf.

LaVeist, T. A. (1996). Why we should continue to study race . . . but do a better job: An essay on race, racism and health. *Ethnicity & Disease, 6,* 21-29.

Long, J. G., & Hylton, K. (2002). Shades of white: An examination of whiteness in sport. *Leisure Studies, 21,* 87-103.

Magill, R. A. (2004). *Motor learning and control: Concepts and applications* (7th ed.). Dubuque, IA: Brown.

Majors, R. (1990). Cool pose: Black masculinity and sports. In M. A. Messner & D. F. Sabo (Eds.), *Sport, men, and the gender order: Critical feminist perspectives* (pp. 109-114). Champaign, IL: Human Kinetics.

Markus, H. (1977). Self-schemata and processing information about the self. *Journal of Personality and Social Psychology, 35,* 63-78.

Martinek, T. (1981). Pygmalion in the gym: A model for the communication of teacher expectations in physical education. *Research Quarterly, 52,* 58-67.

McCullagh, P. (1986). Model status as a determinant of observational learning and performance. *Journal of Sport Psychology, 8*(4), 319-331.

Meaney, K. S., Griffin, K. L., & Hart, M. A. (2005). The effect of model similarity on girls' motor performance. *Journal of Teaching in Physical Education, 24*(2), 165-178.

Meredith, H. V., & Spurgeon, J. H. (1980). Somatic comparisons at age 9 years for South Carolina white girls and girls of other ethnic groups. *Human Biology, 52*(3), 401-411.

Merton, R. K. (1948). The self-fulfilling prophecy. *Antioch Review, 8*(2), 193-210.

Mignano, A., Brewer, B., Winter, C., & Van Raalte, J. (2006). Athletic identity and student involvement of female athletes at NCAA Division III women's and coeducational colleges. *Journal of College Student Development, 47*(4), 457-464.

Miller, P. B. (1998). The anatomy of scientific racism: Racialist responses to black athletic achievement. *Journal of Sport History, 25*(1), 119-151.

Miller, P. S., & Kerr, G. A. (2003). The role experimentation of intercollegiate student athletes. *Sport Psychologist, 17,* 196-219.

Myers, D. G. (1993). *Social psychology.* New York: McGraw-Hill.

Nature Genetics. (2000). Census, race and science. *Nature Genetics, 24,* 97-98.

Oakes, P. J., Haslam, S. A., & Turner, J. C. (1994). *Stereotyping and social reality.* Cambridge, MA: Blackwell.

Payne, V. G., & Isaacs, L. D. (2005). *Human motor development: A lifespan approach.* Boston: McGraw-Hill.

Rastogi, S., Johnston, T. D., Hoeffel, E. M., & Drewery, M. P. Jr. (2011). *The black population: 2010.* Washington, DC: U.S. Department of Commerce, U.S. Bureau of the Census.

Rotich, W. K. (2009). *Like Tweedledum and Tweedledee? Influence of model similarity on efficacy, acquisition of concepts and performance of skills in cricket among middle school children.* Unpublished doctoral dissertation, University of Texas, Austin, TX.

Saporito, S., & Sohoni, D. (2006). Coloring outside the lines: Racial segregation in public schools and their attendance boundaries. *Sociology of Education, 79*(2), 81-105.

Schunk, D. H. (1987). Peer models and children's behavioral change. *Review of Educational Research, 57,* 149-179.

Sellers, R. M., Smith, M. A., Shelton, J. N., Rowley, S. A., & Chavous, T. M. (1998). Multidimensional model of racial identity: A reconceptualization of African American racial identity. *Personality and Social Psychology Review, 2,* 18-39.

Sheldon, J. P., Jayaratne, T. E., & Petty, E. M. (2007). White Americans' genetic explanations for a perceived race difference in athleticism: The relation to prejudice toward stereotyping of Blacks. *Athletic Insight: The Online Journal of Sport Psychology, 9.* www.athleticinsight.com/Vol9Iss3/RaceDifference.htm.

Spencer, M. B., & Markstrom-Adams, C. (1990). Identity processes among racial and ethnic minority children in America. *Child Development, 61,* 290-310.

Steele, C. M., & Aronson, J. (1995). Stereotype threat and the intellectual test performance of African Americans. *Journal of Personality and Social Psychology, 69,* 797-811.

Steinfeldt, J. A., Reed, C., & Steinfeldt, M. C. (2010). Racial and athletic identity of African Americans football players at historically Black colleges and universities and predominately White institutions. *Journal of Black Psychology, 36,* 3-24.

Stone, J., Lynch, C. I., Sjomeling, M., & Darley, J. M. (1999). Stereotype threat effects on black and white athletic performance. *Journal of Personality and Social Psychology, 77,* 1213-1227.

Stone, J., Perry, Z. W., & Darley, J. M. (1997). "White men can't jump": Evidence for the perceptual confirmation of racial stereotypes following a basketball game. *Basic and Applied Social Psychology, 19,* 291-306.

Stryker, S. (1968). Identity salience and role performance: The importance of symbolic interaction theory for family research. *Journal of Marriage and the Family, 30,* 558-564.

Stryker, S. (2007). Identity theory and personality theory: Mutual relevance. *Journal of Personality, 75,* 1083-1102.

Tate, W. (2003). The "race" to theorize education: Who is my neighbor? *Qualitative Studies in Education, 16,* 121-126.

Tatum, B. (1997). *"Why are all the black kids sitting together in the cafeteria?": And other conversations about race.* New York: Basic Books.

Trouilloud, D. O., Sarrazin, P. G., Martinek, T. G., & Guillet, E. (2002). The influence of teacher expectations on student achievement in physical education. *European Journal of Social Psychology, 32,* 591-607.

U.S. Census Bureau. (2000). American FactFinder. http://factfinder2.census.gov/faces/nav/jsf/pages/index.xhtml.

Webb, W. M., Nasco, S. A., Riley, S., & Headrick, B. (1998). Athlete identity and reactions to retirement from sports. *Journal of Sport Behavior, 21,* 338-362.

Wheaton, B., & Beal, B. (2003). "Keeping it real": Subcultural media and discourses of authenticity in alternative sport. *International Review for the Sociology of Sport, 38,* 155-176.

Wiggins, D. K. (1997). "Great speed but little stamina": The historical debate over black athletic superiority. In S. W. Pope (Ed.), *The new American sport history: Recent approaches and perspectives* (pp. 312-338). Urbana, IL: University of Illinois Press.

Wilbon, M. (2002, May 5). To NBA's European stars, "big white stiff doesn't translate." *Washington Post,* 4D.

CHAPTER 15

Amara, M., Aquilina, D., & Henry, I., with PMP Consultants. (2004). Sport and multicultural dialogue: A review of policy in the 25 European Member States, a study undertaken for the European Commission DG Education and Culture. http://ec.europa.eu/sport/library/documents/c3/pmp-study-dual-career_en.pdf.

Andersson, R. (2007). Ethnic residential segregation and integration processes in Sweden. In K. Schönwälder (Ed.), *Residential segregation and the integration of immigrants: Britain, the Netherlands and Sweden.* Discussion Paper SP IV 2007-602 (pp. 61-90). Berlin, Germany: Wissenschaftszentrum Berlin für Sozialforschung gGmbH, Social Science Research Center Berlin.

Askins, K. (2004). Visible communities' use and perceptions of the Peak District and North York Moors National Parks: A preliminary analysis of interview data. Available at Durham E-Theses Online: http://etheses.dur.ac.uk/3169/.

Axén, E., & Lindström, M. (2002). Ethnic differences in self-reported lack of access to a regular doctor: A population based study. *Ethnicity & Health, 7*(3), 195-207.

Bade, K. (2003; Orig. ed. 2000). *Migration in European history.* Oxford: Blackwell.

Bell, S., Morris, N., Findlay, C., Travlou, P., Montarzino, A., Gooch, D., Gregory, G., & Ward Thompson, C. (2004).

Nature for people: The importance of green spaces to East Midlands communities. English Nature Research Reports, No. 567. Peterborough, UK: English Nature.

Bhabha, H. K. (1994). *The location of culture.* London and New York: Routledge.

Bolt, G., Özüekren, A. S., & Phillips, D. (2009). Linking integration and residential segregation. *Journal of Ethnic and Migration Studies, 36*(2), 169-186.

Breedveld, K., Kamphuis, C., & Tiessen-Raaphorst, A. (2008). *Rapportage sport 2008* (p. 93). The Hague: Sociaal en Cultureel Planbureau/W.J.H. Mulier Instituut.

Breuer, C., & Wicker, P. (2008). Sportvereine in Deutschland. Sportentwicklungsbericht 2007/2008. Analyse zur Situation der Sportvereine in Deutschland. www.bisp.de/cln_090/nn_16030/DE/Aktuelles/Nachrichten/2008/Sportentwick__2007__08.html?__nnn=true.

Bruin, S. de. (2006). Voor elk wat wils? *Agora* (4), 23-26.

Bruquetas-Callejo, M., Garcés-Mascareñas, B., Penninx, R., & Scholten, P. (2007). Policymaking related to immigration and integration. The Dutch Case. Working Paper No. 15. *IMISCOE Working Paper: Country Report.* Amsterdam, Netherlands: IMISCOE.

Buijs, A. E., Langers, F., & De Vries, S. (2006). Een andere kijk op groen. Beleving van natuur en landschap in Nederland door allochtonen en jongeren. Rapport 24. Wageningen, The Netherlands.

Burgers, J., & Van der Lugt, H. (2006). Spatial assimilation of minority groups. The case of suburbanising Surinamese in the Rotterdam region. *Journal of Housing and the Built Environment, 21*(2), 127-139.

Clarke, J., van Dam, E., & Gooster, L. (1998). New Europeans: Naturalization and citizenship in Europe. *Citizenship Studies, 2*(1), 43-67.

Countryside Council for Wales. (2005). Access awareness study: Key findings on participation and barriers, CCW. www.ccw.gov.uk/publications--research.aspx.

Dawson, A. J., Sundquist, J., & Johansson, S. E. (2006). The influence of ethnicity and length of time since immigration on physical activity. *Ethnicity & Health, 10*(4), 293-309.

De Haan, J., & Breedveld, K. (2000). *Trends en determinanten in de sport. Eerste resultaten uit het AVO 1999.* The Hague: SCP Werkdokument.

De Hart, J., et al. (2002). *Zekere banden: Sociale cohesie, leefbaarheid en veiligheid.* The Hague: SCP.

Department for Communities and Local Government. (2006). *Managing for diversity: A case study of four local authorities.* London: Department for Communities and Local Government.

Ethnos Research and Consultancy. (2005). What about us? Diversity review part 1: Challenging perceptions: Under-represented visitor needs. http://publications.naturalengland.org.uk/file/290015.

EUMC. (2006). *Muslims in the European Union: Discrimination and Islamophobia.* Vienna: European Monitoring Centre on Racism and Xenophobia.

European Travel Commission (ETC). (2006). Tourism trends for Europe. Brussels (European Travel Commission). Related online version at www.etc-corporate.org/modules.php?name=Content&pa=showpage&pid=100.

Eurostat. (2010). Migration statistics. Retrieved November 16, 2010, from http://epp.eurostat.ec.europa.eu/portal/page/portal/eurostat/home/.

Favell, A. (1998). *Philosophies of integration: Immigration and the idea of citizenship in France and Britain.* London: Macmillan.

Fennema, M., et al. (2000). *Sociaal Kapitaal en Politieke Participatie van Etnische Minderheden.* Amsterdam: IMES.

Fertig, M. (2004). *The societal integration of immigrants in Germany.* Discussion Paper Series, No. 1213. Bonn, Germany: Forschungsinstitut zur Zukunft der Arbeit/Institute for the Study of Labor.

FRA, European Union Agency for Fundamental Rights. (2010). *Racism, ethnic discrimination and exclusion of migrants and minorities in sport: A comparative overview of the situation in the European Union.* Luxembourg: Publications Office of the European Union.

Friberg, J. H. (2006). Social exclusion and participation among young people with immigrant backgrounds. In *Poverty among children, young people and families – a booklet of information and experiences.* Oslo, Norway: Norwegian Ministry of Children and Equality.

Fryer, P. (1984). *Staying power. The history of Black people in Britain.* London: Pluto Press.

Geldrop, M., & van Heerwaarden, Y. (2003). *Uitgaansbeleving van Amsterdamse allochtone jongeren: Marokkaanse, Turkse, Surinaamse en Antilliaanse jongeren aan het woord over uitgaan in Amsterdam.* Amsterdam: DSP-groep BV, Amsterdam i.o. van de gemeente Amsterdam.

Gijsberts, M., & Dagevos, J. (2010). *At home in the Netherlands. Trends in integration of non-Western migrants.* Annual Report on Integration 2009. The Hague: SCP.

Green, G. T., Bowker, J. M., Johnson, C. Y., Cordell, H. K., & Wang, X. (2007). An examination of constraints to wilderness visitation. *Journal of Wilderness, 13,* 1-12.

Gundelach, P. (2010). Democracy and denomination: Democratic values among Muslim minorities and the majority population in Denmark. *Ethnic and Racial Studies, 33*(3), 426-450.

Hofstede, G. J. (2003). *Cultural consequences: Comparing values, behaviours, institutions and organizations across nations* (2nd ed.). London: Sage.

Jay, M., & Schraml, U. (2009). Understanding the role of urban forests for migrants - uses, perception and integrative potential. *Urban Forestry and Urban Greening, 8,* 283-294.

Johnston, R., Forrest, J., & Poulsen, M. (2002). Are there ethnic enclaves/ghettos in English cities? *Urban Studies, 39*(4), 591-618.

Jokovi, E. M. (2000). *Recreatie van Turken, Marokkanen en Surinamers in Rotterdam en Amsterdam; een verkenning van het vrijetijdsgedrag van de 1e en 2e generatie en van de effecten van de etnische cultuur op de vrijetijdsbesteding.* Wageningen, The Netherlands: Alterra.

Jokovi, E. M. (2001). *Recreatie van Turken, Marokkanen en Surinamers in Rotterdam en Amsterdam: En verkenning van het vrijetijdsgedrag en van de effecten van de etnische cultuur op de vrijetijdsbesteding. [Recreation of Turks, Moroccans and Surinamese in Rotterdam and Amsterdam: An exploration of leisure behavior and the effects of ethnic culture on leisure participation]*. Wageningen, The Netherlands: Alterra.

Joppke, C. (1999). How immigration is changing citizenship: A comparative view. *Ethnic and Racial Studies, 22*(4), 629-652.

Joppke, C. (2004). The retreat of multiculturalism in the liberal state: Theory and policy. *British Journal of Sociology, 55*(2), 237-257.

Kelaher, M., Paul, S., Lambert, H., Ahmad, W., Paradies, Y., & Davey Smith, G. (2008). Discrimination and health in an English study. *Social Science & Medicine, 66*, 1627-1636.

Klaver, J., Tromp, E., & Oude Ophuis, R. (2005). *Allochtonen en Vrijwilligerswerk. [Allochtons and volunteering]*. Amsterdam: Regioplan Beleidsonderzoek.

Komen, M. (2004). *Etniciteit en uitgaan in Den Haag*. The Hague: Haagse Hogeschool.

Lagendijk, E., & Van der Gugten, M. (1995). *Sport en allochtonen, feiten, ontwikkelingen en beleid 1986-1995*. The Hague: Ministerie van Volksgezondheid Welzijn en Sport, directie Sport.

Landry, C., & Bianchini, F. (1995). *The creative city: A toolkit for urban innovators*. London: Demos.

Lee, P., & Murie, A. (1999). Spatial and social divisions within British cities: Beyond residualisation. *Housing Studies, 14*(5), 625-640.

Lindström, M. (2005). Ethnic differences in social participation and social capital in Malmö, Sweden: A population-based study. *Social Science & Medicine 60*(7), 1527-1546.

Lindström, M., & Sundquist, J. (2001). Immigration and leisure-time physical inactivity. *Ethnicity & Health, 6*(2), 77-85.

Madge, C. (1997). Public parks and the geography of fear. *Tijdschrift Voor Economische En Sociale Geografie, 88*, 237-250.

Martinez, S. D., & Vreeswijk, A. (2002). Ruimtelijke concentratie van allochtonen. In J. Veenman (Ed.), *De toekomst in meervoud, Perspectief op multicultureel Nederland*. Assen, The Netherlands: Koninklijke Van Gorcum.

Masso, A. (2009). A readiness to accept immigrants in Europe? Individual and country-level characteristics. *Journal of Ethnic and Migration Studies, 35*(2), 251-270.

Morris, N. (2003). *Black and minority ethnic groups and public open space literature review*. OPENspace Research Centre. Edinburgh: Edinburgh College of Art and Heriot-Watt University.

Munck, R. (2009). *Globalization and migration: New issues, new politics*. London: Routledge.

Musterd, S. (2005). Social and ethnic segregation in Europe: Levels, causes and effects. *Journal of Urban Affairs, 27*(3), 331-348.

Muus, P. (2001). International migration and the European Union: Trends and consequences. *European Journal on Criminal Policy and Research, 9*, 31-49.

Natural England. (2010). *Monitor of engagement with the natural environment: The national survey on people and the natural environment*. Annual report 2009-10 survey. London: Natural England.

O'Brien, L., and Morris, J. (2009). *Active England: The woodland projects. Report to the Forestry Commission*. Surrey, UK: Forest Research.

OPENspace. (2006). *Review of the Scottish Forestry Strategy. Consultation process: Focus groups*. Final report. Edinburgh: OPENspace.

Parekh, B. (1996). Minority practices and principles of toleration. *International Migration Review, 30*(1), 251-284.

Peters, K. (2010). Being together in urban parks: Connecting public space, leisure and diversity. *Leisure Sciences 32*(5), 418-433.

Peters, K., Elands, B., & Buijs, A. (2010). Social interactions in urban parks: Stimulating social cohesion? *Urban Forestry and Urban Greening, 9*(2), 93-100.

Peucker, M. (2009). *Racism, xenophobia and structural discrimination in sports*. Country report: Germany. Bamberg, Germany: European Forum for Migration Studies (EFMS).

Philips, D. (2010). Minority ethnic segregation, integration and citizenship: A European perspective. *Journal of Ethnic and Migration Studies, 36*(2), 209-225.

Ratcliffe, P. (2004). *Race, ethnicity and difference: Imagining the inclusive society*. Maidenhead, UK: Open University Press.

Rath, J. (1993). De tegenbedoelde effecten van het minderhedenbeleid. De constructie van minderheden. In G. Pas (Ed.), *Achter de coulissen. Gedachten over de multi-etnische samenleving* (pp. 24-42). Amsterdam: Wetenschappelijk Bureau Groen Links.

Rath, J. (2007). *The transformation of ethnic neighborhoods into places of leisure and consumption*. Working Paper No. 144. Amsterdam: University of Amsterdam, Institute for Migration and Ethic Studies (IMES).

Ravenscroft, N., & Markwell, S. (2000). Ethnicity and the integration and exclusion of young people through urban park and recreation provision. *Managing Leisure 5*(3), 135-150.

Salt, J. (1998). *Current trends in international migration in Europe*. Strasbourg: Council of Europe, CDMG.

Sassen, S. (1991). *The global city: New York, London, Tokyo*. Princeton, NJ: Princeton University Press.

Sauer, M. (2009). *Teilhabe und Orientierungen türkeistämmiger Migrantinnen und Migranten in Nordrhein-Westfalen*. Essen, Germany: Stiftung Zentrum für Türkeistudien.

Schipperijn, J., Ekholm, O., Stigsdotter, A. U. K., Toftager, M., Bentsen, P., Kamper-Jørgensen, F., & Randrup, T. B. (2010). Factors influencing the use of green space: Results from a Danish national representative survey. *Landscape and Urban Planning, 95*(3), 130-137.

Scott Porter Research & Marketing Ltd. (2000). *Sports and minority ethnic communities: Aiming at social inclusion.* Edinburgh: Sport Scotland.

Shaw, S., Bagwell, S., & Karmowska, J. (2004). Ethnoscapes as spectacle: Reimaging multicultural districts as new destinations for leisure and tourism consumption. *Urban Studies, 41*(10), 1983-2000.

Sijtsma, M. (2011). *Negotiating the oppression of discrimination encountered in outdoor leisure: A study of Muslim women in the Netherlands.* MSc thesis, Wageningen University, Leisure, Tourism and Environment.

Soysal, Y. (1994). *Limits to citizenship: Migrants and postnational membership in Europe.* Chicago: University of Chicago Press.

Sport England. (2000). *Sports participation and ethnicity in England: National survey 1999-2000.* London: Sport England.

Sporting Equals. (2000). *Achieving racial equality: A standard for sport.* Commission for Rural Communities State of the Countryside Report 2005. London: Commission for Racial Equality/Sport England.

Statistics Denmark. (2009). Statistical yearbook. www.dst.dk/.

Taylor, C. (1994). Multiculturalisme. (vertaald door Tine Ausma). Amsterdam: Boom.

Taylor, T. (2001). Cultural diversity and leisure: Experiences of women in Australia. *Loisir et Société/Society and Leisure, 24*(2), 535-555.

Te Kloeze, J. W. (2001). Integration through leisure? Leisure time activities and the integration of Turkish families in Arnhem and Enschede in the Netherlands. *World Leisure Journal, 43,* 52-61.

Triadafilopoulos, P. (2011). Illiberal means to liberal ends? Understanding recent immigrant integration policies in Europe. *Journal of Ethnic and Migration Studies, 37*(6), 861-880. (Special issue on "The Limits of the Liberal State.")

Uunk, W. (2002). Concentratie en achterstand: Over de samenhang tussen etnische concentratie en de sociaal-economische positie onder allochtonen en autochtonen. Assen, Netherland: Koninklijke Van Gorcum.

Uzzell, D., Kelay, T., & Leach, R. (2005). "What about us?" Diversity Review evidence–part two. Challenging perceptions: Provider awareness of under-represented groups. University of Surrey. Report to the Countryside Agency. http://publications.naturalengland.org.uk/file/290015.

Van Amersfoort, J. M. M. (1986). Nederland als immigratieland. In L. van den Berg-Eldering (Ed.), *Van gastarbeider tot immigrant. Marokkanen en Turken in Nederland, 1965-1985* (pp. 15-46). Alphen aan den Rijn, The Netherlands: Samson.

Van den Broek, A., & Keuzenkamp, S. (Eds.). (2008). *Het dagelijkse leven van allochtone stedelingen.* The Hague: SCP.

Van Kempen, R., & Murie, A. (2009). The new divided city: Changing patterns in European cities. *Tijdschrift voor Economische en Sociale Geografie, 100*(4), 377-398.

Van Kempen, R., & Van Weesep, J. (1998). Ethnic residential patterns in Dutch cities: Backgrounds, shifts and consequences. *Urban Studies, 35,* 1813-1833.

Vorster, J. M. (2008). Perspectives on the core characteristics of religious fundamentalism today. *Journal for the Study of Religions and Ideologies, 7*(21), 44-65.

Walseth, K. (2006). Young Muslim women and sport: The impact of identity work. *Leisure Studies, 25*(1), 75-94.

Ward, T., Lelkes, O., Sutherland, H., & György Tóth, I. (Eds.). (2009). European inequalities: Social inclusion and income distribution in the European Union (p. 214). Budapest: TÁRKI Social Research Institute.

Ward, V. E. (2000). Immigrant elders: Are we missing them? An examination of leisure participation and identity among immigrant elders. *Journal of Aging and Identity, 5*(4), 197-195.

Ward Thompson, K., et al. (2008). *Participation in outdoor recreation by WAG priority groups.* CCW Policy Research Report No. 08/15. Edinburgh, UK: OPENspace Research Centre.

Yücesoy, E. U. (2006). *Everyday urban public space: Turkish immigrant women's perspective.* Dissertation, Utrecht University.

CHAPTER 16

Abbott, R., Jenkins, D., Haswell-Elkins, M., Fell, K., MacDonald, D., & Cerin, E. (2008). Physical activity of young people in the Torres Strait and Northern Peninsula Region: An exploratory study. *Australian Journal of Rural Health, 16*(5), 278-282.

Allport, G. W. (1954). *The nature of prejudice.* Cambridge, MA: Addison-Wesley.

Ang, I., Brand, J., Noble, G., & Sternberg, J. (2006). Connecting diversity: Paradoxes of multicultural Australia. http://epublications.bond.edu.au/cgi/viewcontent.cgi?article=1020&context=hss_pubs.

Annear, M., Cushman, G., Espiner, S., Gidlow, B., & Toohey, M. (2010). *Advancing an integrated leisure research strategy for New Zealand: An analysis of the perceived research priorities of stakeholders in the arts, outdoor recreation, sport and community recreation sectors.* Land, Environment and People Report No. 21. Canterbury, NZ: Lincoln University.

Arai, S., & Kivel, B. D. (2009). Critical race theory and social justice perspectives on whiteness, difference(s) and (anti)racism: A fourth wave of race research in leisure studies. *Journal of Leisure Research, 41*(4), 459-470.

Atkinson, J. (1991). *Recreation in the aboriginal community: A report to the Department of the Arts, Sport, the Environment, Tourism and Territories.* Canberra, Australia: Australian Government Publishing.

Australia Department of Sport, Recreation and Tourism. (1986). *Aboriginals and recreation* (p. 59). Canberra, Australia: Department of Sport, Recreation and Tourism.

Australian Bureau of Statistics. (1986). Year book Australia, 1986. Retrieved May 20, 2010, from www.abs.gov.au/

AUSSTATS/abs@.nsf/DetailsPage/1301.01986?OpenDocument.

Australian Bureau of Statistics. (2004). Aboriginal and Torres Strait Islander peoples: Aspects of sport and recreation. Retrieved April 5, 2010, from www.ausport.gov.au/__data/assets/pdf_file/0003/276924/ABS-Indigenous_-people-and-sport.pdf.

Australian Bureau of Statistics. (2006a). Aboriginal and Torres Strait Islander Australians: Involvement in arts and culture. Retrieved April 6, 2010, from www.abs.gov.au/ausstats/abs@.nsf/cat/4721.0.

Australian Bureau of Statistics. (2006b). Migrants and participation in sports and physical activity. Retrieved April 7, 2010, from www.ausport.gov.au/__data/assets/pdf_file/0009/286029/ABS_migrants_participation_sport_physical_activity.pdf.

Australian Bureau of Statistics. (2007a). *Attendance at selected cultural venues and events, Australia, 2005–06.* Canberra, Australia: ABS.

Australian Bureau of Statistics. (2007b). *Migrants, general social survey, Australia, 2002.* Canberra, Australia: ABS.

Australian Bureau of Statistics. (2007c). Migrants, participation in sports and physical recreation, Australia, 2005–06. Retrieved October 20, 2010, from www.abs.gov.au/AUSSTATS/subscriber.nsf/log?openagent&34150ds0014_2005-06_mphs_sportsparticipation_migrants.xls&3415.0&Data Cubes&83D7DD8C14FBAFD2CA2578BD0013C774&0&June 2011&29.06.2011&Latest.

Australian Bureau of Statistics. (2007d). Motivators and constraints to participation in sports and physical recreation. Retrieved March 23, 2013, from https://secure.ausport.gov.au/__data/assets/pdf_file/0011/142220/ABS_-_Motivators_and_Constraints_to_particpation_in_Sports_and_Physical_Recreation.pdf.

Australian Bureau of Statistics. (2007e). Survey of involvement in organised sport and physical activity. Retrieved May 14, 2010, from www.abs.gov.au/AUSSTATS/abs@.nsf/Lookup/6285.0Explanatory%20Notes1Apr%202007?OpenDocument.

Australian Bureau of Statistics. (2008a). Australian historical population statistics, 2008. Retrieved May 10, 2010, from www.abs.gov.au/ausstats/abs@.nsf/mf/3105.0.65.001.

Australian Bureau of Statistics. (2008b). Yearbook chapter, 2008: Overcoming Indigenous disadvantage. Retrieved June 30, 2010, from www.abs.gov.au/AUSSTATS/abs@.nsf/Previousproducts/1301.0Feature%20Article9012008?opendocument&tabname=Summary&prodno=1301.0&issue=2008&num=&view=.

Australian Bureau of Statistics. (2009a). *Migrants' attendance at selected cultural venues and events, Australia, 2005–06.* Canberra, Australia: ABS.

Australian Bureau of Statistics. (2009b). National Aboriginal and Torres Strait Islander Social Survey, 2008. Retrieved April 8, 2010, from http://abs.gov.au/AUSSTATS/abs@.nsf/DetailsPage/4714.02008?OpenDocument.

Australian Bureau of Statistics. (2010a). Framework for measuring wellbeing: Aboriginal and Torres Strait Islander peoples, 2010. Retrieved April 6, 2010, from www.abs.gov.au/AUSSTATS/abs@.nsf/Latestproducts/19D9830509A76AE5CA2577BB00151EBA?opendocument.

Australian Bureau of Statistics. (2010b). Indigenous disadvantage and selected measures of well-being. Retrieved March 23, 2013, from www.abs.gov.au/AUSSTATS/abs@.nsf/Lookup/1301.0Feature+Article9012009–10.

Australian Government Independent Sport Panel. (2009). *The future of sport in Australia.* Canberra, Australia: Independent Sport Panel.

Australian Institute of Health and Welfare, & Australian Bureau of Statistics. (2008). *The health and welfare of Australia's Aboriginal and Torres Strait Islander peoples.* Canberra, Australia: ABS.

Beaglehole, A. (2012). Immigration regulation – 1914-1945: Restrictions on non-British immigration. *Te Ara – the Encyclopedia of New Zealand*, from www.TeAra.govt.nz/en/immigration-regulation/page-3.

Beneforti, M., & Cunningham, J. (2002). *Investigating indicators for measuring the health and social impact of sport and recreation programs in Indigenous communities.* Casuarina, Northern Territory, Australia: Cooperative Research Centre for Aboriginal and Tropical Health.

Best, E. (1925). *Games and pastimes of the Maori.* Wellington, NZ: Whitcombe and Tombs.

Brislin, R. W., Lonner, W. J., & Thorndike, R. M. (1973). *Cross-cultural research methods.* New York: Wiley.

Brown, H. (2008). *Nga Taonga Takaro: Maori sports and games.* Auckland, NZ: Penguin.

Brown, M., Guthrie, P., & Growden, G. (2007). *Rugby for dummies* (2nd ed.). Mississauga, ON, Canada: Wiley.

Cairnduff, S. (2001). Sport and recreation for Indigenous youth in the Northern Territory: Scoping research priorities for health and social outcomes. www.ausport.gov.au/__data/assets/pdf_file/0011/375743/2001_Sport_and_Recreation_for_Indigenous_Youth_in_the_Northern_Territory.pdf.

Centre for Multicultural Youth Issues. (2003). Multicultural resource kit for state sporting associations. www.cmy.net.au/Assets/191/1/SSA_Multi_Resource.pdf.

Centre for Multicultural Youth Issues. (2007a). Multicultural youth in Australia: Settlement and transition. www.cmy.net.au/Assets/213/1/youth_in_australia_settlement_and_transition_october_2007.pdf.

Centre for Multicultural Youth Issues. (2007b). Playing for the future: The role of sport and recreation in supporting refugee young people to "settle well" in Australia. www.cmy.net.au/Assets/185/2/PlayingfortheFuture.pdf.

Clarke, A. (2007). *Holiday seasons: Christmas, New Year and Easter in nineteenth-century New Zealand.* Auckland, NZ: Auckland University Press.

Creative New Zealand. (1999). *Arts Every Day Survey, 1997.* Wellington, NZ: Creative New Zealand.

Creative New Zealand. (2008). *New Zealanders and the arts: Attitudes, attendance and participation.* Wellington, NZ: Creative New Zealand.

Cunningham, J., & Beneforti, M. (2005). Investigating indicators for measuring the health and social impact of sport and recreation programs in Australian Indigenous communities. *International Review for the Sociology of Sport, 40*(1), 89-98.

Curthoys, A. (2000). An uneasy conversation: The multi-cultural and the Indigenous. In J. Docker & G. Fischer (Eds.), *Race, colour and identity in Australia and New Zealand* (pp. 21-36). Sydney: UNSW Press.

Curthoys, A., & Moore, C. (1995). Working for the White people: An historiographic essay on Aboriginal and Torres Strait Islander labour. *Labour History, 69,* 1-29.

Daley, C. (2009). Modernity, consumption and leisure. In G. Byrnes (Ed.), *The New Oxford History of New Zealand* (pp. 423-446). South Melbourne, Victoria, Australia: Oxford University Press Australia and New Zealand.

Department of Immigration and Multicultural Affairs. (2001). Immigration Federation to century's end 1901-2000. www.immi.gov.au/media/publications/statistics/federation/federation.pdf.

Dixon, R., Tse, S., Rossen, F., & Sobrun-Maharaj, A. (2010). *Family resilience: The settlement experience for Asian immigrant families in New Zealand.* Wellington, NZ: Families Commission.

Dunn, K., Forrest, J., Pe-Pua, R., Hynes, M., & Maeder-Han, K. (2009). Cities of race hatred? The spheres of racism and anti-racism in contemporary Australian cities. *Cosmopolitan Civil Societies Journal, 1*(1), 1-14.

Dunn, K. M., Kamp, A., Shaw, W. S., Forrest, J., & Paradies, Y. (2010). Indigenous Australians' attitudes towards multiculturalism, cultural diversity, "race" and racism. *Journal of Australian Indigenous Issues, 13*(4), 19-31.

Dunstan, S., Boyd, S., & Crichton, S. (2004). *Migrants' experiences of New Zealand: Pilot survey report, longitudinal immigration survey.* Wellington, NZ: Department of Labour.

Earle, D. (1995). Pacific Islands people in Aotearoa/New Zealand: Existing and emerging paradigms. *Social Policy Journal of New Zealand* (4), 14-23.

Edwards, K. (2009). Traditional games of a timeless land: Play cultures in Aboriginal and Torres Strait Islander communities. *Australian Aboriginal Studies* (2), 32-43.

English, B. (2003). Staggering response to "Beaches For All" petition. Retrieved June 25, 2011, from www.scoop.co.nz/stories/PA0307/S00438.htm.

Floyd, M. (1998). Getting beyond marginality and ethnicity: The challenge for race and ethnic studies in leisure research. *Journal of Leisure Research, 30*(1), 3-22.

Floyd, M., & Gramann, J. (1993). Effects of acculturation and structural assimilation in resource-based recreation: The case of Mexican Americans. *Journal of Leisure Research, 25*(1), 6-21.

Foreshore and Seabed Act 2004. (n.d.). www.legislation.govt.nz/act/public/2004/0093/latest/DLM319846.html#DLM319846.

Fox, K. M. (2007). Aboriginal peoples in North American and Euro-North American leisure. *Leisure/Loisir, 31*(1), 217-243.

Girling, A., Liu, J., & Ward, C. (2010). *Confident, equal or proud? A discussion paper on the barriers Asians face to equality in New Zealand.* Wellington, NZ: Human Rights Commission.

Grattan, M. (2011, August 8). Indigenous spending damned as wasteful. *The Age.* Retrieved August 10, 2011, from www.theage.com.au/national/indigenous-spending-damned-as-wasteful-20110807-1ihrd.html.

Haagen, C. (1994). *Bush toys: Aboriginal children at play.* Canberra, Australia: Aboriginal Studies Press in association with National Museum of Australia

Hanlon, C., & Coleman, D. (2006). Recruitment and retention of culturally diverse people by sport and active recreation clubs. *Managing Leisure, 11*(2), 77-95.

Hill, M. (2011, September 4). Curb white immigrants: Academic. *Sunday Star Times.* Retrieved September 7, 2011, from www.stuff.co.nz/sunday-star-times/news/5561013/Curb-white-immigrants-academic.

Hill, R. (2009). Maori and state policy. In G. Byrnes (Ed.), *The New Oxford History of New Zealand* (pp. 513-536). South Melbourne, Victoria, Australia: Oxford University Press.

Hillary Commission. (1997). *Sport and physical activity survey, 1996.* Wellington, NZ: Hillary Commission.

Hillary Commission. (1999). *Sport and physical activity survey, 1998.* Wellington, NZ: Hillary Commission.

Howe, K. R. (1984). *Where the waves fall: A New South Sea Islands history from first settlement to colonial rule.* Honolulu: University of Hawaii Press.

Huang, L. F. (2009). *The role of leisure in the process of acculturation of Taiwanese migrants in Australia.* Unpublished doctoral dissertation, Griffith University, Brisbane, Australia.

Human Rights and Equal Opportunity Commission (HREOC). (1997). *Bringing them home: Report of the national inquiry into the separation of Aboriginal and Torres Strait Islander children from their families (Australia)* (p. 524). Sydney: HREOC.

Hunt, J., Marshall, A. L., & Jenkins, D. (2008). Exploring the meaning of, the barriers to and potential strategies for promoting physical activity among urban Indigenous Australians. *Health Promotion Journal of Australia, 19*(2), 102-108.

Johnson, C., Bowker, J., & Cordell, H. K. (2005). Acculturation via nature-based outdoor recreation: A comparison of Mexican and Chinese ethnic groups in the United States. *Environmental Practice, 7,* 257-272.

Juniu, S. (2000). The impact of immigration: Leisure experience in the lives of South American immigrants. *Journal of Leisure Research, 32*(3), 358-381.

Kabir, N. (2007). *The Cronulla riot: How one newspaper represented the event.* Paper presented at the Australian Sociological Association Conference. www.tasa.org.au/conferences/conferencepapers07/papers/268.pdf.

Kelly, L. (2012). 2011 Report on the Central Land Council Community Development Program. Retrieved October 13, 2012, from www.clc.org.au/files/pdf/CLC_CDU_2011_Monitoring_Report_compressed.pdf.

Keogh, V. (2002). Multicultural sport: Sustaining a level playing field. www.cmy.net.au/Assets/190/1/Sport_sustaining.pdf.

Kirk, A. (2011, August 8). Review damns dismal return on Indigenous spending. Retrieved August 8, 2011, from www.abc.net.au/news/2011-08-07/cabinet-report-indigenous-programs/2828256.

Laidler, A., & Cushman, G. (1993). Leisure participation in New Zealand. In H. Perkins & G. Cushman (Eds.), *Leisure, recreation and tourism* (pp. 1-14). Auckland, NZ: Longman Paul.

Lovelock, B., Lovelock, K., Jellum, C., & Thompson, A. (2010a). *Migrants' experiences of nature-based recreation in New Zealand*. Manuscript submitted for publication.

Lovelock, B., Lovelock, K., Jellum, C., & Thompson, A. (2010b). *Recent immigrants' recreation experiences of outdoor nature-based settings in New Zealand*. Dunedin, NZ: University of Otago, Centre for Recreation Research.

Lovelock, K., Lovelock, B., Jellum, A., & Thompson, A. (2011). In search of belonging: Immigrant experiences of outdoor nature-based settings in New Zealand. *Leisure Studies, 30*(4), 513-529.

Macdonald, D., Abbott, R., Knez, K., & Nelson, A. (2009). Taking exercise: Cultural diversity and physically active lifestyles. *Sport, Education and Society, 14*(1), 1-19.

Masgoret, A., Merwood, P., & Tausi, M. (2009). *New faces, new futures in New Zealand*. Wellington, NZ: Department of Labour.

McLean, M. (1996). *Maori music*. Auckland, NZ: Auckland University Press.

Ministry of Health. (2004). *New Zealand health survey, 2002-3*. Wellington, NZ: Ministry of Health.

Ministry of Health. (2008). *New Zealand health survey, 2006-7*. Wellington, NZ: Ministry of Health.

Mosely, P. (Ed.). (1997). *Sporting immigrants: Sport and ethnicity in Australia*. Crows Nest, New South Wales, Australia: Walla Walla Press.

Mowatt, R. (2009). Notes from a leisure son: Expanding an understanding of Whiteness in leisure. *Journal of Leisure Research, 41*(4), 511-528.

Musharbash, Y. (2007). Boredom, time, and modernity: An example from Aboriginal Australia. *American Anthropologist, 109*(2), 307-317.

Nelson, A. (2009). Sport, physical activity and urban Indigenous young people. *Australian Aboriginal Studies, 2*, 101-111.

Nelson, A., Abbott, R., & Macdonald, D. (2010). Indigenous Australians and physical activity: Using a social-ecological model to review the literature. *Health Education Research, 25*(3), 498-509.

New Foreshore Bill passed. (2011). http://tvnz.co.nz/politics-news/new-foreshore-bill-passed-4082232.

New Zealand Immigration Service (NZIS). (2004). *Refugee voices: A journey towards resettlement*. Wellington, NZ: Department of Labour.

Oates, A. M. (1979). *Australian Aboriginal recreations* (p. 12). Melbourne, Australia: National Museum of Victoria.

Oliver, P. (2006). What's the score? A survey of cultural diversity and racism in Australian sport. Retrieved November 20, 2010, from www.hreoc.gov.au/racial_discrimination/whats_the_score/index.html.

Paradies, Y., Harris, R., & Anderson, I. (2008). *The impact of racism on Indigenous health in Australia and Aotearoa: Towards a research agenda*. Darwin, Australia: Cooperative Research Centre for Aboriginal Health.

Pascoe, B. (2008). *The little red yellow black book: An introduction to Indigenous Australia* (2nd ed.). Canberra, Australia: Aboriginal Studies Press.

Pate, G. S. (1995). *Prejudice reduction and the findings of research*. Tucson, AZ: University of Arizona, College of Education.

Pearson, D. (2005). Citizenship, identity and belonging: Addressing the mythologies of the unitary nation state in Aotearoa/New Zealand. In J. H. Liu, T. McCreanor, T. McIntosh, & T. Teaiwa (Eds.), *New Zealand identities: Departures and destinations* (pp. 21-37). Wellington, NZ: Victoria University Press.

Pettigrew, T. F., & Tropp, L. R. (2006). A meta-analytic test of intergroup contact theory. *Journal of Personality and Social Psychology, 90*(5), 751-783.

Phillips, J. (1990). Of verandahs and fish and chips and footie on Saturday afternoon: Reflections on 100 years of New Zealand historiography. *New Zealand Journal of History, 24*(2), 131-132.

Public Access New Zealand. (2003). "Beaches for Recreation" petition launched. Retrieved June 25, 2011, from www.publicaccessnewzealand.com/.

Roberts, N. S. (2009). Crossing the color line with a different perspective on Whiteness and (anti)racism: A response to Mary McDonald. *Journal of Leisure Research, 41*(4), 495-509.

Robertson, I. (1975). *Sport and play in aboriginal culture: Then and now*. Salisbury, Australia: Salisbury College of Advanced Education.

Roth, W. E. (1902). *Games, sports and amusements of the North Queensland Aboriginals*. Brisbane, Australia: Government Printing Office.

Sabnani, H. B., & Ponterotto, J. G. (1992). Racial/ethnic minority-specific instrumentation in counseling research: A review, critique, and recommendations. *Measurement and Evaluation in Counseling and Development, 24*, 161-187.

Sallis, J. F., & Owen, N. (1997). Ecological models of health behavior. In K. Glanz, F. M. Lewis, & B. K. Rimer (Eds.), *Health behavior and health education: Theory, research, and practice* (2nd ed., pp. 403-424). San Francisco: Jossey-Bass.

Salmond, A. (1975). *Hui: A Study of Maori ceremonial gatherings*. Wellington, NZ: A.H. & A.W. Reed.

Salter, M. A. (1967). *Games and pastimes of the Australian Aboriginal*. Unpublished master's thesis, University of Alberta, Edmonton, AB.

Schinke, R. J., Hanrahan, S. J., Eys, M. A., Blodgett, A., Peltier, D., Ritchie, S. D., et al. (2008). The development of cross-cultural relations with a Canadian Aboriginal community through sport research. *Quest, 60*(3), 357-369.

Sibley, C. G., & Liu, J. H. (2004). Attitudes towards biculturalism in New Zealand: Social dominance and Pakeha attitudes towards the general principles and resource-specific aspects of bicultural policy. *New Zealand Journal of Psychology, 33*(2), 88-99.

Small Candle Consulting. (2009). Indigenous sport program evaluation report. Retrieved October 22, 2010, from www.dsr.wa.gov.au/indigenoussportprogramevaluationreport.

Special Broadcasting Service. (2011). Our story: Radio. www.sbs.com.au/aboutus/our-story/index/id/10/h/Radio.

Spoonley, P., & Taiapa, C. (2009). *Sport and cultural diversity: Responding to the sports and leisure needs of immigrants and ethnic minorities in Auckland. A report for Auckland Regional Physical Activity and Sport Strategy (ARPASS).* Auckland, NZ: Massey University.

Sport and Recreation New Zealand (SPARC). (2009). *Active New Zealand survey 2007-2008.* Wellington, NZ: SPARC.

Stafford, J., & Williams, M. (2006). *Maoriland: New Zealand literature.* Wellington, NZ: Victoria University Press.

Statistics New Zealand. (2001). *New Zealand time-use survey, 1998-99.* Wellington, NZ: Statistics New Zealand.

Statistics New Zealand. (2010). *QuickStats about culture and identity.* Wellington, NZ: Statistics New Zealand.

Statistics New Zealand. (2011). *New Zealand time-use survey, 2009-10.* Wellington, NZ: Statistics New Zealand.

Stebbins, R. (2006). Serious leisure. In C. Rojek, S. Shaw, & A. Veal (Eds.), *A handbook of leisure studies* (pp. 448-458). Houndsmill, Hampshire, UK: Palgrave Macmillan.

Stodolska, M. (2000a). Changes in leisure participation patterns after immigration. *Leisure Sciences, 22,* 39-63.

Stodolska, M. (2000b). Looking beyond the invisible: Can research on leisure of ethnic and racial minorities contribute to leisure theory? *Journal of Leisure Research, 32*(1), 156-160.

Stodolska, M. (2007). Ethnic enclosure, social networks, and leisure behaviour of immigrants from Korea, Mexico, and Poland. *Leisure/Loisir, 31*(1), 277-324.

Stodolska, M., & Alexandris, K. (2004). The role of recreational sport in the adaptation of first generation immigrants in the United States. *Journal of Leisure Research, 36*(3), 379-413.

Stuart, J., Jose, P., & Ward, C. (2009). *Settling in: Parent-adolescent family dynamics in the acculturation process.* Wellington, NZ: Families Commission.

Tatz, C. (1987). *Aborigines in sport.* Bedford Park, South Australia: Australian Society for Sports History.

Taylor, T. (2001). Cultural diversity and leisure: Experiences of women in Australia. *Loisir & Société/Society & Leisure, 24*(2), 535-555.

Taylor, T. (2003). Diversity management in a multi-cultural society: An exploratory study of cultural diversity and team sport in Australia. *Annals of Leisure Research, 6*(2), 168-188.

Taylor, T., Lock, D., & Darcy, S. (2009). The Janus face of diversity in Australian sport. *Sport in Society, 12*(7), 861-875.

Tcha, S. S., & Lobo, F. (2003). Analysis of constraints to sport and leisure participation: The case of Korean immigrants in Western Australia. *World Leisure Journal, 45*(3), 13-23.

Toohey, C., & Taylor, T. (1997). Sport provision for women of minority cultures in Australia: Whose responsibility? *Women in Sport and Physical Activity Journal, 6*(2), 254-264.

Tsai, E. H. (2000). The influence of acculturation on perception of leisure constraints of Chinese immigrants. *World Leisure Journal, 42*(4), 33-42.

Tsai, E. H., & Coleman, D. J. (1999). Leisure constraints of Chinese immigrants: An exploratory study. *Loisir & Société/Society & Leisure, 22*(1), 243-264.

Tynan, M. (2007). Shifting egalitarianisms and contemporary racism in rural Victorian football: The Rumbalara experience. *Australian Journal of Anthropology, 18*(3), 276-294.

Vamplew, W. (1994). Violence in Australian soccer: The ethnic contribution. In *Ethnicity and soccer in Australia* (pp. 1-15). Campbelltown, New South Wales, Australia: Australian Society for Sports History.

Veal, A. J., & Lynch, R. (2001). *Australian leisure.* Frenchs Forest, New South Wales: Pearson Education Australia.

Victorian Health Promotion Foundation. (2007). *More than tolerance: Embracing diversity for health.* Calton South, Victoria, Australia: VicHealth.

Walker, G., & Deng, J. (2011). Leisure satisfaction and acculturative stress: The case of Chinese-Canadian immigrants. *Journal of Leisure Research, 43*(2), 226-245.

Walker, S., Donn, M., & Laidler, A. (2005). Leisure participation in New Zealand. In G. Cushman, A. Veal, & J. Zuzanek (Eds.), *Free time and leisure participation: International perspectives* (pp. 177-195). Wallingford, Oxfordshire, UK: CABI.

Wearing, S., Goodall, H., Byrne, D., & Kijas, J. (2008). Cultural diversity in the social valuing of parkland: Networking communities and park management. *Australasian Parks and Leisure, 11*(2), 20-29.

Wearne, B., Chesters, J., & Whyte, S. (2005). Lungmarama Yolngu nha: A week in the life of an outreach program. *Australian Aboriginal Studies, 2,* 16-26.

Western Australia Department of Sport and Recreation. (n.d.). How to be more inclusive of people from diverse backgrounds. Retrieved December 14, 2010, from www.dsr.wa.gov.au/assets/files/Clubhouse/16_How_to_be_an_Inclusive_Club.pdf.

Wilson, J. O. (1966). National groups. In A. H. McLintock (Ed.), *An encyclopedia of New Zealand, Vol. 2* (pp. 623-632). Wellington, NZ: R. E. Owen, Government Printer.

Wright, S. C., Aron, A., McLaughlin-Volpe, T., & Ropp, S. A. (1997). The extended contact effect: Knowledge of cross-group friendships and prejudice. *Journal of Personality and Social Psychology, 73*(1), 73-90.

Zubrick, S. R., Silburn, S. R., Lawrence, D. M., Mitrou, F. G., Dalby, R. B., Blair, E. M., et al. (2005). *Western Australian Aboriginal Child Health Survey: The social and emotional well-being of Aboriginal children and young people.* Perth, Australia: Curtin University of Technology and Telethon Institute for Child Health Research.

CHAPTER 17

2001 Survey on Social Life. (n.d.). Retrieved May 25, 2012, from www.pref.okinawa.jp/toukeika/sli/2001/2001_top.html.

Aberson, C. L., & Haag, S. C. (2007). Contact, perspective taking, and anxiety as predictors of stereotype endorsement, explicit attitudes, and implicit attitudes. *Group Processes and Intergroup Relations, 10,* 179-201.

Ainu Association of Hokkaido. (2010). Actual living conditions of the Hokkaido Ainu. Retrieved March 25, 2013, from www.ainu-assn.or.jp/english/eabout03.html.

Allport, G. W. (1954). *The nature of prejudice.* Reading, MA: Addison Wesley.

Amir, Y. (1969). Contact hypothesis in ethnic relations. *Psychological Bulletin, 71,* 319-342.

Amir, Y. (1976). The role of intergroup contact in change of prejudice and race relations. In P. A. Katz (Ed.), *Towards the elimination of racism* (pp. 245-280). New York: Pergamon.

Asakura, T. (2009). Kimchi cross the border. *Research report of the National Museum of Ethnology of Japan, 83,* 59-67.

Association of Gaming Industry of Japan. (2009). Revenues, participants' numbers, and activity frequencies. Retrieved March 25, 2013 from www.nichiyukyo.or.jp/condition/index.php.

Baek, J. S., & Lee, G. H. (2006). Leisure constraints of the immigrant workers in Korea. *The Korea Academic Society of Tourism and Leisure, 18,* 243-259.

Beauchamp, E. (2007). *East Asia: History, politics, sociology, culture.* New York: Routledge.

Berry, J. W., Poortinga, Y. H., Segall, M. H., & Dasen, P. R. (2002). *Cross-cultural psychology: Research and applications* (2nd ed.). Cambridge: Cambridge University Press.

Binder, J., Zagefka, H., Brown, R., Funke, F., Kessler, T., Mummendey, A., Maquil, A., Birman, D., Trickett, E. J., & Vinokurov, A. (2002). Acculturation and adaptation of Soviet Jewish refugee adolescents: Predictors of adjustment across life domains. *American Journal of Community Psychology, 30,* 585-607.

Bullock, C. C., & Mahon, M. J. (1997). *Introduction to recreation services for people with disabilities: A person-centered approach.* Champaign, IL: Sagamore.

Cameron, L., Rutland, A., Brown, R., & Douch, R. (2006). Changing children's intergroup attitudes towards refugees: Testing different models of extended contact. *Child Development, 77,* 1208-1219.

Chen, N. N., Clark, C. D., Gottschang, S. Z., & Jeffery, L. (2001). Introduction. In N. Chen, C. D. Clark, S. Z. Gottschang, & L. Jeffery (Eds.), *China urban.* Durham, NC, and London: Duke University Press.

Chick, G. (1995). The adaptive qualities of leisure: A cross-cultural survey. In C. Simpson & B. Gidlow (Eds.), *Proceedings of the ANZALS Conference, 1995* (pp. 158-163). Canterbury, NZ: Australian and New Zealand Association for Leisure Studies.

Chick, G. (1998). Leisure and culture: Issues for an anthropology of leisure. *Leisure Sciences, 20,* 111-133.

Choi, S. H. (2002). *A study on the influence of the middle-aged generation's recognition of leisure and values of sports on the motives for participation in leisure sports.* Doctoral dissertation, Yonsei University, Seoul, South Korea.

Choi, S. H. (2009). The types of leisure activities and policy implications: Age and household monthly income. *The Korean Women Economists Association, 6,* 111-128.

Cockerham, W., & Yamori, Y. (2001). Okinawa: An exception to the social gradient of life expectancy in Japan. *Asia Pacific Journal of Clinical Nutrition, 10,* 154-158.

Dattilo, J. (2008). *Leisure education program planning: A systematic approach* (3rd ed.). State College, PA: Venture.

Demoulin, S., & Leyens, J. (2009). Does contact reduce prejudice or does prejudice reduce contact? A longitudinal test of the contact hypothesis among majority and minority groups in three European countries. *Journal of Personality and Social Psychology, 96,* 843-856.

Dong, E., & Yi-Kook, J. (2010). *Korean leisure: From tradition to modernity.* Jaipur, India: Rawat Publications.

Dovidio, J. F., Gaertner, S. L., John, M.-S., Halabi, S., Saguy, T., Pearson, A. R., & Riek, B. M. (2008). Majority and minority perspectives in intergroup relations: The role of contact, group representations, threat, and trust in intergroup conflict and reconciliation. In A. Nadler, T. E. Malloy, & J. D. Fisher (Eds.), *The social psychology of intergroup reconciliation* (pp. 227-253). New York: Oxford University Press.

Du, J., Li, X., Qin, Y., & Li, H. (2002). An analysis of the trends of China's outbound tourism [in Chinese]. *Tourism Tribune, 17,* 44-48.

Emerson, M. O., Kimbro, R. T., & Yancey, G. (2002). Contact theory extended: The effects of prior racial contact on current social ties. *Social Science Quarterly, 83,* 745-761.

e-Seoul Statistics. (2009). Foreign nationals make up 2.4% of Seoul population. Retrieved May 25, 2012, from http://news.naver.com/main/read.nhn?mode=LSD&mid=sec&sid1=104&oid=044&aid=0000084799.

Exchange Promotion Division of Okinawa. (n.d.). Number of foreigners. Retrieved May 25, 2013, www.pref.okinawa.jp/site/kankyo/heiwadanjo/danjo/documents/h23p1-p4.pdf.

Fache, W. (1995). Leisure education in community system. In H. Ruskin & A. Sivan (Eds.), *Leisure education towards the 21st century* (pp. 51-78). Provo, UT: Brigham Young University Press.

Fischer, M. J. (2008). Does campus diversity promote friendship diversity? A look at interracial friendships in college. *Social Science Quarterly, 89,* 631-655.

Fischer, R., Maes, J., & Schmitt, M. (2007). Tearing down the "wall in the head"? Culture contact between Germans. *International Journal of Intercultural Relations, 31*, 163-179.

Gao, W., & Smyth, R. (2010). *What keeps China's migrant workers going? Expectations and happiness among China's floating population.* Discussion Paper, Monash University, Department of Economics. Retrieved May 25, 2012, from www.buseco.monash.edu.au/eco/research/papers/2010/1410chinagaosmyth.pdf.

Garcia, B. C. (2004). Rural-urban migration in China: Temporary migrants in search of permanent settlement. *Portal 1* (2). Retrieved May 25, 2012, from http://epress.lib.uts.edu.au/ojs/index.php/portal/article/view/58/35.

Gong, B. (1998). *Chinese leisure.* Shanghai: Shanghai Antique Press.

Gu, S. (1992). Two types of population migration in China: A comparative study. *Chinese Journal of Population Science, 4(1)*, 75-84.

Gustafsson, B., & Sai, D. (2006). *Villages where China's ethnic minorities live.* Institute for the Study of Labor (IZA), Discussion Paper No. 2418. Retrieved May 25, 2012, from http://ftp.iza.org/dp2418.pdf.

Her, S. W. (1999). The study of leisure satisfaction according to swimming participation in middle-aged women. *Korean Society of Leisure & Recreation, 34(1)*, 205-213.

Heo, M. K., & Kwon, Y. (2010). An exploratory study on the leisure behavior of foreign students in Korea using the intercultural communication theory. *The Tourism Sciences Society of Korea, 34*, 135-154.

Heyne, L. A., & Schleien, S. J. (1997). Teaming up with parents to support inclusive recreation. *Parks & Recreation, 32*, 76-81.

Hiwasaki, L. (2000). Ethnic tourism in Hokkaido and the shaping of Ainu identity. *Pacific Affairs, 73*, 393-412.

Hong, S. T. (1995). A study on the better solutions of work and leisure management for overseas workers. *The Korea Academic Society of Tourism and Leisure, 7*, 185-199.

Ito, E., Nogawa, H., Kitamura, K., & Walker, G. J. (2011). The role of leisure in the assimilation of Brazilian immigrants into Japanese society: Acculturation and structural assimilation through judo participation. *International Journal of Sport and Health Science, 9*, 8-14.

Iwasaki, Y., Nishino, H., Onda, T., & Bowling, C. (2007). Leisure research in a global world: Time to reverse the Western domination in leisure research? *Leisure Sciences, 29*, 113-117.

Jackman, M. R., & Crane, M. (1986). "Some of my best friends are black . . .": Interracial friendship and whites' racial attitudes. *Public Opinion Quarterly, 50*, 459-486.

Japan National Tourism Organization. (2013). Experiencing Ainu culture. Retrieved March 25, 2013 from www.jnto.go.jp/eng/indepth/scenic/hokkaido/hokkaido_05.html.

Japanese Ministry of Justice. (2011, June 3). *Statistics of foreign nationals.* Retrieved from www.moj.go.jp/nyuukokukanri/kouhou/nyuukantourokusya toukei110603.html.

Japan Productive Center. (2010). White paper of leisure of Japan. Tokyo.

Jiang, W., & Yamashita, K. (2005). Residential concentration of Chinese newcomers in a public apartment complex in the suburbs of Tokyo: A case of Kawaguchi Shibazono Danchi in Saitama. *Studies in Human Geography, 29*, 33-58.

Kaji, H. (2007). Present-day problems and measures in the pachinko parlor industry (1). *The Social Science, 78*, 23-47 Retrieved May 25, 2013 from http://doors.doshisha.ac.jp/webopac/bdyview.do?bodyid=BD00011612&elmid=Body&lfname=007000780002.pdf&loginflg=on.

Katsuura, M. (2010). On relationship between two leisure activities in the survey of time use and leisure activities. *Bulletin of Japan Statistics Research Institute, 2010*, 27-37.

Kim, S. (2004). *Physical self-concept profile for leisure sport participation.* Doctoral dissertation, Chung-Ang University, Seoul, South Korea.

Knight, J., & Gunatilaka, R. (2010). Great expectations? The subjective well-being of rural urban migrants in China. *World Development, 38(1)*, 113-124.

Korea National Statistical Office. (2005). Population Registration Statistics (in Korean). Retrieved from www.kosis.go.kr. Accessed: October 2005 – April 2006.

Korea Times. (2009, April 12). S. Korea's obesity rate lowest in OECD. Retrieved May 25, 2012, from www.koreatimes.co.kr/www/news/nation/2009/04/113_42993.html.

Kwon, Y. H., & Ko, B. C. (2011). An exploratory study on the leisure constraints of foreign Korean wives. *The Journal of Tourism Studies, 23(1)*, 27-48.

Lee, C. W. (2005). *Modern leisure studies.* Seoul: Daehanmedia.

Lee, G. H., & Kim, S. Y. (2010). Leisure sports policy direction for multicultural society integration. *Journal of Leisure & Wellness, 3(1)*, 21-30.

Lee, J-H. (2007). Sport philosophy: The leisure sport on the view of social-welfare. *Korean Philosophy Society for Sport and Dance, 15*, 149-164.

Leisure activities. (n.d.). 2006 Survey on time use and leisure activities. Retrieved May 25, 2012, from www.stat.go.jp/english/data/shakai/2006/pdf/koudou-a.pdf.

Li, B. (2008). A sociological research on ethnic minorities in the villages of Yunnan Province [in Chinese]. *Industrial & Science Tribune, 7*, 100-101.

Lie, J. (2008). *Zainichi (Koreans in Japan): Diasporic nationalism and postcolonial identity.* Berkeley, CA: University of California Press.

Lieberson, S. (1980). *A piece of the pie: Black and white immigrants since 1880.* Berkeley, CA: University of California Press.

Lin, Y. (1962). *My country and my people.* London: Lowe and Brydone Printers Ltd.

Link, P., Madsen, R. P., & Pickowicz, P. G. (2002). Introduction. In P. Link, R. P. Madsen, & P. G. Pickowicz (Eds.), *Popular China: Unofficial culture in a globalizing society.* New York: Rowman & Littlefield Publishers, Inc.

Liu, H., Yeh, C., Chick, G. E., & Zinn, H. C. (2008). An exploration of meanings of leisure: A Chinese perspective. *Leisure Sciences, 30,* 482-488.

Liu-Farrer, G. (2004). The Chinese social dance party in Tokyo: Identity and status in an immigrant leisure subculture. *Journal of Contemporary Ethnography, 33,* 651-674.

Ma, H.(2010). *Eight "zeros": Leisure status of Chinese peasant workers.* Paper presented at the XVII ISA World Congress of Sociology, Gothenburg, Sweden.

Ma, L., & Biao, X. (1998). Native place, migration and the emergence of peasant enclaves in Beijing. *China Quarterly, 155,* 547-581.

Mannell, R. (2007). Leisure, health and well-being. *World Leisure Journal, 49,* 114-128.

Ministry of Justice of Korea. (2005, July 6). Korean immigration service. Retrieved from www.moj.go.kr/HP/COM/bbs_03/ShowData.do?strNbodCd=noti0040&strWrtNo=85&strAnsNo=A&strFilePath=moj/&strRtnURL=MOJ_40204000&strOrgGbnCd=100000.

Ministry of Justice of Korea. (2008). Annals of Statistics, Immigration and foreign policy. Retrieved from www.moj.go.kr/HP/COM/bbs_03/ListShowData.do?strNbodCd=noti0097&strWrtNo=10&strAnsNo=A&strNbodCd=noti0703&strFilePath=moj/&strRtnURL=MOJ_40402000&strOrgGbnCd=104000&strThisPage=1&strNbodCdGbn.

Ministry of Public Administration and Security. (2012). Report on foreigners in Korea. Retrieved March 6, 2013 from www.mopas.go.kr/gpms/ns/mogaha/user/userlayout/bulletin/userBtView.action?userBtBean.bbsSeq=1022589&userBtBean.ctxCd=1012&userBtBean.ctxType=21010002&userBtBean.categoryCd=.

Mio, J. S., Barker-Hackett, L., & Tumambing, J. (2008). *Multicultural psychology.* New York: McGraw-Hill Higher Education.

Nakamura, Y. (2008). An analysis of the poverty of modern Ainu. *Journal of Education and Social Work, 14,* 15-25.

National Bureau of Statistics of China. (2012). 2009 Migrant work monitoring report. Retrieved May 25, 2012, from www.stats.gov.cn/tjfx/fxbg/t20100319_402628281.htm.

Olzak, S. (1992). *The dynamics of ethnic competition and conflict.* Stanford, CA: Stanford University Press.

Onai, T. (2003). *Education and child-care of Brazilians living in Japan* [in Japanese]. Tokyo: Akashi-shoten.

Organization for Economic Cooperation and Development (OECD). (2012). OECD health data 2012. Retrieved May 25, 2012, from www.oecd.org/document/16/0,2340,en_2649_34631_2085200_1_1_1_1,00.html.

Otten, S., Sassenberg, K., & Kessler, T. (2009). *Intergroup relations: The role of motivation and emotion.* New York: Psychology Press.

Peng, Z., & Zheng, X. (2008). Yichan Yu Lvyou: Chuantong Yu Xiandai de Bingzhi Yu Beili (Heritage and tourism: Juxtaposition and deviation of the tradition and the modern). *Guangxi Minority Studies, 93,* 33-39.

Pettigrew, T. F. (1998). Intergroup contact theory. *Annual Review of Psychology, 49,* 65-85.

Pettigrew, T. F., & Tropp, L. R. (2000). Does intergroup contact reduce prejudice? Recent meta-analytic findings. In S. Oskamp (Ed.), *Reducing prejudice and discrimination* (pp. 93-114). Mahwah, NJ: Erlbaum.

Pettigrew, T. F., & Tropp, L. R. (2006). A meta-analytic test of intergroup contact theory. *Journal of Personality and Social Psychology, 90,* 751-783.

Portal Site of Official Statistics of Japan. (2013). Foreigner registration statistics. Retrieved March 25, 2013 from www.e-stat.go.jp/SG1/estat/List.do?lid=000001074828.

Roth, J. (2005). Political and cultural perspectives on "insider" minorities. In J. Robertson (Ed.), *A companion to the anthropology of Japan* (pp. 73-88). Malden, MA: Blackwell.

Ryang, S. (2005). Koreans in Japan. In C. Ember, M. Ember, & I. Skoggard (Eds.), *Encyclopedia of diasporas: Immigrant and refugee cultures around the world* (pp. 974-982). New York: Springer.

Ryang, S. (2009). Diaspora and Koreans in Japan. In S. Ryang & J. Lie (Eds.), *Diaspora without homeland: Being Korean in Japan* (pp. 1-20). Berkeley, CA, and Los Angeles: University of California Press.

Schlueter, E., & Scheepers, P. (2010). The relationship between outgroup size and anti-outgroup attitudes: A theoretical synthesis and empirical test of group threat and intergroup contact theory. *Social Science Research, 39,* 285-295.

Seol, D. H. (2007). Sociology of the "Mixed-Blood": Hierarchical nationhood of the Koreans. *The Journal of the Humanities, 52,* 125-160. The Institute of the Humanities Yeungnam University.

Seol, D. H., & Lee, G. S. (2011). Family resources, marital satisfaction, and divorce proneness in international marriage couples in Korea. *Korean Regional Sociology, 13(1),* 117-147.

Shan, W. (2009). Comparing ethnic minorities and Han Chinese in China. *East Asian Policy.* Retrieved May 25, 2012, from www.eai.nus.edu.sg/Vol2No2_ShanWei.pdf.

Siddle, R. (1997). Ainu: Japan's indigenous people. In M. Wenier (Ed.), *Japan's minorities: The illusion of homogeneity* (pp. 21-39). New York: Routledge.

Statistics of Korea. (2010). Annual report. Korea immigration service annual report. Retrieved from http://lib1.kostat.go.kr/search/detail/CATTOT000000062362?mainLink=/search/tot?oi=DISP01&os=ASC&briefLink=/search/tot?oi=DISP01&os=ASC/result?si=2_A_st=FRNT_A_q=Korea+Immigration+ServiceMinistry+of+Justice.

Stephan, W. G., & Stephan, C. W. (1985). Intergroup anxiety. *Journal of Social Issues, 41,* 157-176.

Stephan, W. G., Ybarra, O., & Bachman, G. (1999). Prejudice toward immigrants: An integrated threat theory. *Journal of Applied Social Psychology, 29,* 2221-2237.

Stevens, G. (2008). Subject, object and active participant: The Ainu, law, and legal mobilization. *Indigenous Law Journal, 7,* 127-169.

Stodolska, M. (1998). Assimilation and leisure constraints: Dynamics of constraints on leisure in immigrant populations. *Journal of Leisure Research, 30*, 521-551.

Sun, M., & Fan. C. C. (2011). China's permanent and temporary migrants: Differentials and changes, 1990-2000. *Professional Geographer, 63*, 92-112.

Taira, K. (1997). Troubled national identity: The Ryukyuans/Okinawans. In M. Weiner (Ed.), *Japan's minorities: The illusion of homogeneity* (pp. 140-177). New York: Routledge.

Time use. (n.d.). 2006 Survey on time use and leisure activities. Retrieved May 25, 2012, from www.stat.go.jp/english/data/shakai/2006/pdf/jikan-a.pdf.

Tropp, L. R., & Pettigrew, T. F. (2005). Relationships between intergroup contact and prejudice among minority and majority status groups. *Psychological Science, 16*, 951-957.

Van Zomeren, M., Fischer, A. H., & Spears, R. (2007). Testing the limits of tolerance: How intergroup anxiety amplifies negative and offensive responses to out-group-initiated contact. *Personality and Social Psychology Bulletin, 33*, 1686-1699.

Wang, J. (2001). Culture as leisure and culture as capital. *Positions, 9*, 69-104.

Wang, J., & Stringer, L. A. (2000). The impact of Taoism on leisure. *World Leisure, 3*, 33-41.

Weber, I. (2002). Shanghai baby: Negotiating youth self-identity in urban China. *Social Identities, 8*, 347-368.

Willcox, D., Willcox, B., He, Q., Wang, N., & Suzuki, M. (2008). They really are that old: A validation study of centenarian prevalence in Okinawa. *Journal of Gerontology: Biological Sciences, 63*, 338-349.

Wong, E. (2010). China's Han flock to theme parks featuring minorities. *New York Times*, February 23. Retrieved May 25, 2012, from www.nytimes.com/2010/02/24/world/asia/24park.html?_r=1.

Wright, S. C., Aron, A., McLaughlin-Volpe, T., & Ropp, S. A. (1997). The extended contact effect: Knowledge of cross-group friendships and prejudice. *Journal of Personality and Social Psychology, 73*, 73-90.

Xia, Y. (2006). The study on leisure lives of peasant workers in city: A survey from Lucheng Industry District in Wenzhou [in Chinese]. *Market & Demographic Analysis, 12*, 41-49.

Yan, Z. (2007). Leisure time and sport participation of urban migrant workers. *Cultural Construction, 27*, 68-69.

Yang, Y. (2001). *Social exclusion and economic discrimination: The status of migrants in China's coastal rural areas.* China Center for Economic Research, Working Paper No. E2001005.

Yang, Y., & Yang, S. (2005). Characteristics of Chinese Korean and Chinese society in Korea [in Chinese] Retrieved May 25, 2013 from http://qwgzyj.gqb.gov.cn/hwzh/127/379.shtml.

Yin, Y. (2005). The identity of Chinese living in Japan on the media of Chinese [In Japanese]. *Nature-People-Society: Science and the Humanities, 38*, 17-36. Retrieved May 25 2013, from http://library.kanto-gakuin.ac.jp/e-Lib/bdyview.do?bodyid=NI10000196&elmid=Body&lfname=03yin.html.

Yokohama Local Finance Bureaus. (2012). I love China Town YOKOHAMA [In Japanese] Retrieved May 25, 2013 from www.chinatown.or.jp/fact/column/relaytalk03.

Yu, P., & Berryman, D. L. (1996). The relationship among self-esteem, acculturation, and recreation participation of recently arrived Chinese immigrant adolescents. *Journal of Leisure Research, 28*, 251-273.

Zhang, Y. (2003). The creation of overseas Chinese culture in Yokohama: The changing view of Chinese culture through the succession of lion dance. *Forum of International Development Studies, 23*, 223-242.

Zhao, Y. (1999). Labor migration and earnings differences: The case of rural China. *Economic Development & Cultural Change, 47*, 767-782.

Zhou, H. (2003). Changes in leisure life style of ethnic minorities [in Chinese]. *Jianghan Tribune, 12*, 117-119.

Zong, X. (2006). *Tourism development and cultural transformation* [in Chinese]. Beijing: Travel & Tourism Press.

CONCLUSION

Allison, M.T. (1988). Breaking boundaries and barriers: Future directions in cross-cultural research. *Leisure Sciences, 10*(4), 247-259.

American Psychological Association, Presidential Task Force on Immigration. (2012). *Crossroads: The psychology of immigration in the new century.* www.apa.org/topics/immigration/report.aspx.

Arai, S., & Kivel, B. D. (2009). Critical race theory and social justice perspectives on whiteness, difference(s) and (anti) racism: A fourth wave of race research in leisure studies. *Journal of Leisure Research, 41*(4), 459-472.

Brown, B. A., & Frankel, B. G. (1993). Activity through the years: Leisure, leisure satisfaction, and life satisfaction. *Sociology of Sport Journal, 10*, 1-17.

Crawford, D., & Jackson, E. (2005). Leisure constraints theory: Dimensions, directions, and dilemmas. In E. Jackson (Ed.), *Constraints to leisure* (pp. 153-167). State College, PA: Venture.

Floyd, M. F. (1998). Getting beyond marginality and ethnicity: The challenge for race and ethnic studies in leisure research. *Journal of Leisure Research, 30*, 3-22.

Floyd, M. F., Bocarro, J. N., & Thompson, T. D. (2008). Research on race and ethnicity in leisure studies: A review of five major journals. *Journal of Leisure Research, 40*, 1-22.

Gao, G., Ting-Toomey, S., & Gudykunst, W.B. (1996). Chinese communication processes. In M. H. Bond (Ed.), *The handbook of Chinese psychology* (pp. 280-293). Hong Kong: Oxford University Press.

Gibson, R., & Anderson, M. (2008). Touching the void: Art education research in Australia. *Asia Pacific Journal of Education, 28*, 103-112.

Gómez, E. (2002). The Ethnicity and Public Recreation Participation (EPRP) Model. *Leisure Sciences, 24,* 123-142.

Hunt, K., & Ditton, R. (2001). Perceived benefits of recreational fishing to Hispanic-American and Anglo anglers. *Human Dimensions of Wildlife, 6,* 153-172.

Irwin, P. N., Gartner, W. C., & Phelps, C. C. (1990). MexicanAmerican/Anglo cultural differences as recreation style determinants. *Leisure Sciences, 12,* 335-348.

Kitwana, B. (2002). *The hip hop generation: Young Blacks and the crisis in African American culture.* New York: Basic Books.

Kivel, B., Johnson, C., & Scraton, S. (2009). (Re)Theorizing leisure, experience, and race. *Journal of Leisure Research, 41,* 473-493.

Kleiber, D. A., Walker, G. J., & Mannell, R. C. (2011). *A social psychology of leisure* (2nd ed.). State College, PA: Venture.

Kruglanski, A. (2001). That "vision thing": The state of theory in social and personality psychology at the edge of the new millennium. *Journal of Personality and Social Psychology, 80,* 871-875.

Lashua, B., & Fox, K. (2006). Rec needs a new rhythm cuz rap is where we're livin'. *Leisure Sciences, 28*(3), 207-283.

Manning, R. E. (2011). *Studies in outdoor recreation: Search and research for satisfaction* (3rd ed.). Corvallis, OR: Oregon State University Press.

Markovsky, B. (2008). Graduate training in sociological theory and theory construction. *Sociological Perspectives, 51,* 423-447.

Philipp, S. F. (1997). Race, gender, and leisure benefits. *Leisure Sciences, 19,* 191-207.

Popper, K. (1959). *The logic of scientific discovery.* New York: Harper. (Original work published as *Logik der Forschung,* 1935.)

Ryan, R., Bernstein, J., & Brown, K. (2010). Weekends, work, and well-being: Psychological need satisfactions, and day of the week effects on mood, vitality, and physical symptoms. *Journal of Social & Clinical Psychology, 29,* 95-122.

Sell, J., Knottnerus, J. D., & Adcock-Azbill, C. (2012). Disruptions in task groups. *Social Science Quarterly, 93.* http://onlinelibrary.wiley.com/doi/10.1111/j.1540-6237.2012.00879.x/full.

Shinew, K. J., & Floyd, M. F. (2005). Racial inequality and constraints to leisure in the post-Civil Rights era: Toward an alternative framework. In E. Jackson (Ed.), *Constraints to leisure* (pp. 35-51). State College, PA: Venture.

Shinew, K., Stodolska, M., Floyd, M., Hibbler, D., Allison, M., Johnson, C., & Santos, C. (2006). Race and ethnicity in leisure behavior: Where have we been and where do we need to go? *Leisure Sciences, 28,* 403-408.

Spiers, A., & Walker, G. J. (2009). The effects of ethnicity and leisure satisfaction on happiness, peacefulness, and quality of life. *Leisure Sciences, 31,* 84-99.

Stodolska, M. (2007). Social networks, ethnic enclosure, and leisure behavior of immigrants from Korea, Mexico, and Poland. *Leisure/Loisir, 31,* 277-324.

Stodolska, M., & Livengood, J. S. (2006). The effects of religion on the leisure behavior of American Muslim immigrants. *Journal of Leisure Research, 38,* 293-320.

Tienda, M., & Haskins, R. (2011). Immigrant children. *The Future of Children, 21,* 1-266. http://futureofchildren.org/futureofchildren/publications/docs/21_01_FullJournal.pdf.

Tinsley, H. E. A., Tinsley, D. J., & Croskeys, C. E. (2002). Park usage, social milieu, and psychosocial benefits of park use reported by older urban park users from four ethnic groups. *Leisure Sciences, 24,* 199-218.

Vaske, J. J., & Manning, R. E. (2008). Analysis of multiple data sets in outdoor recreation research: Introduction to the special issue. *Leisure Sciences, 30,* 93-95.

Walker, G. J., & Deng, J. (2003/2004). Comparing leisure as a subjective experience with the Chinese experience of rùmí. *Leisure/Loisir, 28,* 245-276.

Walker, G. J., Deng, J., & Dieser, R. (2001). Ethnicity, acculturation, self-construal, and motivations for outdoor recreation. *Leisure Sciences, 23,* 263-283.

Walker, G. J., & Virden, R. J. (2005). Constraints on outdoor recreation. In E. Jackson (Ed.), *Constraints to leisure* (pp. 201-219). State College, PA: Venture.

Washburne, R.F. (1978). Black under-participation in wildland recreation: Alternative explanations. *Leisure Sciences, 1,* 175-189.

Note: The italicized *f* and *t* following page numbers refer to figures and tables, respectively.

South Asian North Americans 108, 174, 183
South Korea. *See* Korea
Spanish 76, 96
sport. *See also* baseball
    activity choices, health and 226
    African Americans in 217-227
    in Australia 250-251, 259
    environmental influences on 225-226
    ethnicity and 215-227
    identity in 222-224
    modeling in 226
    in New Zealand 267
    NFL 217-218
    participation patterns in 217-218
    race and 215-227
    research on 5, 215-227
    rugby union 267
    self-schemata in 221-222
    socialization into 224-225
    stereotypes in 220-221
    theoretical frameworks 218-226
    Whites in 217-219, 221-226
    women in 216
staff, discrimination by 183-184
statistical techniques 30-32
status 155
stereotypes, in sport 220-221
stereotype threat 221
stress 147
structural assimilation 11-12
structural constraints 166-167, 167*f*, 169*f*, 172, 176
structural equation modeling (SEM) 31
success, trajectories of 301
Supreme Court 42, 56-57, 61-62
surveys 29-30
swimming pools, segregation in 41-43
Switzerland 234
symbolic racism 179-180
systemic racism 47-48, 256

T
Taoism 199, 281
tennis 60
territorial constraints 166
theories
    acculturation 11-12
    adaptation 11-12
    assimilation 11-12
    basic needs 154, 158
    Conditioned Attitude Model of Individual Discriminatory Behavior 14-15
    CRT 18, 34-35

cultural capital 17-18
    defined 10
    development of 304
    discrimination 13-15
    diversity in 298-299
    emerging 17-18
    EPRP Model 14-15, 25
    ethnic boundary maintenance 13
    ethnicity hypothesis 11, 18, 172
    frameworks, in leisure research on race and ethnicity 8-19, 25, 304
    future advances in 18-19
    marginality hypothesis 10-11, 13-14, 18, 172
    MSHP 14-15, 33
    OIT 158
    overview of 4, 7-8
    in qualitative research 34-35
    SDT 25, 158-159, 161
    self-construal 15-16
    social capital 17
    social learning 226
    sport 218-226
    TPB 17, 25
    transnationalism 13
theory of planned behavior (TPB) 17, 25
Thoreau, Henry David 55
Three-Fifths Compromise 55
Torres Strait Islanders 248-250, 253*f*, 254
tourism
    ecotourism 121
    in Europe 237
    Indigenous peoples of North America and 120-121
TPB. *See* theory of planned behavior
trajectories of success 301
transcendentalism 197
translators 50
transnational arrangements 93-94
transnationalism 13
travel, in Jewish culture 148-149
Treaty of Waitangi Act 1975 263-266
triangulation 35-36
Turkey 234, 236-237, 239-244
TWS. *See* The Wilderness Society
Type I error 26
Type II error 26

U
undocumented era, of immigration 78-79
United Kingdom 232-234, 236-239, 246
United States (U.S.). *See also* African Americans; Asian North

Americans; Indigenous peoples of North America; Latino Americans; religious minorities, in North America
    discrimination in 177-189, 299
    diversity in 1-2
    Forest Service 173, 200
    immigrants, wilderness and 5, 193-200
    minority access to leisure services in 43-47
    National Park Service 38, 42
    obesity in 202, 214
urban areas, Indigenous peoples in 121-124
U.S. *See* United States

V
values, Muslim 139-140
verbal confrontation 186-187
vertical collectivism 16
vertical individualism 16
violence, racial 59, 61

W
Watson v. Memphis 62
welcomeness, perceptions of 94
Whiteness, normalized 219
Whites
    privilege of 179
    racial frame of 48-49
    in sport 217-219, 221-226
wilderness
    African Americans and 70-71
    Asian North Americans and 193-196, 198-200
    immigrants and 5, 193-200, 271-272
    Indigenous peoples of North America and 115-117
    Latino Americans and 193-194, 196-198, 200
The Wilderness Society (TWS) 195
withdrawal 187
women, in sport 216
World War I 58

Y
Young Men's and Young Women's Hebrew Associations (YMWAs and YWHAs) 149
youth 301-302
youth baseball 18, 34-35

Z
zainichi Chinese 286-288, 294-295
zainichi Koreans 280, 286-288, 291, 294

Monika Stodolska, PhD, is a professor in the department of recreation, sport and tourism at the University of Illinois. She received her PhD in earth and atmospheric sciences from the University of Alberta, Canada. Her research focuses on issues of cultural change and quality of life and their relationship to leisure behavior of ethnic and racial minorities. She explores subjects such as the adaptation processes among minority groups, the effects of leisure on identity development among young immigrants, and transnationalism. Other subjects that are prominent in her research include ethnic and racial discrimination in leisure settings, recreation behavior of minority populations in natural environments, physical activity among minority groups, and constraints on leisure. She also has an emerging research line on new technologies and new media in leisure and recreation. Dr. Stodolska's research has been funded by the USDA Forest Service, Robert Wood Johnson Foundation, and National Recreation and Park Association. Her research has been published in *Journal of Leisure Research, Leisure Sciences, Leisure/Loisir, Annals of Behavioral Medicine, Social Science Quarterly, Journal of Immigrant and Refugee Studies,* and other outlets.

Kimberly J. Shinew, PhD, is a professor in the department of recreation, sport and tourism at the University of Illinois. She received her PhD in parks, recreation and tourism management from Clemson University. Her research focuses on the interrelated effect of race, ethnicity, social class, and gender on leisure preferences and behaviors; the impact of constraints, discrimination, and other factors on access to recreation and leisure services and activities; the roles of leisure spaces and activities in facilitating interaction among diverse groups; and the roles of leisure in encouraging physical activity and active living. Dr. Shinew's research has been funded by the USDA Forest Service, Robert Wood Johnson Foundation, and National Recreation and Park Association. Her research has been published in *Journal of Leisure Research, Leisure Sciences, Sex Roles, Journal of Physical Activity & Health,*

Annals of Behavioral Medicine, Journal of Park and Recreation Administration, Journal of Immigrant and Refugee Studies, Qualitative Research in Sport and Exercise, American Journal of Health Promotion, and other outlets.

Myron F. Floyd, PhD, is a professor in the department of parks, recreation and tourism management at North Carolina State University. Collaborating with colleagues and graduate students, he examines how socioeconomic and cultural factors affect recreation behavior in natural and built environments. He specializes in understanding racial and ethnic disparities in access to parks and urban open space. His most recent work examines the effects of built and natural environments on physical activity and health in low-income and minority communities. Dr. Floyd's research has been supported by government organizations at the state and federal levels, including the U.S. Army Corps of Engineers, USDA Forest Service, USDI National Park Service, and U.S. Fish and Wildlife Service. His research appears in a variety of social science and public health journals, including *Environment and Behavior, Leisure Sciences, Journal of Physical Activity and Health,* and *American Journal of Preventive Medicine.* Dr. Floyd holds degrees from Clemson University (BS, MS) and Texas A&M University (PhD). He is a fellow of the Academy of Leisure Sciences.

Gordon J. Walker, PhD, is a professor in the faculty of physical education and recreation at the University of Alberta. He received his PhD from Virginia Polytechnic Institute and State University. His research program integrates social and cross-cultural psychology and leisure theory. He is particularly interested in how culture and ethnicity affect leisure participation (e.g., gambling, outdoor recreation, physical activity) and behavior (e.g., motivations for, constraints to, experiences during, and outcomes of, leisure). Gordon's research has focused primarily on Chinese, Chinese Canadian, and British Canadian people's leisure, with funding from the Alberta Gambling Research Institute and the Social Science and Humanities Research Council of Canada, resulting in a number of conference abstracts, book chapters, and refereed articles. Gordon was invited to teach two courses on culture and leisure at Shanghai University of Sport in 2009, the same year he was elected as a fellow of the Academy of Leisure Sciences. In 2011 he coauthored the second edition of *A Social Psychology of Leisure* with Doug Kleiber and Roger Mannell. His leisure interests include reading histories and mysteries, adventure traveling (he's visited every continent except Antarctica), and listening to music (blues, classical, and rock—especially the Boss).

ABOUT THE CONTRIBUTORS

Albert Y. Bimper Jr., PhD, is an assistant professor in the ethnic studies department with a concentration in African American studies at Colorado State University. His research focuses on the intersection of race and sport, which spans the study of identity, sociocultural knowledge, developmental needs related to the Black athlete, transition after sport, and exploration of richer learning experiences for student-athlete academic achievement. Bimper cowrote "Diamonds in the Rough: Examining a Case of Successful Black Male Student Athletes in College Sport" in the *Journal of Black Psychology*. He received the Graduate Diversity Award from the North American Society for the Sociology of Sport (NASSS). He received his PhD from the University of Texas, Austin.

Grant Cushman, PhD, is a professor of parks, recreation and tourism at Lincoln University in New Zealand. He has had a long interest in the study of leisure within New Zealand. He was president of the Australian and New Zealand Association for Leisure Studies and coeditor of the *World Leisure Journal* from 2010 to 2012, which enabled him to network with scholars and enhance his scholarship in this field. For one of his publications, Cushman coedited two-volume monographs on international leisure participation research, one titled *Free Time and Leisure Participation: International Perspectives*. He belongs to the Australian and New Zealand Association for Leisure Studies and the World Leisure Organization. He received his PhD from the University of Illinois at Urbana-Champaign.

Jinyang Deng, PhD, is an associate professor in the recreation, parks, and tourism resources program at West Virginia University. He has lived and worked in China, Australia, Canada, and the United States. Deng published "Chinese Acculturation Measurement," an article in *Canadian Ethnic Studies*. He belongs to the Travel and Tourism Research Association and the World Leisure Organization. He earned a BS in forestry from Central South Forestry College (renamed Central South University of Forestry and Technology) in

China (1987), an MS in forest recreation from the same university (1990), and a PhD in recreation and leisure studies from the University of Alberta, Canada (2004).

Erwei Dong, PhD, is an assistant professor in leisure studies at the University of South Alabama. He has conducted field research related to leisure lifestyles, well-being, race and ethnicity, and population health in urban and rural settings. He has conducted leisure lifestyle research projects in six cities in China, three cities and three rural areas in Taiwan, one city in Korea, and one city in Japan. Dong has also been a project manager and research assistant, a Korea Foundation research fellow, and a visiting professor at University of Ryukyus in Japan. He cowrote "Leisure Constraints in Six Chinese Cities" in *Leisure Sciences*. He received his PhD from Pennsylvania State University.

Mariela Fernandez, MS, is a research assistant at the University of Illinois at Urbana-Champaign (UIUC). She has three years of experience conducting or aiding in projects related to diverse populations, including inner-city families from Detroit, Latino urban residents (parents and youth), and Latino rural residents. Her publication "Attracting Hispanics to an African American Recreation Center" (coauthored) is featured in *NRPA Leisure Research Symposium Abstract Proceedings*. It documents the leisure constraints of Hispanic parents while enrolling their children at a public recreation center with a majority African American clientele. Also, her research documents horizontal discrimination between African Americans and Hispanics as well as historical discrimination. The findings of this study are highlighted in her paper in the *Journal of Leisure Research*. She is a member of the Diversity Research Laboratory at UIUC. Fernandez was also a recipient of the Bradberry Youth Development Scholarship and the Hispanic Leaders of Agriculture and the Environment Fellowship at Texas A&M University. She received her master's degree from Texas A&M University.

Karen Fox, PhD, is a professor in the faculty of physical education and recreation at the University of Alberta. She has a long history of working as a community organizer with marginalized groups including Hispanic communities in New Mexico, Ramah Navajo High School in New Mexico, urban Aboriginal communities in Winnipeg and Edmonton, and a Native Hawaiian charter school. Fox also held a Social Science and Humanities Research grant that focused on community processes and leadership among urban Aboriginal hip-hop artists. Her research and scholarship have led to numerous coauthored manuscripts about diversity, including immigrant women and their struggles in a new community and leisure education from a Native Hawaiian perspective, as well as numerous manuscripts related to Indigenous critiques and perspectives on leisure. Fox was also a member of the Edmonton Urban Aboriginal Affairs Council and a volunteer teacher and staff member for Kanu o ka Aina Native Hawaiian Charter School. She is a fellow in the Academy of Leisure Sciences. She received her PhD from the University of Minnesota.

Bob Gidlow, MA, is an associate professor in the department of social science, parks, recreation, tourism and sport at Lincoln University in New Zealand. He supervises a number of PhD students from diverse cultural backgrounds. Gidlow was secretary of the Australian and New Zealand Association for Leisure Studies and was coeditor (with Cushman) of the *World Leisure Journal* from 2010 to 2012. One of his more influential publications is "Bringing Men Back In? Male Recreational Hunters, Divers and Fly-Fishers and the Creation of Recreation Space" in *Annals of Leisure Research*. It is one of the few studies to examine the wider social contexts of individualistic outdoor recreational pursuits. Gidlow also belongs to the Australian and New Zealand Association for Leisure Studies and the World Leisure Organization. He received his MA from the University of Kent at Canterbury.

Louis Harrison Jr., PhD, is a professor at the University of Texas at Austin. He is a well-established scholar in the areas of race, racial identity, and African Americans in sport. He has written a book, seven book chapters, and over 40 refereed journal articles and given more than 75 profes-

sional presentations at national and international conferences and symposia. Harrison cowrote "Living the Dream or Awakening from the Nightmare: Race and Athletic Identity" in *Race Ethnicity and Education*. He received the Charles D. Henry Award from the American Alliance for Health, Physical Education, Recreation and Dance and the E.B. Henderson Award from the Social Justice and Diversity Committee of the American Alliance for Health, Physical Education, Recreation and Dance. Harrison was recently inducted as a fellow in the National Academy of Kinesiology. He received his PhD in kinesiology from Louisiana State University.

Paul Heintzman, PhD, is an associate professor of leisure studies at the University of Ottawa. He received his PhD in recreation and leisure studies from the University of Waterloo with a thesis on the topic of leisure and spiritual well-being. Heintzman is the editor of a special issue of the journal *Leisure/Loisir* on the theme of leisure and spirituality and coeditor of the book *Christianity and Leisure: Issues in a Pluralistic Society*. He is a member of the Canadian Association for Leisure Studies and of the Christian Society for Kinesiology and Leisure Studies. In 2003 he received the Society of Park and Recreation Educators Teaching Innovation Award for creative experiential learning activities developed for a fourth-year class on leisure and spirituality, and in 2007 he was recipient of the Christian Society for Kinesiology and Leisure Studies' Literary Award.

Karla A. Henderson, PhD, is a professor in the department of parks, recreation and tourism management at North Carolina State University. She wrote two editions of the textbook *Dimensions of Choice: Qualitative Approaches to Research in Parks, Recreation, Tourism, Sport, and Leisure,* in 1991 and 2006. She has also done extensive research on leisure and African American and American Indian women. Henderson belongs to the Academy of Leisure Sciences and the American Academy of Park and Recreation Administrators. She has received numerous awards, including the National Recreation and Park Association's Roosevelt Award for Research Excellence, both the World Leisure George Torkildsen Literary Award and the National Recreation and Park Association

Literary Award in 2010, and the Lifetime Achievement Award from North Carolina State University in 2012. She received her PhD from the University of Minnesota and holds a ScD (honoris causa) from the University of Waterloo.

Daniel A. Henhawk, MA, is a doctoral candidate in the department of recreation and leisure studies at University of Waterloo. He has had a lifelong involvement in sport and recreation at various levels. He is currently specializing in Indigenous issues such as colonization and decolonization as these concepts relate to leisure. Henhawk cowrote "Indigenous Qualitative Inquiry: (Re)Awakening, Together, From a Long Colonizing Slumber" in *International Review of Qualitative Research*. He is currently a Social Sciences and Humanities Research Council of Canada award holder for completion of his doctorate. He received his master's degree from the University of Waterloo.

Cassandra Johnson-Gaither, PhD, is a research social scientist and project leader with the Integrating Human and Natural Systems Research Work Unit for the U.S. Forest Service. Her research on race and ethnicity and outdoor leisure spans nearly 20 years. She has published extensively on the topic of ethnic and racial minority engagement with natural resources and the environment, with particular attention to cultural meanings as motivators for natural resource engagement. Johnson-Gaither cowrote "African American Wildland Memories" in *Environmental Ethics*. This piece opens up an aspect of culture that likely influences outdoor recreation choices for African Americans. She belongs to the International Association for Society and Natural Resources and the American Sociological Association. She received her PhD in sociology from the University of Georgia.

Junhyoung Kim, PhD, is an assistant professor in the department of recreation, parks and leisure services administration at Central Michigan University. He has a strong research background in leisure, ethnicity, and health. Kim is involved in research projects intended to examine the value of intergroup contact and acculturation with a diverse sample of groups such as Korean immigrant adolescents and foreigners who immigrated to Korea. He was also a research assistant for the

Wounded Warrior Project at Pennsylvania State University, which explored various aspects of leisure and recreation in relation to healing and the recovery process. One of his more important publications, titled "Exploring the Experience of Intergroup Contact and the Value of Recreation Activities in Facilitating Positive Intergroup Interactions of Immigrants," appeared in *Leisure Sciences*. He received his PhD from Pennsylvania State University.

Monica Li, PhD, is a lecturer at Beijing International Studies University. She has conducted research related to leisure constraints, race and ethnicity, leisure and sociocultural change, and leisure and transnationalism. She was a project manager in Spain for a project focusing on the general goal of capacity building for developing countries on sustainable tourism and social development, a postdoctoral research fellow at Peking University in China, and a research assistant at the University of Illinois at Urbana-Champaign. One of Li's widely cited publications is an article in *Leisure Sciences* titled "Transnationalism, Leisure, and Chinese Graduate Students in the United States." She received her PhD from the University of Illinois at Urbana-Champaign.

Leo McAvoy, PhD, is a professor emeritus at the University of Minnesota. As a professor and researcher for 33 years, he focused on the personal and social benefits of environmental behaviors and the management of human behavior in outdoor recreation settings. He wrote "American Indians, Place Meanings and the Old/New West" in the *Journal of Leisure Research*. McAvoy was also the lead researcher on four collaborative research projects with the USDA Forest Service and American Indian Tribes and Canadian First Nations. He belongs to the National Recreation and Park Association and the National Parks and Conservation Association. McAvoy has received many awards, including the Theodore and Franklin Roosevelt Award for Excellence in Park and Recreation Research from the National Recreation and Park Association, the Association for Experiential Education's Teaching Award, and the Wilderness Education Association's Paul Petzoldt Outdoor Leadership Award. He received his PhD from the University of Minnesota.

Rasul A. Mowatt, PhD, is an associate professor in the department of recreation, park, and tourism studies at Indiana University Bloomington. His research background is in race studies, social justice, critical theory, and cultural studies. He has been a park professional for eight years and a social justice advocate for 22 years. His article, published in the *Journal of Leisure Research* titled "Notes from a Leisure Son: Expanding an Understanding of Whiteness in Leisure," introduced new ways of connecting leisure to social justice movements. He belongs to the National Recreation and Park Association and the National Association for the Advancement of Colored People (NAACP). He received his PhD from the University of Illinois at Urbana-Champaign.

Karin Peters, PhD, is an assistant professor at the Cultural Geography Group at Wageningen University in the Netherlands. She has published frequently in the field of leisure and ethnic diversity, mostly focusing on the Dutch society but also at the European level. One of her articles in *Forest Policy and Economics* is titled "Towards Access for All? Policy and Research on Access of Ethnic Minority Groups to Natural Areas in Four European Countries." Peters has supervised many graduate students on a variety of topics in the field of leisure science. She is also the deputy chair of the Research Network of Sociology and Migration (RN35) of the European Sociological Association. Peters is editor in chief of the journal *Vrijetijdstudies (Leisure Studies)*. She received her PhD from Wageningen University.

Ingrid E. Schneider, PhD, is a professor in the department of forest resources and the director of the University of Minnesota Tourism Center. She coauthored *Diversity and the Recreation Profession,* which advances understanding of organizational change to promote diversity. Schneider belongs to the National Recreation and Park Association and the International Association for Society and Natural Resources. She is a fellow of the Academy of Leisure Sciences. She received her PhD from Clemson University.

David Scott, PhD, is a professor in the department of recreation, park, and tourism sciences at Texas A&M University. His research has examined various aspects of social inequality for 20 years. Scott has published dozens of articles on leisure, supervised graduate students doing research in this area, and contributed numerous invited articles and book chapters related to inequality in leisure. His article "Recreational Specialization: A Critical Look at the Construct" in the *Journal of Leisure Research* broke new ground on ways of thinking about leisure participation. Scott received the Theodore and Franklin Roosevelt Award for Excellence in Recreation and Park Research from the National Recreation and Park Association. He received his PhD from Pennsylvania State University.

Iryna Sharaievska, PhD, is an assistant professor in the department of health, leisure, and exercise science at Appalachian State University. For the past five years, she has conducted research on leisure among diverse population groups, including Latino urban residents, African American teenagers, and Korean and East European women married to American men. She teaches courses in leisure services and diversity. Sharaievska has delivered a number of presentations focused on leisure among diverse groups. She also cowrote "Discrimination in Leisure Settings in Latino Urban Communities" in *Leisure/Loisir*. She is a faculty affiliate of the Diversity Research Laboratory at the University of Illinois at Urbana-Champaign. Sharaievska is also a recipient of the 2011 Christine Ziebarth Howe Award. She received her PhD from the University of Illinois at Urbana-Champaign.

Kindal A. Shores, PhD, is an associate professor in the department of recreation and leisure studies and an adjunct professor in the department of public health at East Carolina University's Brody School of Medicine. She is a certified physical activity and public health intervention specialist (American College of Sports Medicine certification). She is recognized for her expertise in physical activity and cowrote "Rural and Urban Park Use and Park-Based Physical Activity" in *Preventive Medicine*. Dr. Shores is in her seventh year on the faculty at East Carolina University. She draws on her research experience in exercise science and leisure studies to investigate the unique contribution of public parks and recreation to healthy lifestyles. She belongs to the American Alliance for Physical Activity Research and the National Recreation and Park Association. She has MS and PhD degrees in recreation and leisure studies with coursework emphasis in sociology and race studies from Texas A&M University.

Michael Toohey, PhD, is an associate professor at Beijing Institute of Technology. His research interest is in the history of sport and leisure, in particular the role of clubs and societies in 19th-century New Zealand. He cowrote "One Who Does Not Make His Living: Social Class and Cash Amateur Bicycle Racing in Nineteenth Century New Zealand" in the *International Journal of the History of Sport*. This article examines a hitherto underexplored phenomenon in sport history. Toohey received his PhD in social history from Lincoln University in New Zealand.

Eva Hiu-Lun Tsai, PhD, is an adjunct research fellow for Griffith Business School at Griffith University. As an immigrant and a member of an ethnic minority in Australia, she has developed an interest in cross-cultural comparative research and leisure research related to ethnic minorities. She has conducted several studies and published material extensively in this area. Tsai has also taught postgraduate courses at Hong Kong Baptist University and supervised students' dissertations focusing on development and management of leisure and sport of special populations. One of her more important publications is "A Cross-Cultural Study of the Influence of Perceived Positive Outcomes on Participation in Regular Active Recreation: Hong Kong and Australian" in *Leisure Sciences*. She received the University Medal and her PhD from Griffith University.

Xiye Wang, PhD, cowrote "The Effect of Face Concerns on University Students' Leisure Travel: A Cross-Cultural Comparison" in the *Journal of Leisure Research*. She worked with Aboriginal communities in Edmonton, Alberta, Canada, during her postdoctoral studies. Wang obtained her PhD in recreation and leisure studies from the University of Alberta.

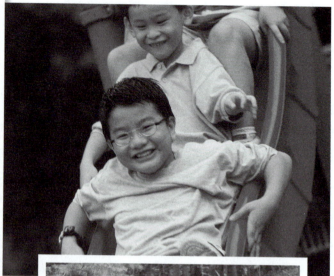